Her fine eyes raised to heaven, as if invoking at that moment the spirit of her mother to regard the vernal offering of her child; while her white hands were folded on her heart, and she softly exclaimed, "Alas! is this the only tribute left for me to pay?"

Children of the Abbey, p. 46.

PHILADELPHIA: PORTER & COATES.

"Lose," continued the figure in a hollow voice, "lose your superstitious fears, and in me behold not an airy inhabitant of the other world, but a sinful, sorrowing, and repentant woman."

Children of the Abbey, p. 467.

PHILADELPHIA: PORTER & COATES.

THE

CHILDREN OF THE ABBEY.

A Tale,

BY

REGINA MARIA ROCHE.

A matchless pair;
With equal virtue formed, and equal grace,
The same, distinguished by their sex alone:
Hers the mild lustre of the blooming morn,
And his the radiance of the risen day.—THOMSON.

ILLUSTRATED BY F. O. C. DARLEY.

PHILADELPHIA:
PORTER & COATES.

THE

CHILDREN OF THE ABBEY.

CHAPTER I.

> "Yellow sheafs from rich Ceres the cottage had crowned,
> Green rushes were strewed on the floor;
> The casements sweet woodbine crept wantonly round,
> And decked the sod seats at the door."—CUNNINGHAM.

AIL, sweet asylum of my infancy! Content and innocence reside beneath your humble roof, and charity unboastful of the good it renders. Hail, ye venerable trees! my happiest hours of childish gaiety were passed beneath your shelter—then, careless as the birds that sung upon your boughs, I laughed the hours away, nor knew of evil.

Here surely I shall be guarded from duplicity; and if not happy, at least in some degree tranquil. Here unmolested may I wait, till the rude storm of sorrow is overblown, and my father's arms are again expanded to receive me.

Such were the words of Amanda, as the chaise (which she had hired at a neighboring village on quitting the mail) turned down a little verdant lane, almost darkened by old trees, whose interwoven branches allowed her scarcely a glimpse of her nurse's cottage, till she had reached the door.

A number of tender recollections rushing upon her mind, rendered her almost unable to alight; but the nurse and her husband, who had been impatiently watching for the arrival of their fondling, assisted her, and the former, obeying the dictates of nature and affection, half stifled her with caresses; the latter respectfully kissed her hand, and dropped a tear of unutterable joy upon it. Lort, he said, he was surprised, to be sure, at the alteration a few years had made in her person—why, it seemed to him as if it was only the other day since he had carried her about in his arms, quite a little fairy. Then he begged to know how his tear old captain was, and Mr. Oscar—and whether the latter was not grown a very fine youth. Amanda, smiling through her tears, endeavored to answer his inquiries; but she was so much affected by her feelings, as to be scarcely able to speak; and when, by her desire, he went out to discharge the chaise, and assist the young man (who had travelled with her from London) to bring in her luggage, her head sunk upon her nurse's bosom, whose arms encircled her waist. "My dear faithful nurse," she sobbed, "your poor child is again returned to seek an asylum from you." "And she is heartily welcome," replied the good creature, crying herself, "and I have taken care to have everything so nice, and so tidy, and so comfortable, that I warrant you the greatest laty in the land need not disdain your apartments; and here are two little girls, as well as myself, that will always be ready to attend, serve, and obey you. This is Ellen, your own foster-sister; and this is Betsey, the little thing I had in the cradle when you went away—and I have besides, though I say it myself that should not say it, two as fine lads as you could wish to see; they are now at work at a farmer's hard by; but they will be here presently. Thank Cot, we are all happy, though obliged to earn our own bread; but 'tis sweeter for that reason, since labour gives us health to enjoy it, and contentment blesses us all." Amanda affectionately embraced the two girls, who were the pictures of health and cheerfulness, and was then conducted into a little parlor, which, with a small bed-chamber adjoining it, was appropriated to her use. The neatness of the room was truly pleasing; the floor was nicely sanded; the hearth was dressed with "flowers and fennel gay;" and the chimney-piece adorned with a range of broken tea-cups, "wisely kept for show;" a clock ticked behind the door; and an ebony cupboard displayed a profusion of the showiest ware the country could produce And now the nurse, on "hospitable thought intent," hurried from Amanda to prepare her dinner. The chicken, as she said herself, was ready to pop down in a minute; Ellen tied the asparagus; and Betsey laid the cloth; Edwin drew his best cider, and, having brought it in himself, retired to entertain his guest in the kitchen (Amanda's travelling companion), before whom he had already set some of his most substantial fare.

Dinner, in the opinion of Amanda, was served in a moment; but her heart was too full to eat, though pressed to do so with the utmost tenderness, a tenderness which, in truth, was the means of overcoming her.

When insulted by malice, or oppressed by cruelty, the heart ca. assume a stern fortitude foreign to its nature; but this seeming apathy vanishes at the voice of kindness, as the rigid frost of winter melts before the gentle influence of the sun, and tears, gushing tears of gratitude and sensibility, express its yielding feelings. Sacred are such tears; they flow from the sweet source of social affection: the good alone can shed them.

Her nurse's sons soon returned from their labor; two fine nut-brown youths. They had been the companions of her infant sports, and she spoke to them with the most engaging affability.

Domestic bliss and rural felicity Amanda had always been accustomed to, till within a short period; her attachment to them was still as strong as ever, and had her father been with her, she would have been happy.

It was now about the middle of June, and the whole country was glowing with luxuriant beauty. The cottage was in reality a comfortable, commodious farm-house; it was situated in North Wales, and the romantic scenery surrounding it was highly pleasing to a disposition like Amanda's, which delighted equally in the sublime and beautiful. The front of the cottage was almost covered with woodbine, intermingled with vines; and the lane already mentioned formed a shady avenue up to the very door; one side overlooked a deep valley, winding amongst hills clad in the liveliest verdure; a clear stream running through it turned a mill in its course, and afforded a salutary coolness to the herds which ruminated on its banks; the other side commanded a view of rich pastures, terminated by a thick grove, whose natural vistas gave a view of cultivated farms, a small irregular village, the spire of its church, and a fine old castle, whose stately turrets rose above the trees surrounding them.

The farm-yard, at the back of the cottage, was stocked with poultry and all the implements of rural industry; the garden was divided from it by a rude paling, interwoven with honeysuckles and wild roses; the part appropriated for vegetables divided from the part sacred to Flora by rows of fruit trees; a craggy precipice hung over it, covered with purple and yellow flowers, thyme, and other odoriferous herbs, which afforded browsage to three or four goats that skipped about in playful gambols; a silver stream trickled down the precipice, and winding round a plantation of shrubs, fell with a gentle murmur into the valley. Beneath a projecting fragment of the rock a natural recess was formed, thickly lined with moss, and planted round with a succession of beautiful flowers.

> "Here, scattered wild, the lily of the vale
> Its balmy essence breathes; here cowslips hang
> The dewy head, and purple violets lurk—
> With all the lowly children of the shade."—THOMSON.

Of those scenes Amanda had but an imperfect recollection; such a faint idea as we retain of a confused but agreeable dream, which, though we cannot explain, leaves a pleasing impression behind.

Peculiar circumstances had driven her from the shelter of a parent's arms, to seek security in retirement at this abode of simplicity and peace. Here the perturbation of fear subsided; but the soft melancholy of her soul at times was heightened, when she reflected, that in this very place an unfortunate mother had expired almost at the moment of giving her birth.

Amanda was now about nineteen; a description of her face and person would not do her justice, as it never could convey a full idea of the ineffable sweetness and sensibility of the former, or the striking elegance and beautiful proportion of the latter.

Sorrow had faded her vivid bloom; for the distresses of her father weighed heavy on her heart, and the blossom drooped with the tree which supported it. Her agonized parent, witnessing this sudden change, sent her into Wales, as much for health as for security; she was ordered goat's whey and gentle exercise; but she firmly believed that consolation on her father's account could alone effect a cure.

Though the rose upon her cheek was pale, and the lustre of her eyes was fled, she was from those circumstances (if less dazzling to the eye) more affecting to the heart. Cold and unfeeling indeed must that one have been, which could see her unmoved; for hers was that interesting face and figure which had power to fix the wandering eye and change the gaze of admiration into the throb of sensibility; nor was her mind inferior to the form that enshrined it.

She now exerted her spirits in gratitude to her humble but benevolent friends. Her arrival had occasioned a little festival at the cottage: the tea things, which were kept more for show than use in the ebony cupboard, were now taken out and carried by her desire to the recess in the garden; whether Mrs. Edwin followed the family with a hot cake, Amanda thought large enough to serve half the principality.

The scene was delightful, and well calculated to banish all sadness but despair; Amanda was therefore cheered; for she was too much the child of piety ever to have felt its baneful influence. In the midst of her troubles she still looked up with confidence to that Power who has promised never to forsake the righteous.

The harmless jest, the jocund laugh went round, and Amanda enjoyed the innocent gaiety; for a benevolent mind will ever derive pleasure from the happiness of others. The declining sun now gave softer beauties to the extensive scenery; the lowing of the cattle was faintly echoed by the neighboring hills; the cheerful carol of the peasant floated on the evening gale, that stole perfumes from the beds of flowers and wafted them around; the busy bees had now completed the delicious labor of the day, and with incessant hummings sought their various hives, while—

> "Every copse
> Deep-tangled, tree irregular, and bush
> Were prodigal of harmony."—Thomson.

To complete the concert, a blind harper, who supported himself by summer rambles through the country, strolled into the garden; and after a plentiful repast of bread and cheese, and nut-brown ale, began playing.

The venerable appearance of the musician, the simple melody of his harp, recalled to Amanda's recollection the tales of other times, in which she had so often delighted: it sent her soul back to the ages of old, to the days of other years, when bards rehearsed the exploits of heroes, and sung the praises of the dead. "While the ghosts of those they sung, came in their rustling winds, and were seen to bend with joy towards the sound of their praise." To proceed, in the beautiful language of Ossian, "The sound was mournful and low, like the song of the tomb; such as Fingal heard, when the crowded sighs of his bosom rose; and, "some of my heroes are low," said the grey-haired King of Morven: "I hear the sound of death on the harp. Ossian, touch the trembling string. Bid the sorrow rise, that their spirits may fly with joy to Morven's woody hills. He touched the harp before the king: the sound was mournful and low. Bend forwards from your clouds," he said, "ghosts of my fathers, bend. Lay by the red terror of your course. Receive the falling chief; whether he comes from a distant land, or rises from the rolling sea, let his robe of mist be near; his spear, that is formed of a cloud; place an half-extinguished meteor by his side, in the form of the hero's sword. And, oh! let his countenance be lovely, that his friends may delight in his presence. Bend from your clouds," he said, "ghosts of my fathers, bend."

The sweet enthusiasm which arose in Amanda's mind, from her present situation, her careful nurse soon put an end to, by reminding her of the heavy dew then falling. Amanda could have stayed for hours in the garden; but resigning her inclination to her nurse's, she immediately accômpanied her into the house. She soon felt inclined to retire to rest; and, after a slight supper of strawberries and cream (which was all they could prevail on her to touch), she withdrew to her chamber, attended by the nurse and her two daughters, whò all thought their services requisite; and it was not without much difficulty Amanda persuaded them to the contrary.

Left to solitude, a tender awe stole upon the mind of Amanda, when she reflected that in this very room her mother had expired. The recollection of her sufferings—the sorrows her father and self had experienced since the period of her death—the distresses they still felt and might yet go through—all raised a sudden agony in her soul, and tears burst forth. She went to the bed, and knelt beside it; "Oh! my mother," she cried, "if thy departed spirit be permitted to look down upon this world, hear and regard the supplications of thy child, for thy protection amidst the snares which may be spread for her. Yet," continued she, after a pause, "that Being, who has taken thee to himself, will, if I continue innocent, extend his guardian care: to Him, therefore, to Him be raised the fervent prayer for rendering abortive every scheme of treachery."

She prayed with all the fervency of devotion; her wandering thoughts were all restrained, and her passions gradually subsided into a calm.

Warmed by a pure and ardent piety, that sacred power which comes with healing on its wings to the afflicted children of humanity, she felt a placid hope spring in her heart, that whispered to it, all would yet be well.

She arose tranquil and animated. The inhabitants of the cottage had retired to repose; and she heard no sound save the ticking of the clock from the outside room. She went to the window, and raising the white calico curtain, looked down the valley; it was illumined by the beams of the moon, which tipped the trees with a shadowy silver, and threw a line of radiance on the clear rivulet. All was still, as if creation slept upon the bosom of serenity. Here, while contemplating the scene, a sudden flutter at the window startled her; and she saw in a moment after a bird flit across, and perch upon a tree whose boughs shaded the casement; a soft serenade was immediately begun by the sweet and plaintive bird of night.

Amanda at length dropped the curtain, and sought repose; it soon blessed her eyelids, and shed a sweet oblivion over all her cares.

> "Sleep on, sweet innocent!
> And when a soul is found sincerely so,
> A thousand liveried angels lacquey it,
> Driving far off all thought of harm or sin."—MILTON.

CHAPTER II.

"Canst thou bear cold and hunger? Can these limbs,
Framed for the tender offices of love,
Endure the bitter gripes of smarting poverty?
When in a bed of straw we shrink together,
And the bleak winds shall whistle round our heads,
Wilt thou talk to me thus,
Thus hush my cares, and shelter me with love?"—OTWAY.

ITZALAN, the father of Amanda, was the descendant of an ancient Irish family, which had, however, unfortunately attained the summit of its prosperity long before his entrance into life; so that little more than a name, once dignified by illustrious actions, was left to its posterity. The parents of Fitzalan were supported by an employment under government, which enabled them to save a small sum for their son and only child, who at an early period became its sole master, by their dying within a short period of each other. As soon as he had in some degree recovered the shock of such calamities, he laid out his little pittance in the purchase of a commission, as a profession best suiting his inclinations and finances.

The war between America and France had then just commenced; and Fitzalan's regiment was amongst the first forces sent to the aid of the former. The scenes of war, though dreadfully affecting to a soul of exquisite sensibility, such as he possessed, had not power to damp the ardor of his spirit; for, with the name, he inherited the hardy resolution of his progenitors.

He had once the good fortune to save the life of a British soldier; he was one of a small party, who, by the treachery of their guides, were suddenly surprised in a wood, through which they were obliged to pass to join another detachment of the army. Their only way in this alarming exigence was to retreat to the fort from whence they had but lately issued: encompassed as they were by the enemy, this was not achieved without the greatest difficulty. Just as they had reached it, Fitzalan saw far behind them, a poor soldier, who had been wounded at the first onset, just overtaken by two Indians. Yielding to the impulse of compassion in which all idea of self was lost, Fitzalan hastily turned to his assistance, and flinging himself between the pursued and the pursuers, he kept them at bay till the poor creature had reached a place of safety. This action, performed at the imminent hazard of his life, secured him the lasting gratitude of the soldier, whose name was Edwin; the same that now afforded an asylum to his daughter.

Edwin had committed some juvenile indiscretions, which highly incensed his parents: in despair at incurring their resentment, he enlisted with a recruiting party in their neighborhood: but, accustomed all his life to peace and plenty, he did not by any means relish his new situation. His gratitude to Fitzalan was unbounded; he considered him as the preserver of his life; and, on the man's being dismissed, who had hitherto attended him as a servant, entreated he might be taken in his place. This entreaty Fitzalan complied with; he was pleased with Edwin's manner; and, having heard the little history of his misfortunes, promised, on their return to Europe, to intercede with his friends for him.

During his stay abroad, Fitzalan was promoted to a captain-lieutenancy; his pay was his only support, which, of necessity, checked the benevolence of a spirit "open as day to melting charity."

On the regiment's return to Europe, he obtained Edwin's discharge, who longed to re-enter upon his former mode of life. He accompanied the penitent himself into Wales, where he was received with the truest rapture.

In grief for his loss, his parents had forgotten all resentment for his errors, which, indeed, had never been very great: they had lost their two remaining children during his absence, and now received him as the sole comfort and hope of their age.

His youthful protector was blest with the warmest gratitude: tears filled his fine eyes, as he beheld the pleasure of his parents, and the contrition of the son; and he departed with that heartfelt pleasure, which ever attends and rewards an action of humanity.

He now accompanied his regiment into Scotland; they were quartered at a fort in a remote part of that kingdom.

Near the fort was a fine old abbey, belonging to the family of Dunreath; the high hills which nearly encompassed it, were almost all covered with trees, whose dark shades gave an appearance of gloomy solitude to the building.

The present possessor, the Earl of Dunreath, was now far advanced in life; twice had he married, in expectation of a male heir to his large estates, and twice he had been disappointed. His first lady had expired immediately after the birth of a daughter. She had taken under her protection a young female, who, by unexpected vicissitudes in her family, was left destitute of support. On the demise of her patroness, she retired from the Abbey to the house of a kinswoman in its vicinity; the Earl of Dunreath, accustomed to her society, felt his solitude doubly augmented by her absence. He had ever followed the dictates of inclination, and would not disobey them now: ere the term of mourning was expired, he offered her his hand, and was accepted.

The fair orphan, now triumphant mistress of the Abbey, found there was no longer occasion to check her natural propensities. Her soul was vain, unfeeling, and ambitious; and her sudden elevation broke down all the barriers which prudence had hitherto opposed to her passions.

She soon gained an absolute ascendancy over her lord—she knew how to assume the smile of complacency, and the accent of sensibility.

Forgetful of the kindness of her late patroness, she treated the infant she had left with the most cruel neglect; a neglect which was, if possible, increased, on the birth of her own daughter, as she could not bear that Augusta (instead of possessing the whole) should only share the affection and estates of her father. She contrived by degrees to alienate the former from the innocent Malvina; and she trusted, she should find means to deprive her of the latter.

Terrified by violence, and depressed by severity, the child looked dejected and unhappy; and this appearance, Lady Dunreath made the Earl believe, proceeded from sulkiness and natural ill-humor. Her own child, unrestrained in any wish of her heart, was, from her playful gaiety, a constant source of amusement to the Earl; her mother had taken care to instruct her in all the little endearments, which, when united with infantine sweetness, allure almost imperceptibly the affections.

Malvina, ere she knew the meaning of sorrow, thus became its prey: but, in spite of envy or ill treatment, she grew up with all the graces of mind and form that had distinguished her mother; her air was at once elegant and commanding; her face replete with sweetness; and her fine eyes had a mixture of sensibility and languor in them, which spoke to the feeling soul.

Augusta was also a fine figure; but unpossessed of the winning graces of elegance and modesty which adorned her sister, her form always appeared decorated with the most studied art, and her large eyes had a confident assurance in them, that seemed to expect and demand universal homage.

The warriors of the fort were welcome visitants at the Abbey, which Lady Dunreath contrived to render a scene of almost constant gaiety, by keeping up a continual intercourse with all the adjacent families, and entertaining all the strangers who came into its neighborhood.

Lord Dunreath had long been a prey to infirmities, which at this period generally confined him to his room; but though his body was debilitated, his mind retained all its active powers.

The first appearance of the officers at the Abbey was at a ball given by Lady Dunreath, in consequence of their arrival near it; the gothic apartments were decorated, and lighted up with a splendor that at once displayed taste and magnificence; the lights, the music, the brilliancy and unusual gaiety of the company, all gave to the spirits of Malvina an agreeable flutter they had never before experienced; and a brighter bloom than usual stole over her lovely cheek.

The young co-heiresses were extremely admired by the military heroes. Malvina, as the eldest, opened the ball with the colonel; her form had attracted the eyes of Fitzalan, and vainly he attempted to withdraw them, till the lively conversation of Augusta, who honored him with her hand, forced him to restrain his glances, and pay her the sprightly attentions so generally expected—when he came to turn Malvina, he involuntarily detained her hand for a moment: she blushed, and the timid beam that stole from her half-averted eyes, agitated his whole soul.

Partners were changed in the course of the evening, and he seized the first opportunity that offered for engaging her; the softness of her voice, the simplicity yet elegance of her language, now captivated his heart, as much as her form had charmed his eyes

Never had he before seen an object he thought half so lovely or engaging; with her he could not support that lively strain of conversation he had done with her sister. Where the heart is much interested, it will not admit of trifling.

Fitzalan was now in the meridian of manhood; his stature was above the common size, and elegance and dignity were conspicuous in it; his features were regularly handsome, and the fairness of his forehead proved what his complexion had been, till change of climate and hardship had embrowned it; the expression of his countenance was somewhat plaintive: his eyes had a sweetness in them that spoke a soul of the tenderest feelings; and the smile that played around his mouth, would have adorned a face of female beauty.

When the dance with Lady Malvina was over, Lady Augusta took care for the remainder of the evening to engross all his attention. She thought him by far the handsomest man in the room, and gave him no opportunity of avoiding her; gallantry obliged him to return her assiduities, and he was by his brother officers set down in the list of her adorers. This mistake he encouraged: he could bear raillery on an indifferent subject: and joined in the mirth, which the idea of his laying siege to the young heiress occasioned.

He deluded himself with no false hopes relative to the real object of his passion; he knew the obstacles between them were insuperable; but his heart was too proud to complain of fate; he shook off all appearance of melancholy, and seemed more animated than ever.

His visits at the Abbey became constant; Lady Augusta took them to herself, and encouraged his attentions: as her mother rendered her perfect mistress of her own actions, she had generally a levee of redcoats every morning in her dressing room. Lady Malvina seldom appeared; she was at those times almost always employed in reading to her father; when that was not the case, her own favorite avocations often detained her in her room; or else she wandered out, about the romantic rocks on the sea-shore; she delighted in solitary rambles, and loved to visit the old peasants, who told her tales of her departed mother's goodness, drawing tears of sorrow from her eyes, at the irreparable loss she had sustained by her death.

Fitzalan went one morning as usual to the Abbey to pay his customary visit; as he went through the gallery which led to Lady Augusta's dressing-room, his eyes were caught by two beautiful portraits of the Earl's daughters; an artist, by his express desire, had come to the Abbey to draw them; they were but just finished, and that morning placed in the gallery.

Lady Augusta appeared negligently reclined upon a sofa, in a verdant alcove; the flowing drapery of the loose robe in which she was habited, set off her fine figure; little Cupids were seen fanning aside her dark-brown hair, and strewing roses on her pillow.

Lady Malvina was represented in the simple attire of a peasant girl, leaning on a little grassy hillock, whose foot was washed by a clear stream, while her flocks browsed around, and her dog rested beneath the shade of an old tree, that waved its branches over her head, and seemed sheltering her from the beams of a meridian sun.

"Beautiful portrait!" cried Fitzalan, "sweet resemblance of a seraphic form!"

He heard a soft sigh behind him; he started, turned, and perceived Lady Malvina; in the utmost confusion he faltered out his admiration of the pictures; and not knowing what he did, fixed his eyes on Lady Augusta's, exclaiming, "How beautiful!" "'Tis very handsome indeed," said Malvina, with a more pensive voice than usual, and led the way to her sister's drawing-room.

Lady Augusta was spangling some ribbon; but at Fitzalan's entrance she threw it aside, and asked him if he had been admiring her picture?—"Yes," he said, "'twas that alone had prevented his before paying his homage to the original." He proceeded in a strain of compliments, which had more gallantry than sincerity in them. In the course of their trifling, he snatched a knot of the spangled ribbon, and pinning it next his heart, declared it should remain there as a talisman against all future impressions

He stole a glance at Lady Malvina; she held a book in her hand; but her eyes were turned towards him, and a deadly paleness overspread her countenance.

Fitzalan's spirits vanished; he started up, and declared he must be gone immediately. The dejection of Lady Malvina dwelt upon his heart; it flattered its fondness, but pained its sensibility. He left the fort in the evening, immediately after he had retired from the mess; he strolled to the sea-side, and rambled a considerable way among the rocks. The scene was wild and solemn; the shadows of evening were beginning to descend; the waves stole with low murmurs upon the shore, and a soft breeze gently agitated the marine plants that grew amongst the crevices of the rocks; already were the sea-fowl, with harsh and melancholy cries, flocking to their nests, some lightly skimming over the water, while others were seen, like dark clouds arising from the long heath on the neighboring hills. Fitzalan pursued his way in deep and melancholy meditation, from which a plaintive Scotch air, sung by the melting voice of harmony itself, roused him. He looked towards the spot from whence the sound proceeded, and beheld Lady Malvina standing on a low rock, a projection of it affording her support. Nothing could be more picturesque than her appearance: she looked like one of the beautiful forms which Ossian so often describes: her white dress fluttered in the wind, and her dark hair hung dishevelled around her. Fitzalan moved softly, and stopped behind her; she wept as she sung, and wiped away her tears as she ceased singing; she sighed heavily. "Ah! my mother," she exclaimed, "why was Malvina left behind you?"—"To bless and improve mankind," cried Fitzalan. She screamed, and would have fallen, had he not caught her in his arms; he prevailed on her to sit down upon the rock, and allow him to support her till her agitation had subsided. "And why," cried he, "should Lady Malvina give way to melancholy, blest as she is with all that can render life desirable? Why seek its indulgence, by rambling about those dreary rocks; fit haunts alone, he might have added, for wretchedness and me? Can I help wondering at your dejection (he continued), when to all appearance (at least) I see you possessed of everything requisite to constitute felicity?"

"Appearances are often deceitful," said Malvina, forgetting in that moment the caution she had hitherto inviolably observed, of never hinting at the ill treatment she received from the Countess of Dunreath and her daughter. "Appearances are often deceitful," she said, "as I, alas! too fatally experience. The glare, the ostentation of wealth, a soul of sensibility would willingly resign for privacy and plainness if they were to be attended with real friendship and sympathy."

"And how few," cried Fitzalan, turning his expressive eyes upon her face, "can know Lady Malvina without feeling friendship for her virtues, and sympathy for her sorrows!" As he spoke, he pressed her hand against his heart, and she felt the knot of ribbon he had snatched from her sister: she instantly withdrew her hand, and darting a haughty glance at him, "Captain Fitzalan," said she, "you were going, I believe, to Lady Augusta; let me not detain you."

Fitzalan's passions were no longer under the dominion of reason; he tore the ribbon from his breast and flung it into the sea. "Going to Lady Augusta!" he exclaimed, "and is her lovely sister then really deceived? Ah! Lady Malvina, I now gaze on the dear attraction that drew me to the Abbey. The feelings of a real, a hopeless passion could ill support raillery or observation: I hid my passion within the recesses of my heart, and gladly allowed my visits to be placed to the account of an object truly indifferent, that I might have opportunities of seeing an object I adored." Malvina blushed and trembled: "Fitzalan," cried she, after a pause, "I detest deceit."

"I abhor it too, Lady Malvina," said he; "but why should I now endeavor to prove my sincerity, when I know it is so very immaterial? Excuse me for what I have already uttered, and believe that though susceptible, I am not aspiring." He then presented his hand to Malvina; she descended from her seat, and they walked towards the Abbey. Lady Malvina's pace was slow, and her blushes, had Fitzalan looked at her, would have expressed more pleasure than resentment: she seemed to expect a still further declaration; but Fitzalan was too confused to speak; nor indeed was it his intention again to indulge himself on the dangerous subject. They proceeded in silence; at the Abbey gate they stopped, and he wished her good-night. "Shall we not soon see you at the Abbey?" exclaimed Lady Malvina in a flurried voice, which seemed to say she thought his adieu rather a hasty one. "No, my lovely friend," cried Fitzalan, pausing, while he looked upon her with the most impassioned tenderness,—"in future I shall confine myself chiefly to the fort." "Do you dread an invasion?" asked she, smiling, while a stolen glance of her eyes gave peculiar meaning to her words. "I long dreaded that," cried he in the same strain, "and my fears were well founded; but I must now muster all my powers to dislodge the enemy." He kissed her hand, and precipitately retired.

Lady Malvina repaired to her chamber, in such a tumult of pleasure as she had never before experienced. She admired Fitzalan from the first evening she beheld him; though his attentions were directed to her sister, the language of his eyes, to her, contradicted any attachment these attentions might have intimated; his gentleness and sensibility seemed congenial to her own. Hitherto she had been the slave of tyranny and caprice; and now, for the first time, experienced that soothing tenderness her wounded feelings had so long sighed for. She was agitated and delighted; she overlooked every obstacle to her wishes; and waited impatiently a further explanation of Fitzalan's sentiments.

Far different were his feelings from hers: to know he was beloved, could scarcely yield him pleasure, when he reflected on his hopeless situation, which forbad his availing himself of any advantage that knowledge might have afforded. Of a union indeed he did not dare to think, since its consequences, he knew, must be destruction; for rigid and austere as the Earl was represented, he could not flatter himself he would ever pardon such a step; and the means of supporting Lady Malvina, in any degree of comfort, he did not possess himself. He determined, as much as possible, to avoid her presence, and regretted continually having yielded to the impulse of his heart, and revealed his love, since he believed it had augmented hers.

By degrees he discontinued his visits at the Abbey; but he often met Lady Malvina at parties in the neighborhood: caution, however, always sealed his lips, and every appearance of particularity was avoided. The time now approached for the departure of the regiment from Scotland, and Lady Malvina, instead of the explanation she so fondly expected, so ardently desired, saw Fitzalan studious to avoid her.

The disappointment this conduct gave rise to, was too much for the tender and romantic heart of Malvina to bear without secretly repining. Society grew irksome; she became more than ever attached to solitary rambles, which gave opportunities of indulging her sorrows without restraint: sorrows, pride often reproached her for experiencing.

It was within a week of the change of garrison, when Malvina repaired one evening to the rock where Fitzalan had disclosed his tenderness: a similarity of feeling had led him thither; he saw his danger, but he had no power to retreat; he sat down by Malvina, and they conversed for some time on indifferent subjects; at last, after a pause of a minute, Malvina exclaimed, "You go then, Fitzalan, never, never, I suppose, to return here again!" "'Tis probable I may not indeed," said he. "Then we shall never meet again," cried she, while a trickling tear stole down her lovely cheek, which, tinged as it was with the flush of agitation, looked now like a half-blown rose moistened with the dews of early morning.

"Yes, my lovely friend," said he, "we shall meet again—we shall meet in a better place; in that heaven," continued he, sighing, and laying his cold, trembling hand upon hers, "which will recompense all our sufferings." "You are melancholy to-night, Fitzalan," cried Lady Malvina, in a voice scarcely articulate.

"Oh! can you wonder at it?" exclaimed he, overcome by her emotion, and forgetting in a moment all his resolutions—"Oh! can you wonder at my melancholy, when I know not but that this is the last time I shall see the only woman I ever loved—when I know, that in bidding her adieu I resign all the pleasure, the happiness of my life."

Malvina could no longer restrain her feelings; she sunk upon his shoulder and wept. "Good heavens!" cried Fitzalan, almost trembling beneath the lovely burthen he supported—"What a cruel situation is mine! But, Malvina, I will not, cannot plunge you in destruction. Led by necessity, as well as choice, to embrace the profession of a soldier, I have no income but what is derived from that profession; though my own distresses I could bear with fortitude, yours would totally unman me; nor would my honor be less injured than my peace, were you involved in difficulties on my account. Our separation is therefore, alas! inevitable."

"Oh! no," exclaimed Malvina, "the difficulties you have mentioned will vanish. My father's affections were early alienated from me; and my fate is of little consequence to him—nay, I have reason to believe he will be glad of an excuse for leaving his large possessions to Augusta; and oh! how little shall I envy her those possessions, if the happy destiny I now look forward to is mine." As she spoke, her mild eyes rested on the face of Fitzalan, who clasped her to his bosom in a sudden transport of tenderness. "But though my father is partial to Augusta," she continued, "I am sure he will not be unnatural to me; and though he may withhold affluence, he will, I am confident, allow me a competence; nay, Lady Dunreath, I believe, in pleasure at my removal from the Abbey, would, if he hesitated in that respect, become my intercessor."

The energy with which Malvina spoke convinced Fitzalan of the strength of her affection. An ecstasy never before felt pervaded his soul at the idea of being so beloved; vainly did prudence whisper, that Malvina might be deluding herself with false hopes, the suggestions of love triumphed over every consideration; and again folding the fair being he held in his arms to his heart, he softly asked, would she, at all events, unite her destiny with his.

Lady Malvina, who firmly believed what she had said to him would really happen, and who deemed a separation from him the greatest misfortune which could possibly befall her, blushed, and faltering yielded a willing consent.

The means of accomplishing their wishes now occupied their thoughts. Fitzalan's imagination was too fertile not soon to suggest a scheme which had a probability of success; he resolved to intrust the chaplain of the regiment with the affair, and request his attendance the ensuing night in the chapel of the Abbey, where Lady Malvina promised to meet them with her maid, on whose secrecy she thought she could rely.

It was settled that Fitzalan should pay a visit the next morning at the Abbey, and give Malvina a certain sign, if he succeeded with the chaplain.

The increasing darkness at length reminded them of the lateness of the hour. Fitzalan conducted Malvina to the Abbey gate, where they separated, each involved in a tumult of hopes, fears, and wishes.

The next morning Lady Malvina brought her work into her sister's dressing room; at last Fitzalan entered; he was attacked by Augusta for his long absence, which he excused by pleading regimental business. After trifling some time with her, he prevailed on her to sit down to the harpsichord; and then glancing to Malvina, he gave her the promised signal.

Her conscious eyes were instantly bent to the ground; a crimson glow was suddenly succeeded by a deadly paleness; her head sunk upon her bosom; and her agitation must have excited suspicions had it been perceived; but Fitzalan purposely bent over her sister, and thus gave her an opportunity of retiring unnoticed from the room. As soon as she had regained a little composure, she called her maid, and, after receiving many promises of secrecy, unfolded to her the whole affair. It was long past the midnight hour ere Malvina would attempt repairing to the chapel; when she at last rose for that purpose she trembled universally; a kind of horror chilled her heart; she began to fear she was about doing wrong, and hesitated; but when she reflected on the noble generosity of Fitzalan, and that she herself had precipitated him into the measure they were about taking, her hesitation was over; and leaning on her maid, she stole through the winding galleries, and lightly descending the stairs, entered the long hall, which terminated in a dark arched passage, that opened into the chapel.

This was a wild and gloomy structure, retaining everywhere vestiges of that monkish superstition which had erected it; beneath were the vaults which contained the ancestors of the Earl of Dunreath, whose deeds and titles were enumerated on gothic monuments; their dust-covered banners waving around in sullen dignity to the rude gale, which found admittance through the broken windows.

The light, which the maid held, produced deep shadows, that heightened the solemnity of the place.

"They are not here," said Malvina, casting her fearful eyes around. She went to the door, which opened into a thick wood; but here she only heard the breeze rustling amongst the trees; she turned from it, and sinking upon the steps of the altar, gave way to an agony of tears and lamentations. A low murmur reached her ear; she started up; the chapel door was gently pushed open, and Fitzalan entered with the chaplain; they had been watching in the wood for the appearance of light. Malvina was supported to the altar, and a few minutes made her the wife of Fitzalan.

She had not the courage, till within a day or two previous to the regiment's departure from Scotland, to acquaint the Earl with her marriage; the Countess already knew it, through the means of Malvina's woman, who was a creature of her own. Lady Dunreath exulted at the prospect of Malvina's ruin; it at once gratified the malevolence of her soul, and the avaricious desire she had of increasing her own daughter's fortune; she had, besides, another reason to rejoice at it; this was, the attachment Lady Augusta had formed for Fitzalan, which, her mother feared, would have precipitated her into a step as imprudent as her sister's, had she not been beforehand with her.

This fear the impetuous passions of Lady Augusta naturally excited. She really loved Fitzalan; a degree of frantic rage possessed her at his marriage; she cursed her sister in the bitterness of her heart, and joined with Lady Dunreath in working up the Earl's naturally austere and violent passions into such a paroxysm of fury and resentment, that he at last solemnly refused forgiveness to Malvina, and bid her never more appear in his presence.

She now began to tread the thorny path of life; and though her guide was tender and affectionate, nothing could allay her anguish for having involved him in difficulties, which his noble spirit could ill brook or struggle against. The first year of their union she had a son, who was called after her father, Oscar Dunreath; the four years that succeeded his birth were passed in wretchedness that baffles description. At the expiration of this period their debts were so increased, Fitzalan was compelled to sell out on half-pay. Lady Malvina now expected an addition to her family; her situation, she hoped, would move her father's heart, and resolved to essay everything, which afforded the smallest prospect of obtaining comfort for her husband and his babes; she prevailed on him, therefore, to carry her to Scotland.

They lodged at a peasant's in the neighborhood of the Abbey; he informed them the Earl's infirmities were daily increasing; and that Lady Dunreath had just celebrated her daughter's marriage with the Marquis of Roseline. This nobleman had passionately admired Lady Malvina; an admiration the Countess always wished transferred to her daughter. On the marriage of Malvina he went abroad; his passion was conquered ere he returned to Scotland, and he disdained not the overtures made for his alliance from the Abbey. His favorite propensities, avarice and pride, were indeed gratified by the possession of the Earl of Dunreath's sole heiress.

The day after her arrival Lady Malvina sent little Oscar, with the old peasant, to the Abbey; Oscar was a perfect cherubim—

"The bloom of opening flowers, unsullied beauty,
Softness and sweetest innocence he wore,
And looked like nature in the world's first spring."

Lady Malvina gave him a letter for the Earl, in which, after pathetically describing her situation, she besought him to let the uplifted hands of innocence plead her cause. The peasant watched till the hour came for Lady Dunreath to go out in her carriage, as was her daily custom: he then desired to be conducted to the Earl, and was accordingly ushered into his presence: he found him alone, and briefly informed him of his errand. The Earl frowned and looked agitated; but did not by any means express that displeasure which the peasant had expected; feeling for himself, indeed, had lately softened his heart; he was unhappy; his wife and daughter had attained the completion of their wishes, and no longer paid him the attention his age required. He refused, however, to accept the letter: little Oscar, who had been gazing on him from the moment he entered the apartment, now ran forward; gently stroking his hand, he smiled in his face, and exclaimed, "Ah! do pray take poor mamma's letter." The Earl involuntarily took it; as he read, the muscles of his face began to work, and a tear dropped from him. "Poor mamma cries too," said Oscar, upon whose hand the tear fell. "Why did your mamma send you to me?" said the Earl. "Because she said," cried Oscar, "that you were my grandpapa—and she bids me love you, and teaches me every day to pray for you." "Heaven bless you, my lovely prattler!" exclaimed the Earl, with sudden emotion, patting his head as he spoke. At this moment Lady Dunreath rushed into the apartment: one of her favorites had followed her, to relate the scene that was going forward within it: and she had returned, with all possible expedition, to counteract any dangerous impression that might be made upon the Earl's mind. Rage inflamed her countenance: the Earl knew the violence of her temper; he was unequal to contention, and hastily motioned for the peasant to retire with the child. The account of his reception excited the most flattering hopes in the bosom of his mother: she counted the tedious hours, in expectation of a kind summons to the Abbey; but no such summons came. The next morning the child was sent to it; but the porter refused him admittance, by the express command of the Earl, he said. Frightened at his rudeness, the child returned weeping to his mother, whose blasted expectations wrung her heart with agony, and tears and lamentations broke from her. The evening was far advanced, when suddenly her features brightened: "I will go," cried she, starting up—"I will again try to melt his obduracy. Oh! with what lowliness should a child bend before an offended parent! Oh! with what fortitude, what patience, should a wife, a mother, try to overcome difficulties which she is conscious of having precipitated the objects of her tenderest affections into!"

The night was dark and tempestuous; she would not suffer Fitzalan to attend her; but proceeded to the Abbey, leaning on the peasant's arm. She would not be repulsed at the door, but forced her way into the hall: here Lady Dunreath met her, and with mingled pride and cruelty, refused her access to her father, declaring it was by his desire she did so. "Let me see him but for a moment," said the lovely suppliant, clasping her white and emaciated hands together—"by all that is tender in humanity, I beseech you to grant my request."

"Turn this frantic woman from the Abbey," said the implacable Lady Dunreath, trembling with passion—"at your peril suffer her to continue here. The peace of your lord is too precious to be disturbed by her exclamations."

The imperious order was instantly obeyed, though, as Cordelia says, "it was a night when one would not have turned an enemy's dog from the door." The rain poured in torrents; the sea roared with awful violence; and the wind raged through the wood, as if it would tear up the trees by the roots. The peasant charitably flung his plaid over Malvina: she moved mechanically along; her senses appeared quite stupefied. Fitzalan watched for her at the door: she rushed into his extended arms, and fainted; it was long ere she showed any symptoms of returning life. Fitzalan wept over her in the anguish and distraction of his soul; and scarcely could he forbear execrating the being who had so grievously afflicted her gentle spirit: by degrees she revived; and, as she pressed him feebly to her breast, exclaimed, "The final stroke is given—I have been turned from my father's door."

The cottage in which they lodged afforded but few of the necessaries, and none of the comforts of life; such, at least, as they had been accustomed to. In Malvina's present situation, Fitzalan dreaded the loss of her life, should they continue in their present abode; but whither could he take her, wanderer as he was upon the face of the earth? At length the faithful Edwin occurred to his recollection: his house, he was confident, would afford them a comfortable asylum, where Lady Malvina would experience all that tenderness and care her situation demanded.

He immediately set about procuring a conveyance, and the following morning Malvina bid a last adieu to Scotland.

Lady Dunreath, in the mean time, suffered torture: after she had seen Malvina turned from the Abbey, she returned to her apartment: it was furnished with the most luxurious elegance, yet could she not rest within it. Conscience already told her, if Malvina died, she must consider herself her murderer; her pale and woe-worn image seemed still before her; a cold terror oppressed her heart, which the horrors of the night augmented; the tempest shook the battlements of the Abbey; and the winds, which howled through the galleries, seemed like the last moans of some wandering spirit of the pile, bewailing the fate of one of its fairest daughters. To cruelty and ingratitude Lady Dunreath had added deceit: her lord was yielding to the solicitations of his child, when she counteracted his intentions by a tale of falsehood. The visions of the night were also dreadful; Malvina appeared expiring before her, and the late Lady Dunreath, by her bedside, reproaching her barbarity. "Oh cruel!" the ghastly figure seemed to say, "is it you, whom I fostered in my bosom, that have done this deed—driven forth my child, a forlorn and wretched wanderer?"

Oh, conscience, how awful are thy terrors! thou art the vicegerent of Heaven, and dost anticipate its vengeance, ere the final

3

hour of retribution arrives. Guilt may be triumphant, but never, never can be happy: it finds no shield against thy stings and arrows. The heart thou smitest bleeds in every pore, and sighs amidst gaiety and splendor.

The unfortunate travellers were welcomed with the truest hospitality by the grateful Edwin; he had married, soon after his return from America, a young girl, to whom, from his earliest youth, he was attached. His parents died soon after his union, and the whole of their little patrimony devolved to him. Soothed and attended with the utmost tenderness and respect, Fitzalan hoped Lady Malvina would here regain her health and peace: he intended, after her recovery, to endeavor to be put on full pay; and trusted he should prevail on her to continue at the farm.

At length the hour came, in which she gave a daughter to his arms. From the beginning of her illness the people about her were alarmed; too soon was it proved their alarms were well founded: she lived after the birth of her infant but a few minutes, and died embracing her husband, and blessing his children.

Fitzalan's feelings cannot well be described: they were at first too much for reason, and he continued some time in perfect stupefaction. When he regained his sensibility, his grief was not outrageous; it was that deep, still sorrow, which fastens on the heart, and cannot vent itself in tears or lamentations: he sat with calmness by the bed, where the beautiful remains of Malvina lay; he gazed without shrinking on her pale face, which death, as if in pity to his feelings, had not disfigured; he kissed her cold lips, continually exclaiming, "Oh! had we never met, she might still have been living." His language was something like that of a poet of her own country:—

"Wee, modest crimson-tippèd flower,
I met thee in a luckless hour."

It was when he saw them about removing her that all the tempest of his grief broke forth. Oh! how impossible to describe the anguish of the poor widower's heart, when he returned from seeing his Malvina laid in her last receptacle: he shut himself up in the room where she had expired, and ordered no one to approach him; he threw himself upon the bed; he laid his cheek upon her pillow, he grasped it to his bosom, he wetted it with tears, because she had breathed upon it. Oh, how still, how dreary, how desolate, did all appear around him! "And shall this desolation never more be enlightened," he exclaimed, "by the soft music of Malvina's voice? Shall these eyes never more be cheered by beholding her angelic face?" Exhausted by his feelings, he sunk into a slumber: he dreamt of Malvina, and thought she lay beside him: he awoke with sudden ecstasy, and, under the strong impression of the dream, stretched out his arms to enfold her. Alas! all was empty void: he started up—he groaned in the bitterness of his soul—he traversed the room with a distracted pace—he sat him down in the little window, from whence he could view the spire of the church (now glistening in the moonbeams) by which she was interred. "Deep, still, and profound," cried he, "is now the sleep of my Malvina—the voice of love cannot awake her from it; nor does she now dream of her midnight mourner."

The cold breeze of night blew upon his forehead, but he heeded it not; his whole soul was full of Malvina, whom torturing fancy presented to his view, in the habiliments of the grave. "And is this emaciated form, this pale face," he exclaimed, as if he had really seen her, "all that remain of elegance and beauty, once unequalled!"

A native sense of religion alone checked the transports of his grief; that sweet, that sacred power, which pours balm upon the wounds of sorrow, and saves its children from despair; that power whispered to his heart, a patient submission to the will of heaven was the surest means he could attain of again rejoining his Malvina.

She was interred in the village church-yard: at the head of her grave a stone was placed, on which was rudely cut,

MALVINA FITZALAN,

ALIKE LOVELY AND UNFORTUNATE.

Fitzalan would not permit her empty title to be on it: "she is buried," he said, "as the wife of a wretched soldier, not as the daughter of a wealthy peer."

She had requested her infant might be called after her own mother; her request was sacred to Fitzalan, and it was baptized by the united names of Amanda Malvina. Mrs. Edwin was then nursing her first girl; but she sent it out, and took the infant of Fitzalan in its place to her bosom.

The money, which Fitzalan had procured by disposing of his commission, was now nearly exhausted; but his mind was too enervated to allow him to think of any project for future support. Lady Malvina was deceased two months, when a nobleman came into the neighborhood, with whom Fitzalan had once been intimately acquainted: the acquaintance was now renewed; and Fitzalan's appearance, with the little history of his misfortunes, so much affected and interested his friend, that, without solicitation, he procured him a company in a regiment, then stationed in England. Thus did Fitzalan again enter into active life; but his spirits were broken, and his constitution injured. Four years he continued in the army; when, pining to have his children (all that now remained of a woman he adored), under his own care, he obtained through the interest of his friend, leave to sell out. Oscar was then eight, and Amanda four; the delighted father, as he held them to his heart, wept over them tears of mingled pain and pleasure.

He had seen in Devonshire, where he was quartered for some time, a little romantic solitude, quite adapted to his taste and finances; he proposed for it, and soon became its proprietor. Hither he carried his children, much against the inclinations of the Edwins, who loved them as their own: two excellent schools in the neighborhood gave them the usual advantages of genteel education; but as they were only day scholars, the improvement, or rather forming of their morals, was the pleasing task of their father. To his assiduous care too they were indebted for the rapid progress they made in their studies, and for the graceful simplicity of their manners: they rewarded his care, and grew up as amiable and lovely as his fondest wishes could desire. As Oscar advanced in life, his father began to experience new cares; for he had not the power of putting him in the way of making any provision for himself. A military life was what Oscar appeared anxious for: he had early conceived a predilection for it, from hearing his father speak of the services he had seen; but though he possessed quite the spirit of a hero, he had the truest tenderness, the most engaging softness of disposition; his temper was, indeed, at once mild, artless, and affectionate. He was about eighteen, when the proprietor of the estate, on which his father held his farm, died, and his heir, a colonel in the army, immediately came down from London to take formal possession: he soon became acquainted with Fitzalan, who, in the course of conversation, one day expressed the anxiety he suffered on his son's account. The Colonel said he was a fine youth, and it was a pity he was not provided for. He left Devonshire, however, shortly after this, without appearing in the least interested about him.

Fitzalan's heart was oppressed with anxiety; he could not purchase for his son, without depriving himself of support. With the nobleman who had formerly served him so essentially, he had kept up no intercourse, since he quitted the army; but he frequently heard of him, and was told he had become quite a man of the world, which was an implication of his having lost all feeling: an application to him, therefore, he feared, would be unavailing, and he felt too proud to subject himself to a repulse.

From this disquietude he was unexpectedly relieved by a letter from the Earl of Cherbury, his yet kind friend, informing him he had procured an ensigncy for Oscar, in Colonel Belgrave's regiment, which he considered a very fortunate circumstance, as the colonel, he was confident, from personally knowing the young gentleman, would render him every service in his power. The Earl chided Fitzalan for never having kept up a correspondence with him, assured him he had never forgotten the friendship of their earlier years; and that he had gladly seized the first opportunity which offered, of serving him in the person of his son; which opportunity he was indebted to Colonel Belgrave for.

Fitzalan's soul was filled with gratitude and rapture; he immediately wrote to the Earl, and the Colonel, in terms expressive of his feelings. Colonel Belgrave received his thanks as if he had really deserved them; but this was not by any means the case: he was a man devoid of sensibility, and had never once thought of serving Fitzalan or his son; his mentioning them was merely accidental.

In a large company, of which the Earl of Cherbury was one, the discourse happened to turn on the Dunreath family, and by degrees led to Fitzalan, who was severally blamed and pitied for his connection with it; the subject was, in the opinion of Colonel Belgrave, so apropos, he could not forbear describing his present situation, and inquietude about his son, who, he said he fancied, must, like a second Cincinnatus, take the ploughshare instead of the sword.

Lord Cherbury lost no part of his discourse; though immersed in politics, and other intricate concerns, he yet retained, and was ready to obey, the dictates of humanity, particularly when they did not interfere with his own interests; he therefore directly conceived the design of serving his old friend.

Oscar soon quitted Devonshire after his appointment, and brought a letter from his father to the Colonel, in which he was strongly recommended to his protection, as one unskilled in the ways of men.

And now all Fitzalan's care devolved upon Amanda; and most amply did she recompense it. To the improvement of her genius, the cultivation of her talents, the promotion of her father's happiness, seemed her first incentive; without him no amusement was enjoyed, without him no study entered upon; he was her friend, guardian, and protector; and no language can express, no heart (except a paternal one), conceive the rapture he felt, at seeing a creature grow under

> his forming hand
> ———— So fair
> That what seemed fair in all the world, seemed now
> Mean, or in her contained.

Some years had elapsed since Oscar's departure, ere Colonel Belgrave returned into their neighborhood; he came soon after his nuptials had been celebrated in Ireland, with a lady of that country, whom Oscar's letters described as possessing every mental and personal charm which could please or captivate the heart. Colonel Belgrave came unaccompanied by his fair bride. Fitzalan, who believed him his benefactor, and consequently regarded him as a friend (still thinking it was through his means Lord Cherbury had served him), immediately waited upon him, and invited him to his house. The invitation, after some time, was accepted; but had he imagined what an attraction the house contained, he would not have long hesitated about entering it: he was a man, indeed, of the most depraved principles; and an object he admired, no tie or situation, however sacred, could guard from his pursuit

Amanda was too much a child, when he was last in the country, to attract his observation; he had, therefore, no idea that the blossom he then so carelessly overlooked, had since expanded into such beauty. How great, then, was his rapture and surprise, when Fitzalan led into the room where he had received him, a tall, elegantly-formed girl, whose rosy cheeks were dimpled with the softest smile of complacence, and whose fine blue eyes beamed with modesty and gratitude upon him! He instantly marked her for his prey; and blessed his lucky stars which had inspired Fitzalan with the idea of his being his benefactor, since that would give him an easier access to the house than he could otherwise have hoped for.

From this time he became almost an inmate of it, except when he chose to contrive little parties at his own for Amanda. He took every opportunity that offered, without observation, to try to ingratiate himself in her favor: those opportunities the unsuspecting temper of Fitzalan allowed to be frequent—he would as soon have trusted Amanda to the care of Belgrave, as to that of her brother; and never, therefore, prevented her walking out with him, when he desired it, or receiving him in the morning, while he himself was absent about the affairs of his farm—delighted to think the conversation or talents of his daughter (for Amanda frequently sung and played for the Colonel) could contribute to the amusement of his friend. Amanda innocently increased his flame, by the attention she paid, which she considered but a just tribute of gratitude for his services: she delighted in talking to him of her dear Oscar, and often mentioned his lady; but was surprised to find he always waived the latter subject.

Belgrave could not long restrain the impetuosity of his passions: the situation of Fitzalan (which he knew to be a distressed one) would, he fancied, forward his designs on his daughter; and what those designs were, he, by degrees, in a retired walk one day, unfolded to Amanda. At first she did not perfectly understand him; but when, with increased audacity, he explained himself more fully, horror, indignation, and surprise took possession of her breast; and, yielding to their feelings, she turned and fled to the house, as if from a monster. Belgrave was provoked and mortified; the softness of her manners had tempted him to believe he was not indifferent to her, and that she would prove an easy conquest.

Poor Amanda would not appear in the presence of her father, till she had, in some degree, regained composure, as she feared the smallest intimation of the affair might occasion fatal consequences. As she sat with him, a letter was brought her; she could not think Belgrave would have the effrontery to write, and opened it, supposing it came from some acquaintance in the neighborhood How great was the shock she sustained, on finding it from him! Having thrown off the mask, he determined no longer to assume any disguise. Her paleness and confusion alarmed her father, and he instantly demanded the cause of her agitation. She found longer concealment was impossible; and, throwing herself at her father's feet, besought him, as she put the letter into his hands, to restrain his passion. When he perused it, he raised her up, and commanded her, as she valued his love or happiness, to inform him of every particular relative to the insult she had received. She obeyed, though terrified to behold her father trembling with emotion. When she concluded, he tenderly embraced her; and, bidding her confine herself to the house, rose, and took down his hat. It was easy to guess whither he was going; her terror increased; and, in a voice scarcely articulate, she besought him not to risk his safety. He commanded her silence, with a sternness never before assumed. His manner awed her; but, wher she saw him leaving the room, her feelings could no longer be controlled—she rushed after him, and flinging her arms round his neck, fainted on it. In this situation the unhappy father was compelled to leave her to the care of a maid, lest her pathetic remonstrances should delay the vengeance he resolved to take on a wretch who had meditated a deed of such atrocity against his peace; but Belgrave was not to be found.

Scarcely, however, had Fitzalan returned to his half-distracted daughter ere a letter was brought him from the wretch, in which he made the most degrading proposals; and bade Fitzalan beware how he answered them, as his situation had put him entirely into his power. This was a fatal truth: Fitzalan had been tempted to make a large addition to his farm, from an idea of turning the little money he possessed to advantage: but he was more ignorant of agriculture than he had imagined; and this ignorance, joined to his own integrity of heart, rendered him the dupe of some designing wretches in his neighborhood: his whole stock dwindled away in unprofitable experiments, and he was now considerably in arrears with Belgrave. The ungenerous advantage he strove to take of his situation, increased, if possible, his indignation; and again he sought him, but still without success.

Belgrave soon found no temptation of prosperity would prevail on the father or daughter to accede to his wishes; he therefore resolved to try whether the pressure of adversity would render them more complying, and left the country, having first ordered his steward to proceed directly against Fitzalan.

The consequence of this order was an immediate execution on his effects; and, but for the assistance of a good-natured farmer, he would have been arrested. By his means, and under favor of night, he and Amanda set out for London; they arrived there in safety, and retired to obscure lodgings. In this hour of distress, Fitzalan conquered all false pride, and wrote to Lord Cherbury, entreating him to procure some employment which would relieve his present distressing situation. He cautiously concealed everything relative to Belgrave—he could not bear that it should be known that he had ever been degraded by his infamous proposals. Oscar's safety, too, he knew depended on his secrecy; as he was well convinced no idea of danger, or elevation of rank, would secure the wretch from his fury, who had meditated so great an injury against his sister.

He had the mortification of having the letter he sent to Lord Cherbury returned, as his lordship was then absent from town; nor was he expected for some months, having gone on an excursion of pleasure to France. Some of these months had lingered away in all the horrors of anxiety and distress, when Fitzalan formed the resolution of sending Amanda into Wales, whose health had considerably suffered, from the complicated uneasiness and terror she experienced on her own and her father's account.

Belgrave had traced the fugitives; and though Fitzalan was guarded against all the stratagems he used to have him arrested.

he found means to have letters conveyed to Amanda, full of base solicitations and insolent declarations, that the rigor he treated her father with was quite against his feelings, and should instantly be withdrawn, if he acceded to the proposals he made for her.

But though Fitzalan had determined to send Amanda into Wales, with whom could he trust his heart's best treasure? At last the son of the worthy farmer who had assisted him in his journey to London, occurred to his remembrance; he came often to town, and always called on Fitzalan. The young man, the moment it was proposed, expressed the greatest readiness to attend Miss Fitzalan. As every precaution was necessary, her father made her take the name of Dunford, and travel in the mail-coach, for the greater security. He divided the contents of his purse with her; and recommending this lovely and most beloved child to the protection of heaven, saw her depart, with mingled pain and pleasure; promising to give her the earliest intelligence of Lord Cherbury's arrival in town, which, he supposed, would fix his future destiny. Previous to her departure, he wrote to the Edwins, informing them of her intended visit, and also her change of name for the present. This latter circumstance, which was not satisfactorily accounted for, excited their warmest curiosity; and not thinking it proper to ask Amanda to gratify it, they, to use their own words, sifted her companion, who hesitated not to inform them of the indignities she had suffered from Colonel Belgrave, which were well known about his neighborhood.

CHAPTER III.

"——Thy grave shall with fresh flowers be dressed,
And the green turf lie lightly on thy breast;
There shall the morn her earliest tears bestow,
There the first roses of the year shall blow."—POPE.

GENTLE noise in her chamber roused Amanda from a light, refreshing slumber, and she beheld her nurse standing by her bed-side with a bowl of goat's whey. Amanda took the salubrious draught with a smile, and instantly starting up, was dressed in a few minutes. She felt more composed than she had done for some time past; the transition from a narrow, dark street to a fine open country, would have excited a lively transport in her mind, but for the idea of her father still remaining in the gloomy situation she had quitted.

On going out, she found the family all busily employed; Edwin and his sons were mowing in a meadow near the house, the nurse was churning, Ellen washing the milk-pails by the stream in the valley, and Betsey turning a cake for her breakfast. The tea-table was laid by a window, through which a woodbine crept, diffusing a delightful fragrance; the bees feasted on its sweetness, and the gaudy butterflies fluttered around it; the refulgent sun gladdened the face of nature; the morning breeze tempered its heat, and bore upon its dewy wings the sweets of opening flowers; birds carolled their matins almost on every spray; and scattered peasants, busied in their various labors, enlivened the extensive prospect.

Amanda was delighted with all she saw, and wrote to her father that his presence was only wanting to complete her pleasure. The young man who had attended her, on receiving her letter, set out for the village, from whence he was to return in a stage-coach to London.

The morning was passed by Amanda in arranging her little affairs, walking about the cottage, and conversing with the nurse relative to past times and present avocations. When the hour for dinner came, by her desire it was carried out into the recess in the garden, where the balmy air, the lovely scene which surrounded her, rendered it doubly delicious.

In the evening she asked Ellen to take a walk with her, to which she joyfully consented. "And pray, Miss," said Ellen, after she had smartened herself up with a clean white apron, her Sunday cap, and a hat loaded with poppy-colored ribbons, smiling as she spoke, at the pretty image her glass reflected, "where shall we go?" "To the church-yard," replied Amanda. "Oh, Lord, Miss!" "won't that be rather a dismal place to go to?" "Indulge me, my dear Ellen," said Amanda, "in showing me the way thither; there is one spot in it my heart wants to visit."

The church-yard lay at the entrance of the little village; the church was a small structure, whose gothic appearance proclaimed its ancient date; it was rendered more venerable by the lofty elms and yews which surrounded it, apparently coeval with itself, and which cast dark shades upon the spots where the "rude forefathers of the hamlet slept," which,

> "With uncouth rhymes and shapeless sculpture decked,
> Implored the passing tribute of a sigh."

And it was a tribute Amanda paid, as she proceeded to the grave of Lady Malvina, which Ellen pointed out; it was overgrown with grass, and the flag, which bore her name, green, from time and damp. Amanda involuntarily sunk on her knees, and kissed the hallowed earth; her eyes caught the melancholy inscription. "Sweet spirit," she said, "heaven now rewards your sufferings. Oh, my mother! if departed spirits are ever allowed to review this world, with love ineffable you may now be regarding your child. Oh, if she is doomed to tread a path as thorny as the one you trod, may the same sweetness and patience that distinguished you, support her through it! with the same pious awe, the same meek submission, may she bow to the designations of her Creator!"

The affecting apostrophe drew tears from the tender-hearted Ellen, who besought her not to continue longer in such a dismal place. Amanda now arose weeping--her spirits were entirely overcome; the busy objects of day had amused her mind, and prevented it from meditating on its sorrows; but, in the calm solitude of the evening, they gradually revived in her remembrance Her father's ill-health, she feared, would increase for want of her tender attentions; and when she thought of his distress, his confinement, his dejection, she felt agony at their separation.

Her melancholy was noticed at the cottage. Ellen informed the nurse of the dismal walk they had taken, which at once accounted for it; and the good woman exerted herself to enliven her dear child, but Amanda, though she faintly smiled, was not to be cheered, and soon retired to bed—pale, languid, and unhappy.

Returning light, in some degree, dispelled her melancholy; she felt, however, for the first time, that her hours would hang heavy on her hands, deprived as she was of those delightful resources which had hitherto diversified them. To pass her time in listless inaction, or idle saunters about the house, was insupportable; and besides, she found her presence in the morning was a restraint on her humble friends, who did not deem it good manners to work before her; and to them, who, like the bees, were obliged to lay up their wintry hoard in summer, the loss of time was irreparable.

In the distraction of her father's affairs, she had lost her books, implements for drawing, and musical instruments; and in the cottage she could only find a bible, a family prayer-book, and a torn volume of old ballads.

"Tear heart, now I think on't," said the nurse, "you may go to the library at Tudor Hall, where there are books enough to keep you a-going, if you lived to the age of Methusalem himself; and very pretty reading to be sure amongst them, or our Parson Howel would not have been going there as often as he did to study, till he got a library of his own. The family are all away; and as the door is open every fine day to air the room, you will not be noticed by nopoty going into it; though, for that matter, poor old Mrs. Abergwilly would make you welcome enough, if you promised to take none of the books away with you. But as I know you to be a little bashful or so, I will, if you choose, step over and ask her leave for you to go." "If you please," said Amanda; "I should not like to go without it." "Well, I shan't be long," continued the nurse, "and Ellen shall show you the way to-day; it will be a pretty pit of a walk for you to take every morning."

The nurse was as good as her word; she returned soon, with Mrs. Abergwilly's permission for Amanda to read in the library whenever she pleased. In consequence of this, she immediately proceeded to the Hall, whose white turrets were seen from the cottage: it was a large and antique building, embosomed in a grove; the library was on the ground-floor, and entered by a spacious folding-door. As soon as she had reached it, Ellen left her, and returned to the cottage; and Amanda began with pleasure to examine the apartment, whose elegance and simplicity struck her with immediate admiration.

On one side was a row of large windows, arched quite in the gothic style; opposite to them were corresponding arches, in whose recesses the bookcases were placed; round these arches were festoons of laurel, elegantly executed in stucco-work; and above them medallions of some of the most celebrated poets: the chimney-piece.

of the finest Italian marble, was beautifully inlaid and ornamented; the paintings on the ceiling were all highly finished, and of the allegorical kind; and it was difficult to determine whether the taste that designed, or the hand that executed them, merited most praise: upon marble pedestals stood a celestial and terrestrial globe, and one recess was entirely hung with maps. It was a room, from its situation and appearance, peculiarly adapted for study and contemplation; all around was solitude and silence, save the rustling of the trees, whose dark foliage cast a solemn shade upon the windows.

Opposite the entrance was another folding-door, which being a little opened, Amanda could not resist the desire she felt of seeing what was beyond it. She entered a large vaulted apartment, whose airy lightness formed a pleasing contrast to the gloomy one she had left. The manner in which it was fitted up, and the musical instruments, declared this to be a music-room. It was hung with pale green damask, spotted with silver, and bordered with festoons of roses, intermingled with light silver sprays; the seats corresponded to the hangings; the tables were of fine inlaid wood; and superb lustres were suspended from the ceiling, which represented, in a masterly style, scenes from some of the pastoral poets; the orchestra, about the centre of the room, was enclosed with a light balustrading of white marble, elevated by a few steps.

The windows of this room commanded a pleasing prospect of a deep romantic dale; the hills through which it wound, displaying a beautiful diversity of woody scenery, interspersed with green pastures and barren points of rocks: a fine fall of water fell from one of the highest of the hills, which, broken by intervening roots and branches of trees, ran a hundred different ways, sparkling in the sunbeams as they emerged from the shade.

Amanda stood long at a window, enjoying this delightful prospect, and admiring the taste which had chosen this room for amusement; thus at once gratifying the eye and ear. On looking over the instruments, she saw a pianoforte unlocked; she gently raised the lid, and touching the keys, found them in tolerable order. Amanda adored music; her genius for it was great, and had received every advantage her father could possibly give it: in cultivating it he had laid up a fund of delight for himself, for "his soul was a stream that flowed at pleasant sounds."

Amanda could not resist the present opportunity of gratifying her favorite inclination. "Harmony and I," cried she, "have long been strangers to each other." She sat down, and played a little tender air: those her father loved, recurred to her recollection, and she played a few of them with even more than usual elegance. "Ah dear and valued object," she mournfully sighed, "why are you not here to share my pleasure?" She wiped away a starting tear of tender remembrance, and began a simple air

Ah gentle Hope, shall I no more
  Thy cheerful influence share?
Oh must I still thy loss deplore,
  And be the slave of care?

The gloom which now obscures my days
  At thy approach would fly,
And glowing fancy would display
  A bright unclouded sky.

Night's dreary shadows fleet away
  Before the orient beam;
So sorrow melts before thy sway,
  Thou nymph of cheerful mien.

Ah! seek again my lonely breast,
  Dislodge each painful fear;
Be once again my heavenly guest,
  And stay each falling tear.

Amanda saw a number of music-books lying about; she examined a few, and found they contained compositions of some of the most eminent masters. They tempted her to continue a little longer at the instrument: when she rose from it, she returned to the library, and began looking over the books, which she found were a collection of the best that past or present times had produced. She soon selected one for perusal, and seated herself in the recess of a window, that she might enjoy the cool breeze, which sighed amongst the trees. Here, delighted with her employment, she forgot the progress of time; nor thought of moving, till Ellen appeared with a request from the nurse, for her immediate return, as her dinner was ready, and she was uneasy at her fasting so long. Amanda did not hesitate to comply with the request; but she resolved henceforth to be a constant visitor to the hall, which contained such pleasing sources of amusement: she also settled in her own mind often to ramble amidst its shades, which were perfectly adapted to her taste. These resolutions she put in practice; and a week passed in this manner, during which she heard from her father, who informed her, that, suspecting the woman with whom he lodged to be in Colonel Belgrave's interest, he proposed changing his abode; he desired her therefore not to write till she heard from him again, and added, "Lord Cherbury was daily expected."

CHAPTER IV.

"Mine eyes were half closed in sleep. Soft music came to mine ear; it was like the rising breeze, that whirls at first, the thistle's beard, that flies, dark shadowy over the grass."—OSSIAN.

MANDA went every morning to the hall, where she alternately played and read: in the evening she again returned to it; but instead of staying in the library, generally took a book from thence, and read at the foot of some old moss-covered tree, delighted to hear its branches gently rustling over her head, and myriads of summer flies buzzing in the sunny ray, from which she was sheltered. When she could no longer see to read, she deposited her book in the place she had taken it from, and rambled to the deepest recesses of the grove: this was the time she loved to saunter carelessly along, while all the jarring passions that obtruding care excited were hushed to peace by the solemnity and silence of the hour, and the soul felt at once composed and elevated: this was the time she loved to think on days departed, and sketch those scenes of felicity which, she trusted, the days to come would realize. Sometimes she gave way to all the enthusiasm of a young and romantic fancy, and pictured to herself the time when the shades she wandered beneath were

——— the haunts of meditation,
The scenes, where ancient bards the inspiring breath
Ecstatic felt, and, from this world retired,
Conversed with angels, and immortal forms,
On gracious errands bent; to save the fall
Of Virtue struggling on the brink of Vice.—THOMSON.

Her health gradually grew better, as the tranquillity of her mind increased: a faint blush again began to tinge her cheek, and her lovely eyes beamed a placid lustre, through their long silken lashes.

She returned one evening from her usual ramble, with one of those unaccountable depressions on her spirits to which, in a greater or lesser degree, almost every one is subject. When she retired to bed, her sleeping thoughts took the tincture of her waking ones, and images of the most affecting nature arose in her mind: she went through the whole story of her mother's sufferings, and suddenly dreamt she beheld her expiring under the greatest torture; and that while she wept her fate the clouds opened, and discovered her adorned with seraphic beauty, bending with a benignant look towards her child, as if to assure her of her present happiness. From this dream Amanda was roused by the softest, sweetest strains of music she had ever heard: she started with amazement; she opened her eyes, and saw a light around her, far exceeding that of twilight. Her dream had made a deep impression on her, and a solemn awe diffused itself over her mind; she trembled universally; but soon did the emotion of awe give way to that of surprise, when she heard on the outside of the window the following lines from Cowley, sung in a manly and exquisitely melodious voice, the music which awoke her being only a symphony to them:—

Awake, awake, my lyre,
And tell thy silent master's humble tale
In sounds that may prevail;
Sounds that gentle thoughts inspire.
Though so exalted she,
And I so lowly be,
Tell her such different notes make all thy harmony.

Hark, how the strings awake,
And though the moving hand approach not near
Themselves with awful fear,
A kind of numerous trembling make.
Now all thy forces try,
Now all thy charms apply,
Revenge upon her ear the conquest of her eye.

Weak lyre, thy virtue sure
Is useless here, since thou art only found
To cure, but not to wound,
And she to wound, but not to cure.

4 *

Too weak, too, wilt thou prove
My passion to remove,
Physic to other ills, thou'rt nourishment to love.

Sleep, sleep again, my lyre,
For thou canst never tell my humble tale,
In sounds that will prevail,
Nor gentle thoughts in her inspire.
All thy vain mirth lay by,
Bid thy strings silent lie,
Sleep, sleep again, my lyre, and let thy master die.

Ere the voice ceased, Amanda had quite shaken off the effects of her dream; and when all again was silent, she drew back the curtain, and saw it was the moon, then at the full, which, beaming through the calico window-curtains, cast such a light around her. The remainder of the night was passed in ruminating on this strange incident: it was evident the serenade was addressed to her; but she had not seen any one since her arrival in the neighborhood from whom she could have expected such a compliment, or, indeed, believed capable of paying it; that the person who paid it was one of no mean accomplishments, from his performance, she could not doubt. She resolved to conceal the incident, but to make such inquiries the next morning as might possibly lead to a discovery. From the answers those inquiries received, the clergyman was the only person whom, with any degree of probability, she could fix on. She had never seen him, and was at a loss to conceive how he knew anything of her, till it occurred he might have seen her going to Tudor Hall, or rambling about it.

From the moment this idea arose, Amanda deemed it imprudent to go to the hall; yet, so great was the pleasure she experienced there, she could not think of relinquishing it without the greatest reluctance. She at last considered, if she had a companion, it would remove any appearance of impropriety. Ellen was generally employed at knitting; Amanda therefore saw, that going to the hall could not interfere with her employment, and accordingly asked her attendance thither, which the other joyfully agreed to.

"While you look over the books," said Ellen, as they entered the library, "I will just step away about a little business." "I beg you may not be long absent," cried Amanda. Ellen assured her she would not, and flew off directly. She had in truth seen, in an enclosure near the hall, Tim Chip, the carpenter, at work, who was the rural Adonis of these shades. He had long selected Ellen for the fair nymph of his affection, which distinction excited not a little jealousy among the village girls, and considerably increased the vanity of Ellen, who triumphed in a conquest that at once gratified her love, and exalted her above her companions.

Amanda entered the music-room. The melodious strains she had heard the preceding night dwelt upon her memory, and she sat down to the piano and attempted them; her ear soon informed her the attempt was successful; and her voice (as the words were familiar to her) then accompanied the instrument— "Heavenly sounds!" exclaimed some one behind her, as she concluded singing. Amanda started in terror and confusion from the chair, and beheld a tall and elegant young man standing by it. "Good heaven!" cried she, blushing and hastily moving to the door, scarcely knowing what she said, "where can Ellen be?" "And do you think," said the stranger, springing forward and intercepting her passage, "I shall let you escape in this manner? No; really, my charming girl, I should be the most insensible of beings if I did not avail myself of the happy opportunity chance afforded of entreating leave to be introduced to you." As he spoke, he gently seized her hand and carried it to his lips. "Be assured, sir," said Amanda, "the chance, as you call it, which brought us together, is to me most unpleasant, as I fear it has exposed me to greater freedom than I have been accustomed to." "And is it possible," said he, "you really feel an emotion of anger? Well, I will relinquish my lovely captive if she condescendingly promises to continue here a few minutes longer, and grants me permission to attend her home." "I insist on being immediately released," exclaimed Amanda. "I obey," cried he, softly pressing her hand, and then resigning it—"you are free; would to Heaven I could say the same!"

Amanda hurried to the grove, but in her confusion took the wrong path, and vainly cast her eyes around in search of Ellen. The stranger followed, and his eyes wandered with hers in every direction they took. "And why," cried he, "so unpropitious to my wish of introduction?—a wish it was impossible not to feel from the moment you were seen." Amanda made no reply, but still hurried on, and her fatigue and agitation were soon too much for her present weak state of health, and, quite overpowered, she was at last compelled to stop, and lean against a tree for support. Exercise had diffused its softest bloom over her cheek; her hair fluttered in the breeze that played around her, and her eyes, with the beautiful embarrassment of modesty, were bent to the ground to avoid the stranger's ardent gaze. He watched her with looks of the most impassioned admiration, and softly exclaimed, as if the involuntary exclamation of rapture, "Good heavens, what an angel! Fatigue has made you ill," he said; "and 'tis your haste to avoid me has occasioned this disorder. Could you look into my heart, you would then find there was no reason to fly me; the emotions that lovely face excites in a soul of sensibility could never be inimical to your safety."

At this moment Amanda perceived Ellen leaping over a style, she had at last left Mr. Chip, after promising to meet him in the evening at the cottage, where the blind harper was to attend to give them a dance. She ran forward, but, on seeing the stranger, started back in the utmost amazement. "Bless me!" said Amanda, "I thought you would never come." "You go, then," said the stranger, "and give me no hope of a second interview. Oh say," taking her hand, "will you not allow me to wait upon you?" "It is utterly impossible," replied Amanda, "and I shall be quite distressed if longer detained." "See, then," said he, opening a gate which led from the grove into the road, "how like a courteous knight I release you from painful captivity. But think not, thou beautiful though cruel fair one," he continued gaily, "I shall resign my hopes of yet conquering thy obduracy."

"Oh, Lord!" cried Ellen, as they quitted the grove, "how did you meet with Lord Mortimer?" "Lord Mortimer?" repeated Amanda, 'Yes, himself, inteed," said Ellen; "and I think in all my porn days I was never more surprised than when I saw him with you, looking so soft and so sweet upon you; to be sure he is a beautiful man, and besides that, the young Lort of Tudor Hall." Amanda's spirits were greatly flurried when she heard he was the master of the mansion, where he had found her seated with as much composure as if possessor of it.

As they were entering the cottage, Ellen, twitching Amanda's sleeve, cried, "Look! look!" Amanda, hastily turning round, perceived Lord Mortimer, who had slowly followed them half way down the lane. On being observed, he smiled, and kissing his hand, retired.

Nurse was quite delighted at her child being seen by Lord Mortimer (which Ellen informed her of): her beauty, she was convinced, had excited his warmest admiration; and admiration might lead (she did not doubt) to something more important. Amanda's heart fluttered with an agreeable sensation, as Ellen described to her mother the tender looks with which Lord Mortimer regarded her. She was at first inclined to believe, that in his lordship she had found the person whose melody so agreeably disturbed her slumbers; but a minute's reflection convinced her this belief must be erroneous: it was evident (or she would have heard of it) that Lord Mortimer had only arrived that day at Tudor-Hall: and even had he seen her before, upon consideration she thought it improbable that he should have taken the trouble of coming in such a manner to a person in a station, to all appearance, so infinitely beneath his own. Yes, it was plain, chance alone had led him to the apartment where she sat; and the common-place gallantry fashionable men are accustomed to, had dictated the language he addressed to her. She half sighed, as she settled the matter thus in her mind, and again fixed on the curate as her serenader. Well, she was determined, if ever he came in her way, and dropped a hint of an attachment, she would immediately crush any hopes he might have the vanity to entertain!

CHAPTER V.

> "The blossoms opening to the day,
> The dews of heaven refined,
> Could nought of purity display
> To emulate his mind."—GOLDSMITH.

FTER tea Amanda asked little Betsey to accompany her in a walk; for Ellen (dressed in all her rural finery) had gone earlier in the evening to the dance. But Amanda did not begin her walk with her usual alacrity: her bonnet was so heavy, and then it made her look so ill, that she could not go out till she had made some alterations in it; still it would not do; a hat was tried on; she liked it better, and at last set out; but not as usual did she pause, whenever a new or lovely feature in the landscape struck her view, to express her admiration: she was often indeed so absorbed in thought, as to start when Betsey addressed her, which was often the case: for little Betsey delighted to have Miss Amanda to trace figures for her in the clouds, and assist her in gathering wild flowers. Scarcely knowing which way they went, Amanda rambled to the village; and feeling herself fatigued, turned into the churchyard to rest upon one of the raised flags.

The graves were ornamented with garlands of cut paper, inter woven with flowers: tributes of love from the village maids to the memory of their departed friends.

As Amanda rested herself, she twined a garland of the wild flowers she had gathered with Betsey, and hung it over the grave of Lady Malvina: her fine eyes raised to heaven, as if invoking at that moment the spirit of her mother, to regard the vernal offering of her child; while her white hands were folded on her heart, and she softly exclaimed, "Alas, is this the only tribute for me to pay!"

A low murmur, as if from voices near, startled her at the instant; she turned with quickness, and saw Lord Mortimer, with a young clergyman, half hid by some trees, attentively observing her. Blushing and confused, she drew her hat over her face, and catching Betsey's hand, hastened to the cottage.

Lord Mortimer had wandered about the skirts of the cottage, in hopes of meeting her in the evening; on seeing the direction she had taken from it, he followed her: and just as she entered the churchyard, unexpectedly met the curate. His company, at a moment so propitious for joining Amanda, he could well have dispensed with; for he was more anxious than he chose to acknowledge to himself, to become acquainted with her.

Lord Mortimer was now in the glowing prime of life: his person was strikingly elegant, and his manners insinuatingly pleasing; seducing sweetness dwelt in his smile, and, as he pleased, his expressive eyes could sparkle with intelligence, or beam with sensibility; and to the eloquence of his language, the harmony of his voice imparted a charm that seldom failed of being irresistible; his soul was naturally the seat of every virtue; but an elevated rank, and splendid fortune, had placed him in a situation somewhat inimical to their interests, for he had not always strength to resist the strong temptations which surrounded him; but though he sometimes wandered from the boundaries of virtue, he had never yet entered upon the confines of vice—never really injured innocence, or done a deed which could wound the bosom of a friend: his heart was alive to every noble propensity of nature; compassion was one of its strongest feelings, and never did his hand refuse obedience to the generous impulse. Among the various accomplishments he possessed, was an exquisite taste for music, which, with every other talent, had been cultivated to the highest degree of possible perfection; his spending many years abroad had given him every requisite advantage for improving it. The soft, melodious voice of Amanda would of itself almost have made a conquest of his heart; but aided by the charms of her face and person, altogether were irresistible.

He had come into Wales on purpose to pay a visit to an old friend in the Isle of Anglesey: he did not mean to stop at Tudor Hall; but within a few miles of it the phaeton, in which he travelled (from the fineness of the weather), was overturned, and he severely hurt. He procured a hired carriage, and proceeded to the hall, to put himself into the hands of the good old housekeeper, Mrs. Abergwilly; who, possessing as great a stock of medical knowledge as Lady Bountiful herself, he believed would cure his bruises with as much, or rather more expedition, than any country surgeon whatever. He gave strict orders that his being at the hall should not be mentioned, as he did not choose, the few days he hoped and believed he should continue there, to be disturbed by visits which he knew would be paid if an intimation of his being there was received. From an apartment adjoining the music room he had discovered Amanda. Though scarcely able to move, at the first sound of her voice he stole to the door, which being a little open, gave him an opportunity of seeing her perfectly; and nothing but his situation prevented his immediately appearing before her, and expressing the admiration she had inspired him with As soon as she departed he sent for the house keeper, to inquire who the beautiful stranger was. Mrs. Abergwilly only knew she was a young lady lately come from London, to lodge at David Edwin's cottage, whose wife had entreated permission for her to read in the library, which, she added, she had given, seeing that his lordship read in his dressing-room; but, if he pleased, she would send Miss Dunford word not to come again— "By no means," his lordship said. Amanda therefore continued her visits as usual, little thinking with what critical regard and fond admiration she was observed. Lord Mortimer daily grew better; but the purpose for which he had come into Wales seemed utterly forgotten; he had a tincture of romance in his disposition, and availed himself of his recovery to gratify it, by taking a lute and serenading his lovely cottage girl. He could no longer restrain his impatience to be known to her; and the next day, stealing from his retirement, surprised her as already related.

As he could not, without an utter violation of good manners, shake off Howel, he contented himself with following Amanda into the church-yard, where, shaded by trees, he and his companion stood watching her unnoticed, till an involuntary exclamation of rapture from his lordship discovered their situation. When she departed, he read the inscription on the tombstone; but, from the difference of names, this gave no insight into any connection between her and the person it mentioned. Howel could give no information of either; he was but a young man, lately appointed to the parsonage, and had never seen Amanda till that evening.

Lord Mortimer was solicitous, even to a degree of anxiety, to learn the real situation of Amanda. As Howel, in his pastoral function, had free access to the houses of his parishioners, it occurred to him that he would be an excellent person to discover it; he therefore, as if from curiosity alone, expressed his wish of knowing who she was, and requested Howel, if convenient, to follow her directly to Edwin's cottage (where, he said, by chance, he heard she lodged), and endeavor to find out from the good people everything about her. This request Howel readily complied with; the face, the figure, the melancholy, and, above all, the employment of Amanda, had interested his sensibility and excited his curiosity.

He arrived soon after her at the cottage, and found her laughing at her nurse, who was telling her she was certain she should see her a great lady. Amanda rose to retire at his entrance; but he, perceiving her intention, declared if he disturbed her, he would immediately depart; she accordingly reseated herself, secretly pleased at doing so, as she thought, either from some look or word of the curate's, she might discover if he really was the person who had serenaded her; from this idea she showed no aversion to enter into conversation with him.

The whole family, nurse excepted, had followed Ellen to the dance; and that good woman thought she could do no less, for the honor of Howel's visit, than prepare a little comfortable supper for him. The benevolence of his disposition, and innocent gaiety of his temper, had rendered him a great favorite amongst his rustic neighbors, whom he frequently amused with simple ballads and pleasant tales. Amanda and he were left *tête-à-tête* while the nurse was busied in preparing her entertainment; and she was soon as much pleased with the elegance and simplicity of his manners, as he was with the innocence and sweetness of hers. The objects about them naturally led to rural subjects, and from them to what might almost be termed a dissertation on poetry: this was a theme peculiarly agreeable to Howel, who wooed the pensive muse beneath the sylvan shade; nor was it less so to Amanda—she was a zealous worshipper of the muses, though diffidence made her conceal her invocations to them. She was led to point out the beauties of her favorite authors, and the soft sensibility of her voice raised a kind of tender enthusiasm in Howel's soul; he gazed and listened, as if his eye could never be satisfied with seeing, or his ear with hearing. At his particular request, Amanda recited the pathetic description of the curate and his lovely daughter from the "Deserted Village"—a tear stole down her cheek as she proceeded. Howel softly laid his hand on hers, and exclaimed, "Good heavens, what an angel!"

"Come, come," said Amanda, smiling at the energy with which he spoke, "you, at least, should have nothing to do with flattery."

"Flattery!" repeated he, emphatically; "Oh heavens! did you but know my sincerity——"

"Well, well," cried she, wishing to change the subject, "utter no expression in future which shall make me doubt it."

"To flatter you," said he, "would be impossible, since the highest eulogium must be inadequate to your merits."

"Again!" said Amanda.

"Believe me," he replied, "flattery is a meanness I abhor; the expressions you denominate as such proceed from emotions I should contemn myself for want of sensibility if I did not experience."

The nurse's duck and green peas were now set upon the table, but in vain did she press Howel to eat; his eyes were too well feasted to allow him to attend to his palate. Finding her entreaties ineffectual in one respect, she tried them in another, and begged he would sing a favorite old ballad; this he at first hesitated to do, till Amanda (from a secret motive of her own) joined in the entreaty; and the moment she heard his voice, she was convinced he was not the person who had been at the outside of her window. After his complaisance to her, she could not refuse him one song. The melodious sounds sunk into his heart; he seemed fascinated to the spot, nor thought of moving till the nurse gave him a hint for that purpose, being afraid of Amanda sitting up too late.

He sighed as he entered his humble dwelling; it was perhaps the first sigh he had ever heaved for the narrowness of his fortune. "Yet," cried he, casting his eyes around, "in this abode, low and humble as it is, a soul like Amanda's might enjoy felicity."

The purpose for which Lord Mortimer sent him to the cottage, and Lord Mortimer himself, were forgotten. His lordship had engaged Howel to sup with him after the performance of his embassy, and impatiently awaited his arrival: he felt displeased, as the hours wore away without bringing him; and, unable at last to restrain the impetuosity of his feelings, proceeded to the parsonage, which he entered a few minutes after Howel. He asked, with no great complacency, the reason he had not fulfilled his engagement. Absorbed in one idea, Howel felt confused, agitated, and unable to frame any excuse; he therefore simply said, what in reality was true, "that he had utterly forgotten it."

"I suppose, then," exclaimed Lord Mortimer, in a ruffled voice, "you have been very agreeably entertained?"

"Delightfully," said Howel.

Lord Mortimer grew more displeased, but his anger was now levelled against himself as well as Howel. He repented and regretted the folly which had thrown Howel in the way of such temptation, and had perhaps raised a rival to himself.

"Well," cried he, after a few hasty paces about the room, "and pray, what do you know about Miss Dunford?"

"About her!" repeated Howel, as if starting from a reverie; "why—nothing."

"Nothing!" re-echoed his lordship.

"No," replied Howel, "except that she is an angel."

Lord Mortimer was now thoroughly convinced all was over with the poor parson; and resolved, in consequence of this conviction, to lose no time himself. He could not depart without inquiring how the evening had been spent, and envied Howel the happy minutes he had so eloquently described.

CHAPTER VI.

"———— Hither turn
Thy graceful footsteps; hither, gentle maid,
Incline thy polished forehead. Let thy eyes
Effuse the mildness of their azure dawn;
And may the fanning breezes waft aside
Thy radiant locks, disclosing, as it bends
With airy softness from the marble neck,
The cheek fair-blooming, and the rosy lip,
Where winning smiles, and pleasure sweet as love,
With sanctity and wisdom, tempering blend
Their soft allurements."—AKENSIDE.

HILE Amanda was at breakfast the next morning, Betsey brought a letter to her; expecting to hear from her father, she eagerly opened it, and, to her great surprise, perused the following lines:—

TO MISS DUNFORD.

Lord Mortimer begs leave to assure Miss Dunford he shall remain dissatisfied with himself till he has an opportunity of personally apologizing for his intrusion yesterday. If the sweetness of her disposition fulfils the promise her face has given of it, he flatters himself his pardon will speedily be accorded: yet never shall he think himself entirely forgiven, if her visits to the library are discontinued. Happy and honored shall Lord Mortimer consider himself, if Tudor Hall contains anything which can amuse or merit the attention of Miss Dunford.

July 17th.

"From Lord Mortimer!" said Amanda, with involuntary emotion. "Well, this really has astonished me." "Oh Lort, my tear!" cried the nurse in rapture.

Amanda waved her hand to silence her, as the servant stood in the outside room. She called Betsey: "Tell the servant," said she——

"Lort!" cried the nurse softly, and twitching her sleeve, "write his lortship a little pit of a note, just to let him see what a pretty scribe you are."

Amanda could not refrain smiling; but disengaging herself from the good woman, she arose, and going to the servant, desired him to tell his lord, she thanked him for his polite attention; but that in future it would not be in her power to go to the library. When she returned to the room, the nurse bitterly lamented her not writing. "Great matters," she said, "had often arisen from small beginnings." She could not conceive why his lortship should be treated in such a manner: it was not the way she had ever served her Edwin. Lort, she remembered if she got but the scrawl of a pen from him, she used to sit up to answer it. Amanda tried to persuade her it was neither necessary or proper for her to write. An hour passed in arguments between them, when two servants came from Tudor Hall to the cottage with a small bookcase, which they sent in to Amanda, and their lord's compliments, that in a few minutes he would have the honor of paying his respects to her.

Amanda felt agitated by this message; but it was the agitation of involuntary pleasure. Her room was always perfectly neat, yet did the nurse and her two daughters now busy themselves with trying, if possible, to put it into nicer order: the garden was ransacked for the choicest flowers to ornament it; nor would they depart till they saw Lord Mortimer approaching. Amanda, who had opened the bookcase, then snatched up a book, to avoid the appearance of sitting in expectation of his coming.

He entered with an air at once easy and respectful, and taking her hand, besought forgiveness for his intrusion the preceding day. Amanda blushed, and faltered out something of the confusion she had experienced from being so surprised; he reseated her, and drawing a chair close to hers, said he had taken the liberty of sending her a few books to amuse her, till she again condescended to visit the library, which he entreated her to do; promising that, if she pleased, both it and the music-room should be sacred to her alone. She thanked him for his politeness; but declared she must be excused from going. Lord Mortimer regarded her with a degree of tender admiration; an admiration heightened by the contrast he drew in his mind between her and the generality of fashionable women he had seen, whom he often secretly censured for sacrificing too largely at the shrine of art and fashion. The pale and varied blush which mantled the cheek of Amanda at once announced itself to be an involuntary suffusion; and her dress was only remarkable for its simplicity; she wore a plain robe of dimity, and an abbey cap of thin muslin, that shaded, without concealing, her face, and gave to it the soft expression of a Madonna; her beautiful hair fell in long ringlets down her back, and curled upon her forehead.

"Good heaven!" cried Lord Mortimer, "how has your idea dwelt upon my mind since last night: if in the morning I was charmed, in the evening I was enraptured. Your looks, your attitude, were then beyond all that imagination could conceive of loveliness and grace; you appeared as a being of another world mourning over a kindred spirit. I felt

"Awe-struck, and as I passed, I worshipped."

Confused by the energy of his words, and the ardent glances he directed towards her, Amanda, scarcely knowing what she did, turned over the leaves of the book she still held in her hand; in doing so, she saw written on the title-page, the Earl of Cherbury. "Cherbury?" repeated she, in astonishment.

"Do you know him?" asked Lord Mortimer.

"Not personally; but I revere, I esteem him; he is one of the best, the truest friends, my father ever had."

"Oh, how happy," exclaimed Lord Mortimer, "would his son be, were he capable of inspiring you with such sentiments as you avow for him."

"His son!" repeated Amanda, in a tone of surprise, and looking at Lord Mortimer.

"Yes," replied he. "Is it then possible," he continued, "that you are really ignorant of his being my father?"

Surprise kept her silent a few minutes; for her father had never given her any account of the earl's family, till about the period he thought of applying to him; and her mind was so distracted at that time on his own account, that she scarcely understood a word he uttered. In the country she had never heard Lord Cherbury mentioned; for Tudor Hall belonged not to him, but to Lord Mortimer, to whom an uncle had bequeathed it.

"I thought, indeed, my lord," said Amanda, as soon as she recovered her voice, "that your lordship's title was familiar to me; though why, from the hurry and perplexity in which particular circumstances involved me, I could not tell."

"Oh, suffer," cried Lord Mortimer, with one of his most insinuating smiles, "the friendship which our parents feel to be continued to their children; let this," taking her soft hand, and pressing his lips to it, "be the pledge of amity between us." He now inquired when the intimacy between her father and his had commenced, and where the former was. But from those inquiries Amanda shrunk. She reflected, that, without her father's permission, she had no right to answer them; and that, in a situation like his and hers, too much caution could not be observed. Besides, both pride and delicacy made her solicitous at present to conceal her father's real situation from Lord Mortimer: she could not bear to think it should be known his sole dependence was on Lord Cherbury, uncertain as it was, whether that nobleman would ever answer his expectations. She repented having ever dropped a hint of the intimacy subsisting between them, which surprise alone had made her do, and tried to waive the subject. In this design Lord Mortimer assisted her; for he had too much penetration not instantly to perceive it confused and distressed her. He requested permission to renew his visit, but Amanda, though well inclined to grant his request, yielded to prudence instead of inclination, and begged he would excuse her; the seeming disparity (she could not help saying) in their situations, would render it very imprudent in her to receive such visits; she blushed, half sighed, and bent her eyes to the ground as she spoke. Lord Mortimer continued to entreat, but she was steady in refusing; he would not depart, however, till he had obtained permission to attend her in the evening to a part of Tudor Grove which she had never yet seen, and he described as particularly beautiful. He wanted to call for her at the appointed hour, but she would not suffer this, and he was compelled to be contented with leave to meet her near the cottage when it came.

With a beating heart she kept her appointment, and found his lordship not many yards distant from the cottage, impatiently waiting her approach. A brighter bloom than usual glowed upon her cheek as she listened to his ardent expressions of admiration; yet not to such expressions, which would soon have sated an ear of delicacy like Amanda's, did Lord Mortimer confine himself; he conversed on various subjects; and the eloquence of his language, the liveliness of his imagination, and the justness of his remarks, equally amused and interested his fair companion. There was, indeed, in the disposition and manners of Lord Mortimer that happy mixture of animation and softness which at once amuses the fancy and attracts the heart; and never had Amanda experienced such minutes as she now passed with him, so delightful in their progress, so rapid in their course. On entering the walk he had mentioned to her, she saw he had not exaggerated its beauties. After passing through many long and shaded alleys, they came to a smooth green lawn, about which the trees rose in the form of an amphitheatre, and their dark, luxuriant, and checkered shades proclaimed that amongst them

> "The rude axe, with heaved stroke,
> Was never heard, the nymphs to daunt,
> Or fright them from their hallowed haunt."—MILTON.

The lawn gently sloped to a winding stream, so clear as perfectly to reflect the beautiful scenery of heaven, now glowing with the gold and purple of the setting sun; from the opposite bank of the stream rose a stupendous mountain, diversified with little verdant hills and dales, and skirted with a wild shrubbery, whose blossoms perfumed the air with the most balmy fragrance. Lord Mortimer prevailed on Amanda to sit down upon a rustic bench, beneath the spreading branches of an oak, enwreathed with ivy;

here they had not sat long, ere the silence, which reigned around, was suddenly interrupted by strains, at once low, solemn, and melodious, that seemed to creep along the water, till they had reached the place where they sat; and then, as if a Naiad of the stream had left her rushy couch to do them homage, they swelled by degrees into full melody, which the mountain echoes alternately revived and heightened. It appeared like enchantment to Amanda; and her eyes, turned to Lord Mortimer, seemed to say, it was to his magic it was owing. After enjoying her surprise some minutes, he acknowledged the music proceeded from two servants of his, who played on the clarinet and French horn, and were stationed in a dell of the opposite mountain. Notwithstanding all her former thoughts to the contrary, Amanda now conceived a strong suspicion that Lord Mortimer was really the person who had serenaded her; that she conceived pleasure from the idea, is scarcely necessary to say; she had reason soon to find she was not mistaken. Lord Mortimer solicited her for the Lady's song in Comus, saying the present situation was peculiarly adapted to it; on her hesitating, he told her she had no plea to offer for not complying, as he himself had heard her enchanting powers in it. Amanda started, and eagerly inquired when or by what means. It was too late for his lordship to recede; and he not only confessed his concealment near the music-room, but his visit to her window. A soft confusion, intermingled with pleasure, pervaded the soul of Amanda at this confession: and it was some time ere she was sufficiently composed to comply with Lord Mortimer's solicitations for her to sing; she at last allowed him to lead her to the centre of a little rustic bridge thrown over the stream, from whence her voice could be sufficiently distinguished for the music to keep time to it, as Lord Mortimer had directed. Her plaintive and harmonious invocation, answered by the low breathing of the clarinet, which appeared like the softest echo of the mountain, had the finest effect imaginable, and "took the imprisoned soul, and wrapped it in Elysium."

Lord Mortimer, for the first time in his life, found himself at a loss to express what he felt: he conducted her back to the seat, where, to her astonishment, she beheld fruits, ices, and creams, laid out, as if by the hand of magic, for no mortal appeared near the spot. Dusky twilight now warned her to return home; but Lord Mortimer would not suffer her to depart till she had partaken of this collation.

He was not by any means satisfied with the idea of only beholding her for an hour or two of an evening; and when they came near the cottage, desired to know whether it was to chance alone he was in future to be indebted for seeing her. Again he entreated permission to visit her sometimes of a morning, promising he would never disturb her avocations, but would be satisfied merely to sit and read to her, whenever she chose to work, and felt herself inclined for that amusement: Amanda's refusals grew fainter; and at last she said, on the above-mentioned conditions, he might sometimes come. That he availed himself of this permission, is scarcely necessary to say; and from this time few hours passed without their seeing each other.

The cold reserve of Amanda by degrees wore away; from her knowledge of his family she considered him as more than a new or common acquaintance. The emotions she felt for him, she thought sanctioned by that knowledge, and the gratitude she felt for Lord Cherbury for his former conduct to her father, which claimed, she thought, her respect and esteem for so near and valuable a connection of his; the worth, too, she could not avoid acknowledging to herself, of Lord Mortimer, would, of itself alone, have authorized them. Her heart felt he was one of the most amiable, most pleasing of men; she could scarcely disguise, in any degree, the lively pleasure she experienced in his society; nay, she scarcely thought it necessary to disguise it, for it resulted as much from innocence as sensibility, and was placed to the account of friendship. But Lord Mortimer was too penetrating not soon to perceive he might ascribe it to a softer impulse: with the most delicate attention, the most tender regard, he daily, nay, hourly, insinuated himself into her heart, and secured for himself an interest in it, ere she was aware, which the efforts of subsequent resolution could not overcome. He was the companion of her rambles, the alleviator of her griefs; the care which so often saddened her brow always vanished at his presence, and in conversing with him she forgot every cause of sorrow.

He once or twice delicately hinted at those circumstances which at his first visit she had mentioned, as sufficiently distressing to bewilder her recollection. Amanda, with blushes, always shrunk from the subject, sickening at the idea of his knowing that her father depended on his for future support. If he ever addressed her seriously on the subject of the regard he professed for her (which, from his attentions, she could not help sometimes flattering herself would be the case), then, indeed, there would be no longer room for concealment: but, except such a circumstance took place, she could not bring herself to make any humiliating discovery

Tudor Grove was the favorite scene of their rambles; sometimes she allowed him to lead her to the music-room; but as these visits were not frequent, a lute was brought from it to the cottage, and in the recess in the garden she often sung and played for the enraptured Mortimer; there, too, he frequently read for her, always selecting some elegant and pathetic piece of poetry, to which the harmony of his voice gave additional charms; a voice, which sunk into the heart of Amanda, and interested her sensibility even more than the subject he perused.

Often straying to the valley's verge, as they contemplated the lovely prospect around, only bounded by distant and stupendous mountains, Lord Mortimer, in strains of eloquence, would describe the beautiful scenes and extensive landscapes beyond them; and, whenever Amanda expressed a wish (as she sometimes would from thoughtless innocence) of viewing them, he would softly sigh, and wish he was to be her guide to them; as to point out beauties to a refined and cultivated taste like hers, would be to him the greatest pleasure he could possibly experience. Seated sometimes on the brow of a shrubby hill, as they viewed the scattered hamlets beneath, he would expatiate on the pleasure he conceived there must be in passing a tranquil life with one lovely and beloved object: his insidious eyes, turned towards Amanda, at these minutes, seemed to say, she was the being who could realize all the ideas he entertained of such a life; and when he asked her opinion of his sentiments, her disordered blushes, and faltering accents, too plainly betrayed her conscious feelings. Every delicacy which Tudor Hall contained, was daily sent to the cottage, notwithstanding Amanda's prohibition to the contrary; and sometimes Lord

Mortimer was permitted to dine with her in the recess. Three weeks spent in this familiar manner, endeared and attached them to each other more than months would have done, passed in situations liable to interruption.

CHAPTER VII.

"———— She alone
Heard, felt, and seen, possesses every thought,
Fills every sense, and pants in every vein.
Books are but formal dullness, tedious friends,
And sad amid the social band he sits,
Lonely and unattentive. From his tongue
The unfinished period falls, while, bore away
On swelling thought his wafted spirit flies
To the vain bosom of his distant fair."—THOMSON.

OWEL was no stranger to the manner in which hours rolled away at the cottage; he hovered round it, and seized every interval of Lord Mortimer's absence to present himself before Amanda; his emotions betrayed his feelings, and Amanda affected reserve towards him, in hopes of suppressing his passion; a passion, she now began to think, when hopeless, must be dreadful.

Howel was a prey to melancholy; but not for himself alone did he mourn; fears for the safety and happiness of Amanda added to his dejection; he dreaded that Lord Mortimer, perhaps, like too many of the fashionable men, might make no scruple of availing himself of any advantage which could be derived from a predilection in his favor.

He knew him, it is true, to be amiable; but in opposition to that, he knew him to be volatile, and sometimes wild, and trembled for the unsuspecting credulity of Amanda. "Though lost to me," exclaimed the unhappy young man, "oh never, sweetest Amanda, mayest thou be lost to thyself!"

He had received many proofs of esteem and friendship from Lord Mortimer; he therefore studied how he might admonish without offending, and save Amanda without injuring himself. It at last occurred to him that the pulpit would be the surest way of effecting his wishes, where the subject, addressed to all, might particularly strike the one for whom it was intended, without appearing as if designed for that purpose; and timely convince him, if, indeed, he meditated any injurious design against Amanda, of its flagrance.

On the following Sunday, as he expected, Lord Mortimer and Amanda attended service; his lordship's pew was opposite the one she sat in, and we fear his eyes too often wandered in that direction

The youthful monitor at last ascended the pulpit; his text was from Jeremiah, and to the following effect:—

"She weepeth sore in the night, and her tears are on her cheeks; among all her lovers she hath none to comfort her; all her friends have dealt treacherously with her, they are become her enemies."

After a slight introduction, in which he regretted that the declension of moral principles demanded such an exhortation as he was about to give, he commenced his subject: he described a young female, adorned with beauty and innocence, walking forward in the path of integrity, which a virtuous education had early marked for her to take, and rejoicing as she went with all around her; when, in the midst of happiness, unexpected calamity suddenly surprised and precipitated her from prosperity into the deepest distress: he described the benefits she derived in this trying period from early implanted virtue and religion; taught by them (he proceeded) the lovely mourner turns not to the world for consolation—no, she looks up to her Creator for comfort, whose supporting aid is so particularly promised to afflicted worth. Cheered by them, she is able to exert her little talents of genius and taste, and draw upon industry for her future support; her active virtues, he thinks the best proof of submission she can give to the will of Heaven; and in these laudable exertions she finds a conscious peace, which the mere possession of fortune could never bestow. While thus employed, a son of perfidy sees and marks her for his prey, because she is at once lovely and helpless: her unsuspecting credulity lays her open to his arts, and his blandishments by degrees allure her heart. The snare which he has spread at last involves her; with the inconstancy of libertinism he soon deserts her; and again is she plunged into distress. But mark the difference of her first and second fall: conscience no longer lends its opposing aid to stem her sorrow, despair instead of hope arises; without one friend to soothe the pangs of death, one pitying soul to whisper peace to her departing spirit; insulted, too, perhaps, by some unfeeling being, whom want of similar temptations alone, perhaps, saved from similar imprudences, she sinks an early victim to wretchednesss.

Howel paused; the fulness of his heart mounted to his eyes, which involuntarily turned and rested upon Amanda. Interested by his simple and pathetic eloquence, she had risen, and leaned over the pew, her head resting on her hand, and her eyes fastened on his face. Lord Mortimer had also risen, and alternately gazed upon Howel and Amanda, particularly watching the latter, to see how the subject would affect her. He at last saw the tears trickling down her cheeks: the distresses of her own situation, and the stratagems of Belgrave, made her, in some respect, perceive a resemblance between herself and the picture Howel had drawn. Lord Mortimer was unutterably affected by her tears, a faint sickness seized him, he sunk upon the seat, and covered his face with his handkerchief, to hide his emotion; but by the time service was over it was pretty well dissipated: Amanda returned home, and his lordship waited for Howel's coming out of church. "What the devil, Howel," said he, "did you mean by giving us such an exhortation? Have you discovered any little affair going on between some of your rustic neighbors?" The parson colored, but remained silent; Lord Mortimer rallied him a little more, and then departed; but his gaiety was only assumed.

On his first acquaintance with Amanda, in consequence of what he heard from Mrs. Abergwilly, and observed himself, he had been tempted to think she was involved in mystery: and what, but impropriety, he thought, could occasion mystery. To see so young, so lovely, so elegant a creature an inmate of a sequestered cottage, associating with people (in manners at least) so infinitely beneath her; to see her trembling and blushing, if a word was dropped that seemed tending to inquire into her motives for retirement; all these circumstances, I say, considered, naturally excited a suspicion injurious to her in the mind of Lord Mortimer; and he was tempted to think some deviation from prudence had, by depriving her of the favor of her friends, made her retire to obscurity; and that she would not dislike an opportunity of emerging from it, he could not help thinking. In consequence of these ideas, he could not think himself very culpable in encouraging the wishes her loveliness gave rise to: besides, he had some reason to suspect she desired to inspire him with these wishes; for Mrs. Abergwilly told him she had informed Mrs. Edwin of his arrival; an information he could not doubt her having immediately communicated to Amanda; therefore her continuing to come to the hall seemed as if she wished to throw herself in his way. Mrs. Edwin had indeed been told of his arrival, but concealed it from Amanda, that she should not be disappointed of going to the hall, which she knew, if once informed of it, she would not go to.

'Tis true, Lord Mortimer saw Amanda wore (at least) the semblance of innocence: but this could not remove his suspicions, so often had he seen it assumed, to hide the artful stratagems of a depraved heart.

Ah! why will the lovely female, adorned with all that heaven and earth can bestow to render her amiable, overleap the modesty of nature, and by levity and boldness lose all pretensions to the esteem which would otherwise be an involuntary tribute.

Nor is it herself alone she injures; she hurts each child of purity, helps to point the sting of ridicule, and weave the web of art.

We shun the blazing sun, but court his tempered beams; the rose, which glares upon the day, is never so much sought as the bud enwrapt in the foliage; and, to use the expression of a late much-admired author, "The retiring graces have ever been reckoned the most beautiful."

He had never heard the Earl mention a person of the name of Dunford; and he knew not, or rather suspected, little credit was to be given to her assertion of an intimacy between them, particularly as he saw her, whenever the subject was mentioned, shrinking from it in the greatest confusion.

Her reserve he imputed to pretence; and flattering himself it would soon wear off, determined, for the present at least, to humor her affectation.

With such ideas, such sentiments, had Lord Mortimer's first visits to Amanda commenced: but they experienced an immediate change as the decreasing reserve of her manners gave him greater and more frequent opportunities of discovering her mental perfections; the strength of her understanding, the justness of her remarks, the liveliness of her fancy, above all, the purity which mingled in every sentiment, and the modesty which accompanied every word, filled him with delight and amazement; his doubts gradually lessened, and at last vanished, and with them every design, which they alone had ever given rise to. Esteem was now united to love, and real respect to admiration: in her society he only was happy, and thought not, or rather would not suffer himself to think, on the consequences of such an attachment. It might be said, he was entranced in pleasure, from which Howel completely roused him, and made him seriously ask his heart, what were its intentions relative to Amanda. Of such views as he perceived Howel suspected him of harboring his conscience entirely acquitted him; yet so great were the obstacles he knew in the way of an union between him and Amanda, that he almost regretted (as every one does, who acts against their better judgment) that he had not fled at the first intimation of his danger. So truly formidable indeed did these obstacles appear, that he at times resolved to break with Amanda, if he could fix upon any plan for doing so, without injuring his honor, after the great attention he had paid her.

Ere he came to any final determination, however, he resolved to try and discover her real situation: if he even left her, it would be a satisfaction to his heart to know whether his friendship could be serviceable: and if an opposite measure was his plan, it could never be put in execution without the desired information. He accordingly wrote to his sister, Lady Araminta Dormer, who was then in the country with Lord Cherbury, requesting she would inquire from his father whether he knew a person of the name of Dunford; and if he did, what his situation and family were. Lord Mortimer begged her ladyship not to mention the inquiries being dictated by him, and promised at some future period to explain the reason of them. He still continued his assiduities to Amanda, and at the expected time received an answer to his letter; but how was he shocked and alarmed, when informed, Lord Cherbury never knew a person of the name of Dunford! His doubts began to revive; but before he yielded entirely to them, he resolved to go to Amanda, and inquire from her, in the most explicit terms, how, and at what time, her father and the Earl had become acquainted: determined, if she answered him without embarrassment, to mention to his sister whatever circumstances she related, lest a forgetfulness of them alone had made the Earl deny his knowledge of Dunford. Just as he was quitting the grove with this intent, he espied Edwin and his wife coming down a cross-road from the village, where they had been with poultry and vegetables. It instantly occurred to him that these people, in the simplicity of their hearts, might unfold the real situation of Amanda, and save him the painful necessity of making inquiries, which she, perhaps, would not answer, without his real motives for making them were assigned, which was what he could not think of doing.

Instead, therefore, of proceeding, he stopped till they came up to him, and then with the most engaging affability addressed them, inquiring whether they had been successful in the disposal of their goods. They answered bowing and courtesying, and he then insisted that, as they appeared tired, they should repair to the hall, and rest themselves. This was too great an honor to be refused; and they followed their noble conductor, who hastened forward to order refreshment into a parlor for them. The nurse, who in her own way was a cunning woman, instantly suspected, from the great and uncommon attention of Lord Mortimer, that he wanted to inquire into the situation of Amanda. As soon as she saw him at some distance, "David," cried she, "as sure as eggs are eggs," (unpinning her white apron, and smoothing it nicely down as she spoke), "this young lort wants to have our company, that he may find out something apout Miss Amanda. Ah, pless her pretty face, I thought how it would be; but we must be as cunning as foxes, and not tell too much nor too little, because if we told too much it would offend her, and she would ask us how we got all our intelligence, and would not think us over and above genteel, when she heard we had sifted Jemmy Hawthorn for it, when he came down from London with her. All we must do is just to drop some hints, as it were, of her situation, and then his lortship, to be sure, will make his advantage of them, and ask her everything apout herself, and then she will tell him of her own accord: so, David, mind what you say, I charge you." "Ay, ay," cried David, "leave me alone; I'll warrant you you'll always find an old soldier 'cute enough for anypoty."

When they reached the hall, they were shown into a parlor, where Lord Mortimer was expecting them: with difficulty he made them sit down at the table, where meat and wine were laid out for them. After they had partaken of them, Lord Mortimer began with asking Edwin some questions about his farm (for he was a tenant on the Tudor estate), and whether there was anything wanting to render it more comfortable. "No," Edwin replied, with a low bow, thanking his honorable lordship for his inquiry. Lord Mortimer spoke of his family. "Ay, Cot pless the poor things," Edwin said, "they were, to be sure, a fine thriving set of children." Still Lord Mortimer had not touched on the subject nearest his heart. He felt embarrassed and agitated. At last, with as much composure as he could assume, he asked how long they imagined Miss Dunford would stay with them. Now was the nurse's time to speak. She had hitherto sat simpering and bowing "That depended on circumstances," she said. "Poor tear young laty, though their little cottage was so obscure, and so unlike anything she had before been accustomed to, she made herself quite happy with it." "Her father must miss her society very much," exclaimed Lord Mortimer. "Tear heart, to be sure he does," cried nurse. "Well, strange things happen every tay; but still I never thought what did happen would have happened, to make the poor old gentleman and his daughter part." "What happened?" exclaimed Lord Mortimer, starting and suddenly stopping in the middle of the room, for hitherto he had been walking backwards and forwards. "'Twas not her business," the nurse replied, "by no manner of means, to be speaking about the affairs of her petters; put for all that she could not help saying, because, she thought it a pity his lortship, who was so good and so affable, should remain in ignorance of everything; that Miss Amanda was not what she appeared to be; no, if the truth was told, not the person she passed for at all; but, Lort, she would never forgive me," cried the nurse, "if your lortship told her it was from me your lortship heard this. Poor tear thing, she is very unwilling to have her situation known, though she is not the first poty who has met with a pad man; and shame and sorrow be upon him who tistrest herself and her father."

Lord Mortimer had heard enough: every doubt, every suspicion was realized; and he was equally unable and unwilling to inquire further. It was plain Amanda was unworthy of his esteem; and to inquire into the circumstances which occasioned that unworthiness, would only have tortured him. He rung the bell abruptly, and ordering Mrs. Abergwilly to attend the Edwins, withdrew immediately to another room. Now there was an opportunity for Lord Mortimer to break with Amanda, without the smallest imputation on his honor. Did it give him pleasure? No: it filled him with sorrow, disappointment, and anguish: the softness of her manners, even more than the beauty of her person, had fascinated his soul, and made him determine, if he found her worthy (of which indeed he had then but little doubt) to cease not, till every obstacle which could impede their union should be overcome. He was inspired with indignation at the idea of the snare he imagined she had spread for him; thinking her modesty all a pretext to draw him into making honorable proposals. As she sunk in his esteem, her charms lessened in his fancy; and he thought it would be a proper punishment for her, and a noble triumph over himself, if he conquered, or at least resisted his passion, and forsook her entirely. Full of this idea, and influenced by resentment for her supposed deceit, he resolved, without longer delay, to fulfil the purpose which had brought him into Wales, namely, visiting his friend; but how frail is resolution and resentment when opposed to tenderness! Without suffering himself to believe there was the least abatement of either in his mind, he forbid the carriage, in a few minutes after he had ordered it, merely, he persuaded himself, for the purpose of yet more severely mortifying Amanda: as his continuing a little longer in the neighborhood, without noticing her, might, perhaps, convince her, she was not quite so fascinating as she believed herself to be. From the time his residence at Tudor Hall was known, he had received constant invitations from the surrounding families, which, on Amanda's account, he uniformly declined. This he resolved should no longer be the case: some were yet unanswered, and these he meant to accept, as means indeed of keeping him steady in his resolution of not seeing her, and banishing her in some degree from his thoughts. But he could not have fixed on worse methods than these for effecting either of his purposes: the society he now mixed among was so different from that he had lately been accustomed to, that he was continually employed in drawing comparisons between them. He grew restless; his unhappiness increased; and he at last felt, that if he desired to experience any comfort, he must no longer absent himself from Amanda; and also that, if she refused to accede to the only proposals now in his power to make her, he would be miserable; so essential did he deem her society to his happiness; so much was he attached from the softness and sweetness of her manners. At the time he finally determined to see her again, he was in a large party at a Welsh baronet's where he had dined; and on the rack of impatience to put his determination in practice, he retired early, and took the road to the cottage.

Poor Amanda, during this time, was a prey to disquietude: the first day of Lord Mortimer's absence, she felt a little uneasiness, but strove to dissipate it, by thinking business had detained him. The next morning she remained entirely at home, every moment expecting to behold him; but this expectation was totally destroyed, when from the outside room she heard one of the nurse's sons tell of all the company he had met going to Sir Lewis ap Shenkin's, and amongst the rest Lord Mortimer, whose servants had told him, the day before their lord dined at Mr. Jones's, where there was a deal of company, and a grand ball in the evening. Amanda's heart almost died within her at these words; pleasure then, not business, had prevented Lord Mortimer from coming to her; these amusements which he had so often declared were tasteless to him, from the superior delight he experienced in her society. Either he was insincere in such expressions, or had now grown indifferent. She condemned herself for ever having permitted his visits, or received his assiduities; she reproached him for ever having paid those assiduities, knowing, as he must, the insincerity or inconstancy of his nature. In spite of wounded pride, tears of sorrow and disappointment burst from her; and her only consolation was, that no one observed her. Her hours passed heavily away; she could not attend to anything; and in the evening walked out to indulge, in a lonely ramble, the dejection of her heart: she turned from Tudor Hall, and took (without knowing it indeed) the very road which led to the house where Lord Mortimer had dined. With slow and pensive steps she pursued her way, regardless of all around her, till an approaching footstep made her raise her eyes, and she beheld, with equal surprise and confusion, the very object who was then employing her thoughts. Obeying the impulse of pride, she hastily turned away; till, recollecting that her precipitately avoiding him would at once betray her sentiments, she paused to listen to his passionate inquiries after her health: having answered them with involuntary coldness, she again moved on; but her progress was soon stopped by Lord Mortimer; snatching her hand, he insisted on knowing why she appeared so desirous to avoid him. Amanda made no reply to this, but desired he would let her go. "Never," he exclaimed, "till you wear another face to me. Oh! did you know the pain I have suffered since last we met, you would from pity, I am sure, treat me with less coldness." Amanda's heart throbbed with sudden pleasure; but she soon silenced its emotion, by reflecting that a declaration of uneasiness, at the very time he was entering into gaiety, had something too inconsistent in it to merit credit. Hurt by supposing he wanted to impose on her, she made yet more violent efforts to disengage her hand; but Lord Mortimer held it too firmly for her to be successful; he saw she was offended, and it gave him flattering ideas of the estimation in which he stood with her, since to resent his neglect was the most convincing proof he could receive of the value she set upon his attention. Without hurting her feelings by a hint, that he believed the alteration in her manner occasioned his absence, in indirect terms he apologized for it, saying what indeed was partly true, that a letter lately received had so ruffled his mind he was quite unfit for her society, and had therefore availed himself of those hours of chagrin and uneasiness to accept invitations, which at some time or other he must have done, to avoid giving offence; and by acting as he had done, he reserved the precious moments of returning tranquillity for her he adored. Ah! how readily do we receive any apology, do we admit of any excuse, that comes from a beloved object! Amanda felt as if a weight was suddenly removed from her heart; her eyes were no longer bent to the earth, her cheek no longer pale; and a smile, the smile of innocence and love, enlivened all her features. She seemed suddenly to forget her hand was detained by Lord Mortimer, for no longer did she attempt to free it; she suffered him gently to draw it within his, and lead her to the favorite haunt in Tudor Grove.

Pleased, yet blushing and confused, she heard Lord Mortimer, with more energy than he had ever yet expressed himself with, declare the pain he suffered the days he saw her not. From his ardent, his passionate expressions, what could the innocent Amanda infer, but that he intended, by uniting his destiny to hers, to secure to himself a society he so highly valued; what could she infer, but that he meant immediately to speak in explicit terms? The idea was too pleasing to be received in tranquillity, and her whole soul felt agitated. While they pursued their way through Tudor Grove, the sky, which had been lowering the whole day, became suddenly more darkened, and by its increasing gloom foretold an approaching storm. Lord Mortimer no longer opposed Amanda's returning home; but scarcely had they turned for that purpose, ere the vivid lightning flashed across their path, and the thunder awfully reverberated amongst the hills. The hall was much nearer than the cottage, and Lord Mortimer, throwing his arm round Amanda's waist, hurried her to it; but ere they reached the library, whose door was the first they came to, the rain began pouring with violence. Lord Mortimer snatched off Amanda's wet hat and cloak; the rest of her clothes were quite dry; and immediately ordered tea and coffee, as she refused any other refreshments: he dismissed the attendants, that he might, without observation or restraint, enjoy her society. As she presided at the tea-table, his eyes, with the fondest rapture, were fastened on her face, which never had appeared more lovely; exercise had heightened the pale tint of her cheek, over which her glossy hair curled in beautiful disorder; the unusual glow gave a greater radiance to her eyes, whose soft confusion denoted the pleasure she experienced from the attention of Lord Mortimer. He restrained not, he could not restrain, the feelings of his soul "Oh, what happiness!" he exclaimed. "No wonder I found all society tasteless, after having experienced yours. Where could I find such softness, yet such sensibility; such sweetness, yet such animation; such beauty, yet such apparent unconsciousness of it? Oh, my Amanda, smoothly must that life glide on, whose destiny you shall share!"

Amanda endeavored to check these transports, yet secretly they filled her with delight, for she regarded them as the sincere effusions of honorable love. Present happiness, however, could not render her forgetful of propriety: by the time tea was over, the evening began to clear, and she protested she must depart. Lord Mortimer protested against this for some time longer, and at last brought her to the window, to convince her there was still a slight rain falling. He promised to see her home as soon as it was over, and entreated, in the mean time, she would gratify him with a song. Amanda did not refuse; but the raptures he expressed, while she sung, she thought too violent, and rose from the piano when she had concluded, in spite of his entreaties to the contrary. She insisted on getting her hat and cloak, which had been sent to Mrs. Abergwilly to dry: Lord Mortimer at last reluctantly went out to obey her.

Amanda walked to the window: the prospect from it was lovely; the evening was now perfectly serene; a few light clouds alone floated in the sky, their lucid skirts tinged with purple rays from the declining sun; the trees wore a brighter green, and the dew-drop that had heightened their verdure, yet glittered on their sprays; across a distant valley was extended a beautiful rainbow, the sacred record of Heaven's covenant with man. All nature appeared revived and animated; the birds now warbled their closing lays, and the bleating of the cattle was heard from the neighboring hills. "Oh! how sweet, how lovely is the dewy landscape!" exclaimed Amanda, with that delight which scenes of calm and vernal nature never fail of raising in minds of piety and tenderness.

"'Tis lovely, indeed!" repeated Lord Mortimer, who returned at the moment, assuring her the things would be sent in directly. "I admire the prospect," continued he, "because you gaze upon it with me; were you absent, like every other charm, it would lose its beauty, and become tasteless to me. Tell me," cried he, gently encircling her waist, "why this hurry, why this wish to leave me? Do you expect elsewhere to meet with a being who will value your society more highly than I do? Do you expect to meet with a heart more fondly, more firmly attached to you than mine? Oh, my Amanda, if you do, how mistaken are such expectations!"

Amanda blushed, and averted her head, unable to speak.

"Ah, why," continued he, pursuing her averted eyes with his, "should we create uneasiness to ourselves, by again separating?"

Amanda looked up at these words with involuntary surprise in her countenance. Lord Mortimer understood it: he saw she had hitherto deluded herself with thinking his intentions towards her very different from what they really were; to suffer her longer to deceive herself would, he thought, be cruelty. Straining her to his beating heart, he imprinted a kiss on her tremulous lips, and softly told her, that the life, which without her would lose half its charms, should be devoted to her service; and that his fortune, like his heart, should be in her possession. Trembling while she struggled to free herself from his arms, Amanda demanded what he meant: her manner somewhat surprised and confused him; but recollecting this was the moment for explanation, he, though with half-averted eyes, declared his hopes—his wishes and intentions. Surprise—horror—and indignation, for a few minutes overpowered Amanda; but suddenly recovering her scattered senses, with a strength greater than she had ever before felt, she burst from him, and attempted to rush from the room. Lord Mortimer caught hold of her. "Whither are you going, Amanda?" exclaimed he, affrighted by her manner.

"From the basest of men," cried she, struggling to disengage herself.

He shut the door, and forced her back to a chair: he was shocked—amazed—and confounded by her looks: no art could have assumed such a semblance of sorrow as she now wore; no feelings but those of the most delicate nature, have expressed such emotion as she now betrayed: the enlivening bloom of her cheeks was fled, and succeeded by a deadly paleness; and her soft eyes, robbed of their lustre, were bent to the ground with the deepest expression of woe. Lord Mortimer began to think he had mistaken, if not her character, her disposition; and the idea of having insulted either purity or penitence, was like a dagger to his heart. "Oh, my love!" he exclaimed, laying his hand on her trembling one, "what do you mean by departing so abruptly?"

"My meaning, my Lord," cried she, rising and shaking his hand from hers, "is now as obvious as your own—I seek, for ever, to quit a man who, under the appearance of delicate attention, meditated so base a scheme against me. My credulity may have yielded you amusement, but it has afforded you no triumph: the tenderness which I know you think, which I shall not deny your having inspired me with, as it was excited by imaginary virtues, so it vanished with the illusion which gave it birth; what then was innocent, would now be guilty. Oh, heavens!" continued Amanda, clasping her hands together, in a sudden agony of tears, "is it me, the helpless child of sorrow, Lord Mortimer sought as a victim to illicit love! Is it the son of Lord Cherbury destined such a blow against the unfortunate Fitzalan?"

Lord Mortimer started. "Fitzalan!" repeated he. "Oh! Amanda, why did you conceal your real name? And what am I to infer from your having done so?"

"What you please, my Lord," cried she. "The opinion of a person I despise can be of little consequence to me; yet," continued she, as if suddenly recollecting herself, "that you may have no plea for extenuating your conduct, know that my name was concealed by the desire of my father, who, involved in unexpected distress, wished me to adopt another, till his affairs were settled."

"This concealment has undone me," exclaimed Lord Mortimer: "it has led me into an error, I shall never cease repenting. Oh! Amanda, deign to listen to the circumstances which occasioned this error; and you will then, I am sure, think me at least less culpable than I now appear to be; you will then, perhaps, allow me to make some atonement."

"No, my Lord," cried Amanda, "willingly I will not allow myself to be deceived: for without deceit, I am convinced you could mention no circumstance which could possibly palliate your conduct, or what you so gently term an error. Had I, my Lord, by art or coquetry, sought to attract your notice, your crime would have been palliated; but when you pursued, I retired; and the knowledge of your being Lord Cherbury's son first induced me to receive your visits. I suffered their continuance, because I thought you amiable: sad mistake! Oh! cruel, ungenerous Mortimer, how have you abused my unsuspecting confidence!"

As she ended these words, she moved towards the door. Awed by her manner, confounded by her reproaches, tortured by remorse, and half offended at her refusing to hear his vindication, he no longer attempted to prevent her quitting the apartment; he followed her, however, from it. "What do you mean, my Lord," asked she, "by coming after me?"

"I mean to see you safely home," replied he, in a tone of proud sullenness.

"And is it Lord Mortimer," cried she, looking steadfastly in his face, "pretends to see me safe?"

He stamped, struck his hand violently against his forehead, and exclaimed, "I see—I see—I am despicable in your eyes; but, Amanda, I cannot endure your reproaches. Pause for a few minutes, and you will find I am not so deserving of them as you imagine."

She made no reply, but quickened her pace: within a few yards of the cottage Lord Mortimer caught her, with a distracted air. "Amanda," said he, "I cannot bear to part with you in this manner: you think me the veriest villain on earth; you will drive me from your heart; I shall become abhorrent to you."

"Most assuredly, my Lord," replied she, in a solemn voice.

"Cannot compunction then extenuate my error?"

"'Tis not compunction, 'tis regret you feel, for finding your designs unsuccessful."

"No: by all that is sacred, 'tis remorse for ever having meditated such an injury. Yet I again repeat, if you listen to me, you will find I am not so culpable as you believe. Oh! let me beseech you to do so; let me hope that my life may be devoted to you alone, and that I may thus have opportunities of apologizing for my conduct. Oh! dearest Amanda," kneeling before her, "drive me not from you in the hour of penitence."

"You plead in vain, my Lord," cried she, breaking from him.

He started in an agony from the ground, and again seized her. "Is it thus," he exclaimed, "with such unfeeling coldness I am abandoned by Amanda? I will leave you, if you only say I am not detested by you; if you only say the remembrance of the sweet hours we have spent together will not become hateful to you."

He was pale and trembled; and a tear wet his cheek. Amanda's began to flow: she averted her head, to hide her emotion; but he had perceived it. "You weep, my Amanda," said he, "and you feel the influence of pity!"

"No, no," cried she, in a voice scarcely articulate: "I will acknowledge," continued she, "I believe you possessed of sensibility; and an anticipation of the painful feelings it will excite on the reflection of your conduct to me, now stops my further reproaches. Ah! my Lord, timely profit by mental correction, nor ever again encourage a passion which virtue cannot sanction or reason justify."

> "Thus spoke the angel;
> And the grave rebuke, severe in youthful beauty,
> Added grace invincible."

Amanda darted from Lord Mortimer; and entering the cottage, hastily closed the door. Her looks terrified the nurse, who was the only one of the family up, and who, by means of one of her sons, had discovered that Amanda had taken refuge from the thunder-storm in Tudor Hall.

Amanda had neither hat nor cloak on; her face was pale as death; her hair, blown by the wind, and wet from the rain, hung dishevelled about her; and to the inquiries of her nurse she could only answer by sobs and tears. "Lack a tay," said the nurse, "what ails my sweet chilt?"

Relieved by tears, Amanda told her nurse she was not very well, and that she had been reflecting on the great impropriety there was in receiving Lord Mortimer's visits, whom she begged her nurse, if he came again, not to admit.

The nurse shook her head, and said she supposed there had been some quarrel between them; but if Lord Mortimer had done anything to vex her tear chilt, she would make him pay for it. Amanda charged her never to address him on such a subject; and having made her promise not to admit him, she retired to her chamber faint, weary, and distressed. The indignity offered her by Colonel Belgrave had insulted her purity and offended her pride, but he had not wounded the softer feelings of her soul; it was Mortimer alone had power to work them up to agony.

The charm which had soothed her sorrows was fled; and while she glowed with keen resentment, she wept from disappointed tenderness. "Alas! my father," she cried, "is this the secure retreat you fondly thought you had discovered for me! Sad mistake! Less had I to dread from the audacious front of vice, than the insidious form of virtue: delicacy shrinking from one, immediately announced the danger; but innocence inspired confidence in the other; and credulity, instead of suspicion, occupied the mind. Am I doomed to be the victim of deception—and, except thy honest tender heart, my father, find every other fraught with deceit and treachery to me? Alas! if in the early season of youth, perpetual perfidy makes us relinquish candor and hope, what charms can the world retain? The soul sickening, recoils within itself, and no longer startles at dissolution. Belgrave aimed at my peace—but Mortimer alone had power to pierce 'the vital vulnerable heart.' Oh, Mortimer! from you alone the blow is severe—you, who, in divine language I may say were my guide, my companion, and my familiar friend."

Lord Mortimer was now a prey to all the pangs which an ingenuous mind, oppressed with a consciousness of error, must ever feel: the most implacable vengeance could not devise a greater punishment for him, than his own thoughts inflicted; the empire of inordinate passion was overthrown, and honor and reason regained their full and natural ascendancy over them. When he reflected on the uniform appearance of innocence Amanda had always worn, he wondered at his weakness in ever having doubted its reality—at his audacity, in ever having insulted it; when he reflected on her melancholy, he shuddered as if having aggravated it. "Your sorrows, as well as purity, my Amanda," he cried, "should have rendered you a sacred object to me."

A ray of consolation darted into his mind at the idea of prevailing on her to listen to the circumstances which had led him into a conduct so unworthy of her and himself: such an explanation, he trusted, would regain her love and confidence, and make her accept, what he meant immediately to offer—his hand: for pride and ambition could raise no obstacles to oppose this design of reparation; his happiness depended on its being accepted. Amanda was dearer to him than life, and hope could sketch no prospect, in which she was not the foremost object. Impetuous in his passions, the lapse of the hours was insupportably tedious; and the idea of waiting till the morning to declare his penitence, his intention, and again implore her forgiveness, filled him with agony: he went up to the cottage, and laid his hand upon the latch; he hesitated; even from the rustics he wished to conceal his shame and confusion. All within and without the cottage was still; the moonbeams seemed to sleep upon the thatch, and the trees were unagitated by a breeze.

"Happy rustics!" exclaimed Lord Mortimer. "Children of content and undeviating integrity, sleep presses sweetly on your eye-lids. My Amanda too rests, for she is innocent."

He descended to the valley, and saw a light from her window: he advanced within a few yards of it, and saw her plainly walk about with an agitated air—her handkerchief raised to her eyes, as if she wept. His feelings rose almost to frenzy at this sight, and he execrated himself for being the occasion of her tears. The village clock struck one: good heavens! how many hours must intervene ere he could kneel before the lovely mourner, implore her soft voice to accord his pardon, and (as he flattered himself would be the case), in the fulness of reconciliation, press her to his throbbing heart, as the sweet partner of his future days. The light was at last extinguished; but he could not rest, and continued to wander about like a perturbed spirit till the day began to dawn, and he saw some early peasants coming to their labors.

CHAPTER VIII.

"Oh let me now, into a richer soil,
Transplant thee safe, where vernal suns and showers
Diffuse their warmest, largest influence;
And of my garden be the pride and joy."—THOMSON.

HE moment he thought he could see Amanda, Mortimer hastened to the cottage; the nurse, as she had promised, would not reproach him, though she strongly suspected his having done something to offend her child; that her sullen air declared her dissatisfaction. "Miss Fitzalan was too ill," she said, "to see company:" (for Lord Mortimer had inquired for Amanda by her real name, detesting the one of Dunford, to which, in a great degree, he imputed his unfortunate conduct to her.) The nurse spoke truth in saying Amanda was ill; her agitation was too much for her frame, and in the morning she felt so feverish she could not rise; she had not spirits, indeed, to attempt it. Sunk to the lowest ebb of dejection, she felt solitude alone congenial to her feelings. Hitherto the morning had been impatiently expected; for, with Mortimer, she enjoyed its

"Cool, its fragrant, and its silent hour."

But no Mortimer was now desired. In the evening he made another attempt; and finding Ellen alone, sent in a supplicatory message by her to Amanda. She was just risen, and Mrs. Edwin was making tea for her; a flush of indignation overspread her pale face, on receiving his message. "Tell him," said she, "I am astonished at his request, and never will grant it. Let him seek elsewhere a heart more like his own, and trouble my repose no more."

He heard her words, and in a fit of passion and disappointment flew out of the house. Howel entered soon after, and heard from Ellen an account of the quarrel: a secret hope sprung in his heart at this intelligence, and he desired Ellen to meet him in about half an hour in the valley, thinking by that time he could dictate some message to send by her to Amanda.

As the parson had never paid Miss Fitzalan any of those atten

7 *

tions which strike a vulgar eye, and had often laughed and familiarly chatted with Ellen, she took it into her head he was an admirer of hers; and if being the object of Chip's admiration excited the envy of her neighbors, how much would that increase when the parson's predilection was known? She set about adorning herself for her appointment; and while thus employed the honest, faithful Chip entered, attired in his holiday clothes, to escort her to a little dance. Ellen bridled up at the first intimation of it; and, delighted with the message Amanda had sent to Lord Mortimer, which in her opinion was extremely eloquent, she resolved now to imitate it.

"Timothy," said she, drawing back her head, "your request is the most improperest that can be conceived, and it is by no means convenient for me to adhere to it. I tell you, Tim," cried she, waving the corner of her white apron, for white handkerchief she had not, "I wonder at your presumptioness in making it; cease your flattering expressions of love, look out amongst the inferiority for a heart more like your own, and trouble my pleasure no more."

Chip paused a moment, as if wanting to comprehend her meaning. "The short and the long of it then, Nell," said he, "is, that you and I are to have nothing more to say to each other."

"True," cried his coquettish mistress.

"Well, well, Nell," said he, half crying, "the time may come when you will repent having served a true-hearted lad in this manner." So saying, he ran from the house.

Ellen surveyed herself with great admiration, and expected nothing less than an immediate offer of the parson's hand. She found him punctual to his appointment, and after walking some time about the valley, they sat down together upon a little bank. "Ellen," said he, taking her hand, "do you think there is any hope for me?"

"Nay, now intead, Mr. Howel," cried she, with affected coyness, "that is such a strange question."

"But the quarrel, perhaps," said he, "may be made up."

"No, I assure you," replied she, with quickness, "it was entirely on your account it ever took place."

"Is it possible!" exclaimed he, pleasure sparkling in his eyes; "then I may re-urge my passion."

"Ah, tear now, Mr. Howel, you are so very pressing.

"Do you think," said he, "she is too ill to see me?"

"Who too ill?"

"Why, Miss Fitzalan." (For, the moment Ellen knew Lord Mortimer was acquainted with Amanda's name, she thought there was no longer reason for concealing it from any one, and had informed Howel of it.)

"Miss Fitzalan!" repeated she, staring and changing color.

"Yes, Ellen, the dear, lovely Miss Fitzalan, whom I adore more than language can express, or imagination conceive."

Adieu to Ellen's airy hopes: her chagrin could not be concealed; and tears burst from her. The curate tenderly inquired the cause of her emotion; though vain, she was not artful, and could not disguise it. "Why, really, you made such speeches, I thought—and then you looked so. But it is no matter: I pelieve all men are teceitful."

From her tears and disjointed sentences, he began to suspect something, and his gentle mind was hurt at the idea of giving her pain; anxious, however, to receive his doom from Amanda, he again asked, if she thought he could see her.

Ellen answered him snappishly, she could not tell; and hurried to the cottage, where a flood of tears soon relieved her distress. To be dressed so charmingly, and for no purpose, was a pity: she therefore resolved on going to the dance, consoling herself with the old saying of having more than one string to her bow; and that if Chip was not as genteel, he was quite as personable a man as the curate. Walking down the lane, she met a little boy, who gave her a letter from Chip; full of the idea of its containing some overtures for a reconciliation, she hastily broke it open, and read to the following effect:—

Ellen:—After your cruelty, I could not bear to stay in the village, as I never could work another stroke with a light heart; and every tree and meadow would remind me of the love my dear girl once bore her poor Chip. So, before this comes to hand, I shall be on my way to enter one of the King's ships, and Heaven knows whether we shall ever meet again; but this I know, I shall always love Ellen, though she was so cruel to her own faithful Tim Chip.

Thus did the vanity of Ellen receive a speedy punishment. Her distress for some days was unabated; but at last yielded to the mild arguments of Amanda, and the hopes she inspired of seeing the wandering hero again.

Howel at last obtained an interview, and ventured to plead his passion. Amanda thanked him for his regard, but declared her inability of returning it as he wished; assuring him, however, at the same time, of her sincere friendship.

"This then shall suffice," said he. "Neither sorrow nor disappointment are new to me; and when they oppress me, I will turn to the idea of my angel friend, and forget, for some moments at least, my heavy burthen."

Lord Mortimer made several attempts for again seeing Amanda, but without success; he then wrote, but his letters were not more successful. In despair at finding neither letters nor messages received by Amanda, he at last, by stratagem, effected an interview. Meeting one of the young Edwins returning from the post-town with a letter, he inquired, and heard it was for Miss Fitzalan; a little persuasion prevailed on the young man to relinquish it, and Lord Mortimer flew directly to the cottage. "Now," cried he, "the inexorable girl must appear, if she wishes to receive her letter."

The nurse informed Amanda of it; but she, suspecting it to be a scheme, refused to appear. "By Heaven, I do not deceive her!" exclaimed Lord Mortimer; "nor will I give the letter into any hands but hers." "This, my Lord," said Amanda, coming from her chamber, "is really cruel; but give me the letter," impatiently stretching out her hand for it. "Another condition remains to be complied with," cried he, seizing her soft hand, which she, however, instantly withdrew; "you must read it, Miss Fitzalan, in my presence." "Good Heavens, how you torment me!" she exclaimed. "Do you comply then?" "Yes," she replied, and received the letter from him. The pity and compunction of his lordship increased as he gazed on her pale face, while her eyes eagerly ran over the contents of the letter, which were as follows:—

TO MISS FITZALAN.

To be able to communicate pleasure to my Amanda, rewards me for tedious months of wretchedness. Dry up your tears, sweet child of early sorrow, for the source of grief exists no longer: Lord Cherbury has been kind beyond my warmest expectations, and has given me the ineffable delight, as far as pecuniary matters can do, of rendering the future days of Amanda happy. In my next, I shall be more explicit; at present, I have not a moment I can call my own, which must excuse this laconic letter. The faithful Edwins will rejoice in the renewed fortune of their dear Amanda's affectionate father.

Jermyn Street. AUGUSTUS FITZALAN.

The emotions of Amanda were irrepressible: the letter dropped from her trembling hands, and her streaming eyes were raised to heaven. "Oh bless him!" she exclaimed. "Gracious Heaven, bless the benefactor of my father for this good deed! May sorrow or misfortune never come across his path."

"And who, may I ask," said Lord Mortimer, "merits so sweet a prayer from Amanda?"

"See," cried she, presenting him the letter, as if happy at the moment to have such a proof of the truth of what she had alleged to him.

Lord Mortimer was affected by the letter: his eyes filled with tears, and he turned aside to hide his emotion; recovering himself, he again approached her. "And while you so sweetly pray for the felicity of the father," said he, "are you resolved on dooming the son to despair? If sincere penitence can extenuate error, and merit mercy, I deserve to be forgiven."

Amanda rose, as if with an intention of retiring, but Lord Mortimer caught her hand. "Think not," cried he, "I will lose the present opportunity, which I have so long desired, and with such difficulty obtained, of entering into a vindication of my conduct: however it may be received by you, it is a justice I owe my own character to make: for as I never wilfully injured innocence, so I cannot bear to be considered as its violator. Amidst the wildness, the extravagance of youth, which with compunction I acknowledge being too often led into, my heart still acquitted me of ever committing an act which could entail upon me the pangs of conscience. Sacred to me has virtue ever been, how lowly soever in situation."

The idea of his being able to vindicate himself scarcely afforded less pleasure to Amanda than it did to Lord Mortimer. She suffered him to reseat her, while he related the circumstances which had led him astray in his opinion of her. Oh! how fervent was the rapture that pervaded Amanda's heart, when, as she listened to him, she found he was still the amiable, the generous, the noble character her fancy had first conceived him to be. Tears of pleasure, exquisite as those she had lately shed, again fell from her; for oh! what delight is there in knowing that an object we cannot help loving we may still esteem. "Thus," continued Lord Mortimer, "have I accounted for my error: an error which, except on account of your displeasure, I know not whether I should regret, as it has convinced me, more forcibly than any other circumstance could have done, of the perfections of your mind, and has, besides, removed from mine, prejudices which causelessly I did not entertain against your sex. Was every woman in a similar situation to act like you,

> ——Such numbers would not in vain,
> Of broken vows and faithless men complain.

To call you mine is the height of my wishes; on your decision I rest for happiness. Oh! my Amanda, let it be a favorable decision, and suffer me to write to Mr. Fitzalan, and request him to bestow on me the greatest treasure one being could possibly receive from another—a woman lovely and educated as you have been."

When he mentioned appealing to her father, Amanda could no longer doubt the sincerity of his intentions. Her own heart pleaded as powerfully as his solicitations did for pardoning him; and if she did not absolutely extend her hand, she at least suffered it to be taken without any reluctance. "I am forgiven, then," said Lord Mortimer, pressing her to his bosom. "Oh, my Amanda, years of tender attention can never make up for this goodness!"

When his transports were a little abated, he insisted on writing immediately to Fitzalan. As he sealed the letter, he told Amanda he had requested an expeditious answer. The happiness of the youthful pair was communicated to the honest rustics, whom Lord Mortimer liberally rewarded for their fidelity to his Amanda, and whom she readily excused for their ambiguous expressions to him, knowing they proceeded from simplicity of heart, and a wish of serving her, yet without injuring themselves, by betraying the manner in which they had procured intelligence of her situation.

The day after the reconciliation, Lord Mortimer told Amanda he was compelled, for a short time, to leave her; with that reluctance, he hoped, he said, she could readily conceive; but the visit, which he had come into Wales for the purpose of paying, had been so long deferred, his friend was growing impatient, and threatened to come to Tudor Hall to see what detained him there. To prevent such a measure, which he knew would be a total interruption to the happiness he enjoyed in her society, Lord Mortimer added he meant to pass a few days with him, hoping by the time he returned there would be a letter from Mr. Fitzalan, which would authorize his immediate preparations for their nuptials. Amanda wished, but could not totally hide, the uneasiness she felt at the prospect of a separation; the idea, however, of his speedy return, rendered it but transient, and he departed in a few hours after he had mentioned his intention.

Amanda had never before experienced such happiness as she now enjoyed. She now saw herself on the point of being elevated to a situation, by a man, too, whom she adored, which would give her ample opportunities of serving the dearest connections of her heart, and of gratifying the benevolence of her disposition, and the elegance of her taste. Oh, how delightful to think she should be able to soothe the declining period of her father's life, by providing for him all the requisite indulgences of age! oh, how delightful to think she should be accessory to her dear Oscar's promotion! how rapturous to imagine at her approach the drooping children of misery would brighten with pleasing presages of relief, which she should amply realize! Such were Amanda's anticipations of what she termed the blessings of an affluent fortune; felicity, in her opinion, was to be diffused to be enjoyed. Of Lord Cherbury's sanction to the attachment of his son, she entertained not a doubt; her birth was little inferior to his, and fortune was entirely out of the question—for a liberal mind, she thought, could never look to that, when on one side was already possessed more than sufficient for even the luxuries of life. Such were the ideas of the innocent and romantic Amanda—ideas which made her seem to tread on air, and which she entertained till subsequent experience convinced her of their fallacy.

CHAPTER IX.

> "Alas! the story melts away my soul!
> That best of fathers, how shall I discharge
> The gratitude and duty which I owe him?
> —By laying up his counsels in your heart."—CATO.

AMANDA was sitting in the recess in the garden, the fourth evening of Lord Mortimer's absence, when suddenly she heard the rattling of a carriage. Her heart bounded, and she flew into the house; at the very moment a chaise stopped at the door, from which, to her inexpressible amazement, her father descended.

Transfixed to the spot, it was many minutes ere she had power to bid him welcome, or return the fond caresses he bestowed upon her. "I am come, Amanda," said he, eagerly interrupting the joyful speeches of the Edwins, "to take you away with me; and one hour is all I can give you to prepare yourself." "Good Heaven!" said Amanda, starting, "to take me away immediately?" "Immediately," he repeated. "And as I know you are attached to this good girl," turning to Ellen, "I shall be happy, if her parents permit, to procure her attendance for you."

The Edwins, who would have followed themselves, or allowed any of their family to follow Fitzalan and his daughter round the world, gladly consented to her going; and the girl, exclusive of her attachment to Amanda, which was very great, having pined ever since her lover's departure, rejoiced at the idea of a change of scene.

Not so Amanda: it made her suffer agony; to be torn from Lord Mortimer in the hour of reconciliation and explanation, was more than she could support with fortitude. Her father, perhaps, had not received his letter; it was but justice then to him and Lord Mortimer to reveal her situation. She left her trunk half-packed, and went out for that purpose; but as she stood before him with quivering lips and half-averted eyes, at a loss to begin, he took her hand, and softly exclaimed: "My love, let us for the present waive every subject; the moments are precious; hasten to put on your habit, or we shall be too late at the stage where I propose resting to-night." Amanda turned in silence to her chamber to comply with his desire; tears ran down her cheeks, and for the first time she conceived the idea of being hurried away to avoid Lord Mortimer; but why, she could not think—honor as well as tenderness, she thought, demanded her acquainting him with the cause of her precipitate journey; but, when she took up a pen for that purpose, her hand was unsteady, and she was so much disturbed by the nurse and her daughters, who ran backwards and forwards in all the bustle of preparation, that she could not write: her father prevented a second effort, for he was continually coming to her chamber-door urging her to be quick, and thus prevented her delivering any message to the nurse for Lord Mortimer; so great was his eagerness to depart, he would not suffer the horses to be taken from the chaise, or any refreshment to be brought him by the Edwins, notwithstanding their pressing entreaties: neither would he answer their interrogatories as to where he was going, saying they should know hereafter. The parting embrace was at last given and received with a heavy heart—Amanda was handed to the carriage—silence prevailed—all the travellers were equally though differently affected; the cottage and the spire of the village church had awakened the most affecting remembrances in the mind of Fitzalan, and tears fell from him to the memory of his unfortunate Malvina: sighs burst from Amanda as she viewed the white turrets of Tudor Hall, and Ellen sobbed on passing the forsaken cottage of poor Chip. From all these affecting and beloved objects the rapidity of the carriage soon conveyed them; but the impressions they left upon their minds were not so easily eradicated. Fitzalan was the first to break the unsocial silence, and it seemed as if he did so for the purpose of rousing the dejection of his daughter: a cross road from the cottage shortly brought them to Conway Ferry, which they were obliged to pass, and here, had Amanda's mind been at ease, she would have felt truly gratified by viewing the remains of gothic magnificence which Castle Conway exhibited; as it was, she could not behold them unmoved, and, whilst she admired, gave the passing tribute of a sigh to grandeur and decay. They only continued in Conway till a carriage was provided for them, and soon came beneath the stupendous projections of Penmaenmawr; this was a scene as new as awful to

Amanda: "Well, Cot in heaven pless their souls," Ellen said, "what a telil of a way they should be in if one of them huge stones rolled down upon the carriage." They stopped not again until they reached Bangor Ferry, where they were to rest for the night. Amanda's strength and spirits were now so entirely exhausted, that had not a glass of wine been immediately procured her, she would have fainted from weakness; this a little revived her, and the tears she shed relieved in some degree the oppressions of her heart; her father left her and Ellen together, while he went to give directions about the journey of the ensuing day.

Amanda went to the window and threw up the sash; the air from the mountains she thought refreshed her; the darkness of the hour was opposed by a bright moon, which cast a trembling radiance upon the water, and by its partial gleams exhibited a beautiful scene of light and shade, that had Amanda been in another frame of mind she would infinitely have admired; the scene too was almost as still as it was lovely, for no voice was heard except a low murmur from voices below stairs: while she stood here in a deep reverie, the paddling of oars suddenly roused her, and she beheld a boat on the opposite shore, which in a few minutes gained the one where she was, and she saw coming from it to the inn a large party of gentlemen, whose air and attendants announced them to be men of fashion; they seemed by their discourse to be a convivial party; the light was too dim to allow their faces to be discerned, but in the figure of one Amanda thought she perceived a strong resemblance to Lord Mortimer; her heart throbbed, she leaned forward to endeavor to distinguish more plainly, and at the moment heard his well-known voice ordering his groom to have the horses ready at twelve o'clock, as he would take the advantage of such fine weather to set off at that hour for Tudor Hall; the party were then ushered into a room contiguous to the one occupied by Amanda, while the bustling of the waiters, and the clattering of knives, forks, and plates, announced the preparations for a late dinner. Oh! what were now the agitations of Amanda, to think that in one moment she could inform Lord Mortimer of her situation; but the transport the idea gave was relinquished almost as soon as felt, as such a measure she thought might perhaps for ever disoblige her father. In this tumult of doubt and perplexity he found her; and by his conduct convinced her that he not only knew of Lord Mortimer's being in the house, but wished her to avoid him; for he instantly led her from the window, and, shutting it down, darted, for the first time in his life, a severe frown at her; a dagger in the breast of Amanda could scarcely have given her more pain—a cold horror ran through her veins, and she was oppressed by as many fears as if she had been conscious of offending him. The supper he had ordered was a little retarded by the late dinner of his gay neighbors; he would have had it in another room had another been disengaged; vainly did his timid companions try to eat—Amanda was sick, and Ellen frightened, though she knew not why; the waiter was dismissed, and the most unsocial silence prevailed.

Unbounded gaiety reigned in the next apartment, from which every sound could plainly be distinguished. Dinner over, the exhilarating juice went round, and bumper toasts were called. Lord Mortimer at last was asked for a fair nymph. "I will give you," exclaimed he, in a voice which denoted his being uncommonly elevated, "an Angel!"—Amanda's heart beat violently, and her cheeks glowed. "A name for this celestial beauty!" demanded one of the party: "Amanda," cried his lordship. "Oh, faith, Mortimer, that won't do;" said another of his companions; "this angel shall not pass without the rest of her name." "Miss Fitzalan, then," exclaimed his lordship. "Oh! oh!" cried a new voice, with a loud laugh, after due honor had been paid to the toast, "I begin to unravel a mystery; upon my soul I could not conceive till this instant what had kept you so long at the hall; for I had seen the maiden part of the household, and knew the metal there not very attractive; but this Amanda, I suppose, is the rosy daughter of some poor curate in its vicinity, who for"—"Beware!" interrupted Lord Mortimer in an agitated voice, "of what you say; give me no reason to repent having introduced a name so valued into this company—the situation of Miss Fitzalan is not exactly what you suppose; but let this suffice for you to know—it is such as secures her from every species of impertinence; and were it even less protected, her own elegance and propriety would elevate her above receiving any." The face of Fitzalan, during this conversation, was crimsoned over, and he again darted a frown at the trembling Amanda, which almost petrified her; he told her that she and Ellen must retire immediately to rest, as they had a long journey before them the ensuing day, which would require their rising early. Amanda, for the first time in her life, wished to be relieved from his presence, and gladly rose to obey him; he attended her himself to the room prepared for her, which was directly over that where the gentlemen sat; to think of rest was impossible; the severity of her father's looks, and her precipitate journey—she knew not whither—but evidently for the purpose of avoiding Lord Mortimer, filled the thoughts of Amanda with confusion and distress: Ellen essayed artless consolation: "What the tefil do you think," said she, "if I was to go down to give his lortship an intimation of your peing here; you could easily contrive to see him in the garden, or else we could pring him up here, and if the captain surprised us, we could pop him in a moment behind the curtain." Amanda motioned her to silence, unwilling to lose the smallest sound of Lord Mortimer's voice, and determined, anxious as she was to see him, never to act in opposition to her father. At length the horses were led from the stable, and the convivial party descended to them. Amanda softly raised the window, and saw Lord Mortimer eagerly vault upon the saddle; he gave a hasty adieu to the friends, and galloped off; they mounted at the same time, but took a contrary direction. Amanda leaned out till she could no longer hear the clattering of the horses' hoofs; her heart sunk as the sound died upon her ear; she wept as she retired from the window; the idea of Mortimer's disappointment aggravated her grief; she no longer opposed Ellen's efforts to undress her; exhausted by fatigue, sleep soon closed her eyes, and fancy again transported her to Tudor Hall and Mortimer.

By the first dawn of day a knock at her chamber-door roused her from this pleasing illusion, and she heard her father desiring her to rise immediately. Drowsy as she was, she instantly obeyed the summons, and awaking Ellen, they were ready to attend him in a few minutes; a boat was already prepared, and on gaining the opposite side they found a carriage in waiting. Day was now just dawning; a gray mist enveloped the mountains, and cast a shade of obscurity upon all the inferior objects: at length the atmosphere began to brighten—the lucid clouds in the east were tinged with golden radiance, and the sun in beautiful and refulgent majesty arose, gladdening the face of nature with his potent beams; the trees, the shrubs, seemed waving their dewy heads in sign of grateful homage, while their winged inhabitants, as they soared in the air, poured forth the softest notes of melody. Amanda, in spite of sadness, beheld the charming scene with admiration; and Fitzalan contemplated it with delight. "All nature," he exclaimed, "points out to man the gratitude due to the Divine dispenser of good; hardened must that heart be against the feelings of sensibility, which the harmony and fragrance of this early hour awakens not to a perfect sense of it!" Amanda assented to his remark more by a smile than words, for she was ill able to speak. They stopped not till they reached Gwintey, where they breakfasted, and then proceeded, without resting again, to Holyhead, which place Fitzalan announced as they entered it. And now, Amanda first conceived the idea of being brought to another kingdom, which her father soon confirmed her in—for, as soon as they alighted, he inquired when a packet would sail, and heard with evident pleasure about six in the afternoon. He directly desired three passages to be engaged; and, having ordered an early dinner, dismissed Ellen into another room; and seating himself by Amanda, he took her hand, and with a tender voice thus addressed her: "To give pain to your gentle heart has inflicted torture on mine; but honor compelled me to the conduct which I have adopted, and which, I trust and believe, Amanda will excuse when she knows my motive for it, which in due order she shall hear.

"On Lord Cherbury's arrival in town, I was immediately informed of it, according to the promise of his domestics, and directly sent him my letter; scarcely had he read it, ere, with all the ardor of true friendship, he came and brought me to his house, where we might securely reflect on what was to be done. His lordship soon formed a plan that at once inspired me with gratitude and pleasure, as it promised me competence without depriving me of independence—this was to accept the agency of a considerable estate in the north of Ireland, which he possessed in right of his wife, the late Countess of Cherbury, who was an Irish heiress. He proposed my residing in the mansion house, offering to advance a sum sufficient to answer all demands and exigencies; and striving to lighten the obligations he conferred upon me, by declaring he had long been seeking a man of well-known probity, as his last agent had gone off considerably in arrears to him. I accepted his generous offer, and soon freed myself from the power of Belgrave. I now felt a tranquillity I was long a stranger to, and was busied in preparing to come down to you, when Lord Mortimer's letter, like a clap of thunder, broke the happy calm I enjoyed. Gracious heaven! I shuddered to think, that at the very period Lord Cherbury was building up my fortunes, the hopes he entertained for this darling son were in a way of being destroyed, through means of a connection of mine; he had hinted to me his having already settled upon a splendid alliance for Lord Mortimer, which he also hinted his heart was set on: this the infatuated young man had himself some knowledge of; for in his rash letter he entreated my secrecy relative to his proposal for you till beyond the reach of mortals to separate you: no doubt he would never have asked my consent, had he thought he could have procured you without it; he took me, I suppose, for some needy and ambitious creature, who would, though at the expense of integrity, grasp an opportunity of elevating a child to rank and fortune; but never was an erring mortal more mistaken, though dearer to me than the air I breathe—though the lovely child of my lost Malvina—though a cherubim, whose innocent endearments often raised in me, as Prospero says—

> An undergoing stomach—to bear up
> Against what should ensue.

I would rather see you breathless at my feet, than, by conscious and apparent meanness, deserve and incur the malevolence of calumny. I committed the letter to the flames, and requested Lord Cherbury's final commands; being desirous to commence my journey without longer delay, as your delicate state of health, I said, made me anxious to have you immediately under my own care; he complied with my request, and I travelled post, resolved to separate you and Lord Mortimer—even if prepared for the altar: nor was I alone actuated to this by gratitude to Lord Cherbury, or consideration for my own honor—no, with these, a regard for your peace equally influenced me—a soul of sensibility and refinement like yours could never, I know, be happy if treated with repulsive coldness by the family of her husband; particularly if her conscience told her she merited that coldness by entering it clandestinely. Could I bear to think that you—so lovely in person—so amiable in manners—so illustrious in descent—should be called an artful and necessitous contriver? an imputation, which, most undoubtedly, your union with Lord Mortimer would have incurred. No, to the God who gave you to my care, I hold myself responsible, as far as in my power, for preserving your peace—to the mother, whose last words implored my tenderness for her offspring, I hold myself accountable—to me she still exists—I think her ever near—and ere I act, always reflect whether such an action would meet her approbation. Such is the respect virtue excites—it lives when the frail texture of mortality is dissolved. Your attachment, when repelled by reason and fortitude, will soon vanish; as for Lord Mortimer, removed from the flame which warmed his heart, he will soon forget it ever played around it—should he, however, be daring enough to persevere, he will find my resolution unalterable. Honor is the only hereditary possession that ever came to me uninjured; to preserve it in the same state has been ever my unremitted study—it irradiated the gloomy morning of care, and I trust it will gild the setting hours of existence."

Amanda's emotions deprived her of speech or acting—she sat a pale statue, listening to her father's firm and rapid language, which announced the abolition of her hopes; ignorant of her inability to speak, he felt hurt at her silence; and rising abruptly, walked about the room with a disordered air. "I see—I see," cried he at last, looking mournfully upon her, "I am destined to be unhappy; the little treasure which remained from the wreck of felicity, I had hoped (vain hope!) would have comforted and consoled me for what then was lost" "Oh! my father!" exclaimed Amanda, suddenly starting and sighly deeply, "how you pierce my heart!" His pale, emaciated looks seemed to declare him sinking beneath a burden of care; she started up, and flung herself into his arms. "Dearest, best of fathers!" she exclaimed, in a voice broken by sobs, "what is all the world to me in comparison of you? Shall I put Lord Mortimer, so lately a stranger, in competition with your happiness? Oh no! I will henceforth try to regulate every impulse of my heart according to your wishes." Fitzalan burst into tears—

the enthusiasm of virtue warmed them both—hallowed are her raptures, and amply do they recompense the pain attendant on her sacrifices.

Dinner was brought in, to which they sat down in their usual social manner; and Amanda, happy in her father's smiles, felt a ray of returning cheerfulness. The evening was delightfully serene when they went on board, and the vessel, with a gentle motion, glided over the glittering waves; sickness soon compelled Amanda and Ellen to retire from the deck; yet, without a sigh, the former could not relinquish the prospect of the Welsh mountains. By the dawn of next morning the vessel entered the bay of Dublin, and Fitzalan shortly after brought Amanda from the cabin to contemplate a scene which far surpassed all her ideas of sublimity and beauty, a scene which the rising sun soon heightened to the most glowing radiance; they landed at the Marine Hotel, where they breakfasted, and then proceeded in a carriage to a hotel in Capel street, where they proposed staying a few days for the purpose of enjoying Oscar's company, whose regiment was quartered in Dublin, and making some requisite purchases for their journey to the north. As the carriage drove down Capel street, Amanda saw a young officer standing at the corner of Mary's Abbey, whose air very much resembled Oscar's; her heart palpitated; she looked out and perceived the resemblance was a just one, for it was Oscar himself—the carriage passed too swiftly for him to recognise her face; but he was astonished to see a fair hand waving to him; he walked down the street, and reached the hotel just as they were entering it.

CHAPTER X.

"And whence, unhappy youth, he cried,
The sorrows of thy breast?"—GOLDSMITH.

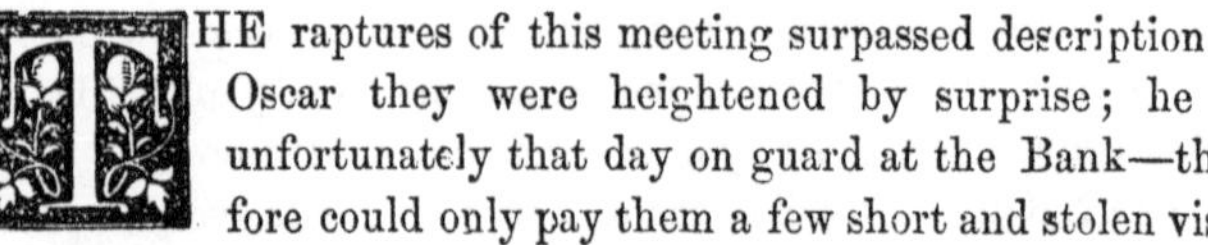

THE raptures of this meeting surpassed description; to Oscar they were heightened by surprise; he was unfortunately that day on guard at the Bank—therefore could only pay them a few short and stolen visits; but the next morning, the moment he was relieved, he came to them. Fitzalan had given Amanda money to purchase whatever she deemed necessary for her convenience and amusement, and Oscar attended her to the most celebrated shops to make her purchases: having supplied herself with a pretty fashionable assortment for her wardrobe, she procured a small collection of books, sufficient, however, from their excellence, to form a little library in themselves, and every requisite for drawing; nor did she forget the little wants and vanities of Ellen; they returned about dinner time to the hotel, where they found their father, who had been transacting business for Lord Cherbury in different parts of the town. We may now suppose him in the possession of happiness, blessed as he was in the society of his children, and the certainty of a competence; but, alas! happiness has almost ever an attendant drawback, and he now experienced one of the most corroding kind from the alteration he witnessed in his son. Oscar was improved in his person, but his eyes no longer beamed with animation, and the rose upon his cheek was pale; his cheerfulness no longer appeared spontaneous, but constrained, as if assumed for the purpose of veiling deep and heartfelt sorrow.

Fitzalan, with all the anxiety and tenderness of a parent, delicately expressed his wish of learning the source of his uneasiness, that by so doing he might be better qualified to alleviate it, hinting at the same time, in indirect terms, that if occasioned by any of the imprudences which youth is sometimes inadvertently led into, he would readily excuse them, from a certainty that he who repented never would again commit them. Oscar started from the remotest hint of divulging his uneasiness: he begged his father, however, to believe (since he had unfortunately perceived it) that it was not derived from imprudence; he pretended to say it was but a slight chagrin, which would soon wear away of itself if not renewed by inquiries. Fitzalan, however, was too much affected by the subject to drop it as readily as Oscar wished. After regarding him for a few minutes with an attention as mournful as fixed, while they sat round the table after dinner, he suddenly exclaimed, "Alas! my dear boy, I fear things are worse within than you will allow." "Now, indeed, Oscar," cried Amanda, sweetly smiling on him, anxious to relieve him from the embarrassment these words had involved him in, and to dissipate the deep gloom of her father's brow, "though never in the wars, I fancy you are not quite heart whole." He answered her with affected gaiety, but, as if wishing to change the discourse, suddenly spoke of Colonel Belgrave, who, at present, he said, was absent from the regiment; occupied by his own feelings, he observed not the glow which mantled the cheeks of his father and sister at that name.

"You know Mrs. Belgrave," said Amanda, endeavoring to regain her composure. "Know her!" repeated he, with an involuntary sigh, "oh, yes!" Then, after the pause of a few minutes, turning to his father, "I believe I have already informed you, sir," he said, "that she is the daughter of your brave old friend, General Honeywood, who, I assure you, paid me no little attention on your account; his house is quite the temple of hospitality, and she the little presiding goddess." "She is happy, I hope," said Amanda. "Oh, surely," replied Oscar, little thinking of the secret motive his sister had for asking such a question, "she possesses what the world thinks necessary to constitute felicity."

Fitzalan had accounted to his son for leaving Devonshire, by saying the air had disagreed with Amanda; he told him of the friendship of Lord Cherbury, from which he said he trusted shortly to be able to have him promoted. "Be assured, my dear Oscar," he cried, "most willingly would I relinquish many of the comforts of life to attain the ability of hastening your advancement, or adding to your happiness." "My happiness!" Oscar mournfully repeated; tears filled his eyes; he could no longer restrain them; and starting up, hurried to a window. Amanda followed, unutterably affected at his emotion: "Oscar, my dear Oscar," said she as she flung her arms round his neck, "you distress me beyond example." He sat down, and leaning his head on her bosom, as she stood before him, his tears fell through her handkerchief. "Oh, heavens!" exclaimed Fitzalan, clasping his hands together, "what a sight is this! Oh! my children, from your felicity alone could I ever derive any; if the hope I entertained of that felicity is disappointed, the heart which cherished it must soon be silent." He arose and went to them: "yet," continued he, "amidst the anguish of this moment, I feel a ray of pleasure at perceiving an affection so strong and tender between you; it will be a mutual consolation and support when the feeble help and protection I can give is finally removed; oh! then, my Oscar," he proceeded, while he folded their united hands in his, "become the soothing friend and guardian of this dear, this amiable, this too lovely girl—let her not too severely feel—too bitterly mourn—the loss of an unhappy father!"

Amanda's tears began to stream, and Oscar's for a few minutes were increased. "Excuse me," at last he said, making an effort to exert himself, to his father, "and be assured, to the utmost of my ability, I will ever obey your wishes, and fulfil your expectations; I am ashamed of the weakness I have betrayed—I will yield to it no more—forget therefore your having seen it, or at least remember it with pain, as I solemnly assure you, no effort on my part shall be untried to conquer it entirely; and now let the short time we have to continue together be devoted to cheerfulness."

Soon after this he mentioned Parker's performance in Marlborough Green, and proposed, as it was now the hour, taking Amanda there; the proposal was not objected to, and Ellen, who they knew would particularly delight in such an amusement, was committed to the care of Oscar's servant, a smart young soldier, who escorted her with much gallantry; the Green was extremely crowded, particularly with officers, whose wandering glances were soon attracted to Amanda, as one of the most elegant girls present. Oscar was soon surrounded by them, and compelled, not only to gratify their curiosity by discovering who she was, but their gallantry by introducing them to her. Their compliments soon diverted her attention from the exhibition, and Ellen, who sat behind her on a bench, afforded innocent mirth by her remarks. "Pless her soul and poty too," she said, "it was the most comical and wonderfulest sight she had ever seen in her porn days." A string of redcoats would have attended Amanda to the hotel had not Oscar prevented it.

The next day was devoted to visiting the public buildings, the park, and a few of the most beautiful places in its vicinage. On the ensuing morn Fitzalan and Amanda continued their journey to the north, where Oscar assured them he expected leave to visit them the following summer, after the reviews were over: as he helped his sister in the carriage she put a pocketbook into his hand (given by her father for that purpose), which contained something to replenish his purse.

Ere we attend the travellers, or rather while they are journeying along, we shall endeavor to account for the dejection of Oscar.

CHAPTER XI.

> "From the loud camp retired and noisy court,
> In honorable ease and rural sport;
> The remnant of his days he safely passed,
> Nor found they lagged too slow nor flew too fast.
> He made his wish with his estate comply,
> Joyful to live, yet not afraid to die:
> One child he had—a daughter chaste and fair,
> His age's comfort, and his fortune's heir."—PRIOR.

OSCAR'S regiment, on his first joining it in Ireland, was quartered in Enniskellen, the corps was agreeable, and the inhabitants of the town hospitable and polite. He felt all the delight of a young and enterprising mind, at entering, what appeared to him, the road to glory and pleasure; many of his idle mornings were spent in rambling about the country, sometimes accompanied by a party of officers, and sometimes alone.

In one of his solitary excursions along the beautiful banks of Lough Erne, with a light fusee on his shoulder, as the woods, that almost descended to the very edge of the water, abounded in game; after proceeding a few miles he felt quite exhausted by the heat, which, as it was now the middle of summer, was intense; at a little distance he perceived an orchard, whose glowing apples promised a delightful repast; knowing that the fruit in many of the neighboring places was kept for sale, he resolved on trying if any was to be purchased here, and accordingly opened a small gate, and ascended through a grass grown path in the orchard, to a very plain white cottage, which stood upon a gentle sloping lawn, surrounded by a rude paling, he knocked against the door with his fusee, and immediately a little rosy girl appeared; "tell me, my pretty lass," cried he, "whether I can purchase any of the fine apples I see here." "Anan!" exclaimed the girl with a foolish stare. Oscar glancing at the moment into the passage, saw, from a half-closed door, nearly opposite to the one at which he stood, a beautiful fair face peeping out; he involuntarily started, and pushing aside the girl, made a step into the passage; the room door directly opened, and an elderly woman, of a genteel figure and pleasing countenance, appeared. "Good Heaven!" cried Oscar, taking off his hat, and retreating, "I fear I have been guilty of the highest impertinence; the only apology I can offer for it is by saying it was not intentional. I am quite a stranger here, and having been informed most of the orchards hereabouts contained fruit for sale, I intruded under that idea." "Your mistake, sir," she replied, with a benevolent smile, "is too trifling to require an apology; nor shall it be attended with any disappointment to you."

She then politely showed him into the parlor, where, with equal pleasure and admiration, he contemplated the fair being of whom before he had but a transient glance: she appeared to be scarcely seventeen, and was, both as to face and figure, what a painter would have chosen to copy for the portrait of a little playful Hebe; though below even the middle size, she was formed with the nicest symmetry; her skin was of a dazzling fairness, and so transparent, that the veins were clearly discernible; the softest blush of nature shaded her beautifully-rounded cheeks; her mouth was small and pouting, and whenever she smiled a thousand graces sported round it; her eyes were full and of a heavenly blue, soft, yet animated, giving, like the expression of her whole countenance, at once an idea of innocence, spirit, and sensibility; her hair, of the palest and most glossy brown, hung carelessly about her, and, though dressed in a loose morning-gown of muslin, she possessed an air of fashion and even consequence; the easy manner in which she bore the looks of Oscar, proclaimed her at once not unaccustomed to admiration, nor displeased with that she now received; for that Oscar admired her could not but be visible, and he sometimes fancied he saw an arch smile playing over her features, at the involuntary glances he directed towards her.

A fine basket of apples, and some delicious cider, was brought to Oscar, and he found his entertainer as hospitable in disposition as she was pleasing in conversation.

The beautiful interior of the cottage by no means corresponded with the plainness of the exterior; the furniture was elegantly neat, and the room ornamented with a variety of fine prints and landscapes; a large folding glass door opened from it into a pleasure-garden.

Adela, so was the charming young stranger called, chattered in the most lively and familiar terms, and at last running over to the basket, tossed the apples all about the table, and picking out the finest presented them to Oscar. It is scarcely necessary to say he received them with emotion: but how transient is all sublunary bliss! A cuckoo-clock, over Oscar's head, by striking three, reminded him that he had passed near two hours in the cottage. "Oh, Heavens!" cried he, starting, "I have made a most unconscionable intrusion; you see, my dear ladies," bowing respectfully to both, "the consequence of being too polite and too fascinating." He repeated his thanks in the most animated manner, and snatching up his hat, departed, yet not without casting

"One longing, lingering look behind."

The sound of footsteps after him in the lawn made him turn, and he perceived the ladies had followed him thither. He stopped again to speak to them, and extolled the lovely prospect they had from that eminence of the lake and its scattered islands. "I presume," said Adela, handling the fusee on which he leaned, "you were trying your success to-day in fowling?" "Yes; but, as you may perceive, I have been unsuccessful." "Then, I assure you," said she, with an arch smile, "there is choice game to be found in our woods." "Delicious game, indeed!" cried he, interpreting the archness of her look, and animated by it to touch her hand, "but only tantalizing to a keen sportsman, who sees it elevated above his reach." "Come, come," exclaimed the old lady, with a sudden gravity, "we are detaining the gentleman." She took her fair companion by the arm, and hastily turned to the cottage. Oscar gazed after them a moment, then, with a half-smothered sigh, descended to the road. He could not help thinking this incident of the morning very like the novel adventures he had sometimes read to his sister Amanda as she sat at work; and, to complete the resemblance, thought he, I must fall in love with the little heroine. Ah! Oscar, beware of such imprudence! guard your heart with all your care against tender impressions, till fortune has been more propitious to you! Thus would my father speak, mused Oscar, and set his own misfortunes in terrible array before me, were he now present: well, I must endeavor to act as if he were here to exhort me. Heigh ho! proceeded he, shouldering his fusee, glory for some time to come must be my mistress!

The next morning the fusee was again taken down, and he sallied out, carefully avoiding the officers, lest any of them should offer to accompany him; for he felt a strange reluctance to their participating in either the smiles of Adela or the apples of the old lady. Upon his arrival at the orchard, finding the gate open, he advanced a few steps up the path, and had a glimpse of the cottage, but no object was visible. Oscar was too modest to attempt entering it uninvited; he therefore turned back, yet often cast a look behind him; no one, however, was to be seen. He now began to feel the heat oppressive, and himself fatigued with his walk, and sat down upon a moss-covered stone, on the margin of the lake, at a little distance from the cottage, beneath the spreading branches of a hawthorn; his hat and fusee were laid at his feet, and a cool breeze from the water refreshed him; upon its smooth surface a number of boats and small sail-vessels were now gliding about in various directions, and enlivened the enchanting prospect which was spread upon the bosom of the lake: from contemplating it he was suddenly roused by the warble of a female voice; he started, turned, and beheld Adela just by him "Bless me!" cried she, "who would have thought of seeing you here; why, you look quite fatigued, and, I believe, want apples to-day as much as you did yesterday?" Then, sitting down on the seat he had resigned, she tossed off her bonnet, declaring it was insupportably warm, and began rummaging a small work-bag she held on her arm. Oscar snatching the bonnet from the ground, Adela flung apples into it, observing it would make an excellent basket He sat down at her feet, and never, perhaps, felt such a variety of emotions as at the present moment: his cheeks glowed with a brighter color, and his eyes were raised to hers with the most ardent admiration; yet not to them alone could he confine the expression of his feelings; they broke in half-formed sentences from his lips, which Adela heard with the most perfect composure, desiring him either to eat or pocket his apples quickly, as she wanted her bonnet, being in a great hurry to return to the cottage, from which she had made a kind of stolen march. The apples were instantly committed to his pocket, and he was permitted to tie on the bonnet. A depraved man might have misinterpreted the gaiety of Adela, or at least endeavored to take advantage of it; but the sacred impression of virtue, which nature and education had stamped upon the heart of Oscar, was indelibly fixed, and he neither suspected, nor, for worlds, would have attempted injuring, the innocence of Adela: he beheld her (in what indeed was a true light) as a little playful nymph, whose actions were the offspring of innocence.

"I assure you," exclaimed she, rising, "I am very loth to quit this pleasant seat; but, if I make a much longer delay, I shall find the lady of the cottage in anxious expectation." "May I advance?" said Oscar, as he pushed open the gate for her. "If you do," replied she, "the least that will be said from seeing us together, is, that we were in search of each other the whole of the morning." "Well," cried Oscar, laughing at this careless speech, "and if they do say so, it would not be doing me injustice." "Adieu, adieu," said she, waving her hand, "not another word for a kingdom."

What a compound of beauty and giddiness it is! thought Oscar, watching her till she entered the cottage. As he returned from the sweet spot he met some laborers, from whom he inquired concerning its owner, and learned she was a respectable widow lady of the name of Marlowe.

On Oscar's return from Enniskellen, he heard from the officers that General Honeywood, an old veteran, who had a fine estate about fourteen miles from the town, was that morning to pay his compliments to them, and that cards had been left for a grand *fête* and ball, which he annually gave on the 1st of July, to commemorate one of the glorious victories of King William. Every person of any fashion in and about the neighborhood was on such occasions sure of an invitation; and the officers were pleased with theirs, as they had for some time wished for an opportunity of seeing the General's daughter, who was very much admired.

The General, like a true veteran, retained an enthusiastic attachment for the profession of arms, to which not only the morning, but the meridian of his life had been devoted, and which he had not quitted till compelled by a debilitated constitution. Seated in his paternal mansion he began to experience the want of a faithful companion, who would heighten the enjoyments of the tranquil hour, and soothe the infirmities of age: this want was soon supplied by his union with a young lady in the neighborhood, whose only dowry was innocence and beauty. From the great disparity of their ages it was concluded she had married for convenience; but the tenor of her conduct changed this opinion, by proving the General possessed her tenderest affections: a happier couple were not known; but this happiness was terminated as suddenly as fatally by her death, which happened two years after the birth of her daughter; all the General's love was then centered in her child. Many of the ladies in the neighborhood, induced by the well-known felicity his lady had enjoyed, or by the largeness of his fortune, made attempts to engage him again in matrimonial toils; but he fought shy of them all, solemnly declaring, "he would never bring a stepmother over his dear girl." In her infancy, she was his plaything, and as she grew up his comfort; caressed, flattered, adored from her childhood, she scarcely knew the meaning of harshness and contradiction; a naturally sweet disposition, and the superintending care of an excellent woman, prevented any pernicious effect from such excessive indulgence as she received; to disguise or duplicity she was a perfect stranger; her own feelings were never concealed, and others she supposed equally sincere in revealing theirs: true, the open avowal of her regard or contempt often incurred the imputation of imprudence; but had she even heard it she would have only laughed at it—for the General declared whatever she said was right, and her own heart assured her of the innocence of her intentions. As she grew up the house again became the seat of gaiety; the General, though very infirm, felt his convivial spirit revive: he delighted in the society of his friends, and could still

"Shoulder his crutch, and show how fields were won!"

Oscar, actuated by an impulse, which if he could, he, at least, did not strive to account for, continued daily to parade before the orchard, but without again seeing Adela.

At length the day for General Honeywood's entertainment arrived, and the officers, accompanied by a large party, set off early for Woodlawn, the name of the General's seat. It was situated on the borders of the lake, where they found barges waiting to convey them to a small island, which was the scene of the morning's amusement: the breakfast was laid out amidst the ruins of an ancient building, which, from the venerable remains of its gothic elegance, was most probably, in the days of religious enthusiasm, the seat of sacred piety: the old trees in groups formed a thick canopy overhead, and the ivy that crept along the walls filled up many of the niches where the windows had formerly been; those that still remained open, by descending to the ground, afforded a most enchanting prospect of the lake; the long succession of arches, which composed the body of the chapel, were in many places covered with creeping moss, and scattered over with wall-flowers blue hair-bells, and other spontaneous productions of nature; while between them were placed seats and breakfast-tables, ornamented in a fanciful manner.

The officers experienced a most agreeable surprise on entering; but how inferior were their feelings to the sensations which Oscar felt, when, introduced with the party by the General to his daughter, he beheld in Miss Honeywood the lovely Adela! She seemed to enjoy his surprise, and Mrs. Marlowe, from the opposite side of the table, beckoned him to her with an arch look; he flew round, and she made room for him by herself: "Well, my friend," cried she, "do you think you shall find the General's fruit as tempting as mine?" "Ah!" exclaimed Oscar, half sighing, half smiling, "Hesperian fruit, I fear, which I can never hope to obtain." Adela's attention, during breakfast, was too much engrossed by the company to allow her to notice Oscar more than by a few hasty words and smiles. There being no dancing till the evening, the company, after breakfast, dispersed according to their various inclinations.

The island was diversified with little acclivities, and scattered over with wild shrubs, which embalmed the air; temporary arbors of laurel, intermingled with lilies, were erected and laid out with fruits, ices, and other refreshments; upon the edge of the water a marquee was pitched for the regimental band, which Colonel Belgrave had politely complimented the General with: a flag was hoisted on it, and upon a low eminence a few small field-pieces were mounted: attendants were everywhere dispersed, dressed in white streamers, ornamented with a profusion of orange-colored ribbons; the boatmen were dressed in the same livery; and the barges, in which several of the party were to visit the other islands, made a picturesque appearance with their gay streamers fluttering in the breeze; the music, now softly dying away upon the water, now gradually swelling on the breeze, and echoed back by the neighboring hills, added to the pleasures of the scene.

Oscar followed the footsteps of Adela; but at the very moment in which he saw her disengaged from a large party, the Genera hallooed to him from a shady bank on which he sat; Oscar could not refuse the summons; and, as he approached, the General, extending his hand, gave him a cordial squeeze, and welcomed him as the son of a brave man he had once intimately known. "I recollected the name of Fitzalan," said he, "the moment I heard it mentioned; and had the happiness of learning from Colonel Belgrave I was not mistaken in believing you to be the son of my old friend." He now made several inquiries concerning Fitzalan, and the affectionate manner in which he mentioned him was truly pleasing to Oscar. "He had once," he said, "saved his life at the imminent danger of his own, and it was an obligation, while that life remained, he could not forget."

Like Don Guzman in Gil Blas, the General delighted in fighting over his battles, and now proceeded to enumerate many incidents which happened during the American war, when he and Fitzalan served in the same regiment. Oscar could well have dispensed with such an enumeration; but the General, who had no idea that he was not as much delighted in listening as he was in speaking, still went on. Adela had been watching them some time; her patience at length, like Oscar's, being exhausted, she ran forward and told her father "he must not detain him another minute, for they were going upon the lake; and you know, papa," cried she, "against we come back, you can have all your battles arranged in proper form, though, by the bye, I don't think it is the business of an old soldier to intimidate a young one with such dreadful tales of iron wars." The General called her saucy baggage, kissed her with rapture, and saw her trip off with his young friend, who seized the favorable opportunity to engage her for the first set in the evening. About four the company assembled in the Abbey to dinner; the band played during the repast; the toasts were proclaimed by sound of trumpet, and answered by an immediate discharge from the Mount. At six the ladies returned to Woodlawn to change their dresses for the ball, and now

"Awful beauty put on all its charms."

Tea and coffee were served in the respective rooms, and by eleven the ball-room was completely crowded with company, at once brilliant and lively, particularly the gentlemen, who were not a little elevated by the General's potent libations to the glorious memory of him whose victory they were celebrating.

Adela, adorned in a style superior to what Oscar had yet seen, appeared more lovely than he had even at first thought her; her dress, which was of thin muslin, spangled, was so contrived as to give a kind of aerial lightness to her figure. Oscar reminded her of the promise of the morning, at the very moment the colonel approached for the purpose of engaging her. She instantly informed him of her engagement to Mr. Fitzalan. "Mr. Fitzalan!" rereated the colonel, with the haughty air of a man who thought he had reason to be offended; "he has been rather precipitate, indeed; but, though we may envy, who shall wonder at his anxiety to engage Miss Honeywood?"

Dancing now commenced, and the elegant figure of Adela never appeared to greater advantage; the transported General watched every movement, and, "incomparable, by Jove!—what a sweet angel she is!" were expressions of admiration which involuntarily broke from him in the pride and fondness of his heart. Oscar, too, whose figure was remarkably fine, shared his admiration, and he declared to Colonel Belgrave, he did not think the world could produce such another couple. This assertion was by no means pleasing to the Colonel; he possessed as much vanity, perhaps, as ever fell to the share of a young belle conscious of perfections, and detested the idea of having any competitor (at least such a powerful one as Oscar) in the good graces of the ladies. Adela, having concluded the dance, complained of fatigue, and retired to an alcove, whither Oscar followed her. The window commanded a view of the lake, the little island, and the ruined Abbey; the moon in full splendor cast her silvery light over all those objects, giving a softness to the landscape, even more pleasing than the glowing charms it had derived from the radiancy of day. Adela in dancing had dropped the bandeau from her hair; Oscar took it up, and still retained it. Adela now stretched forth her hand to take it. "Allow me," cried he, gently taking her hand, "to keep it; to-morrow you would cast it away as a trifle, but I would treasure it as a relic of inestimable value; let me have some memento of the charming hours I have passed to-day." "Oh, a truce," said Adela, "with such expressions (who did not, however, oppose his putting her bandeau in his bosom); they are quite commonplace, and have already been repeated to hundreds, and will again, I make no doubt." "This is your opinion?" "Yes, really." "Oh, would to Heaven," exclaimed Oscar, "I durst convince you how mistaken a one it is." Adela, laughing, assured him that would be a difficult matter. Oscar grew pensive. "I think," cried he, "if oppressed by misfortune, I should of all places on earth like a seclusion in the old Abbey." "Why, really," said Adela, "it is tolerably calculated for a hermitage; and if you take a solitary whim, I beg I may be apprised of it in time, as I should receive peculiar pleasure in preparing your mossy couch and frugal fare." "The reason for my liking it," replied he, "would be the prospect I should have from it of Woodlawn." "And does Woodlawn," asked Adela, "contain such particular charms, as to render a view of it so very delightful?"

At this moment they were summoned to call a new dance—a summons, perhaps, not agreeable to either, as it interrupted an interesting tête-à-tête. The Colonel engaged Adela for the next set; and though Oscar had no longer an inclination to dance, to avoid particularity he stood up, and with a young lady who was esteemed extremely handsome. Adela, as if fatigued, no longer moved with animation, and suddenly interrupted the Colonel in a gallant speech he was making to her, to inquire, "if he thought Miss

O'Neal (Oscar's partner) pretty—so very pretty as she was generally thought?" The Colonel was too keen not to discover at once the motive which suggested this inquiry. "Why, faith," cried he, after examining Miss O'Neal some minutes through an opera glass, "the girl has charms, but so totally eclipsed at present," looking languishingly at Adela, "in my eyes, that I cannot do them the justice they may perhaps merit: Fitzalan, however, by the homage he pays her, seems as if he would make up for the deficiency of every other person." Adela turned pale, and took the first opportunity of demanding her bandeau from Oscar; he, smilingly, refused it, declaring it was a trophy of the happiness he had enjoyed that day, and that the General should have informed her a soldier never relinquished such a glorious memento." "Resign mine," replied Adela, "and procure one from Miss O'Neal."—"No!" cried he, "I would not pay her charms and my own sincerity so bad a compliment, as to ask what I should not in the least degree value." Adela's spirits revived, and she repeated her request no more.

The dancing continued after supper, with little intermission, till seven, when the company repaired to the saloon to breakfast, after which they dispersed. The General particularly and affectionately bid Oscar farewell, and charged him to consider Woodlawn as his head-quarters. "Be assured," said the good-natured old man, "the son of my brave, worthy, and long respected friend, will ever be valuable to my heart and welcome to my home; and would to heaven, in the calm evening of life, your father and I had pitched our tents nearer each other."

From this period Oscar became almost an inmate of his house, and the General shortly grew so attached to him, that he felt unhappy if deprived of his society; the attentions he received from Oscar were such as an affectionate son would pay a tender father; he supported his venerable friend whenever he attempted to walk, attended him in all the excursions he made about his domain, read to him when he wanted to be lulled to sleep, and listened, without betraying any symptoms of fatigue, to his long and often truly tiresome stories of former battles and campaigns; in paying these attentions Oscar obeyed the dictates of gratitude and esteem, and also gratified a benevolent disposition, happy in being able

"To rock the cradle of declining age."

But his time was not so entirely engrossed by the General as to prevent his having many hours to devote to Adela; with her he alternately conversed, read, and sung, rambled with her through romantic paths, or rode along the beautiful borders of Lough Erne, was almost her constant escort to all the parties she went to in the neighborhood, and frequently accompanied her to the hovels of wretchedness, where the woes which extorted the soft tear of commiseration he saw amply relieved by her generous hand; admiring her as he did before, how impossible was it for Oscar, in these dangerous tête-à-têtes, to resist the progress of a tender passion—a passion, however, confined (as far at least as silence could confine it) to his own heart. The confidence which he thought the General reposed in him, by allowing such an intercourse with his daughter, was too sacred in his estimation to be abused; but though his honor resisted, his health yielded to his feelings.

Adela, from delighting in company, suddenly took a pensive turn; she declined the constant society she had hitherto kept up, and seemed in a solitary ramble with Oscar to enjoy more pleasure than the gayest party appeared to afford her; the favorite spot they visited almost every evening was a path on the margin of the lake, at the foot of a woody mountain; here often seated, they viewed the sun sinking behind the opposite hills; and while they enjoyed the benignancy of his departing beams, beheld him tinge the trembling waves with gold and purple; the low whistle of the ploughman returning to his humble cottage, the plaintive carol of birds from the adjacent grove, and the low bleating of cattle from pastures which swelled above the water, all these, by giving the softest and most pleasing charms of nature to the hour, contrived to touch, yet more sensibly, hearts already prepossessed in favor of each other. Adela would sometimes sing a little simple air, and carelessly leaning on the arm of Oscar, appear to enjoy perfect felicity. Not so poor Oscar: the feelings of his soul at these moments trembled on his lips, and to repress them was agony.

An incident soon occurred which endeared him yet more to the General. Driving one day in a low phaeton along a road cut over a mountain, the horses, frightened by a sudden firing from the lake, began rearing in the most frightful manner; the carriage stood near a tremendous precipice, and the servants, appalled by terror, had not power to move. Oscar saw that nothing but an effort of desperate resolution could keep them from destruction; he leaped out, and, rushing before the horses, seized their heads, at the eminent hazard of being tumbled down the precipice, on whose very verge he stood; the servants, a little relieved from their terror, hastened to his assistance; the traces were cut, and the poor General, whose infirmities had weakened his spirits, conveyed home in almost a state of insensibility. Adela, perceiving him from her dressing-room window, flew down, and learning his danger, fell upon his neck in an agony of mingled joy and terror; her caresses soon revived him, and as he returned them, his eyes eagerly sought his deliverer. Oscar stood near, with mingled tenderness and anxiety in his looks; the General took his hand, and whilst he pressed it along with Adela's to his bosom, tears fell on them. "You are both my children!" he exclaimed; "the children of my love, and from your felicity I must derive mine." This expression Oscar conceived to be a mere effusion of gratitude, little thinking what a project relative to him had entered the General's head, who had first, however, consulted and learned from his daughter it would be agreeable to her. This generous, some will say romantic, old man, felt for Oscar the most unbounded love and gratitude, and as the best proof of both, he resolved to bestow on this young soldier his rich and lovely heiress, who had acknowledged to her father her predilection for him. He knew his birth to be noble, his disposition amiable, and his spirit brave; besides, by this union he should secure the society of Adela. He wished her married, yet dreaded, whenever that event took place, he should be deprived of her; but Oscar, he supposed, bound to him by gratitude, would, unlike others, accede to his wishes of residing at Woodlawn during his lifetime. His project he resolved on communicating to Colonel Belgrave, whom, on Oscar's account, he regarded, as Oscar had said (what indeed he believed), that he was partly indebted to him for his commission.

What a thunder-stroke was this to Belgrave, who arrived at Woodlawn the morning after the resolution was finally settled, and was asked to accompany the General, about a little business, to the summer-house in the garden. Poor Oscar trembled; he felt a presentiment he should be the subject of discourse, and had no doubt but the General meant to complain to Colonel Belgrave, as a person who had some authority over him, about his great particularity to Miss Honeywood.

Rage, envy, and surprise, kept the Colonel silent some minutes after the General had ended speaking; dissimulation then came to his aid, and he attempted, though in faltering accents, to express his admiration of such generosity; yet to bestow such a treasure, so inestimable, on such a man, when so many of equal rank and fortune sighed for its possession; upon a man, too, or rather a boy, from whose age it might be expected his affections would be variable. "Let me tell you, Colonel," said the General, hastily interrupting him, and striking his stick upon the ground, as he rose to return to the house, "there can be little danger of his affections changing when such a girl as Adela is his wife; so touch no more upon that subject, I entreat you: but you must break the affair to the young fellow, for I should be in such a confounded flurry I should set all in confusion, and beat an alarm at the first onset."

The gloom and embarrassment which appeared in the countenance of the Colonel, filled Oscar with alarms; he imagined them excited by friendship for him. After what the General had said, he sighed to hear particulars, and longed, for the first time, to quit Woodlawn. The Colonel was indeed in a state of torture; he had long meditated the conquest of Adela, whose fortune and beauty rendered her a truly desirable object; to resign her without one effort of circumventing Oscar was not to be thought of. To blast his promised joys, even if it did not lead to the accomplishment of his own wishes, he felt would give him some comfort, and he resolved to leave no means untried for doing so.

They set off early in the morning for Enniskellen, and Belgrave sent his servant on before them, that there might be no restraint on the conversation he found Oscar inclined to begin.

CHAPTER XII.

> "Sincerity!
> Thou first of virtues, let no mortal leave
> Thy onward path, although the earth should gape,
> And from the gulf of hell destruction cry
> To take dissimulation's winding way."—DOUGLAS.

ELL, Colonel," said Oscar, "I fancy I was not mistaken in thinking the General wanted to speak with you concerning me; I am convinced you will not conceal any particulars of a conversation it may be so essential to my honor to hear." "Why, faith," cried the Colonel, delighted to commence his operations, "he was making a kind of complaint about you; though he acknowledges you a brave lad, yet, hang him, he has not generosity enough to reward that bravery with his daughter, or any of his treasure." "Heaven is my witness!" exclaimed the unsuspicious Oscar, "I never aspired to either; I always knew my passion for his daughter as hopeless as fervent, and my esteem for him as disinterested as sincere; I would have sooner died than abused the confidence he reposed in me, by revealing my attachment; I see, however, in future, I must be an exile to Woodlawn." "Not so, neither," replied the Colonel; "only avoid such particularity to the girl; I believe in my soul she has more pride than susceptibility in her nature; in your next visit, therefore, which, for that purpose, I would have you soon make, declare, in a cavalier manner, your affections being engaged previous to your coming to Ireland; this declaration will set all to rights with the General; he will no longer dread you on his daughter's account; you will be as welcome as ever to Woodlawn, and enjoy, during your continuance in the country, the society you have hitherto been accustomed to." "No," said Oscar, "I cannot assert so great a falsehood." "How ridiculous!" replied the Colonel; "for heaven's sake, my dear boy, drop such romantic notions; I should be the last man in the world to desire you to invent a falsehood which could injure any one; but no priest in Christendom would blame you for this." "And suppose I venture it, what will it do but bind faster round my heart chains already too galling, and destroy in the end all remains of peace."

"Faith, Fitzalan," said the Colonel, "by the time you have had a few more love affairs with some of the pretty girls of this kingdom, you will talk no more in this way; consider, and be not too scrupulous, how disagreeable it will be to resign the General's friendship, and the pleasing society you enjoyed at Woodlawn; besides, it will appear strange to those who knew your former intimacy: in honor, too, you are bound to do as I desire you, for should the girl have been imprudent enough to conceive an attachment for you, this will certainly remove it: for pride would not allow its continuance after hearing of a favorite rival; and the General will be essentially served." "My dear Colonel," said Oscar, his eyes suddenly sparkling, "do you think she has been imprudent enough to conceive a partiality for me?" "I am sure," said the Colonel, "that is a question I cannot possibly answer; but, to give my opinion, I think, from her gay, unembarrassed manner, she has not." "I suppose not, indeed," cried Oscar, mournfully sighing: "why then should I be guilty of a falsehood for a person who is already indifferent to me?" "I have told you my reason," replied the Colonel, coldly; "do as you please." They were now both silent, but the conversation was soon renewed, and many arguments passed on both sides. Oscar's heart secretly favored the Colonel's plan, as it promised the indulgence of Adela's society; to be an exile from Woodlawn was insupportable to his thoughts; reason yielded to the vehemence of passion, and he at last fell into the snare the perfidious Belgrave had spread, thus, by a deviation from truth, forfeiting the blessings a bounteous Providence had prepared for him.

Oh! never let the child of integrity be seduced from the plain and undeviating path of sincerity: oh! never let him hope by illicit means to attain a real pleasure; the hope of obtaining any good through such means will, like a meteor of the night, allure but to deceive.

Soon after his fatal promise to the Colonel, a self-devoted victim, he accompanied him to Woodlawn; on their arrival, Miss Honeywood was in the garden, and Oscar, trembling, went to seek her; he found her sitting in a flower-woven arbor—

"Herself the fairest flower."

Never had she looked more lovely; the natural bloom of her cheeks was heightened by the heat, and glowed beneath the careless curls that fell over them; and her eyes, the moment she beheld Oscar, beamed with the softest tenderness, the most bewitching sensibility. "My dear, dear Fitzalan!" cried she, throwing aside the book she had been reading, and extending her hand, "I am glad to see you; I hope you are come to take up your residence for some time at Woodlawn." "You hope!" repeated Oscar, mournfully. "I do, indeed! but, bless me, what is the matter? You look so pale and thin, you look but the shadow of yourself, or rather like a despairing shepherd, ready to hang himself on the first willow tree he meets." "I am indeed unhappy!" cried Oscar; "nor will you wonder at my being so when I acknowledge I at this present time feel a passion which I must believe hopeless." "Hopeless! well, now, I insist on being your confidant, and then," smiling somewhat archly, "I shall see what reason you have so despair." "Agreed," exclaimed Oscar; "and now to my story:" then pausing a minute, he started up. "No," continued he, "I find it impossible to tell it——; let this dear, this estimable object," drawing a miniature of his sister from his bosom, "speak for me, and declare whether he who loves such a being can ever lose that love, or help being wretched at knowing it is without hope."

Adela snatched it hastily from him, and by a sudden start betrayed her surprise; words indeed are inadequate to express her heart-rending emotions as she contemplated the beautiful countenance of her imaginary rival: and was Oscar, then—that Oscar whom she adored—whose happiness she had hoped to constitute—whose fortune she delighted to think she should advance—really attached to another; alas! too true, he was—of the attachment she held a convincing proof in her hand; she examined it again and again, and in its mild beauties thought she beheld a striking proof of the superiority over the charms she herself possessed; the roses forsook her cheeks, a mist overspread her eyes, and with a shivering horror she dropped it from her hand. Oscar had quitted the arbor to conceal his agonies. "Well," said he, now returning with forced calmness, "is it not worthy of inspiring the passion I feel?" Unable to answer him, she could only point to the place where it lay, and hastened to the house. "Sweet image!" cried Oscar, taking it from the ground, "what an unworthy purpose have I made you answer!—alas! all is now over—Adela—my Adela!—is lost for ever!—lost—ah, heavens! had I ever hopes of possessing her?—oh, no! to such happiness never did I dare to look forward."

Adela, on reaching the parlor which opened into the garden, found her father there. "Ah! you little baggage, do I not deserve a kiss for not disturbing your *tête-à-tête?* Where is that young rogue, Fitzalan?" "I beg, I entreat, sir," said Adela, whose tears could no longer be restrained, "you will never mention him again to me; too much has already been said about him." "Nay, pr'ythee, my little girl," exclaimed the General, regarding her with surprise, "cease thy sighs and tears, and tell me what's the matter." "I am hurt," replied she, in a voice scarcely articulate, "that so much has been said about Mr. Fitzalan, whom I can never regard in any other light than that of a common acquaintance." The Colonel, who had purposely lingered about the wood, now entered. Adela started, and precipitately retreated through another door. "Faith, my dear Colonel," said the General, "I am glad you are come; the boy and girl have had a little skirmish; but, like other love quarrels, I suppose it will soon be made up—so let me know how the lad bore the announcement of his good fortune." "It fills a rational mind with regret," exclaimed the Colonel, seating himself gravely, and inwardly rejoicing at the success of his stratagem, "to find such a fatality prevalent among mankind as makes them reject a proffered good, and sigh for that which is unattainable; like wayward children, neglecting their sports to pursue a rainbow, and weeping as the airy pageant mocks their grasp." "Very true, indeed," said the General; "very excellent, upon my word; I doubt if the chaplain of a regiment ever delivered such a pretty piece of morality; but, dear Colonel," laying his hand on his knee, "what did the boy say?" "I am sorry, sir," he replied, "that what I have just said is so applicable to him. He acknowledged the lady's merit, extolled her generosity—but pleaded a prior attachment against accepting your offer, which even one more exalted would not tempt him to forego, though he knows not whether he will ever succeed in it." "The devil he did!"

exclaimed the General, as soon as rage and surprise would allow him to speak. "The little impertinent puppy! the ungrateful young dog! a prior attachment!—reject my girl—my Adela—who has had such suitors already; so, I suppose I shall have the whole affair blazed about the country; I shall hear from every quarter how my daughter was refused; and by whom?—why, by a little Ensign, whose whole fortune lies in his sword-knot. A fine game I have played, truly; but if the jackanapes opens his lips about the matter, may powder be my poison if I do not trim his jacket for him!" "Dear General," said the Colonel, "you may depend on his honor; but even supposing he did mention the affair, surely you should know it would not be in his power to injure Miss Honeywood—amiable—accomplished—in short, possessed, as she is, of every perfection. I know men, at least one man of consequence, both from birth and fortune, who has long sighed for her, and who would, if he received the least encouragement, openly avow his sentiments." "Well," cried the General, still panting for breath, "we will talk about him at some future time; for I am resolved on soon having my little girl married, and to her own liking, too."

Oscar and Adela did not appear till dinner time; both had been endeavoring to regain composure; but poor Oscar had been far less successful than Adela in the attempt; not that she loved less, for indeed her passion for him was of the tenderest nature, and she flattered herself with having inspired one equally ardent in his breast. Sanctioned by her father, she thought it would constitute the felicity of their lives, and looked forward with a generous delight to the period when she should render her beloved Fitzalan prosperous and independent. The disappointment she experienced, as the first she had ever met, sat heavy on her heart, and the gay visions of youth were in one moment clouded by melancholy; but her pride was as great as her sensibility, and as its powerful impulse pervaded her mind, she resolved to afford Oscar no triumph by letting him witness her dejection; she therefore wiped away all traces of tears from her eyes, checked the vain sigh that struggled at her heart, and dressed herself with as much attention as ever. Her heavy eyes, her colorless cheeks, however, denoted her feelings; she tried, as she sat at table, to appear cheerful, but in vain; and, on the removal of the cloth, immediately retired, as no ladies were present.

The General was a stranger to dissimulation, and as he no longer felt, he no longer treated Oscar with his usual kindness. When pale, trembling, and disordered, he appeared before him, he received him with a stern frown, and an air scarcely complaisant. This increased the agitation of Oscar: every feeling of his soul was in commotion; he was no longer the life of their company; their happiness and mirth formed a striking contrast to his misery and dejection; he felt a forlorn wretch—a mere child of sorrow and dependence; scalding tears dropped from him as he bent over his plate; he could have cursed himself for such weakness: fortunately it was unnoticed. In losing the General's attention, he seemed to lose that of his guests; his situation grew too irksome to be borne; he rose, unregarded, and a secret impulse led him to the drawing-room. Here Adela, oppressed by the dejection of her spirits, had flung herself upon a couch, and gradually sunk into a slumber: Oscar stepped lightly forward, and gazed on her with a tenderness as exquisite as a mother would have felt in viewing her sleeping babe; her cheek, which rested on her fair hand, was tinged with a blush, by the reflection of a crimson curtain through which the sun darted, and the traces of a tear were yet discernible upon it. "Never!" cried Oscar, with folded hands, as he hung over the interesting figure, "never may any tear, except that of soft sensibility for the woes of others, bedew the cheek of Adela—perfect as her goodness be her felicity—may every blessing she now enjoys be rendered permanent by that Power who smiles benignly upon innocence like hers! Oh! Adela, he who now prays for your felicity never will lose your idea, he will cherish it in his heart, to ameliorate his sorrows, and, from the dreary path which may be appointed for him to tread, sometimes look back to happier scenes!" Adela began to stir; she murmured out some inarticulate words, and, suddenly rising from the couch, beheld the motionless form of Fitzalan: haughtily regarding him, she asked the meaning of such an intrusion. "I did not mean indeed to intrude," said he; "but when I came and found you, can you wonder at my being fascinated to the spot?" The plaintive tone of his voice sunk deep into Adela's heart; she sighed heavily, and turning away seated herself in a window. Oscar followed; he forgot the character he had assumed in the morning, and gently seizing her hand, pressed it to his bosom: at this critical minute, when mutual sympathy appeared on the point of triumphing over duplicity, the door opened, and Colonel Belgrave appeared; from the instant of Oscar's departure, he had been on thorns to follow him, fearful of the consequences of a *tête-à-tête*, and was attended by the rest of the gentlemen.

Oscar was determined on not staying another night at Woodlawn, and declared his intention by asking Colonel Belgrave if he had any commands for Enniskellen, whither he meant to return immediately. "Why, hang it, boy," cried the General, in a rough grumbling voice, "since you have stayed so long, you may as well stay the night; the clouds look heavy over the lake, and threaten a storm." "No, sir," said Oscar, coloring, and speaking in the agitation of his heart, "the raging of a tempest would not make me stay." Adela sighed, but pride prevented her speaking. Fitzalan approached her: "Miss Honeywood," said he—he stopped—his voice was quite stifled. Adela, equally unable to speak, could only encourage him to proceed by a cold glance. "Lest I should not," resumed he, "have the happiness of again visiting Woodlawn, I cannot neglect this opportunity of assuring you that the attention, the obligations I have received in it, never can be forgotten by me; and that the severest pang my heart could possibly experience would result from thinking I lost any part of the friendship you and the General honored me with." Adela bent her head, and Oscar, seeing that she either would not, or could not speak, bowed to the General, and hurried from the room; the tears he had painfully suppressed gushed forth, and at the bottom of the stairs he leaned against the bannisters for support; while he cast his eyes around, as if bidding a melancholy farewell to the scene of former happiness, a hasty footstep advanced: he started, and was precipitately retreating, when the voice of the butler stopped him; this was an old veteran, much attached to Oscar, and his usual attendant in all his fowling and fishing parties. As he waited at tea, he heard Oscar's declaration of departing with surprise, and followed him for the purpose of expressing that and his concern. "Why, Lord now, Mr. Fitzalan," cried he, "what do you mean by leaving us so oddly? But if you are so positive about going to Enniskellen to-night, let me order Standard to be prepared for you." Oscar for some time had had the command of the stables · but knowing as he did that he had lost the General's favor, he could no longer think of taking those liberties which kindness had once invited him to: he wrung the hand of his humble friend, and snatching his hat from the hall table, darted out of the house: he ran till he came to the mountain path, on the margin of the lake. "Never," cried he, distractedly striking his breast, "shall I see her here again! oh, never, never, my beloved Adela! shall your unfortunate Fitzalan wander with you through those enchanting scenes: oh! how transient was this gleam of felicity!"

Exhausted by the violence of his feelings, he fell into a kind of torpid state against the side of the mountain; the shadows of night were thickened by a coming storm; a cold blast howled amongst the hills, and agitated the gloomy waters of the lake; the rain, accompanied by sleet, began to fall, but the tempest raged unregarded around the child of sorrow, the wanderer of the night. Adela alone,

"Heard, felt, or seen,"

pervaded every thought. Some fishermen approaching to secure their boats drove him from this situation, and he flew to the woods which screened one side of the house: by the time he reached it the storm had abated, and the moon, with a watery lustre, breaking through the clouds, rendered, by her feeble rays, the surrounding and beloved scenes just visible.

Adela's chamber looked into the wood, and the light from it riveted Oscar to a spot exactly opposite the window. "My Adela," he exclaimed, extending his arms as if she could have heard and flown into them; then dejectedly dropping them, "she thinks not on such a forlorn wretch as me; oh, what comfort to lay my poor distracted head for one moment on her soft bosom, and hear her sweet voice speak pity to my tortured heart!" Sinking with weakness from the conflicts of his mind, he sought an old roofless root-house in the centre of the wood, where he and Adela had often sat. "Well," said he, as he flung himself upon the damp ground, "many a brave fellow has had a worse bed; but God particularly protects the unsheltered head of the soldier and the afflicted." The twittering of the birds roused him from an uneasy slumber, or rather lethargy, into which he had fallen; and starting up he hastened to the road, fearful, as day was beginning to dawn, of being seen by any of General Honeywood's workmen. It was late ere he arrived at Enniskellen, and before he gained his room he was met by some of the officers, who viewed him with evident astonishment; his regimentals were quite spoiled; his fine hair, from which the rain had washed all the powder, hung dishevelled about his shoulders; the feather of his hat was broken, and the disorder of his countenance was not less suspicious than that of his dress: to their inquiries he stammered out something of a fall, and extricated himself with difficulty from them.

In an obscure village, fifteen miles from Enniskellen, a detachment of the regiment lay; the officer who commanded it disliked his situation extremely; but company being irksome to Oscar, it was just such a one as he desired, and he obtained leave to relieve him: the agitation of his mind, aided by the effects of the storm he had been exposed to, was too much for his constitution: immediately on arriving at his new quarters he was seized with a violent fever; an officer was obliged to be sent to do duty in his place, and it was long ere any symptoms appeared which could flatter those who attended him with hopes of his recovery; when able to sit up he was ordered to return to Enniskellen, where he could be immediately under the care of the regimental surgeon.

Oscar's servant accompanied him in the carriage, and as it drove slowly along he was agreeably surprised by a view of Mrs. Marlowe's orchard; he could not resist the wish of seeing her, and making inquiries relative to the inhabitants of Woodlawn; for with Mrs. Marlowe, I should previously say, he had not only formed an intimacy, but a sincere friendship. She was a woman of the most pleasing manners, and to her superintending care Adela was indebted for many of the graces she possessed, and at her cottage passed many delightful hours with Oscar.

The evening was far advanced when Oscar reached the orchard, and leaning on his servant, slowly walked up the hill: had a spectre appeared before the old lady, she could not have seemed more shocked than she now did, at the unexpected and emaciated appearance of her young friend. With all the tenderness of a fond mother, she pressed his cold hands between her own, and seated him by the cheerful fire which blazed on her hearth, then procured him refreshments that, joined to her conversation, a little revived his spirits; yet, at this moment, the recollection of the first interview he ever had with her, recurred with pain to his heart. "Our friends at Woodlawn, I hope," cried he—he paused —but his eyes expressed the inquiry his tongue was unable to make. "They are well and happy," replied Mrs. Marlowe; "and you know, I suppose, of all that has lately happened there?" "No, I know nothing; I am as one awoke from the slumbers of the grave." "Ere I inform you, then," cried Mrs. Marlowe, "let me, my noble Oscar, express my approbation, my admiration of your conduct, of that disinterested nature which preferred the preservation of constancy to the splendid independency offered to your acceptance." "What splendid independency did I refuse?" asked Oscar, wildly staring at her. "That which the General offered." "The General!" "Yes, and appointed Colonel Belgrave to declare his intentions." "Oh Heavens!" exclaimed Oscar, starting from his chair; "did the General indeed form such intentions, and has Belgrave then deceived me? He told me my attentions to Miss Honeywood were noticed and disliked! he filled my soul with unutterable anguish, and persuaded me to a falsehood which has plunged me into despair!" "He is a monster!" cried Mrs. Marlowe, "and you are a victim to his treachery." "Oh no! I will fly to the General, and open my whole soul to him; at his feet I will declare the false ideas of honor which misled me; I shall obtain his forgiveness, and Adela will yet be mine." "Alas! my child," said Mrs. Marlowe, stopping him as he was hurrying from the room, "it is now too late; Adela can never be yours; she is married, and married unto Belgrave." Oscar staggered back a few paces, uttered a deep groan, and fell senseless at her feet. Mrs. Marlowe's cries brought in his servant, as well as her own, to his assistance; he was laid upon a bed, but it was long ere he showed any signs of recovery; at length, opening his heavy eyes, he sighed deeply, and exclaimed "she is lost to me for ever!"

The servants were dismissed, and the tender-hearted Mrs. Marlowe knelt beside him. "Oh! my friend," said she, "my heart sympathizes in your sorrow; but it is from your own fortitude, more than my sympathy, you must now derive resources of support." "Oh, horrible! to know the cup of happiness was at my lips, and that it was my own hand dashed it from me." "Such, alas!" said Mrs. Marlowe, sighing, as if touched at the moment with a similar pang of self-regret, "is the waywardness of mortals; too often do they deprive themselves of the blessings of a bounteous Providence by their own folly and imprudence—oh! my friend, born as you were with a noble ingenuity of soul, never let that soul again be sullied by the smallest deviation from sincerity." "Do not aggravate my sufferings," said Oscar, "by dwelling on my error." "No, I would sooner die than be guilty of such barbarity; but admonition never sinks so deeply on the heart as in the hour of trial. Young, amiable as you are, life teems, I doubt not, with various blessings to you—blessings which you will know how to value properly, for early disappointment is the nurse of wisdom." "Alas!" exclaimed he, "what blessings?" "These, at least," cried Mrs. Marlowe, "are in your own power—the peace, the happiness, which ever proceeds from a mind conscious of having discharged the incumbent duties of life, and patiently submitted to its trials." "But do you think I will calmly submit to his baseness?" said Oscar, interrupting her. "No; Belgrave shall never triumph over me with impunity!" He started from the bed, and, rushing into the outer room, snatched his sword from the table on which he had flung it at his entrance. Mrs. Marlowe caught his arm. "Rash young man!" exclaimed she, "whither would you go—is it to scatter ruin and desolation around you? Suppose your vengeance was gratified, would that restore your happiness? Think you that Adela, the child of virtue and propriety, would ever notice the murderer of her husband, how unworthy, soever, that husband might be? Or that the old General, who so fondly planned your felicity, would forgive, if he could survive, the evils of his house, occasioned by you?" The sword dropped from the hand of the trembling Oscar. "I have been blameable," cried he, "in allowing myself to be transported to such an effort of revenge; I forgot everything but that; and as to my own life, deprived of Adela, it appears so gloomy as to be scarcely worth preserving."

Mrs. Marlowe seized this moment of yielding softness to advise and reason with him; her tears mingled with his, as she listened to his relation of Belgrave's perfidy; tears augmented by reflecting, that Adela, the darling of her care and affections, was also a victim to it. She convinced Oscar, however, that it would be prudent to confine the fatal secret to their own breasts; the agitation of his mind was too much for the weak state of his health; the fever returned, and he felt unable to quit the cottage. Mrs. Marlowe prepared a bed for him, trusting he would soon be able to remove, but she was disappointed; it was long ere Oscar could quit the bed of sickness; she watched over him with maternal tenderness, while he, like a blasted flower, seemed hastening to decay.

The General was stung to the soul by the rejection of his offer, which he thought would have inspired the soul of Oscar with rapture and gratitude; never had his pride been so severely wounded —never before had he felt humbled in his own eyes: his mortifying reflections the Colonel soon found means to remove, by the most delicate flattery, and the most assiduous attention, assuring the General that his conduct merited not the censure, but the applause of the world. The sophistry which can reconcile us to ourselves is truly pleasing; the Colonel gradually became a favorite, and when he insinuated his attachment for Adela, was assured he should have all the General's interest with her. He was now more anxious than ever to have her advantageously settled; there was something so humiliating in the idea of her being rejected, that it drove him at times almost to madness: the Colonel possessed all the advantages of fortune; but these weighed little in his favor with the General (whose notions we have already proved very disinterested), and much less with his daughter; on the first overture about him she requested the subject might be entirely dropped; the mention of love was extremely painful to her. Wounded by her disappointment in the severest manner, her heart required time to heal it; her feelings delicacy confined to her own bosom; but her languid eyes, and faded cheeks, denoted their poignancy. She avoided company, and was perpetually wander ing through the romantic and solitary paths which she and Oscar had trod together; here more than ever she thought of him, and feared she had treated her poor companion unkindly; she saw him oppressed with sadness, and yet she had driven him from her by the repulsive coldness of her manner—a manner, too, which, from its being so suddenly assumed, could not fail of conveying an idea of her disappointment; this hurt her delicacy as much as her tenderness, and she would have given worlds, had she possessed them, to recall the time when she could have afforded consolation to Oscar, and convinced him that solely as a friend she regarded him. The Colonel was not discouraged by her coldness; he was in the habit of conquering difficulties, and doubted not he should overcome any she threw in his way; he sometimes, as if by chance, contrived to meet her in her rambles; his conversation was always amusing, and confined within the limits she had prescribed; but his eyes, by the tenderest expression, declared the pain he suffered from this proscription, and secretly pleased Adela, as it convinced her of the implicit deference he paid to her will.

Some weeks had elapsed since Oscar's voluntary exile from Woodlawn, and sanguine as were the Colonel's hopes, he found without a stratagem they would not be realized, at least as soon as he expected: fertile in invention, he was not long in concerting one. He followed Adela one morning into the garden, and found her reading in the arbor; she laid aside the book at his entrance, and they chatted for some time on indifferent subjects. The Colonel's servant at last appeared with a large packet of letters, which he presented to his master, who, with a hesitating air, was about putting them into his pocket, when Adela prevented him:—"Make no ceremony, Colonel," said she, "with me; I shall resume my book till you have perused your letters." The Colonel bowed for her permission and began; her attention was soon drawn from her book by the sudden emotion he betrayed; he started, and exclaimed, "Oh, heavens! what a wretch!" then, as if suddenly recollecting his situation, looked at Adela, appeared confused, stammered out a few inarticulate words, and resumed his letter; when finished, he seemed to put it into his pocket, but in reality dropped it at his feet for the basest purpose. He ran over the remainder of the letters, and rising, entreated Adela to excuse his leaving her so abruptly, to answer some of them. Soon after his departure, Adela perceived an open letter lying at her feet; she immediately took it up with an intention of returning to the house with it, when the sight of her own name, in capital letters, and in the well-known hand of Fitzalan, struck her sight; she threw the letter on the table; an universal tremor seized her; she would have given any consideration to know why she was mentioned in a correspondence between Belgrave and Fitzalan: her eye involuntarily glanced at the letter; she saw some words in it which excited still more strongly her curiosity; it could no longer be repressed; she snatched it up, and read as follows:—

TO COLONEL BELGRAVE.

You accuse me of insensibility to, what you call the matchless charms of Adela, an accusation I acknowledge I merit; but why, because I have been too susceptible to those of another, which, in the fond estimation of a lover (at least), appear infinitely superior. The General's offer was certainly a most generous and flattering one, and has gratified every feeling of my soul, by giving me an opportunity of sacrificing, at the shrine of love, ambition and self-interest; my disinterested conduct has confirmed me in the affections of my dear girl, whose vanity I cannot help thinking a little elevated by the triumph I have told her she obtained over Adela; but this is excusable indeed when we consider the object I relinquished for her. Would to heaven the General was propitious to your wishes; it would yield me much happiness to see you, my first and best friend, in possession of a treasure you have long sighed for. I shall, no doubt, receive a long lecture from you for letting the affair relative to Adela be made known, but faith, I could not resist telling my charmer. Heaven grant discretion may seal her lips; if not, I suppose I shall be summoned to formidable combat with the old General. Adieu! and believe me,

Dear Colonel, ever yours,

OSCAR FITZALAN.

"Wretch!" cried the agitated Adela, dropping the letter (which it is scarcely necessary to say was an infamous forgery) in an agony of grief and indignation, "is this the base return we meet for our wishes to raise you to prosperity? Oh! cruel Fitzalan, is it Adela—who thought you so amiable, and who never thoroughly valued wealth, till she believed it had given her the power of conducing to your felicity—whom you hold up as an object of ridicule for unfeeling vanity to triumph over?" Wounded pride and ten derness raised a whirl of contending passions in her breast; she sunk upon the bench, her head rested on her hand, and sighs and tears burst from her. She now resolved to inform Fitzalan she knew the baseness of his conduct, and sting his heart with keen reproaches: now resolved to pass it over in silent contempt. While thus fluctuating, the Colonel softly advanced and stood before her: in the tumult of her mind she had quite forgot the probability of his returning, and involuntarily screamed and started at his appearance. By her confusion, she doubted not but he would suspect her of having perused the fatal letter. Oppressed by the idea, her head sunk on her bosom, and her face was covered with blushes. "What a careless fellow I am!" said the Colonel, taking up the letter, which he then pretended to perceive; he glanced at Adela. "Curse it!" continued he, "I would rather have had all the letters read than this one." He suspects me, thought Adela; her blushes faded, and she fell back on her seat, unable to support the oppressive idea of having acted against the rules of propriety. Belgrave flew to support her: "Loveliest of women!" he exclaimed, and with all the softness he could assume, "what means this agitation?" "I have been suddenly affected," answered Adela, a little recovering, and, rising, she motioned to return to the house. "Thus," answered the Colonel, "you always fly me; but go, Miss Honeywood; I have no right, no attraction, indeed, to detain you; yet, be assured," and he summoned a tear to his aid, while he pressed her hand to his bosom, "a heart more truly devoted to you than mine you can never meet; but I see the subject is painful, and again I resume the rigid silence you have imposed on me; go, then, most lovely and beloved, and since I dare not aspire to a higher, allow me, at least, the title of your friend." "Most willingly," said Adela, penetrated by his gentleness. She was now tolerably recovered, and he prevailed on her to walk instead of returning to the house; she felt soothed by his attention; his insidious tongue dropped manna; he gradually stole her thoughts from painful recollections; the implicit respect he paid her will flattered her wounded pride, and her gratitude was excited by knowing he resented the disrespectful mention of her name in Fitzalan's letter; in short, she felt esteem and respect for him—contempt and resentment for Oscar. The Colonel was too penetrating not to discover her sentiments, and too artful not to take advantage of them. Had Adela, indeed, obeyed the real feelings of her heart, she would have declared against marrying; but pride urged her to a step which would prove to Fitzalan his conduct had not affected her. The General rejoiced at obtaining her consent, and received a promise that for some time she should not be separated from him. The most splendid preparations were made for the nuptials; but though Adela's resentment remained unabated, she soon began to wish she had not been so precipitate in obeying it; an involuntary repugnance rose in her mind against the connection she was about forming, and honor alone kept her from declining it for ever: her beloved friend, Mrs. Marlowe, supported her throughout the trying occasion, and, in an inauspicious hour, Adela gave her hand to the perfidious Belgrave.

About a fortnight after her nuptials, she heard from some of the officers of Oscar's illness; she blushed at his name. "Faith," cried one of them, "Mrs. Marlowe is a charming woman; it is well he got into such snug quarters: I really believe elsewhere he would have given up the ghost." "Poor fellow," said Adela, sighing heavily, yet without being sensible of it. Belgrave rose, he caught her eye, a dark frown lowered on his brow, and he looked as if he would pierce into the recesses of her heart: she shuddered, and, for the first time, felt the tyranny she had imposed upon herself. As Mrs. Marlowe chose to be silent on the subject, she resolved not to mention it to her; but she sent every day to invite her to Woodlawn, expecting by this to hear something of Oscar; but she was disappointed. At the end of a fortnight, Mrs. Marlowe made her appearance; she looked pale and thin. Adela gently reproved her for her long absence, trusting this would oblige her to allege the reason of it; but no such thing. Mrs. Marlowe began to converse on indifferent subjects; Adela suddenly grew peevish, and sullenly sat at her work.

In a few days after Mrs. Marlowe's visit, Adela, one evening, immediately after dinner, ordered the carriage to the cottage; by this time she supposed Oscar had left it, and flattered herself, in the course of conversation, she should learn whether he was perfectly recovered ere he departed. Proposing to surprise her friend she stole by a winding path to the cottage, and softly opened the parlor door; but what were her feelings, when she perceived Oscar sitting at the fireside with Mrs. Marlowe, engaged in a deep conversation! She stopped, unable to advance. Mrs. Marlowe embraced and led her forward. The emotions of Oscar were not inferior to Adela's. He attempted to rise, but could not. A glance from the expressive eyes of Mrs. Marlowe, which seemed to conjure him not to yield to a weakness which would betray his real sentiments to Adela, somewhat reanimated him. He rose, and tremblingly approached her. "Allow me, madam," cried he, "to ——" The sentence died unfinished on his lips; he had not power to offer congratulations on an event which had probably destroyed the happiness of Adela, as well as his own. "Oh! a truce with compliments," said Mrs. Marlowe, forcing herself to assume a cheerful air; "prithee, good folks, let us be seated, and enjoy, this cold evening, the comforts of a good fire." She forced the trembling, the almost fainting, Adela to take some wine, and, by degrees, the flutter of her spirits and Oscar's abated, but the sadness of their countenances, the anguish of their souls, increased. The cold formality, the distant reserve they both assumed, filled each with sorrow and regret. So pale, so emaciated, so woe-begone did Fitzalan appear, so much the son of sorrow and despair, that had he half murdered Adela, she could not at that moment have felt for him any other sentiments than those of pity and compassion. Mrs. Marlowe, in a laughing way, told her of the troubles she had had with him: "for which, I assure you," said she, "he rewards me badly; for the moment he was enlarged from the nursery, he either forgot or neglected all the rules I had laid down for him. Pray do join your commands to mine, and charge him to take more care of himself." "I would, most willingly," cried Adela, "if I thought they would influence him to do so." "Influence!" repeated Oscar, emphatically; "oh, heavens!" then starting up, he hurried to the window, as if to hide and to indulge his melancholy. The scene he viewed from it was dreary and desolate. It was now the latter end of autumn; the evening was cold, a savage blast howled from the hills, and the sky was darkened by a coming storm. Mrs. Marlowe roused him from his deep reverie. "I am sure," said she, "the prospect you view from the window can have no great attractions at present." "And yet," cried he, "there is something sadly pleasing in it: the leafless trees, the fading flowers of autumn, excite in my bosom a kind of mournful sympathy; they are emblems to me of him whose tenderest hopes have been disappointed; but, unlike him, they, after a short period, shall again flourish with primeval beauty." "Nonsense," exclaimed Mrs. Marlowe; "your illness has affected your spirits; but this gloom will vanish long before my orchard reassumes its smiling appearance, and haply attracts another smart redcoat to visit an old woman." "Oh! with what an enthusiasm of tenderness," cried Oscar, "shall I ever remember the dear, though dangerous, moment I first entered this cottage!" "Now, no flattery, Oscar," said Mrs. Marlowe; "I know your fickle sex too well to believe I have made a lasting impression; why, the very first fine old woman you meet at your ensuing quarters, will, I dare say, have similar praise bestowed on her." "No," replied he, with a languid smile; "I can assure you, solemnly, the impression which has been made on my heart will never be effaced." He stole a look at Adela; her head sunk upon her bosom, and her heart began to beat violently. Mrs. Marlowe wished to change the subject entirely; she felt the truest compassion for the unhappy young couple, and had fervently desired their union; but since irrevocably separated, she wished to check any intimation of a mutual attachment, which now could answer no purpose but that of increasing their misery. She rung for tea, and endeavored by her conversation to enliven the tea-table; the effort, however, was not seconded. "You have often," cried she, addressing Adela, as they again drew their chairs round the fire, "desired to hear the exact particulars of my life; unconquerable feelings of regret hitherto prevented my acquiescing in your desire; but, as nothing better now offers for passing away the hours, I will, if you please, relate them." "You will oblige me by so doing" cried Adela; "my curiosity, you know, has been long excited '

CHAPTER XIII.

> "But mine the sorrow, mine the fault,
> And well my life shall pay;
> I'll seek the solitude he sought,
> And stretch me where he lay."—GOLDSMITH.

O begin, then, as they say in a novel, without further preface, I was the only child of a country curate, in the southern part of England, who, like his wife, was of a good, but reduced family. Contented dispositions and an agreeable neighborhood, ready on every occasion to oblige them, rendered them, in their humble situations, completely happy. I was the idol of both their hearts; every one told my mother I should grow up a beauty, and she, poor simple woman, believed the flattering tale. Naturally ambitious, and somewhat romantic, she expected nothing less than my attaining, by my charms, an elevated situation; to fit me to it, therefore, according to her idea, she gave me all the showy, instead of solid, advantages of education. My father being a meek, or rather an indolent man, submitted entirely to her direction; thus, without knowing the grammatical part of my own language, I was taught to gabble bad French by myself; and, instead of mending or making my clothes, to flourish upon catgut and embroider satin. I was taught dancing by a man who kept a cheap school for that purpose in the village; music I could not aspire to, my mother's finances being insufficient to purchase an instrument; she was therefore obliged to content herself with my knowing the vocal part of that delightful science, and instructed me in singing a few old-fashioned airs, with a thousand graces, in her opinion at least.

To make me excel by my dress, as well as my accomplishments, all the misses of the village, the remains of her finery were cut and altered into every form which art or ingenuity could suggest; and, Heaven forgive me, but my chief inducement in going to church on a Sunday was to exhibit my flounced silk petticoat and painted chip hat.

When I attained my sixteenth year, my mother thought me, and supposed every one else must do the same, the most perfect creature in the world. I was lively, thoughtless, vain, and ambitious to an extravagant degree; yet, truly innocent in my disposition, and often, forgetting the appearance I had been taught to assume, indulged the natural gaiety of my heart, and in a game of hide-and-go-seek, amongst the haycocks in a meadow, by moonlight, enjoyed perfect felicity.

Once a week, accompanied by my mother, I attended the dancing-master's school, to practise country dances. One evening we had just concluded a set, and were resting ourselves, when an elegant youth, in a fashionable riding dress, entered the room. His appearance at once excited admiration and surprise; never shall I forget the palpitation of my heart at his approach; every girl experienced the same, every cheek was flushed, and every eye sparkled with hope and expectation. He walked round the room, with an easy, unembarrassed air, as if to take a survey of the company; he stopped by a very pretty girl, the miller's daughter—good heavens! what were my agonies! My mother, too, who sat beside me, turned pale, and would actually, I believe, have fainted, had he taken any farther notice of her; fortunately he did not, but advanced. My eyes caught his; he again paused, looked surprised and pleased, and, after a moment, passed in seeming consideration, bowed with the utmost elegance, and requested the honor of my hand for the ensuing dance. My politeness had hitherto only been in theory; I arose, dropped him a profound courtesy, assured him the honór would be all on my side, and I was happy to grant his request. He smiled, I thought, a little archly, and coughed to avoid laughing; I blushed, and felt embarrassed; but he led me to the head of the room to call a dance, and my triumph over my companions so exhilarated my spirits, that I immediately lost all confusion.

I had been engaged to a young farmer, and he was enraged, not only at my breaking my engagement without his permission, but at the superior graces of my partner, who threatened to be a formidable rival to him. "By jingo!" said Clod, coming up to me in a surly manner, "I think, Miss Fanny, you have not used me quite genteelly; I don't see why this here fine spark should take the lead of us all." "Creature!" cried I, with an ineffable look of contempt, which he could not bear, and retired grumbling. My partner could no longer refrain from laughing; the simplicity of my manners, notwithstanding the airs I endeavored to assume, highly delighted him. "No wonder," cried he, "the poor swain should be mortified at losing the hand of his charming Fanny."

The dancing over, we rejoined my mother, who was on thorns to begin a conversation with the stranger, that she might let him know we were not to be ranked with the present company. "I am sure, sir," said she, "a gentleman of your elegant appearance must feel rather awkward in the present party; it is so with us, as, indeed, it must be with every person of fashion; but, in an obscure little village like this, we must not be too nice in our society, except, like a hermit, we could do without any." The stranger assented to whatever she said, and accepted an invitation to sup with us; my mother instantly sent an intimation of her will to my father, to have, not the fatted calf, indeed, but the fatted duck prepared; and he and the maid used such expedition, that, by the time we returned, a neat, comfortable supper was ready to lay on the table. Mr. Marlowe, the stranger's name, as he informed me, was all animation and affability: it is unnecessary to say, that my mother, father, and myself, were all complaisance, delight, and attention. On departing, he asked, and obtained, permission, of course, to renew his visit the next day; and my mother immediately set him down as her future son-in-law.

As everything is speedily communicated in such a small village as we resided in, we learned on the preceding evening he had stopped at the inn, and, hearing music, had inquired from whence it proceeded, and had gone out of curiosity to the dance. We also learned that his attendants reported him to be heir to a large fortune; this report, vain as I was, was almost enough of itself to engage my heart; judge, then, whether it was not an easy conquest to a person, who, besides the above-mentioned attraction, possessed those of a graceful figure and cultivated mind. He visited continually at our cottage; and I, uncultivated as I was daily strengthened myself in his affections. In conversing with him, I forgot the precepts of vanity and affectation, and obeyed the dictates of nature and sensibility. He soon declared the motives of his visits to me—"to have immediately demanded my hand" he said, "would have gratified the tenderest wish of his soul; but, in his present situation, that was impossible—left, at an early age, destitute and distressed, by the death of his parents, an old whimsical uncle, married to a woman equally capricious, had adopted him as heir to their large possessions—he found it difficult," he said, "to submit to their ill-humor, and was confident, if he took any step against their inclinations, he should for ever forfeit their favor; therefore, if my parents would allow a reciprocal promise to pass between us, binding each to each, the moment he became master of expected fortune, or obtained an independence, he would make me a partaker of it." They consented, and he enjoined us to the strictest secrecy, saying, "one of his attendants was placed about him as a kind of spy. He had hitherto deceived him with respect to us, declaring my father was an intimate friend, and that his uncle knew he intended visiting him." But my unfortunate vanity betrayed the secret it was so material for me to keep. I was bound indeed not to reveal it. One morning a young girl, who had been an intimate acquaintance of mine till I knew Marlowe, came to see me "Why, Fanny," cried she, "you have given us all up for Mr. Marlowe; take care, my dear, he makes you amends for the loss of all your other friends." "I shall take your advice," said I, with a smile, and a conceited toss of my head. "Faith, for my part," continued she, "I think you were very foolish not to secure a good settlement for yourself with Clod." "With Clod!" repeated I, with the utmost haughtiness. "Lord, child, you forget who I am!" "Who are you?" exclaimed she, provoked at my insolence; "oh, yes, to be sure, I forget that you are the daughter of a poor country curate, with more pride in your head than money in your purse." "Neither do I forget," said I, "that your ignorance is equal to your impertinence; if I am the daughter of a poor country curate, I am the affianced wife of a rich man, and as much elevated by expectation, as spirit, above you."

Our conversation was repeated throughout the village, and reached the ears of Marlowe's attendant, who instantly developed the real motive which detained him so long in the village. He wrote to his uncle an account of the whole affair; the consequence of this was a letter to poor Marlowe, full of the bitterest reproaches, charging him, without delay, to return home. This was like a thunder-stroke to us all; but there was no alternative between obeying, or forfeiting his uncle's favor. "I fear, my dear Fanny," cried he, as he folded me to his bosom, a little before his departure, "it will be long ere we shall meet again; nay, I also fear I shall be obliged to promise not to write; if both these fears are realized, impute not either absence or silence to a want of the tenderest affection for you." He went, and with him all my happiness! My mother, shortly after his departure, was attacked by a nervous fever, which terminated her days; my father, naturally of weak spirits and delicate constitution, was so shocked by the sudden death of his beloved and faithful companion, that he sunk beneath his grief. The horrors of my mind I cannot describe; I seemed to stand alone in the world, without one friendly hand to prevent my sinking into the grave, which contained the dearest objects of my love. I did not know where Marlowe lived, and, even if I had, durst not venture an application, which might be the means of ruining him. The esteem of my neighbors I had forfeited by my conceit; they paid no attention but what common humanity dictated, merely to prevent my perishing; and that they made me sensibly feel. In this distress, I received an invitation from a school-fellow of mine, who had married a rich farmer about forty miles from our village, to take up my residence with her till I was sufficiently recovered to fix on some plan for future subsistence. I gladly accepted the offer, and, after paying a farewell visit to the grave of my regretted parents, I set off in the cheapest conveyance I could find to her habitation, with all my worldly treasure packed in a portmanteau.

With my friend I trusted I should enjoy a calm and happy asylum till Marlowe was able to fulfil his promise, and allow me to reward her kindness; but this idea she soon put to flight, by informing me, as my health returned, I must think of some method for supporting myself. I started, as at the utter annihilation of all my hopes; for, vain and ignorant of the world, I imagined Marlowe would never think of me if once disgraced by servitude. I told her I understood little of anything except fancy work. She was particularly glad, she said, to hear I knew that, as it would, in all probability, gain me admittance to the service of a rich old lady in the neighborhood, who had long been seeking for a person who could read agreeably and do fancy works, with which she delighted to ornament her house. She was a little whimsical, to be sure, she added, but well-timed flattery might turn those whims to advantage; and, if I regarded my reputation, I should not reject so respectable a protection. There was no alternative; I inquired more particularly about her, but how great was my emotion, when I learned she was the aunt of Marlowe. My heart throbbed with exquisite delight at the idea of being in the same house with him; besides, the service of his aunt would not, I flattered myself, degrade me as much in his eyes as that of another person's; it was necessary, however, my name should be concealed, and I requested my friend to comply with my wish in that respect. She rallied me about my pride, which she supposed had suggested the request, but promised to comply with it; she had no doubt but her recommendation would be sufficient to procure me immediate admittance, and, accordingly, taking some of my work with me, I proceeded to the habitation of Marlowe. It was an antique mansion, surrounded with neat-clipped hedges, level lawns, and formal plantations. Two statues, cast in the same mould, and resembling nothing either in heaven, earth, or sea, stood grinning horribly upon the pillars of a massy gate, as if to guard the entrance from impertinent intrusion. On knocking, an old porter appeared. I gave him my message, but he, like the statues, seemed stationary, and would not, I believe, have stirred from his situation to deliver an embassy from the King. He called, however, to a domestic, who, happening to be a little deaf, was full half an hour before he heard him; at last, I was ushered up stairs into an apartment, from the heat of which one might have conjectured it was under the torrid zone. Though in the middle of July, a heavy hot fire burned in the grate; a thick carpet, representing birds, beasts, and flowers, was spread on the floor, and the windows, closely screwed down, were heavy with wood-work, and darkened with dust. The master and mistress of the mansion, like Darby and Joan, sat in arm-chairs on each side of the fire; three dogs, and as many cats, slumbered at their feet. He was leaning on a spider-table, poring over a voluminous book, and she was stitching a counterpane. Sickness and ill-nature were visible in each countenance. "So!" said she, raising a huge pair of spectacles at my entrance, and examining me from head to

12

foot, "you are come from Mrs. Wilson's; why, bless me, child, you are quite too young for any business; pray, what is your name, and where do you come from?" I was prepared for these questions, and told her the truth, only concealing my real name, and the place of my nativity. "Well, let me see those works of yours," cried she. I produced them, and the spectacles were again drawn down. "Why, they are neat enough, to be sure," said she, "but the design is bad—very bad, indeed: there is taste, there is execution!" directing me to some pictures, in heavy gilt frames, hung round the room. I told her, with sincerity, "I had never seen anything like them." "To be sure, child," exclaimed she, pleased at what she considered admiration in me, "it is running a great risk to take you; but if you think you can conform to the regulations of my house, I will, from compassion, and as you are recommended by Mrs. Wilson, venture to engage you; but, remember, I must have no gad-about, no fly-flapper, no chatterer, in my family. You must be decent in your dress and carriage, discreet in your words, industrious at your work, and satisfied with the indulgence of going to church on a Sunday." I saw I was about entering upon a painful servitude; but the idea of its being sweetened by the sympathy of Marlowe a little reconciled me to it.

On promising all she desired, everything was settled for my admission into her family, and she took care I should perform the promises I made her. I shall not recapitulate the various trials I underwent from her austerity and peevishness; suffice it to say, my patience, as well as taste, underwent a perfect martyrdom. I was continually seated at a frame, working pictures of her own invention, which were everything that was hideous in nature. I was never allowed to go out, except on a Sunday to church, or on a chance evening when it was too dark to distinguish colors.

Marlowe was absent on my entering the family, nor durst I ask when he was expected. My health and spirits gradually declined from my close confinement. When allowed, as I have before said, of a chance time to go out, instead of enjoying the fresh air, I have sat down to weep over scenes of former happiness. I dined constantly with the old housekeeper. She informed me, one day, that Mr. Marlowe, her master's young heir, who had been absent some time on a visit, was expected home on the ensuing day Fortunately, the good dame was too busily employed to notice my agitation. I retired as soon as possible from the table, in a state of indescribable pleasure. Never shall I forget my emotions, when I heard the trampling of his horse's feet, and saw him enter the house! Vainly I endeavored to resume my work; my hands trembled, and I sunk back on my chair, to indulge the delightful idea of an interview with him, which I believed to be inevitable. My severe task-mistress soon awakened me from my delightful dream; she came to tell me: "I must confine myself to my own and the housekeeper's room, which, to a virtuous, discreet maiden, such as I appeared to be, she supposed would be no hardship, while her nephew, who was a young, perhaps rather a wild young man, remained in the house: when he again left it, which would soon be the case, I should regain my liberty." My heart sunk within me at her words, but, when the first shock was over, I consoled myself by thinking I should be able to elude her vigilance. I was, however, mistaken; she and the housekeeper were perfect Arguses. To be in the same house with Marlowe yet, without his knowing it, drove me almost distracted.

I at last thought of an expedient, which, I hoped, would effect the discovery I wanted. I had just finished a piece of work, which my mistress was delighted with. It was an enormous flower-basket, mounted on the back of a cat, which held beneath its paw a trembling mouse. The raptures the old lady expressed at seeing her own design so ably executed encouraged me to ask permission to embroider a picture of my own designing, for which I had the silks lying by me. She complied, and I set about it with alacrity. I copied my face and figure as exactly as I could, and, in mourning drapery and a pensive attitude, placed the little image by a rustic grave, in the church-yard of my native village, at the head of which, half embowered in trees, appeared the lovely cottage of my departed parents. These well-known objects, I thought, would revive, if indeed she was absent from it, the idea of poor Fanny in the mind of Marlowe. I presented the picture to my mistress, who was pleased with the present, and promised to have it framed. The next day while I sat at dinner, the door suddenly opened, and Marlowe entered the room. I thought I should have fainted. My companion dropped her knife and fork with great precipitation, and Marlowe told her he was very ill, and wanted a cordial from her. She rose with a dissatisfied air, to comply with his request. He, taking this opportunity of approaching a little nearer, darted a glance of pity and tenderness, and softly whispered—"To-night, at eleven o'clock, meet me in the front parlor."

You may conceive how tardily the hours passed till the appointed time came, when, stealing to the parlor, I found Marlowe expecting me. He folded me to his heart, and his tears mingled with mine, as I related my melancholy tale. "You are now, my Fanny!" he cried, "entirely mine; deprived of the protection of your tender parents, I shall endeavor to fulfil the sacred trust they reposed in my honor, by securing mine to you, as far as lies in my power. I was not mistaken," continued he, "in the idea I had formed of the treatment I should receive from my flinty-hearted relations on leaving you. Had I not promised to drop all correspondence with you, I must have relinquished all hopes of their favor. Bitter, indeed," cried he, while a tear started in his eye, "is the bread of dependence. Ill could my soul submit to the indignities I received; but I consoled myself throughout them, by the idea of future happiness with my Fanny. Had I known her situation (which, indeed, it was impossible I should, as my uncle's spy attended me wherever I went), no dictate of prudence would have prevented my flying to her aid!" "Thank Heaven, then, you were ignorant of it," said I. "My aunt," he proceeded, "showed me your work, lavishing the highest encomiums on it. I glanced my eye carelessly upon it, but, in a moment, how was that careless eye attracted by the well-known objects presented to it! this, I said to my heart, can only be Fanny's work. I tried to discover from my aunt whether my conjectures were wrong, but without success. When I retired to dress, I asked my servant if there had been any addition to the family during my absence; he said a young woman was hired to do fine works, but she never appeared among the servants."

Marlowe proceeded to say, "he could not bear I should longer continue in servitude, and that without delay he was resolved to unite his fate to mine." I opposed this resolution a little; but soon, too self-interested, I fear, acquiesced in it. It was agreed I should inform his aunt my health would no longer permit my continuing in her family, and that I should retire to a village six miles off, where Marlowe undertook to bring a young clergyman, a particular friend of his, to perform the ceremony. Our plan, as settled, was carried into execution, and I became the wife of Marlowe. I was now, you will suppose, elevated to the pinnacle of happiness; I was so, indeed, but my own folly precipitated me from it. The secrecy I was compelled to observe mortified me exceedingly, as I panted to emerge from the invidious cloud which which had so long concealed my beauty and accomplishments from a world that I was confident, if seen, would pay them the homage they merited. The people with whom I lodged had been obliged by Marlowe, and, therefore, from interest and gratitude, obeyed the injunction he gave them, of keeping my residence at their house a secret; they believed, or affected to believe, I was an orphan committed to his care, whom his uncle would be displeased to know he had taken under his protection. Three or four times a week I received stolen visits from Marlowe, when, one day (after a month had elapsed in this manner) standing at the parlor window, I saw Mrs. Wilson walking down the village. I started back, but too late to escape her observation; she immediately bolted into the room with all the eagerness of curiosity. I bore her first interrogatories tolerably well, but when she upbraided me for leaving the excellent service she had procured for me, for duplicity in saying I was going to another, and for my indiscretion in respect to Marlowe, I lost all command of my temper, and, remembering the inhumanity with which she had forced me into servitude, I resolved to mortify her completely, by assuming all the airs I had heretofore so ridiculously aspired to. Lolling in my chair, with an air of the most careless indifference, I bid her no longer petrify me with her discourse. This raised all the violence of rage, and she plainly told me, " from my conduct with Marlowe, I was unworthy her notice." "Therefore," cried I, forgetting every dictate of prudence, " his wife will neither desire nor receive it in future." "His wife!" she repeated, with a look of scorn and incredulity. I produced the certificate of my marriage; thus, from an impulse of vanity and resentment, putting myself in the power of a woman, a stranger to every liberal feeling, and whose mind was inflamed with envy towards me. The hint I forced myself at parting to give her, to keep the affair secret, only determined her more strongly to reveal it. The day after her visit, Marlowe entered my apartment—pale, agitated, and breathless, he sunk into a chair. A pang, like conscious guilt, smote my heart, and I trembled as I approached him. He repulsed me when I attempted to touch his hand. "Cruel, inconsiderate woman!" he said, "to what dreadful lengths has your vanity hurried you; it has drawn destruction upon your own head as well as mine!" Shame and remorse tied my tongue; had I spoken, indeed, I could not have vindicated myself, and I turned aside and wept. Marlowe, mild, tender, and adoring, could not long retain resentment; he started from his chair, and clasped me to his bosom. "Oh, Fanny!" he cried, "though you have ruined me, you are still dear as ever to me."

This tenderness affected me even more than reproaches, and tears and sighs declared my penitence. His expectations relative to his uncle were finally destroyed, on being informed of our marriage, which Mrs. Wilson lost no time in telling him. He burned his will, and immediately made another in favor of a distant relation. On hearing this intelligence, I was almost distracted; I flung myself at my husband's feet, implored his pardon, yet declared I could never forgive myself. He grew more composed upon the increase of my agitation, as if purposely to soothe my spirits, assuring me, that, though his uncle's favor was lost, he had other friends on whom he greatly depended. We set off for London, and found his dependence was not ill-placed; for, soon after his arrival, he obtained a place of considerable emolument in one of the public offices. My husband delighted in gratifying me, though I was often both extravagant and whimsical, and almost ever on the wing for admiration and amusement. I was reckoned a pretty woman, and received with rapture the nonsense and adulation addressed to me. I became acquainted with a young widow, who concealed a depraved heart under a specious appearance of innocence and virtue, and by aiding the vices of others, procured the means of gratifying her own; yet so secret were all her transactions, that calumny had not yet attacked her, and her house was the rendezvous of the most fashionable people. My husband, who did not dislike her manner, encouraged our intimacy, and at her parties I was noticed by a young nobleman, then at the head of the ton. He declared I was one of the most charming objects he had ever beheld, and, for such a declaration, I thought him the most polite I had ever known. As Lord T. condescended to wear my chains, I must certainly, I thought, become quite the rage. My transports, however, were a little checked by the grave remonstrances of my husband, who assured me Lord T. was a famous, or rather an infamous libertine; and that, if I did not avoid his lordship's particular attentions, he must insist on my relinquishing the widow's society. This I thought cruel, but I saw him resolute, and promised to act as he desired—a promise I never adhered to, except when he was present. I was now in a situation to promise an increase of family, and Marlowe wished me to nurse the child. The tenderness of my heart seconding his wish, I resolved on obeying it; but when the widow heard my intention she laughed at it, and said it was absolutely ridiculous, for the sake of a squalling brat, to give up all the pleasures of life; besides, it would be much better taken care of in some of the villages about London. I denied this; still, however, she dwelt on the sacrifices I must make, the amusements I must give up, and at last completely conquered my resolution. I pretended to Marlowe my health was too delicate to allow me to bear such a fatigue, and he immediately sacrificed his own inclinations to mine. I have often wondered at the kind of infatuation with which he complied with all my desires. My little girl, almost as soon as born, was sent from me; but, on being able to go out again, I received a considerable shock, from hearing my noble admirer was gone to the Continent, owing to a trifling derangement in his affairs. The vain pursuits of pleasure and dissipation were still continued. Three years passed in this manner, during which I had a son, and my little girl was brought home. I have since often felt astonished at the cold indifference with which I regarded my Marlowe, and our lovely babe, on whom he doated with all the enthusiasm of tenderness. Alas! vanity had then absorbed my heart, and deadened every feeling of nature and sensibility; it is the parent of self-love and apathy, and degrades those who harbor it below humanity.

Lord T. now returned from the Continent; he swore my idea had never been absent from his mind, and that I was more charming than ever; while I thought him, if possible, more polite and engaging. Again my husband remonstrated. Sometimes I seemed to regard these remonstrances, sometimes protested I would not submit to such unnecessary control. I knew, indeed, that my intentions were innocent, and believed I might safely indulge my vanity, without endangering either my reputation or peace. About this time Marlowe received a summons to attend a dying friend four miles from London. Our little girl was then in a slight fever, which had alarmed her father, and confined me most unwillingly, I must confess, to the house. Marlowe, on the point of departing, pressed me to his breast: "My heart, my beloved Fanny!" said he, "feels unusually heavy. I trust the feeling is no presentiment of approaching ill. Oh! my Fanny! on you and my babe, I rest for happiness—take care of our little cherub, and above all (his meek eye encountering mine), take care of yourself, that, with my accustomed rapture, I may, on my return, receive you to my arms." There was something so solemn, and so tender, in this address, that my heart melted, and my tears mingled with those which trickled down his pale cheeks. For two days I attended my child assiduously, when the widow made her appearance. She assured me I should injure myself by such close confinement, and that my cheeks were already faded by it. She mentioned a delightful masquerade which was to be given that night, and for which Lord T. had presented her with tickets for me and herself; but she declared, except I would accompany her, she would not go. I had often wished to go to a masquerade; I now, however, declined this opportunity of gratifying my inclination, but so faintly, as to prompt a renewal of her solicitations, to which I at last yielded; and, committing my babe to the care of a servant, set off with the widow to a warehouse to choose dresses. Lord T. dined with us, and we were all in the highest spirits imaginable: about twelve we went in his chariot to the Haymarket, and I was absolutely intoxicated with his flattery, and the dazzling objects around me. At five we quitted this scene of gaiety. The widow took a chair; I would have followed her example, but my Lord absolutely lifted me into his chariot, and there began talking in a strain which provoked my contempt, and excited my apprehensions. I expressed my displeasure in tears which checked his boldness, and convinced him he had some difficulties yet to overcome ere he completed his designs. He made his apologies with so much humility, that I was soon appeased, and prevailed on to accept them. We arrived at the widow's house in as much harmony as we left it; the flags were wet, and Lord T. insisted on carrying me into the house. At the door I observed a man muffled up, but as no one noticed him, I thought no more about it. We sat down to supper in high spirits, and chatted for a considerable time about our past amusements. His Lordship said: "After a little sleep we should recruit ourselves by a pleasant jaunt to Richmond, where he had a charming villa." We agreed to his proposal, and retired to rest. About noon we arose; and, while I was dressing myself for the projected excursion, a letter was brought in to me. "Good Lord! Halcot!" exclaimed I, turning to the widow, "if Marlowe is returned, what will become of me?" "Oh! read, my dear creature!" cried she impatiently, "and then we can think of excuses." "I have the letter here," continued Mrs Marlowe, laying her hand to her breast, and drawing it forth after a short pause, "I laid it to my heart to guard it against future folly."

THE LETTER.

The presages of my heart were but too true—we parted never to meet again. Oh! Fanny, beloved of my soul, how are you lost to yourself and Marlowe! The independence, splendor, riches, which I gave up for your sake, were mean sacrifices, in my estimation, to the felicity I fondly expected to have enjoyed with you through life. Your beauty charmed my mind, but it was your simplicity captivated my heart. I took, as I thought, the perfect child of innocence and sincerity to my bosom; resolved, from duty, as well as from inclination, to shelter you in that bosom, to the utmost of my power, from every adverse storm. Whenever you were indisposed, what agonies did I endure! yet, what I then dreaded, could I have possibly foreseen, would have been comparative happiness to my present misery; for, oh! my Fanny, far preferable would it have been to behold you in the arms of death than infamy.

I returned immediately after witnessing the last pangs of my friend—oppressed with the awful scene of death, yet cheering my spirits by an anticipation of the consolation I should receive from my Fanny's sympathy. Good God! what was my horror, when I found my little babe, instead of being restored to health by a mother's care, nearly expiring through her neglect! The angel lay gasping on her bed, deserted by the mercenary wretch to whose care she was consigned. I inquired, and the fatal truth rushed upon my soul; yet, when the first tumult of passion had subsided, I felt that, without yet stronger proofs, I could not abandon you. Alas! too soon did I receive those proofs. I traced you, Fanny, through your giddy round, till I saw you borne in the arms of the vile Lord T. into the house of his vile paramour. You will wonder, perhaps, I did not tear you from his grasp. Could such a procedure have restored you to me, with all your unsullied innocence, I should not have hesitated; but that was impossible, and my eyes then gazed upon Fanny for the last time. I returned to my motherless babe, and, I am not ashamed to say, I wept over it with all the agonies of a fond and betrayed heart.

Ere I bid an irrevocable adieu, I would, if possible, endeavor to convince you that conscience cannot always be stifled—that illicit love is constantly attended by remorse and disappointment; for, when familiarity, or disease, has diminished the charms which excited it, the frail fetters of admiration are broken by him who looks only to an exterior for delight; if, indeed, your conscience should not be awakened till this hour of desertion comes, when it does arrive, you may, perhaps, think of Marlowe. Yes, Fanny, when your cheeks are faded by care, when your wit is enfeebled by despondency, you may think of him whose tenderness would have outlived both time and change, and supported you, without abatement, through every stage of life.

To stop short in the career of vice is, they say, the noblest effort of virtue. May such an effort be yours; and may you yet give joy to the angels of heaven, who, we are taught to believe, rejoice over them that truly repent! That want should strew no thorns in the path of penitence, all that I could take from my babe I have assigned to you. Oh! my dear culprit, remember the precepts of your early youth—of those who, sleeping in the dust, are spared the bitter tear of anguish, such as I now shed—and, ere too late, expiate your errors. In the solitude to which I am hastening, I shall continually pray for you; and when my child raises its spotless hands to Heaven, it shall implore its mercy for erring mortals; yet, think not it shall ever hear your story. Oh! never shall the blush of shame, for the frailties of one so near, tinge its ingenuous countenance. May the sincerity of your repentance restore that peace and brightness to your life, which, at present, I think you must have forfeited, and support you with fortitude through its closing period! As a friend, once dear, you will ever exist in the memory of

MARLOWE.

As I concluded the letter, my spirits, which had been gradually receding, entirely forsook me, and I fell senseless on the floor. Mrs. Halcot and Lord T. took this opportunity of gratifying their curiosity by perusing the letter, and when I recovered, I found myself supported between them. "You see, my dear angel," cried Lord T., "your cruel husband has entirely abandoned you; but grieve not, for in my arms you shall find a kinder asylum than he ever afforded you." "True," said Mrs. Halcot; "for my part, I think she has reason to rejoice at his desertion."

I shall not attempt to repeat all I said to them in the height of my distraction. Suffice it to say, I reproached them both as the authors of my shame and misery; and, while I spurned Lord T. indignantly from my feet, accused Mrs. Halcot of possessing neither delicacy nor feeling. Alas! accusation or reproach could not lighten the weight on my heart—I felt a dreadful consciousness of having occasioned my own misery. I seemed as if awaking from a disordered dream, which had confused my senses; and the more clearly my perception of what was right returned, the more bitterly I lamented my deviation from it. To be reinstated in the esteem and affection of my husband, was all of felicity I could desire to possess. Full of the idea of being able to effect a reconciliation, I started up; but, ere I reached the door, sunk into an agony of tears: recollecting that ere this he was probably far distant from me. My base companions tried to assuage my grief, and make me in reality the wretch poor Marlowe supposed me to be. I heard them in silent contempt, unable to move, till a servant informed me a gentleman below stairs desired to see me. The idea of a relenting husband instantly occurred, and I flew down; but how great was my disappointment only to see a particular friend of his! Our meeting was painful in the extreme. I asked him if he knew anything of Marlowe, and he solemnly assured me he did not. When my confusion and distress had a little subsided, he informed me that in the morning he had received a letter from him, with an account of our separation, and the fatal cause of it. The letter contained a deed of settlement on me of a small paternal estate, and a bill of fifty pounds, which Marlowe requested his friend to present himself to me. He also added my clothes were sent to his house, as our lodgings had been discharged. I did not find it difficult to convince this gentleman of my innocence, and, putting myself under his protection, was immediately conveyed to lodgings in a retired part of the town. Here he consoled me with assurances of using every effort to discover the residence of my husband. All, alas! proved unsuccessful; and my health gradually declined. As time wore away, my hope yet left still undiminished my desire of seeing him. Change of air was at last deemed requisite to preserve my existence, and I went to Bristol. I had the good fortune to lodge in the house with an elderly Irish lady, whose sweet and benevolent manner soon gained my warmest esteem, and tempted me to divulge my melancholy tale, where so certain of obtaining pity. She had also suffered severely from the pressure of sorrow; but hers, as it proceeded not from imprudence, but the common vicissitudes of life, was borne without that degree of anguish mine occasioned. As the period approached for her return to her native country, I felt the deepest regret at the prospect of our separation, which she, however, removed, by asking me to reside entirely with her. Eight years had elapsed since the loss of my husband, and no latent hope of his return remained in my heart sufficiently strong to tempt me to forego the advantages of such society. Ere I departed, however, I wrote to several of his friends, informing them of the step I intended taking, and, if any tidings of Marlowe occurred, where I was to be found. Five years I passed with my valuable friend in retirement, and had the pleasure of thinking I contributed to the ease of her last moments. This cottage, with a few acres adjoining it, and four hundred pounds, was all her wealth, and to me she bequeathed it, having no relations whose wants gave them any claim upon her.

The events I have just related will, I hope, strengthen the moral so many wish to impress upon the minds of youth, namely—that, without a strict adherence to propriety, there can be no permanent pleasure; and that it is the actions of early life must give to old age either happiness and comfort, or sorrow and remorse. Had I attended to the admonitions of wisdom and experience, I should have checked my wanderings from prudence, and preserved my happiness from being sacrificed at the shrine of vanity; then, instead of being a solitary in the world, I might have had my little fireside enlivened by the partner of my heart, and, perhaps, my children's children sporting around; but suffering is the proper tax we pay for folly; the frailty of human nature, the prevalence of example, the allurements of the world, are mentioned by many as extenuations for misconduct. Though virtue, say they, is willing, she is often too weak to resist the wishes they excite. Mistaken idea! and blessed is that virtue which, opposing, ends them. With every temptation we have the means of escape; and woe be to us if we neglect those means, or hesitate to disentangle ourselves from the snare which vice or folly may have spread around us. Sorrow and disappointment are incident to mortality, and when not occasioned by any conscious imprudence, should be considered as temporary trials from Heaven to improve and correct us, and therefore cheerfully be borne. A sigh stole from Oscar as she spoke, and a tear trickled down the soft cheek of Adela. "I have," continued Mrs. Marlowe, "given you, like an old woman, a tedious tale; but that tediousness, with every other imperfection I have acknowledged, I rest upon your friendship and candor to excuse."

CHAPTER XIV.

"Denied her sight, he often crept
Beneath the hawthorn's shade;
To mark the spot in which she wept—
In which she wept and prayed."—MALLET.

HE night was waning fast, and Adela rose to depart as her friend concluded her story; yet it required an effort of resolution to retire. Mrs. Marlowe, however, was too well convinced of the expediency and propriety of this to press her longer stay, though the eyes of Oscar, suddenly turned to her, seemed to entreat she would do so. The night was dark and wet, which prevented Mrs. Marlowe from accompanying Adela to the carriage. Not so Oscar; he took the umbrella from the servant, who held it for his mistress, and bid him hasten on to have the carriage-door opened. "Oscar," cried Mrs. Marlowe, extremely unwilling to allow even this short *tête-à-tête*, "Mrs. Belgrave will dispense with your gallantry, for you are really too great an invalid to venture out such a night as this." Adela attempted to dissuade him from it, but her voice was so low and faltering as scarcely to be articulate. Oscar gently seized her hand, and pulled it under his arm; he felt it tremble as he did so. The touch became contagious; an universal tremor affected his frame, and never, perhaps, had he and Adela experienced a moment of greater unhappiness. Adela at last found herself obliged to speak, conscious that her silence must appear particular, and said, she feared he would be injured by his attentions to her. More fatally injured than he already was, he might have replied, he could not be; but, he checked the words ready to burst from his lips, and only answered that he would be unfit for a soldier, if he could not endure the inclemency of the wintry blast. The light from the globes of the carriage gave him a view of her pale lovely cheeks, and he saw she was weeping. Confused at the idea of betraying her distress, she averted her head, and hastily ascended the steps; yet, for a moment, her trembling hand rested upon Oscar's, as if, in this manner, she would have given the adieu she had not the power of pronouncing. Lost in agony, he remained, like a statue, on the spot where she had left him, till roused by the friendly voice of Mrs. Marlowe, who, alarmed at his long absence, came to seek him. Soothed by her kind solicitude, he directly returned with her to the house, where his indignation against the perfidious Belgrave again broke forth. He execrated him, not only as the destroyer of his peace, but a peace infinitely more precious than his own—that of the charming Adela.

Mrs. Marlowe essayed every art of consolation, and, by sympathy and mildness, at last subdued the violence of his feelings; she acknowledged the loss he sustained in being deprived of Adela; but, since irrevocable, both virtue and reason required him to struggle against his grief, and conceal it. By their sacred dictates, she entreated him to avoid seeing Adela. He felt she was right in the entreaty, and solemnly promised to comply with it; her friendship was balm to his wounded heart, and her society the only pleasure he was capable of enjoying. Whenever he could absent himself from quarters he retired to her, and frequently spent three or four days at a time in her cottage. By discontinuing his visits in the gay neighborhood of Woodlawn, he avoided all opportunities of seeing Adela, yet often, on a clear frosty night, has he stole from the fireside of Mrs. Marlowe to the beloved and beautiful haunts about the lake, where he and Adela passed so many happy hours together. Here he indulged in all the luxury of woe; and such are the pleasures of virtuous melancholy, that Oscar would not have resigned them for any of the common-place enjoyments of life.

Often did he wander to the grove from whence he had a view of Adela's chamber, and if a lucky chance gave him a glimpse of her, as she passed through it, a sudden ecstasy would pervade his bosom; he would pray for her felicity, and return to Mrs. Marlowe, as if his heart was lightened of an oppressive weight. That tender friend flattered herself, from youth and the natural gaiety of his disposition, his attachment, no longer fed by hope, would gradually decline; but she was mistaken—the bloom of his youth was faded, and his gaiety converted into deep despondency. Had he never been undeceived with regard to the General and Adela, pride, no doubt, would quickly have lessened the poignancy of his feelings; but when he reflected on the generous intentions of the one, on the sincere affection of the other, and the supreme happiness he might have enjoyed, he lost all fortitude. Thus, by perpetually brooding over the blessings once within his reach, losing all relish for those which were yet attainable, his sorrow, instead of being ameliorated, was increased, by time. The horror and indignation with which he beheld Belgrave, after the first knowledge of his baseness, could scarcely be restrained. Though painful, he was pleased the effort had proved a successful one, as, exclusive of his sacred promise to Mrs. Marlowe, delicacy on Adela's account induced him to bear his wrongs in silence. He could not, however, be so great a hypocrite as to profess any longer esteem or respect for the Colonel, and when they met, it was with cold politeness on both sides.

The unfortunate Adela pined in secret. Her interview with Oscar had destroyed the small remainder of her peace. His pale and emaciated figure haunted her imagination; in vain, by dwelling on his unkind letter, did she endeavor to lessen her tenderness. She felt the emotion of pity stronger than that of resentment, and that the friendship of Oscar would have been sweeter to her soul than the love or attention of any other object. By obeying the impulse of passion, she feared she had doomed herself to wretchedness. Belgrave was a man whom, upon mature deliberation, she never could have chosen. The softness of his manners gradually vanished when the purpose for which they had been assumed was completed. Unfeeling and depraved, the virtues of Adela could excite no esteem in his bosom, and the love (if it can merit that appellation) which he felt for her, quickly subsided after their marriage; but as the General retained the greatest part of his fortune in his own power, he continued tolerably guarded in his conduct. A slave, however, to the most violent passions, he was often unable to control them; and, forgetful of all prudential motives, delighted at those times in mortifying Adela by sly sarcasms on her attachment for Oscar. Though deeply wounded, she never complained; she had partly forged her chains, and resolved to bear them without repining. Tranquil in appearance, the poor General, who was not penetrating, thought his darling perfectly happy. Such, however, was not the opinion of those who visited at Woodlawn. The rose of health no longer spread its beautiful tints on the cheek of Adela, nor were her eyes irradiated by vivacity.

The Colonel never went to Enniskellen except about military business, but he made frequent excursions to the metropolis and other parts of the kingdom in pursuit of pleasure. Adela felt relieved by his absence; and the General, satisfied at his not attempting to take her along with him, never murmured at it. The period now arrived for the departure of the regiment. Adela had not seen Oscar since the interview at Mrs. Marlowe's. She declined going to the reviews which preceded the change of garrison, and sincerely hoped no chance would again throw him in her way. Oscar sickened at the idea of quitting the country without seeing her. He knew she was not to accompany the Colonel. The officers were going to pay a farewell visit to Woodlawn, and he could not resist being of the party. They were shown into the drawing-room, where Adela and the General sat. She was startled at the appearance of Oscar, but though a blush tinged her pale face, she soon recovered her composure, and entered into conversation. The General pressed them to stay to dinner, but they had many visits to pay and begged to be excused. "My dear Fitzalan," said the General, who had long dropped his displeasure, "I wish you happiness and success, and hope I shall soon hear of your being at the head of a company; remember, I say soon—for I am an old veteran, and should be sorry to drop into the trench till I had heard of the good fortune of my friends. Your father was a brave fellow, and, in the speedy advancement of his son, should receive a reward for his past services." Oscar pressed the General's hand to his breast. He cast his tearful eyes on Adela; she sighed, and bent hers to the ground. "Be assured, sir," he cried, "no gratitude can be more fervent than that your goodness has inspired me with; no wishes can be more sincere than mine for the happiness of the inhabitants of Woodlawn." "Ineffectual wishes," softly exclaimed Adela; "happiness, from one of its inhabitants at least, has, I fear, fled for ever."

The General's wishes for the success of Oscar may be considered as mere words of course, since not enforced by more substantial proofs of regard; but, in reality, soon after his daughter's marriage, in his usual blunt manner, he had mentioned to the Colonel his giving a thousand or two to help the promotion of Oscar. Belgrave, who could not bear that the man whom he had injured should have a chance of obtaining equal rank with himself, opposed this truly generous design, by saying, "Oscar was taken under the patronage of Lord Cherbury, and that the General's bounty might therefore, at some future period, be better applied in serving a person without his interest." To this the General assented, declaring that he never yet met with a brave soldier or his offspring in distress without feeling and answering the claim they had upon his heart.

Oscar obtained a ready promise from Mrs. Marlowe of corresponding with him. He blushed and faltered as he besought her sometimes to acquaint him with the health of their friends at Woodlawn. Change of scene produced no alteration in him. Still pining with regret, and lanquid from ill-health, his father and sister found him. The comforts of sympathy could not be his, as the anguish which preyed on his heart he considered of too sacred a nature to divulge. He hoarded up his grief, like a miser hoarding up his treasure, fearful that the eye of suspicion should glance at it, as he pressed his lovely sister to his heart. Had he imagined she was the object of Colonel Belgrave's licentious passion, the bounds he had hitherto prescribed to his resentment would in a moment have been overturned, and he would, had it been necessary, have pursued the monster round the world, to avenge the injury he had meditated, as well as the one he had committed.

We shall now bid adieu to Oscar for the present, and, drawing on our boots of seven leagues, step after Fitzalan and Amanda

---

CHAPTER XV.

"Confessed from yonder slow extinguished clouds,
All ether softening, sober evening takes
Her wonted station in the middle air;
A thousand shadows at her back."—THOMSON.

ASTLE CARBERRY, to which our travellers were going, was a large gothic pile, erected in the rude and distant period when strength more than elegance was deemed necessary in a building. The depredations of war, as well as time, were discernible on its exterior; some of its lofty battlements were broken, and others mouldering to decay, while about its ancient towers

"The rank grass waved its head,
And the moss whistled to the wind."

It stood upon a rocky eminence overhanging the sea, and commanding a delightful prospect of the opposite coast of Scotland; about it were yet to be traced irregular fortifications, a moat, and remains of a drawbridge, with a well, long since dry, which had been dug in the rock to supply the inhabitants in times of siege with water. On one side rose a stupendous hill, covered to the very summit with trees, and scattered over with relics of druidical antiquity; before it stretched an extensive and gently swelling lawn, sheltered on each side with groves of intermingled shade, and refreshed by a clear and meandering rivulet, that took its rise from the adjoining hill, and murmured over a bed of pebbles.

After a pleasant journey, on the evening of the fourth day, our travellers arrived at their destined habitation. An old man and woman, who had the care of it, were apprised of their coming, and on the first approach of the carriage, opened the massy door, and waited to receive them: they reached it when the sober gray of twilight had clad every object. Amanda viewed the dark and stupendous edifice, whose gloom was now heightened by the shadows of evening, with venerable awe. The solitude, the silence which reigned around, the melancholy murmur of the waves as they dashed against the foot of the rocks, all heightened the sadness of her mind; yet it was not quite an unpleasing sadness, for with it was now mingled a degree of that enthusiasm which plaintive and romantic spirits are so peculiarly subject to feel in viewing the venerable grandeur of an ancient fabric renowned in history. As she entered a spacious hall, curiously wainscoted with oak, ornamented with coats of arms, spears, lances, and old armor, she could not avoid casting a retrospective eye to former times, when, perhaps, in this very hall, bards sung the exploits of those heroes, whose useless arms now hung upon the walls. She wished, in the romance of the moment, some gray bard near her, to tell the deeds of other times—of kings renowned in our land—of chiefs we behold no more. In the niches in the hall were figures of chieftains, large as life, and rudely carved in oak. Their frowning countenances struck a sudden panic upon the heart of Ellen. "Cot pless their souls," she said, "what the tefil did they do there, except to frighten the people from going into the house."

They were shown into a large parlor, furnished in an old-fashioned manner, and found a comfortable supper prepared for them. Oppressed with fatigue, soon after they had partaken of it, they retired to rest. The next morning, immediately after breakfast, Amanda, attended by the old woman and Ellen, ranged over the Castle. Its interior was quite as gothic as its exterior; the stairs were winding, the galleries intricate, the apartments numerous, and mostly hung with old tapestry, representing Irish battles, in which the chiefs of Castle Carberry were particularly distinguished. Their portraits, with those of their ladies, occupied a long gallery, whose arched windows cast a dim religious light upon them. This was terminated by a small apartment in the centre of one of the towers that flanked the building. The room was an octagon, and thus commanded a sea and land prospect, uniting at once the sublime and beautiful in it. The furniture was not only modern but elegant, and excited the particular attention and inquiries of Amanda. The old woman informed her this had been the dressing-room of the late Countess of Cherbury, both before and after her marriage: "one of the sweetest, kindest ladies," continued she, "I ever knew; the Castle has been quite deserted since she died—alack-a-day! I thought my poor heart would have broke when I heard of her death. Ah! I remember the night I heard the Banshee crying so pitifully." "And pray what is that?" interrupted Amanda. "Why, a little woman, no higher than a yard, who wears a blue petticoat, a red cloak, and a handkerchief round her head; and when the head of any family, especially a great family, is to die, she is always heard, by some of the old followers, bemoaning herself." "Lort save us!" cried Ellen, "I hope his lortship, the Earl, won't take it into his head to die while we are here, for I'd as lief see one of the fairies of Penmaenmawr, as such a little old witch." "Well, proceed," said Amanda. "So, as I was saying, I heard her crying dismally one night in a corner of the house. So, says I to my husband, Johnaten, says I, I am sure we shall hear something about my good lord or lady. And sure enough we did the next day, and ever since we have seen none of the family." "Did you ever see the young lord?" asked Amanda, with involuntary precipitation. "See him! aye, that I did, when he was about eight years old; there is his picture (pointing to one which hung over the chimney); my lady had it done by a fine English painter, and brought it over with her. It is the moral of what he then was." The eager eyes of Amanda were instantly turned to it, and she traced, or at least imagined she did so, a resemblance still between it and him. The painter seemed as if he had had the description of Pity in his mind when he drew the picture; for Lord Mortimer was portrayed, as she is represented in the beautiful allegory, sheltering a trembling dove in his bosom from a ferocious hawk. Oh! Mortimer! thought Amanda, thy feeling nature is here ably delineated! The distressed, or the helpless, to the utmost of your power, you would save from the gripe of cruelty and oppression. Her father had desired her to choose pleasant apartments for her own immediate use, and she accordingly fixed on this and the room adjoining it, which had been Lady Cherbury's chamber. Her things were brought hither, and her books, works, and implements for drawing, deposited in rich inlaid cabinets. Pleased with the arrangements she had made, she brought her father, as soon as he was at leisure, to view them. He was happy to find her spirits somewhat cheerful and composed, and declared in future he would call this Amanda's Tower. Accompanied by him, she ascended to the battlements of the Castle, and was delighted with the extensive and variegated prospect she beheld from them. A spacious edifice, at some distance, embowered in a grove of venerable oaks, attracted her admiration. Her father told her that was Ulster Lodge, a seat belonging to the Marquis of Roslin, who was an Irish as well as a Scotch Peer, and had very extensive possessions in Ireland. Fitzalan added, he had been inquiring of the old man about the neighborhood, and learned from him that, at the expiration of every three or four years, the Marquis usually came over to Ulster Lodge, but had never yet been accompanied by the Marchioness, or Lady Euphrasia Sutherland, who was his only child.

The domestic economy of Castle Carberry was soon settled. A young man and woman were hired, as Johnaten and his wife, Kate, were considered little more than supernumeraries. Ellen was appointed to attend Amanda, and do whatever plain work was required. Fitzalan felt a pleasing serenity diffused over his mind, from the idea of being in some degree independent, and in the way of making some provision for his children. The first shock of a separation from Lord Mortimer being over, the cheerfulness of Amanda gradually returned, the visions of hope again revived in her mind, and she indulged a secret pleasure at living in the house he had once occupied. She considered her father as particularly connected with his family, and doubted not, from this circumstance, she should sometimes hear of him. She judged of his constancy by her own, and believed he would not readily forget her. She acknowledged her father's motives for separating them were equally just and delicate; but firmly believed, if Lord Mortimer (as she flattered herself he would) confessed a partiality in her favor to his father, that, influenced by tenderness for his son, friendship for her father, and the knowledge of her descent, he would immediately give up every idea of another connection, and sanction theirs with his approbation. No obstacle appeared to such an union but want of fortune, and that want she could never suppose would be considered as one by the liberal-minded Lord Cherbury, who had himself an income sufficient to gratify even luxurious wishes. Her time was agreeably diversified by the sources of amusements she drew from herself. Her father, whose supreme felicity consisted in contributing to her pleasure, purchased a delightful harp for her in Dublin, which arrived a few days after them, at Castle Carberry, and with its dulcet lays she often charmed, not only his spirit, but her own, from every mortal care. She loved to rise early, and catch the first beams of the sun, as she wandered over the dewy lawn, where the lowing cattle cropped the flowery herbage, and the milkmaid sung her plaintive ditty.

With her father she took long walks about the adjacent country. He had visited every scene before, and now pointed out whatever was worthy her attention: the spots where the heroes of former ages had fallen, where the mighty stones of their fame were raised, that the children of the North might hereafter know the places where their fathers fought; that the hunter, as he leaned upon a mossy tomb, might say, here fought the heroes of other years, and their fame shall last for ever!

Amanda, too, often rambled by herself, particularly among the rocks, where were several natural grottos, strewed with shells and seaweeds. Here, of a mild day, she loved to read, and listen to the low murmurs of the tide. The opposite Scottish hills, among which her mother first drew breath, often attracted and fixed her attention, frequently drawing tears from her eyes, by awaking in her mind the recollection of that mother's sufferings.

On a morning, when she sat at work in her apartment, Ellen, who was considered more as a friend than a servant, sometimes sat with her; the conversation not unfrequently turned on nurse Edwin's cottage, from which Ellen, with an arch simplicity, would advert to Tudor Hall, thence naturally to Lord Mortimer, and conclude with poor Chip, exclaiming: "What a pity true love should ever be crossed!"

CHAPTER XVI.

"Some take him for a tool
That knaves do work with, called a fool;
Fools are known by looking wise,
As men find woodcocks by their eyes."—HUDIBRAS.

HE solitude of Castle Carberry was interrupted in less than a fortnight by visits and invitations from the neighboring families. The first they accepted was to dinner at Mr. Kilcorban's. He was a man of large fortune, which, in the opinion of many, compensated for the want of polished manners, and a cultivated mind; but others, of a more liberal way of thinking, could not possibly excuse those deficiencies, which were more apparent from his pretending to every excellence; and more intolerable from his deeming himself authorized, by his wealth and consequence, to say and do almost whatever he pleased. His Lady was, like himself, a compound of ignorance, pride, and vanity. Their offspring was numerous, and the three who were sufficiently old to make their appearance, were considered, by their parents and themselves, as the very models of elegance and perfection. The young heir had been sent to the University; but, permitted to be his own master, he had profited little by his residence there. Enough, however, perhaps he thought, for a man of fortune, who wanted not professional knowledge. His face was coarse, his person inelegant, and his taste in adorning himself preposterously ridiculous. Fashion, Hoyle, and the looking-glass, were his chief studies, and, by his family and self, he was considered quite the thing.

The young ladies were supposed to be very accomplished, because they had instructors in almost every branch of education; but, in reality, they understood little more than the names of what they were attempted to be taught. Nature had not been lavish of her gifts. Of this, however, they were conscious, and patched, powdered, and painted in the very extremity of the mode. Their mornings were generally spent in rolling about in a coach and six with their mamma, collecting news and paying visits; their evenings were constantly devoted to company, without which they declared they could not exist. They sometimes affected languor and sentiment, talked of friendship, and professed for numbers, the most sincere; yet, to the very girls they pretended to regard, delighted in exhibiting their finery, if certain they could not purchase the same, and would feel mortified by seeing it.

Mr. Kilcorban had indulged his family in a trip to Bath one autumn, and, in so doing, had afforded a never-failing subject for conversation; upon every occasion this delightful excursion was mentioned—the novelties they saw, the admiration they excited, the elegant intimacies they formed, the amazing sum they expended, were all described and exaggerated.

Lady Greystock, an ancient widow, was at present on a visit to them. She had known Fitzalan in his youth, and now, with pleasure, renewed her intimacy with him; and the account she gave of his family and connections, prepossessed the neighborhood in his favor. She was a shrewd, sensible woman; the dignity of her person commanded respect, but the sarcastic expression of her countenance prevented her conciliating esteem.

An old chariot belonging to the Earl of Cherbury, which had been for years unemployed in the coach-house, was brought forth, for the purpose of conveying Fitzalan and his daughter on their visits. After a good deal of rubbing and washing, it was found tolerably decent, and they proceeded in it to Mr. Kilcorban's, which was about two miles from Castle Carberry. A numerous party was already assembled. While Amanda was paying her compliments to Mrs. Kilcorban and Lady Greystock, a general whisper relative to her took place among the younger part of the company, who had formed themselves into a group quite distant from the rest. One gentleman swore, "she was a devilish fine girl!" He was seconded in the remark by another, who extolled her complexion. "You are a simpleton," cried a young lady, who was reckoned a great wit; "I would engage for half a crown to get as fine a color in Dublin." Her companions laughed, and declared she only spoke truth in saying so. Mr. Bryan Kilcorban, who leaned on her chair, said, "A bill should be brought into the house to tax such complexions; for kill me," continued he, "the ladies are so irresistible from nature, it is quite unconscionable to call in art as an auxiliary." He then stalked over to Amanda, who sat by Lady Greystock; lolling over her chair, he declared, "he thought the tedious hours would never elapse till again blessed with her presence. "Of her," he said, "it was sufficient to have but one glimpse to make him pant for the second." A summons to dinner relieved her from this nonsense. Luxury and ostentation were conspicuous in the fare and decorations of the table, and Amanda never felt any hours so tedious as those she passed at it. When the ladies returned to the drawing-room, the Miss Kilcorbans, and their companions, began to examine and admire her dress. "What a pretty pattern this gown is worked in!" said one. "What a sweet, becoming cap this is," cried a second. "Well, certainly the English milliners have a great deal of taste, my dear," said Miss Kilcorban, whispering to Amanda. "I have a monstrous favor to ask of you," drawing her at the same instant to the window. "I am sure," said Amanda, "any in my power to grant I shall with pleasure." "Oh! really, then, it is in your power. It is only to refuse the pattern of your cap to any girls who may ask you for it, and to give it me and my sister. You cannot conceive how we dote on being the first in the fashion, one is so stared at, and so envied. I detest anything when it becomes common You cannot think how we are teased every summer, when we return from Dublin, for fashions; but we always make it a point to refuse. I must tell you a delightful trick I played a friend of mine. She received a large present of the most beautiful muslins from India, which she laid by till I returned from town, supposing I would let her see my things, as I always told her I was extremely fond of her Well, I lent her a gown, which was quite old-fashioned, but assured her it was the very newest mode. She accordingly had her beautiful muslins cut in imitation of it, and so spoiled them from making any other habit. Well, we met at an assize ball, where all the elegant people of the county were assembled, and, I declare, I never saw so ridiculous a figure as she made. When she found herself unlike every one in the room, I really thought she would have fainted, and that my sister and I should have expired with laughing. Poor thing! the tears absolutely trickled down her cheeks. Do not you think it was a charming trick?" "Very much so," said Amanda; "I think it gave a striking specimen of your humor." "Well, my dear," exclaimed Miss Kilcorban, without minding the marked emphasis of Amanda's last words, "if you allow us, my sister and I will call on you to-morrow to look over your things." "It would be giving yourselves a great deal of unnecessary trouble," replied Amanda, coolly, who did not by any means relish this forward proposal; "my things can boast of little but simplicity, and I am always my own milliner." "Really! well, I protest you have a great deal of taste; my maid, who is very handy, would, I think, be able to make up things in pretty much the same style, if you were obliging enough to give her patterns. If you do, perhaps you will add to the favor, and allow us to say they are the newest Bath fashions. Was you ever at Bath?" "No." "Oh! then I assure you, you have a monstrous pleasure to come; it is the sweetest place on earth—quite a paradise! I declare I thought I should have died with grief at leaving it. Papa has been inexorable ever since to our entreaties for a second trip. He says the first cost too much money. Indeed, it was an enormous sum; only think how much." "I am the worst person in the world," said Amanda, "for guessing," sick of her impertinent volubility, and moving from the window. The evening was fine, and the grounds about the house beautiful; she therefore proposed a walk. At this proposal, the young ladies, who had hitherto been in deep confab, looked at each other, and remained silent for some minutes. Miss Kilcorban, then, who had no notion of gratifying the inclination of her guest, by the sacrifice of her own, said, "it blew a little, and that her hair would be ruined, and the Marchelle powder blown from it by such a walk." Another young lady, looking down at her white satin slippers, vowed "she would not venture into the grass for worlds." A third declared, "when once dressed, she could not bear to be tumbled." Amanda had too much politeness to repeat her wish, and it was, therefore, unanimously agreed upon among the fair coterie, that they should continue in the drawing-room, to be in statu quo for the reappearance of the beaux.

Lady Greystock now beckoned to our heroine to take a seat by her. She gladly obeyed. "Well, my dear," said her ladyship, "I hope you have had enough of these country misses—those would-be misses of the ton." Amanda smiled assentingly. "Heaven defend me, or any one I like," continued her ladyship, "from their clack! The confusion of Babel was, I really believe, inferior to that their tongues create, yet some people have the absurdity to reckon these girls accomplished Poor Mrs. Kilcorban torments one with the perfections of her daughters; against they are disposed of, which she imagines will be very soon, she has a new brood of graces training up to bring out. Mercy on me! what a set of hoydens. I would lay my life, at this very instant they are galloping about the nursery like a parcel of wild colts, tearing or tormenting an unfortunate French governess, who was formerly fille de chambre to a woman of quality, and does not understand even the grammatical part of her own language." "Mrs. Kilcorban's opinion of her children," said Amanda, "is natural, considering the partiality of a parent." "Yes; but not more bearable on that account," replied her ladyship; "and I should endeavor to open her eyes to her folly, if I thought her acquaintances would forgive my depriving them of such a fund of amusement."

Mr. Bryan Kilcorban, with some gentlemen, now entered the room, and advanced to Amanda. "So," said he, "you have got by the dowager; hang me, but I would let my beard grow, if all women resembled her in their dispositions." "By way of appearing sagacious, I suppose," said her ladyship, who was extremely quick, and had caught the last words. "Alas! poor youth, no embellishments on the exterior would ever be able to make us believe the tenement within well furnished." Her ladyship was now summoned to a whist-table, and Miss Kilcorban immediately took her vacant seat. "My dear creature!" said she, "are you not bored to death? Lady Greystock is a queer piece, I can assure you. I suppose she was asking some favor from you, such as to work her an apron or handkerchief. She is noted everywhere for requesting such little jobs, as she calls them; indeed, we should never put up with the trouble she gives us, but that she is vastly rich, and papa's relation, and has no one so nearly connected with her as we are." "All very good reasons for your complaisance," replied Amanda; "but should you not be more careful in concealing them?" "Oh, Lord! no! every one knows them as well as we do ourselves. She was here last summer, and took a fancy to the pattern of an apron of mine; and made me the reasonable request of working one like it for her. All this she pretended was to prevent my being idle. Well, I said I would, and wrote up to the Moravian House in Dublin, where I had got mine, for one exactly like it. In due time I received and presented it to the dowager, certain that, in return, I should receive a few of her diamond pins, which she had often heard me admire. They are the prettiest I ever saw, and quite unfit for her, but she had the cruelty to disappoint me." "Upon my faith!" cried Mrs. Kilcorban, who had taken a chair at the other side of Amanda, and listened with evident pleasure to her daughter's voluble speech, "Lady Greystock is an odd being; I never met with any one like her in all my travels through England, Ireland, and Wales; but she is a great orator, and possesses the gift of the gab in a wonderful degree."

"Ah, indeed," thought Amanda; "and you and your fair daughters resemble her in that respect." After tea, she was prevailed on to sit down to commerce; but she soon grew as tired of the party as of the game, and lost on purpose to be released. She had hoped for a little more chat with Lady Greystock; but her ladyship was passionately fond of cards, and at all times would have preferred the pleasures of a card-table to the eloquence of a Cicero. Kilcorban, on finding her disengaged, tormented her with many absurd compliments. A challenge to a brag-table at length relieved her from his nonsense, and she loitered about the card-tables till they broke up for supper.

Amanda always expressed to her father her sentiments of any company she had been in; and those she now delivered, on quitting the party, perfectly coincided with his. He laughed at the account which the Kilcorbans had given of Lady Greystock, to whom he knew they paid the most extravagant flattery, in hopes of obtaining some of her large fortune.

CHAPTER XVII.

"Remote from man, with God they passed their days,
Prayer all their business, all their pleasure praise."—PARNEL.

HE following evening they were engaged to spend at a farmer's. The invitation was given with such humility, yet pressed with such warmth, that they could not avoid accepting it, and accordingly, soon after dinner, walked to the house, which was about a mile from Castle Carberry. It was a low thatched building—every appendage to it bespoke neatness and comfort. It was situated in a beautiful meadow, enclosed from the road by a hawthorn hedge, and on the opposite side lay an extensive common, on which stood the stupendous and venerable ruins of an abbey, called St. Catherine's. They appeared a melancholy monument of the power of time over strength and grandeur; and while they attacted the observation of the curious, excited a sigh in the bosom of sensibility.

The farmer's family consisted of three daughters and two sons, who were now dressed in their best array. They had assembled a number of their neighbors, among whom was a little fat priest, called Father O'Gallaghan—considered the life of every party—and a blind piper. The room was small, and crowded with furniture as well as company. It was only divided from the kitchen by a short passage, and the steam of hot cakes, and the smoke of a turf fire, which issued thence, soon rendered it distressingly warm. Amanda got as near the window as possible, but still could not procure sufficient air; and as everything for tea was not quite ready, asked one of the Miss O'Flannaghans if she would accompany her to St. Catherine's. She answered in the affirmative. The priest, who had been smirking at her ever since her entrance, now shook his fat sides, and said he wished he could get her initiated there; "for it would do my soul good," cried he, "to confess such a pretty little creature as you are. Though faith, I believe I should find you like Paddy McDenough, who used to come to confession every Easter, though the devil a thing the poor man had to confess about at all at all. So, says I to him, Paddy, my jewel, says I, I believe I must make a saint of you, and lay you on the altar." "Oh! honey, father!" cried he, "not yet awhile, till I get a new suit of clothes on, which I shall by next Michaelmas." Amanda left them all laughing at this story, and her father engaged in conversation with some farmers, who were desiring his interest with Lord Cherbury, for new leases on moderate terms.

Amanda had about a quarter of a mile to walk across the common; the ground was marshy and uneven, and numerous stumps of trees denoted its having once been a noble forest, of which no memorial but these stumps, and a few tall trees immediately near the abbey remained, that stretched their venerable arms around it, as if to shade that ruin whose progress they had witnessed, and which Amanda found well worthy of inspection. She was equally astonished at its elegance and extent; with sacred awe traversing the spacious cloisters, the former walks of holy meditation, she pursued her way through winding passages, where vestiges of cells were yet discernible, over whose mouldering arches the grass waved in rank luxuriance, and the creeping ivy spread its gloomy foliage, and viewed with reverence the graves of those who had once inhabited them; they surrounded that of the founder's which was distinguished by a cross, and Miss O'Flannaghan related the traditions that were current concerning him. He was a holy monk who had the care of a pious lady's conscience; she, on her deathbed, had a remarkable dream, or vision, in which she thought an angel appeared, and charged her to bequeath her wealth to her confessor, who would, no doubt, make a much better use of it than those she designed it for. She obeyed the sacred injunction, and the good man immediately laid the foundation of this abbey, which he called after his benefactress, and to which he, and the community he belonged to, removed. The chapel was roofless, but still retained many relics of superstitious piety, which had escaped, in a tolerable degree, both time and weather. Saints and martyrs were curiously cut over the places where the altars and cisterns for holy water had once stood, to which Amanda passed through a long succession of elegant arches, among which were a number of tomb-stones, with curious devices, and unintelligible inscriptions. Half hid by grass and weeds, on a flag, which she perceived must have been lately placed there, she saw some faded flowers strewn, and looking at her companion, saw a tear dropping from her on them She gently asked the cause of it, and heard a favorite brother was interred there. The girl moved from the spot, but Amanda, detained by an irrepressible emotion, stayed a minute longer to contemplate the awful scene. All was silent, sad, and solitary; the grass-grown aisles looked long untrodden by human foot, the green and mouldering walls appeared ready to crumble into atoms, and the wind, which howled through their crevices, sounded to the ear of fancy as sighs of sorrow for the desolation of the place. Full of moralizing melancholy, the young, the lovely Amanda, hung over the grave of her companion's youthful brother; and taking up the withered flower, wet with the tear of sisterly affection, dropped another on it, and cried, "Oh! how fit an emblem is this of life! how illustrative of these words—

'Man comes forth as a flower in the field, and is soon cut down.'"

Miss O'Flannaghan now led her through some more windings, when, suddenly emerging from them, she found herself, to her great surprise, in a large garden, entirely encompassed by the ruins, and in the centre of it stood a long low building, which her companion informed her was a convent; a folding door at the side opened into the chapel, which they entered, and found a nun praying.

Amanda drew back, fearful of disturbing her; but Miss O'Flannaghan accosted her without ceremony, and the nun returned the salutation with the most cordial good humor. She was fifty, as Amanda afterwards heard, for she never could, from her appearance, have conceived her to be so much. Her skin was fair, and perfectly free from wrinkle; the bloom and down upon her cheeks as bright and as soft as that upon a peach; though her accent at once proclaimed her country, it was not unharmonious; and the cheerful obligingness of her manner amply compensated the want of elegance. She wore the religious habit of the house, which was a loose flannel dress, bound round her waist by a girdle, from which hung her beads and a cross; a veil of the same stuff descended to the ground, and a mob cap, and forehead cloth, quite concealed her hair.* Miss O'Flannaghan presented Amanda to

---

* The Abbey and the Nun, which the Author has attempted to describe, were such as she really saw, but in a different part of Ireland from that which she has mentioned.

her as a stranger, who wished to see everything curious in the chapel. "Ah! my honey," cried she, "I am sorry she is come at a time when she will see us all in the dismals, for you know we are in mourning for our prioress (the altar was hung in black): but, my dear (turning to Amanda), do you mean to come here next Sunday? for if you do, you will find us all bright again." Upon Amanda's answering in the negative, she continued, "Faith, and I am sorry for that, for I have taken a great fancy to you, and when I like a person, I always wish them as great a chance of happiness as I have myself." Amanda, smiling, said, she believed none could desire a greater, and the nun obligingly proceeded to show her all the relics and finery of the chapel; among the former was a head belonging to one of the eleven thousand virgin martyrs, and the latter, a chest full of rich silks, which pious ladies had given for the purpose of dressing the altar. Pulling a drawer from under it, she displayed a quantity of artificial flowers, which she said were made by the sisters and their scholars. Amanda wished to make a recompense for the trouble she had given, and finding they were to be sold, purchased a number, and having given some to Miss O'Flannaghan, whom she observed viewing them with a wishful eye, she left the rest with the nun, promising to call for them the next day. "Ay, do," said she, "and you may be sure of a sincere welcome. You will see a set of happy poor creatures, and none happier than myself. I entered the convent at ten; I took the vows at fifteen, and from that time to the present, which is a long stretch, I have passed a contented life, thanks be to our blessed lady!" raising her sparkling eyes to heaven. They ascended a few steps to the place where the community sat. It was divided from the body of the chapel by a slight railing. Here stood the organ. The nun sighed as she looked at it. "Poor sister Agatha," cried she, "we shall never get such another organist. She was always fit indeed for the heavenly choir. Oh! my dear," turning to Amanda, "had you known her, you would have loved her. She was our late prioress, and elected to that office at twenty-nine, which is reckoned an early age for it, on account of the cleverness it requires. She had held it but two years when she died, and we never were so comfortable as during her time, she managed so well. The mourning in the chapel, as I have already told you, will be over for her next Sunday; but that which is in our hearts will not be so speedily removed." Miss O'Flannaghan now reminded Amanda it was time to return, to which, with secret reluctance, she consented. The nun pressed her to stay to tea; but, on hearing of her engagement, only reminded her of the promised visit. In their walk back, her companion informed Amanda that the society consisted of twelve nuns. Their little fortunes, though sunk in one common fund, were insufficient to supply their necessities, which compelled them to keep a day-school, in which the neighboring children were instructed in reading, writing, plain-work, embroidery, and artificial flowers. She also added, that the nuns were allowed to go out, but few availed themselves of that liberty, and that, except in fasting, they were strangers to the austerities practised in foreign convents.

For such a society Amanda thought nothing could be better adapted than their present situation. Sheltered by the ruins, like the living entombed among the dead, their wishes, like their views, were bounded by the mouldering walls, as no object appeared beyond them which could tempt their wandering from their usual limits. The dreary common, which met their view, could not be more bleak and inhospitable than the world in general would have proved to these children of poverty and nature.

Father O'Gallaghan met the ladies at the door, and, familiarly taking Amanda's hand, said, "Why, you have stayed long enough to be made a nun of. Here (said he) the cakes are buttered, the tea made, and we are all waiting for you. Ah! you little rogue," smirking in her face, "by the head of St. Patrick, those twinklers of yours were not given for the good of your soul. Here you are come to play pell-mell among the hearts of the honest Irish lads Ah, the devil a doubt but you will have mischief enough to answer for by and by, and then I suppose you will be coming to me to confess and absolve you; but remember, my little honey, if you do, I must be paid beforehand." Amanda disengaged her hand, and entered the parlor, where the company, by a display of pocket-handkerchiefs on their laps, seemed prepared to make a downright meal of the good things before them. The Miss O'Flannaghans, from the toils of the tea-table, at last grew as red as the ribbon with which they were profusely ornamented. The table at length removed, the chairs arranged, and benches placed in the passage for the old folks, the signal for a dance was given by the piper's playing an Irish jig. The farmer's eldest son, habited in his new sky-blue coat, his hair combed sleek on his forehead, and his complexion as bright as a full-blown poppy, advanced to our heroine, and begged, with much modesty, and many bows, she would do him the favor to stand up with him. She hesitated a little, when Father O'Gallaghan, giving her a tap, or rather slap, on the shoulder, made her start suddenly from her seat. He laughed heartily at this, declaring he liked to see a girl alive and merry. As he could not join in the dance, he consoled himself with being master of the ceremonies, and insisted on Amanda's dancing and leading off the priest in his boots. She felt little inclined to comply; but she was one of those who can sacrifice their own inclination to that of others. Being directed in the figure by the priest, she went down the dance, but the floor being an earthen one, by the the time she had concluded it, she begged they would excuse her sitting the remainder of the evening, she felt so extremely fatigued. She and Fitzalan would gladly have declined staying supper, but this they found impossible, without either greatly mortifying, or absolutely offending, their hospitable entertainers.

The table was covered with a profusion of good country fare, and none seemed to enjoy it more truly than the priest. In the intervals of eating, his jests flew about in every direction. The scope he gave to his vivacity exhilarated the rest, so that, like Falstaff, he was not only witty himself, but a promoter of wit in others. "Pray, father," said a young man to him, "what do you give in return for all the good cheer you get?" "My blessing, to be sure," replied he. "What better could I give?" "Ay, so you may think, but that is not the case with us all, I promise you. It is so pithy, I must tell you a story about that same thing called a priest's blessing. A poor man went one day to a priest, who had the name of being very rich and very charitable; but as all we hear is not Gospel, so the poor man doubted a little the truth of the latter report, and resolved on trying him. 'Father,' says he, 'I have met with great losses. My cabin was burned, my pigs stolen, and my cow fell into a ditch and broke her neck; so I am come to ask your reverence, for the love of heaven, to lend me a crown.' 'A crown!' repeated the angry and astonished priest. 'O! you rogue, where do you think I could get money to lend, except, like yourself, I had pilfered and stolen?' 'Oh! that is neither here nor there,' replied the man. 'You know I cleared the score on my conscience with you long ago, so tell me, father, if you will lend me half-a-crown?' 'No, nor a shilling.' 'Well, a farthing, then; anything from such a good man as you.' 'No,' said the priest, 'not a mite.' 'Mayn't I have your blessing?' then asked the man. 'Oh! that you shall, and welcome,' replied he, smiling. 'Why, then, Father,' returned the other, 'I would refuse it if you forced it upon me; for, do you see, had it been worth one farthing, you would have refused it to me.'"

"You have put me in mind of a very curious story," exclaimed another young man, as this one concluded his. "A young knight went into a chapel in Spain one morning, where he observed a monk standing in a supplicating attitude, with a box in his hand. He asked him what this was for, and learned, to collect money for praying the souls of fifty Christians out of purgatory, whom the Moors had murdered. The knight threw a piece of money into the box, and the monk, after repeating a short prayer, exclaimed, 'There is one soul redeemed.' The knight threw in a second, and the priest, after the same ceremony, cried, 'There is another free.' Thus they both went on, one giving, and the other praying, till, by the monk's account, all the souls were free. 'Are you sure of this?' inquired the knight. 'Ay,' replied the priest, 'they are all assembled together at the gate of heaven, which St. Peter gladly opened for them, and they are now joyfully seated in Paradise.' 'From whence they cannot be removed, I suppose,' said the knight 'Removed!' repeated the astonished priest. 'No, the world itself might be easier moved.' 'Then, if you please, holy father, return me my ducats; they have accomplished the purpose for which they were given, and, as I am only a poor cavalier, without a chance of being as happily situated, at least for some years, as the souls we have mutually contributed to release, I stand in great need of them.'"

Fitzalan was surprised at the freedom with which they treated the priest; but he laughed as merrily as the rest at their stories, for he knew that, though they sometimes allowed themselves a little latitude, they neither wished nor attempted to shake off his power.

Fitzalan and Amanda withdrew as early as possible from the party, which, if it wanted every other charm, had that of novelty, at least, to them. The next morning Amanda repaired to the convent, and inquired for Sister Mary, the good-natured nun she had seen the preceding evening. She immediately made her appearance, and was delighted at seeing Amanda. She conducted her to the school-room, where the rest of the nuns and the pupils were assembled; and Amanda was delighted with the content and regularity which appeared in the society, as well as the obliging eagerness they showed to gratify her curiosity. They led her through the house, which contained a number of apartments, every nun having one to herself, furnished with a bed, chair, table, and crucifix, and then to the parlor, where their new prioress sat. She was a woman far advanced in life. Had a painter wanted to personify benevolence, he might have chosen her for a model—so soft, so benignant was her countenance. Sorrow, as well as time, had marked it deeply; but the mild expression of her eyes announced the most perfect resignation to that sorrow. She received Amanda with the truest politeness and most friendly warmth; and Amanda felt impressed with real reverence for her, whilst she acknowledged in her mind there could not be a happier situation for her than her present. She thought it a pity the world had been deprived of a woman who would have proved such an ornament to it. Sister Mary disappeared, but returned in a few minutes with cakes and currant-wine, which she forced Amanda to take. The good sister was enchanted with her young visitor, and having no idea of concealing her feelings, she openly expressed her admiration. "Dear mother," said she, addressing the prioress, "is she not a lovely creature? What pretty eyes she has got, and what sweet little hands! Oh, if our blessed lady would but touch her heart, and make her become one of us, I should be so happy." The prioress smiled; she was not so great an enthusiast as Sister Mary. "It would be a pity," said she, "so sweet a flower should be hid amidst the ruins of St Catherine's."

Amanda made an addition to her flowers; she was thanked by the nuns, and entreated to favor them often with a visit. Just as she reached Castle Carberry, she saw the Kilcorbans' carriage stop at it, from which Lady Greystock and the young ladies alighted. They both spoke at once, and so extremely fast that Amanda scarcely understood what they said. They declared a thousand impertinent visitors had prevented their coming the preceding morning and looking at the things she had obligingly promised to show them. Amanda recollected no such promise, but would not contradict them, and permitted their taking what patterns they liked. Lady Greystock smiled sarcastically at her young kinswomen, and expressed a wish to see the castle. Amanda led her through it. Her ladyship was particularly pleased with the dressing-room. Here the young ladies, with rude and eager curiosity, examined everything; but her ladyship, who was full as curious as themselves, could not condemn freedoms she took herself. Observing a petticoat in a tambour-frame, she admired the pattern; and hearing it was designed by Amanda, extolled her fine taste, and declared she should of all things like to have one worked in the same. This hint was too plain to pass unnoticed. Amanda wished to oblige, particularly any one advanced in life, and told her ladyship she would work one for her. Lady Greystock smiled most graciously at this, and pressing her hand, declared she was a charming girl. The Miss Kilcorbans winked slily, and, taking her hand in turn, assured her they had conceived a most ardent friendship for her, and hoped she would often favor them with her company. Amanda answered those insincere professions with cool civility, and the visitors departed.

CHAPTER XVIII.

"Oh! fields, oh! woods, when, when, shall I be made
The happy tenant of your shade!"—COWLEY.

SOLITUDE to Amanda was a luxury, as it afforded her opportunities of indulging the ideas on which her heart delighted to dwell; she yet believed she should see Lord Mortimer, and that Lord Cherbury's sanctioning their attachment would remove the delicate scruples of her father. From soothing his passing hours, beguiling her own with the accomplishments she possessed, and indulging the tender suggestions of hope, a pleasure arose she thought ill exchanged for the trifling gaiety of the parties she was frequently invited to; she was never at a loss for amusement within Castle Carberry, or about its domain; the garden became the object of her peculiar care; its situation was romantic, and long neglect had added to its natural wildness. Amanda in many places discovered vestiges of taste, and wished to restore all to primeval beauty. The fruit-trees were matted together, the alleys, grass-grown, and the flowers, choked with weeds; on one side lay a small wilderness, which surrounded a gothic temple, and on the other green slopes with masses of naked rock projecting through them; a flight of rugged steps, cut in the living rock, led to a cave on the summit of one of the highest, a cross rudely carved upon the wall, and the remains of a matted couch, denoted this having formerly been a hermitage; it overhung the sea, and all about it were tremendous crags, against which the waves beat with violence. Over a low-arched door was a smooth stone, with the following lines engraved upon it:—

"The pilgrim oft
At dead of night, amid his orisons hears
Aghast the voice of time—disparting towers
Tumbling all precipitate down, dashed
Rattling around, loud thundering to the moon."—DYER.

Under Amanda's superintending care, the garden soon lost its rude appearance, a new couch was procured for the hermitage, which she ornamented with shells and sea-weeds, rendering it a most delightful recess; the trees were pruned, the alleys cleared of opposing brambles, and over the wall of the gothic temple she hung the flowers she had purchased at St. Catherine's, in fanciful wreaths.

She often ascended the devious path of the mountain, which stretched beyond Castle Carberry, and beheld the waves glittering in the sunbeams, from which its foliage sheltered her. But no visionary pleasures, no delightful rambles, no domestic avocations made her forgetful to the calls of benevolence; she visited the haunts of poverty, and relieved its necessities to the utmost of her power; the wretchedness so often conspicuous among many of the lower rank, filled her not only with compassion, but surprise, as she had imagined that liberty and a fruitful soil were generally attended with comfort and prosperity. Her father, to whom she communicated this idea, informed her that the indigence of the peasants proceeded in a great degree from the emigration of their landlords. "Their wealth," said he, "is spent in foreign lands, instead of enriching those from whence it was drawn; policy should sometimes induce them to visit their estates; the revenue of half a year spent on them would necessarily benefit the poor wretches whose labors have contributed to raise it; and by exciting their gratitude, add inclination to industry, and consequently augment their profits.

"The clouds which are formed by mists and exhalations, return to the places from whence they were drawn in fertilizing showers and refreshing dews, and almost every plant enriches the soil from which it sprung. Nature, indeed, in all her works, is a glorious precedent to man; but while enslaved by dissipation, he cannot follow her example, and what exquisite sources of enjoyment does he lose—to lighten the toils of labor, to cheer the child of poverty, to raise the drooping head of merit—oh! how superior to the revels of dissipation, or the ostentation of wealth.

"Real happiness is forsaken for a gaudy phantom called pleasure; she is seldom grasped but for a moment—yet in that moment has power to fix envenomed stings within the breast. The heart which delights in domestic joys, which rises in pious gratitude to heaven, which melts at human woe, can alone experience true pleasure The fortitude with which the peasants bear their suffer ings should cure discontent of its murmurs; they support adversity without complaining, and those who possess a pile of turf against the severity of the winter, a small strip of ground planted with cabbage and potatoes, a cow, a pig, and some poultry, think themselves completely happy, though one wretched hovel shelters all alike."

Oh! how rapturous! thought Amanda—the idea of Lord Mortimer's feeling recurring to her mind—to change such scenes; to see the clay-built hovel vanish, and a dwelling of neatness and convenience rise in its stead; to wander, continued she, with him whose soul is fraught with sensibility, and view the projects of benevolence realized by the hand of charity; see the faded cheek of misery regain the glow of health,

"The desert blossom as the rose,"

and content and cheerfulness sport beneath its shades.

From such an ecstatic reverie as this, Amanda was roused one morning by the entrance of the Kilcorbans and Lady Greystock into the dressing-room where she was working. "Oh! my dear!" cried the eldest of the young ladies, "we have such enchanting news to tell you. Only think, who is coming down here immediately—your uncle and aunt and cousin. An express came this morning from Dublin, where they now are, to the steward at Ulster Lodge, to have everything prepared against next week for them. "I declare," said Miss Alicia, "I shall quite envy you the delightful amusement you will have with them." Amanda blushed, and felt a little confused. "You will have no reason, then, I fancy," replied she, "for I really do not know them." "Oh, Lord!" exclaimed Mrs. Kilcorban, "well, that is very comical, not to know your own relations; but perhaps they always lived in Scotland, and you were afraid to cross the sea to pay them a visit." "If that was the only fear she had," said Lady Greystock, with a satirical smile, "she could easily have surmounted it: besides would it not have held good with respect to one place as well as another?" "Well, I never thought of that," cried Mrs. Kilcorban: "but pray, miss, may I ask the reason why you do not know them by letter?" "It can be of very little consequence to you, madam," replied Amanda, coolly, "to hear it." "They say Lady

Euphrasia Sutherland is very accomplished," exclaimed Miss Kilcorban; "so a correspondence with her would have been delightful. I dare say you write sweetly yourself; so if ever you leave Castle Carberry, I beg you will favor me with letters, for of all things, I doat on a sentimental correspondence." "No wonder," said Lady Greystock, "you are so particularly well qualified to support one." "But, my dear!" resumed Miss Kilcorban, "we are to give the most enchanting ball that ever was given in this world! Papa says we shall have full liberty to do as we please respecting it." "It will be a troublesome affair, I am afraid," said Mrs. Kilcorban. "We are to have confectioners and French cooks from Dublin," continued her daughter, without minding this interruption. "Everything is to be quite in style and prepared against the third night of the Marquis and Marchioness's arrival; so, my dear, you and your papa will hold yourselves in readiness for our summons." Amanda bowed. "My sister and I are to have dancing dresses from town, but I will not give you an idea of the manner in which we have ordered them to be made. I assure you, you will be absolutely surprised and charmed when you see them. All the elegant men in the country will be at our entertainment. I dare say you will be vastly busy preparing for it." "Nature," said Lady Greystock, "has been too bounteous to Miss Fitzalan, to render such preparations necessary." "Oh, Lord!" cried the young ladies, with a toss of their heads, "Miss Fitzalan is not such a fool, I suppose, as to wish to appear unlike every one else in her dress, but," rising with their mamma, and saluting her much more formally than they had done at their entrance, "she is the best judge of that."

Fitzalan had never seen the Marchioness since his marriage, nor did he ever again wish to behold her. The inhumanity with which she had treated her lovely sister—the malice with which she had augmented her father's resentment against that poor sufferer, had so strongly prepossessed his mind with ideas of the selfishness and implacability of hers, as to excite sentiments of distaste and aversion for her. He considered her as the usurper of his children's rights—as accessory to the death of his adored Malvina, and consequently the author of the agonies he endured—agonies which time, aided by religion, could scarcely conquer.

15 *

CHAPTER XIX.

> "Oh love, how are thy precious, sweetest minutes
> Thus ever crossed, thus vexed with disappointments;
> Now pride, now fickleness, fantastic quarrels,
> And sullen coldness give us pain by turns."—ROWE.

T the expected time, the Marquis and his family arrived with great splendor at Ulster Lodge, which was immediately crowded with visitors of the first consequence in the county, among whom were the Kilcorbans, whose affluent fortune gave them great respectability. Mr. Kilcorban wished, indeed, to be first in paying his compliments to the Marquis, who had a borough in his disposal he was desirous of being returned for. Disappointed the last time he set up as one of the candidates for the county, this was his only chance of entering that house he had long been ambitious for a seat in. He knew, indeed, his oratorical powers were not very great—often saying, he had not the gift of the gab like many of the honorable gentlemen; but then he could stamp and stare, and look up to gods and goddesses* for their approbation, with the best of them; and, besides, his being a member of parliament would increase his consequence, at least in the country.

The female part of his family went from Ulster Lodge to Castle Carberry, which they entered with a more consequential air than ever, as if they derived new consequence from the visit they had been paying. Instead of flying up to Amanda, as usual, the young ladies swam into the room, with, what they imagined, a most bewitching elegance, and, making a sliding courtesy, flung themselves upon a sofa, exactly opposite a glass, and alternately viewed themselves, and pursued their remarks on Lady Euphrasia's dress. "Well, certainly, Alicia," said Miss Kilcorban, "I will have a morning gown made in imitation of her ladyship's: that frill of fine lace about the neck is the most becoming thing in nature; and the pale blue lining sweetly adapted for a delicate complexion." "I think, Charlotte," cried Miss Alicia, "I will have my tambour muslin in the same style, but lined with pink to set off the work."

* Ladies were admitted to the gallery of the Irish House of Commons.

"This aunt of yours, my dear," exclaimed Mrs. Kilcorban, "is really a personable-looking woman enough, and her daughter a pretty little sort of body."

"Oh! they are charming creatures," cried both the young ladies; "so elegant, so irresistibly genteel."

"Your ideas and mine, then," said Lady Greystock, "differ widely about elegance and irresistibility, if you ascribe either to the ladies in question. Mr. Kilcorban," continued she, turning to Amanda, "feared, I believe, my Lord Marquis would fly across the sea in a few hours; and that he might catch him ere he took wing, never ceased tormenting us, from the time breakfast was over till we entered the carriage, to make haste, though he might have known it was quite too early for fine folks to be visible.

"Well, we posted off to Ulster Lodge, as if life and death depended on our despatch. Mr. Kilcorban was ushered into the Marquis's study, and we into an empty room, to amuse ourselves, if we pleased, with portraits of the Marquis's ancestors; whilst bells in all quarters were tingling—maids and footmen running up and down stairs—and cats, dogs, monkeys, and parrots, which I found composed part of the travelling retinue, were scratching, barking, chattering, and screaming, in a room contiguous to the one we occupied. At length a fine, perfumed jessamy made his appearance, and saying the ladies were ready to have the honor of receiving us, skipped up stairs like a harlequin. The Marchioness advanced about two steps from her couch to receive us, and Lady Euphrasia half rose from her seat, and, after contemplating us for a minute, as if to know whether we were to be considered as human creatures or not, sunk back into her former attitude of elegant languor, and continued her conversation with a young nobleman who had accompanied them from England."

"Well, I hope you will allow he is a divine creature," exclaimed Miss Kilcorban, in an accent of rapture. "Oh! what eyes he has," cried her sister; "what an harmonious voice! I really never beheld any one so exquisitely handsome!"

"Lord Mortimer, indeed," said Lady Greystock—Amanda started, blushed, turned pale, panted as if for breath, and stared as if in amazement. "Bless me, Miss Fitzalan," asked her ladyship, "are you ill?" "No, madam," replied Amanda, in a trembling voice; "'tis only—'tis only a little palpitation of the heart I am subject to. I have interrupted your ladyship; pray proceed." "Well," continued Lady Greystook, "I was saying that Lord Mortimer was one of the most elegant and engaging young men I had ever beheld. His expressive eyes seemed to reprove the folly of his fair companion; and her neglect made him doubly assiduous, which to me was a most convincing proof of a noble mind."

How did the heart of Amanda swell with pleasure at this warm eulogium on Lord Mortimer! The tear of delight, of refined affection, sprung to her eye, and could scarcely be prevented falling.

"Lord, Madam," cried Miss Kilcorban, whose pride was mortified at Amanda's hearing of the cool reception they had met with, "I can't conceive the reason you ascribe such rudeness and conceit to Lady Euphrasia; 'tis really quite a misconstruction of the etiquette necessary to be observed by people of rank."

"I am glad, my dear," replied Lady Greystock, "you are now beginning to profit by the many lessons I have given you on humility."

"I assure you, Miss," said Mrs. Kilcorban, "I did not forget to tell the Marchioness she had a niece in the neighborhood. I thought, indeed, she seemed a little shy on the subject; so I suppose there has been a difference in the families, particularly as you don't visit her; but, at our ball, perhaps, everything may be settled." Amanda made no reply to this speech, and the ladies departed.

Her bosom, as may well be supposed, was agitated with the most violent perturbations on hearing of Lord Mortimer's being in the neighborhood. The pleasure she felt at the first intelligence gradually subsided on reflecting he was an inmate, probably a friend of those relations who had contributed to the destruction of her mother; and who, from the character she had heard of them, it was not uncharitable to think, would feel no great regret, if her children experienced a destiny equally severe. Might they not infuse some prejudices against her into his bosom; to know she was the child of the unfortunate Malvina, would be enough to provoke their enmity; or, if they were silent, might not Lady

Euphrasia, adorned with every advantage of rank and fortune, have won, or at least soon win, his affections?

Yet scarcely did these ideas obtrude, ere she reproached herself for them as injurious to Lord Mortimer, from whose noble nature she thought she might believe his constancy never would be shaken, except she herself gave him reason to relinquish it.

She now cheered her desponding spirits, by recalling the ideas she had long indulged with delight, as her residence was still a secret to the Edwins, whose letters to their daughter were, by Fitzalan's orders, constantly directed to a distant town, from whence hers, in return, were sent. She concluded chance had informed Lord Mortimer of it, and flattered herself, that to avoid the suspicion which a solitary journey to Ireland might create in the mind of Lord Cherbury, he had availed himself of the Marquis's party, and come to try whether she was unchanged, and her father would sanction their attachment, ere he avowed it to the Earl.

Whilst fluctuating between hope and fear, Ellen, all pale and breathless, ran into the room, exclaiming, "He is come! he is come! Lord Mortimer is come!"

"Oh, heavens!" sighed Amanda, sinking back in her chair, and dropping her trembling hands before her. Ellen, alarmed, blamed herself for her precipitation, and, flying to a cabinet, snatched a bottle of lavender water from it, which she plentifully sprinkled over her, and then assisted her to a window. "I was so flurried," cried the good-natured girl, as she saw her mistress recovering, "I did not know what I was about. Heaven knows, the sight of poor Chip himself could not have given me more pleasure. I was crossing the hall when I saw his lortship alighting; and to be sure, if one of the old warriors had stepped out of his niche—and the tefil take them all, I say, for they grin so horribly they frighten me out of my wits if I go through the hall of a dark evening—so if one of them old fellows, as I was saying, had jumped out, I could not have peen more startled, and pack I ran into the little parlor, and there I heard his lortship inquiring for my master; and to be sure the sound of his voice did my heart good, for he is an old friend, as one may say. So as soon as he went into the study, I stole up stairs; and one may guess what he and my master are talking apout, I think."

The emotion of Amanda increased. She trembled so she could not stand. She felt as if her destiny, her future happiness, depended on this minute. In vain she endeavored to regain composure. Her spirits were wound up to the highest pitch of expectation, and the agitations inseparable from such a state were not to be repressed.

She continued near an hour in this situation, when the voice of Mortimer struck her ear. She started up, and, standing in the centre of the room, saw him walking down the lawn with her father, who left him when he had reached the gate, where his servants and horses were. The chill of disappointment pervaded the heart of Amanda, and a shower of tears fell from her. Ellen, who had remained in the room, was almost as much disappointed as her mistress. She muttered something about the inconstancy of men. They were all, for her part, she pelieved, alike; all like Mr. Chip—captious on every occasion. The dinner bell now summoned Amanda. She dried her eyes, and tied on a little straw hat to conceal their redness. With much confusion she appeared before her father. His penetrating eye was instantly struck with her agitation and pallid looks, and he conjectured she knew of the visit he had received. On receiving that visit, he wondered not at the strength of her attachment. The noble and ingenuous air of Lord Mortimer had immediately prepossessed Fitzalan in his favor. He saw him adorned with all those perfections which are calculated to make a strong and permanent impression on a heart of sensibility, and he gave a sigh to the cruel necessity which compelled him to separate two beings of such congenial loveliness; but as that necessity neither was or could be overcome, he rejoiced that Lord Mortimer, instead of visiting him on account of his daughter, had merely come on affairs relative to the castle, and had inquired for her with a coolness which seemed to declare his love totally subdued. Not the smallest hint relative to the letter in which he had proposed for her dropped from him, and Fitzalan concluded his affections were transferred to some object more the favorite of fortune than his portionless Amanda.

This object, he was inclined to believe, was Lady Euphrasia Sutherland, from what Lord Cherbury had said concerning the splendid alliance he had in view for his son, and from Lord Mortimer's accompanying the Roslin family to Ireland.

He felt he had not fortitude to mention those conjectures to Amanda. He rather wished she should imbibe them from her own observation; and pride, he then trusted, would come to her aid, and stimulate her to overcome her attachment. Dinner passed in silence. When the servant was withdrawn, he resolved to relieve the anxiety which her looks informed him pressed upon her heart, by mentioning the visit of Lord Mortimer. He came, he told her, merely to see the state the castle was in, and thus proceeded: "Lord Mortimer is, indeed, an elegant and sensible young man, and will do honor to the house from which he is descended. He had long wished, he told me, to visit this estate, which was endeared to him by the remembrance of his juvenile days, but particularly by its being the place of his mother's nativity, and her favorite residence; and the opportunity of travelling with an agreeable party, had determined him no longer to defer gratifying this wish.

"He mentioned his mother in terms of the truest respect and tenderness; and his softened voice, his tearful eye, proclaimed his heart the mansion of sensibility. His virtues, like his praises, will do honor to her memory. He had been told the castle was in a very ruinous state, and was agreeably surprised to find it in as good order as could be expected from its ancient date. He desired to see the garden, which had been laid out under the direction of his mother. He expected not to have found a vestige of her taste remaining, and was consequently charmed to find himself mistaken. Every spot appeared to remind him of some happy hour, especially the gothic temple. 'How many happy minutes have I passed in this place,' said his lordship, after a silence for some time, 'with the best of women.'—Upon my word, Amanda," continued Fitzalan, "you have ornamented it in a very fanciful manner. I really thought his lordship would have stolen some of your lilies or roses, he examined them so accurately." Amanda blushed, and her father still perceiving expectation in her eyes, thus went on: "His lordship looked at some of the adjacent grounds; and as he has mentioned what improvements he thought necessary to be made in them, I fancy he will not repeat his visit, or stay much longer in the kingdom."

In a few minutes after this conversation Fitzalan repaired to his library, and Amanda to the garden. She hastened to the temple. Never had she before thought it so picturesque, or such an addition to the landscape. The silence of Lord Mortimer on entering it, she did not, like her father, believe proceeded altogether from retracing scenes of former happiness with his mother. "No," said she, "in this spot he also, perhaps, thought of Amanda."

True, he had mentioned her with indifference to her father, but that might (and she would flatter herself it did) proceed from resentment, excited by her precipitate flight from Wales, at a period when his received addresses gave him a right to information about all her actions, and by her total neglect of him since. Their first interview, she trusted, would effect a reconciliation, by producing an explanation. Her father then, she flattered herself, tender as he was, depending on her for happiness, and prepossessed in Lord Mortimer's favor, would no longer oppose their attachment, but allow Lord Cherbury to be informed of it, who she doubted not, would, in this as well as every other instance, prove himself truly feeling and disinterested.

Thus did Amanda, by encouraging ideas agreeable to her wishes, try to soften the disappointment she had experienced in the morning. Fitzalan, on meeting his daughter at tea, was not surprised to hear she had been in the gothic temple, but he was to see her wear so cheerful an appearance. He was no stranger to the human heart, and he was convinced some flattering illusion could alone have enabled her to shake off the sadness with which, but an hour before, she had been oppressed. The sooner such an illusion was removed, the better; and to allow her to see Lord Mortimer, he imagined would be the most effectual measure for such a purpose.

The more he reflected on that young nobleman's manner, and what he himself had heard from Lord Cherbury, the more he was convinced Lady Euphrasia Sutherland was not only the object destined for Lord Mortimer, but the one who now possessed his affections; and believed his visit to Castle Carberry had been purposely made, to announce the alteration of his sentiments by the coldness of his conduct, and check any hopes which his appearance in the neighborhood might have created.

He had hesitated about Amanda's accepting the invitation to the Kilcorbans' ball; but he now determined she should go, impressed with the idea of her being there convinced of the change in Lord Mortimer's sentiments—a conviction he deemed necessary to produce one in her own.

Amanda impatiently longed for this night, which she believed would realize either her hopes or fears.

CHAPTER XX.

"A crimson blush her beauteous face o'erspread,
Varying her cheeks by turns with white and red;
The driving colors, never at a stay,
Run here and there, and flush and fade away;
Delightful change! thus Indian ivory shows,
Which with the bordering paint of purple glows,
Or lilies damasked by the neighboring rose."—DRYDEN.

HE wished-for night at length arrived, and Amanda arrayed herself for it with a fluttering heart. The reflection of her mirror did not depress her spirits: hope had increased the brilliancy of her eyes, and given an additional glow to her complexion. Ellen, who delighted in the charms of her dear young lady, declared many of the Irish ladies would have reason to envy her that night; and Fitzalan when he entered the parlor was struck with her surpassing loveliness. He gazed on her with a rapture that brought tears into his eyes, and felt a secret pride at the idea of the Marchioness beholding this sweet descendant of her neglected sister—

"Into such beauty spread and blown so fair,
Though poverty's cold wind, and crushing rain,
Beat keen and heavy on her tender years."

"No," said he to himself, "the titled Euphrasia, if she equals, cannot at least surpass my Amanda—meekness and innocence dwell upon the brow of my child; but the haughty Marchioness will teach pride to lower upon Lady Euphrasia."

Amanda, on reaching Grangeville, found the avenue full of carriages. The lights dispersed through the house gave it quite the appearance of an illumination. It seemed, indeed, the mansion of gaiety and splendor. Her knees trembled as she ascended the stairs. She wished for time to compose herself, but the door opened, her name was announced, and Mrs. Kilcorban came forward to receive her. The room, though spacious, was extremely crowded. It was decorated in a fanciful manner with festoons of flowers, intermingled with variegated lamps. Immediately over the entrance was the orchestra, and opposite to it sat the Marchioness and her party. The heart of Amanda beat, if possible, with increased quickness on the approach of Mrs. Kilcorban, and her voice was lost in her emotions. Recollecting, however, that the scrutinizing eyes of Lord Mortimer, and her imperious relations, were now on her, she almost immediately recovered composure, and with her usual elegance walked up the room. Most of the company were strangers to her, and she heard a general buzz of "Who is she?" accompanied with expressions of admiration from the gentlemen, among whom were the officers of a garrison town near Grangeville. Confused by the notice she attracted, she hastened to the first seat she found vacant, which was near the Marchioness.

Universal, indeed, was the admiration she had excited among the male part of the company, by her beauty, unaffected graces, and simplicity of dress.

She wore a robe of plain white lutestring, and a crape turban, ornamented with a plume of drooping feathers. She had no appearance of finery, except a chain of pearls about her bosom, from which hung her mother's picture, and a light wreath of embroidered laurel, intermingled with silver blossoms, round her petticoat. Her hair, in its own native and glossy hue, floated on her shoulders, and partly shaded a cheek where the purity of the lily was tinted with the softest bloom of the rose. On gaining a seat, her confusion subsided. She looked up, and the first eyes she met were those of Lord Mortimer (who leaned on Lady Euphrasia Sutherland's chair), fastened on her face with a scrutinizing earnestness, as if he wished to penetrate the recesses of her heart, and discover whether he yet retained a place in it. She blushed, and looking from him, perceived she was an object of critical attention to the Marchioness and Lady Euphrasia. There was a malignant expression in their countenances, which absolutely shocked her; and she felt a sensation of horror at beholding the former, who had so largely contributed to the sorrows of her mother. "Can it be possible," said Lady Euphrasia, replying to a young and elegant officer who stood by her, in a tone of affectation, and with an impertinent sneer, "that you think her handsome?" "Handsome," exclaimed he with warmth, as if involuntarily repeating her ladyship's word, "I think her bewitchingly irresistible. They told me I was coming to the land of saints;" but, glancing his sparkling eyes around, and fixing them on Amanda; "I find it is the land of goddesses."

The Marchioness haughtily frowned—Lady Euphrasia smiled satirically, tossed her head, and played with her fan. The propensities to envy and ill-nature, which the Marchioness had shown in her youth, were not less visible in age. As they were then excited on her own account, so were they now on her daughter's. To engross praise and admiration for her, she wished beauty blasted, and merit extirpated; nor did she ever fail, when in her power, to depreciate one, and cast an invidious cloud of calumny over the other. She beheld Amanda with envy and hatred. Notwithstanding her partiality to her daughter, she could not avoid seeing her vast inferiority, in point of personal charms, to her young relation. True, Lady Euphrasia possessed a fortune, which would always insure her attention; but it was that unimpassioned and studied attention selfishness dictates, the mere tribute of flattery. How different from the spontaneous attention which Amanda excited, who, though portionless and untitled, was beheld with admiration, followed with praise, and courted with assiduity.

Lady Euphrasia's mind was the counterpart of her mother's; but in figure she resembled her father. Her stature was low, her features contracted, and though of the same age as Amanda, their harsh expression made her appear much older. Though blessed with the abundant gifts of fortune, she was unhappy, if, from any one's manner, she conceived that they thought nature had not been quite so liberal to her. In the domestic circle, constant flattery kept her in good humor; but when out she was frequently chagrined at seeing women, infinitely below her in rank and fortune, more noticed than herself.

At the ball she supposed she should have appeared as little less, at least, than a demi-goddess. Art and fashion were exhausted in adorning her, and she entered the room with all the insolence of conscious rank and affectation of beauty. As she walked she appeared scarcely able to support her delicate frame, and her languishing eyes were half closed. She could, however, see there was a number of pretty women present, and felt disconcerted. The respect, however, which she was paid, a little revived her; and having contrived to detain Lord Mortimer by her chair and Sir Charles Bingley, the young officer already mentioned, who was colonel of a regiment quartered in an adjacent town, she soon felt her spirits uncommonly exhilarated by the attentions of two of the most elegant men in the room; and, like a proud sultana in the midst of her slaves, was enjoying the compliments she extorted from them by her prefatory speeches, when the door opened, and Amanda, like an angel of light, appeared to dissolve the mists of vanity and self-importance. Lord Mortimer was silent, but his speaking eyes confessed his feelings. Sir Charles Bingley, who had no secret motive to conceal his, openly avowed his admiration, to which Lady Euphrasia replied as has been already mentioned.

All the rapture Sir Charles expressed Lord Mortimer felt. His soul seemed on the wing to fly to Amanda—to utter its feelings—to discover hers, and chide her for her conduct. This first emotion of tenderness, however, quickly subsided, on recollecting what that conduct had been—how cruelly, how ungratefully she had used him. Fled in the very moment of hope and expectation, leaving him a prey to distrust, anxiety, and regret, he dreaded some fatal mystery—some improper attachment (experience had rendered him suspicious), which neither she nor her father could avow; for never did he imagine that the scrupulous delicacy of Fitzalan alone had effected their separation. He still adored Amanda; he neither could nor desired to drive her from his thoughts, except well assured she was unworthy of being harbored in them, and felt unutterable impatience to have her mysterious conduct explained. From Tudor Hall he had repaired to London, restless and unhappy. Soon after his arrival there, the

Marquis proposed his accompanying him to Ireland. This he declined, having reason to think Lord Cherbury meditated an alliance for him with his family. The Earl expressed regret at his refusal. He said he wished he would join the Marquis's party, as he wanted his opinion relative to the state of Castle Carberry, where a man of integrity then resided, who would have any alterations or repairs he might think necessary executed in the most eligible manner. He mentioned the name of Fitzalan. Lord Mortimer was surprised and agitated. He concealed his emotions, however, and with apparent carelessness, asked a few questions about him, and found that he was indeed the father of Amanda. She was not mentioned, nor did he dare to inquire concerning her; but he immediately declared that since his father wished it so much, he would accompany the Marquis. This was extremely pleasing to that nobleman, and he and Lord Cherbury had in reality agreed upon a union between him and Lady Euphrasia, and meant soon openly to avow their intention. Lord Mortimer suspected, and Lady Euphrasia was already apprised of, it; and from vanity, was pleased at the idea of being connected with a man so universally admired. Love was out of the question, for she had not sufficient sensibility to experience it.

He, cautious of creating hopes which he never meant to realize, treated her only with the attention which common politeness demanded, and on every occasion seemed to prefer the Marchioness's conversation to hers, intending by this conduct to crush the projected scheme in embryo, and spare himself the mortification of openly rejecting it. Had his heart even been disengaged, Lady Euphrasia could never have been his choice. If Amanda in reality proved as amiable as he had once reason to believe her, he considered himself bound, by every tie of honor as well as love, to fulfil the engagement he had entered into with her. He resolved, however, to resist every plea of tenderness in her favor, except he was thoroughly convinced she still deserved it. He went to Castle Carberry purposely to make a display of indifference, and prevent any ideas being entertained of his having followed her to Ireland. He deemed himself justifiable in touching her sensibility (if, indeed, she possessed any for him) by an appearance of coldness and inattention; but determined, after a little retaliation of this kind on her, for the pain she had made him endure, to come to an explanation, and be guided by its result relative to his conduct in future to her.

The character of a perfect stranger was the one he was to support throughout the evening; but her loveliness, and the gallantry of Sir Charles Bingley, tempted him a thousand times to break through the restraint he had imposed on himself.

The Marchioness and Lady Euphrasia were not the only persons displeased by the charms of Amanda. The Miss Kilcorbans saw, with evident mortification, the admiration she excited, which they had flattered themselves with chiefly engrossing; their disappointment was doubly severe, after the pain, trouble, and expense they had undergone in ornamenting their persons; after the suggestions of their vanity, and the flattering encomiums of their mamma, who presided herself at their toilet, every moment exclaiming, 'Well, well, heaven help the men to-night, girls!"

They fluttered across the room to Amanda, sweeping at least two yards of painted tiffany after them; assured her they were extremely glad to see her, but were afraid she was unwell, as she never looked so ill. Amanda assured them she was conscious of no indisposition, and the harmony of her features remained undisturbed. Miss Kilcorban, in a half whisper, declared the Marchioness had never smiled since she had entered the room, and feared her mamma had committed a great mistake in inviting them together. The rudeness of this speech shocked Amanda. An indignant swell heaved her bosom, and she was about replying to it as it deserved, when Miss Alicia stopped her by protesting she believed Lord Mortimer dying for Lady Euphrasia. Amanda involuntarily raised her eyes at this speech; but, instead of Lord Mortimer, beheld Sir Charles Bingley, who was standing behind the young ladies. "Am I pardonable," cried he, smiling, "for disturbing so charming a trio? but a soldier is taught never to neglect a good opportunity: and one so propitious as the present for the wish of my heart might not again offer." The Miss Kilcorbans bridled up at this speech; played their fans, and smiled most graciously on him, certainly concluding he meant to engage one or other for the first set. Passing gently between them, he bowed gracefully to Amanda, and requested the honor of her hand. She gave an assenting smile, and he seated himself beside her till the dancing commenced. The sisters cast a malignant glance over them, and swam off with a contemptuous indifference.

Lady Euphrasia had expected Sir Charles and Lord Mortimer would have been competitors for her hand, and was infinitely provoked by the desertion of the former to her lovely cousin. He was a fashionable and animated young man, whom she had often honored with her notice in England, and wished to enlist in the train of her supposed adorers. Lord Mortimer could scarcely restore her good humor by engaging her. Almost immediately after him, young Kilcorban advanced for the same purpose, and Lord Mortimer sincerely regretted he had been beforehand with him. The little fop was quite chagrined at finding her ladyship engaged; but entreated the next set he might have the supreme honor and ecstatic felicity of her hand. This, with the most impertinent affectation, she promised, if able to endure the fatigue of another dance.

Amanda was next couple to Lady Euphrasia, and endeavored therefore to calm her spirits, which the rudeness of Miss Kilcorban had discomposed, and attend to the lively conversation of Sir Charles, who was extremely pleasing and entertaining. Lord Mortimer watched them with jealous attention. His wandering glances were soon noticed by Lady Euphrasia, and her frowns and sarcastic speeches evinced her displeasure at them. He tried to recollect himself, and act as politeness required. She, not satisfied with fixing his attention, endeavored to attract Sir Charles's. She spoke to him across Amanda; but all her efforts were here ineffectual. He spoke and laughed with her ladyship, but his eyes could not be withdrawn from the angelic countenance of his partner. Amanda's hand trembled as, in turning, she presented it to Lord Mortimer; but, though he extended his, he did not touch it. There was a slight in this which pierced Amanda's heart. She sighed, unconscious of doing so herself. Not so Sir Charles. He asked her, smiling, to where, or whom, that sigh was wafted. This made Amanda recall her wandering thoughts. She assumed an air of sprightliness, and went down the dance with much animation. When finished, Sir Charles led her to a seat near the one Lady Euphrasia and Lord Mortimer occupied. She saw the eyes of his lordship often directed towards her, and her heart fluttered at the pleasing probability of being asked to dance by him. Sir Charles regretted that the old-fashioned custom of not changing partners was over, and declared he could not leave her till she had promised him her hand for the third set. This she could not refuse, and he left her with reluctance, as the gentlemen were again standing up, to seek a partner. At the same moment Lord Mortimer quitted Lady Euphrasia. Oh! how the bosom of Amanda throbbed when she saw him approach and look at her. He paused. A faintishness came over her. He cast another glance on her, and passed on. Her eye followed him, and she saw him take out Miss Kilcorban. This, indeed, was a disappointment. Propriety, she thought, demanded his dancing the first set with Lady Euphrasia, but, if not totally indifferent, surely he would not have neglected engaging her for the second. "Yes," said she to herself, "he has totally forgotten me. Lady Euphrasia is now the object, and he only pays attention to those who can contribute to her amusement." Several gentlemen endeavored to prevail on her to dance, but she pleaded fatigue, and sat solitary in a window, apparently regarding the gay assembly, but in reality too much engrossed by painful thoughts to do so. The woods, silvered by the beams of the moon, recalled the venerable shades of Tudor Hall to memory, where she had so often rambled by the same pale beams, and heard vows of unchangeable regard—vows registered in her heart, yet now without the hope of having them fulfilled. The dancing over, the company repaired to another room for refreshments. Amanda, absorbed in thought, heeded not their almost total desertion, till young Kilcorban, capering up to her, declared she looked as lonesome as a hermit in his cell, and, laughing in her face, turned off with a careless impertinence. He had not noticed her before that night. He was indeed one of those little fluttering insects who bask in the rays of fortune, and court alone her favorites. Elated by an acquaintance with the Marchioness and Lady Euphrasia, he particularly neglected Amanda, not only from deeming them more worthy of his attention, but from perceiving he could take no step more certain of gaining their favor. His words made Amanda sensible of the singularity of her situation. She arose immediately, and went to the other room. Every seat was already occupied

Near the door sat Lady Euphrasia and the Miss Kilcorbans. Lord Mortimer leaned on the back of her ladyship's chair, and young Kilcorban occupied one by her side, which he never attempted offering to Amanda. She stood, therefore, most unpleasantly by the door, and was exceedingly confused at hearing a great many, in a whispering way, remarking the strangeness of her not being noticed by so near a relation as the Marchioness of Roslin. A general titter at her situation prevailed among Lady Euphrasia's party, Lord Mortimer excepted. "Upon my word," said young Kilcorban, looking at Amanda, "some ladies study attitudes which would be as well let alone." "For the study of propriety," replied her ladyship, who appeared to have unbended from her haughtiness, "she would do admirably for the figure of Hope." "If she had but an anchor to recline on," rejoined he. "Yes," answered her ladyship, "with her floating locks and die-away glances." "Or else, Patience on a monument," cried he. "Only she has no grief here to smile at," returned Lady Euphrasia. "Pardon me there," said he; "she has the grief—not, indeed, that I believe she would smile at it—of being totally eclipsed by your ladyship." "Or, what do you think," cried Lord Mortimer, whose eyes sparkled with indignation during this dialogue, "of likening her to Wisdom, pitying the follies of human kind, and smiling to see the shafts of malice recoiling from the bosom of innocence and modesty, with contempt, on those who levelled them at it?"

Amanda heard not these words, which were delivered in rather a low voice. Her heart swelled with indignation at the impertinence directed to her, and she would have quitted the room but that the passage was too much crowded for her to pass. Sir Charles Bingley, occupied in attending the young lady with whom he had danced, observed not Amanda till this moment. He instantly flew to her. "Alone—and standing!" said he; "why did I not see you before?—you look fatigued." She was pale with emotion. "Kilcorban," continued he, "I must suppose you did not see Miss Fitzalan, or your seat would not have been kept." Then catching him by the arm, he raised him nimbly from his chair, and directly carried it to Amanda; and having procured her refreshments, seated himself at her feet, exclaiming, "this is my throne, let kings come bow to it." Her lovely and unaffected graces had excited Sir Charles's admiration; but it was the neglect with which he saw her treated, diffused such a soothing tenderness through his manner as he now displayed. It hurt his sensibility, and had she even been plain in her appearance, would have rendered her the peculiar object of his attention. He detested the Marchioness and her daughter for their rancorous envy, as much as he despised the Kilcorbans for their mean insolence. The Marchioness told him a long tale of the shocking conduct of Amanda's parents, whose ill qualities she declared her looks announced her to possess, and endeavored to depreciate her in his favor; but that was impossible.

"Lord!" said Lady Euphrasia, rising as she spoke, "let me pass; this scene is sickening." Lord Mortimer remained behind her. He loitered about the room, and his looks were often directed towards Amanda. Her hopes began to revive. The lustre rekindled in her eyes, and a soft blush again stole over her cheek. Though engaged to Sir Charles, she felt she should be pleased to have Lord Mortimer make an overture for her hand. The company were now returning to the ball-room, and Sir Charles took her hand to lead her after them. At that moment Lord Mortimer approached. Amanda paused as if to adjust some part of her dress. He passed on to a very beautiful girl, whom he immediately engaged, and led from the room. She followed them with her eyes, and continued without moving, till the fervent pressure Sir Charles gave her hand, restored her to recollection.

When the set with him was finished, she would have left the house directly, had her servant been there; but after putting up the horses, he had returned to Castle Carberry, and she did not expect him till a very late hour. She declared her resolution of dancing no more, and Sir Charles having avowed the same, they repaired to the card-room, as the least crowded place they could find. Lady Greystock was playing at the table, with the Marquis and Marchioness. She beckoned Amanda to her, and having had no opportunity of speaking before, expressed her pleasure at then seeing her. The Marquis examined her through his spectacles. The Marchioness frowned, and declared, "she would take care, in future, to avoid parties subject to such disagreeable intruders." This speech was too pointed not to be remarked. Amanda wished to appear undisturbed, but her emotions grew too powerful to be suppressed, and she was obliged to move hastily from the table. Sir Charles followed her. "Cursed malignity," cried he, endeavoring to screen her from observation, while tears trickled down her cheeks; "but, my dear Miss Fitzalan, was your beauty and merit less conspicuous, you would have escaped it; 'tis the vice of little minds to hate that excellence they cannot reach." "It is cruel, it is shocking," said Amanda, "to suffer enmity to outlive the object who excited it, and to hate the offspring on account of the parent—the original of this picture," and she looked at her mother's, "merited not such conduct." Sir Charles gazed on it;—it was wet with the tears of Amanda. He wiped them off, and pressing the handkerchief to his lips, put it in his bosom.

At this instant Lord Mortimer appeared. He had, indeed, been for some time an unnoticed observer of the progress of this tête-à-tête. As soon as he perceived he had attracted their regard, he quitted the room.

"His lordship is like a troubled spirit to-night, wandering to and fro," said Sir Charles; "I really believe everything is not right between him and Lady Euphrasia." "Something, then," cried Amanda, "is in agitation between him and her ladyship?" "So says the world," replied Sir Charles, "but I do not always give implicit credit to its reports. I have known Lord Mortimer this long time; and from my knowledge of him, should never have supposed Lady Euphrasia Sutherland a woman capable of pleasing him; nay, to give my real opinion, I think him quite uninterested about her ladyship. I will not say so much as to all the other females present. I really imagined several times to-night, from his glances to you, he was on the point of requesting an introduction, which would not have pleased me perfectly. Mortimer possesses more graces than those which merely meet the eye, and is a rival I should by no means like to have."

Amanda, confused by this discourse, endeavored to change it, and at last succeeded. They conversed pleasantly together on different subjects, till they went to supper, when Sir Charles still continued his attention. Lord Mortimer was, or at least appeared to be, entirely engrossed with Lady Euphrasia, who from time to time tittered with the Miss Kilcorbans, and looked satirically at

Amanda. On quitting the supper-room, she found her servant in the hall, and immediately desired him to have the carriage drawn up. Sir Charles, who held her hand, requested her to stay a little longer, yet acknowledged it was self alone which dictated the request, as he knew she would not promote her own pleasure by complying with it. As he handed her into the carriage, he told her he should soon follow her example in retiring, as the scene, so lately delightful, in losing her, would lose all its charms. He entreated, and obtained permission, to wait on her the next morning.

How different was now the appearance of Amanda, to what it had been at her departure from Castle Carberry! Pale, trembling, and languid, her father received her into his arms—for, till she returned, he could not think of going to rest—and instantly guessed the cause of her dejection. His heart mourned for the pangs inflicted on his child's. When she beheld him gazing on her with mingled woe and tenderness, she tried to recruit her spirits; and after relating a few particulars of the ball, answered the minute inquiries he made relative to the conduct of the Marchioness and Lady Euphrasia. He appeared unutterably affected on hearing it. "Merciful power," exclaimed he, "what dispositions! But you are too lovely, too like your mother, my Amanda, in every perfection, to escape their malice. Oh! may it never injure you as it did her. May that Providence, whose protection I daily implore for the sweet child of my love, the source of earthly comfort, render every wish, every scheme which may be formed against her, abortive; and oh! may it yet bless me with the sight of her happiness."

Amanda retired to her chamber, inexpressibly affected by the language of her father. "Yes," cried she, her heart swelling with pity and gratitude to him, "my sorrow in future shall be concealed, to avoid exciting his. The pain inflicted by thy inconstancy, Mortimer, shall be hid within the recesses of my heart, and never shall the peace of my father be disturbed by knowing the loss of mine."

The gray dawn was now beginning to advance, but Amanda had no inclination for repose. As she stood at the window, she heard the solemn stillness of the scene frequently interrupted by the distant noise of carriages, carrying home the weary sons and daughters of dissipation. "But a few hours ago," said she, "and how gay, how animated was my soul; how dull, how cheerless now! Oh! Mortimer, but a few hours ago, and I believed myself the beloved of thine heart, but the flattering illusion is now over, and I no longer shall hope, or thou deceive." She changed her clothes, and, flinging herself on the bed, from mere fatigue, at length sunk into a slumber.

CHAPTER XXI.

"Love reigns a very tyrant in my heart,
Attended on his throne by all his guard
Of furious wishes, fears, and nice suspicions."—OTWAY.

HE next morning brought Sir Charles Bingley to Castle Carberry. Fitzalan was out, but Amanda received him in her dressing-room. He told her, with evident concern, he was on the point of setting off for the metropolis, to embark from thence immediately for England, having received letters that morning, which recalled him there. He regretted that their intimacy, or rather friendship, as with insinuating softness he entreated permission to call it, was interrupted at its very commencement—declared it gave him more pain than she could imagine, or he express—and that his return to Ireland would be expedited for the purpose of renewing it, and requested he might be flattered with an assurance of not being totally forgotten during his absence. Amanda answered him as if she supposed mere politeness had dictated the request. Her father, she said, she was sure, would be happy to see him, if he returned again to their neighborhood. At his entrance, he said, could stay but a few minutes, yet he remained about two hours, and when he arose to depart, declared he had reason to think the castle an enchanted one. He found it difficult to get from it; "yet, unlike the knights of old," continued he, "I wish not to break the spell which detained me in it."

Day after day elapsed, and no Lord Mortimer appeared. Amanda, indeed, heard frequently of him, and always as the admirer of Lady Euphrasia. Frequently, too, she heard about the family at Ulster Lodge, their superb entertainments, and those given in the neighborhood to them. The Kilcorbans seemed to have given her up entirely. Lady Greystock was the only one of the family who continued to pay her any attention. She called once or twice at Castle Carberry to see whether her apron was finished, and tell all the news she had picked up, to Amanda. The resolution which Amanda had formed of concealing her melancholy from her father, she supported tolerably well, but she only indulged it more freely in solitude. The idea of Lord Mortimer's union with Lady Euphrasia haunted her imagination and embittered every moment. "Yes," she would exclaim (as she wandered through the garden, which had been converted from a rude wilderness into a scene of beauty by her superintending care), "I have planted flowers, but another shall enjoy their sweets. I have planted roses for Mortimer to strew in the path of Lady Euphrasia;—I have adorned the landscape, and she shall enjoy its beauty!"

About three weeks after the ball, as she sat at work one morning in the dressing-room, beguiling her thoughts with a little plaintive song, she heard the door softly open behind her: she supposed it to be Ellen; but not finding any one advance, turned round and perceived not Ellen indeed, but Lord Mortimer himself. She started from her chair:—the work dropped from her hands, and she had neither power to speak or move.

"I fear I have surprised and alarmed you," said Lord Mortimer. "I ask pardon for my intrusion, but I was informed I should find Mr. Fitzalan here."

"He is in the study, I believe, my Lord," replied Amanda, coolly, and with restored composure. "I will go and inform him your lordship wishes to see him."

"No," exclaimed he, "I will not suffer you to have so much trouble: my business is not so urgent as to require my seeing him immediately." He reseated Amanda, and drew a chair near her.

She pretended to be busy with her work, whilst the eyes of Lord Mortimer were cast round the room, as if viewing well-known objects, which at once pleased and pained his sensibility, by awakening the memory of past delightful days. "This room," said he, softly sighing, "I well remember; it was the favorite retirement of one of the most amiable of women."

"So I have heard," replied Amanda, "the virtues of Lady Cherbury are remembered with the truest gratitude by many in the vicinity of the castle."

"I think," cried Lord Mortimer, gazing upon Amanda with the softest tenderness, "the apartment is still occupied by a kindred spirit."

Amanda's eyes were instantly bent on the ground, and a gentle sigh heaved her bosom; but it was rather the sigh of regret than pleasure; with such an accent as this Lord Mortimer was wont to address her at Tudor Hall, but she had now reason to think it only assumed, for the purpose of discovering whether she yet retained any sensibility for him. Had he not treated her with the most pointed neglect? was he not the declared admirer of Lady Euphrasia? had he not confessed, on entering the room, he came to seek not her, but her father? These ideas rushing through her mind, determined her to continue no longer with him; delicacy, as well as pride, urged her to this, for she feared, if she longer listened to his insinuating language, it might lead her to betray the feelings of her heart; she therefore arose, and said she would acquaint her father his lordship waited for him.

"Cold, insensible Amanda," cried he, snatching her hand, to prevent her departing, "is it thus you leave me? when we parted in Wales, I could not have believed we should ever have had such a meeting as this."

"Perhaps not, my Lord," replied she, somewhat haughtily, "but we have both thought more prudently since that period."

"Then why," said he, "did not prudence teach you to shun a conduct which could create suspicion?"

"Suspicion, my Lord!" repeated Amanda, with a kind of horror in her look.

"Pardon me," cried he, "the word is disagreeable; but, Miss Fitzalan, when you reflect on the manner in which you have acted to me;—your precipitate, your clandestine departure, at the very period when a mutual acknowledgment of reciprocal feelings should have been attended with the most explicit candor on both sides, you cannot wonder at unpleasant conjectures and tormenting doubts obtruding on my mind."

"Is it possible, my Lord," said Amanda, "you never conceived the reason of my departure? Is it possible reflection never pointed it out?"

"Never, I solemnly assure you; nor shall I be happy till I know it." He paused, as if for a reply; but Amanda, agitated by his words, had not power to speak. Whilst he stood silent, trembling, and apparently embarrassed, she heard her father's voice, as he ascended the stairs. This instantly restored hers. "I must go, my Lord," cried she, starting, and struggling to withdraw her hand. "Promise then to meet me," he said, "this evening at St. Catherine's, by seven, or I will not let you go. My soul will be in tortures till I have your actions explained." "I do promise," said Amanda. Lord Mortimer released her, and she retired into her chamber just time enough to avoid her father.

Again her hopes began to revive. Again she believed she was not mistaken in supposing Lord Mortimer had come into Ireland on her account. His being mentioned as the admirer of Lady Euphrasia, she supposed owing to his being a resident in the house with her. About herself, had he been indifferent, he never could have betrayed such emotions. His looks, as well as language, expressed the feelings of a heart tenderly attached and truly distressed. Lest any circumstance had happened, which would prevent a renewal of that attachment, she felt as much impatience as he manifested, to give the desired explanation of her conduct.

His lordship was scarcely gone, ere Lady Greystock made her appearance. Amanda supposed, as usual, she only came to pay a flying visit: how great then was her mortification and surprise, when her ladyship told her she was come to spend the day quite in the family way with her, as the ladies of Grangeville were so busy preparing for a splendid entertainment they were to be at the ensuing day, that they had excluded all visitors, and rendered the house quite disagreeable.

Amanda endeavored to appear pleased, but to converse she found almost impossible, her thoughts were so engrossed by an absent object. Happily her ladyship was so very loquacious herself, as at all times to require a listener more than a speaker. She was, therefore, well satisfied with the taciturnity of her fair companion. Amanda tried to derive some comfort from the hope that her ladyship would depart early in the evening, to which she flattered herself she would be induced by the idea of a comfortable whist party at home. But six o'clock struck, and she manifested no inclination to move. Amanda was in agony. Her cheek was flushed with agitation. She rose and walked to the window, to conceal her emotion, whilst her father and Lady Greystock were conversing. The former at last said, he had some letters to write, and begged her ladyship to excuse his absence for a few minutes. This she most graciously promised to do, and pulling out her knotting, requested Amanda to read to her till tea-time. Amanda took up a book, but was so confused, she scarcely knew what, or how she read.

"Softly, softly, my dear child," at last exclaimed her ladyship, whose attention could by no means keep pace with the rapid manner in which she read. "I protest you post on with as much expedition as my Lady Blerner's poneys on the circular." Amanda blushed, and began to read slowly; but when the clock struck seven her feelings could no longer be repressed. "Good Heaven!" cried she, letting the book drop from her hand, and starting from her chair, "this is too much." "Bless me! my dear!" said Lady Greystock, staring at her, "What is the matter?" "Only a slight headache, madam," answered Amanda, continuing to walk about the room.

Her busy fancy represented Lord Mortimer, now impatiently waiting for her—thinking in every sound which echoed among the desolate ruins of St. Catherine's he heard her footsteps; his soul melting with tenderness at the idea of a perfect reconciliation, which an unsatisfied doubt only retarded. What would he infer from her not keeping an appointment so ardently desired, so solemnly promised, but that she was unable to remove that doubt to his satisfaction. Perhaps he would not credit the reason she could assign for breaking her engagement. Perhaps, piqued at her doing so, he would not afford her an opportunity of accounting for it, or the apparent mystery of her late conduct? To retain his doubts would be to lose his tenderness, and, at last, perhaps, expe.

her from his heart. She thought of sending Ellen to acquaint him with the occasion of her detention at home; but this idea existed but for a moment. An appointment she concealed from her father she could not bear to divulge to any other person; it would be a breach of duty and delicacy, she thought. "No," said she to herself, "I will not, from the thoughtlessness and impetuosity which lead so many of my sex astray, overstep the bounds of propriety, and to reinstate myself in the esteem of one person lose that of others; and, above all, that of my own heart. If Lord Mortimer refuses to hear my justification, he will act neither agreeably to candor or justice, and pride must aid in repelling my regret." "You look strangely, indeed, my dear," said Lady Greystock, who was attentively watching her, whilst those ideas were rising in her mind. Amanda recollected the remarks which might be made on her behavior; and, apologizing for the manner in which she had acted, took her seat with some degree of composure. Fitzalan soon after entered the room, and tea was made; when over, Lady Greystock declared they were a snug party for three-handed whist. Amanda would gladly have excused herself from being of the party, but politeness made her conceal her reluctance; but extreme dejection was noticed both by Fitzalan and her ladyship. The latter imputed it to regret, at not being permitted by her father to accept an invitation she had received for a ball the ensuing evening.

"Don't fret about it, my dear creature," said she, laying down her cards, to administer the consolation she supposed Amanda required; "'tis not by frequenting balls and public places a girl always stands the best chance of being provided for; I, for my part, have been married three times, yet never made a conquest of any one of my husbands in a public place. No, it was the privacy of my life partly obtained for me so many proofs of good fortune." Fitzalan and Amanda laughed. "I shall never be dissatisfied with staying at home," said the latter, "though without either expecting or desiring to have my retirement recompensed as your ladyship's was." "One prize will satisfy you then," said Fitzalan. "Ah!" cried Lady Greystock, "it is Lady Euphrasia Sutherland will obtain the capital one. I don't know where such another young man as Lord Mortimer is to be found." "Then your ladyship supposes," said Fitzalan, "there is some truth in the reports circulated, relative to him and Lady Euphrasia." "I assure you there is," said she; "and I think the connection will be a very eligible one. Their births, their fortunes, are equal." But ah, thought Amanda, how unlike their dispositions. "I dare say," proceeded her ladyship, "Lady Euphrasia will have changed her title before this time next year."

Fitzalan glanced at Amanda; her face was deadly pale, and she put him and Lady Greystock out in the game by the errors she committed. At last the carriage from Grangeville arrived, and broke up a party Amanda could not much longer have supported. Her father perceived the painful efforts she made to conceal her distress. He pitied her from his soul, and, pretending to think she was only indisposed, entreated her to retire to her chamber. Amanda gladly complied with this entreaty, and began to meditate on what Lady Greystock had said. Was there not a probability of its being true? Might not the indifference Lord Mortimer had manifested on his first arrival in the neighborhood have really originated from a change of affections? Might not the tenderness he displayed in the morning have been concerted with the hope of its inducing her to gratify his curiosity, by relating the reason of her journey from Wales, or please his vanity by tempting her to give some proof of attachment? But she soon receded from this idea. Lady Greystock was not infallible in her judgment. Reports of approaching nuptials, Amanda knew, had often been raised without any foundation for them. The present report, relative to Lord Mortimer and Lady Euphrasia, might be one of that nature. She could not believe him so egregiously vain, or so deliberately base, as to counterfeit tenderness merely for the purpose of having his curiosity or vanity gratified. She felt, however, truly unhappy, and could derive no consolation but from the hope that her suspense, at least, would soon be terminated.

She passed a restless night; nor was her morning more composed. She could not settle to any of her usual avocations. Every step she heard, she started in expectation of instantly seeing Lord Mortimer; but he did not appear. After dinner she walked out alone, and took the road to St. Catherine's. When she reached the ruins, she felt fatigued, and sat down upon a flag in the chapel to rest herself. "Here," said she, pensively leaning her head upon her hand, "Mortimer waited for me; perhaps with tender impatience. Here, too, he perhaps accused me of neglect or deceit." She heard a rustling behind her, and turning, perceived Sister Mary.

"You are welcome, my dear soul," cried the good-natured nun, running forward, and sitting down by her; "but why did you not come in to see us?" continued she, affectionately kissing her. Amanda said, "such was her intention, but feeling a little indisposed, she had remained in the air, in hopes of growing better." "Oh, Jesu!" cried the sister, "you do indeed look ill, I must go and get you a cordial from our prioress, who is quite a doctress, I assure you."

Amanda caught her gown as she was running away, and assured her she was better.

"Well, then," said she, resuming her seat, "I must tell you of an odd thing which happened here last night. I came out to walk about the ruins between the lights—that is, as one may say, when it is neither dark or light. As the air was cold, I wrapped my veil about me, and had just turned the cloisters, when I heard a quick foot pacing after me. Well, I, supposing it to be one of the sisters, walked slowly, that she might easily overtake me. But you may guess my surprise when I was overtaken, not by one of them indeed, but by one of the finest and most beautiful young men I ever beheld. Lord, how he did start when he saw me, just for all the world as if I was a ghost; he looked quite wild, and flew off muttering something to himself. Well, I thought all this strange, and was making all the haste I could to the convent, when he appeared again coming from under that broken arch; and he bowed and smiled so sweetly, and held his hat in his hand so respectfully, whilst he begged my pardon for the alarm he had given me; and then he blushed and strove to hide his confusion with his handkerchief, while he asked me if I had seen here a young lady about the ruins that evening, as a particular friend had informed him she would be there, and desired him to escort her home. 'Why, my dear sir,' says I, 'I have been about this place the whole evening, and here has neither been man, woman, nor child, but you and myself; so the young lady changed her mind, and took another ramble.' 'So I suppose,' said he, and he looked so pale, and so melancholy, I could not help thinking it was a sweetheart he had been seeking; so by way of giving him a bit of comfort, 'Sir,' says I, 'if you will leave any marks of the young lady you were seeking with me, I will watch here myself a little longer for her; and if she comes I will tell her how uneasy you were at not finding her, and be sure to despatch her after you.' 'No, he thanked me,' he said, 'but it was of very little consequence his not meeting her, or indeed whether he ever met her again,' and went away." "Did he?" said Amanda. "Bless me!" exclaimed the nun, "you are worse, instead of better."

Amanda acknowledged she was, and rising, requested she would excuse her not paying her compliments that evening at the nunnery.

Sister Mary pressed her to drink tea with the prioress, or at least take some of her excellent cordial; but Amanda refused both requests, and the affectionate nun saw her depart with reluctance.

Scarcely had she regained the road, ere a coach and six, preceded and followed by a number of attendants, approached with such quickness that she was obliged to step aside to avoid it. Looking in at the window as it passed, she saw Lord Mortimer and Lady Euphrasia seated in it, opposite to each other; she saw they both perceived her, and that Lady Euphrasia laughed, and put her head forward to stare impertinently at her. Amanda was mortified that they had seen her: there was something at that moment humiliating in the contrast between their situation and hers—she, dejected and solitary, they adorned and attended with all the advantages of fortune. But in the estimation of a liberal mind, cried she, the want of such advantages can never lessen me—such a mind as I flatter myself Lord Mortimer possesses. Ah! if he thinks as I do, he would prefer a lonely ramble in the desolate spot I have just quitted, to all the parade and magnificence he is about witnessing. The night passed heavily away. The idea of Lord Mortimer's devoting all his attention to Lady Euphrasia, could not be driven from her mind.

The next morning, the first object she saw, on going to the window, was a large frigate lying at anchor near the castle. Ellen entered her chamber, and sighing heavily, as she always did, indeed, at the sight of a ship, said, "she wished it contained her wandering sailor." Amanda indulged a hope that Lord Mortimer would appear in the course of the day, but she was disappointed She retired, after tea, in the evening to her dressing-room, and, seated in the window, enjoyed a calm and beautiful scene. Not a cloud concealed the bright azure of the firmament; the moon spread a line of silvery radiance over the waves, that stole with a melancholy murmur upon the shore; and the silence which reigned around was only interrupted by the faint noise of the mariners on board the frigate, and their evening drum. At last Amanda heard the paddling of oars, and perceived a large boat coming from the ship, rowed by sailors in white shirts and trowsers, their voices keeping time to their oars. The appearance they made was picturesque, and Amanda watched them till the boat disappeared among the rocks. The supper bell soon after summoned her from the window; but scarcely had she retired to her chamber for the night, ere Ellen, smiling, trembling, and apparently overcome with joy, appeared.

"I have seen him," cried she, hastily; "oh, madam, I have seen poor Chip himself, and he is as kind and as true-hearted as ever. I went this evening to the village to see old Norah, to whom you sent the linen, for she is a pleasing kind of poty, and does not laugh like the rest at one for their Welsh tongue; so when I was returning home, and at a goot tistance from her cabin, I saw a great number of men coming towards me, all dressed in white. To pe sure, as I heerd a great teal apout the white poys, I thought these were nothing else, and I did so quake and tremble, for there was neither hole, or bush, or tree on the spot, that would have sheltered one of the little tiny fairies of Penmaenmawr. Well, they came on, shouting and laughing, and merrier than I thought such rogues ought to be; and the moment they espied me, they gathered round me, and began pulling me about; so I gave a great scream, and tirectly a voice (Lort, how my heart jumped at it) cried out, 'that is Ellen;' and to pe sure poor Chip soon had me in his arms; and then I heard they were sailors from the frigate, come to get fresh provisions at the village; so I turned pack with them, and they had a great bowl of whiskey punch, and a whole sight of cakes, and Chip told me all his adventures; and he was so glad when he heard I lived with you, pecause he said you were a sweet, mild young laty, and he was sure you would sometimes remind me of him; and he hopes soon to get his tischarge, and then—" "You are to be married," said Amanda, interpreting the blushes and hesitation of Ellen. "Yes, matam, and I assure you Chip is not altered for the worse py a seafaring life. His voice, inteed, is a little of the roughest, but he told me that was owing to his learning the poatswain's whistle. Poor fellow, he sails to-morrow night. The ship is on the Irish station, and they are to coast it to Dublin."

"Happy Ellen!" said Amanda, as she retired from her chamber, "thy perturbations and disquietudes are over; assured of the affection of thy village swain, peace and cheerfulness will resume their empire in thy breast."

The next evening at twilight, Amanda went down to the beach with her father to see the fishermen drawing their seines on shore, on which their hopes, and the comfort of their families, depended. Whilst Fitzalan conversed with them, Amanda seated herself on a low rock to observe their motions. In the murmur of the waves there was a gentle melancholy, in unison with her present feelings From a pensive meditation, which had gradually rendered her inattentive to the scene before her, she was suddenly roused by voices behind her. She started from her seat, for in one of them she imagined she distinguished the accent of Lord Mortimer. Nor was she mistaken. He was descending a winding path near her, accompanied by a naval officer. To pass without seeing her was impossible; and as he approached her, he stopped, apparently hesitating whether or not he should address her. In a few minutes his hesitation ended, with waving his handkerchief, as if to bid her adieu, whilst he proceeded to a small boat which had been for some time lying in a creek among the rocks, and which, on receiving him and his companion, immediately rowed to the frigate Amanda trembled. Her heart beat violently. Ellen had informed her the frigate was to sail that night; and what could induce Lord Mortimer to visit it at such an hour, except an intention of departing in it.

Uncertainty is dreadful. She grew sick with anxiety before her father returned to the castle. On entering it, she immediately repaired to her chamber, and calling Ellen hastily, demanded if Chip's intelligence was true?

"Alas! yes," replied Ellen, weeping violently; "and I know the reason you inquire. You saw Lort Mortimer going to the ship. I saw him myself, as I stood on the beach talking to Chip, who was one of the sailors that came in the boat for his lortship and the captain; and to be sure the sight left my eyes when I saw my lort departing, pecause I knew he was going away in anger at the treatment he supposed he received from you."

"From me?" exclaimed Amanda.

"Oh! you will never forgive me for acting so padly as I have done by you," sobbed Ellen; "put inteed the sight of poor Chip drove everything from my memory put himself. Last night, as I was going to Norah's, I overtook Lort Mortimer on the road, who was walking quite sorrowfully, as I may say, py himself; so to pe sure I thought I could do no less in good manners than drop him a courtesy as I passed; so up he came to me tirectly: 'And, my good girl, how are you?' said he; and he smiled so sweetly, and looked so handsome; and then he took my hand, and to pe sure his hand was as soft as any velvet. 'And pray, Ellen,' said he, 'is Miss Fitzalan at home, and disengaged?' I told him you was, and Cot knows, my Lort, said I, and melancholy enough, too. I left her in the tressing-room window, looking out at the waves, and listening to the winds. 'Well, hasten home,' cried he, 'and tell her she will oblige me greatly py meeting me immediately at the rocks peyond the castle.' I promised him I would, and he put, nay, inteed, forced five guineas into my hand, and turned off another road, charging me not to forget; put as I was so near Norah's, I thought I might just step in to see how she did, and when I left her, I met poor Chip, and Lort knows I am afraid he would have made me forget my own tear father and mother."

"Oh, Ellen!" cried Amanda, "how could you serve me so?"

"Oh, tear!" said Ellen, redoubling her tears, "I am certainly one of the most unfortunate girls in the world; put, Lort, now, Miss Amanda, why should you be so sorrowful; for certain my lort loves you too well always to pe angry. There is poor Chip now, though he thought I loved Parson Howel, he never forgot me."

Ellen's efforts at consolation were not successful, and Amanda dismissed her, that, unnoticed and unrestrained, she might indulge the tears which flowed at the idea of a long, a lasting separation, perhaps, from Lord Mortimer. Offended, justly offended, as she supposed, with her, the probability was she would be banished from his thoughts, or, if remembered, at least without esteem or tenderness: thus might his heart soon be qualified for making another choice. She walked to the window, and saw the ship already under weigh. She saw the white sails fluttering in the breeze, and heard the shouts of the mariners. "Oh, Mortimer!" cried she, "is it thus we part? is it thus the expectations you raised in my heart are disappointed? You go hence, and deem Amanda unworthy a farewell. You gaze, perhaps, at this moment on Castle Carberry, without breathing one sigh for its inhabitants. Ah, had you loved sincerely, never would the impulse of resentment have conquered the emotion of tenderness. No, Mortimer, you deceived me, and perhaps yourself, in saying I was dear to you. Had I been so, never could you have acted in this manner." Her eyes followed the course of the vessel, till it appeared like a speck in the horizon. "He is gone," said she, weeping afresh, and withdrawing herself from the window; "he is gone, and if ever I meet him again, it will probably be as the husband of Lady Euphrasia."

CHAPTER XXII.

"Think'st thou I'll make a life of jealousy,
To follow still the changes of the moon
With fresh surmises? No; to be once in doubt
Is to be resolved. But yet
I'll see before I doubt: when I doubt, prove,
And on the proof there is no more but this—
Away at once with love or jealousy."—SHAKSPEARE.

LORD MORTIMER had, in reality, departed with sentiments very unfavorable to Amanda. He had waited impatiently at St. Catherine's, in the fond expectation of having all his doubts removed by a candid explanation of the motives which caused her precipitate journey from Wales. His soul sighed for a reconciliation: his tenderness was redoubled by being so long restrained. The idea of folding his beloved Amanda to his bosom, and hearing that she deserved all the tenderness and sensibility which glowed in that bosom for her, gave him the highest pleasure; but when the appointed hour passed, and no Amanda appeared, language cannot express his disappointment. Almost distracted by it, he ventured to inquire concerning her from Sister Mary; and, long after the friendly nun had retired to the convent, continued to wander about the ruins, till the shadows of night had enveloped every object from his view. "She fears to come, then," exclaimed he, quitting the desolate spot, oppressed with the keenest anguish; "she fears to come, because she cannot satisfy my doubts. I witnessed her agitation, her embarrassment, this morning, when I hinted at them. The mystery which separated us will not be explained, and it is vain to think we shall ever meet, as I once flattered myself we should."

This thought seemed to strike at all his hopes. The distress and disorder of his mind was depicted on his countenance, and escaped not the observation and raillery of the Marchioness and Lady Euphrasia; but their raillery was in vain, and unanswered by him; he was absorbed in a train of pensive reflections, which they had neither power to remove or disturb.

Most unwillingly he accompanied them the ensuing day to a splendid entertainment given purposely for them in the neighborhood. The unexpected sight of Amanda, as she stood on a little elevated bank, to avoid the carriage, caused a sudden emotion of surprise and delight in his bosom. The utmost powers of eloquence could not have pleaded her cause so successfully as her own appearance at that minute did. The languor of her face, its mild and seraphic expression, her pensive attitude, and the timid modesty with which she seemed shrinking from observation, all touched the sensibility of Lord Mortimer, awakened his softest feelings, revived his hopes, and made him resolve to seek another opportunity of demanding an explanation from her. The sudden color which flushed his cheeks, and the sparkling of his eyes, as he looked from the carriage, attracted the notice of his companions. They smiled maliciously at each other, and Lady Euphrasia declared, "She supposed the girl was stationed there to try and attract admiration, which, perhaps, her silly old father had told her she merited—or else to meet with adventures." Lord Mortimer drew in his head, and the contrast between her ladyship and the fair being he had been looking at, never struck him so forcibly as at that moment, and lessened one as much as it elevated the other in his estimation.

He wandered near the castle the next evening, in hopes of meeting Amanda. His disappointment was diminished by seeing Ellen, who, he was confident, would be faithful to the message intrusted to her. With this confidence he hastened to the rocks, every moment expecting the appearance of Amanda. Her image, as it appeared to him the preceding day, dwelt upon his imagination, and he forcibly felt how essential to his peace was a reconciliation with her. An hour elapsed, and his tenderness again began to give way to resentment. It was not Ellen, but Amanda he doubted. He traversed the beach in an agony of impatience and anxiety; a feverish heat pervaded his frame, and he trembled with agitation. At length he heard the distant sound of the supper-bell at Ulster Lodge, which never rang till a late hour. All hopes of seeing Amanda were now given up, and every intention of meeting her at a future period relinquished. She avoided him designedly, it was evident. He would have cursed himself for betraying such anxiety about her, and his wounded pride revolted from the idea of seeking another interview. "No! Amanda!" he exclaimed, as he passed the castle, "you can no longer have any claim upon me. Mysterious appearances in the most candid mind will raise suspicions. In giving you an opportunity for accounting for such appearances, I did all that candor, tenderness, sensibility, and honor could dictate; and, instead of again making efforts to converse with you, I must now make others, which, I trust, will be more successful, entirely to forget you."

The next morning he accompanied the Marquis in his barge to the frigate, where he was agreeably surprised to find in the commander an old friend of his, Captain Somerville, who returned to Ulster Lodge with his visitors, and there, in a half jesting, half serious manner, asked Lord Mortimer to accompany him on his intended cruise. This his lordship instantly promised he would, with pleasure. He was completely tired of the Roslin family, and was, besides, glad of an opportunity of convincing Amanda he was not quite so fascinated to her as she perhaps believed, by his quitting the neighborhood ere their departure. As he descended to the boat, the sight of Amanda shook his resolution. She seemed destined to cross his path, merely to give him disquietude. An ardent wish sprung in his heart to address her, but it was instantly suppressed, by reflecting how premeditately she had avoiding him; pride, therefore, prompted him to pass her in silence; yet, as the boat receded from the shore, his eyes were riveted to the spot on which she stood, and when he could no longer see her white gown fluttering in the wind, he gave a sigh to the remembrance of the happy days he had passed with her at Tudor Hall; and another to the idea, that such hours would never more be enjoyed by him.

The family at Ulster Lodge were both mortified and disappointed by his departure, though he, perceiving their displeasure, had endeavored to lessen it, by promising to wait their arrival in Dublin, and return with them to England. His departure seemed a tacit intimation that he was not as much attached to Lady Euphrasia as they wished him to be. A suspicion of this nature had, indeed, for some time pervaded their minds, and also that his affections were elsewhere disposed of: they had reason to believe that the person who possessed them dwelt in the vicinity of the Lodge, from the great alteration which took place in his manner, immediately after his arrival at it. In hopes of discovering who this was, they watched him critically at all the parties he frequented with him, but soon found it was not the present, but the absent objects had the power of exciting emotions in him. At the name of Amanda Fitzalan or her father they observed him color, and frequently saw him contemplate Castle Carberry, as if it contained a being infinitely dear to him; to Amanda, therefore, they feared he was attached, and supposed the attachment commenced at the Kilcorbans' ball, where they had noticed his impassioned glances at this hated, because too lovely relation. The most unbounded rage took possession of their souls; they regretted ever having come to Ireland, where they supposed Lord Mortimer had first seen Amanda, as Lord Cherbury had mentioned the children of Fitzalan being strangers to him or his family. They knew the passions of Lord Cherbury were impetuous, and that ambition was the leading principle of his soul. Anxious for an alliance between his family and theirs, they knew he would ill brook any obstacle which should be thrown in the way of its completion, and therefore resolved, if Lord Mortimer, at their next meeting, appeared averse to the wishes of his father, to acquaint the Earl with the occasion of his son's disinclination, and represent Fitzalan and his daughter as aiding and abetting each other, in an insidious scheme to entangle the affections of Lord Mortimer, and draw him into a marriage; a scheme which, to a man of the world (as they knew Lord Cherbury to be), would appear so very probable as to gain implicit credit. This they knew would convert the esteem he felt for Fitzalan into hatred and contempt; his favor would consequently be withdrawn, and the father and child again sunk into indigent obscurity. To think that Amanda, by dire necessity, should be reduced to servitude; to think the elegance of her form should be disguised by the garb of poverty, and the charms of her face faded by misery, were ideas so grateful, so ecstatic to their hearts, that to have them realized, they felt they could with pleasure relinquish the attentions of Lord Mortimer, to have a pretext for injuring Fitzalan with his father: though not quite assured their suspicions were well founded, they would never have hesitated communicating them as such to Lord Cherbury; but for their own satisfaction they wished to know what reason they had to entertain them. Lady Greystock was the only person they observed on a footing of intimacy with Amanda, and through her means flattered themselves they might make the desired discovery. They therefore began to unbend from their haughtiness, and make overtures for an intimacy with her; overtures which she received with delight, and in their present attention forgot their past neglect, which had given her such disgust. As they became intimate with her, they were much amused by a shrewd manner she possessed of telling stories, and placing the foibles and imperfections of their visitors in the most conspicuous and ludicrous light; particularly of such visitors as were not agreeable to them. With the foibles of human nature she was well acquainted, also with the art of turning those foibles to her own advantage. She perceived the egregious vanity of the Marchioness and Lady Euphrasia, and by administering large portions of what Sterne styles the delicious essence of the soul, to them, soon became an immense favorite

After an injunction of secrecy, the Marchioness communicated her fears relative to Lord Mortimer and Amanda, which, she pretended, regard for one and pity for the other, had excited; as an attachment either of an honorable or dishonorable nature, she knew Lord Cherbury would never pardon. To know, therefore, how far matters had proceeded between them, would be some satisfaction, and might, perhaps, be the means of preventing the ill consequences she dreaded. Lady Greystock was not to be imposed on; she perceived it was not pity for Amanda, but envy and jealousy, which had excited the fears of the Marchioness. If Lord Mortimer was attached to Amanda, from his sentiments and manner, she was convinced it was an attachment of the purest nature. She carefully concealed her thoughts, however, affected to enter into all the alarms of the Marchioness, and, as she saw she was expected to do, promised all in her power should be done for discovering what attachment subsisted between his lordship and Miss Fitzalan. For this purpose she began to grow constant in her visits at Castle Carberry, often spending whole days in the most familiar manner with Amanda, and endeavoring, by various methods, to beguile her of the secrets of her heart. Sometimes she rallied her on her melancholy; sometimes expressed pity for it in strains of the most soothing tenderness; would frequently relate little fictitious and embellished anecdotes of her own youth, in which she said she had suffered the most exquisite misery, from an unfortunate entanglement; would then advert to Lord Mortimer; express her wonder at his precipitate departure, and her admiration of his virtues, declaring, if ever Lady Euphrasia gained his heart, which she much doubted, she must be considered as one of the most fortunate of women.

Delicacy sealed the lips of Amanda and guarded her secret. She believed her passion to be hopeless, and felt that to be offered consolation on such a subject, would, to her feelings, be truly humiliating. But though she could command her words, she could not her feelings, and they were visibly expressed in her countenance. She blushed whenever Lord Mortimer was mentioned; looked shocked if a union between him and Lady Euphrasia was hinted at; and smiled if a probability was suggested of its never taking place. Lady Greystock, at last, relinquished her attempts at betraying Amanda into a confession of her sentiments; indeed, she thought such a confession not very requisite, as her countenance pretty clearly developed what they were; and she deemed herself authorized to inform the Marchioness that she was sure something had passed between Lord Mortimer and Amanda, though what she could not discover, from the circumspection of the latter. The Marchioness was enraged, and more determined than ever on involving Amanda in destruction, if Lord Mortimer hesitated a moment in obeying the wishes of his father, by uniting himself to Lady Euphrasia.

CHAPTER XXIII.

"And to be plain, 'tis not your person
My stomach's set so sharp and fierce on:
But 'tis your better part, your riches,
That my enamored heart bewitches."—HUDIBRAS.

MONTH after the departure of Lord Mortimer the Roslin family left Ulster Lodge. Amanda sighed, as she saw them pass, at the idea of the approaching meeting, which might, perhaps, soon be followed by an event that would render her fond remembrance of Lord Mortimer improper. Many of the families about the castle were already gone to town for the winter. Those who remained in the country till after Christmas, among whom were the Kilcorbans, had so entirely neglected Amanda, from the time the Marchioness arrived in the neighborhood, that they could not think of renewing their visits, confident as they were, from the proper dignity of her and Fitzalan's manner, that they would be unwelcome.

The weather was now often too severe to permit Amanda to take her usual rambles; and the solitude of the castle was heightened by her own melancholy ideas, as well as by the dreariness of the season. No more the magic hand of hope sketched scenes of flattering brightness, to dissipate the gloominess of the present ones. The prospects of Amanda's heart were as dreary, as desolate, as those she viewed from the windows of the castle. Her usual avocations no longer yielded delight. Every idea, every occupation was embittered by the reflection of being lessened in the estimation of Lord Mortimer. Her health declined with her peace, and again Fitzalan had the anguish of seeing sorrow nipping his lovely blossom. The rose forsook her cheek, and her form assumed a fragile delicacy, which threatened the demolition of his earthly happiness. He was not ignorant of the cause of her dejection, but he would not shock her feelings by hinting it. Every effort, which tenderness could suggest, he essayed to cheer her, but without any durable effect; for though she smiled when he expressed a wish to see her cheerful, it was a smile transient as the gleamings of a wintry sun, and which only rendered the succeeding gloom more conspicuous.

At this period of distress, Lady Greystock, who continued her visits at the castle, made a proposal, which Fitzalan eagerly embraced. This was to take Amanda with her to London, whither she was obliged to go directly, about a lawsuit carrying on between her and the nephew of her late husband.

Change of scene, Fitzalan trusted, would remove from Amanda's mind the dejection which oppressed it, and consequently aid the restoration of her health. Of Lord Mortimer's renewing his addresses, he had not the slightest apprehension, as he neglected the opportunities he might have had in the country for such a purpose. Fitzalan, it may be remembered, knew not that his lordship had ever deviated from his indifference, and he believed it occasioned by a transfer of his affections to Lady Euphrasia. He was also ignorant of the great intimacy between the Roslin family and Lady Greystock, and consequently of the probability there was, from such an intimacy, of Amanda's being often in the way of Lord Mortimer. If she met him, he was confident it would be as the husband or favored lover of Lady Euphrasia; and, in either of these characters, he was certain, from the rectitude and purity of her principles, she would be more than ever impressed with the necessity of conquering her attachment; whilst the pain attending such a conviction would be lessened, and probably soon removed by surrounding objects, and the gay scenes she must engage in from being the companion of Lady Greystock, who had a numerous and elegant acquaintance in London.

Her ladyship appeared to him, as she did to many others, a

pleasing, rational woman—one to whose care his heart's best treasure might safely be consigned. He was induced to accept her protection for his Amanda, not only on account of her present but future welfare. His own health was extremely delicate. He deemed his life very precarious, and flattered himself Lady Greystock, by having his beloved girl under her care, would grow so attached to her, as to prove a friend if he should be snatched away ere his newly-obtained independence enabled him to make a provision for her. In indulging this hope, his heart could not reproach him for anything mean or selfish. Her ladyship had frequently assured him all her relations were very distant ones, and in affluent circumstances, so that if his Amanda received any proof of kindness from her, she could neither injure nor encroach on the rights of others.

This, however, was not the case, though carefully concealed from him, as well as many others, by her ladyship. Her education had either given birth to, or strengthened, the artful propensities of her disposition. She had been one of the numerous offspring of a gentleman in the southern part of Ireland, whose wife, a complete housewife, knowing his inability of giving his daughters fortunes, determined to bring them up so as to save one for their future husbands.

At the age of nineteen, Miss Bridget, by her reputation for domestic cleverness, attracted the notice of a man of easy independence in the neighborhood, who, being a perfect Nimrod, wanted somebody to manage those concerns at home, which he neglected for the field and kennel; and in obtaining Miss Bridget, he procured this valuable acquisition. His love of sport, with his life, was fatally terminated the second year of his marriage, by his attempting to leap a five-bar gate. A good jointure devolved to his widow, and the office of consoling her to the rector of the parish, a little fat elderly man, who might have sat very well for the picture of Boniface. So successful were his arguments, that he not only expelled sorrow from her heart, but introduced himself into it, and had the felicity of receiving her hand as soon as her weeds were laid aside. Four years they lived in uninterrupted peace, but too free an enjoyment of the good things of this life undermined the constitution of the rector. He was ordered to

Bath, where his mortal career was shortly terminated, and his whole fortune was left to his wife.

In the house where she lodged was an ancient baronet, who had never been married. His fortune was considerable, but his manner so strange and whimsical, that he appeared incapable of enjoying the advantages it would have afforded to others. Notwithstanding his oddities, he was compassionate; and as the fair relict was unaccompanied by a friend, he waited on her for the purpose of offering consolation, and any service in his power. This attention instantly inspired her with an idea of trying to make him feel tenderer sentiments than those of pity for her. His title and fortune were so attractive, that neither his capricious disposition, nor the disparity of their ages, he being sixty, and she only eight-and-twenty, could prevent her ardently desiring a connection between them. Her efforts to effect this were long unsuccessful; but perseverance will almost work miracles. Her constant good humor, and unremitted solicitude about him, who was in general an invalid, at last made an impression on his flinty heart, and in a fit of sudden gratitude he offered her his hand, which was eagerly accepted.

The presumptive heir to the baronet's large possessions was the son and only child of a deceased sister. At the period this unexpected alliance took place, he was about twenty, pleasing in his person, and engaging in his manner, and tenderly beloved by his uncle. This love, Lady Greystock saw, if it continued, would frustrate her wish of possessing the baronet's whole property. Various schemes fluctuated in her mind relative to the manner in which she should lay the foundation for Rushbrook's ruin. Ere she could determine on one, chance discovered a secret which completely aided her intentions.

In the neighborhood of the baronet's country residence, Rushbrook had formed an attachment for the daughter of a man, against whom his uncle entertained the most inveterate enmity. A union with this girl, she was well convinced, would ruin him. She therefore gave him to understand she knew of his attachment, and sincerely pitied his situation, encouraging his love by the most flattering eulogiums on his adored Emily; declared her regret that hearts so congenial should be separated; and at last intimated that if they wished to unite, she was convinced she would soon be able to obtain Sir Geoffry's forgiveness for such a step. Her artful insinuations hurried the unsuspicious pair into the snare she had spread for them. The consequence of this was what she expected.

Sir Geoffry's rage was unappeasable, and he solemnly vowed never more to behold his nephew. Lady Greystock wished to preserve, if possible, appearances to the world, and prevailed on him to give her five hundred pounds for Rushbrook, to which she added five of her own, and presented the notes to him, with an assurance of pleading his cause whenever she found a favorable opportunity for doing so.

He purchased an ensigncy in a regiment on the point of embarking for America, where he felt he would rather encounter distress than among those who had known him in affluence.

Her ladyship now redoubled her attention to Sir Geoffry, and at last prepossessed him so strongly with the idea of her affection for him, that he made a will, bequeathing her his whole fortune, which she flattered herself with soon enjoying. But the constitution of Sir Geoffry was stronger than she imagined, and policy obliged her to adhere to a conduct which had gained his favor, as she knew the least alteration of it would, to his capricious temper, be sufficient to make him crush all her hopes.

Fifteen years passed in this manner, when a friend of Rushbrook's advised him no longer to be deluded by the promises Lady Greystock still continued to make, of interceding in his favor, but to write himself to his uncle for forgiveness, which the duty he owed his family, and the distress of his situation, should prompt him to immediately. Rushbrook accordingly wrote a most pathetic letter, and his friend, as he had promised, delivered it himself to the baronet. The contents of the letter, and the remonstrance of his visitor, produced a great change in the sentiments of the baronet. Tenderness for a nephew he had adopted as his heir from his infancy began to revive, and he seriously reflected, that by leaving his fortune to Lady Greystock, he should enrich a family unconnected with him, whilst the last branch of his own was left to obscurity and wretchedness. Pride recoiled from such an idea, and he told the gentleman he would consider about a reconciliation with his nephew.

The conversation between them, which Lady Greystock had contrived to overhear, filled her with dismay; but this was increased almost to distraction, when an attorney being sent for, she repaired again to her hiding-place, and heard a new will dictated entirely in Rushbrook's favor.

Sir Geoffry was soon prevailed on to see his nephew, but Mrs. Rushbrook and the children were not suffered to appear before him. They were, however, supplied with everything requisite for making a genteel appearance, and accompanying the regiment (again ordered abroad) with comfort.

Soon after their departure, Sir Geoffry sunk into a sudden state of insensibility, from which no hopes of his ever recovering could be entertained. The situation was propitious to the designs of Lady Greystock; none but creatures of her own were admitted to his chamber. An attorney was sent for, who had often transacted business for her, relative to her affairs in Ireland; and a good bribe easily prevailed on him to draw up a will she dictated, similar to that before made in her favor. The baronet was raised in her arms, whilst the attorney guided his almost lifeless hand in signing it; and two clerks set their names as witnesses. Sir Geoffry expired almost immediately after this scheme was executed.

Rushbrook's friend, who had been appointed to act for him, if this event took place whilst he was abroad, now appeared. A will found in Sir Geoffry's cabinet was read, by which it appeared Mr. Rushbrook was his sole heir. The exultation of the peruser, however, was of short continuance; her ladyship's attorney appeared, and declared the will was rendered null by one of later date, which he had drawn up in Sir Geoffry's last moments, by his express desire. Consternation and surprise pervaded the mind of Rushbrook's friend; he saw the will was too well attested for him to dispute it, yet he suspected foul play, and lost no time in communicating his suspicion to Rushbrook.

Her ladyship settled her affairs most expeditiously and returned with delight to her native country, after a very long absence from it. Most of her near relations were dead, but she had many distant ones, who, prompted by the knowledge of her large fortune, eagerly reminded her of their affinity, and vied with each other in paying her attention. This was extremely pleasing to her ladyship, who was fond of pleasure at other people's expense. For herself she had laid down rules of the most rigid economy, which she strictly adhered to. From the many invitations she received she was seldom a resident in her own house; she judged of others by herself, and ascribed the attentions she received to their real source, self-interest, which she laughed secretly to think she should disappoint.

She was remarkable (as Miss Kilcorban informed Amanda) for asking young people to do little matters for her, such as making her millinery, working ruffles, aprons, and handkerchiefs.

The tranquillity she enjoyed for two years after Sir Geoffry's death was a little interrupted by his nephew's arrival from America, and commencing a suit directly against her by the advice of his friends and some eminent lawyers, on the supposition that the will by which she inherited had been made when his uncle was in a state of imbecility.

Lady Greystock, however, received but a trifling shock from this; she knew he had no money to carry on such an affair, and that his advocates would lose their zeal in his cause, when convinced of the state of his finances. On being obliged to go to London to attend the suit, it immediately occurred that Amanda would be a most pleasing companion to take along with her, as she would not only enliven the hours she must sometimes pass at home, but do a number of little things in the way of dress, which would save a great deal of expense.

Amanda, on the first proposal of accompanying her, warmly opposed it; she felt unutterable reluctance to leave her father, and assured him she would, by exerting herself, prove that a change of scene was not requisite for restoring her cheerfulness. Fitzalan knew her sincerity in making this promise, but he also knew her inability of performing it; his happiness, he declared, depended on her complying with this request: he even said his own health would probably be established by it, as during her absence he would partake of the amusements of the country, which he had hitherto declined on her account. This assertion prevailed on her to consent, and immediate preparations were made for her journey.

as the invitation had not been given till within a few days of her ladyship's intended departure. As she went by Holyhead, Fitzalan determined on sending Ellen to her parents till Amanda returned from England, which determination pleased Ellen exceedingly, as she longed to see her family, and tell them particulars of Chip. As the hour approached for quitting her father, the regret and reluctance of Amanda increased; nor were his feelings less oppressive, though better concealed: but when the moment of parting came, they could no longer be suppressed; he held her with a trembling grasp to his heart, as if life would forsake it. On her departure, the gloom on his mind seemed like a presentiment of evil; he repented forcing her from him, and scarcely could he refrain from saying they must not part.

Lady Greystock, who in every scene and every situation preserved her composure, hinted to him the injury he was doing his daughter by such emotions; and mentioned how short their separation would be, and what benefit would accrue to Amanda from it.

This last consideration recalled to his mind instantly com posed him, and he handed them to her ladyship's chariot, which was followed by a hired chaise containing her woman and Ellen; he then sighed her a last adieu, returned to his solitary habitation to pray, and, in spite of all his efforts, weep for his darling child.

Amanda's tears streamed down her pale cheek, and never did she experience a pang of such sorrow as that she felt, when, the chaise descending a hill, she caught the last glimpse of Castle Carberry.

She perceived, however, that her ladyship had no relish for a gloomy companion, and therefore endeavored to recover her spirits, and enter into conversation.

Lady Greystock had a number of friends in that part of Ireland, and therefore never stopped at an inn.

"I always, my dear," said she to Amanda, "make use of the friendship professed for me, and thus endeavor to render the great road of life delightful."

They arrived the third day in Sackville Street, where her ladyship had a house, and two days after embarked for England. They slept the first night they landed at Holyhead, and the next morn ing pursued their journey

CHAPTER XXIV.

"A song, a flower, a name, at once restore
Those long connected scenes when first they moved
The attention ————."—AKENSIDE.

HE dejection of Amanda gradually declined, as the idea of seeing Lord Mortimer again revived. It revived not, however, without hopes, fears, and agitations. Sometimes she imagined she should find him devoted to Lady Euphrasia; then again believed his honor and sincerity would not allow him to give her up so suddenly, and that this apparent indifference proceeded from resentment, which would vanish if an opportunity once offered (and she trusted there would) for explaining her conduct. She endeavored to calm the emotions these ideas gave rise to, by reflecting that a short time now would most probably terminate her suspense.

They stopped for the night, about five o'clock, at an inn about a mile from Tudor Hall. After dinner, Amanda informed Lady Greystock she wished to accompany Ellen to her parents. To this her ladyship made no objection, on finding she did not want the carriage. She charged her, however, not to forget the hour of tea, by which time she would be refreshed by a nap, and ready to engage her at a game of picquet.

They set out unattended, as Ellen refused the ostler's offer of carrying her portmanteau, saying she would send for it the next day. This she did by Amanda's desire, who wished, unobserved to pursue a walk, in which she promised herself a melancholy indulgence, from reviewing the well-known scenes endeared by tender recollections.

A mournful, yet not undelightful, sensation attends the contemplation of scenes where we once enjoyed felicity—departed joys are ever remembered with an enthusiasm of tenderness which soothes the sorrow we experience for their loss.

Such were the present feelings of Amanda; while Ellen, undisturbed by regrets for the past, pointed out, with pleasure, the dwellings of her intimates and friends. Yet when she came to Chip's deserted cottage, she stopped, and a tear stole from her eye, accompanied at the same time by a smile, which seemed to say, "though thou art now lonely and cheerless, the period is approaching when comfort and gaiety shall resume their stations within thee; when the blaze of thy fire and thy taper shall not only diffuse cheerfulness within, but without, and give a ray to the desolate or benighted traveller, to guide him to thy hospitable shelter!"

Amanda, leaning on Ellen's arm, proceeded slowly in her walk. The evening was delightful. The blue vault of heaven was spangled with stars, and the air, without being severely cold, was clear and refreshing. Their road, on one side, was skirted with the high woods of Tudor Hall. Amanda gazed on them with emotion; but when she came to the gate which Lord Mortimer had opened for her departure at their first interview, the softness of her heart could no longer be resisted: she stopped, leaned pensively upon it, and wept. The evergreens, with which the woods abounded, prevented their wearing a desolate appearance. She wished to have pierced into their most sequestered gloom, but she had no time to indulge this wish; nor did she, indeed, believe her companion, who was tinctured with superstitious fears, would have accompanied her. "When the glow of vegetation again revives," said she to herself, "when the blossoms and the flowers again spread their spangled foliage to the sun, and every shade resounds with harmony, where, alas! will Amanda be?—far distant, in all probability, from these delightful scenes, perhaps neglected and forgotten by their master!"

The awful murmurs of the wind rustling through the trees, joined to the solemn sound of a neighboring waterfall, began to excite fears in Ellen's breast. She laid her trembling hand on Amanda, and besought her, for the love of Cot, to hasten to the cottage. The road still wound round the wood; and lights from a small village, which lay on its borders, cast various shadows upon the trees; whilst the hum of distant voices floated upon the gale, and fancy pictured joyous groups of rustics assembling round their fires, to enjoy refreshment after the labors of the day.

"Peaceful people," said Amanda, "when the wants of nature are satisfied, no care or trouble obtrudes upon your minds. Tired, but not exhausted with the toils of the day, with preparing the bosom of the earth for the ethereal mildness of the spring, you seek and enjoy a calm repose."

In the lane which led to her nurse's cottage, Amanda paused for a moment. Down this lane Lord Mortimer had once pursued her. She looked towards the mansion of Tudor Hall. She endeavored to discern the library, but all was dark and dismal, except the wing, which Ellen informed her was occupied by the domestics. Through the window of Edwin's cottage, they saw all the family seated round a blazing fire, chatting and laughing. The transport of Ellen's heart overcame every idea of caution. She hastily unlatched the door, and flung herself into her parents' arms. Their surprise and joy was unbounded, aud Amanda was received and welcomed with as much tenderness as their child, without ever asking the reason of her sudden appearance. The first question was, "Would she not stay with them?" and her answer filled them with regret and disappointment. Perceiving them about procuring her refreshments, "she declared she had not a minute to stay. The time allotted for her walk was already exceeded, and she feared Lady Greystock would be offended at being left so long at an inn by herself." She therefore hastily presented some little presents she had brought for the family, and was bidding them farewell, when poor Ellen, who, from so long residing with her young lady, almost adored her, suddenly flung herself into her arms, and clinging round her neck, as if to prevent a separation, which, till the moment of its arrival, she thought she could have supported, exclaimed:—

"Oh, my tear young laty, we are going to part, and my heart sinks within me at the idea. Even Chip himself, if he was here, could not console me. I know you are not happy, and that increases my sorrow. Your sweet cheek is pale, and I have often seen you cry when you thought no poty was minding you. If you who are so goot are not happy, how can a peing like me hope to be so? Oh, may I soon pe plest with seeing you return the mistress of Tudor Hall, married to the sweetest, handsomest of noblemen, who, I know, in my soul, loves you, as well inteed he may, for where would he see the fellow of my young laty? Then Chip and I will be so happy, for I am sure you and my lort will shelter our humble cottage."

Amanda pressed the affectionate girl to her breast, and mingled tears with hers, while she softly whispered to her not to hint at such an event; "but be assured, my dearest Ellen," continued she, "that I shall ever rejoice at your felicity, which, to the utmost of my power, I would promote, and hope soon to hear of your union with Chip."

"Alack-a-tay!" said her nurse; "are you going away, when I thought you come to stay among us? and then, perhaps, my Lort would have come, and then there would have peen such a happy meeting. Why, I verily thought he would have gone distracted when he found you, as one may say, run away; and to pe sure I did pity him, and should have made no scruple to tell him where you were, had I known it myself, which he suspected, for he offered me a sight of money if I would discover. Then there is Parson Howel; why he has peen like unto nothing put a ghost since you went away; and he does so sigh, and he comes almost every tay to ask me apout you, and whether I think or know Lord Mortimer is with you. He will be in such grief to think you were here without his seeing you."

"Well," said Amanda, endeavoring to appear cheerful, "we may all yet have a happy meeting."

She then repeated her farewell, and, leaning on the arm of old Edwin, returned to the inn, where she again bid him adieu; and hastening to her ladyship, found her just awaking from a comfortable slumber. They drank tea, and, after playing for about an hour at picquet, retired to rest. Amanda, who enjoyed but little repose, rose early in the morning, and, finding her ladyship not quite ready, went down to the court to walk about till she was; where, to her great surprise, the first object she perceived was Howel, leaning pensively against a gate opposite the house. He flew over, and, catching her hand, exclaimed, "You are surprised, but, I trust, not displeased. I could not resist such an opportunity of seeing you once more, after all I have suffered from your precipitate journey, and the probability of never more beholding you. I have been watching here, in expectation of this happiness, since the first dawn of day."

"I am sorry," said Amanda, gravely, "your time was so ill employed."

"How coldly you speak," cried he. "Ah! could you read my heart, you would see so little presumption in it, that you would, I am confident, pity, though you could not relieve, its feelings. Every spot you loved to frequent, I have haunted since your departure. Your mother's grave has often been the scene of pensive meditation. Nor has it wanted its vernal offering; the loveliest flowers of my garden I have wove into wreaths, and hung them over it, in fond remembrance of her angel daughter."

The plaintive sound of Howel's voice, the dejection of his countenance, excited the softest feelings of sensibility in Amanda's bosom. But she grew confused by the tenderness of his expression, and, saying she was happy to see him, tried to disengage her hand, that she might retire.

"Surely," said he, still detaining it a few moments, "you might grant me without reluctance—you, who are going to enjoy every happiness and pleasure, going to meet the favored——"

Amanda anticipated the name he was about uttering, and her confusion redoubled. She attempted again, yet in vain, to withdraw her hand, and turned to see whether any one was observing them. How great was her mortification, on perceiving Lady Greystock leaning from a window, exactly over their heads! She smiled significantly at Amanda, on being seen; and, the carriage being ready, said, "She would attend her below stairs." Howel now relinquished Amanda's hand. He saw she looked displeased; and expressed such sorrow, accompanied with such submissive apologies for offending her, that she could not avoid according him her pardon. He handed both her and Lady Greystock into the carriage, and looked a melancholy adieu as it drove off.

"Upon my word, a pretty smart young fellow!" said Lady Greystock. "Though impatient this long time to set out, I could not think of interrupting the interesting tête-à-tête I saw between you and him. I suppose you have been a resident in this part of the country before, from your seeming to know this tender swain so well."

Amanda wished to avoid acknowledging this. If known, she feared it would lead to a discovery, or at least excite a suspicion of her intimacy with Lord Mortimer, which she was desirous of concealing, while in this uncertainty concerning him.

"Your ladyship has heard, I believe," replied she, "that Ellen's mother nursed me?" "Yes, my dear," answered her ladyship, with some smartness; "but if your acquaintance even commenced with this youth in infancy, I fancy it has been renewed since that period."

Amanda blushed deeply, and, to hide her confusion, pretended to be looking at the prospect from the window. Lady Greystock's eyes pursued hers. Tudor Hall was conspicuous from the road, and Amanda involuntarily sighed as she viewed it.

"That is a fine domain," said Lady Greystock; "I presume you have visited it, and know its owner?"

Amanda could not assert a falsehood, neither could she evade the inquiries of Lady Greystock; and therefore not only confessed its being the estate of Lord Mortimer, but her own residence near it the preceding summer. Her ladyship immediately conjectured it was then the attachment between her and Lord Mortimer had commenced; and the blushes, the hesitation, and the unwillingness of Amanda, in owning her visit to Wales, all confirmed this conjecture. She tried, however, to insinuate herself into her full confidence, by warm expressions of esteem, and by hinting, that from the disposition of Lord Mortimer, she could not believe he ever did, or ever would, think seriously of Lady Euphrasia; this, she hoped, would either induce or betray Amanda to open her whole heart; but she was disappointed. She flattered herself, however, with thinking she had discovered enough to satisfy the Marchioness, if she, as Lady Greystock feared she would, expressed any disapprobation at seeing Amanda her companion. She intended saying, that Fitzalan had absolutely forced her under her protection.

They arrived late in the evening of the third day at Pall Mall, where her ladyship's agent had previously taken lodgings for them.

Lady Greystock, though immersed in business against the approaching trial, neglected no means of amusement; and, the day after her arrival, sent a card of inquiry to the Roslin family, as the most eligible mode of informing them of it. The next morning, as she expected, she received a visit from them. Amanda was sitting in the window when the carriage drove up to the door. She instantly arose, and left the room, determined neither to expose herself to their impertinence, or appear solicitous for their notice, by staying in their company uninvited. Lady Greystock soon informed them of Amanda's having accompanied her to London; and they, as she expected, expressed both surprise and displeasure at it. As she had settled in her own mind, she, therefore, told them, "that Fitzalan had urged her to take his daughter under her care, with entreaties she could not resist. Entreaties," she added, with a significant look, "she believed he had good reason for making." She then related all she suspected, or rather had discovered, relative to the attachment between Lord Mortimer and Amanda having commenced the preceding summer in Wales.

The Marchioness and Lady Euphrasia instantly concluded she was sent to London for the purpose of having it completed by a marriage. This, however, they determined to prevent. The Marchioness felt the most inveterate hatred against her; and also, that, to prevent her being advantageously settled, even if that settlement threatened not to interfere with the one she had projected for her daughter, she could undertake almost any project Though she abhorred the idea of noticing her, yet she was tempted now to do so, from the idea that it would better enable her to watch her actions. This idea she communicated in a hasty whisper to Lady Euphrasia, who, approving it, she told Lady Greystock, "as Miss Fitzalan was her guest, she would, on that account, permit her to be introduced to them." Amanda was accordingly sent for. On entering the room, Lady Greystock took her hand, and presented her to the Marchioness and Lady Euphrasia. The former, half rising, with a coldness she could not conquer, said, "Whenever Lady Greystock honored her with a visit, she should be happy to see Miss Fitzalan along with her." The latter only noticed her by a slight bow; and when Amanda drew a chair near the sofa on which she sat, or rather reclined, she continued staring in her face, and alternately humming an Italian air, and caressing a little dog she had brought with her. The unembarrassed elegance of Amanda's air and manner surprised and mortified them, as they expected to have seen her covered with confusion, at an introduction so unexpected. To their haughty souls, nothing was more delightful than the awe and deference which vulgar and illiberal minds are so apt to pay to rank and fortune. They were provoked to see, in Amanda, conscious dignity, instead of trembling diffidence. As she sat by Lady Euphrasia, the Marchioness could not help secretly confessing she was a dangerous rival to her daughter; for never did her lovely features and ingenuous countenance appear to such advantage, as when contrasted to Lady Euphrasia's. The Marchioness withdrew soon after her entrance, unable longer to restrain the malignant passions which envy had excited.

Both she and Lady Euphrasia were convinced that to communicate their suspicions at present to Lord Cherbury, about her and his son, would not answer the end proposed, for it could be of little consequence, they reflected, to withdraw the esteem of the father, if that of the son continued, who, independent in his notions, and certain of the fortunes of his ancestors, might not hesitate to gratify himself. The point, therefore, was, by some deep-laid scheme, to ruin Amanda in the estimation of Lord Mortimer; and if in the power of mortals to contrive and execute such a scheme, they gave themselves credit for being able to effect it.

The blow at her fond hopes, they resolved, should be followed by one against the peace of Fitzalan, on whom they knew, whenever they pleased, they could draw the resentment of Lord Cherbury. Thus should they completely triumph over the lovely Amanda—plunge two beings they detested into poverty and wretchedness—destroy expectations which interfered with their own, and secure an alliance with a man they had long wished united to their family.

From the unaltered indifference of Lord Mortimer to Lady Euphrasia, they were convinced of his predilection for another, flattering themselves that nothing but a prior attachment could have rendered him insensible to the attractions of her ladyship. To render the object of this attachment contemptible in his sight, they believed would produce the transfer of affections they so long desired. The haughty soul of Lady Euphrasia would never have permitted her to think of accepting Lord Mortimer after his neglect of her, but by the opportunity she should have by such an acceptance of triumphing over Amanda. From this idea, she entered warmly into all her mother's plans.

Lord Cherbury had never yet spoken explicitly to his son concerning the union he had projected for him. He often, indeed, dropped hints about it, which he always found either neglected, or purposely misunderstood; and from these circumstances was pretty sensible of the disinclination Lord Mortimer felt to his wishes. He knew he entertained high notions of the independence which a rational mind has a right to maintain, and that in an affair of such consequence, as Mortimer frequently said he considered a matrimonial connection to be, he would neither be controlled by the opinion of others or merely allured by the advantages of fortune.

To avoid a disagreeable argument with a son he not only loved, but respected, he sought rather, by indirect means, to involve him in an entanglement with the Roslin family, than come to an open explanation with him. For this purpose he contrived parties as often as possible with them in public; where, by Lord Mortimer's being seen with Lady Euphrasia, reports might be raised of an intended alliance between them—reports which he himself propagated among some particular friends, with a desire of having them circulated, but an injunction of secrecy as to their author. These reports would, he trusted, on reaching Lord Mortimer, lead to a discussion of the affair; and then he meant to say, as Lord Mortimer had partly contributed to raise them himself by his attendance on Lady Euphrasia, he could not possibly, with honor, recede from realizing them; yet often did his lordship fear his scheme would prove abortive—for he well knew the cool judgment and keen penetration of his son. This fear always inspired him with horror, for he had a motive for desiring the union which he durst not avow.

Lord Mortimer quickly indeed discerned what his father's views were in promoting his attendance on Lady Euphrasia. He therefore avoided her society whenever it was possible to do so without absolute rudeness, and contradicted the reports he almost continually heard of an intended alliance between them in the most solemn manner. He had always disliked her, but latterly that dislike was converted into hatred, from the malevolence of her conduct towards Amanda; and he felt that, even were his heart free, he never could devote it to her—or give his hand where it must be unaccompanied with esteem. He wished to avoid a disagreeable conversation with Lord Cherbury, and flattered himself his unaltered indifference to her ladyship would at length convince his lordship of the impossibility of accomplishing his projected scheme; and that consequently it would be dropped ere openly avowed, and he saved the painful necessity of absolutely rejecting a proposal of his father's.

In the evening Lady Greystock and Amanda received cards for dinner the next day at the Marquis of Roslin's. Amanda made no objection to this invitation. Her father had often declared, if the Marchioness made an overture for an intimacy with his children, he would not reject it, as he always deemed family quarrels highly prejudicial to both parties, with regard to the opinion of the world. Besides, had she objected to it, she should either have been a restraint on Lady Greystock, or left to total solitude; and the idea also stole upon her mind that she should lose a chance of seeing Lord Mortimer, whom she supposed a frequent guest of the Marquis's. Her heart fluttered at the idea of soon beholding him, and the bright glow of animation which overspread her countenance in consequence of this idea attracted the observation of Lady Greystock, who congratulated her on the alteration that was already visible in her looks; and inferred from thence that she was so well recovered of her fatigue as to be able to contrive a little trimming for her against the next day. This Amanda cheerfully undertook, and having a quick execution as well as an elegant taste, soon made progress in it which delighted her ladyship, who, to divert her whilst she worked, related some of the many entertaining anecdotes with which her memory was stored.

Though Amanda submitted her beautiful hair to the hands of a friseur, she departed not from the elegant simplicity always conspicuous in her dress. Her little ornaments were all arranged with taste, and an anxious wish of appearing to advantage. So lovely, indeed, did she appear to Lady Greystock, that her ladyship began seriously to fear she should not be forgiven by the Marchioness or Lady Euphrasia, for having introduced such an object to their parties.

About six they reached Portman Square, and found a large party assembled in the drawing-room. After the first compliments were over and Amanda introduced to the Marquis—not, indeed, as a near relation, but an utter stranger—a gentleman stepped up to the Marchioness, and addressing her in a low voice, was immediately presented by her to Amanda, as the Earl of Cherbury.

"My dear young lady," said he, "allow me to express the pleasure I feel at seeing the daughter of my worthy friend, Mr. Fitzalan. Allow me also to increase that pleasure," continued he, taking her hand, and leading her to a very lovely girl who sat at some distance, "by presenting Miss Fitzalan to Lady Araminta Dormer, and desiring their friendship for each other."

Surprised, confused, yet delighted by notice so little expected, the heart of Amanda heaved with emotion; her cheeks mantled with blushes, and the tear of sensibility trembled in her eye. She was not, however, so embarrassed as to be incapable of expressing her acknowledgments to his lordship for his attention, and also to assure him she had early been taught, and sensibly felt, the claims he had upon her gratitude and respect. He bowed, as if to prevent a further mention of obligations, and left her seated by his daughter, who had expressed her pleasure at being introduced to her, not in the supercilious style of Lady Euphrasia, but in the sweet accents of affability and tenderness.

The conduct of Lord Cherbury had drawn all eyes upon Amanda; and the Marchioness and Lady Euphrasia regarded her with peculiar malignancy. The idea, however, that they could, whenever they pleased, deprive her of his notice, a little lessened the jealousy and mortification it had excited.

"Pray, who is this little creature," exclaimed Miss Malcolm (who was a relation of the Marquis's, and, from being extremely ugly, extremely rich, and extremely ill-natured, was an immense favorite of Lady Euphrasia's), "that puts one in mind of a country miss, on her first appearance at a country assembly, blushing and trembling at every eye she meets?"

"Some kind of a far-off relation of my mother's," replied Lady Euphrasia, "whom that old dowager, Lady Greystock, picked up in the wilds of Ireland, and has absolutely forced upon our notice; though I assure you, from compassion, we should have taken the poor creature long ago under our protection, but for the shocking conduct of her family to the Marchioness, and the symptoms she has already betrayed of following their example. It is really ridiculous sending her to London. I dare say her silly old father has exhausted all his ways and means in trying to render her decent, comforting himself, no doubt, with the hope of her entrapping some young fool of quality, who may supply his wants as well as hers."

"Ay, I suppose all the stock in the farm was sold to dress her out," cried young Freelove, a little, trifling fop, who leaned on the back of her ladyship's chair. He was a ward of Lord Cherbury, and his fortune considerable; but nature had not been quite as bounteous to him as the blind goddess. Both his mind and person were effeminate to a degree of insignificance. All he aimed at was—being a man of fashion. His manners, like his dress were therefore regulated by it, and he never attempted to approve of anything, or any creature, till assured they were quite the ton. He had danced attendance for some time on Lady Euphrasia, and she encouraged his assiduities in hopes of effecting a change in Lord Mortimer's manner. But had his lordship even been a passionate lover, poor Freelove was not calculated to inspire him with jealousy. "I declare," continued he, surveying Amanda through an opera-glass which dangled from his button-hole, "if her father has nothing to support him but the hope of her making a conquest of importance, he will be in a sad way, for, 'pon my soul, I can see nothing the girl has to recommend her, except novelty; and that, you know, is a charm which will lessen every day. All she can possibly expect, is an establishment for a few months with some tasteless being, who may like the simplicity of her country look."

"And more than she merits," exclaimed Miss Malcolm; "I have no patience with such creatures forcing themselves into society quite above them."

"I assure you," said Lady Euphrasia, "you would be astonished at her vanity and conceit, if you knew her. She considers herself a first-rate beauty, though positively any one may see she is quite the reverse, and pretends to the greatest gentleness and simplicity. Then she has made some strange kind of people (to be sure they must be) believe she is accomplished; though, I dare say, if she can read tolerably, and scrawl out a decent letter, 'tis the utmost she can do."

"We will quiz her after dinner about her accomplishments," said Freelove, "and have a little fun with her."

"Ay, do," cried Miss Malcolm. "We will ask her to play and sing," said her ladyship; "for I assure you she pretends to excel in both; though, from her father's poverty, I am certain she can know little of either. I shall enjoy her confusion of all things, when her ignorance is detected."

Whilst this conversation was passing, Amanda, in conversing with Lady Araminta, experienced the purest pleasure. Her ladyship was the "softened image" of Lord Mortimer. Her voice was modulated to the same harmony as his, and Amanda gazed and listened with rapture. On her confusion abating, her eye had wandered round the room in quest of his lordship, but he was not in it. At every stir, near the door, her heart fluttered at the idea of seeing him; nor was this idea relinquished till summoned to dinner. She fortunately procured a seat next Lady Araminta, which prevented her thinking the time spent at dinner tedious. In the evening the rooms were crowded with company, but Lord Mortimer appeared not among the brilliant assembly. Yet the pang of disappointment was softened to Amanda by his absence, intimating that he was not anxious for the society of Lady Euphrasia. True, business, or a prior engagement, might have prevented his coming; but she, as is natural, fixed on the idea most flattering to herself.

Lady Euphrasia, in pursuance of the plan laid against Amanda, led the way to the music-room, attended by a large party; as Freelove had intimated to some of the beaux and belles, her ladyship and he were going to quiz an ignorant Irish country girl. Lady Euphrasia sat down to the harpsichord, that she might have a better pretext for asking Amanda to play. Freelove seated himself by the latter, and began a conversation which, he thought, would effectually embarrass her; but it had quite a contrary effect, rendering him so extremely ridiculous as to excite a universal laugh at his expense.

Amanda soon perceived his intention in addressing her; and, also, that Lady Euphrasia and Miss Malcolm were privy to it, having caught the significant looks which passed among them. Though tremblingly alive to every feeling of modesty, she had too much sense, and real nobleness of soul, to allow the illiberal sallies of impertinence to divest her of composure.

"Have you seen any of the curiosities of London, my dear?" exclaimed Freelove, lolling back in his chair, and contemplating the lustre of his buckles, unconscious of the ridicule he excited

"I think I have," said Amanda, somewhat archly, and glancing at him, "quite an original in its kind." Her look, as well as the emphasis on her words, excited another laugh at his expense, which threw him into a momentary confusion.

"I think," said he, as he recovered from it, "the Monument and the Tower would be prodigious fine sights to you, and I make it a particular request that I may be included in your party whenever you visit them, particularly the last place."

"And why," replied Amanda, "should I take the trouble of visiting wild beasts, when every day I may see animals equally strange, and not half so mischievous?"

Freelove, insensible as he was, could not mistake the meaning of Amanda's words, and he left her with a mortified air, being, to use his own phrase, "completely done up."

Lady Euphrasia, now rising from the harpsichord, requested Amanda to take her place at it, saying, with an ironical air, "her performance (which indeed was shocking) would make hers appear to amazing advantage."

Diffident of her own abilities, Amanda begged to be excused. But when Miss Malcolm, with an earnestness even oppressive, joined her entreaties to Lady Euphrasia's, she could no longer refuse.

"I suppose," said her ladyship, following her to the instrument, "these songs," presenting some trifling ones, "will answer you better than the Italian music before you?"

Amanda made no reply, but turned over the leaves of the book to a lesson much more difficult than that Lady Euphrasia had played. Her touch at first was tremulous and weak, but she was too susceptible of the powers of harmony not soon to be inspired by it; and gradually her style became so masterly and elegant, as to excite universal admiration, except in the bosoms of those who had hoped to place her in a ludicrous situation. Their invidious scheme, instead of depressing, had only served to render excellence conspicuous; and that mortification they destined for another, fell upon themselves. When the lesson was concluded, some gentlemen who either were, or pretended to be, musical connoisseurs, entreated her to sing. She chose a plaintive Italian air, and the exquisite taste and sweetness with which she sung, equally astonished and delighted. Nor was admiration confined to the accomplishments she displayed. The soft expression of her countenance, which seemed accordant to the harmonious sounds that issued from her lips, was viewed with pleasure, and praised with energy; and she rose from the harpsichord covered with blushes from the applause which stole around her. The gentlemen gathered round Lady Euphrasia, to inquire who the beautiful stranger was, and she gave them pretty much the same account she had already done to Miss Malcolm.

The rage and disappointment of that young lady, and her ladyship, could scarcely be concealed. "I declare, I never knew anything so monstrously absurd," exclaimed Lady Euphrasia, "as to let a girl in her situation learn such things, except, indeed, it was to qualify her for a governess, or an opera singer."

"Ay, I suppose," said Miss Malcolm, "we shall soon hear her quavering away at one of the theatres; for no person of fashion would really intrust her children to so confident a creature."

The fair object of their disquietude gladly accompanied Lady Araminta into another room. Several gentlemen followed, and crowded about her chair, offering that adulation which they were accustomed to find acceptable at the shrine of beauty. To Amanda, however, it was irksome, not only from its absurd extravagance, but as it interrupted her conversation with Lady Araminta. The Marchioness, however, who critically watched her motions, soon relieved her from the troublesome assiduities of the beaux, by placing them at card-tables. Not, indeed, from any good-natured motive, but she could not bear that Amanda should have so much attention paid her, and flattered herself she would be vexed by losing it.

In the course of conversation, Lady Araminta mentioned Ireland. She had a faint remembrance of Castle Carberry, she said, and had been half tempted to accompany the Marquis and his family in their late excursion. Her brother, she added, had almost made her promise to visit the castle with him the ensuing summer. "You have seen Lord Mortimer, to be sure?" continued her ladyship.

"Yes, madam," faltered Amanda, while her face was overspread with a crimson hue. Her ladyship was too penetrating not to perceive her confusion, and it gave rise to a conjecture of something more than a slight acquaintance being between his lordship and Amanda. The melancholy he had betrayed on his return from Ireland had excited the raillery of her ladyship, till convinced, by the discomposure he showed whenever she attempted to inquire into the occasion of it, that it proceeded from a source truly interesting to his feelings. She knew of the alliance her father had projected for him with the Roslin family—a project she never approved of, for Lady Euphrasia was truly disagreeable to her; and a soul like Mortimer's, tender, liberal, and sincere, she knew could never experience the smallest degree of happiness with a being so uncongenial in every respect as was Lady Euphrasia to him. She loved her brother with the truest tenderness, and secretly believed he was attached in Ireland. She wished to gain his confidence, yet would not solicit it, because she knew she had it not in her power essentially to serve him. Her arguments, she was convinced, would have little weight with Lord Cherbury, who had often expressed to her his anxiety for a connection with the Roslin family. With the loveliness of Amanda's person, with the elegance of her manner, she was immediately charmed. As she conversed with her, esteem was added to admiration, and she believed that Mortimer would not have omitted mentioning to her the beautiful daughter of his father's agent, had he not feared betraying too much emotion at her name. She appeared to Lady Araminta just the kind of woman he would adore; just the being that would answer all the ideas of perfection (romantic ideas she had called them) which he had declared necessary to captivate his heart. Lady Araminta already felt for her unspeakable tenderness In the softness of her looks, in the sweetness of her voice, there were resistless charms; and she felt, that if oppressed by sorrow, Amanda Fitzalan, above all other beings, was the one she would select to give her consolation. The confusion she betrayed at the mention of Mortimer, made her ladyship suspect she was the cause of his dejection. She involuntarily fastened her eyes upon her face, as if to penetrate the recesses of her heart, yet with a tenderness which seemed to say she would pity the secret she might there discover.

Lord Cherbury, at this moment of embarrassment to Amanda, approached. He said, "He had just been making a request, and an apology to Lady Greystock, and was now come to repeat them to her. The former was, to meet the Marquis's family at his house the next day at dinner; and the latter was, to excuse so unceremonious an invitation, which he had been induced to make on Lady Araminta's account, who was obliged to leave town the day after the next, and had, therefore, no time for the usual etiquette of visiting."

Amanda bowed. This invitation was more pleasing than one of more form would have been. It seemed to indicate friendship, and a desire to have the intimacy between her and his daughter cultivated. It gave her also a hope of seeing Lord Mortimer. All these suggestions inspired her with uncommon animation, and she entered into a lively conversation with Lord Cherbury, who had infinite vivacity in his look and manner. Lady Araminta observed the attention he paid her with pleasure. A prepossession in her favor, she trusted, might produce pleasing consequences.

Lady Greystock at length rose to depart. Amanda received an affectionate adieu from Lady Araminta; and Lord Cherbury attended the ladies to their carriage. On driving off, Lady Greystock observed, what a charming polite man his lordship was; and, in short, threw out such hints, and entered into such a warm eulogium on his merits, that Amanda began to think he would not find it very difficult to prevail on her ladyship to enter once more the temple of Hymen.

Amanda retired to her chamber in a state of greater happiness than for a long period before she had experienced; but it was a happiness which rather agitated than soothed the feelings; particularly hers, which were so susceptible of every impression, that

> "They turned at the touch of joy or woe,
> And turning trembled too."

Her present happiness was the offspring of hope, and therefore peculiarly liable to disappointment; a hope derived from the attention of Lord Cherbury, and the tenderness of Lady Araminta, that the fond wishes of her heart might yet be realized; wishes, again believed from hearing of Lord Mortimer's dejection, which his sister had touched upon, and from his absenting himself from the Marquis's, which were not uncongenial to those he himself entertained. She sat down to acquaint her father with the particulars of the day she had passed: for her chief consolation in her absence from him, was, in the idea of writing and hearing constantly. Her writing finished, she sat by the fire, meditating on the interview she expected would take place on the ensuing day, till the hoarse voice of the watchmen, proclaiming past three o'clock, roused her from her reverie. She smiled at the abstraction of her thoughts, and retired to bed to dream of felicity.

So calm were her slumbers—so delightful her dreams—that Sol had long shot his timorous ray into her chamber ere she awoke. Her spirits still continued serene and animated. On descending to the drawing-room, she found Lady Greystock just entering it. After breakfast, they went out in her ladyship's carriage to different parts of the town. All was new to Amanda, who, during her former residence in it, had been entirely confined to lodgings in a retired street. She wondered at, and was amused by, the crowds continually passing and repassing. About four they returned to dress. Amanda began the labors of the toilet with a beating heart; nor were its quick pulsations decreased on entering Lady Greystock's carriage, which in a few minutes conveyed her to Lord Cherbury's house in St. James's Square. She followed her ladyship with tottering steps; and the first object she saw on entering the drawing-room was Mortimer standing near the door.

CHAPTER XXV.

"Begone my cares; I give you to the winds."—Rowe.

N the drawing-room were already assembled the Marquis, Marchioness, Lady Euphrasia, Miss Malcolm, and Freelove. Lady Araminta perceived in the hesitating voice of Amanda the emotions which agitated her, and which were not diminished when Lord Cherbury, taking her trembling hand, said—

"Mortimer, I presume you have already seen Miss Fitzalan in Ireland?"

"I have, my Lord," replied Mortimer, bowing, and at the same time approaching to pay his compliments.

"Every eye in the room, except Lord Cherbury's and Freelove's, was now turned upon his lordship and Amanda, and thought, in the expressive countenances of both, enough could be read to confirm their suspicions of a mutual attachment subsisting between them.

Amanda, when seated, endeavored to recover from her confusion. Miss Malcolm, to prevent Lord Mortimer's taking a seat by her, which she thought she perceived him inclined to do, beckoned him to her, and contrived to engage him in trifling chat, till they were summoned to dinner. On receiving his hand, which he could not avoid offering, to lead her to the parlor, she cast a look of exultation at Amanda. Lady Araminta, perceiving all the gentlemen engaged, good-humoredly put her arm within Amanda's, and said she would be her chaperon on the present occasion. Lord Mortimer quitted Miss Malcolm the moment he had procured her a seat, though she desired him to take one between her and Lady Euphrasia, and, passing to the other side, placed himself by Amanda. This action pleased her as much as it mortified them. It embarrassed her, however, a little; but perceiving the scrutinizing earnestness with which the Marchioness and Lady Euphrasia regarded her, she exerted her spirits, and was soon able to join in the general conversation which Lord Mortimer promoted.

The unexpected arrival of Amanda in London astonished, and

notwithstanding his resentment, delighted him. His sister, when they were alone in the morning, had mentioned her with all the fervency of praise. Her plaudits gave to him a sensation of satisfied pride, which convinced him he was not less than ever interested about Amanda. Since his return from Ireland, he had been distracted by incertitude and anxiety about her. The innocence, the purity, the tenderness she had displayed, were perpetually recurring to his memory. It was impossible, he thought, they could be feigned, and he began to think the apparent mystery of her conduct she could satisfactorily have explained—that designedly she had not avoided him—and that, but for the impetuosity of his own passions, which had induced his precipitate departure, he might, ere this, have had all his doubts removed. Tortured with incessant regret for this departure, he would have returned immediately to Ireland, but at this period found it impossible to do so, without exciting inquiries from Lord Cherbury, which, at present, he did not choose to answer. He had planned an excursion thither the ensuing summer with Lady Araminta, determined no longer to endure his suspense. He now almost believed the peculiar interposition of Providence had brought Amanda to town, thus affording him another opportunity of having his anxiety relieved, and the chief obstacle, perhaps to his, and he flattered himself also, to her happiness, removed; for, if assured her precipitate journey from Wales was occasioned by no motive she need blush to avow, he felt he should be better enabled to combat the difficulties he was convinced his father would throw in the way of their union. Notwithstanding Lady Araminta's endeavors to gain his implicit confidence, he resolved to withhold it from her, lest she should incur even the temporary displeasure of Lord Cherbury, by the warm interest he knew she would take in his affairs, if once informed of them.

Amanda looked thinner and paler than when he had seen her in Ireland—yet, if possible, more interesting from these circumstances; and, from the soft glance she had involuntarily directed towards him at her entrance, he was tempted to think he had, in some degree, contributed to rob her lovely cheek of its bloom; and this idea rendered her dearer than ever to him. Scarcely could he restrain the rapture he felt on seeing her within the necessary bounds; scarcely could he believe the scene which had given rise to his happiness real. His heart, at the moment melting with tenderness, sighed for the period of explanation, which he trusted, which he hoped, would also be the period of reconciliation.

The gentlemen joined the ladies about teatime, and as no additional company was expected, Lady Euphrasia proposed a party to the Pantheon. This was immediately agreed to. Amanda was delighted at the proposal, as it not only promised to gratify her curiosity, but to give Lord Mortimer an opportunity of addressing her, as she saw he wished, but vainly attempted, at home. The Marquis and Lord Cherbury declined going. Lady Greystock, who had not ordered her carriage till a much later hour, accepted a place in the Marchioness's.

Neither Lady Euphrasia nor Miss Malcolm could bear the idea of Lord Mortimer and Amanda going in the same carriage, as the presence of Lady Araminta, they were convinced, would not prevent their using an opportunity so propitious for conversing as they wished. Lady Euphrasia, therefore, with sudden eagerness declared she and Miss Malcolm would resign their seats in the Marchioness's carriage to Miss Fitzalan and Freelove for the pleasure of accompanying Lady Araminta in hers. The Marchioness, who conjectured her daughter's motive for this new arrangement, seconded it, to the secret regret of Amanda, and the visible chagrin of Lord Mortimer. Amanda, however, consoled herself for this disappointment by reflecting on the pleasure she should enjoy in a few minutes, when freed from the disagreeable observation of the Marchioness and Lady Euphrasia; her reflections were not in the least interrupted by any conversation being addressed to her. The Marchioness and Lady Greystock chatted together, and Freelove amused himself humming a song, as if for the purpose of mortifying Amanda by his inattention. When the carriage stopped, he assisted the former ladies out; but as if forgetting such a being existed as Amanda, he went on with them. She was descending the steps when Lord Mortimer pressed forward, and snatching her hand, softly exclaimed: "We have met again, and neither envy nor malice shall again separate us." A beautiful glow overspread the countenance of Amanda: her hand trembled in his, and she felt, in that moment, recompensed for her former disappointment.

and elevated above the little insolence of Freelove. Lord Mortimer handed her to his sister, who was waiting to receive her, and they proceeded to the room. Lady Euphrasia entered it with a temper unfitted for enjoyment. She was convinced the whole soul of Mortimer was devoted to Amanda, and she trembled from the violent and malignant feelings that conviction excited. From the moment he entered the carriage till he quitted it he had remained silent, notwithstanding all her efforts and Miss Malcolm's to force him into conversation. He left them as soon as they reached the Pantheon to watch the Marchioness's carriage, which followed theirs, and on rejoining Amanda he attached himself entirely to her, without any longer appearing anxious to conceal his predilection for her. He had, indeed, forgotten the necessity there was for concealing it; all his feelings, all his ideas, were engrossed by ecstasy and tenderness. The novelty, the brilliancy of the scene, excited surprise and pleasure in Amanda, and he was delighted with the animated description she gave of the effect it produced upon her mind. In her he found united, exalted sense, lively fancy, and an uncorrupted taste: he forgot that the eyes of jealousy and malevolence were on them; he forgot every object but herself.

But, alas! poor Amanda was doomed to disappointment this evening. Lady Greystock, according to a hint she had received, after a few rounds, stepped up to her, and declared she must accompany her to a seat, as she was convinced her health was yet too weak to bear much fatigue. Amanda assured her she was not in the least fatigued, and that she would prefer walking; besides, she had half-promised Lord Mortimer to dance with him. This Lady Greystock absolutely declared, she would not consent to, though Lady Araminta, on whose arm Amanda leaned, pleaded for her friend, assuring her ladyship "she would take care Miss Fitzalan should not injure herself."

"Ah, you young people," said Lady Greystock, "are so carried away with spirits, you never reflect on consequences; but I declare, as she is intrusted to my care, I could not answer it to my conscience to let her run into any kind of danger."

Lady Araminta remonstrated with her ladyship, and Amanda would have joined, but that she feared her real motive for doing so would have been discovered. She perceived the party were detained from proceeding on her account, and immediately offered her arm to Lady Greystock, and accompanied her and the Marchioness to a seat Lady Euphrasia, catching hold of Lady Araminta's arm, hurried her, at the same instant, into the crowd; and Miss Malcolm, as if by chance, laid her hand on Lord Mortimer, and thus compelled him to attend her party. She saw him, however, in the course of the round, prepared to fly off; but when they had completed it, to her inexpressible joy, the situation of Amanda made him relinquish his intention, as to converse with her was utterly impossible; for the Marchioness had placed her between Lady Greystock and herself, and, under the pretence of frequently addressing her ladyship, was continually leaning across Amanda, so as to exclude her almost from observation, thus rendering her situation, exclusive of the regret at being separated from Lord Mortimer and Lady Araminta, highly disagreeable. The Marchioness enjoyed a malicious joy in the uneasiness she saw she gave Amanda. She deemed it but a slight retaliation for the uneasiness she had given Lady Euphrasia—a trifling punishment for the admiration she had excited.

Amanda, indeed, whilst surveying the scene around her with wonder and delight, had herself been an object of critical attention and inquiry. She was followed, universally admired, and allowed to be the finest girl that had appeared for a long season.

Relieved of her presence, Lady Euphrasia's spirits began to revive, and her good-humor to return. She laughed maliciously with Miss Malcolm at the disappointment of Lord Mortimer and Amanda. After a few rounds, Sir Charles Bingley, in company with another gentleman, passed them. He was, to use Miss Malcolm's own phrase, "an immense favorite with her," and she had long meditated and attempted the conquest of his heart. The attention which politeness obliged him to show, and the compliments she sometimes compelled him to pay, she flattered herself, were intimations of the success of her scheme. Lady Euphrasia, notwithstanding her intentions relative to Lord Mortimer, and her professed friendship for Miss Malcolm, felt an ardent desire to have Sir Charles enrolled in the list of her admirers, and both ladies determined he should not again pass without noticing them. They accordingly watched his approach, and when they again met, addressed him in a manner that, to a man at all interested about either, would have been truly flattering. As this, however, was not the young baronet's case, after paying his compliments in a general way to the whole party, he was making his parting bow, when his companion, pulling him by the sleeve, bid him observe a beautiful girl sitting opposite to them. They had stopped near the Marchioness's seat, and it was to Amanda Sir Charles's eyes were directed.

"Gracious heaven!" cried he, starting, while his cheek was suffused with a glow of pleasure; "can this be possible? Can this in reality," advancing to her seat, "be Miss Fitzalan? This surely," continued he, "is a meeting as fortunate as unexpected. But for it, I should have been posting back to Ireland in a day or two."

Amanda blushed deeply at his thus publicly declaring her power of regulating his actions. Her confusion restored that recollection his joyful surprise had deprived him of, and he addressed the Marchioness and Lady Greystock. The former haughtily bowed, without speaking; and the latter, laughing significantly, said, "she really imagined ecstasy on Miss Fitzalan's account had made him forget any one else was present." The situation of Amanda was tantalizing in an extreme degree to Sir Charles. It precluded all conversation, and frequently hid her from his view, as the Marchioness and Lady Greystock still continued their pretended whispers. Sir Charles had some knowledge of the Marchioness's disposition, and quickly perceived the motive of her present conduct.

"Your ladyship is kind," said he, "in trying to hide Miss Fitzalan, as no doubt you are conscious 'tis not a slight heart-ache she would give to some of the belles present this evening. But why," continued he, turning to Amanda, "do you prefer sitting to walking?"

Amanda made no answer; but a glance from her expressive eyes to the ladies informed him of the reason.

Lady Euphrasia and Miss Malcolm, provoked at the abrupt departure of Sir Charles, had hurried on; but scarcely had they proceeded a few yards ere envy and curiosity induced them to turn back. Lady Araminta perceived their chagrin, and secretly enjoyed it. Sir Charles, who had been looking impatiently for their approach, the moment he perceived them, entreated Amanda to join them.

"Let me," cried he, presenting his hand, "be your knight on the present occasion, and deliver you from what may be called absolute captivity."

She hesitated not to accept his offer. The continual buzz in the room, with the passing and repassing of the company, had made her head giddy. She deemed no apology requisite to her companions; and, quitting her seat, hastened forward to Lady Araminta, who had stopped for her. A crowd at that moment, intervening between them, retarded her progress. Sir Charles, pressing her hand with fervor, availed himself of this opportunity to express his pleasure at their unexpected meeting.

"Ah! how little," cried he, "did I imagine there was such happiness in store for me this evening."

"Sir Charles," said Amanda, endeavoring, though in vain, to withdraw her hand, "you have learned the art of flattering since your return to England."

"I wish," cried he, "I had learned the art of expressing, as I wish, the sentiments I feel."

Lord Mortimer, who had made way through the crowd for the ladies, at this instant appeared. He seemed to recoil at the situation of Amanda, whose hand was yet detained in Sir Charles's, while the soft glow and confusion of her face gave at least a suspicion of the language she was listening to.

On rejoining the party she hoped again to have been joined by Lord Mortimer; but, even if inclined for this, Sir Charles totally prevented him. His lordship deserted them, yet almost continually contrived to intercept the party, and his eyes were always turned on Amanda and Sir Charles. He was really displeased with her. He thought she might as well have left her seat before as after Sir Charles's appearance, and he resolved to watch her closely. She was asked to dance by Sir Charles, and several other gentlemen, but refused, and Lady Araminta, on her account, followed her example. Lady Euphrasia and Miss Malcolm either were too much discomposed, or not asked by gentlemen they liked, to join the festive group.

Amanda, from being disappointed, soon grew languid, and endeavored to check, with more than usual seriousness, the ardent expressions of Sir Charles, who repeatedly declared, "he had hurried over the affairs which brought him to England entirely on her account, as he thought every day an age until they again met."

She was rejoiced when Lady Araminta proposed returning home. Lady Euphrasia and Miss Malcolm had no longer a desire to accompany her ladyship, as they believed Lord Mortimer already gone, and she and Amanda therefore returned alone. Sir Charles was invited to supper, an invitation he joyfully accepted, and promised to follow her ladyship as soon as he had apprised the party he came with of his intention.

Lady Araminta and Amanda arrived some time before the rest of the party. Her ladyship said, "that her leaving town was to attend the nuptials of a particular friend," and was expressing her hopes, that on her return, she should often be favored with the company of Amanda, when the door suddenly opened and Lord Mortimer entered. He looked pleased and surprised, and taking a seat on the sofa between them, exclaimed, as he regarded them with unutterable tenderness, "surely one moment like this is worth whole hours such as we have lately spent. May I," looking at Amanda, "say that chance is now as propitious to me as it was some time ago to Sir Charles Bingley? Tell me," continued he, "were you not agreeably surprised to-night?"

"By the Pantheon, undoubtedly, my lord."

"And by Sir Charles Bingley?"

"No. He is too slight an acquaintance either to give pleasure by his presence or pain by his absence."

This was just what Lord Mortimer wanted to hear. The looks of Amanda, and, above all, the manner in which she had received the attentions of Sir Charles, evinced her sincerity. The shadow of jealousy removed, Lord Mortimer recovered all his animation. Never does the mind feel so light, so truly happy, as when a painful doubt is banished from it.

"Miss Fitzalan," said Lady Araminta, recurring to what

Amanda had just said, "can see few beings, like herself, capable of exciting immediate esteem. For my own part, I cannot persuade myself that she is an acquaintance of but two days, I feel such an interest in her welfare, such a sisterly regard." She paused, and looked expressively on her brother and Amanda. His fine eyes beamed the liveliest pleasure.

"Oh, my sister," cried he, "encourage that sisterly affection Who so worthy of possessing it as Miss Fitzalan? and who but Amanda," continued he, passing his arm round her waist, and softly whispering to her, "shall have a right to claim it?"

The stopping of the carriages now announced the return of the party, and terminated a scene, which, if much longer protracted, might, by increasing their agitation, have produced a full discovery of their feelings. The ladies were attended by Sir Charles and Freelove. The Marquis and Lord Cherbury had been out, but returned about this time; and soon after supper the company departed—Lady Araminta tenderly bidding Amanda farewell.

The cares which had so long pressed upon the heart of Amanda, and disturbed its peace, were now vanished. The whisper of Lord Mortimer had assured her that she was not only the object of his tenderest affection, but most serious attention. The regard of Lady Araminta flattered her pride, as it implied a tacit approbation of her brother's choice.

The next morning, immediately after breakfast, Lady Greystock went out to her lawyer, and Amanda was sitting at work in the dressing-room, when Sir Charles Bingley was announced. He now expressed, if possible, more pleasure at seeing her than he had done the preceding night; congratulated himself at finding her alone, and repeatedly declared, from their first interview, her image had never been absent from his mind. The particularity and ardor of his expressions Amanda wished, and endeavored, to repress. She had not the ridiculous and unfeeling vanity to be delighted with an attachment she could not return; besides, his attentions were unpleasing, as she believed they gave uneasiness to Lord Mortimer. She therefore answered him with cold and studied caution, which, to his impetuous feelings, was insupportable Half resenting, half rallying it, he snatched her hand, in spite of her efforts to prevent him, and was declaring he could not bear it, when the door opened, and Lord Mortimer appeared. Had Amanda been encouraging the regard of Sir Charles, she could not have betrayed more confusion. Lord Mortimer retreated a few steps, in evident embarrassment; then bowing coolly, again advanced and took a seat. Sir Charles started up, with a look which seemed to say he had been most unpleasantly interrupted, and walked about the room. Amanda was the first who broke silence. She asked, in a hesitating voice, "Whether Lady Araminta was yet gone?" "No," his lordship gravely replied; "but in a few minutes she proposed setting out, and he meant to accompany her part of the way." "So, till her ladyship was ready," cried Sir Charles, with quickness, "that no time might be lost, you come to Miss Fitzalan?"

Lord Mortimer made no reply. He frowned, and rising directly, slightly saluted Amanda, and retired.

Convinced, as she was, that Lord Mortimer had made the visit for the purpose of speaking more explicitly than he had yet done, she could not entirely conceal her chagrin, or regard Sir Charles without some displeasure. It had not, however, the effect of making him shorten his visit. He continued with her till Lady Greystock's return, to whom he proposed a party that evening for the opera, and obtained permission to wait upon her ladyship at tea, with tickets, notwithstanding Amanda declared her disinclination to going. She wished to avoid the public, as well as private, attentions of Sir Charles; but both she found impossible to do. The impression which the charms of her mind and form had made on him was of too ardent, too permanent a nature, to be erased by her coldness. Generous and exalted in his notions, affluent and independent in his fortune, he neither required any addition of wealth, nor was under any control which could prevent his following his inclinations. His heart was bent on a union with Amanda. Though hurt by her indifference, he would not allow himself to be discouraged by it. Time and perseverance, he trusted and believed, would conquer it. Unaccustomed to disappointment, he could not, in an affair which so materially concerned his happiness, bear the idea of proving unsuccessful. Had Amanda's heart been disengaged, he would probably have succeeded as he wished; for he was calculated to please, to inspire admiration and esteem; and Amanda felt a real friendship for him, and sincerely grieved that his ardent regard could not be reduced to as temperate a medium as hers.

Lady Greystock had a numerous and brilliant acquaintance in London, amongst whom she was continually engaged. Sir Charles was well known to them, and therefore almost constantly attended Amanda wherever she went. His unremitted and particular attention excited universal observation; and he was publicly declared the professed admirer of Lady Greystock's beautiful companion. The appellation was generally bestowed on her by the gentlemen; as many of Lady Greystock's female intimates declared, from the appearance of the girl, as well as her distressed situation, they wondered Sir Charles Bingley could ever think about her, for her ladyship had represented her as a person in the most indigent circumstances, on which account she had taken her under her protection. All that envy, hatred, and malice could suggest against her, Miss Malcolm said. The Marchioness and Lady Euphrasia, judging of her by themselves, supposed that as she was not sure of Lord Mortimer she would accept of Sir Charles; and though this measure would remove all apprehensions relative to Lord Mortimer, yet the idea of the wealth and consequence she would derive from it, almost distracted them. Thus does envy sting the bosoms which harbor it.

Lord Mortimer again resumed his reserve. He was frequently in company with Amanda, but never even attempted to pay her any attention; yet his eyes, which she often caught riveted on her, though the moment she perceived them they were withdrawn, seemed to say that the alteration in his manner was not produced by any diminution of tenderness. He was, indeed, determined to regulate his conduct by hers to Sir Charles. Though pained and irritated by his assiduities, he had too much pride to declare a prior claim to her regard—a woman who could waver between two objects, he deemed unworthy of either. He therefore resolved to leave Amanda free to act, and put her constancy to a kind of test. Yet, notwithstanding all his pride, we believe, if not pretty well convinced that this test would have proved a source of triumph to himself, he never would have submitted to it. The period for Lady Araminta's return was now arrived, and Amanda was anxiously expecting her, when she heard from Lady Euphrasia that her ladyship had been ill in the country, and would not therefore leave it for some time. This was a severe disappointment to Amanda, who had hoped, by her ladyship's means, to have seen less of Sir Charles and more of Lord Mortimer.

CHAPTER XXVI.

"And why should such, within herself, she cried,
Lock the lost wealth, a thousand want beside."—PARNELL.

MANDA was sitting alone in the drawing-room one morning, when a gentleman was shown into it, to wait for Lady Greystock. The stranger was about the middle period of life; his dress announced him a military man, and his thread-bare coat seemed to declare that whatever laurels he had gathered they were barren ones. His form and face were interesting; infirmity appeared to press upon one, and sorrow had deeply marked the other, yet without despoiling it of a certain expression which indicated the hilarity nature had once stamped upon it. His temples were sunk, and his cheek faded to a sickly hue. Amanda felt immediate respect and sensibility for the interesting figure before her. The feelings of her soul, the early lessons of her youth, had taught her to reverence distress; and never, perhaps, did she think it so peculiarly affecting, as when in a military garb.

The day was uncommonly severe, and the stranger shivered with the cold.

"I declare, young lady," cried he, as he took the chair which Amanda had placed for him by the fire, "I think I should not tremble more before an enemy, than I do before this day. I don't know but what it is as essential for a subaltern officer to stand cold as well as fire."

Amanda smiled, and resumed her work. She was busily employed making a trimming of artificial flowers for Lady Greystock, to present to a young lady, from whose family she had received some obligations. This was a cheap mode of returning them, as Amanda's materials were used.

"Your employment is an entertaining one," said the stranger, "and your roses literally without thorns; such, no doubt, as you expect to gather in your path through life."

"No," replied Amanda, "I have no such expectation."

"And yet," said he, "how few at your time of life, particularly if possessed of your advantages, could make such a declaration."

"Whoever had reflection undoubtedly would," replied Amanda.

"That I allow," cried he, "but how few do we find with reflection?—from the young it is banished, as the rigid tyrant that would forbid the enjoyment of the pleasures they pant after;—and from the old it is too often expelled, as an enemy to that forgetfulness which can alone insure their tranquillity."

"But in both, I trust," said Amanda, "you will allow there are exceptions."

"Perhaps there are; yet often, when conscience has no reason to dread, sensibility has cause to fear reflection, which not only revives the recollection of happy hours, but inspires such a regret for their loss, as almost unfits the soul for any exertions; 'tis indeed beautifully described in these lines—

> "Still importunate and vain,
> To former joys recurring ever,
> And turning all the past to pain."

Amanda attentively watched him, and thought what he said appeared particularly applicable to himself, as his countenance assumed a more dejected expression. He revived, however, in a few moments.

"I have, my dear young lady," continued he, smiling, "beguiled you most soberly, as Lady Grace says, into conversation. I have, however, given you an opportunity of amusing your fancy by drawing a comparison between an old veteran and a young soldier; but though you may allow him more animation, I trust you will not do me so much injustice as to allow him more taste: while he merely extolled the lustre of your eyes, I should admire the mildness which tempered that lustre; while he praised the glow of your cheek, I should adore that sensibility which had power, in a moment, to augment or diminish it."

At this instant Lady Greystock entered the room—she entered

it with the swell of importance, and a haughty expression of contempt in her features.

The stranger rose from his chair, and his paleness increased.

"So, Mr. Rushbrook," at last drawled out her ladyship. "So, sir: but pray be seated," waving her hand at the same time.

Amanda now retired: she had lingered a few moments in the room, under the pretence of putting her work out of her ladyship's way, to discover who the stranger was.

Rushbrook had been represented to her as artful, treacherous, and contemptible. His appearance was almost a sufficient refutation of those charges, and she began to think they never would have been laid against him by any other being than Lady Greystock, from a desire of depreciating her adversary. In her ladyship she had seen much to dislike since she resided with her; she saw that the temper, like the person, is often allowed to be in dishabille at home.

She felt even warmly interested about Rushbrook; she had heard of his large family; and, from his appearance, she conjectured they must be in distress. There was a kind of humorous sadness in his manner which affected her even more than a settled melancholy perhaps would have done, as it implied the efforts of a noble heart to repel sorrow; and if there cannot be a more noble, neither, surely, can there be a more affecting, sight than that of a good and brave man struggling with adversity.

As she leaned pensively against the window, reflecting on the various inequalities of fortune, yet still believing they were designed by a wise Providence, like hill and valley, mutually to benefit each other, she saw Rushbrook cross the street; his walk was the slow and lingering walk of dejection and disappointment. He raised his hand to his eyes, Amanda supposed to wipe away his tears, and her own fell at the supposition. The severity of the day had increased; a heavy shower of snow was falling, against which poor Rushbrook had no shelter but his threadbare coat. Amanda was unutterably affected; and when he disappeared from her sight, she fell into a sentimental soliloquy, something in the style of Yorick.

"Was I mistress," exclaimed she, as she beheld the splendid carriages passing and repassing, "was I mistress of one of those carriages, an old soldier like Rushbrook should not be exposed to the inclemency of a wintry sky; neither should his coat be threadbare, or his heart oppressed with anguish! If I saw a tear upon his cheek I would say it had no business there, for comfort was about revisiting him." As she spoke, the idea of Lord Mortimer occurred. Her tears were suspended, and her cheek began to glow.

"Yes, poor Rushbrook!" she exclaimed, "perhaps the period is not far distant when a bounteous Providence, through the hands of Amanda, may relieve thy wants; when Mortimer himself may be her assistant in the office of benevolence!"

Lady Greystock's woman now appeared, to desire she would come down to her lady. She immediately obeyed the summons, with a secret hope of hearing something of the conference. Her ladyship received her with an exulting laugh.

"I have good news to tell you, my dear," exclaimed she; "that poor wretch, Rushbrook, has lost the friend who was to have supported him in the lawsuit; and the lawyers, finding the sheet-anchor gone, have steered off, and left him to shift for himself. The miserable creature and his family must certainly starve. Only think of his assurance. He came to say, indeed, he would now be satisfied with a compromise." "Well, madam?" said Amanda.

"Well, madam, repeated her ladyship, mimicking her manner; "I told him I must be a fool indeed, if ever I consented to such a thing, after his effrontery in attempting to litigate the will of his much-abused uncle, my dear, good Sir Geoffry. No, no; I bid him proceed in the suit, as all my lawyers were prepared; and, after so much trouble on both sides, it would be a pity the thing came to nothing." "As your ladyship, however, knows his extreme distress, no doubt you will relieve it." "Why, pray," said her ladyship, smartly, "do you think he has any claim upon me?" "Yes," replied Amanda, "if not upon your justice, at least upon your humanity." "So you would advise me to fling away my money upon him?" "Yes," replied Amanda, smiling, "I would. And, as your ladyship likes the expression, have you fling it away profusely." "Well, well," answered she, "when you arrive at my age, you will know the real value of wealth." "I trust, madam,' said Amanda, with spirit, "I know its real value already. We only estimate it differently."

"And pray," asked her ladyship, with a sneer, "how may you estimate it?"

"As the means, madam, of dispensing happiness around us. Of giving shelter to the houseless child of want, and joy to the afflicted heart; as a sacred deposit intrusted to us by an Almighty Power for those purposes, which, if so applied, will nourish placid and delightful reflections, that, like soothing friends, will crowd around us in the bed of sickness or death, alleviating the pains of one, and the terrors of the other."

"Upon my word," exclaimed Lady Greystock, "a fine flowery speech, and well calculated for a sentimental novel or a moral treatise for the improvement of youth. But I advise you, my dear, in future, to keep your queer and romantic notions to yourself, or else it will be suspected you have made romances your study; for you have just spoken as one of their heroines would have done."

Amanda made no reply; yet as she beheld her ladyship seated in an easy-chair, by a blazing fire, with a large bowl of rich soup before her, which she took every morning, she could not forbear secretly exclaiming: "Hard-hearted woman! engrossed by your own gratifications, no ray of compassion can soften your nature for the misfortunes of others. Sheltered yourself from the tempest, you see it falling, without pity, on the head of wretchedness; and, while you feast on luxuries, think without emotion on those who want even common necessaries."

In the evening they went to a large party at the Marchioness's; but though the scene was gay and brilliant, it could not remove the pensiveness of Amanda's spirits. The emaciated form of Rushbrook, returning to his desolate family, dwelt upon her mind. A little, she thought, as she surveyed the magnificence of the apartments, and the splendor of the company which crowded them, a little from this parade of vanity and wealth, would give relief to many a child of indigence. Never had the truth of the following lines so forcibly struck her imagination:—

"Ah, little think the gay, licentious proud,
Whom pleasure, power, and affluence surround;
They who their thoughtless hours in giddy mirth

And wanton, often cruel, riot waste;
Ah, little think they, while they dance along,
How many feel, this very moment, death,
And all the sad variety of pain.
How many drink the cup
Of baleful grief, or eat the bitter bread
Of misery, sore pierced by wintry winds?
How many shrink into the sordid hut
Of cheerless poverty!"

From such reflections as these she was disturbed by the entrance of Sir Charles Bingley. As usual, he took his station by her, and in a few minutes after him Lord Mortimer appeared. A party for vingt-un was formed, in which Amanda joined, from a wish of avoiding the assiduities of Sir Charles; but he took care to secure a seat next hers, and Lord Mortimer sat opposite to them.

"Bingley," said a gentleman, after they had been some time at the table, "you are certainly the most changeable fellow in the world. About three weeks ago you were hurrying everything for a journey to Ireland, as if life and death depended on your expedition, and here I still find you loitering about the town."

"I deny the imputation of changeableness," replied the Baronet; "all my actions are regulated," and he glanced at Amanda, "by one source, one object."

Amanda blushed, and caught, at that moment, a penetrating look from Lord Mortimer. Her situation was extremely disagreeable. She dreaded his attentions would be imputed to encouragement from her; she had often tried to suppress them, and she resolved her next efforts should be more resolute.

Sir Charles reached Pall Mall the next morning just as Lady Greystock was stepping into her chariot, to acquaint her lawyer of Rushbook's visit. She informed him that Miss Fitzalan was in the drawing-room, and he flew up to her.

"You find," said he, "by what you heard last night, that my conduct has excited some surprise. I assure you my friends think I must absolutely be deranged, to relinquish so suddenly a journey I appeared so anxious to take. Suffer me," continued he, taking her hand, "to assign the true reason for this apparent change."
"Sir Charles," replied Amanda, "'tis time to terminate this trifling."

"Oh let it then be terminated," said he, with eagerness, "by your consenting to my happiness, by your accepting a hand, tendered to you with the most ardent affections of my heart."

With equal delicacy and tenderness, he then urged her acceptance of proposals which were as disinterested as the most romantic generosity could desire them to be.

Amanda felt really concerned that he had made them; the grateful sensibility of her nature was hurt at the idea of giving him pain. "Believe me, Sir Charles," said she, "I am truly sensible of the honor of your addresses; but I should deem myself unworthy of the favorable opinion which excited them, if I delayed a moment assuring you that friendship was the only return in my power to make for them."

The impetuous passions of Sir Charles were now all in commotion. He started from his chair and traversed the apartment in breathless agitation. "I will not, Miss Fitzalan," said he, resuming his seat again, "believe you inflexible. I will not believe that you can think I shall so easily resign an idea which I have so long cherished with rapture."

"Surely, Sir Charles," somewhat alarmed, "you cannot accuse me of having encouraged that idea?"

"Oh no," sighed he passionately, "to me you were always uniformly cold." "And from whence then proceeded such an idea?"

"From the natural propensity we all have to deceive ourselves, and to believe that whatever we wish will be accomplished. Ah! Miss Fitzalan, deprive me not of so sweet a belief. I will not at present urge you to any material step to which you are averse; I will only entreat for permission to hope that time, perseverance, unremitted attention, may make some impression on you, and at last produce a change in my favor."

"Never, Sir Charles, will I give rise to a hope which I think cannot be realized. A little reflection will convince you you should not be displeased at my being so explicit. We are, at this moment, both, perhaps, too much discomposed to render a longer conference desirable. Pardon me, therefore, if I now terminate it, and, be assured, I shall never lose a grateful remembrance of the honor you intended me, or forget the friendship I professed for Sir Charles Bingley."

She then withdrew, without any obstruction from him. Regret

and disappointment seemed to have suspended his faculties; but it was a momentary suspension, and on recovering them he quitted the house.

His pride, at first, urged him to give up Amanda for ever; but his tenderness soon opposed this resolution. He had, as he himself acknowledged, a propensity to believe, that whatever he wished was easy to accomplish; this propensity proceeded from the easiness with which his inclinations had hitherto been gratified. Flattering himself that the coldness of Amanda proceeded more from natural reserve than particular indifference to him, he still hoped she might be induced to favor him. She was so superior, in his opinion, to every woman he had seen, so truly calculated to render him happy, that, as the violence of offended pride abated, he resolved, without another effort, not to give her up. Without knowing it, he had rambled to St. James's Square, and having heard of the friendship subsisting between Lord Cherbury and Fitzalan, he deemed his lordship a proper person to apply to on the present occasion, thinking, that if he interested himself in his favor, he might yet be successful. He accordingly repaired to his house, and was shown into an apartment where the Earl and Lord Mortimer were sitting together. After paying the usual compliments, "I am come, my Lord," said he, somewhat abruptly, "to entreat your interest in an affair which materially concerns my happiness, and trust your lordship will excuse my entreaty, when I inform you it relates to Miss Fitzalan."

The Earl, with much politeness, assured him, "He should feel happy in an opportunity of serving him," and said, "he did him but justice in supposing him particularly interested about Miss Fitzalan, not only as the daughter of his old friend, but from her own great merit."

Sir Charles then acquainted him with the proposals he had just made her, and her absolute rejection of them; and expressed his hope that Lord Cherbury would try to influence her in his favor.

"'Tis very extraordinary, indeed," cried his lordship, "that Miss Fitzalan should decline such an honorable, such an advantageous proposal. Are you sure, Sir Charles, there is no prior attachment in the case?"

"I never heard of one, my Lord, and I believe none exists"

Lord Mortimer's countenance lowered at this, but, happily, its gloom was unperceived.

"I will write to-day," said the Earl, "to Mr. Fitzalan, and mention your proposal to him in the terms it deserves Except authorized by him, you must, Sir Charles, excuse my personal interference in the affair. I have no doubt, indeed, but he will approve of your addresses, and you may then depend on my seconding them with all my interest."

This promise satisfied Sir Charles, and he soon after withdrew. Lord Mortimer was now pretty well convinced of the state of Amanda's heart. Under this conviction, he delayed not many minutes, after Sir Charles's departure, going to Pall Mall; and having particularly inquired whether Lady Greystock was out, and being answered in the affirmative, he ascended to the drawing-room, to which Amanda had again returned.

CHAPTER XXVII.

"Go bid the needle its dear north forsake,
To which with trembling reverence it does bend;
Go bid the stones a journey upward make:
Go bid the ambitious flame no more ascend;
And when these false to their old motions prove,
Then will I cease thee, thee alone to love."—COWLEY.

IN an emotion of surprise at so unexpected a visit, the book she was reading dropped from Amanda, and she arose in visible agitation.

"I fear," said his lordship, "I have intruded somewhat abruptly upon you; but my apology for doing so must be my ardent wish of using an opportunity so propitious for a mutual eclaircissement—an opportunity I might, perhaps, vainly seek again."

He took her trembling hand, led her to the sofa, and placed himself by her. As a means of leading to the desired eclaircissement, he related the agonies he had suffered at returning to Tudor Hall, and finding her gone—gone in a manner so inexplicable, that the more he reflected on it the more wretched he grew. He described the hopes and fears which alternately fluctuated in his mind during his continuance in Ireland, and which often drove him into a state nearly bordering on distraction. He mentioned the resolution, though painful in the extreme, which he had adopted on the first appearance of Sir Charles Bingley's particularity; and finally concluded by assuring her, notwithstanding all his incertitude and anxiety, his tenderness had never known diminution.

Encouraged by this assurance, Amanda, with restored composure, informed him of the reason of her precipitate journey from Wales, and the incidents which prevented her meeting him in Ireland, as he had expected. Though delicacy forbade her dwelling, like Lord Mortimer, on the wretchedness occasioned by their separation, and mutual misapprehensions of each other, she could not avoid touching upon it sufficiently, indeed, to convince him she had been a sympathizing participator in all the uneasiness he had suffered.

Restored to the confidence of Mortimer, Amanda appeared dearer to his soul than ever. Pleasure beamed from his eyes as he pressed her to his bosom, and exclaimed, "I may again call you my own Amanda; again sketch scenes of felicity, and call upon you to realize them." Yet, in the midst of this transport, a sudden gloom clouded his countenance; and, after gazing on her some minutes, with pensive tenderness, he fervently exclaimed, "Would to Heaven, in this hour of perfect reconciliation, I could say that all obstacles to our future happiness were removed." Amanda involuntarily shuddered, and continued silent.

"That my father will throw difficulties in the way of our union, I cannot deny my apprehension of," said Lord Mortimer; "though truly noble and generous in his nature, he is sometimes, like the rest of mankind, influenced by interested motives. He has long, from such motives, set his heart on a connection with the Marquis of Roslin's family. Though fully determined in my intentions, I have hitherto forborne an explicit declaration of them to him, trusting that some propitious chance would yet second my wishes, and save me the painful necessity of disturbing the harmony which has ever subsisted between us."

"Oh! my Lord!" said Amanda, turning pale, and shrinking from him, "let me not be the unfortunate cause of disturbing that harmony. Comply with the wishes of Lord Cherbury, marry Lady Euphrasia, and let me be forgotten."

"Amanda," cried his lordship, "accuse not yourself of being the cause of any disagreement between us. Had I never seen you, with respect to Lady Euphrasia, I should have felt the same inability to comply with his wishes. To me her person is not more unpleasing than her mind. I have long been convinced that wealth alone was insufficient to bestow felicity, and have ever considered the man who could sacrifice his feelings at the shrine of interest or ambition, degraded below the standard of humanity; that to marry, merely from selfish considerations, was one of the most culpable, most contemptible actions which could be committed To enter into such a union, I want the propensities which can alone ever occasion it, namely a violent passion for the enjoyments only attainable through the medium of wealth. Left at an early age uncontrolled master of my own actions, I drank freely of the cup of pleasure, but found it soon pall upon my taste. It was, indeed, unmixed with any of those refined ingredients which can only please the intellectual appetite, and might properly be termed the cup of false instead of real pleasure. Thinking, therefore, as I do, that a union without love is abhorrent to probity and sensibility, and that the dissipated pleasures of life are not only prejudicial but tiresome, I naturally wish to secure to myself domestic happiness; but never could it be experienced except united to a woman whom my reason thoroughly approved, who should at once possess my unbounded confidence and tenderest affection. Who should be, not only the promoter of my joys, but the assuager of my cares. In you I have found such a woman, such a being, as I candidly confess, some time ago, I thought it impossible to meet with. To you I am bound by a sentiment even stronger than love—by honor—and with real gratitude acknowledge my obligations in being permitted to atone, in some degree, for my errors relative to you. But I will not allow my Amanda to suppose these errors proceeded from any settled depravity of soul. Allowed to be, as I have before said, my own master at an early period, from the natural thoughtlessness of youth, I was led into scenes which the judgment of riper years has since severely condemned Here, too, often I met with women whose manners, instead of checking, gave a latitude to freedom; women, too, who, from their situations in life, had every advantage that could be requisite for improving and refining their minds. From conversing with them I gradually imbibed a prejudice against the whole sex, and under that prejudice first beheld you, and feared either to doubt or to believe the reality of the innocence you appeared to possess.

"Convinced at length, most fully, most happily convinced of its reality, my prejudices no longer remained; they vanished like mists before the sun—or rather like the illusions of falsehood before the influence of truth. Were those, my dear Amanda, of your sex, who, like you, had the resistless power of pleasing, to use the faculties assigned them by a bounteous Providence in the cause of virtue, they would soon check the dissipation of the times.

"'Tis impossible to express the power a beautiful form has over the human mind; that power might be exerted for nobler purposes. Purity speaking from love-inspiring lips would, like the voice of Adam's heavenly guest, so sweetly breathe upon the ear as insensibly to influence the heart; the libertine it corrected would, if not utterly hardened, reform; no longer would he glory in his vices, but touched and abashed, instead of destroying, worship female virtue.

"But I wander from the purpose of my soul. Convinced as I am of the dissimilarity between my father's inclinations and mine, I think it better to give no intimation of my present intentions which, if permitted by you, I am unalterably determined on fulfilling, as I should consider it as highly insulting to him to incur his prohibition, and then act in defiance of it, though my heart would glory in avowing its choice. The peculiar circumstances I have just mentioned will, I trust, induce my Amanda to excuse a temporary concealment of it, till beyond the power of mortals to separate us—a private and immediate union, the exigency of situation, and the security of felicity demands. I shall feel a trembling apprehension till I call you mine: life is too short to permit the waste of time in idle scruples and unmeaning ceremonies. The eye of suspicion has long rested upon us, and would, I am convinced, effect a premature discovery, if we took not some measure to prevent it.

"Deem me not too precipitate, my Amanda," passing his arm gently round her waist, "if I ask you to-morrow night, for the last sweet proof of confidence you can give me, by putting yourself under my protection. A journey to Scotland is unavoidable—in the arrangements I shall make for it, all that is due to delicacy I shall consider."

"Mention it no more, my lord," said Amanda, in a faltering accent; "no longer delude your imagination or mine with the hopes of being united."

Hitherto she had believed the approbation of Lord Cherbury to the wishes of his son would be obtained, the moment he was convinced how essential their gratification was to his felicity. She judged of him by her father, who, she was convinced, if situations were reversed, would bestow her on Mortimer without hesitation. These ideas so nourished her attachment, that, like the vital parts of existence, it at length became painfully, almost fatally, susceptible of every shock. Her dream of happiness was over the moment she heard Lord Cherbury's consent was not to be asked, from a fear of its being refused. 'Twas misery to be separated from Lord Mortimer, but it was guilt and misery to marry him clandestinely, after the solemn injunction her father had given her against such a step. The shock of disappointment could not be borne with composure; it pressed like a cold dead weight upon her heart. She trembled, and, unable to support herself, sunk against the shoulder of Lord Mortimer, while a shower of tears proclaimed her agony. Alarmed by her emotion, Lord Mortimer hastily demanded its source, and the reason of the words which had just escaped her.

"Because, my lord," replied she, "I cannot consent to a clandestine measure, nor bear you should incur the displeasure of Lord Cherbury on my account. Though Lady Euphrasia Sutherland is not agreeable, there are many women who, with equal rank and fortune, possess the perfections suited to your taste. Seek for one of these—choose from among them a happy daughter of prosperity, and let Amanda, untitled, unportioned, and unpleasing to your father, return to an obscurity which owes its comforts to his fos tering bounty." "Does this advice," asked Lord Mortimer, "proceed from Amanda's heart?" "No," replied she, hesitatingly, and smiling through her tears, "not from her heart, but from a better counsellor, her reason."

"And shall I not obey the dictates of reason," replied he, "in uniting my destiny to yours? Reason directs us to seek happiness through virtuous means; and what means are so adapted for that purpose, as a union with a beloved and amiable woman? No, Amanda; no titled daughter of prosperity, to use your own words, shall ever attract my affections from you. 'Imagination cannot form a shape, besides your own, to like of;' a shape which even if despoiled of its graces, would enshrine a mind so transcendently lovely, as to secure my admiration. In choosing you as the partner of my future days, I do not infringe the moral obligation which exists between father and son; for as, on one hand, it does not require weak indulgence; so, on the other, it does not demand implicit obedience, if reason and happiness must be sacrificed by it. Nothing would have tempted me to propose a private union but the hope of escaping many disagreeable circumstances by it. If you persist, however, in rejecting it, I shall openly avow my intentions, for a longer continuance of anxiety and suspense I cannot support."

"Do you think, then," said Amanda, "I would enter your family amidst confusion and altercation? No, my Lord, rashly or clandestinely I never will consent to enter it."

"Is this the happiness I promised myself would crown our reconciliation?" exclaimed Lord Mortimer, rising hastily and traversing the apartment. "Is an obstinate adherence to rigid punctilio the only proof of regard I shall receive from Amanda? Will she make no trifling sacrifice to the man who adores her, and whom she professes to esteem?"

"Any sacrifice, my lord, compatible with virtue and filial duty, most willingly would I make; but beyond these limits I must not, cannot, will not step. Cold, joyless, and unworthy of your acceptance would be the hand you would receive if given against my conviction of what was right. Oh, never may the hour arrive in which I should blush to see my father; in which I should be accused of injuring the honor intrusted to my charge, and feel oppressed with the consciousness of having planted thorns in the breast that depended on me for happiness."

"Do not be too inflexible, my Amanda," cried Lord Mortimer, resuming his seat, "nor suffer too great a degree of refinement to involve you in wretchedness; felicity is seldom attained without some pain; a little resolution on your side would overcome any difficulties that lay between us and it; when the act was past my father would naturally lose his resentment, from perceiving its inefficacy, and family concord would speedily be restored. Araminta adores you; with rapture would she receive her dear and lovely sister to her bosom; your father, happy in your happiness, would be convinced his notions heretofore were too scrupulous, and that in complying with my wishes, you had neither violated your own delicacy nor tarnished his honor."

"Ah, my lord, your arguments have not the effect you desire. I cannot be deluded by them, to view things in the light you wish To unite myself clandestinely to you would be to fly in the face of parental authority; to be proposed to Lord Cherbury, when almost certain of a refusal, would not only subject me to insult, but dissolve the friendship which has hitherto subsisted between his lordship and my father. Situated as we are, our only expedient is to separate; 'tis absurd to think longer of a connection against which there are such obstacles; the task of trying to forget will be easier to you, my Lord, than you now perhaps imagine; the scenes you must be engaged in are well calculated to expunge painful remembrances; in the retirement my destiny has doomed me to, my efforts will not be wanting to render me equally successful."

The tears trickled down Amanda's pale cheeks as she spoke; she believed that they must part, and the belief was attended with a pang of unutterable anguish: pleased and pained by her sensibility, Lord Mortimer bent forward and looked in her face.

"Are these tears," said he, "to enforce me to the only expedient you say remains? Ah, my Amanda," clasping her to his breast, "the task of forgetting you could never be accomplished—could never be attempted; life would be tasteless if not spent with you; never will I relinquish the delightful hope of a union yet taking place A sudden thought," resumed he, after pausing a few minutes, "has just occurred. I have an aunt, the only remaining sister of Lord Cherbury, a generous, tender, exalted woman; I have ever been her particular favorite; my Amanda, I know, is the very kind of being she would select, if the choice devolved on her, for my wife: she is now in the country; I will write immediately, inform her of our situation, and entreat her to come up to town to use her influence with my father in our favor. Her fortune is large, from the bequest of a rich relation; and from the generosity of her disposition, I have no doubt she would render the loss of Lady Euphrasia's fortune very immaterial to her brother. This is the only scheme I can possibly devise for the completion of our happiness, according to your notions, and I hope it meets your approbation."

It appeared, indeed, a feasible one to Amanda; and as it could not possibly excite any ideas unfavorable to her father's integrity, she gave her consent to its being tried.

Her heart felt relieved of an oppressive load, as the hope revived that it might be accomplished. Lord Mortimer wiped away her tears; and the cloud which hung over them both being dispersed, they talked with pleasure of future days. Lord Mortimer described the various schemes he had planned for their mode of life. Amanda smiled at the easiness with which he contrived them, and secretly wished he might find it as easy to realize as to project.

"Though the retired path of life," said he, "might be more agreeable to us than the frequented and public one, we must make some little sacrifice of inclination to the community to which we belong. On an elevated station and affluent fortune there are claims from subordinate ranks which cannot be avoided without injuring them. Neither should I wish to hide the beautiful gem I shall possess in obscurity; but, after a winter of what I call moderate dissipation, we will hasten to the sequestered shades of Tudor Hall." He dwelt with pleasure on the calm and rational joys they should experience there; nor could forbear hinting at the period when new tendernesses, new sympathies, would be awakened in their souls; when little prattling beings should frolic before them, and literally strew roses in their paths. He expressed his wish of having Fitzalan a constant resident with them;

and was proceeding to mention some alterations he intended at Tudor Hall, when the return of Lady Greystock's carriage effectually disturbed him. Lord Mortimer, however, had time to assure Amanda, ere she entered the room, that he had no doubt but everything would be soon settled according to their wishes, and that he would take every opportunity her ladyship's absence gave him of visiting her.

"So, so," said Lady Greystock, coming into the room, "this has been Miss Fitzalan's levee-day. Why, I declare, my dear, now that I know of the agreeable tète-à-têtes you can enjoy, I shall feel no uneasiness at leaving you to yourself."

Amanda blushed deeply; and Lord Mortimer thought in this speech he perceived a degree of irony which seemed to say all was not right in the speaker's heart towards Amanda, and on this account he felt more anxious than ever to have her under his own protection. Animated by the idea that this would soon be the case, he told her ladyship, smiling, "she should be obliged to him or any other person who could relieve her mind from uneasiness," and departed. This had been a busy and interesting day to Amanda, and the variety of emotions it had given rise to produced a languor in her mind and frame she could not shake off.

Her expectations were not as sanguine as Lord Mortimer's. Once severely disappointed, she dreaded again to give too great a latitude to hope. Happiness was in view, but she doubted much whether it would ever be within her reach; yet the pain of suspense she endeavcred to alleviate by reflecting that every event was under the dirertion of a superior Being, who knew best what would constitute the felicity of His creatures.

Lady Greystock learned from her maid the length of Lord Mortimer's visit, and she was convinced from that circumstance, as well as from the looks and absent manner of Amanda, that something material had happened in the course of it. In the evening they were engaged to a party, and ere they separated after dinner to dress for it, a plain-looking woman was shown into the room, whom Amanda instantly recollected to be the person at whose house she and her father had lodged on quitting Devonshire to secrete themselves from Colonel Belgrave. This woman had been bribed to serve him, and had forced several letters upon Amanda, who, therefore, naturally abhorred the sight of a person that had joined in so infamous a plot against her; and to her exclamation of surprise and pleasure only returned a cool bow, and directly left the room. She was vexed at seeing this woman. The conduct of Colonel Belgrave had hitherto been concealed, from motives of pride and delicacy; and to Lady Greystock, of all other beings, she wished it not revealed. Her only hope of its not being so was that this woman, on her own account, would not mention it, as she must be conscious that her efforts to serve him were not undiscovered.

Mrs. Jennings had been housekeeper to Lady Greystock during her residence in England, and so successfully ingratiated herself into her favor that, though dismissed from her service, she yet retained it. Lady Greystock was surprised to see she and Amanda knew each other, and inquired minutely how the acquaintance had commenced. The manner in which she mentioned Amanda, convinced Mrs. Jennings she was not high in her estimation, and from this conviction she thought she might safely assert any falsehood she pleased against her. As she knew enough of her lady's disposition to be assured she never would contradict an assertion to the prejudice of a person she disliked by what she designed saying, she trusted anything Amanda might say against her would appear malicious, and that she should also be revenged for the disdainful air with which she had regarded her.

She told her ladyship, "that near a year back Miss Fitzalan had been a lodger of hers, as also an old officer, she called her father; but had she known what kind of people they were, she never would have admitted them into her house. Miss was followed by such a set of gallants, she really thought the reputation of her house would have been ruined. Among them was a Colonel Belgrave, a sad rake, who, she believed, was the favorite. She was determined on making them decamp, when suddenly Miss went off, nobody knew where, but it might easily be guessed. She did not travel alone, for the Colonel disappeared at the same time."

The character of Fitzalan, and the uniform propriety of Amanda's conduct, forbade Lady Greystock's giving implicit credit to what Mrs. Jennings said. She perceived in it the exaggerations of malice and falsehood, occasioned, she supposed, by disappointed avarice, or offended pride. She resolved, however to relate all she heard to the Marchioness, without betraying the smallest doubt of its veracity.

It may appear strange that Lady Greystock, after taking Amanda, unsolicited, under her protection, should, without any cause for enmity, seek to injure her—but Lady Greystock was a woman devoid of principle. From selfish motives she had taken Amanda, and from selfish motives she was ready to sacrifice her. Her ladyship had enjoyed so much happiness in her matrimonial connections, that she had no objection again to enter the lists of Hymen, and Lord Cherbury was the object at which her present wishes pointed. The Marchioness had hinted, in pretty plain terms, that if she counteracted Lord Mortimer's intentions respecting Amanda, she would forward hers relative to Lord Cherbury.

She thought what Mrs. Jennings had alleged would effectually forward their plans, as she knew, if called upon, she would support it. The next morning she went to Portman Square, to communicate her important intelligence to the Marchioness and Lady Euphrasia.

Joy and exultation sat upon their features at receiving this interesting communication, which opened so charming a prospect of separating Lord Mortimer from Amanda, by giving them the power of injuring her character. This joy and exultation they deemed requisite for some time to conceal. They considered their measures would be more successful for being gradually brought about, and, therefore, resolved rather to undermine, than directly strike at the peace of Amanda

Like Lady Greystock, they disbelieved Mrs. Jennings's tale; but, like her ladyship, confined this disbelief to their own bosoms. In the manner, the appearance of Amanda, there was an innocence, a mildness, that denoted something holy dwelt within her breast, and forbade the entrance of any impure or wayward passions; besides, from a gentleman who had resided in Devonshire, they learned the distress Fitzalan was reduced to, by Belgrave's revenge for the virtue of his daughter. This gentleman was now, however, on the continent, and they had no fear of their allegations against Amanda being contradicted, or their schemes against her being overthrown.

After some consultation, it was agreed, as a means of expediting their plot, that Lady Greystock and Amanda should immediately remove to the Marchioness's house. By this change of abode, too, Lord Mortimer would be prevented taking any material step relative to Amanda, till the period arrived, when his own inclination would, most probably, render any further trouble on that account unnecessary.

Lady Greystock, on her return to Pall Mall, after a warm eulogium on the friendship of the Marchioness, mentioned the invitation she had given them to her house, which she declared she could not refuse, as it was made from an ardent desire of enjoying more of their society than she had hitherto done, during their short stay in London. She also told Amanda, that both the Marchioness and Lady Euphrasia had expressed a tender regard for her, and a wish of proving to the world, that any coolness which existed between their families was removed, by her becoming their guest.

This projected removal was extremely disagreeable to Amanda, as it not only terminated the morning interviews which were to take place between her and Lord Mortimer, during the absence of Lady Greystock with her lawyers, but threatened to impose a restraint upon her looks, as well as actions, being confident, from the views and suspicions of Lady Euphrasia, she should be continually watched with the closest circumspection. Her part, however, was acquiescence. The lodgings were discharged, and the next morning they took up their residence under the Marquis of Roslin's roof, to the infinite surprise and mortification of Lord Mortimer, who, like Amanda, anticipated the disagreeable consequences which would result from it.

The altered manners of the Marchioness and Lady Euphrasia surprised Amanda. They received her not merely with politeness, but affection; recapitulated all Lady Greystock had already said concerning their regard; bade her consider herself entirely at home in their house, and appointed a maid solely to attend her.

Notwithstanding their former cool, even contemptuous conduct, Amanda, the child of innocence and simplicity, could not believe the alteration in their manners feigned; she rather believed that her own patience and humility had at length conciliated their regard. The idea pleased her, and like every other, which she supposed could give her father satisfaction, it was instantly communicated to him.

She found herself most agreeably mistaken relative to the restraint she had feared. She was perfect mistress of her own time and actions; and when she saw Lord Mortimer no lowering looks nor studied interference, as heretofore, from the Marchioness or Lady Euphrasia, prevented their frequently conversing together. The Marchioness made her several elegant presents, and Lady Euphrasia frequently dropped the formal appellation of Miss Fitzalan for the more familiar one of Amanda.

Sir Charles Bingley, agreeable to his resolution of not relinquishing Amanda without another effort for her favor, still persisted in his attentions, and visited constantly at the Marquis's.

Amanda had been about a fortnight in Portman Square, when she went one night with the Marchioness, Lady Euphrasia, Miss Malcolm, and Lady Greystock to the Pantheon. Lord Mortimer had told her, that if he could possibly leave a particular party he was engaged to, he would be there. She, therefore, on that account, wished to keep herself disengaged; but immediately on her entrance she was joined by Sir Charles Bingley, and she found she must either dance with him as he requested, or consent to listen to his usual conversation; and she chose the first, as being least particular. The dancing over, Sir Charles was conducting her to get some refreshment, when a gentleman, hastily stepping forward, saluted him by his name. Amanda started at the sound of the voice; she raised her eyes, and with equal horror and surprise beheld Colonel Belgrave.

She turned pale, trembled, and involuntarily exclaimed, "Gracious Heaven!" Her soul recoiled at his sight, as if an evil genius had suddenly darted into her path to blast her hopes of happiness. Sickening with emotion, her head grew giddy, and she caught Sir Charles's arm, to prevent her falling.

Alarmed by her paleness and agitation, he hastily demanded the cause of her disorder, willing to believe, notwithstanding what he had seen, that it did not proceed from the sight of Colonel Belgrave. "O take me, take me from this room!" was all, in faltering accents, Amanda could pronounce, still leaning on him for support. Colonel Belgrave inquired tenderly what he could do to serve her, and at the same time attempted to take her hand. She shrunk from his touch with a look expressive of horror, and again besought Sir Charles to take her from the room, and procure her a conveyance home. Her agitation now became contagious. It was visible to Sir Charles that it proceeded from seeing Colonel Belgrave, and he trembled as he supported her.

Belgrave offered his services in assisting to support her from the room, but she motioned with her hand to repulse him.

At the door they met Lord Mortimer entering. Terrified by the situation of Amanda, all caution, all reserve forsook him, and his rapid and impassioned inquiries betrayed the tender interest she had in his heart. Unable to answer them herself, Sir Charles replied for her, saying, "She had been taken extremely ill after dancing," and added, "he would resign her to his lordship's protection while he went to procure her a chair."

Lord Mortimer received the lovely trembler in his arms. He softly called her his Amanda, the beloved of his soul, and she began to revive. His presence was at once a relief and comfort to her, and his language soothed the perturbations of her mind; but as she raised her head from his shoulder, she beheld Colonel Belgrave standing near them. His invidious eyes fastened on her. She averted her head, and, saying the air would do her good, Lord Mortimer led her forward, and took this opportunity of expressing his wishes for the period when he should be at liberty to watch over her with guardian care, soothe every weakness and soften every care.

In a few minutes Sir Charles returned, and told her he had procured a chair. She thanked him with grateful sweetness for his attention, and requested Lord Mortimer to acquaint the ladies with the reason of her abrupt departure. His lordship wished himself to have attended her to Portman Square, but she thought it would appear too particular, and would not suffer him. She retired to her room immediately on her return, and endeavored, though unsuccessfully, to compose her spirits.

The distress she suffered from Belgrave's conduct had left an impression on her mind which could not be erased. The terror his presence inspired was too powerful for reason to conquer, and raised the most gloomy presages in her mind. She believed him capable of any villany. His looks had declared a continuance of illicit love. She trembled at the idea of his stratagems being renewed. Her apprehensions were doubly painful from the necessity of concealment, lest those dearer to her than existence should be involved in danger on her account. To heaven she looked up for protection, and the terrors of her heart were somewhat lessened, conscious that heaven could render the aims of Belgrave against her peace as abortive as those against her innocence had been.

Sir Charles Bingley parted from Lord Mortimer immediately after Amanda's departure, and returned arm in arm with Belgrave to the room. "Belgrave," said he abruptly, after musing some minutes, "you know Miss Fitzalan?"

Belgrave answered not hastily. He appeared as if deliberating on the reply he should give. At last, "I do know Miss Fitzalan," cried he; "her father was my tenant in Devonshire; she is one of the loveliest girls I ever knew." "Lovely, indeed," said Sir Charles, with a deep and involuntary sigh; "but it is somewhat extraordinary to me that, instead of noticing you as a friend or acquaintance, she should look alarmed and agitated, as if she had seen an enemy." "My dear Bingley," exclaimed Belgrave, "surely at this time of day you cannot be a stranger to the unaccountable caprices of the female mind." "'Tis very extraordinary to me, I own," resumed Sir Charles, "that Miss Fitzalan should behave as she did to you. Were you and her family ever very intimate?"

An invidious smile lurked on Belgrave's countenance at this question.

"Belgrave," exclaimed Sir Charles, passionately, "your manner appears so mysterious that it distracts me. If friendship will not induce you to account for it, my intentions relative to Miss Fitzalan will compel me to insist on your doing so." "Come, come, Bingley," replied the Colonel, "this is not a country for extorting confession. However, seriously, you might depend on my honor, exclusive of my friendship, to conceal nothing from you in which you were materially interested." So saying, he snatched away his arm, rushed into the crowd, and instantly disappeared.

This assurance, however, could not calm the disquietude of Sir Charles. His soul was tortured with impatience and anxiety for an explanation of the mystery, which the agitation of Amanda, and the evasive answers of Belgrave had betrayed. He sought the latter through the room till convinced of his departure, and resolved the next morning to entreat him to deal candidly with him.

Agreeably to this resolution, he was preparing, after breakfast, for his visit, when a letter was brought him which contained the following lines:—

"If Sir Charles Bingley has the least regard for his honor or tranquillity, he will immediately relinquish his intentions relative to Miss Fitzalan. This caution comes from a sincere friend—from a person whom delicacy, not want of veracity, urges to this secret mode of giving it."

Sir Charles perused and re-perused the letter, as if doubting the evidence of his eyes. He at last flung it from him, and clasping his hands together exclaimed: "This is indeed a horrible explanation." He took up the detested paper. Again he examined the characters, and recognised the writing of Colonel Belgrave. He hastily snatched up his hat, and with the paper in his hand, flew directly to his house. The Colonel was alone.

"Belgrave," said Sir Charles, in almost breathless agitation, "are you the author of this letter?" presenting it to him.

Belgrave took it, read it, but continued silent.

"Oh! Belgrave!" exclaimed Sir Charles, in a voice trembling with agony, "pity and relieve my suspense." "I am the author of it," replied Belgrave, with solemnity; "Miss Fitzalan and I were once tenderly attached. I trust I am no deliberate libertine; but, when a lovely, seducing girl was thrown purposely in my way——" "Oh, stop," said Sir Charles, "to me any extenuation of your conduct is unnecessary; 'tis sufficient to know that Miss Fitzalan and I are for ever separated." His emotion overpowered him. He leaned on a table, and covered his face with a handkerchief.

"The shock I have received," said he, "almost unmans me. Amanda was, alas! I must say is, dear, inexpressibly dear to my soul. I thought her the most lovely, the most estimable of women;

and the anguish I now feel, is more on her account than my own. I cannot bear the idea of the contempt which may fall upon her. Oh, Belgrave, 'tis melancholy to behold a human being, so endowed by nature as she is, insensible or unworthy of her blessings. Amanda," he continued, after a pause, "never encouraged me; I therefore cannot accuse her of intending deceit."

"She never encouraged you," replied Belgrave, "because she was ambitious of a higher title. Amanda, beneath a specious appearance of innocence, conceals a light disposition and a designing heart. She aspires to Mortimer's hand, and may probably succeed, for his language and attentions to her last night were those of a tender lover."

"I shall return immediately to Ireland," said Sir Charles, "and endeavor to forget I have ever seen her. She has made me indeed experience all the fervency of love, and bitterness of disappointment. What I felt for her, I think I shall never again feel for any woman.

> "—— I'll lock up all the gates of love,
> And on my eyelids shall conjecture hang,
> To turn all beauty into thoughts of harm,
> And never more shall it be gracious."

Sir Charles Bingley and Colonel Belgrave, in early life, had contracted a friendship for each other which time had strengthened in one, but reduced to a mere shadow in the other. On meeting the Colonel unexpectedly in town, Sir Charles had informed him of his intentions relative to Amanda. His heart throbbed at the mention of her name. He had long endeavored to discover her. Pride, love, and revenge, were all concerned in the accomplishment of his designs, which disappointment had only stimulated. He was one of those determined characters which never relinquish a purpose, "though heaven and earth that purpose crossed." The confidence Sir Charles reposed in him, joined to his warm and unsuspicious temper, convinced him he would be credulous enough to believe any imputation he should cast on Amanda. He therefore lost no time in contriving this execrable scheme, without the smallest compunction for destroying the reputation of an innocent girl, or injuring the happiness of an amiable man.

Removed from the protection of her father, he believed his destined victim could not escape the snare he should spread for her; and as a means of expediting his success, under the appearance of feeling, urged Sir Charles's return to Ireland.

The easy credit which Sir Charles gave to the vile allegations of Belgrave, cannot be wondered at, when his long intimacy and total ignorance of his real character are considered. He knew Belgrave to be a gay man, but he never imagined him to be a hardened libertine. Besides, he never could have supposed any man would have been so audacious, or sufficiently base, as to make such an assertion as Belgrave had done against Amanda, without truth for its support.

The errors of his friend, though the source of unspeakable anguish to him, were more pitied than condemned, as he rather believed they proceeded from the impetuosity of passion, than the deliberation of design, and that they were long since sincerely repented of.

Amanda could not be forgotten; the hold she had on his heart could not easily be shaken off; and like the recording angel, he was often tempted to drop a tear over her faults, and obliterate them for ever from his memory. This, however, was considered the mere suggestion of weakness, and he ordered immediate preparations to be made for his return to Ireland.

CHAPTER XXVIII.

> "Oh how this tyrant doubt torments my breast!
> My thoughts, like birds, who frighted from their rest,
> Around the place where all was hushed before,
> Flutter, and hardly settle any more."—OTWAY.

LORD MORTIMER, distressed by the indisposition of Amanda, hastened, at an earlier hour than usual (for his morning visits), to Portman Square, and was ushered into Lady Euphrasia's dressing-room, where she and Miss Malcolm, who had continued with her the preceding night, were sitting tête-à-tête at breakfast. His lordship was a welcome visitor, but it was soon obvious on whose account he had made his appearance, for scarcely were the usual compliments over, ere he inquired about Miss Fitzalan.

Lady Euphrasia said she was still unwell, and had not yet left her apartment. "She has not recovered her surprise of last night," exclaimed Miss Malcolm, with a malicious smile. "What surprise?" asked his lordship. "Dear me," replied Miss Malcolm, "was not your lordship present at the time she met Colonel Belgrave?" "No," said Lord Mortimer, changing color, "I was not present. But what has Colonel Belgrave to say to Miss Fitzalan?" asked he, in an agitated voice. "That is a question your lordship must put to the young lady herself," answered Miss Malcolm. "Now, I declare," cried Lady Euphrasia, addressing her friend, "'tis very probable her illness did not proceed from seeing Colonel Belgrave—you know she never mentioned being acquainted with him, though her father was his tenant in Devonshire."

Lord Mortimer grew more disturbed, and rose abruptly.

Lady Euphrasia mentioned their intention of going that evening to the play, and invited him to be of the party. He accepted her invitation, and retired.

His visible distress was a source of infinite mirth to the young ladies, which they indulged the moment he quitted the room. The circumstance relative to Belgrave, the Marchioness had informed them of, as she and Lady Greystock were near Amanda when she met him.

Lord Mortimer was unhappy. The mind which has once harbored suspicion will, from the most trivial circumstance, be tempted again to give admission to the unpleasing guest—nor was it a trivial circumstance which discomposed the too susceptible heart of Mortimer. The sudden illness of Amanda, her extraordinary agitation, her eagerness to quit the room, the close, though silent attendance of Belgrave—all these, I say, when recalled to recollection, gave an air of probability to Miss Malcolm's insinuation, that her disorder was occasioned by seeing him. From residing more constantly in England than Sir Charles Bingley had done, he had had more opportunities of learning Belgrave's real character, which he knew to be that of a professed libertine. It was strange, he thought, that when Amanda informed him she once resided in Devonshire, she should concea her father being the Colonel's tenant He began to think her reluctance to a clandestine and immediate marriage might have proceeded from some secret attachment, and not from the strict adherence to filial duty, which had exalted her so much in his opinion.

Yet the idea was scarcely formed, ere he endeavored to suppress it. He started, as if from an uneasy dream, and wondered how he could have conceived this, or any other idea, injurious to Amanda. He felt a degree of remorse at having allowed her, for a moment, to be lessened in his opinion—her tenderness, her purity, he said to himself, could not be feigned; no, she was a treasure greater than he deserved to possess; nor would he, like a wayward son of error, fling away the happiness he had so long desired to obtain.

The calm this resolution produced was but transient. Doubts had been raised, and doubts could not be banished; he was inclined to think them unjust, yet had not power to dispel them. Vainly he applied to the ideas which had heretofore been such consolatory resources of comfort to him—namely, that his father would consent to his union with Amanda, through the interference of his aunt, and the felicity he should enjoy in that union. An unusual heaviness clung to his heart, which, like a gloomy sky, cast a shade of sadness over every prospect. Thoughtful and pensive he reached home, just as Sir Charles Bingley was entering the door, who informed him he had just received a note from Lord Cherbury, desiring his immediate presence.

Lord Mortimer attended him to the Earl, who acquainted him, that he had received a letter from Mr. Fitzalan, in which he expressed a warm sense of the honor Sir Charles did his family, by addressing Miss Fitzalan; and that to have her united to a character so truly estimable, would give him the truest happiness, from the conviction that hers would be secured by such a union "He has written to his daughter expressing his sentiments," continued Lord Cherbury. "I have therefore no doubt, Sir Charles, but that everything will succeed as you wish." "I am sorry, my Lord," cried Sir Charles, with an agitated voice, and a cheek flushed with emotion, "that I ever troubled your lordship in this affair, as I have now, and for ever, relinquished all ideas of a union with Miss Fitzalan." "The resolution is really somewhat extraordinary and sudden," replied the Earl, "after the conversation which so lately passed between us." "Adopted, however, my Lord, from a thorough conviction that happiness could never be attained in a union with that young lady." Sir Charles's tenderness for Amanda was still undiminished; he wished to preserve her from censure, and thus proceeded: "Your lordship must allow I could have little chance of happiness in allying myself to a woman who has resolutely and uniformly treated me with indifference. Passion blinded my reason when I addressed your lordship relative to Miss Fitzalan; but its mists are now dispersed, and sober reflection obliges me to relinquish a scheme, whose accomplishment could not possibly give me satisfaction." "You are certainly the best judge of your own actions, Sir Charles," replied the Earl "My acting in the affair proceeded from a wish to serve you, as well as from my friendship for Captain Fitzalan. I must suppose your conduct will never disparage your own honor, or cast a slight upon Miss Fitzalan." "That, my Lord, you may be assured of," said Sir Charles, with some warmth; "my actions and their motives have hitherto, and will ever, I trust, bear the strictest investigation. I cannot retire without thanking your lordship for the interest you took in my favor. Had things succeeded as I then hoped and expected, I cannot deny but I should have been much happier than I am at present." He then bowed and retired.

Lord Mortimer had listened with astonishment to Sir Charles's relinquishment of Amanda. Like his father, he thought it a sudden and extraordinary resolution. He was before jealous of Amanda's love; he was now jealous of her honor. The agitation of Sir Charles seemed to imply even a cause more powerful than her coldness for resigning her. He recollected that the Baronet and the Colonel were intimate friends. Distracted by apprehensions, he rushed out of the house, and overtook Sir Charles ere he had quitted the square.

"Why, Bingley," cried he, with affected gaiety, "I thought you too valiant a knight to be easily overcome by despair; and that without first trying every effort to win her favor, you never would give up a fair lady you had set your heart on." "I leave such efforts for your lordship," replied Sir Charles, "or those who have equal patience" "But, seriously, Bingley, I think this sudden resignation of Miss Fitzalan somewhat strange. Why, last night I could have sworn you were as much attached to her as ever. From Lord Cherbury's friendship for Captain Fitzalan, I think her, in some degree, under his protection and mine. And as the particularity of your attentions attracted observation, I think your abruptly withdrawing them requires explanation." "As Lord Cherbury was the person I applied to relative to Miss Fitzalan," exclaimed Sir Charles, "and as he was satisfied with the motive I assigned for my conduct, be assured, my Lord, I shall never give another to you." "Your words," retorted Lord Mortimer, with warmth, "imply that there was another motive for your conduct than the one you avowed. What horrid inference may not be drawn from such an insinuation? Oh! Sir Charles! reputation is a fragile flower, which the slightest breath may injure." "My Lord, if Miss Fitzalan's reputation is never injured but by my means, it will ever continue unsullied."

"I cannot, indeed," resumed Lord Mortimer, "style myself her guardian, but I consider myself her friend: and from the feelings of friendship, shall ever evince my interest in her welfare, and resent any conduct which can possibly render her an object of censure to any being." "Allow me to ask your lordship one question," cried Sir Charles, "and promise, on your honor, to answer it." "I do promise," said Lord Mortimer. "Then, my Lord, did you ever really wish I should succeed with Miss Fitzalan?"

Lord Mortimer colored. "You expect, Sir Charles, I shall answer you on my honor? Then, really, I never did." "Your passions and mine," continued Sir Charles, "are impetuous. We had better check them in time, lest they lead us to lengths we may hereafter repent of. Of Miss Fitzalan's fame, be assured, no man can be more tenacious than I should. I love her with the truest ardor. Her acceptance of my proposals would have given me felicity. My suddenly withdrawing them can never injure her, when I declare my motive for so doing was her indifference. Lord Cherbury is satisfied with the reason I have assigned for resigning her. He is conscious that no man of sensibility could experience happiness with a woman in whose heart he knew he had no interest This, I suppose, your lordship will also allow." "Certainly," replied Lord Mortimer. "Then, it strikes me, my Lord, that it is your conduct, not mine, which has a tendency to injure Miss Fitzalan. That it is your words, not mine, which convey an insinuation against her. You really appear as if conscious some other cause existed, which would have made me relinquish her, without the one I have already assigned for doing so."

Lord Mortimer was instantly convinced of the justice of what Sir Charles said. He began to fear his warmth would really prove prejudicial to Amanda, betray the doubts which had obtruded on his mind, and communicate them to those who might not be equally influenced by tenderness and delicacy to conceal them.

"You are right, Sir Charles," said he, "in what you have said; "passion, like a bad advocate, hurts the cause in which it is engaged. From my knowledge of your character, I should have been convinced your honor would have prevented any improper conduct. You are going to Ireland. Permit me, Sir Charles, to offer you my best wishes for your future happiness."

Sir Charles took Lord Mortimer's extended hand. He respected and esteemed his lordship, and a mutual interchange of good wishes took place between them, as this was the last interview they expected for a long time.

The indisposition of Amanda was more of the mental than the bodily kind, and on the first intimation of a party to the play she agreed to join it, in hopes the amusement would remove her dejection. Her father's letter, relative to Sir Charles Bingley, had given her some uneasiness; but as he left her free to act she contented herself with using the negative he allowed her, by a solemn resolution of never acting contrary to his inclinations, and answered his letter to this purpose.

Lord Mortimer and Freelove attended the ladies in the evening to the play. His lordship found an opportunity of tenderly inquiring after Amanda's health. When they were seated in the house, he perceived a lady in another box to whom he wished to speak, and accordingly left his party. This lady offered him a seat by herself, which he accepted. She was a stranger to Amanda, young, and extremely beautiful. Amanda, however, had none of that foolish weakness which could make her dread a rival in every new face, or feel uneasiness at Lord Mortimer's attention to any woman but herself. Assured that his affections for her were founded on the basis of esteem, and that she should retain them while worthy of esteem, she could, without being discomposed by the agreeable conversation he appeared to be enjoying, fix her attention on the stage; so entirely, indeed, that she observed not, from time to time, the glances Lord Mortimer directed towards her. Not so his fair companion. She noticed the wanderings of his eyes, and her own involuntarily pursued their course. She was speaking at the moment, but suddenly stopped, and Lord Mortimer saw her change color. He turned pale himself, and, in a faltering voice, asked her, "if she knew the lady she had been long looking at?" "Know her?" replied she; "oh, heavens! but too well."

Lord Mortimer trembled universally, and was compelled to have recourse to his handkerchief to hide his emotion.

It was by Adela, the lovely and neglected wife of Belgrave, he was sitting. She had been a short time in London, and her acquaintance with Lord Mortimer commenced at a ball, where she had danced with him. He was not one of those kind of men who, when in love, had neither eyes nor ears but for the object of that love. He could see perfections in other women besides his Amanda, and was particularly pleased with Mrs. Belgrave. He instantly perceived she knew Amanda; also, that that knowledge was attended with pain. The well-known profligacy of her husband intruded on his memory, and he shuddered at the dreadful thoughts which rose in his mind.

Curiosity had directed the eyes of Adela to Amanda, but admiration, and an idea of having somewhere before seen her face, riveted them upon her; at last the picture Oscar Fitzalan had shown occurred to her recollection, and she was immediately convinced it was no other than the original of that picture she now saw. Shocked at the sight of a person who, as she thought, had stepped (though innocently) between her and felicity, and distressed by the emotions which past scenes, thus recalled, gave rise to, she entreated Lord Mortimer to conduct her from the box, that she might return home.

He complied with her request, but stopped in the lobby, and entreated her to tell him "where she had known the lady she had so attentively regarded." Adela blushed, and would, if possible, have evaded the question; but the earnestness of his lordship's manner compelled her to answer it. She said "she had no personal knowledge of the lady, but recollected her face, from having seen her picture with a gentleman." "And who was the gentleman?" asked Lord Mortimer, with a forced smile and a faltering voice. "That," replied Adela, with involuntary quickness, "I will not tell." "I should apologize, indeed," cried Lord Mortimer, recollecting himself, "for a curiosity which may appear impertinent." He led her to a chair, and deliberated whether he should not follow her example in quitting the house.

Miss Malcolm had first made him uneasy: uneasiness introduced doubts which Sir Charles Bingley had increased, and Mrs. Belgrave almost confirmed. He dreaded a horrid confirmation of his fears; the picture, like Othello's handkerchief, was a source of unspeakable anguish. The agitation that Mrs. Belgrave had betrayed on mentioning it, joined to her concealment of the gentleman she had seen it with, tempted him to believe he was no other than her husband.

Yet, that he might not be accused of yielding rashly to jealousy, he resolved to confine his suspicions, like his pangs, to his own bosom, except assured they were well founded. A little time, he supposed, would determine the opinion he should form of Amanda. If he found she encouraged Belgrave, he resolved to leave her without an explanation; if, on the contrary, he saw that she avoided him, he meant to mention the circumstance of the picture to her, yet so as not to hurt her feelings, and be regulated by her answer relative to his future conduct. He returned, at last, to the box, and procured a seat behind her. He had not occupied it long ere Colonel Belgrave (who, from a retired part of the house, where he sat with some female friends, had observed Amanda) entered the next box, and made his way to the pillar against which she leaned. He endeavored to catch her eyes, but the noise he made on entering put her on her guard, and she instantly averted her face. Her embarrassment was visible to her party, and they all, Lord Mortimer excepted, enjoyed it. Scarcely could he refrain from chastising the audacity of Belgrave's looks, who continued to gaze on Amanda, though he could not see her face. Nothing but the discovery which such a step would produce could have prevented his lordship, in his present irritable state of mind, from chastising what he deemed the height of insolence.

At last the hour came for relieving Amanda from a situation extremely painful to her. As Lord Mortimer sat next the Marchioness, he was compelled to offer her his hand. Freelove led Lady Euphrasia; Lady Greystock and Miss Malcolm followed her, and Amanda was the last who quitted the box. A crowd in the lobby impeded their progress. Amanda was close behind the Marchioness, when Belgrave forced his way to her, and attempted to take her hand at the very moment Lord Mortimer turned to look at her, who heard him say, "Dear, though unkind, Amanda, why this cruel change in your conduct?"

The eyes of Mortimer flashed fire. "Miss Fitzalan," said he, in a voice trembling through passion, "if you will accept my arm, I will make way for you, or at least secure you from impertinence." Amanda, though trembling and confounded by his looks, hesitated not to accept his offer. Belgrave knew his words alluded to him. At present, however, he resolved not to resent them, convinced, that if he did, his views on Amanda would be defeated. From that moment her beauty was not more powerful in stimulating his designs than his desire of revenge on Lord Mortimer. He saw he was fondly attached to Amanda, and he believed his proud heart would feel no event so afflictive as that which should deprive him of her.

Lord Mortimer handed Amanda in silence to the carriage; he was pressed to return to supper, but refused. The ladies found the Marquis and Lord Cherbury together. Amanda retired to her chamber immediately after supper; the presence of Belgrave had increased the dejection which she hoped the amusements of the theatre would have dissipated; she now indeed longed for the period when she should be entitled to the protection of Lord Mortimer; when she should no longer dread the audacity or stratagems of Belgrave. Lord Cherbury, on her retiring, expressed his regret at her coldness to Sir Charles Bingley, by which she had lost a most honorable and advantageous attachment.

This was an opportunity not to be neglected by the Marchioness, for commencing her operations against Fitzalan. A glance to Lady Greystock was the signal to begin.

"To those,' said Lady Greystock, "who are ignorant of Miss Fitzalan's real motives for refusing Sir Charles, it must appear, no doubt, extraordinary; but ambitious people are not easily satisfied; indeed, I cannot blame her so much for entertaining aspiring notions as those who instilled them into her mind."

Lord Cherbury stared, and requested an explanation of her words.

"Why, I declare, my Lord," cried she, "I do not know but that it will be more friendly to explain than conceal my meaning. When once informed of the young lady's views, your lordship may be able to convince her of that fallacy, and prevail on her not to lose another good opportunity of settling herself in consequence of them; in short, my Lord, Miss Fitzalan, prompted by her father, has cast her eyes on Lord Mortimer. Presuming on your friendship, he thought a union between them might easily be accomplished. I do not believe Lord Mortimer, at first, gave any encouragement to their designs; but when the girl was continually thrown in his way, it was impossible not to notice her at last. I really expressed a thorough disapprobation to her coming to London, knowing their motives for desiring the excursion, but her father never ceased persecuting me till I consented to take her under my protection." "Upon my word," cried the Marquis, who was not of the ladies' privy council, though if he had it is probable he would not have objected to their schemes, "Captain Fitzalan must have had some such motive as this Lady Greystock has mentioned for sending his daughter to London, or else he would not have been so ridiculous as to put himself at the expense of fitting her out for company she has no right to enter." "I never thought," exclaimed Lord Cherbury, whose mind was irritated to the most violent degree of resentment against his injured friend, "that Captain Fitzalan could have acted with such duplicity. He knew the views I entertained for my son, and there is a mean treachery in his attempting to counteract them." "Nay, my Lord," said Lady Greystock, "you are a father yourself, and must make allowances for the anxiety of a parent to establish a child." "No, madam," he replied; "I can make no allowance for a deviation from integrity, or for a sacrifice of honor and gratitude at the shrine of interest. The subject has discomposed me, and I must beg to be excused for abruptly retiring; nothing, indeed, I believe, can wound one so severely as deceit, where one reposed implicit confidence."

The ladies were enraptured at the success of their scheme. The passion of Lord Cherbury could scarcely be smothered in their presence. On the head of Fitzalan they knew it would burst with full violence. They did not mention Belgrave; relative to him they resolved to affect profound ignorance.

The passions of Lord Cherbury were impetuous. He had, as I have already hinted, secret motives for desiring a connection between his family and the Marquis's; and the idea of that desire being defeated drove him almost to distraction. He knew his son's passions, though not so easily irritated as his own were, when once irritated, equally violent. To remonstrate with him concerning Miss Fitzalan, he believed, would be unavailing; he therefore resolved, if possible, to have her removed out of his way ere he apprised him of the discovery he had made of his attachment. He entertained not a doubt of Lady Greystock's veracity; from his general knowledge of mankind, he believed self the predominant consideration in every breast. His feelings were too violent not to seek an immediate vent, and ere he went to bed, he wrote a bitter and reproachful letter to Fitzalan, which concluded with an entreaty, or rather a command, to send without delay for his daughter. A dreadful stroke this for poor Fitzalan.

> "After all his wanderings round this world of care
> And all his griefs,"

He hoped he had at last found a spot where his latter days might close in tranquillity.

The innocent Amanda was received the next morning with smiles by those who were preparing a plot for her destruction.

Whilst at breakfast, a servant informed Lady Greystock a young woman wanted to speak to her. "Who is she?" asked her ladyship; "did she not send up her name?" "No, my Lady; but she said she had particular business with your ladyship."

The Marchioness directed she might be shown up; and a girl about seventeen was accordingly ushered into the room. Her figure was delicate, and her face interesting, not only from its innocence, but the strong expression of melancholy diffused over it. She appeared trembling with confusion and timidity, and the poverty of her apparel implied the source of her dejection.

"So, child," said Lady Greystock, after surveying her from head to foot, "I am told you have business with me." "Yes, madam," replied she, in an accent so low as scarcely to be heard; "my father, Captain Rushbrook, desired me to deliver a letter to your ladyship."

She presented it, and endeavored to screen herself from the scrutinizing and contemptuous glances of Lady Euphrasia by pulling her hat over her face.

"I wonder, child," said Lady Greystock, as she opened the letter, "what your father can write to me about. I don't suppose it can be about the affair he mentioned the other day. Why, really," continued she, after she had perused it, "I believe he takes me for a fool. I am astonished, after his insolent conduct, how he can possibly have the assurance to make application to me for relief. No, no, child, he neglected the opportunity he had of securing me his friend. 'Twould really be a sin to give him the power of bringing up his family in idleness. No, no, child, he must learn you, and the other little dainty misses he has, to do something for yourselves."

The poor girl blushed; a tear trembled in her eye; she tried to suppress it, but it forced its way, and dropped into her bosom. Amanda, inexpressibly shocked, could support the scene no longer. She retired precipitately, and descended to the parlor. Sympathy, as well as compassion, made her feel for this daughter of affliction, for she herself knew what it was to feel the "insolence of prosperity, the proud man's scorn, and all those ills which patient merit of the unworthy takes."

In a few minutes Miss Rushbrook quitted the drawing-room, and stopped in the hall to wipe away her tears. Amanda had been watching for her, and now appeared. She started, and was hurrying away, when Amanda caught her hand, and leading her softly into the parlor, endeavored, with angelic sweetness, to calm her emotion. Surprised at this unexpected attention, and overcome by her feelings, the poor girl sunk on her chair, and dropping her head on Amanda's bosom, wet it with a shower of tears, as she exclaimed: "Alas! my unfortunate parents, how can I return to behold your misery? The grave is the only refuge for you and your wretched children!" "You must not encourage such desponding thoughts," said Amanda. "Providence, all bounteous and all powerful, is able in a short time to change the gloomiest scene into one of brightness. Tell me," she continued, after a pause, "where do you reside?" "At Kensington." "Kensington!" repeated Amanda. "Surely, in your present situation, you are unable to take such a walk." "I must attempt it, however," replied Miss Rushbrook.

Amanda walked from her to the window, revolving a scheme which had just darted into her mind. "If you know any house," said she, "where you could stay for a short time, I would call on you in a carriage, and leave you at home."

This offer was truly pleasing to the poor weak trembling girl, but she modestly declined it, from the fear of giving trouble. Amanda besought her not to waste time in such unnecessary scruples, but to give her the desired information. She accordingly informed her there was a haberdasher's in Bond Street, mentioning the name, where she could stay till called for.

This point settled, Amanda, fearful of being surprised, conducted her softly to the hall-door, and immediately returned to the drawing-room, where she found Lady Euphrasia just beginning Rushbrook's letter, for her mother's amusement. Its style evidently denoted the painful conflicts there were between pride and distress, ere the former could be sufficiently subdued, to allow an application for relief to the person who occasioned the latter. The sight of a tender and beloved wife, languishing in the arms of sickness, and surrounded by a family, under the pressure of the severest want, had forced him to a step, which, on his own account, no necessity could have compelled him to take. He and his family, he said, had drank of the cup of misery to the very dregs. He waived the claims of justice; he only asserted those of humanity, in his present application to her ladyship; and these, he flattered himself, she would allow. He had sent a young petitioner in his behalf, whose tearful eye, whose faded cheek, were sad evidences of the misery he described.

The Marchioness declared she was astonished at his insolence in making such an application, and Lady Euphrasia protested the letter was the most ridiculous stuff she had ever read.

Amanda, in this, as well as in many other instances, differed from her ladyship; but her opinion, like a little project she had in view about the Rushbrooks, was carefully concealed.

Out of the allowance her father made her for clothes and other expenses about ten guineas remained, which she had intended laying out in the purchase of some ornaments for her appearance at a ball, to be given in the course of the ensuing week by the Duchess of B——, and, for which, at the time of invitation, Lord Mortimer had engaged her for his partner. To give up going to this ball, to consecrate to charity the money devoted to vanity, was her project; and most fortunate did she deem the application of Rushbrook, ere her purchase was made, and she consequently prevented from giving her mite. Her soul revolted from the inhumanity of the Marchioness, her daughter, and Lady Greystock. Exempt from the calamities of want themselves, they forgot the pity due to those calamities in others. If this coldness, this obduracy, she cried, within herself, is the effect of prosperity; if thus it closes the avenues of benevolence and compassion, oh! never may the dangerous visitor approach me—for ill should I think the glow of compassion and sensibility exchanged for all its gaudy pleasures.

The ladies had mentioned their intention of going to an auction, where, to use Lady Euphrasia's phrase, "they expected to see all the world." Amanda excused herself from being of the party, saying, "she wanted to make some purchases in the city." Her excuse was readily admitted, and when they retired to their respective toilets, she sent for a coach, and being prepared against it come, immediately stepped into it, and was driven to Bond Street, where she found Miss Rushbrook, with trembling anxiety, waiting her arrival.

On their way to Kensington, the tenderness of Amanda at once conciliated the affection, and gained the entire confidence of her young companion. She related the little history of her parents' sorrows. Her father, on returning from America, with his wife and six children, had been advised by Mr. Heathfield, the friend who had effected a reconciliation between him and his uncle, to commence a suit against Lady Greystock, on the presumption that the will, by which she enjoyed Sir Geoffry's fortune, was illegally executed. He offered him his purse to carry on the suit, and his house for an habitation. Rushbrook gratefully and gladly accepted both offers, and having disposed of his commission, to discharge some present demands against him, he and his family took up their residence under Mr. Heathfield's hospitable roof. In the midst of the felicity enjoyed beneath it, in the midst of the hopes their own sanguine tempers, and the flattering suggestions of the lawyers had excited, a violent fever carried off their benevolent friend, ere a will was executed, in which he had promised largely to consider Rushbrook. His heir, narrow and illiberal, had long feared that his interest would be hurt by the affection he entertained for Rushbrook; and, as if in revenge for the pain this fear had given, the moment he had the power he showed his malignant disposition, sold all the furniture of the house at Kensington, and as a great favor told Rushbrook he might continue in it till the expiration of the half year, when it was to be given up to the landlord. The lawyers understanding the state of his finances, soon informed him he could no longer expect their assistance. Thus, almost in one moment, did all his pleasing prospects vanish, and,

> "Like the baseless fabric of a vision,
> Left not a rack behind."

As a duty he owed his family, he tried whether Lady Greystock would make a compromise between justice and avarice, and afford him some means of support. Her insolence and inhumanity shocked him to the soul; and as he left her presence, he resolved never to enter it again, or apply to her. This last resolution, however, only continued till the distresses of the family grew so great as to threaten their existence, particularly that of his wife, who, overpowered by grief, had sunk into a languishing illness, which every day increased for want of proper assistance.

In hopes of procuring her some, he was tempted again to apply to Lady Greystock. The youth and innocence of his daughter would, he thought, if anything could do it, soften her flinty heart. Besides, he believed that pleasure, at finding his pretensions to the fortune entirely withdrawn, would influence her to administer from it to his wants.

"We have," said Miss Rushbrook, as she concluded her simple narration, "tried, and been disappointed in our last resource What will become of us, I know not; we have long been strangers to the comforts, but even the necessaries of life we cannot now procure." "Comfort," cried Amanda, "often arrives when least expected. To despair, is to doubt the goodness of a Being who has promised to protect all his creatures."

The carriage had now reached Kensington, and within a few yards of Rushbrook's habitation. Amanda stopped it. She took Miss Rushbrook's hand, and as she slipped a ten pound note into it, exclaimed: "I trust the period is not far distant, when the friendship we have conceived for each other may be cultivated under more fortunate auspices."

Miss Rushbrook opened the folded paper. She started, and "the hectic of a moment flushed her cheek." "Oh! madam!" she cried, "your goodness," tears impeded her further utterance.

"Do not distress me," said Amanda, again taking her hand, "by mentioning such a trifle; was my ability equal to my inclination, I should blush to offer it to your acceptance. As it is, consider it as but as the foretaste of the bounty which heaven has, I doubt not, in store for you."

She then desired the door to be opened, and told her companion she would no longer detain her. Miss Rushbrook affectionately kissed her hand, and exclaimed, "You look like an angel, and your goodness is correspondent to your looks. I will not, madam, refuse your bounty. I accept it with gratitude, for those dearer to me than myself. But ah! may I not indulge a hope of seeing you again. You are so kind, so gentle, madam, that every care is lulled into forgetfulness whilst conversing with you."

"I shall certainly see you again as soon as possible," replied Amanda.

Miss Rushbrook then quitted the carriage, which Amanda ordered back to town, and bid the coachman drive as fast as possible. They had not proceeded far, when the traces suddenly gave way, and the man was obliged to dismount, and procure assistance from a public-house on the road, in repairing them. This occasioned a delay, which greatly distressed Amanda. She wished to get home before the ladies, lest, if this was not the case, her long absence should make Lady Greystock, who was remarkably inquisitive, inquire the reason of it; and to tell her she had a strong objection, convinced, as she was, that her ladyship's knowing she relieved objects so extremely disagreeable to her, would occasion a quarrel between them, which would either render a longer residence together impossible or highly disagreeable. And to leave London at the present crisis, when everything relative to Lord Mortimer was drawing to a conclusion, was not to be thought of without the greatest pain.

At length the coachman remounted his box, and the velocity with which he drove, flattered her with the hope of reaching home as soon as she wished. Tranquillized by this hope, she again indulged her imagination with ideas of the comfort her little bounty had probably given Rushbrook and his dejected family. So sweet to her soul was the secret approbation which crowned her charity; so preferable to any pleasure she could have experienced at a ball, that even the disappointment she believed Lord Mortimer would feel from her declining it, was overlooked in the satisfaction she felt from the action she had performed. She was convinced he would inquire her reason for not going, which she determined at present to conceal. It would appear like ostentation, she thought, to say that the money requisite for her appearance at the ball was expended in charity, and perhaps excite his generosity in a manner which delicacy at present forbade her allowing.

She asked the footman who handed her from the carriage whether the ladies were returned; and on being answered in the affirmative, inquired the hour, and learned it was just dinner time. Flurried by this intelligence she hastened to her chamber, followed by the maid appointed to attend her, who said Lady Greystock had inquired for her as soon as she came home. Amanda dressed herself with unusual expedition, and repaired to the drawing-room, where, in addition to the family party, she found Lord Mortimer, Freelove, Miss Malcolm, and some other ladies and gentlemen assembled.

"Bless me, child," said Lady Greystock the moment she entered the room, "where have you been the whole day?" "I declare, Miss Fitzalan," exclaimed Lady Euphrasia, "I believe you stole a march somewhere upon us this morning." "Well," cried Miss Malcolm, laughing, "your ladyship must know that people generally have some important reason for stolen marches which they do not choose to divulge."

Amanda treated this malicious insinuation with the silent contempt it merited; and on Lady Greystock's again asking her where she had been, said, in a low hesitating voice, "in the city."

"In the city!" repeated Lord Mortimer.

This sudden exclamation startled her. She looked at him, and perceived him regarding her with the most scrutinizing earnestness. She blushed deeply, as if detected in a falsehood, and immediately bent her eyes to the ground.

The conversation now changed, but it was sometime ere Amanda's confusion subsided.

Lord Mortimer, indeed, had a reason for his exclamation she little thought of. He had met the Marchioness and her companions, by appointment, at the auction, but soon grew weary of his situation, which the presence of Amanda could alone have rendered tolerable. He pleaded business as an excuse for withdrawing, and hurrying home, ordered his phaeton, and proceeded towards Kensington. As he passed the coach in which Amanda sat, at the time the traces were mending, he carelessly looked into it, and directly recognised her. Lady Euphrasia had informed him she excused herself from their party on account of some business in the city. He never heard of her having any acquaintance in or about Kensington, and was at once alarmed and surprised by discovering her. He drove to some distance from the carriage, and as soon as it began to move, pursued it with equal velocity till it reached town, and then giving his phaeton in charge to the servant, followed it on foot, till he saw Amanda alight from it at the Marquis of Roslin's. Amanda had escaped seeing his lordship by a profound meditation in which she was engaged at the moment, as she pensively leaned against the side of the coach. Lord Mortimer walked back with increased disorder to meet his phaeton. As he approached it, he saw Colonel Belgrave by it, on horseback, admiring the horses, which were remarkably fine, and asking to whom they belonged. His acquaintance with the Colonel had hitherto never exceeded more than a passing bow. Now prompted by an irresistible impulse, he saluted him familiarly; inquired "whether he had had a pleasant ride that morning, and how far he had been." "No farther than Kensington," replied the Colonel.

This answer was confirmation strong to all the fears of Lord Mortimer. He turned pale, dropped the reins which he had taken, with an intention of remounting, and, without even noticing the Colonel, flew from the place, and arrived at home almost in a state of distraction. He was engaged to dine at the Marquis's, but in the first violence of his feelings, resolved on sending an apology. Ere the servant, however, summoned for that purpose had entered his apartment, he changed his resolution. "I will go," said he; "though appearances are against her, she may, perhaps," (and he tried to derive some comfort from the idea), "be able satisfactorily to account for her being at Kensington."

Tortured by conflicting passions, alternately hoping and doubting, he arrived in Portman Square.

Lady Greystock and Lady Euphrasia dwelt with wonder on the length of Amanda's morning excursion. When she entered the room, he thought she appeared embarrassed; and that, on Lady Greystock's addressing her, this embarrassment increased. But when she said she had been in the city, her duplicity, as he termed it, appeared so monstrous to him, that he could not forbear an involuntary repetition of her words. So great, indeed, was the indignation it excited in his breast, that he could scarcely forbear reproaching her as the destroyer of his and her own felicity. Her blush appeared to him, not the ingenuous coloring of innocence, but the glow of shame and guilt. It was evident to him that she had seen Belgrave that morning; that he was the occasion of all the mystery which had appeared in her conduct, and that it was the knowledge of the improper influence he had over her heart which made Sir Charles Bingley so suddenly resign her.

"Gracious Heaven!" said he to himself, "who, that looked upon Amanda, could ever suppose duplicity harbored in her breast? Yet that too surely it is, I have every reason to suppose. Yet a little longer I will bear a torturing state of suspense, nor reveal my doubts till thoroughly convinced they are well founded."

He sat opposite to her at dinner, and his eyes were directed towards her with that tender sadness which we feel on viewing a beloved object we know ourselves on the point of losing for ever.

His melancholy was quickly perceived by the penetrating Marchioness and Lady Euphrasia. They saw, with delight, that the poison of suspicion, infused into his mind, was already beginning to operate. They anticipated the success of all their schemes. Their spirits grew uncommonly elevated; and Lady Euphrasia determined, whenever she had the power, to revenge, on the susceptible nature of Mortimer, all the uneasiness he had made her suffer, and to add, as far as malice could add to it, to the misery about to be the lot of Amanda.

The dejection of Lord Mortimer was also observed by Amanda. It excited her fears and affected her sensibility. She dreaded that his aunt had refused complying with his request relative to her interference with his father, or that the Earl had been urging him to an immediate union with Lady Euphrasia. Perhaps he now wavered between love and duty. The thought struck a cold damp upon her heart. Yet no, cried she, it cannot be; if inclined to change, Lord Mortimer would at once have informed me.

In the evening there was a large addition to the party; but Lord Mortimer sat pensively apart from the company. Amanda, by chance, procured a seat next his. His paleness alarmed her, and she could not forbear hinting her fears that he was ill.

"I am ill, indeed," sighed he, heavily. He looked at her as he spoke, and beheld her regarding him with the most exquisite tenderness. But the period was past for receiving delight from such an appearance of affection; an affection, he had reason to believe was never more than feigned for him; and, also, from his emotions when with her, that he should never cease regretting the deception. His passions, exhausted by their own violence, had sunk into a calm, and sadness was the predominant feeling of his soul. Though he so bitterly lamented, he could not, at the moment, have reproached her perfidy. He gazed on her with mournful tenderness, and to the involuntary expression of regret, which dropped from her on hearing he was ill, only replied, by saying, "Ah!

Amanda, the man that really excites your tenderness must be happy."

Amanda, unconscious that any sinister meaning lurked beneath these words, considered them as an acknowledgment of the happiness he himself experienced from being convinced of her regard, and her heart swelled with pleasure at the idea.

Any further conversation between them was interrupted by Miss Malcolm, who, in a laughing manner, seated herself by Lord Mortimer, to rally him, as she said, into good spirits.

CHAPTER XXIX.

> "But yet I say,
> If imputation and strong circumstances,
> Which lead directly to the door of truth,
> Will give you satisfaction, you may have it."—SHAKSPEARE.

ROM that evening, to the day destined for the ball, nothing material happened. On the morning of that day, as Amanda was sitting in the drawing-room with the ladies, Lord Mortimer entered. Lady Euphrasia could talk of nothing else but the approaching entertainment, which, she said, was expected to be the most brilliant thing that had been given that winter.

"I hope your ladyship," said Amanda, who had not yet declared her intention of staying at home, "will be able to-morrow to give me a good description of it." "Why, I suppose," cried Lady Euphrasia, "you do not intend going without being able to see and hear yourself?" "Certainly," replied Amanda, "I should not, but I do not intend going." "Not going to the ball to-night?" exclaimed Lady Euphrasia. "Bless me, child," said Lady Greystock, "what whim has entered your head to prevent your going?" "Dear Lady Greystock," said Lady Euphrasia, in a tone of unusual good humor, internally delighted at Amanda's resolution, "don't tease Miss Fitzalan with questions." "And you really do not go?" exclaimed Lord Mortimer, in an accent expressive of surprise and disappointment. "I really do not, my

Lord." "I declare," said the Marchioness, even more delighted than her daughter at Amanda's resolution, as it favored a scheme she had long been projecting, "I wish Euphrasia was as indifferent about amusement as Miss Fitzalan: here she has been complaining of indisposition the whole morning, yet I cannot prevail on her to give up the ball."

Lady Euphrasia, who never felt in better health and spirits, would have contradicted the Marchioness, had not an expressive glance assured her there was an important motive for this assertion

"May we not hope, Miss Fitzalan," said Lord Mortimer, "that a resolution so suddenly adopted as yours may be as suddenly changed?" "No, indeed, my Lord, nor is it so suddenly formed as you seem to suppose."

Lord Mortimer shuddered as he endeavored to account for it in his own mind; his agony became almost insupportable; he arose and walked to the window where she sat.

"Amanda," said he, in a low voice, "I fear you forget your engagement to me."

Amanda, supposing this alluded to her engagement for the ball, replied, "she had not forgotten it." "For your inability or disinclination to fulfil it, then," said he, "will you not account?" "Most willingly, my Lord." "When?" asked Lord Mortimer, impatiently, for, unable longer to support his torturing suspense, he determined, contrary to his first intention, to come to an immediate explanation relative to Belgrave. "To-morrow, my Lord," replied Amanda, "since you desire it, I will account for not keeping my engagement, and I trust," a modest blush mantling her cheeks as she spoke, "that your lordship will not disapprove of my reasons for declining it."

The peculiar earnestness of his words, Lord Mortimer imagined, had conveyed their real meaning to Amanda

"Till to-morrow, then," sighed he, heavily, "I must bear disquietude."

His regret, Amanda supposed, proceeded from disappointment at not having her company at the ball: she was flattered by it, and pleased at the idea of telling him her real motive for not going, certain it would meet his approbation, and open another source of benevolence to poor Rushbrook

In the evening, at Lady Euphrasia's particular request, she attended at her toilet, and assisted in ornamenting her ladyship At ten she saw the party depart, without the smallest regret for not accompanying them: happy in self-approbation, a delightful calm was diffused over her mind: a treacherous calm, indeed, which, lulling her senses into security, made the approaching storm burst with redoubled violence on her head; it was such a calm as Shakspeare beautifully describes:—

> "We often see against some storm
> A silence in the heavens; the rack stand still,
> The bold winds speechless, and the orb below
> As hush as death."

She continued in Lady Euphrasia's dressing-room, and took up the beautiful and affecting story of Paul and Mary, to amuse herself. Her whole attention was soon engrossed by it; and, with the unfortunate Paul, she was shedding a deluge of tears over the fate of his lovely Mary, when a sudden noise made her hastily turn her head, and with equal horror and surprise, she beheld Colonel Belgrave coming forward. She started up, and was springing to the door, when, rushing between her and it, he caught her in his arms, and forcing her back to the sofa, rudely stopped her mouth.

"Neither cries or struggles, Amanda," said he, "will be availing; without the assistance of a friend, you may be convinced, I could not have entered this house, and the same friend will, you may depend on it, take care that our tête-à-tête is not interrupted."

Amanda shuddered at the idea of treachery; and being convinced, from what he said, she could not expect assistance, endeavored to recover her fainting spirits, and exert all her resolution.

"Your scheme, Colonel Belgrave," said she, "is equally vile and futile. Though treachery may have brought you hither, you must be convinced that, under the Marquis of Roslin's roof, who, by relationship, as well as hospitality, is bound to protect me, you dare not, with impunity, offer me any insult. The Marquis will be at home immediately; if, therefore, you wish to preserve the semblance of honor, retire without further delay." "Not to retire so easily," exclaimed Belgrave, "did I take such pains, or watch so anxiously for this interview. Fear not any insult; but, till I have revealed the purpose of my soul, I will not be forced from you. My love, or rather adoration, has known no abatement by your long concealment; and now that chance has so happily thrown you in my way, I will not neglect using any opportunity it may offer." "Gracious heaven!" said Amanda, while her eyes flashed with indignation, "how can you have the effrontery to avow your insolent intentions—intentions which long since you must have known would ever prove abortive?" "And why, my Amanda," said he, again attempting to strain her to his breast, while she shrunk from his grasp, "why should they prove abortive? why should you be obstinate in refusing wealth, happiness, the sincere, the ardent affection of a man, who, in promoting your felicity, would constitute his own? My life, my fortune, would be at your command: my eternal gratitude would be yours for any trifling sacrifice the world might think you made me. Hesitate no longer about raising yourself to affluence, which, to a benevolent spirit like yours must be so peculiarly pleasing. Hesitate not to secure independence to your father, promotion to your brother; and, be assured, if the connection I formed in an ill-fated hour, deceived by a specious appearance of perfection, should ever be dissolved, my hand, like my heart, shall be yours." "Monster!" exclaimed Amanda, beholding him with horror, "your hand, was it at your disposal, like your other offers, I should spurn with contempt. Cease to torment me," she continued, "lest, in my own defence, I call upon those who have power, as well as inclination, to chastise your insolence. Let this consideration, joined to the certainty that your pursuit must ever prove unavailing, influence your future actions; for, be assured, you are in every respect an object of abhorrence to my soul."

As she spoke, exerting all her strength, she burst from him, and attempted to gain the door. He flung himself between her and it, his face inflamed with passion, and darting the most malignant glances at her.

Terrified by his looks, Amanda tried to avoid him; and when he caught her again in his arms, she screamed aloud. No one appeared; her terror increased.

"Oh, Belgrave!" cried she, trembling, "if you have one principle of honor, one feeling of humanity remaining, retire. I wil pardon and conceal what is past, if you comply with my request." "I distress you, Amanda," said he, assuming a softened accent, "and it wounds me to the soul to do so, though you, cruel and inexorable, care not what pain you occasion me. Hear me calmly, and be assured I shall attempt no action which can offend you."

He led her again to the sofa, and thus continued:—

"Misled by false views, you shun and detest the only man who has had sufficient sincerity to declare openly his intentions; inexperience and credulity have already made you a dupe to artifice. You imagined Sir Charles Bingley was a fervent admirer of yours, when, be assured, in following you he only obeyed the dictates of an egregious vanity, which flattered him with the hope of gaining your regard, and being distinguished by it. Nothing was farther from his thoughts, as he himself confessed to me, than seriously paying his addresses to you; and had you appeared willing, at last, to accept them, be assured he would soon have contrived some scheme to disengage himself from you. The attentions of Lord Mortimer are prompted by a motive much more dangerous than that which instigated Sir Charles. He really admires you, and would have you believe his views are honorable; but beware of his duplicity. He seeks to take advantage of the too great confidence you repose in him. His purpose once accomplished, he would sacrifice you to Lady Euphrasia; and I know enough of her malevolent disposition to be convinced she would enjoy her triumph over so lovely a victim. Ah, my dear Amanda, even beauty and elegance like yours would not, on the generality of mankind, have power to make them forego the advantages annexed to wealth—on Lord Mortimer, particularly, they would fail of that effect. His ambition and avarice are equal to his father's; and though his heart and soul, I am confident, revolt from the mind and person of Lady Euphrasia, he will unite himself to her, for the sake of possessing her fortune, and thus increasing his own power of procuring the gratifications he delights in. As my situation is known, I cannot be accused of deception, and whatever I promise, will be strictly fulfilled. Deliberate therefore no longer, my Amanda, on the course you shall pursue." "No," cried she, "I shall, indeed, no longer deliberate about it."

As she spoke she started from her seat. Belgrave again seized her hand. At this moment a knocking was heard at the hall door, which echoed through the house. Amanda trembled, and Belgrave paused in a speech he had begun. She supposed the Marquis had returned. It was improbable he would come to that room; and even if he did, from his distrustful and malignant temper, she knew not whether she should have reason to rejoice at or regret his presence. But how great was her confusion when, instead of his voice, she heard those of the Marchioness and her party! In a moment the dreadful consequences which might ensue from her present situation rushed upon her mind. By the forced attentions of the Marchioness and Lady Euphrasia, she was not long deceived, and had reason to believe, from the inveterate dislike they bore her, that they would rejoice at an opportunity like the present for traducing her fame; and with horror she saw that appearances, even in the eyes of candor, would be against her. She had positively, and unexpectedly, refused going to the ball. She had expressed delight at the idea of staying at home. Alas! would not all these circumstances be dwelt upon? What ideas might they not excite in Lord Mortimer, who already showed a tendency to jealousy? Half wild at the idea, she clasped her hands together and exclaimed, in a voice trembling with anguish, "Merciful heaven, I am ruined for ever!"

"No, no," cried Belgrave, flinging himself at her feet, "pardon me, Amanda, and I never more will molest you. I see your principles are invincible. I admire, I revere your purity, and never more will I attempt to injure it. I was on the point of declaring so when that cursed knock came to the door. Compose yourself, and consider what can be done in the present emergency. You will be ruined if I am seen with you. The malicious devils you live with would never believe our united asseverations of your innocence. Conceal me, therefore, if possible, till the family are settled; the person who let me in will then secure my retreat, and I swear solemnly never more to trouble you."

Amanda hesitated between the confidence her innocence inspired, and the dread of the unpleasant construction malice might put on her situation. She heard the party ascending the stairs. Fear conquered her reluctance to concealment, and she motioned to

Belgrave to retire to a closet adjoining the dressing-room. He obeyed the motion, and closed the door softly after him.

Amanda, snatching up her book, endeavored to compose herself; but the effort was ineffectual—she trembled universally—nor was her agitation diminished when, from the outside of the door, Lady Euphrasia called to her to open it. She tottered to it, and almost fainted on finding it locked—with difficulty she opened it, and the whole party, followed by the Marquis, entered.

"Upon my word, Miss Fitzalan," said the Marchioness, "you were determined no one should disturb your meditations. I fear we have surprised you; but poor Euphrasia was taken ill at the ball, and we were obliged to return with her." "Miss Fitzalan has not been much better, I believe," said Lady Euphrasia, regarding her attentively. "Good Lord, child!" cried Lady Greystock, "what is the matter with you? why, you look as pale as if you had seen a ghost." "Miss Fitzalan is fond of solitude," exclaimed the Marquis, preventing her replying to Lady Greystock. "When I returned home about an hour ago, I sent to request her company in the parlor, which honor, I assure you, I was refused."

The message, indeed, had been sent, but never delivered to Amanda.

"I assure you, my Lord," said she, "I heard of no such request." "And pray, child, how have you been employed all this time?" asked Lady Greystock. "In reading, madam," faltered out Amanda, while her death-like paleness was succeeded by a deep blush. "You are certainly ill," said Lord Mortimer, who sat beside her, in a voice expressive of regret at the conviction. "You have been indulging melancholy ideas, I fear," continued he softly, and taking her hand, "for surely—surely to-night you are uncommonly affected."

Amanda attempted to speak. The contending emotions of her mind prevented her utterance, and the tears trickled silently down her cheeks. Lord Mortimer saw she wished to avoid notice, yet scarcely could he forbear requesting some assistance for her.

Lady Euphrasia now complained of a violent headache. The Marchioness wanted to ring for remedies. This Lady Euphrasia opposed; at last, as if suddenly recollecting it, she said, "in the closet there was a bottle of eau-de-luce, which she was certain would be of service to her."

At the mention of the closet, the blood ran cold through the veins of Amanda; but when she saw Lady Euphrasia rise to enter it, had death, in its most frightful form, stared her in the face, she could not have betrayed more horror. She looked towards it with a countenance as expressive of wild affright as Macbeth's, when viewing the chair on which the spectre of the murdered Banquo sat. Lord Mortimer observing the disorder of her looks, began to tremble. He grasped her hand with a convulsive motion, and exclaimed:

"Amanda, what means this agitation?"

A loud scream from Lady Euphrasia broke upon their ears, and she rushed from the closet, followed by Belgrave.

"Gracious Heaven!" exclaimed Lord Mortimer, dropping Amanda's hand, and rising precipitately.

Amanda looked around—she beheld every eye fastened on her with amazement and contempt. The shock was too much for her to support. A confused idea darted into her mind that a deep-laid plot had been concerted to ruin her; she faintly exclaimed, "I am betrayed," and sunk back upon the sofa.

Lord Mortimer started at her exclamation. "Oh Heavens!" cried he, as he looked towards her; unable to support the scene that would ensue in consequence of this discovery, he struck his forehead in an agony, and rushed out of the room. In the hall he was stopped by Mrs. Jane, the maid appointed by the Marchioness to attend Amanda.

"Alack-a-day, my Lord," said she, in a whimpering voice, "something dreadful, I am afraid, has happened above stairs. Oh dear! what people suffer sometimes by their good nature. I am sure, if I thought any harm would come of granting Miss Fitzalan's request, she might have begged and prayed long enough, before I would have obliged her." "Did she desire you to bring Colonel Belgrave to this house?" asked Lord Mortimer. "Oh, to be sure she did, my Lord, or how should I ever have thought of such a thing? She has been begging and praying long enough for me to contrive some way of bringing him here; and she told me a piteous story, which would have softened a stone, of his being a sweetheart of hers before he was married." "Merciful powers!" cried Lord Mortimer, clasping his hands together, "how have I been deceived."

He was hurrying away, when Mrs. Jane caught his coat. "I shall lose my place," said she, sobbing, "that I shall, most certainly; for my Lord and Lady never will forgive my bringing any one in such a way into the house. I am sure, I thought no great harm in it, and did it quite from good nature; for, indeed, how could one resist the poor, dear young lady; she cried, and said she only wanted to bid farewell to her dear Belgrave."

Lord Mortimer could hear no more. He shook her from him, and hurried from the house.

Amanda's faculties suffered but a momentary suspension; as she opened her eyes, her composure and fortitude returned.

"I am convinced," said she, rising and advancing to the Marquis, "it will shock your lordship to hear, that it is the treachery of some person under your roof has involved me in my present embarrassing situation. For my own justification, 'tis necessary to acknowledge that I have long been the object of a pursuit from Colonel Belgrave, as degrading to his character as insulting to mine. When he broke so unexpectedly upon me to-night, he declared, even with effrontery declared, he had a friend in this house who gave him access to it. As your guest, my Lord, I may expect your lordship's protection; also that an immediate inquiry be made for the abettor in this scheme against me, and a full discovery of it extorted—that should the affair be mentioned, it may be explained, and my fame cleared of every imputation." "That, madam," said the Marquis, with a malicious sneer, "would not be quite so easy a matter as you may perhaps suppose. Neither the world nor I am so credulous as you imagine. Your story, madam, by no means hangs well together. There is no person in my house would have dared to commit the act you accuse them of, as they must know the consequence of it would be immediate dismission from my service. Had not Colonel Belgrave been voluntarily admitted, he never would have been concealed;—no, madam, you would have rejoiced at the opportunity our presence gave you of punishing his temerity. Innocence is bold; 'tis guilt alone is timorous."

The truth of part of his speech struck forcibly on Amanda; but how could she explain her conduct?—how declare it was her dread of the Marchioness and Lady Euphrasia's malice which had made her consent to conceal him.

"Oh, I see," said she, in the agony of her soul—"I see I am the dupe of complicated artifice." "I never in my life," cried the Marchioness, "met with such assurance—to desire the Marquis to be her champion." "As she was intrusted to my care, however," exclaimed Lady Greystock, "I think it necessary to inquire into the affair. Pray, sir," turning to the Colonel, "by what means did you come here?"

The Colonel, with undiminished assurance, had hitherto stood near the fatal closet leaning on a chair.

"That, madam," replied he, "I must be excused revealing. Let me, however, assure your ladyship 'tis not on my own account I affect concealment." Here he glanced at Amanda. "Those parts of my conduct, however, which I choose to conceal, I shall always be ready to defend." "Sir," cried the Marquis haughtily, "no explanation or defence of your conduct is here required; I have neither right nor inclination to interfere in Miss Fitzalan's concerns."

The Colonel bowed to the circle, and was retiring, when Amanda flew to him and caught his arm. "Surely, surely," said she, almost gasping for breath, "you cannot be so inhuman as to retire without explaining this whole affair. Oh, Belgrave, leave me not a prey to slander. By all your hopes of mercy and forgiveness hereafter, I conjure you to clear my fame."

"My dear creature," said he, in a low voice, yet loud enough to be heard by the whole party, "anything I could say would be unavailing. You find they are determined not to see things in the light we wish them viewed. Compose yourself, I beseech you, and be assured, while I exist, you never shall want comfort or affluence."

He gently disengaged himself as he spoke, and quitted the room, leaving her riveted to the floor in amazement at his insolence and perfidy.

"I am sure," said Lady Greystock, "I shall regret all my life the hour in which I took her under my protection; though, indeed, from what I heard soon after my arrival in London, I should have despatched her back to her father, but I felt a foolish pity for her. I was in hopes, indeed, the society I had introduced her to would have produced a reformation, and that I might be the means of saving a young creature from entire destruction." "From what I have already suffered by her family, nothing should have tempted me to take her under my roof," exclaimed the Marchioness. "Was she my relation," cried the Marquis, "I should long since have come to a determination about her; as yours, madam," turning to the Marchioness, "I shall not attempt forming one; I deem it, however, absolutely necessary to remove Lady Euphrasia Sutherland from the house till the young lady chooses to quit it. I shall therefore order the carriage to be ready at an early hour for the villa."

"I shall certainly accompany your lordship," cried the Marchioness, "for I cannot endure her sight; and though she deserves it, it shall not be said that we turned her from the house." "The only measure she should pursue," exclaimed Lady Greystock, "is to set off as soon as possible for Ireland; when she returns to obscurity the affair may die away." "It may, however," said Amanda, "be yet revived to cover with confusion its contrivers. To Heaven I leave the vindication of my innocence. Its justice is sure, though sometimes slow, and the hour of retribution often arrives when least expected. Much as I have suffered—much as I may still suffer, I think my own situation preferable to theirs who have set their snares around me. The injurer must ever feel greater pangs than the injured—the pangs of guilt and remorse. I shall return to my obscurity, happy in the consciousness that it is not a shelter from shame, but a refuge from cruelty I seek. But can I be surprised at meeting cruelty from those who have long since waived the ties of kindred?—from those," and she glanced at Lady Greystock, "who have set aside the claims of justice and humanity?"

The Marchioness trembled with rage at this speech, and as Amanda retired from the room, exclaimed, "intolerable assurance."

Amanda repaired immediately to her chamber. She tottered as she walked and the housekeeper and Mrs. Jane, who, with some other servants, had assembled out of curiosity near the door, followed her thither.

The emotions she had so painfully suppressed now burst forth with violence. She fell into an agony of tears and sobs which impeded her breathing. The housekeeper and Jane loosened her clothes and supported her to the bed. In a short time she was sufficiently recovered to be able to speak, and requested they would engage a carriage for her against the next day, at an early hour, that she might commence her journey to Ireland. This they promised, and at her desire retired.

Success, but not happiness, had crowned the Marchioness's scheme. She triumphed in the disgrace she had drawn upon Amanda, but feared that disgrace was only temporary. She had entangled her in a snare, but dreaded not having secured her in it. She distrusted those who had assisted her designs—for the guilty will ever suspect each other. They might betray her, or Colonel Belgrave might repent; but such evils, if they did ever arrive, were probably far distant. In the interim, all she desired to accomplish might be effected. Long had she been meditating on some plan which should ruin Amanda for ever—not only in the opinion of Lord Mortimer, but in the estimation of the world. With the profligacy of Colonel Belgrave she was well acquainted, and inclined from it to believe that he would readily join in any scheme which could give him a chance of possessing Amanda. On discovering her residence, he had ordered his valet, who was a trusty agent in all his villanies, to endeavor to gain access to the house, that he might discover whether there was a chance of introducing him there. The valet obeyed his orders, and soon attached himself to Mrs. Jane, whom the Marchioness had placed about Amanda, from knowing she was capable of any deceitful part She was introduced to Belgrave, and a handsome present secured her in his interest.

She communicated to the Marchioness the particulars of their interview. From that period they had been seeking to bring about such a scene as was at last acted; for the conduct of Amanda had hitherto defeated their intentions. Her staying from the ball at last gave the wished-for opportunity.

Lady Euphrasia was apprised of the whole plot, and the hint of her indisposition was given in the morning, that no suspicion might be entertained in the evening, when mentioned as a plea for returning home earlier than was intended.

Colonel Belgrave was introduced into the closet by Mrs. Jane, through a door that opened from the lobby; and whilst Amanda sat pensively reading, he stole out, and secured the other door, as already mentioned.

When Lady Euphrasia declared she was too ill to continue at the ball, Lord Mortimer offered to attend her home. Had he not done so, the Marchioness intended to have asked him.

The Marquis was persuaded that Amanda was an artful and dangerous rival to his daughter, and he hated her from that consideration. The laws of hospitality obliged him to treat her with politeness, but he gladly seized the first opportunity that offered for expressing his dislike.

Lady Greystock saw through the plot, but she professed her belief of Amanda's guilt, which was all the Marchioness required.

The Marquis left the ladies together, while he went to give orders about his early journey. Soon after his departure a loud knocking was heard, which announced a visitor; and from the lateness of the hour, they conjectured, and were right in doing so, that it must be Lord Mortimer.

After traversing several streets, in an agony no language could describe, he returned to Portman Square. His fancy presented Amanda to his view, overwhelmed with shame, and sinking beneath the keen reproaches levelled at her. In the idea of her sufferings, all resentment for the supposed perfidy was forgotten. Human nature was liable to err, and the noblest efforts that nature could make, was to pardon such errors. To speak comfort to this fallen angel, he felt would relieve the weight which pressed upon his own breast. Pale and disordered he entered the room, and found the ladies apparently much affected.

"My dear lord," said the Marchioness, "I am glad you are come back. As a friend of the family, you may perhaps honor us with your advice on the present occasion." "Indeed," exclaimed Lady Greystock, "I suppose his lordship is at as a great a loss to know what can be done as we are. Was the Colonel in a situation to make any reparation—but a married man, only think, how horrible!" "Execrable monster!" cried Lord Mortimer, starting from his seat, and traversing the room, "it were a deed of kindness to mankind to extirpate him from the earth; but say," continued he, and his voice faltered as he spoke, "where is the unfortunate——," he could not pronounce the name of Amanda. "In her own room," replied the Marchioness. "I assure you, she behaved with not a little insolence, on Lady Greystock advising her to return home. For my part, I shall let her act as she pleases."

She then proceeded to mention the Marquis's resolution of leaving the house till she had quitted it, and that he insisted on their accompanying him.

"To return to her father is certainly the only eligible plan she can pursue," said Lord Mortimer; "but allow me," continued he, "to request that your ladyship will not impute to insolence any expression which dropped from her. Pity her wounded feelings, and soften her sorrows." "I declare," cried Lady Euphrasia, "I thought I should have fainted from the pity I felt for her." "You pitied her, then," said Lord Mortimer, sitting down by her ladyship, "you pitied and soothed her afflictions?" "Yes, indeed," replied she.

If ever Lady Euphrasia appeared pleasing in the eyes of Lord Mortimer, it was at this moment, when he was credulous enough to believe she had shed the tear of pity over his lost Amanda. He took her hand. "Ah! my dear Lady Euphrasia," said he, in an accent of melting softness, "perhaps even now she needs consolation. A gentle female friend would be a comfort to her wounded heart."

Lady Euphrasia immediately took the hint, and said she would go to her.

He led her to the door. "You are going," cried he, "to perform the office of an angel—to console the afflicted. Ah! well does it become the young and gentle of your sex to pity such misfortunes."

Her ladyship retired, but not indeed to the chamber of the forlorn Amanda. In her own she vented the rage of her soul, in something little short of execrations against Lord Mortimer, for the affection she saw he still retained for Amanda.

On her ladyship's retiring, Lady Greystock mentioned every

particular she had heard from Mrs. Jennings, and bitterly lamented her having ever taken Amanda under her protection. The subject was too painful to be long endured by Lord Mortimer. He had heard of the early hour fixed for their journey, and saying he would no longer keep the ladies from repose, precipitately retired. He gave his man directions to watch their motions, and inform him when they left town.

Exhausted by the violence of her emotions, a temporary forgetfulness stole over the senses of Amanda, on her being left to solitude. In this state she continued till roused by a bustle in the house. She started, listened, and heard the sound of a carriage. Supposing it to be the one she had ordered for her departure, she sprang from the bed, and, going to the window, saw, instead of one for her, the Marquis's, into which he was handing the ladies. As soon as it drove from the door, she rang the bell, and the housekeeper immediately appeared, as Mrs. Jane had attended the Marchioness to the villa. Amanda inquired "whether a carriage, as she directed, had been engaged for her."

The housekeeper replied, "the hour in which she spoke was too late for such a purpose, but she had now sent about one."

Amanda endeavored to exert herself, and was packing up her clothes, when a maid entered the chamber, and said, "Lord Mortimer was below, and wished to speak to her."

Tumultuous joy pervaded the mind of Amanda. She had believed it probable she should not see him again before her departure for Ireland, from whence she had determined writing to him the particulars of the affair. His visit seemed to announce he thought not unfavorably of her. She supposed he came to assure her that his opinion of her integrity was unshaken—"and I shall yet triumph," cried she, in the transport of the idea, "over malice and treachery."

She sprung past the maid; her feet scarce touched the ground, and in a moment she found herself in the arms of Lord Mortimer, which involuntarily opened to receive her, for, trembling, weak, and disordered, she would else, on seeing him, have sunk to the floor. He supported her to a sofa. In a little time she raised her head from his shoulder, and exclaimed, "Oh! you are come! I know you are come to comfort me." "Would to Heaven," he answered, "I were capable of either giving or receiving comfort The period, however, I trust, may yet arrive when we shall both at least be more composed. To mitigate your sorrows would lessen my own; for never, oh, never! can my heart forget the love and esteem it once bore Amanda." "Once bore her!" repeated Amanda. "Once bore her, Lord Mortimer! do you say? Then you wish to imply they no longer exist?"

The tone of anguish in which she spoke pierced the heart of Lord Mortimer. Unable to speak, he arose, and walked to the window, to hide his emotion. His words, his silence, all conveyed a fatal truth to Amanda. She saw a dreadful and eternal separation effected between her and Lord Mortimer. She beheld herself deprived of reputation, loaded with calumny, and no longer an object of love, but of detestation and contempt. Her anguish was almost too great to bear, yet the pride of injured innocence made her wish to conceal it; and, as Lord Mortimer stood at the window, she determined to try and leave the room without his knowledge, but ere she gained the door her head grew giddy, her strength failed, she staggered, faintly screamed on finding herself falling, and sunk upon the floor.

Lord Mortimer wildly called for assistance. He raised and carried her back to the sofa; he strained her to his bosom, kissed her pale lips, and wept over her.

"I have wounded your gentle soul, my Amanda," cried he, "but I have tortured my own by doing so. Ah! still dearest of women, did the world compassionate your errors as I compassionate them, neither contempt nor calumny would ever be your portion. How pale she looks!" said he, raising his head to gaze upon her face; "how like a lovely flower untimely faded! Yet were it happiness for her never to revive; a soul like hers, originally noble, must be wretched under the pressure of scorn. Execrable Belgrave! the fairest work of Heaven is destroyed by you. Oh! my Amanda, my distress is surely severe—though anguish rives my heart for your loss, I must conceal it—the sad luxury of grief will be denied me, for the world would smile if I could say I now lamented you."

Such were the effusions of sorrow which broke from Lord Mortimer over the insensible Amanda. The housekeeper, who had been listening all this time, now appeared, as if in obedience to his call, and offered her assistance in recovering Amanda. Heavy sighs at length gave hopes of her restoration. Lord Mortimer, unable to support her pathetic lamentations, determined to depart ere she was perfectly sensible.

"Miss Fitzalan," said he to the housekeeper, "will wish, I am convinced, to quit this house immediately. I shall take upon myself to procure her a carriage, also a proper attendant, for her journey, which, I flatter myself, she will be able to commence in a few hours. Be kind, be gentle to her, my good woman, and depend on my eternal gratitude. When she is recovered, deliver her this letter."

The housekeeper promised to observe his injunctions, and he departed.

To Ireland, with Amanda, he intended sending an old female servant, who had formerly been an attendant of his mother's, and his own man. He was shocked at the conduct of the Marchioness and Lady Greystock, and thought them guilty of the highest inhumanity in thus deserting Amanda. The letter he had put into the housekeeper's hands excited her curiosity so strongly that she was tempted to gratify it. Amanda was not in a situation to perceive what she did, the letter could easily be sealed again, and, in short, without longer hesitation, she opened it. How great was her amazement, on finding it contained a bank-note for five hundred pounds. The words were as follows:—

Consider me, Amanda, in the light of a brother; as such accept my services; to serve you, in any manner, will be a source of consolation, which, I flatter myself, you will be happy to allow me. 'Tis necessary you should return immediately to your father; hesitate not, then, about using the enclosed. Your complying with my request will prove that you yet retain a friendship for MORTIMER.

"What a sum," cried the housekeeper, as she examined the note; "what a nice little independency would this, in addition to what I have already saved, be for an honest woman! What a pity it is such a creature as it is designed for should possess it!" The housekeeper, like her lady, was fertile in invention: to be sure there was some danger in her present scheme, but for such a prize it was worth her while to run some risk. Could she but get

Amanda off ere the carriage from Lord Mortimer arrived, she believed all would succeed as she could wish. Amanda, ignorant as she was of Lord Mortimer's intentions, would not, consequently, be influenced by them, to oppose anything she could do. Full of this idea, she ran out, and calling a footman, high in her favor, desired him immediately to procure a travelling chaise for Miss Fitzalan. She then returned to Amanda, who was just beginning to move.

"Come, come," cried she, going to her, and roughly shaking her shoulder, "have done with those tragedy airs, and prepare yourself against the carriage you ordered, comes: it will be at the door in a few minutes."

Amanda looked round the room. "Is Lord Mortimer gone, then?" said she. "Lord, to be sure he is," cried the housekeeper; "he left you on the floor, and, as he went out, he said you should never have another opportunity of deceiving him."

A sudden frenzy seemed to seize Amanda; she wrung her hands, called upon Lord Mortimer in the impassioned language of despair, and flung herself on the ground, exclaiming, "This last stroke is more than I can bear."

The housekeeper grew alarmed, lest her agitation should retard her departure; she raised her forcibly from the ground, and said, "she must compose herself to begin her journey, which was unavoidable, as the Marchioness had given absolute orders to have her sent from the house early in the morning."

"Accursed house!" said Amanda, whose reason was restored by the strenuous remonstrances of the housekeeper: "Oh, that I had never entered it!" She then told her companion, "if she would assist her, as she was almost too weak to do anything for herself, she would be ready against the carriage came." The housekeeper and maid accordingly attended her to her chamber; the former brought her drops, and the latter assisted in putting on her habit, and packing up her clothes. Amanda having secured her trunks, desired they might be sent, by the first opportunity, to Castle Carberry; she had left a great many clothes there, so took nothing at present with her but a small quantity of linen. She had but a few guineas in her purse; her watch, however, was valuable; and if she had money enough to carry her to Dublin, she knew there she might procure a sufficient sum on it to carry her home.

At last the carriage came; with a trembling frame, and half-broken heart, Amanda entered it. She saw Nicholas, the footman, who had procured it, ready mounted to attend her. She told him it was unnecessary to do so; but he declared he could not think of letting so young a lady travel unprotected. She was pleased at his attention: she had shuddered at the idea of her forlorn situation, and now dropped a tear of sweet sensibility at finding she was not utterly deserted by every human being. The carriage took the road to Parkgate, as Amanda chose to embark from thence, the journey being so much nearer to it than to Holyhead. It was now about eight o'clock; after travelling four hours, the chaise stopped at a small house on the roadside, which appeared to be a common ale-house. Amanda was unwilling to enter it; but the horses were here to be changed; and she was shown into a dirty parlor, where, almost sinking with weakness, she ordered tea to be immediately brought in. She was much astonished, as she sat at the tea-table, to see Nicholas enter the room with a familiar air, and seat himself by her. She stared at him at first, supposing him intoxicated; but perceiving no signs of this in his countenance, began to fear that the insults she had received at the Marquis's made him think himself authorized to treat her with this insolence. She arose abruptly, and, summoning all her resolution to her aid, desired him to retire, adding, "If his attendance was requisite she would ring for him."

Nicholas also quitted his seat, and following her, caught her in his arms, exclaiming, "Bless us, how hoity toity you are grown."

Amanda shrieked, and stamped on the floor in an agony of terror and indignation.

"Why, now really," said he, "after what happened at home, I think you need not be so coy with me." "Oh, save me, Heaven, from this wretch!" was all the affrighted Amanda could articulate.

The door opened. A waiter appeared, and told Nicholas he was wanted without. Nicholas released Amanda, and ran directly from the room. Amanda sunk upon a chair, and her head turned giddy at the idea of the dangers with which she was surrounded. She saw herself in the power of a wretch—perhaps wretches, for the house seemed a proper place for scenes of villany—without the means of delivering herself. She walked to the window. A confused idea of getting through it, and running from the house, darted into her mind, but she turned from it in agony at seeing a number of countrymen drinking before it. She now could only raise her feeble hands to heaven to supplicate its protection.

She passed some minutes in this manner, when the lock turned and made her shudder, but it was the landlady alone who entered. She came, she said, with Nicholas's respectful duty, and he was sorry he was obliged to go back to town without seeing her safe to her journey's end.

"Is he really gone?" asked Amanda, with all the eagerness of joy. "Yes," the woman said; "a person had followed him from London on purpose to bring him back." "Is the carriage ready?" cried Amanda. She was informed it was. "Let me fly, then," said she, running to the door; "let me fly, or the wretch may return." The landlady impeded her progress to tell her the bill was not yet settled. Amanda pulled out her purse, and besought her not to detain her. This the woman had no desire to do. Things were therefore settled without delay between them, and Amanda was driven with as much expedition as she could desire from the terrifying mansion. The chaise had proceeded about two miles, when, in the middle of a solitary road, or rather lane, by the side of a wood, it suddenly stopped. Amanda, alarmed at every incident, hastily looked out, and inquired what was the matter; but how impossible to describe her terror when she beheld Colonel Belgrave, and Nicholas standing by him! She shrunk back, and entreated the postillion to drive on; but he heeded not her entreaty. Nicholas opened the door, and Belgrave sprang into the carriage. Amanda attempted to burst open the door at the opposite side; but he caught her to his bosom, and the horses set off at full speed. Colonel Belgrave's valet had been secreted by Mrs. Jane the preceding night in the house, that he might be able to give his master intelligence of all that passed within it, in consequence of his being discovered in the closet. On hearing the family were gone to the Marquis's villa, Belgrave believed he could easily prevail on the domestics to deliver up Amanda to him. Elated with this hope, he reached the house, attended by his valet, just after she had quitted it. The housekeeper hesitated to inform him of the road she had taken till she had procured what she knew would be the consequence of her hesitation—a large bribe. Horses were then immediately procured, and Belgrave and his servant set off in pursuit of Amanda. The sight of a travelling chaise at the little inn already mentioned, prompted their inquiries; and on finding the chaise waited for Amanda, the Colonel retired to a private room, sent for Nicholas, and secured him in his interest. It was settled they should repair to the wood, by which the postilion was bribed to pass, and from thence proceed to a country-house of the Colonel's. Their scheme accomplished, Nicholas, happy in the service he had done, or rather the reward he had obtained for that service, again turned his face towards London.

The carriage and attendants Lord Mortimer procured for Amanda arrived even earlier than the housekeeper had expected, and she blessed her lucky stars for the precipitancy with which she had hurried off Amanda. They were followed by his lordship himself, whose wretched heart could not support the idea of letting Amanda depart without once more beholding her. Great was his dismay, his astonishment, when the housekeeper informed him she was gone.

"Gone!" he repeated, changing color.

The housekeeper said that, without her knowledge, Miss Fitzalan had a chaise hired, and the moment it came to the door stepped into it, notwithstanding she was told his lordship meant to provide everything proper for her journey himself. "But she said, my Lord," cried the housekeeper, "she wanted none of your care, and that she could never get fast enough from a house, or from people, where and by whom she had been so ill treated."

Lord Mortimer asked if she had any attendant, and whether she took the letter

The housekeeper answered both these questions in the affirmative. "Truly, my Lord," she continued, "I believe your lordship said something in that letter which pleased her, for she smiled on opening it, and said, 'Well, well, this is something like comfort.'"

"And was she really so mean?" he was on the point of asking, but he timely checked a question which was springing from a heart that sickened at finding the object of its tenderest affections unworthy in every respect of possessing them. Every idea of this kind soon gave way to anxiety on her account. His heart misgave him at her undertaking so long a journey under the protection of a common servant; and, unable to endure his apprehensions, he determined instantly to pursue and see her safe himself to the destined port.

The woman, who had hitherto sat in the chaise, was ordered to return home. He entered it with eagerness, and promised liberally to reward the postilions if they used expedition. They had changed horses but once when Lord Mortimer saw Nicholas approaching, whom, at the first glance, he knew. He stopped the carriage, and called out, "Where have you left Miss Fitzalan?" "Faith, my Lord," cried Nicholas, instantly stopping and taking off his hat, "in very good company. I left her with Colonel Belgrave, who was waiting, by appointment, on the road for her." "Oh! horrible infatuation!" said Lord Mortimer, "that nothing can snatch her from the arms of infamy."

The postilion desired to know whether he should return to London.

Lord Mortimer hesitated, and at last desired him to go on according to his first directions. He resolved to proceed to Parkgate and discover whether Amanda had returned to Ireland. They had not proceeded far when they overtook a travelling chaise. As Lord Mortimer passed, he looked into it, and beheld Amanda reclined on the bosom of Belgrave. He trembled universally, closed his eyes, and sighed out the name of the perfidious Amanda. When they had got some way before the other chaise, he desired the postilion to strike off into another road, which, by a circuit of a few miles, would bring them back to London. Amanda, it was evident, had put herself under the protection of Belgrave, and to know whether she went to Ireland was now of little consequence to him, as he supposed her unreclaimable. But how impossible to describe his distress and confusion when almost the first object he beheld, on alighting in St. James's Square, was his aunt, Lady Martha Dormer, who, in compliance with his urgent request, had hastened to London. Had a spectre crossed his sight he could not have been more shocked.

"Well, my dear Frederick," said her ladyship, "you see I lost no time in obeying your wishes. I have flown hither, I may indeed say, on the wings of love. But where is this little divinity of thine? I long to have a peep at her goddess-ship."

Lord Mortimer, inexpressibly shocked, turned to the window.

"I shall see, to be sure," cried her ladyship, "quite a little paragon. Positively, Frederick, I will be introduced this very evening." "My dear aunt, my dear Lady Martha," said Lord Mortimer, impatiently, "for Heaven's sake spare me!" "But tell me," she continued, "when I shall commence this attack upon your father's heart?" "Never! never!" sighed Mortimer, half distracted. "What! you suppose he will prove inflexible? But I do not despair of convincing you to the contrary. Tell me, Frederick, when the little charmer is to be seen?" "Oh, God!" cried Mortimer, striking his forehead, "she is lost," said he, "she is lost for ever!"

Lady Martha was alarmed. She now, for the first time, noticed the wild and pallid looks of her nephew. "Gracious Heaven!" she exclaimed, "what is the matter?"

The dreadful explanation Lord Mortimer now found himself under a necessity of giving. The shame of acknowledging he was so deceived, the agony he suffered from that deception, joined to the excessive agitation and fatigue he had suffered the preceding night, and the present day, so powerfully assailed him at this moment, that his senses suddenly gave way, and he actually fainted on the floor.

What a sight for the tender Lady Martha! She saw something dreadful had happened, and what this was Lord Mortimer, as soon as recovered, informed her.

He then retired to his chamber. He could neither converse nor bear to be conversed with. His fondest hopes were blasted, nor could he forego the sad indulgence of mourning over them in solitude. He felt almost convinced that the hold Amanda had on his affections could not be withdrawn; he had considered her as scarcely less than his wife, and had she been really such, her present conduct could not have given him more anguish. Had she been snatched from him by the hand of death; had she been wedded to a worthy character, he could have summoned fortitude to his aid; but to find her the prey of a villain, was a stroke too horrible to bear, at least for a long period, with patience.

CHAPTER XXX.

> "And let a maid thy pity share,
>
> . . . .
>
> Who seeks for rest, but finds despair
>
> Companion of her way."—GOLDSMITH.

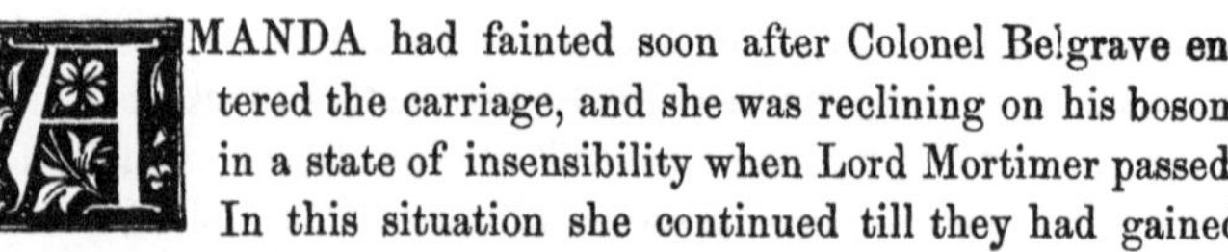

AMANDA had fainted soon after Colonel Belgrave entered the carriage, and she was reclining on his bosom in a state of insensibility when Lord Mortimer passed. In this situation she continued till they had gained a solitary road, when the carriage stopped, and water, procured from an adjacent cottage, being sprinkled on her face, she recovered; but either by arguments or actions she was now unable to oppose Belgrave. She felt a weakness through her whole frame, which she believed the forerunner of death, and a languor on her mind that almost deprived it of the perception of misery.

The refreshments offered to her she could only refuse by a motion of her hand; and in this manner they proceeded till about nine o'clock at night, when they entered an extensive wood, in the very centre of which stood Colonel Belgrave's mansion. He carried Amanda himself into it, and laid her upon a sofa in a large parlor. Some female domestics appeared with drops and cordials, to try and recover her from the almost lifeless state in which she lay. One of them presented a letter to the Colonel, which excited no little perturbation in his mind. It came express to inform him that his uncle, whose estate and title he was heir to, lay at the point of death, and that his presence was immediately required.

The Colonel was not so absolutely engrossed by love as to be incapable of attending to his interest. An addition of fortune was extremely agreeable, as his affairs were somewhat deranged; and, as Amanda was not in a situation at present to comply with any overtures he should make, his resolution was immediately formed to set off without delay, and against his return he trusted Amanda would be not only recovered, but willing to accede to his wishes.

He dismissed the woman who had brought her a little to herself, and taking her hand informed her of the painful necessity he was under of departing for a short time. He also mentioned his hopes, that on his return he should have no obstacle thrown in the way of his happiness by her. "You must be sensible, my dear Amanda," said he, with coolness, "that your reputation is as much gone as if you had complied with my wishes; since it is sacrificed, why not enjoy the advantages that may, that will certainly attend the reality of that sacrifice?" "Monster!" cried Amanda, "your arts may have destroyed my fame, but my innocence bids defiance to your power." "Conquer your obstinacy, Amanda," replied he, "against I return, or I shall not promise but what I may be at last irritated. As you will have no occasion for money here, you must excuse me, my dear creature, if I take your purse into my own keeping. My domestics may be faithful, when they have no inducement to the contrary; but no bribery, no corruption, you know." He then very deliberately took Amanda's purse and watch from her pocket, and deposited them in his own. He had already given directions to his servants concerning their treatment of Amanda, and now ordered them to carry her to a chamber, and make her take some refreshment.

"Reflect, Amanda," said he, ere she retired, "on your present situation, and timely estimate the advantages I offer to your acceptance; wealth, pleasure, the attentions of a man who adores you, are not to be despised. Upon my soul it grieves me to leave you, but the joys of meeting will, I trust, pay the pangs of absence."

As he spoke, he attempted to embrace her, but she faintly shrieked, and shrunk from his grasp. He looked provoked; but as he had no time to lose, he reserved a declaration of his anger for another opportunity, and directly set off for his uncle's.

Amanda was supported to a chamber, and lay down in her clothes on a bed. They offered her bread and wine, but she was too sick to touch any. To remonstrate with the insolent looking creatures who surrounded her she knew would be unavailing, and she turned her face on the pillow to stifle her sobs, as she believed they would exult in her distress. Death she thought approaching, and the idea of being separated from the dear objects who would have soothed its last pangs, was dreadful. Her father in agony, and Oscar, her beloved brother, bewailing her with tears of sorrow, were the images fancy presented to her view.

"Dear objects of my love," she softly exclaimed, "Amanda shall no more behold you, but her last sigh will be breathed for you. Ah! why, why," she cried, "did I suffer myself to be separated from my father?"

A young woman leaned over Amanda, and surveyed her with the most malignant scrutiny. She was daughter to Belgrave's steward, and neither she nor her father possessed sufficient virtue to make them reject the offers Belgrave made them on her account. His attachment to her was violent, but transient, and in the height of it he made her mistress of the mansion she now occupied, which character she maintained with tyrannic sway over the rest of the domestics. Belgrave was really ignorant of the violence of her temper, and had no idea she would dare dispute his inclinations, or disobey his orders. He believed she would be subservient to both, and from this belief, gave Amanda particularly into her charge.

But scarcely had he departed, ere she swore, "that let the consequence be what it would, the vile wretch he had brought into the house to insult her should never remain in it. She shall tramp," cried she, "though I follow her myself when he returns; for such a little hussey shall never triumph over me."

The servants, ignorant and timorous, did not attempt to oppose her.

"Come, madam," said she, suddenly seizing Amanda's arm, and pulling her from the pillow, "have done with these languishing airs, and march." "What do you mean?" cried Amanda, trembling at her inflamed countenance. "Why, I mean you shall quit this house directly; and I wonder Colonel Belgrave could have the assurance to bring such a creature as you into it." "You mistake, indeed," said Amanda; "treachery, not inclination, brought me into it, and I am not what you suppose. If, as you say, you will allow me to depart, I shall ever regard you as my friend; and in every prayer I offer up to Heaven for myself, you shall be remembered." "Oh, dear! but you shall not impose upon me so easily. Come," continued she, turning to a maid, "and help me to conduct this fine lady to the hall door." "Gracious

Heaven!" said Amanda, who by this time was taken, or rather dragged from the bed, "what are you about doing with me? Though I rejoice to quit the house, yet surely, surely," she cried, and her soul recoiled at the idea, "without a guide at this hour of the night, you will not turn me from it."

She then mentioned Colonel Belgrave's having deprived her of her purse and watch, and besought the woman in the most pathetic terms, to supply her with a small sum, which she solemnly assured her should be returned as soon as she reached her friends; and ended with saying, she should depart with gratitude and joy if she complied with her request, and allowed some one to guide her to a place where she might procure a carriage."

"Such madams as you," replied the imperious woman, "are never at a loss for means of procuring money, or a place to go to. I see through your art well enough; you want me to pity you, that I may let you stay till your Colonel returns. But who would be fool then, I wonder? The tables, I warrant, would soon be turned upon me. No, no; out you go this moment." So saying, she rudely seized Amanda, and assisted by another woman, hurried her down stairs, and out of the house directly: they carried her to an intricate part of the wood, and then ran back, leaving the helpless mourner leaning against a tree.

Amanda looked around her. Dark and awful were the shades of the wood. No light appeared but what came from a few wandering stars, which only served to render darkness visible. "Have mercy upon me, Heaven!" groaned Amanda, as she felt herself sinking to the earth. The cold acted as a kind of restorative, and almost immediately revived her. She rested her head against a little bank, and as she thus reclined, a tender sadness pervaded her soul at the idea of her father's sorrow when he heard of her fate. "When he hears," cried she, "that I was driven from the house, as unworthy of pity or protection from any being, that his Amanda, whom he cherished in his bosom, as the darling of his age, was denied the pity he would have shown the greatest wretch that crawls upon the earth, and that she perished without shelter, it will break his heart entirely. Poor Oscar, too—alas! I shall be a source of wretchedness to both. Will Lord Mortimer lament when he hears of my fate? Alas! I cannot believe that he will

He that could leave me in the arms of insensibility, and so readily believe ill of me, must have a heart steeled against compassion for my sufferings. But my unhappy father and brother will never doubt my innocence, and by them I shall be tenderly and truly mourned."

The idea of their sufferings at last recalled her wandering thoughts, and pity for those sufferings made her endeavor to support her own, that she might be able to make some efforts for preserving a life so precious to them. Besides, as she reflected, she could not but attribute her expulsion from the house of infamy to the immediate interposition of Providence in her favor; and whilst her heart swelled with gratitude at the idea, her fortitude gradually returned. She arose, but the vigor of her nerves was not equal to the ardor of her intentions. She walked on, and as she proceeded, the gloom grew more profound, the paths were intricate, and her progress was often impeded by the roots of trees, and the branches that grew about them. After wandering about a considerable time, she at last began to think that, instead of gaining the skirts, she had penetrated into the very centre of the wood, and that to quit it till morning would be impossible. Yielding to this idea, or rather to her excessive weariness, she was seeking for a place to sit down on, when a faint light glimmered before her. She instantly darted through the path from whence it gleamed, and found herself at the extremity of the wood, and that the light proceeded from a small hamlet contiguous to it. Thither she walked, as fast as her trembling limbs would carry her. A profound stillness reigned around, only interrupted by the hoarse and hollow barking of some distant dogs, which, in such an hour, had something particularly solemn in it. The stillness, and sudden disappearance of lights from various windows, convinced Amanda that every cottage was closed for the night; "and were they open," said she, "I perhaps should be denied access to any, deprived as I am of the means of rewarding kindness." She shuddered at the idea of passing a night unsheltered. "It is now, indeed," said she, "I really know what it is to feel for the houseless children of want." She moved softly along. The echo of her own steps alarmed her. She had nearly reached the end of the hamlet, when, before a neat cottage, divided from the others by a clump of old trees, she saw a venerable man, who might well have passed for an ancient hermit. His gray locks thinly shaded his forehead; an expression of deep and pensive thought was visible in his countenance; his arms were folded on his breast, and his eyes were raised with a tender melancholy to heaven, as if that heaven he contemplated was now the abode of some kindred and lamented spirit. Surely such a being, thought she, will pity me. She approached him—stood close to him, yet was unnoticed. Thrice she attempted to speak, and thrice her heart failed her At last she summoned all her courage to her aid, and faintly articulated, "Pity——," she could add no more, but fainted at his feet. The stranger's mind was fraught with all the benevolence his countenance depictured. The transient glance he had caught of Amanda interested every tender feeling. He called to his servant, an elderly woman, his only companion in the cottage, to assist him in conveying her in. This woman's heart was as tender as her master's, and the youth, the beauty, and forlorn situation of Amanda, equally excited their wonder and pity. It was many minutes ere she opened her eyes, and when she did, her senses were quite bewildered. "And my father! alas! my father, I shall never more behold him," was all she could articulate.

She was supported to a small chamber; the old woman undressed her, put her to bed, and sat up with her the remainder of the night. Amanda often started; she raved continually of Belgrave, the author of her woes, and betrayed the strongest horror. "The wound he had inflicted on her heart," she said, "the hand of death could only heal." She mentioned the cruelty of the Marchioness, called upon her father to save her from destruction, and reproached Mortimer for aiding to overwhelm her in disgrace. She continued in this situation three days, during which the old man and his faithful servant watched her with unremitted attention. A neighboring apothecary was summoned to her aid, and a girl from one of the cottages procured to sit up with her at night. The old man frequently knelt by the bedside, watching with anxiety for a favorable symptom. Her incoherent expressions pierced him to the heart: he felt, from mournful sympathy, for the father she so pathetically mentioned, and invoked Heaven to restore her to him.

The afternoon of the third day, Amanda, after a long slumber, awoke, perfectly restored to her senses; it was many minutes, however, after her awaking, ere she recollected all the circumstances that had caused her present situation. She at last opened the curtain, and perceived the old woman, whom we shall hereafter call Eleanor, seated by the bed-side.

"I fear," said she, with a languid smile, "I have been the occasion of a great deal of trouble." "No, no," replied the kind Eleanor, delighted to hear her speak so calmly, and drawing back a little of the curtain at the same time to observe her looks.

Amanda inquired how long she had been ill. Eleanor informed her, and added, "Heaven, my dear child, was kind to you, in throwing you in my master's way, who delights in befriending the helpless." "Heaven will reward him," exclaimed Amanda.

The chamber was gloomy; she requested one of the shutters might be opened. Eleanor complied with her desire, and a ray of the declining sun darting through the casement, cheered her pensive heart. She perfectly remembered the venerable figure she had beheld on the threshold of the cottage, and was impatient to express her gratitude to him. The next day, she trusted, would give her an opportunity of doing so, as she then resolved, if possible, to rise. The wish of her soul was to be with her father ere he could receive any intimation of what had happened. She resolved to communicate to her benevolent host the incidents which had placed her in such a situation; and she flattered herself, on hearing them, he would accommodate her with the means of returning to Ireland: if unable (unwilling she could not think she should find him) to do this, she then intended writing to her father. This measure, however, she fervently trusted, she should have no occasion to take, as she well knew the shock such a letter would give him.

Contrary to the inclination of Eleanor, she rose the next day, and, as soon as she was dressed, sent to request Mr. Howel's company. Eleanor had informed her of her master's name. The chamber was on a ground floor: before the windows were a row of neat white cottages, and behind them rose a range of lofty hills, covered to the very summit with trees, now just bursting into verdure. Before the cottage ran a clear murmuring rivulet, at which some young girls were washing clothes, whilst others spread them upon hedges, and all beguiled their labor with singing, chatting, and laughing together.

"Ah! happy creatures!" cried Amanda, "screened by your native hills, you know nothing of the vices or miseries of the great world: no snares lurk beneath the flowery paths you tread, to wring your hearts with anguish, and nip the early blossoms of your youth."

The old man appeared, and interrupted her meditations. When he beheld the pale face of Amanda, beaming with angelic sweetness; when he saw her emaciated hand extended towards him, while her soft voice uttered her grateful acknowledgments, his emotions could not be suppressed: he pressed her hand between his: tears rolled down the furrows of his face, and he exclaimed, "I thank the Almighty for reviving this sweet flower."

A deep sob from Amanda proved how much he had affected her feelings.

He was alarmed, and hastily endeavored to compose his own, out of regard to hers.

When a little composed, with grateful sweetness she continued to thank him for his kindness. "Pity," said she, "is a sweet emotion to excite; yet from you, without esteem, it would be humiliating; and esteem I cannot flatter myself with obtaining, till I have accounted for being a wretched wanderer." She then gave a brief account of her father and the events of her life.

"Ah! my dear," cried the old man, as she finished her narrative, "you have reason, indeed, to regret your knowledge of Belgrave; but the sorrow he has occasioned you, I believe and trust, will be but transient. That which he has given me, will be lasting as my life. You look astonished. Alas! but for him, I might now have been blessed with a daughter as lovely and as amiable as Fitzalan's. I see you are too delicate to express the curiosity my words have inspired, but I shall not hesitate to gratify it. My relation will draw the tear of pity from your eye; but the sorrows of others often reconcile us to our own.

CHAPTER XXXI.

> "'And oft as ease and health retire,
> To breezy lawn or forest deep,
> The friend shall view yon whitening spire,
> And 'mid the varied landscape weep;
> But thou who own'st that earthy bed,
> Ah! what will every dirge avail?"
> —COLLINS'S ODE ON THOMSON.

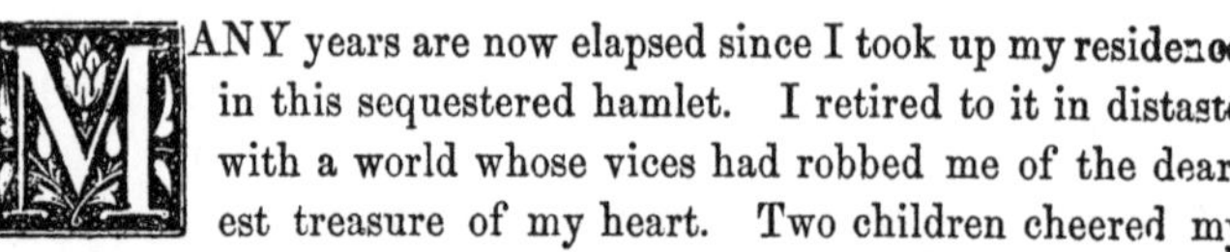

ANY years are now elapsed since I took up my residence in this sequestered hamlet. I retired to it in distaste with a world whose vices had robbed me of the dearest treasure of my heart. Two children cheered my solitude, and in training them up to virtue, I lost the remembrance of half my cares. My son, when qualified, was sent to Oxford, as a friend had promised to provide for him in the church; but my daughter was destined to retirement, not only from the narrowness of my income, but from a thorough conviction it was best calculated to insure her felicity. Juliana was the child of innocence and content. She knew of no greater happiness than that of promoting mine, of no pleasures but what the hamlet could afford, and was one of the gayest, as well as the loveliest, of its daughters. One fatal evening I suffered her to go, with some of her young companions, to a rustic ball, given by the parents of Belgrave to their tenants, on coming down to Woodhouse, from which they had been long absent. The graces of my child immediately attracted the notice of their son. Though young in years, he was already a professed libertine. The conduct of his father had set him an example of dissipation which the volatility of his own disposition too readily inclined him to follow. His heart immediately conceived the basest schemes against Juliana, which the obscurity of her situation prompted him to think might readily be accomplished. From this period he took every opportunity of throwing himself in her way. My suspicions, or rather my fears, were soon excited; for I knew not then the real depravity of Belgrave; but I knew that an attachment between him and my daughter would prove a source of uneasiness to both, from the disparity fortune had placed between them. My task in convincing

Juliana of the impropriety of encouraging such an attachment was not a difficult one. But, alas! I saw the conviction was attended with a pang of anguish, which pierced me to the soul.

Belgrave, from the assumed softness and delicacy of his manners, had made an impression on her heart, which was not to be erased. Every effort, however, which prudence could suggest, she resolved to make, and, in compliance with my wishes, avoided Belgrave. This conduct soon convinced him it would be a difficult matter to lull my caution, or betray her innocence. And finding all his attempts to see, or convey a letter to her, ineffectual, he departed with his parents from Woodhouse.

Juliana heard of his departure with a forced smile; but a starting tear, and a colorless cheek, too clearly denoted to me the state of her mind. I shall not attempt to describe my sufferings on witnessing hers. With my pity was mixed a degree of veneration for that virtue which, in so young a mind, could make such exertions against a passion disapproved of by a parent. The evening of his departure, no longer under any restraint, she walked out alone, and instinctively, perhaps, took the road to Woodhouse. She wandered to its deepest glooms, and there gave way to emotions which, from her efforts to suppress them, were become almost too painful to support. The gloom of the wood was heightened by the shades of evening, and a solemn stillness reigned around, well calculated to inspire pensive tenderness. She sighed the name of Belgrave in tremulous accents, and lamented their ever having met. A sudden rustling among the trees startled her, and the next moment she beheld him at her feet, exclaiming, "We have met, my Juliana, never more to part."

Surprise and confusion so overpowered her senses, as to render her for some time unable to attend to his raptures. When she grew composed, he told her he was returned to make her honorably his; but to effect this intention, a journey from the hamlet was requisite. She turned pale at these words, and declared she never would consent to a clandestine measure. This declaration did not discourage Belgrave; he knew the interest he had in her heart, and this knowledge gave an energy to his arguments, which gradually undermined the resolution of Juliana. Already, he said, she had made a sufficient sacrifice to filial duty; surely something was now due to love like his, which, on her account, would cheerfully submit to innumerable difficulties. As he was under age, a journey to Scotland was unavoidable, he said, and he would have made me his confidant on the occasion, but that he feared my scrupulous delicacy would have opposed his intentions, as contrary to parental authority. He promised Juliana to bring her back to the hamlet immediately after the ceremony; in short, the plausibility of his arguments, the tenderness of his persuasions, and the secret impulses of her heart, at last produced the effect he wished, and he received a promise from her to put herself under his protection that very night.

But oh! how impossible to describe my agonies the ensuing morning when, instead of my child, I found a letter in her room informing me of her elopement; they were such as a fond parent, trembling for the fame and happiness of his child, may conceive My senses must have sunk beneath them had they long continued, but Belgrave, according to his promise, hastened back my child; and as I sat solitary and pensive in the apartment she so often had enlivened, I suddenly beheld her at my feet, supported by Belgrave, as his wife. So great a transition from despair to comfort was almost too powerful for me to support. I asked my heart was its present happiness real; I knelt, I received my child in my arms; in those feeble arms I seemed to raise her with my heart to Heaven in pious gratitude for her returning unsullied. Yet, when my first transports were abated, I could not help regretting her ever having consented to a clandestine union. I entreated Belgrave to write, in the most submissive terms, to his father. He promised to comply with my entreaty, yet hinted his fears that his compliance would be unattended with the success I hoped. He requested, if this should be the case, I would allow his wife to reside in the cottage till he was of age. Oh, how pleasing a request to my heart! a month passed away in happiness, only allayed by not hearing from his father At the expiration of that time he declared he must depart, having received orders to join his regiment, but promised to return as soon as possible; he also promised to write, but a fortnight elapsed and no letter arrived.

Juliana and I grew alarmed, but it was an alarm that only proceeded from fears of his being ill. We were sitting one morning at breakfast, when the stopping of a carriage drew us from the table.

"He is come!" said Juliana, "he is come!" and she flew to open the door; when, instead of her expected Belgrave, she beheld his father, whose dark and haughty visage proclaimed that he came on no charitable intent. Alas! the occasion of his visit was too soon explained; he came to have the ties which bound his son to Juliana broken. My child, on hearing this, with firmness declared, that she was convinced any scheme his cruelty might devise to separate them, the integrity, as well as the tenderness of his son, would render abortive.

"Be not too confident of that, young lady," cried he, smiling maliciously. He then proceeded to inform her that Belgrave, so beloved, and in whose integrity she so much confided, had himself authorized his intentions, being determined to avail himself of non-age, to have the marriage broke.

Juliana could hear no more; she sunk fainting on the bosom of her wretched father. Oh, what a situation was mine, when, as I clasped her wildly to my heart and called upon her to revive, that heart whispered me it was cruelty to wish she should! Alas! too soon she did, to a keen perception of misery. The marriage was dissolved, and health and happiness fled from her together; yet, from compassion to me, I saw she struggled to support the burthen of existence. Every remedy which had a chance of prolonging it, I administered. But, alas! sorrow was rooted in her heart, and it was only its removal, which was impossible, that could have effected her recovery Oh! how often have I stolen from my bed to the door of her apartment, trembling, lest I should hear the last groan escape her lips! How often have I then heard her deep convulsive sobs, and reproached myself for selfishness at the moment for wishing the continuance of her being, which was only wishing the continuance of her misery! Yes, I have then said, I resign her, my Creator, unto thee. I resign her from a certainty, that only with thee she can enjoy felicity. But, alas! in a moment frail nature has triumphed over such a resignation, and, prostrate on the ground, I have implored heaven, either to spare the child, or take the father along with her.

She saw me unusually depressed one day, and proposed a walk, with a hope that any exertion from her might recruit my spirits But when I saw my child, in the very bloom of life, unable to sustain her feeble frame; when I felt her leaning on my almost nerveless arm for support, oh! how intolerable was the anguish that rived my heart!—in vain, by soft endearments, she strove to mitigate it. I averted my face and wept. She motioned to go towards Woodhouse; we had got within sight of the wood, when she complained of fatigue, and sat down. She had not been many minutes in this situation, when she beheld, coming from the wood, Belgrave, and a young girl she knew to be the steward's daughter. The familiar manner in which they appeared conversing, left little room to doubt of the footing on which they were. The hectic glow of Juliana's complexion gave place to a deadly paleness. She arose and returned with me in silence to the cottage, from whence, in less than a week, she was borne to her grave.

Eight years, continued he, after a pause of some minutes, have elapsed since her death, yet is her worth, her beauty, and her sufferings still fresh in the remembrance of the inhabitants of the hamlet. In mine, oh! Miss Fitzalan! how painfully, how pleasingly, do they still exist! No noisome weed is allowed to intermingle in the high grass which has overgrown her grave, at the head of which some kind hand has planted a rose-tree, whose roses blossom, bloom, and die upon the sacred spot. My child is gone before me to that earthly bed, to which I hoped she would have smoothed my passage. Every spot in and about the cottage, continually recall her to my view. The ornaments of this little room were all the work of that hand, long since mouldered into dust. In that bed—he stopped, he groaned, and tears burst from him—in that bed, resumed he (in a few minutes, though with a broken voice), she breathed her last sigh; in that spot I knelt and received the last pressure of her clay-cold lips! Of a calm night, when all is hushed to repose, I love to contemplate that heaven, to which I have given an angel—an angel to whom, I hope, shortly to be reunited; without such a hope, surely, of all men breathing, I should be the most wretched! Oh! how cruel is it then, in those, who, by raising doubts of an hereafter, attempt to destroy such a hope Ye sons of error, hide the impious doubts within your hearts; nor with wanton barbarity endeavor to deprive the miserable of their last comfort. When this world presents nothing but a dreary prospect, how cheering to the afflicted to reflect on that future one, where all will be bright and happy! When we mourn over the lost friends of our tenderest affections, oh! how consolatory to think we shall be re-united to them again! How often has this thought suspended my tears and stopped my sighs! Inspired by it with sudden joy, often have I risen from the cold bed where Juliana lies, and exclaimed: "Oh death! where is thy sting! Oh grave! where is thy victory!" both lost in the certainty of again beholding my child.

Amanda shed tears of soft compassion for the fate of Juliana, and the sorrows of her father, and felt, if possible, her gratitude to Heaven increased, for preserving her from the snares of such a monster of deceit and barbarity as Belgrave.

Howel relieved the anxiety she labored under about the means of returning home, by assuring her he would not only supply her with a sum sufficient for that purpose, but see her to Parkgate himself.

His name struck Amanda—it recalled to remembrance her Welsh friend. She inquired, and heard that the young and tender curate was indeed the son of her benefactor. "The softness of Henry's disposition," said his father, "particularly qualifies him for the sacred function, which prevents his having occasion to mingle in the concerns of the great world. He writes me word that he is the simple shepherd of a simple flock."

One day was all Amanda would devote to the purpose of recruiting her strength. Nothing could prevail on her longer to defer her journey. A chaise was accordingly procured, into which, at the first dawn of day, she and Howel stepped, followed by the blessings of the affectionate Eleanor, who, from her own wardrobe, had supplied Amanda with a few necessaries to take along with her. The church-yard lay about a quarter of a mile from the hamlet. It was only divided from the road by a low and broken wall. Old trees shaded the grass-grown grave, and gave a kind of solemn gloominess to the place.

"See," said Howel, suddenly taking Amanda's hand, and letting down the glass, "see the bed where Juliana reposes."

The grave was distinguished by the rose-tree at its head. The morning breeze gently agitated the high and luxuriant grass which covered it. Amanda gazed on it with inexpressible sadness, but the emotions it excited in her breast she endeavored to check, in pity to the wretched father, who exclaimed, while tears trickled down his pale and furrowed cheeks, "There lies my treasure."

She tried to divert him from his sorrows by talking of his son. She described his little residence, which he had never seen. Thus, by recalling to his recollection the blessings he yet possessed, checking his anguish for those he had lost.

The weakness of Amanda would not allow them to travel expeditiously. They slept one night on the road, and the next day, to her great joy, arrived at Parkgate, as she had all along dreaded a pursuit from Belgrave. A packet was to sail about four o'clock in the afternoon. She partook of a slight repast with her benevolent friend, who attended her to the boat, and with starting tears gave and received an adieu. She promised to write as soon as she reached home, and assured him his kindness would never be obliterated from her heart. He watched her till she entered the ship, then returned to the inn, and immediately set off for the hamlet, with a mind somewhat cheered by the consciousness of having served a fellow-creature.

CHAPTER XXXII.

"The breezy call of incense-breathing morn;
The swallow twittering from its straw-built shed;
The cock's shrill clarion, or the echoing horn,
No more shall rouse him from his lowly bed."—GRAY.

THE weakness which Amanda felt in consequence of her late illness, and the excessive sickness she always suffered at sea, made her retire to bed immediately on entering the packet, where she continued till the evening of the second day, when, about five o'clock, she was landed at the marine hotel. She directly requested the waiter to procure her a messenger to go into town, which being done, she sent to engage a place in the northern mail-coach, that went within a few miles of Castle Carberry If a place could not be procured, she ordered a chaise might be hired, that would immediately set out with her, as the nights were moon-light; but to her great joy the man speedily returned and informed her he had secured a seat in the coach, which she thought a much safer mode of travelling for her than in a hired carriage without any attendant. She took some slight refreshment, and then proceeded to tho mail hotel, from whence, at eleven o'clock, she set out in company with an old gentleman, who very composedly put on a large woollen night-cap, buttoned up his great coat, and fell into a profound sleep. He was, perhaps, just such a kind of companion as Amanda desired, as he neither teased her with insipid conversation or impertinent questions, but left her undisturbed to indulge her meditations during the journey. The second evening, about eight o'clock, she arrived at the nearest town to Castle Carberry, for which she directly procured a chaise and set off. Her spirits were painfully agitated. She dreaded the shock her father would receive from hearing of her sufferings, which it would be impossible to conceal from him. She trembled at what they would both feel on the approaching interview. Sometimes she feared he had already heard of her distress, and a gloomy presage rose in her mind of the anguish she should find him in on that account. Yet again, when she reflected on the fortitude he had hitherto displayed in his trials, under the present, she trusted, he would not lose it; and that he would not only support himself, but her, and bind up those wounds in her heart which perfidy, cruelty, and ingratitude had made. And oh! thought she to herself, when I find myself again in his arms, no temptation shall allure me from them—allure me into a world where my peace and fame have already suffered such a wreck. Thus, alternately fluctuating between hope and fear, Amanda pursued the road to Castle Carberry; but the latter sensation was predominant in her mind.

The uncommon gloominess of the evening added to her dejection—the dark and lowering clouds threatened a violent storm—already a shower of sleet and rain was falling, and everything looked cold and cheerless. Amanda thought the cabins infinitely more wretched than when she had first seen them. Many of their miserable inhabitants were now gathering their little flocks together, and driving them under shelter from the coming storm. The laborers were seen hastening to their respective homes, whilst the ploughboy, with a low and melancholy whistle, drove his slow and wearied team along. The sea looked rough and black, and as Amanda drew nearer to it, she heard it breaking with fury against the rocks. She felt herself extremely ill. She had left the hamlet ere her fever was subdued, and fatigue, joined to want of rest, now brought it back with all its former violence. She longed for rest and quiet, and trusted and believed these would conquer her malady.

The chaise stopped at the entrance of the lawn, as she wished to have her father prepared for her arrival by one of the servants. On alighting from it, it returned to town, and she struck into the grove, and by a winding path reached the castle. Her limbs trembled, and she knocked with an unsteady hand at the door. The sound was awfully reverberated through the building. Some minutes elapsed and no being appeared, neither could she perceive a ray of light from any of the windows. The wind blew the rain directly in her face, and her weakness increased, so that she could scarcely stand. She recollected a small door at the back of the castle, which led to the apartments appropriated to the domestics. She walked feebly to this, to try and gain admittance, and found it open. She proceeded through a long dark passage, on each side of which were small rooms, till she came to the kitchen. Here she found the old woman sitting (to whom the care of the castle was usually consigned), before a large turf fire. On hearing a footstep, she looked behind, and when she saw Amanda, started, screamed, and betrayed symptoms of the utmost terror.

"Are you frightened at seeing me, my good Kate?" cried Amanda. "Oh, holy Virgin!" replied Kate, crossing her breast, "one could not help being frightened, to have a body steal unawares upon them."

"My father is well, I hope?" said Amanda.

"Alack-a-day," cried Kate, "the poor dear Captain has gone through a sea of troubles since you went away." "Is he ill?" exclaimed Amanda. "Ill, ay, and the Lord knows he has reason enough to be ill. But, my dear jewel, do you know nothing at all of what has happened at the castle since you went away?" "No, nothing in the world." "Heaven help you, then," said Kate; "but, my dear soul, sit down upon this little stool, and warm yourself before the fire, for you look pale and cold, and I will tell you all about it. You must know, about three weeks ago, my Johnaten brought the Captain a letter from the post-office; he knew by the mark it was a letter from England, and so, when he comes into the kitchen to me, 'Kate,' says he, 'the Captain has got something now to cheer his spirits, for he has heard from Miss, I am sure.' So, to be sure, I said I was glad of it, for, you must know, my dear, he was low in spirits, and peaking, as one may say, for a few days before. Well, it was always my custom, when he got a letter from England, to go to him as soon as I thought he had read it, and ask about you; so I put on a clean apron, and up I goes to the parlor, and I opened the door, and walked in. Well, sir, says I, I hope there is good news from Miss?

"The Captain was sitting with the letter open before him on a table; he had a handkerchief to his eyes, but when I spoke he took it down, and I saw his face, which generally looked so pale, now quite flushed.

"'This letter, my good Kate,' says he, 'is not from my daughter, but I am glad you are come, for I wanted to speak to you. I am going to leave the castle, and I want you to look over all the things, and see they are in the same state as when I came to it. I shall then settle with the servants I hired, and discharge them.' I was struck all of a heap. The Lord forbid you should be going to leave us, sir, says I.

"The Captain got up—he walked to the window—he sighed heavily, and I saw a tear upon his cheek. He spoke to me again, and begged I would do as he had desired me. So, with a heavy heart, I went and told my Johnaten the sad tidings, who was as sorry as myself, for he loved the Captain dearly, not only from his being so mild a gentleman, but because he was a soldier, as he himself had been in his youth—and a soldier has always a love for one of his cloth. And Johnaten had often said he knew the Captain in America, and that he was a brave officer and a real gentleman.

"Well, the Captain came out to us, and said he was to be Lord Cherbury's agent no longer. And being a good penman, he settled all his own accounts and the servants in the course of the day, and discharged them, giving them both characters, which I warrant will soon get them good places again. Well, he said he must set off for England the next day. So everything was got ready; but in the middle of the night he was seized with spasms in his stomach. He thought himself dying, and at last rung the bell; and as good luck would have it, my Johnaten heard it, and went up to him directly. Had he been without relief much longer, I think he would have died. Johnaten called me up. I had a choice bottle of old brandy lying by me, so I soon blew up a fire, and heating a cup of it, gave it to him directly. He grew a little easier, but was too bad in the morning to think of going on his journey, which grieved him sadly. He got up, however, and wrote a large packet, which he sent by Johnaten to the post-office; packed up some things in a trunk, and put his seal upon his desk. He said he would not stay in the castle on any account, so he went out as soon as Johnaten came back from the post-office, leaning upon his arm, and got a little lodging at Thady Byrne's cabin." "Merciful heaven!" exclaimed the agonized and almost fainting Amanda, "support and strengthen me in this trying hour! enable me to comfort my unfortunate father: preserve me from sinking, that I may endeavor to assist him." Tears accompanied this fervent ejaculation, and her voice was lost in sobs.

"Alack-a-day," said the good-natured Kate, "now don't take it so sadly to heart, my jewel; all is not lost that is in danger, and there is as good fish in the sea as ever were caught; and what though this is a stormy night, to-morrow may be a fine day. Why, the very first sight of you will do the Captain good. Come, cheer up; I will give you some nice hot potatoes for your supper, for you see the pot is just boiling, and some fresh-churned buttermilk; and by the time you have eaten it, Johnaten perhaps may come back—he is gone to town to get some beef for our Sunday dinner—and then I will go with you to Thady's myself."

"No, no," cried Amanda, "every minute I now stay from my father seems an age. Too long has he been neglected—too long without a friend to soothe or attend him. Oh grant, gracious Heaven! grant," raising her clasped hands, "that I may not have returned too late to be of use to him!"

Kate pressed her to stay for Johnaten's return; but the agony of suspense she endured till she saw her father, made her regardless of walking alone, though the hour was late, dark, and tempestuous. Kate, finding her entreaties vain, attended her to the door, and assured her, if Johnaten returned soon, she would go over herself to the cabin, and see if she could do anything for her. Amanda pressed her hand, but was unable to speak. Ill, weak, and dispirited, she had flattered herself, on returning to her father, she should receive relief, support, and consolation; instead of which, heart-broken as she was, she now found she must give, or at least attempt giving them herself. She had before experienced distress, but the actual pressure of poverty she had never yet felt. Heretofore she had always a comfortable asylum to repair to, but now she not only found herself deprived of that, but of all means of procuring one, or even the necessaries of life. But if she mourned for herself, how much more severely did she mourn for her adored father! Could she have procured him comfort—could she in any degree have alleviated his situation—the horrors of her own would have been lessened; but of this she had not the slightest means or prospect. Her father, she knew, possessed the agency too short a time to be enabled to save any money, particularly as he was indebted to Lord Cherbury ere he obtained it. She knew of no being to whom she could apply in his behalf. Lord Cherbury was the only person on whom he depended in his former misfortunes for relief. His friendship, it was evident, by depriving her father of the agency, was totally lost; and to the disconsolate Amanda no way appeared of escaping "want, worldly want, that hungry meagre fiend, who was already close at their heels, and followed them in view."

The violence of the storm had increased, but it was slight in comparison of that which agitated the bosom of Amanda. The waves dashed with a dreadful noise against the rocks, and the angry spirit of the waters roared. The rain fell heavily, and soon soaked through the thin clothing of Amanda. She had about half a mile to walk, through a rugged road, bounded on one side by rocks, and on the other by wild and dreary fields. She knew the people with whom her father lodged; they were of the lowest order, and on her first arrival at Castle Carberry, in extreme dis tress, from which she had relieved them. She recollected their cabin was more decent than many others she had seen, yet still a most miserable dwelling. Wretched as it was, she was glad when she reached it, for the violence of the storm, and the loneliness of the road, had terrified her. The cabin was but a few yards from the beach. There were two windows in front. On one side a pile of turf, and on the other a shed for the pigs, in which they now lay grunting The shutters were fastened on the windows, to prevent their being shaken by the wind; but through the crevices Amanda saw light, which convinced her the inhabitants were not yet retired to repose. She feared her suddenly appearing before her father, in his present weak state, might have a dangerous effect upon him, and she stood before the cabin, considering how she should have her arrival broke to him. She at last tapped gently at the door, and then retreated a few steps from it, shivering with the wet and cold. In the beautiful language of Solomon, she might have said, "Her head was filled with dew, and her locks with the drops of the night." As she expected, the door was almost instantly opened. A boy appeared, whom she knew to be the son of the poor people. She held up her handkerchief, and beckoned him to her. He hesitated, as if afraid to advance, till she called him softly by his name. This assured him. He approached, and expressed astonishment at finding she was the person who had called him. She inquired for her father, and heard he was ill, and then asleep. She desired the boy to enter the cabin before her, and caution his parents against making any noise that might disturb him. He obeyed her, and she followed him.

She found the father of the family blowing a turf fire, to hasten the boiling of a large pot of potatoes. Three ragged children were sitting before it, watching impatiently for their supper. Their mother was spinning, and their old grandmother making bread. The place was small and crowded. Half the family slept below, and the other half upon a loft, to which they ascended by a ladder, and upon which a number of fowls were now familiarly roosting, cackling at every noise made below. Fitzalan's room was divided from the rest of the cabin by a thin partition of wood plastered with pictures of saints and crosses

"Save you kindly, madam," said the mistress of the mansion to Amanda, on entering it.

Byrne got up, and, with many scrapes, offered her his little stool before the fire. She thanked him, and accepted it. His wife, notwithstanding the obligations she lay under to her, seemed to think as much respect was not due to her as when mistress of the castle, and therefore never left her seat, or quitted her spinning, on her entrance.

"My poor father is very ill," said Amanda. "Why, indeed, the Captain has had a bad time of it," answered Mrs. Byrne, jogging her wheel. "To be sure he has suffered some little change; but your great folks, as well as your simple folks, must look to that in this world; and I don't know why they should not, for they are not better than the others, I believe."

"Arrah, Norah, now," said Byrne, "I wonder you are not shy of speaking so to the poor young lady."

Amanda's heart was surcharged with grief—she felt suffocating. She arose, unlatched the door, and the keen, cold air a little revived her. Tears burst forth, she indulged them freely, and they lightened the load on her heart. She asked for a glass of water. A glass was not readily to be procured. Byrne told her she had better take a noggin of butter-milk. This she refused, and he brought her one of water.

She now conquered the reluctance she felt to speak to the uncouth Mrs. Byrne, and consulted her on the best method of mentioning her arrival to her father. Mrs. Byrne said he had been in bed some time, but his sleep was often interrupted, and she would now step into the chamber, and try if he was awake. She accordingly did so, but returned in a moment, and said he still slept.

Amanda wished to see him in his present situation, to judge how far his illness had affected him: she stepped softly into the room. It was small and low, lighted by a glimmering rush-light, and a declining fire. The furniture was poor and scanty; in one corner stood a wooden bedstead, without curtains or any shade, and on this, under miserable bed-clothes, lay poor Fitzalan. Amanda shuddered, as she looked round this chamber of wretchedness. "Oh! my father," she cried to herself, "is this the only refuge you could find?" She went to the bed, she leaned over it, and beheld his face. It was deadly pale and emaciated; he moaned in his sleep, as if his mind was dreadfully oppressed. Suddenly he began to move; he sighed, "Amanda, my dearest child, shall I never more behold you?"

Amanda was obliged to hasten from the room, to give vent to her emotions. She sobbed, she wrung her hands, and in the bitterness of her soul exclaimed, "Alas! alas! I have returned too late to save him."

They soon after heard him stir. She requested Mrs. Byrne to go in, and cautiously inform him she was come. She complied, and in a moment Amanda heard him say, "Thank Heaven, my darling is returned." "You may now go in, miss," said Mrs. Byrne, coming from the room. Amanda went in. Her father was raised in the bed; his arms were extended to receive her. She threw herself into them. Language was denied them both, but tears, even more expressive than words, evinced their feelings. Fitzalan first recovered his voice. "My prayer," said he, "is granted. Heaven has restored my child to smooth the pillow of sickness, and soothe the last moments of existence." "Oh, my father!" cried Amanda, "have pity on me, and mention not those moments. Exert yourself for your child; who in this wide world has she but thee to comfort, support, and befriend her?" "Indeed," said he, "for your sake I wish they may be far distant." He held her at a little distance from him; he surveyed her face, her form, her altered complexion. Her fallen features appeared to shock him. He clasped her again to his bosom. "The world, my child, I fear," cried he, "has used thee most unkindly." "Oh, most cruelly," sobbed Amanda. "Then, my girl, let the reflection of that world, where innocence and virtue will meet a proper reward, console you. Here they are often permitted to be tried; but as gold is tried and purified by fire, so are they by adversity. 'Those whom God loves, He chastises.' Let this idea give you patience and fortitude under every trial. Never forego your dependence on Him, though calamity should pursue you to the very brink of the grave; but be comforted by the assurance He has given, that those who meekly bear the cross He lays upon them, shall be rewarded; that He will wipe away all tears from their eyes and swallow up death in victory. Though a soldier from my youth, and accustomed to all the licentiousness of camps, I never forgot my Creator; and I now find the benefit of not having done so. Now, when my friends desert, the world frowns upon me, when sickness and sorrow have overwhelmed me, religion stands me in good stead; consoles me for what I lost, and softens the remembrance of the past, by presenting prospects of future brightness."

So spoke Fitzalan the pious sentiments of his soul, and they calmed the agitations of Amanda. He found her clothes were wet, and insisted on her changing them directly. In the bundle the good Eleanor gave her, was a change of linen, and a cotton wrapper, which she now put on, in a small closet, or rather shed, adjoining her father's room. A good fire was made up, a better light brought in, and some bread and wine from a small cupboard in the room, which contained Fitzalan's things, set before her, of which he made her immediately partake. He took a glass of wine himself from her, and tried to cheer her spirits. "He had been daily expecting her arrival," he said, "and had had a pallet and bedclothes kept airing for her. He hoped she would not be dissatisfied with sleeping in the closet." "Ah! my father," she cried, "can you ask your daughter such a question?" She expressed her fears of injuring him, by having disturbed his repose. "No," he said, "it was a delightful interruption. It was a relief from pain and anxiety."

Lord Cherbury, he informed her, had written him a letter, which pierced him to the soul. "He accused me," said he, "of endeavoring to promote a marriage between you and Lord Mortimer; of treacherously trying to counteract his views, and take advantage of his unsuspecting friendship. I was shocked at these accusations. But how excruciating would my anguish have been had I really deserved them. I soon determined upon the conduct I should adopt, which was to deny the justice of his charges, and resign his agency—for any further dealings with a man who could think me capable of meanness or duplicity, was not to be thought of. My accounts were always in a state to allow me to resign at a moment's warning. It was my intention to go to England, put them into Lord Cherbury's hands, and take my Amanda from a place where she might meet with indignities as little merited by her as those her father had received were by him. A sudden and dreadful disorder, which I am convinced the agitation of my mind brought on, prevented my executing this intention. I wrote, however, to his lordship, acquainting him with my resignation of his agency, and transmitting my accounts and arrears. I sent a letter to you at the same time, with a small remittance for your immediate return, and then retired from the castle; for I felt a longer continuance in it would degrade me to the character of a mean dependant, and intimate a hope of being reinstated in my former station; which, should Lord Cherbury now offer, I should reject, for ignoble must be the mind which could accept of favors from those who doubted its integrity. Against such conduct my feelings revolt. Poverty, to me, is more welcome than independence, when purchased with the loss of esteem."

Amanda perceived her father knew nothing of her sufferings, but supposed her return occasioned by his letter. She therefore resolved, if possible, not to undeceive him, at least till his health was better. The night was far advanced, and her father, who saw her ill, and almost sinking with fatigue, requested her to retire to rest. She accordingly did. Her bed was made up in the little closet. Mrs. Byrne assisted her to undress, and brought her a bowl of whey, which, she trusted, with a comfortable sleep, would carry off her feverish symptoms, and enable her to be her father's nurse. Her rest, however, was far from being comfortable. It was broken by horrid dreams, in which she beheld the pale and emaciated figure of her father suffering the most exquisite tortures; and when she started from these dreams, she heard his deep moans, which were like daggers going through her heart. She arose once or twice, supposing him in pain, but when she went to his bed she found him asleep, and was convinced, from that circumstance, his pain was more of the mental than the bodily kind. She felt extremely ill. Her bones were sore from the violent motion of the carriage, and she fancied rest would do her good; but when, towards morning, she was inclined to take some, she was completely prevented by the noise the children made on rising. Fearful of neglecting her father, she arose soon after herself, but was scarcely able to put on her clothes from excessive weakness. She found him in bed, but awake. He welcomed her with a languid smile, and extending his hand, which was reduced to mere skin and bone, said, "that joy was a greater enemy to repose than grief, and had broken his earlier than usual that morning." He made her sit down by him. He gazed on her with unutterable tenderness. "In Divine language," cried he, "I may say—'Let me see thy countenance; let me hear thy voice: but sweet is thy voice, and thy countenance is comely, and my soul has pleasure in gazing on it.'" The kettle was already boiling. He had procured a few necessaries for himself, such as tea-things and glasses. Amanda placed the tea-table by the bed-side, and gave him his breakfast. Whilst receiving it from her, his eyes were raised to Heaven, as if in thankful gratitude for the inestimable blessing he still possessed in such a child. After breakfast, he said he would rise, and Amanda retired into the garden till he was dressed, if that could deserve the appellation, which was only a slip of ground planted with cabbages and potatoes, and enclosed with loose stones and blackberry bushes. The spring was already advanced. The day was fine. The light and fleecy clouds were gradually dispersing, and the sky, almost as far as the eye could reach, was of a clear blue. The dusky green of the blackberry bushes was enlivened by the pale purple of their blossoms. Tufts of primroses grew beneath their shelter. The fields, which rose with a gentle swell above the garden, were covered with a vivid green, spangled with daisies, buttercups, and wild honeysuckles, and the birds, as they fluttered from spray to spray, with notes of gladness hailed the genial season.

But neither the season nor its charms could now, as heretofore, delight Amanda. She felt forlorn and disconsolate; deprived of the comforts of life, and no longer interested in the objects about her, she sat down upon a stone at the end of the garden, and she thought the fresh breeze from the sea cooled the feverish heat of her blood. "Alas!" she said to herself, "at this season last year, how different was my situation from the present!" Though not in affluence, neither was she then in absolute distress; and she had besides the comfortable hope of having her father's difficulties removed. Like Burns' mountain daisy, she had then cheerfully glinted forth amidst the storm, because, she thought that storm would be soon overblown; but now, she saw herself on the point of being finally crushed beneath the rude pressure of poverty.

She recollected the words which had escaped her when she last saw Tudor Hall, and she thought they were dictated by something like a prophetic spirit. She had then said, as she leaned upon a little gate which looked into the domain: "When these woods again glow with vegetation; when every shade resounds with harmony, and the flowers and the blossoms spread their foliage to the sun, ah! where will Amanda be! far distant, in all probability, from these delightful shades; perhaps deserted and forgotten by their master."

She was indeed far distant from them; deserted, and if not forgotten, at least only remembered with contempt by their master—remembered with contempt by Lord Mortimer. It was an idea of intolerable anguish. His name was no more repeated as a charm to soothe her grief; his idea increased her misery.

She continued indulging her melancholy meditations, till informed by one of the children the Captain was ready to receive her. She hastened in, and found him in an old high-backed chair, and the ravages of care and sickness were now more visible to her than they had been the night before. He was reduced to a mere skeleton. "The original brightness of his form" was quite gone, and he seemed already on the very brink of the grave. The agony of Amanda's feelings was expressed on her countenance—he perceived and guessed its source. He endeavored to compose and comfort her. She mentioned a physician; he tried to dissuade her from the idea of bringing one, but she besought him in compassion to her to consent, and overcome by her earnestness, he at last promised the ensuing day she should do as she wished.

It was now Sunday, and he desired the service of the day to be read. A small bible lay on the table before him, and Amanda complied with his desire.

In the first lesson were these words: "Leave thy fatherless children to me, and I will be their father." The tears gushed from Fitzalan; he laid his hand, which appeared convulsed with agitation, on the book. "Oh! what words of comfort!" cried he, "are these; what transport do they convey to the heart of a parent burthened with anxiety! Yes, merciful Power, I will, with grateful joy, commit my children to thy care, for thou art the friend who will never forsake them." He desired Amanda to proceed; her voice was weak and broken, and the tears, in spite of her efforts to restrain them, stole down her cheeks.

When she had concluded, her father drew her towards him, and inquired into all that had passed during her stay in London. She related to him, without reserve, the various incidents she had met with previous to her going to the Marchioness's; acknowledged the hopes and fears she experienced on Lord Mortimer's account, and the argument he had made use of to induce her to a clandestine union, with her positive refusal to such a step.

A beam of pleasure illumined the pallid face of Fitzalan. "You acted," said he, "as I expected; and I glory in my child, and feel more indignation than ever against Lord Cherbury for his mean suspicions." Amanda was convinced those suspicions had been infused into his mind by those who had struck at her peace and fame. This idea, however, as well as their injuries to her, she meant if possible to conceal. When her father, therefore, desired her to proceed in her narrative, her voice began to falter, her mind became disturbed, and her countenance betrayed her agitation. The remembrance of the dreadful scenes she had gone through at the Marchioness's made her involuntarily shudder, and she wished to conceal them for ever from her father, but found it impossible to evade his minute and earnest inquiries.

"Gracious Heaven!" said he, on hearing them, "what complicated cruelty and deceit; inhuman monsters! to have no pity on one so young, so innocent, so helpless. The hand of sorrow has indeed pressed heavy on thee, my child; but, after the Marchioness's former conduct, I cannot be surprised at any action of hers."

He gave her a note to discharge her debt to Howel, and begged she would immediately write and return his grateful acknowledgments for his benevolence. She feared he inconvenienced himself by parting with the note; but he assured her he could spare it extremely well, as he had been an economist, and had still sufficient money to support them a few months longer in their present situation.

Amanda now inquired when he had heard from her brother.

She said he had not answered her last letter, and that his silence had made her very uneasy.

"Alas! poor Oscar!" exclaimed Fitzalan, "he has not been exempt from his portion of distress."

He took a letter, as he spoke, from his pocket-book, and presented it to Amanda. She opened it with a trembling hand, and read as follows:—

My dear Father,—Particular circumstances prevented my answering your last letter as soon as I could have wished; and, indeed, the intelligence I have to communicate makes me almost averse to write at all. As my situation, however, must sooner or later be known to you, I think it better to inform you of it myself, as I can, at the same time, reconcile you, I trust, in some degree to it, by assuring you I bear it patiently, and that it has not been caused by any action which can degrade my character as a man or a soldier. I have long, indeed, had a powerful enemy to cope with, and, it will no doubt surprise you to hear, that that enemy is Colonel Belgrave. An interference in the cause of humanity provoked his insolence and malignity. Neither his words nor looks were bearable, and I was irritated by them to send him a challenge. Had I reflected, the probable consequences of such a step must have occurred and prevented my taking it; but passion blinded my reason, and in yielding to its dictates do I hold myself alone culpable throughout the whole affair. I gave him the opportunity his malicious heart had long desired, of working my ruin. I was, by his order, put under an immediate arrest. A court-martial was held, and I was broke for disrespect to a superior officer; but it was imagined by the whole corps I should have been restored. I, however, knew too much of Belgrave's disposition to believe this would be the case; but never shall he triumph in the distress he has caused by witnessing it. I have already settled on the course I shall pursue, and ere this letter reaches you I shall have quitted my native kingdom. Forgive me, my dear sir, for not consulting you relative to my conduct. But I feared, if I did, your tenderness would interfere to prevent it, or lead you to distress yourself on my account; and to think that you and my dear sister were deprived of the smallest comfort, by my means, would be a source of intolerable anguish to me. Blessed as I am with youth, health, and fortitude, I have no doubt but I shall make my way through the rugged path of life extremely well. A parting visit I avoided, from the certainty of its being painful to us both. I shall write as soon as I reach my place of destination. I rejoice to hear Amanda is so happily situated with Lady Greystock: may your suffering and her merit be rewarded as they deserve! Suffer not, I entreat, too tender an anxiety for my interest to disturb your repose. I again repeat I have no doubt but what I shall do well. That Providence, in which I trust, will, I humbly hope, support me through every difficulty, and again unite me to the friends so valuable to my heart Farewell, my dear father, and, be assured, with unabated respect and gratitude, I subjoin myself your affectionate son, OSCAR FITZALAN.

This letter was a cruel shock to Amanda. She hoped to have procured her brother's company, and that her father's melancholy and her own would have been alleviated by it. Sensible of the difficulties Oscar must undergo, without friends or fortune, the tears stole down her cheeks, and she almost dreaded she could no more behold him.

Her father besought her to spare him the misery of seeing those tears. He leaned upon her for comfort and support, he said, and bid her not disappoint him. She hastily wiped away her tears; and though she could not conquer, tried to suppress, her anguish.

Johnaten and Kate called, in the course of the day, to know if they could be of any service to Fitzalan. Amanda engaged Johnaten to go to town the next morning for a physician, and gave Kate the key of a wardrobe where she had left some things, which she desired her to pack up and send to the cabin in the evening. Mrs. Byrne gave them one of her fowls for dinner, and Fitzalan assumed an appearance of cheerfulness, and the evening wore away somewhat better than the preceding part of the day had done.

Johnaten was punctual in obeying Amanda's commands, and brought a physician the next morning to the cabin. Fitzalan appeared much worse, and Amanda rejoiced that she had been resolute in procuring him advice.

She withdrew from the room soon after the physician had entered it, and waited without in trembling anxiety for his appearance. When he came out she asked, with a faltering voice, his opinion, and besought him not to deceive her from pity to her feelings.

He shook his head, and assured her he would not deviate from truth for the world. The Captain was indeed in a ticklish situation, he said, but the medicines he had ordered, and sea bathing, he doubted not, would set all to rights; it was fortunate, he added, she delayed no longer sending for him; mentioned twenty miraculous cures he had performed; admired the immense fine prospect before the door, and wished her good morning, with what he thought quite a degagee and irresistible air.

She was willing to believe his assurances of her father's recovery; as the drowning wretch will grasp at every straw, she eagerly embraced the shadow of comfort, and in the recovery of her father, looked forward to consolation for all her sorrows. She struggled against her own illness, that no assiduous attention might be wanting to him; and would have sat up with him at night, had he not positively insisted on her going to bed.

The medicines he was ordered he received from her hands, but with a look which seemed to express his conviction of their inefficacy. All, however, she wished him to do, he did, and often raised his eyes to Heaven, as to implore it to reward her care, and yet a little longer spare him to this beloved child, whose happiness so much depended on the prolongation of his existence.

Four days passed heavily away, and the assurances of the physician, who was punctual in his attendance, lost their effect upon Amanda. Her father was considerably altered for the worse, and unable to rise, except for a few minutes in the evening, to have his bed made. He complained of no pain or sickness, but seemed sinking beneath an easy and gradual decay. It was only at intervals he could converse with his daughter. His conversation was then calculated to strengthen her fortitude and resignation, and prepare her for an approaching melancholy event. Whenever she received a hint of it, her agony was inexpressible; but pity for her feelings could not prevent her father from using every opportunity that occurred for laying down rules and precepts which might be serviceable to her when without a guide or protector. Sometimes he adverted to the past, but this was only done to make her more cautious of the future.

He charged her to avoid any further intimacy with Lord Mortimer, as an essential measure for the restoration of her peace, the preservation of her fame, and the removal of Lord Cherbury's unjust suspicions, "who will find at last," continued he, "how much he wronged me, and may, perhaps, feel compunction when beyond his power to make reparation."

To all he desired, Amanda promised a religious observance; she thought it unnecessary in him, indeed, to desire her to avoid Lord

Mortimer, convinced as she was that he had utterly abandoned her; but the grief this desertion occasioned, she believed she should soon overcome was her father once restored to health, for then she would have no time for useless regrets or retrospections, but be obliged to pass every hour in active exertions for his support and comfort.

A week passed away in this manner at the cabin—a week of wretchedness to Amanda, who perceived her father growing weaker and weaker. She assisted him, as usual, to rise one evening for a few minutes; when dressed, he complained of an oppression in his breathing, and desired to be supported to the air. Amanda with difficulty led him to the window, which she opened, and seated him by it, then knelt before him, and putting her arms round his waist, fastened her eyes with anxious tenderness upon his face.

The evening was serenely fine; the sun was setting in all its glory, and the sea, illumined by its parting beams, looked like a sheet of burnished silver.

"What a lovely scene!" cried Fitzalan faintly; "with what majesty does the sun retire from the world! the calmness which attends its departure is such, I think, as must attend the exit of a good man." He paused for a few minutes, then raising his eyes to heaven, exclaimed—"Merciful Power! had it pleased thee, I could have wished yet a little longer to have been spared to this young creature; but thy will, not mine, be done! Confiding in thy mercy, I leave her with some degree of fortitude."

Amanda's tears began to flow as he spoke. He raised his hand, on which they fell, and, kissing them off, exclaimed—"Precious drops! My Amanda, weep not too bitterly for me—like a weary traveller, think that rest must now be acceptable to me."

She interrupted him, and conjured him to change the discourse. He shook his head mournfully, pressed her hands between his, and said:—

"Yet a little longer, my child, bear with it;" then bade her assure her brother, whenever they met, which he trusted and believed would be soon, he had his father's blessing,—"the only legacy," he cried, "I can leave him, but one, I am confident, he merits, and will value. To you, my girl, I have no doubt he will prove a friend and guardian. You may both, perhaps, be amply recompensed for all your sorrows. Providence is just in all its dealings, and may yet render the lovely offspring of my Malvina truly happy."

He appeared exhausted by speaking, and Amanda assisted him to lie down, entreating him, at the same time, to take some drops. He consented, and while she was pouring them out at a little table, her back to the bed, she heard a deep groan. The bottle dropped from her hand, she sprang to the bed, and perceived her father lying senseless on the pillow. She imagined he had fainted, and screamed out for assistance. The woman of the cabin, her husband, and mother, all rushed into the room. He was raised up, his temples and hands chafed, and every remedy within the house applied for his recovery, but in vain—his spirit had forsaken its tenement of clay for ever.

Amanda, when convinced of this, wrung her hands together; then, suddenly opening them, she clasped the lifeless body to her breast, and sunk fainting beside it.

CHAPTER XXXIII.

HE remained a considerable time in a state of insensibility, and, when recovered, she found herself in a bed laid upon the floor in a corner of the outside room. Her senses were at first confused—she felt as if waking from a disagreeable dream, but in a few minutes a perfect recollection of what had passed returned. She saw some one sitting by the bed—she raised herself a little, and perceived Sister Mary. "This is, indeed, a charitable visit," cried she, extending her hand, and speaking in a low broken voice. The good-natured nun jumped from her seat on hearing her speak, and embraced her most tenderly. Her caresses affected Amanda inexpressibly—she dropped her head upon her breast, and wept with a vehemence which relieved the oppression of her heart.

Sister Mary said she had never heard of her return to the country, till Mrs. Byrne came to St. Catherine's for a few sprigs of rosemary to strew over the poor Captain. She had returned with her then to the cabin, to try if she could be of any service, and to invite her, in the name of the prioress and the whole sisterhood, to the convent.

Amanda thanked her for her kind invitation, which, she said, she must decline accepting for a few days, till she had performed all her duties, which, in a voice half stifled by sobs, she added, "the grave would soon terminate." She was sorry, she said, that they had undressed her, and requested Sister Mary to assist her in putting on her clothes. The sister tried to dissuade her from this, but soon found she was determined to spend the remainder of the night in her father's apartment. She accordingly dressed her—for Amanda's trembling hands refused their accustomed office—and made her take a glass of wine and water, ere she suffered her to move towards the door. Amanda was astonished, as she approached it, to hear a violent noise, like the mingled sounds of laughing and singing. Her soul recoiled at the tumult, and she asked Sister Mary, with a countenance of terror, "what it meant?" She replied, "it was only some friends and neighbors doing honor to the Captain." Amanda hastily opened the door, anxious to terminate the suspense these words occasioned, but, how great was her horror, when she perceived a set of the meanest rustics assembled round the bed, with every appearance of inebriety, laughing, shouting, and smoking. What a savage scene for a child, whose heart was bursting with grief! She shrieked with horror, and, flinging herself into the arms of Sister Mary, conjured her to have the room cleared.

Sister Mary, from being accustomed to such scenes, felt neither horror nor disgust: she complied, however, with the request of Amanda, and besought them to depart, saying: "that Miss Fitzalan was a stranger to their customs, and besides, poor thing, quite beside herself with grief." They began to grumble at the proposal of removing; they had made preparations for spending a merry night, and Mrs. Byrne said, "if she had thought things would have turned out in this way, the Captain might have found some other place to die in—for the least one could have, after his giving them so much trouble, was a little enjoyment with one's neighbors at the latter end." Johnaten and Kate, who were among the party, joined their entreaties to Sister Mary's, and she, to tempt them to compliance, said, "that in all probability they would soon have another and a better opportunity for making merry than the present." They at length retired, and Sister Mary and Amanda were left alone in the chamber of death. The dim light which remained cast a glimmering shade upon the face of Fitzalan, that added to its ghastliness. Amanda now indulged in all the luxury of grief, and found in Sister Mary a truly sympathetic friend, for the good nun was famed throughout the little circle of her acquaintance for weeping with those that wept, and rejoicing with those that rejoiced. She obtained a promise from Amanda of accompanying her to St. Catherine's as soon as her father was interred; and in return for this she gave an assurance of continuing with her till the last melancholy offices were over, and also, that with the assistance of Johnaten, she would see everything proper provided. This was some comfort to Amanda, who felt herself at present unequal to any exertion; yet, notwithstanding her fatigue and illness, she persevered in her resolution of sitting up with her father every night, dreading that, if she retired to bed, a scene of riot would again ensue, which, in her opinion, was sacrilege to the dead. She went to bed every morning and was nursed with the most tender attention by Sister Mary, who also insisted on being her companion at night. This, however, was but a mere matter of form, for the good sister was totally unable to keep her eyes open, and slept as comfortably upon the earthen floor, with her gown made into a pillow for her head, as if laid upon down: then was poor Amanda left to her own reflections, and the melancholy contemplation of her beloved father's remains. The evening of the fourth day after his decease was fixed upon for his interment; with streaming eyes and a breaking heart, Amanda beheld him put into the coffin, and in that moment felt as if he had again died before her. A small procession attended, consisting of the people of the house, Johnaten and Kate, and a few respectable farmers, to whom Fitzalan had endeared himself during his short abode at Castle Carberry; the men had scarfs and hat-bands, and the women hoods.

Johnaten, who had been a soldier in his youth, resolved to pay him some military honors, and placed his hat and sword upon the coffin. Amanda, by the most painful efforts, supported the preparations for his removal; but when she saw the coffin actually raised to be taken out, she could no longer restrain her feelings; she shrieked in the agony of her soul, a sickness, almost deadly, seized her, and she fell fainting upon Sister Mary's bosom.

CHAPTER XXXIV.

"Oh, let me unlade my breast,
Pour out the fulness of my soul before you,
Show every tender, every grateful thought,
This wondrous goodness stirs. But 'tis impossible,
And utterance all is vile; since I can only
Swear you reign here, but never tell how much."—ROWE.

ISTER MARY recovered her with difficulty, but found it impossible to remove her from the cabin till she was more composed. In about two hours its inhabitants returned, and the car having arrived which she had ordered to convey Amanda to St. Catherine's, she was placed upon it in a state scarcely animate, and, supported by Sister Mary, was conveyed to that peaceful asylum. On arriving at it she was carried immediately into the prioress's apartment, who received and welcomed her with the most tender affection and sensibility—a tenderness which roused Amanda from the stupefaction into which she appeared sinking, and made her weep violently. She felt relieved from doing so, and, as some return for the kindness she received, endeavored to appear benefited by it. She therefore declined going to bed, but lay down upon a little matted couch in the prioress's room. The tea-table was close by it. As she refused any other refreshment, she obtained this by a promise of eating something with it. None of the sisterhood—Sister Mary excepted—were admitted; and Amanda felt this delicate attention and respect to her sorrows with gratitude. She arrived on the eve of their patron saint at the convent, which was always celebrated with solemnity. After tea, therefore, the prioress and Sister Mary were compelled to repair to the chapel; but she removed the reluctance they felt to leave her alone by complaining of being drowsy. A pillow being laid under her head by Sister Mary, soon after they quitted her she fell into a profound slumber, in which she continued till awoke by distant music, so soft, so clear, so harmonious, that the delightful sensations it gave her she could only compare to those which she imagined a distressed and pensive soul would feel when, springing from the shackles of mortality, it first heard the heavenly sounds that welcomed it to the realms of bliss. The chapel from which those celestial sounds proceeded was at the extremity of the house, so that they sometimes swelled upon her ear, sometimes faintly sunk upon it. The pauses in the organ, which was finely played, were filled up by the sweet, though less powerful strains of the sisterhood, who sung a hymn in honor of their saint.

> "No one was here exempt,
> No voice but well could join melodious part."

'Tis a foretaste of heaven, thought Amanda. She heard a deep sigh behind her. She turned her head hastily, and perceived a figure standing near, which bore a strong resemblance to Lord Mortimer. She was alarmed. She could not believe it was him. The light which the small and heavy-arched window admitted was imperfect, and she rose from the couch to be better assured it was or was not him. A second glance convinced her. She might have believed her eyes at first. Trembling and astonished, she sunk upon a seat, excleaiming, "Gracious heaven! what can have brought Lord Mortimer hither?"

He made no reply, but, kneeling before her, took her hands in his, pressed them to his forehead and lips, and laid his head upon them.

"Why," cried Amanda, unutterably affected by the emotions he betrayed, "why, my Lord, are you come hither?" "To try," he replied, in a voice scarcely articulate, "whether Miss Fitzalan will yet consider me as her friend." "That, my Lord," said she, "depends upon circumstances; but while your lordship remains in your present position, what they are I cannot explain."

Lord Mortimer instantly rose and seated himself beside her. "Now, tell me," said he, "what those circumstances are." "The first, my Lord, is to exculpate my father in the opinion of Lord Cherbury, and, by declaring the commencement and progress of our acquaintance, eradicate from his lordship's mind the injurious suspicions he entertained against him. This, perhaps, you will say is useless, considering those suspicions can no longer wound him; but, my Lord, I deem it an incumbent duty on me to remove from his memory the obloquy on my account cast on it." "I promise you most solemnly," said Lord Mortimer, "you shall be obeyed. This is a debt of justice, which I had resolved to pay ere I received your injunction for doing so. It is but lately I heard of the unjust charges made against him, nor do I now know what fiend gave rise to them." "The same, perhaps," exclaimed Amanda, "who spread such complicated snares for my destruction, and involved me in every horror but that which proceeds from conscious guilt. Oh, my Lord! the second circumstance I allude to is, if you should hear my name treated with scorn and contempt by those few—those very few—whom I had reason to esteem, and to believe esteemed me, that you would kindly interpose in my justification, and say I merited not the aspersions cast upon me. Believe me innocent, and you will easily persuade others I am so. You shake your head, as much as to say you cannot think me so, after the proofs you have seen to the contrary. Ah, my Lord! the proofs were contrived by malice and treachery, to ruin me in the estimation of my friends, and by perfidy, to force me into a crime, of which I already bear the appearance and the stigma. Surely, in this solemn hour, which has seen my beloved father consigned to his kindred earth, when, with a mind harassed by sorrow, and a body worn out with fatigue, I feel as if standing on the verge of the grave, I should be the most abandoned of wretches, if I could assert my innocence without the consciousness of really possessing it. No, my Lord; by such a falsehood I should be not only wicked, but foolish, in depriving myself of that happiness hereafter which will so fully recompense my present miseries." "Oh, Amanda!" cried Lord Mortimer, who had been walking backward and forward in an agitated manner while she spoke, "you would almost convince me against the evidence of my own senses." "Almost," she repeated. "Then I see, my Lord, you are determined to disbelieve me. But why, since so prejudiced against me, have you come hither? Was it merely to be assured of my wretchedness? to hear me say that I stand alone in the world, without one being interested about my welfare; that my present asylum is bestowed by charity; and that, if my life be prolonged, it must be spent in struggling against constitution, sorrow, and ill fame, to procure a subsistence." "No, no," exclaimed Lord Mortimer, flinging himself at her feet; "never shall you suffer such misery. Were you even the being I was tempted to think you some time ago, never would Mortimer suffer the woman his heart doated on to feel such calamity. I do not, I cannot believe you would deceive me. There is an irresistible eloquence in your words that convinces me you have been the victim of treachery, and I its dupe. I cannot give you a more convincing proof of my confidence in you, than by again renewing my entreaties to have one fame, one fate, one fortune ours."

The resolution which Amanda had forced to support her through the painful scene she guessed would ensue the moment she saw Lord Mortimer, now vanished, and she burst into a flood of tears. She saw his conduct in the most generous, the most exalted light. Notwithstanding appearances were so much against her, he was willing to rely solely on her own asseveration of innocence, and to run every risk on her account, that by a union he might shelter her from the distresses of her present situation. But while her sensibility was affected by his expressions, her pride was alarmed lest he should impute her ardent desire of vindicating herself to the expectation of having his addresses renewed. In broken accents she endeavored to remove such an idea, if it had arisen, and to convince him that all further intimacy between them must now be terminated. Lord Mortimer ascribed the latter part of her speech to the resentment she felt against him for ever entertaining doubts of her worth. She desired him to rise, but he refused till he was forgiven. "My forgiveness is yours indeed, my Lord," said she, "though your suspicions wounded me to the soul. I can scarcely wonder at your entertaining them, when I reflect on the different situations in which I was found, which, if your lordship can spare a little longer time, or deem it worth devoting to such a purpose, as well as I am able I will account for being involved in" Lord Mortimer declared his ardent desire to hear those particulars, which nothing but a fear of fatiguing or agitating her could have prevented his before expressing. He then seated himself by her.

and taking her cold and emaciated hand in his, listened to her little narrative.

She briefly informed him of her father's residing in Devonshire after the death of her mother, of the manner in which they became acquainted with Colonel Belgrave, of his having ingratiated himself into their friendship, by pretending to be Oscar's friend, and then plunging them in distress, when he found they not only resisted but resented his villanous designs. She related the artful manner in which Lady Greystock had drawn her from her father's protection, and the cold and insolent reception she met from the Marchioness and her daughter, when introduced by the above-mentioned lady, the enmity the Marchioness bore her father, the sudden alteration in her behavior, the invitation to her house so unexpected and unnecessary, all tended to inspire a belief that she was concerned in contriving Colonel Belgrave's admittance to the house, and had also given Lord Cherbury reason to suspect the integrity of her father.

Lord Mortimer here interrupted Amanda, to mention the conversation which passed between him and Mrs. Jane in the hall.

She raised her hands and eyes to heaven with astonishment at such wickedness, and said, "Though she always suspected the girl's integrity, from a certain sycophant air, she never imagined she could be capable of such baseness."

Lord Mortimer again interrupted her, to mention what Lady Greystock had told him concerning Mrs. Jennings, as also what the housekeeper had said of the note he gave her for Amanda.

"Good God!" said Amanda, "when I hear of all the enemies I had, I almost wonder I escaped so well." She then resumed her narrative, accounted for the dislike Mrs. Jennings had to her, and explained the way in which she was entrapped into Colonel Belgrave's power, the almost miraculous manner in which she was freed from his house, the friendship she received from Howel, and the situation in which she arrived at Castle Carberry, and found her father. The closing scene she could not describe, for sighs and sobs impeded her utterance. Lord Mortimer gently folded her to his breast. He called her his dear, his unfortunate, his lovely girl, more precious than ever to his heart, and declared he never again would quit her till she had given him a right to espouse her quarrels, and secure her from the machinations of her enemies. Her warm tears wet his cheek as she exclaimed, "that could never be."

"My promise is already past," cried she. "That which was given to the living shall not be forfeited to the dead; and this, my Lord, by design, is the last time we must ever meet." "What promise?" exclaimed Lord Mortimer. "Surely no one could be so inhuman as to extort a promise from you to give me up?" "It was not inhumanity extorted it," replied Amanda, "but honor, rectitude, and discretion; without forfeiting those never can I violate it. There is but one event could make me acquiesce in your wishes, that is, having a fortune adequate to yours to bring you, because then Lord Cherbury could ascribe no selfish motive to my conduct; but as such an event is utterly improbable, I might almost say impossible, it is certain we shall never be united. Any further intercourse between us, you must therefore be convinced, would injure me. Disturb not, therefore, my Lord, my retirement; but ere you depart, allow me to assure you you have lightened the weight on my heart by crediting what I have said. Should I not recover from the illness which now preys upon me, it will cheer my departing spirit to know you think me innocent; and, if I live, it will support me through many difficulties, and often, perhaps, after the toils of a busy day, shall I comfort myself by reflecting that those I esteem, if they think of me, it is with their wonted regard."

Lord Mortimer was affected by the manner in which she spoke, his eyes began to glisten, and he was again declaring he would not suffer her to sacrifice happiness at the shrine of a too scrupulous and romantic generosity, when the door opened, and the prioress and Sister Mary (who had been detained in the chapel by a long discourse from the priest) entered, bearing lights.

Lord Mortimer started in much confusion, retreated to one of the windows, and drew out his handkerchief to conceal the emotions Amanda had excited. She was unable to speak to the prioress an Sister Mary, who stared round them, and then at each other, not certain whether they should advance or retreat. Lord Mortimer in a few moments recovered his composure, and advancing to the prioress, apologized for his intrusion into her apartment; but said ne had the honor of being a friend of Miss Fitzalan's, and could not resist his wish of inquiring in person after her health as soon as he arrived in the country.

The prioress, who had once seen a good deal of the polite world, received his address with ease and complaisance. Sister Mary went over to Amanda, and found her weak, trembling, and weeping. She expressed the utmost concern at seeing her in such a situation, and immediately procured her a glass of wine, which she insisted on her taking. The lights now gave Lord Mortimer an opportunity of contemplating the depredations which grief and sickness had made upon her. Her pale and sallow complexion, her heavy and sunken eyes, struck him with horror. He could not conceal his feelings. "Gracious Heaven!" cried he, going to the couch, and taking her hand, "I fear you are very ill."

She looked mournfully in his face without speaking; but this look was sufficient to assure him he was not mistaken. The efforts she had made to converse with him, and the yet greater efforts she made to banish him for ever from her, quite exhausted her; after the various miseries she had gone through, how soothing to her soul would have been the attentions of Lord Mortimer, how pleasing, how delightful, the asylum she should have found in his arms! But no temptation, no distress, she resolved should ever make her disobey the injunction of her adored father.

"She is very bad indeed," said Sister Mary, "and we must get her to bed as soon as possible." "She requires rest and repose indeed," said Lord Mortimer; "but tell me, my dear Miss Fitzalan (taking her hand) if I have those good ladies' permission for calling here to-morrow, will you, if able to rise, see me?" "I cannot, indeed," said Amanda; "I have already declared this must be our last interview, and I shall not retract from what I have said." "Then," exclaimed Lord Mortimer, regardless, or rather forgetful, of those who heard him, from the agitation and warmth of his feelings, "I shall, in one respect at least, accuse you of dissimulation, that of feigning a regard for me you never felt." "Such an accusation is now of little consequence," replied Amanda; "perhaps you had better think it just." "Cruel, inexorable girl, to refuse seeing me, to wish to have the anxiety which now preys upon my heart prolonged!"

"Young man," said the prioress, in an accent of displeasure, seeing the tears streaming down Amanda's cheeks, "respect her sorrows."

"Respect them, madam," repeated he; "Oh! Heaven, I respect, I venerate them; but will you, my dear lady, when Miss Fitzalan is able, prevail on her to communicate the particulars of our acquaintance; and will you then become my advocate, and persuade her to receive my visits?" "Impossible, sir," said the prigress, "I shall never attempt to desire a larger share of confidence from Miss Fitzalan than she desires to bestow upon me. From my knowledge of her I am convinced her conduct will be always guided by discretion; she has greatly obliged me by choosing this humble retreat for her residence; she has put herself under my protection, and I shall endeavor to fulfil that sacred trust by securing her from any molestation." "Well, madam," said Lord Mortimer, "I flatter myself Miss Fitzalan will do me justice in declaring my visits proceeded from wishes, which, though she may disappoint, she cannot disapprove. I shall no longer intrude upon your time or hers, but will still hope I shall find you both less inflexible."

He took up his hat, he approached the door; but when he glanced at Amanda, he could not depart without speaking to her, and again went to the couch.

He entreated her to compose and exert herself; he desired her forgiveness for any warmth he had betrayed, and he whispered to her that all his earthly happiness depended on her restoration to health, and her becoming his. He insisted on her now giving him her hand as a pledge of amity between them. She complied; but when presuming on this he again asked her consent to repeat his visits, he found her inexorable as ever, and retired, if not with a displeased, a disappointed countenance. Sister Mary attended him from the apartment. At the door of the convent he requested her to walk a few paces from it with him, saying he wanted to speak to her. She consented, and remembering he was the person who frightened her one evening amongst the ruins, determined now, if she had a good opportunity, to ask what had then brought him thither?

Lord Mortimer knew the poverty of the convent, and feared

Amanda might want many things, or its inhabitants be distressed to procure them for her; he therefore pulled out a purse and presenting it to Sister Mary, requested she would apply it for Miss Fitzalan's use, without mentioning anything about it to her. Sister Mary shook the purse. "Oh! Jesu Maria," exclaimed she, "how heavy it is!"

Lord Mortimer was retiring, when, catching hold of him, she cried, "Stay, stay, I have a word or two to say to you. I wonder how much there is in this purse?"

Lord Mortimer smiled, "If not enough for the present emergencies," said he, "it shall soon be replenished."

Sister Mary sat down on a tomb-stone, and very deliberately counted the money into her lap. "Oh! mercy," said she, "I never saw so many guineas together before in all my life!"

Again Lord Mortimer smiled, and was retiring; but again stopping him, she returned the gold into the purse, and declared, "she neither would or durst keep it."

Lord Mortimer was provoked at this declaration, and, without replying to it, walked on. She ran nimbly after him, and, dropping the purse at his feet, was out of sight in a moment. When she returned to the prioress's apartment, she related the incident, and took much merit to herself for acting so prudently. The prioress commended her very much, and poor Amanda, with a faint voice, said, "she had acted quite right."

A little room, inside the prioress's chamber, was prepared for Amanda, into which she was now conveyed, and the good-natured Sister Mary brought her own bed, and laid it beside hers.

CHAPTER XXXV.

"With dirges due, and sad array,
Slow through the church-way path I saw him borne."

IT will now be necessary to account for the sudden appearance of Lord Mortimer at the convent. Our reader may recollect that we left him in London, in the deepest affliction for the supposed perfidy of

Amanda—an affliction which knew no diminution from time; neither the tenderness of his aunt, Lady Martha Dormer, nor the kind consideration his father showed for him, who, for the present, ceased to importune him about Lady Euphrasia, could have any lenient effect upon him—he pined in thought, and felt a distaste to all society. He at last began to think, that though Amanda had been unhappily led astray, she might, ere this, have repented of her error, and forsaken Colonel Belgrave. To know whether she had done so, or whether she could be prevailed upon to give him up, he bel eved, would be an alleviation of his sorrows. No sooner had he persuaded himself of this, than he determined on going to Ireland, without delay, to visit Captain Fitzalan, and, if she was not returned to his protection, advise with him about some method of restoring her to it.

He told Lord Cherbury he thought an excursion into Wales would be of service to him. His lordship agreed in thinking it might, and, secretly delighted that all danger relative to Amanda was over, gladly concurred in whatever could please his son, flattering himself that, on his return to London, he would no longer raise any objections to an alliance with the fair Scotch heiress.

Lord Mortimer travelled with as much expedition to Holyhead as if certain that perfect happiness, not a small alleviation of misery, would be the recompense of his journey. He concealed from his aunt the real motives which actuated him to it, blushing, even to himself, at the weakness which he still felt relative to Amanda. When he crossed the water he again set off post, attended on horseback only by his own man. Within one mile of Castle Carberry he met the little mournful procession approaching, which was attending poor Fitzalan to his last home. The carriage stopped to let them pass, and in the last of the group he perceived Johnaten, who, at the same moment, recognised him. Johnaten, with much surprise in his countenance, stepped up to the carriage, and, after bowing, and humbly hoping his lordship was well, with a melancholy shake of his head, informed him whose remains he was following.

"Captain Fitzalan dead!" repeated Lord Mortimer, with a face as pale as death, and a faltering voice, while his heart sunk within him at the idea that his father was, in some degree, accessory to the fatal event: for, just before he left London, Lord Cherbury had informed him of the letter he wrote to Fitzalan, and this, he believed, joined to his own immediate family misfortunes, had precipitated him from the world. "Captain Fitzalan dead!" he exclaimed. "Yes, and please you, my Lord," said Johnaten, wiping away a tear, "and he has not left a better or braver man behind him. Poor gentleman, the world pressed hard upon him." "Had he no tender friend about him?" asked Lord Mortimer. "Were neither of his children with him?" "Oh! yes, my Lord, poor Miss Amanda." "She was with him!" said Lord Mortimer, in an eager accent. "Yes, my Lord, she returned here about ten days ago, but so sadly altered, I think she won't stay long behind him. Poor thing, she is going fast, indeed, and the more's the pity, for she is a sweet creature."

Lord Mortimer was inexpressibly shocked. He wished to hide his emotions, and waved his hand to Johnaten to depart; but Johnaten either did not, or would not, understand the motion, and he was obliged, in broken accents, to say, "he would no longer detain him."

The return of Amanda was to him a conviction that she had seen her error in its true light. He pictured to himself the affecting scene which must have ensued between a dying father and a penitent daughter, so loved, so valued, as was Amanda; her situation, when she received his forgiveness and benediction; he represented her to himself as at once bewailing the loss of her father, and her offences, endeavoring, by prayers, by tears, by sighs, to obliterate them in the sight of Heaven, and render herself fit to receive its awful fiat.

He heard she was dying; his soul recoiled at the idea of seeing her shrouded in her native clay, and yet he could not help believing this the only peaceful asylum she could find, to be freed from the shafts of contempt and malice of the world. He trembled lest he should not behold the lovely penitent while she was capable of observing him; to receive a last adieu, though dreadful, would yet, he thought, lighten the horrors of an eternal separation and perhaps too, it would be some comfort to her departing spirit to know from him he had pardoned her; and conscious, surely, he thought to himself, she must be of needing pardon from him, whom she had so long imposed on by a specious pretext of virtue. He had heard from Lord Cherbury that Captain Fitzalan had quitted the castle; he knew not, therefore, at present, where to find Amanda, nor did he choose to make any inquiries till he again saw Johnaten.

As soon as the procession was out of sight, he alighted from the carriage, and ordering his man to discharge it, on arriving at Castle Carberry, he took a path across the fields, which brought him to the side of the churchyard where Fitzalan was to be interred.

He reached it just as the coffin was lowering into the earth. A yew-tree, growing by the wall against which he leaned, hid him from observation. He heard many of the rustics mentioning the merits of the deceased in terms of warm, though artless, commendation, and he saw Johnaten receiving the hat and sword (which, as military trophies, he had laid upon the coffin), with a flood of tears.

When the churchyard was cleared, he stepped across the broken wall to the silent mansion of Fitzalan. The scene was wild and dreary, and a lowering evening seemed in unison with the sad objects around. Lord Mortimer was sunk in the deepest despondence. He felt awfully convinced of the instability of human attainments, and the vanity of human pursuits, not only from the ceremony he had just witnessed, but his own situation. The fond hopes of his heart, the gay expectations of his youth, and the hilarity of his soul, were blasted, never, he feared, to revive. Virtue, rank, and fortune, advantages so highly prized by mankind, were unable to give him comfort, to remove the malady of his heart, to administer one oblivious antidote to a mind diseased.

"Peace to thy shade, thou unfortunate soldier," exclaimed he, after standing some time by the grave with folded arms. "Peace to thy shade—peace which shall reward thee for a life of toil and trouble. Happy should I have deemed myself, had it been my lot to have lightened thy grief, or cheered thy closing hours. But those who were dearer to thee than existence I may yet serve, and thus make the only atonement now in my power for the injustice, I fear, was done thee. Thy Amanda, and thy gallant son, shall be my care, and his path, I trust, it will be in my power to smooth through life"

A tear fell from Lord Mortimer upon the grave, and he turned mournfully from it towards Castle Carberry. Here Johnaten was arrived before him, and had already a large fire lighted in the dressing-room poor Amanda, on coming to the castle, had chosen for herself. Johnaten fixed on this for Lord Mortimer, as the parlors had been shut up ever since Captain Fitzalan's departure, and could not be put in any order till the next day; but it was the worst place Lord Mortimer could have entered, as not only itself but everything in it reminded him of Amanda; and the grief it excited at his first entrance was so violent as to alarm not only his man (who was spreading a table with refreshments), but Johnaten, who was assisting him. He soon checked it, however; but when he again looked round the room, and beheld it ornamented with works done by Amanda, he could scarcely prevent another burst of grief as violent as the first.

He now learned Amanda's residence; and so great was his impatience to see her that, apprehensive the convent would soon be closed, he set off, fatigued as he was, without recruiting himself with any refreshment. He intended to ask for one of the ladies of St. Catherine's, and entreat her, if Amanda was then in a situation to be seen, to announce his arrival to her; but after rapping repeatedly with a rattan against the door, the only person who appeared to him was a servant girl. From her he learned the ladies were all in the chapel, and that Miss Fitzalan was in the prioress's apartment. He asked, "Was she too ill to be seen?" The girl replied, "No"—for having only entered the room to leave the kettle in it, at a time when Amanda was composed, she imagined she was very well. Lord Mortimer then told her his name, and desired her to go up to Miss Fitzalan and inquire whether she would see him. The girl attempted not to move. She was in reality so struck of a heap by hearing that she had been talking to a lord, that she knew not whether she was standing on her head or her heels. Lord Mortimer imputing her silence to disinclination to comply with his request, put a guinea into her hand, and entreated her to be expeditious. This restored her to animation, but ere she reached the room she forgot his title, and being ashamed to deliver a blundering message to Miss Fitzalan, or to appear stupid to Lord Mortimer, she returned to him, pretending she had delivered his message, and that he might go up. She showed him the door, and when he entered he imputed the silence of Amanda, and her not moving, to the effects of her grief. He advanced to the couch, and was not a little shocked on seeing her eyes closed—concluding from this that she had fainted, but her easy respiration soon convinced him that this was a mistake, and he immediately concluded that the girl had deceived him. He leaned over her till she began to stir, and then retreated behind her, lest his presence, on her first awaking, should alarm her.

What took place in the interview between them has already been related. Notwithstanding appearances were so much against her, and no explanation had ensued relative to them, from the moment she asserted her innocence with solemnity he could no longer doubt it; and yielding at once to its conviction, to his love, to his pity for her, he again renewed his overtures for a union. Hearing of the stratagems laid for her destruction, the dangers she had escaped, the distresses she had experienced, made him more anxious than ever for completing it, that by his constant protection he might secure her from similar trials, and by his tenderness and care restore her to health, peace, and happiness. He longed for the period of her triumphing over the perfidious Marchioness, and the detestable Lady Euphrasia, by being raised to that station they had so long attempted to prevent her attaining, and thus proving to them that virtue, sooner or later, will counteract the designs of vice. He felt a degree of rapture at the idea of his being no longer obliged to regret the ardent, the unabated affection he felt for her. His transports were somewhat checked when she solemnly declared a union between them impossible, and forbade his seeing her again. He was piqued by the steadiness with which she repeated this resolution, but her present weak state prevented his betraying any resentment, and he flattered himself he would be able to conquer her obstinacy. He could not now, indeed, despair of any event after the unexpected restoration of Amanda to his esteem, and the revival of those hopes of felicity, which in the certainty of having lost her had faded away. He returned, as Johnaten said, an altered man, to the castle. He no longer experienced horror at entering the dressing-room which displayed so many vestiges of his Amanda's taste.

He resolved on an immediate union as the surest proof he could give her of his perfect confidence in her sincerity, not allowing himself to suppose she would continue firm in the resolution she had recently avowed to him. He then intended setting off for London, and sparing neither time, trouble, nor expense to obtain from the inferior agents in the plot laid against her, a full avowal of the part they had themselves acted in it, and all they knew relative to those performed by others. This was not designed for his own satisfaction. He wanted no confirmation of what Amanda asserted, as his proposal to marry her immediately demonstrated; it was to cover with confusion those who had meditated her destruction, and add to the horrors they would experience when they found her emerging from obscurity—not as Miss Fitzalan, but as Lady Mortimer. Such proofs of her innocence would also prevent malice from saying he was the dupe of art, and he was convinced, for both their sakes, it was requisite to procure them. He would then avow his marriage, return for his wife, introduce her to his friends, and, if his father kept up any resentment against them longer than he expected, he knew in Lady Martha Dormer's house, and at Tudor Hall, he would find not only an eligible, but pleasant residence. Those delightful schemes kept him awake half the night, and when he fell asleep it was only to dream of happiness and Amanda.

In the morning, notwithstanding the prohibition he had received to the contrary, he went to inquire how she was, and to try and see her. The girl who had answered his repeated knocks the preceding evening, appeared, and told him Miss Fitzalan was very bad. He began to think that this must be a pretext to avoid seeing him, and to come at the truth was slipping a bribe into her hand, when Sister Mary, who had been watching them from an adjoining room, appeared, and stopped this measure. She repeated what the girl had just said, and, in addition to it, declared that even if Miss Fitzalan was up she would not see him, and that he must come no more to St. Catherine's, as both Miss Fitzalan and the prioress would resent such conduct exceedingly; and that, if he wanted to inquire after the health of the former, he might easily send a servant. and it would be much better done than to come frisking over there every moment.

Lord Mortimer was seriously displeased with this unceremonious speech. "So, I suppose," cried he, "you want to make a real nun of Miss Fitzalan, and to keep her from all conversation." "And a happy creature she would be were she to become one of us," replied Sister Mary; "and as to keeping her from conversation, she might have as much as she pleased with any one. Indeed, I believe the poor thing likes you well enough; the more's her misfortune for doing so." "I thank you, madam," cried Lord Mortimer; "I suppose it one of your vows to speak truth; if so, I must acknowledge you keep it religiously." "I have just heard her," proceeded Sister Mary, without minding what he had said, "tell the prioress a long story about you and herself, by which I find it was her father's desire she should have nothing more to say to you, and I dare say the poor gentleman had good reasons for doing so. I beg, my Lord, you will come no more here, and, indeed, I think it was a shame for you to give money to the simpleton who answered you. Why, it was enough to turn the girl's head, and set her mad after one fal-lal or other."

Lord Mortimer could not depart without an effort to win Sister Mary over to his favor, and engage her to try and persuade Miss Fitzalan to permit his visits, but she was inflexible; he then entreated to know if Amanda was so ill as to be unable to rise. She assured him she was, and, as some little consolation to the distress she perceived this assurance gave him, said he might send when he pleased to inquire after her health, and she would take care to answer the messenger herself.

Lord Mortimer began now to be seriously alarmed lest Captain Fitzalan had prevailed on his daughter to make a solemn renunciation of him. If this was the case, he knew nothing could prevail on her to break her promise. He was half distracted with doubt and anxiety, which were scarcely supportable, when he reflected that they could not for some time be satisfied, since, even if he wrote to her for that purpose, she could not at present be able to answer his letter; again he felt convinced of the instability of earthly happiness, and the close connection there has ever been between pleasure and pain.

CHAPTER XXXVI

"Thy presence only 'tis can make me blest,
Heal my unquiet mind, and tune my soul."—OTWAY.

HE fatigue, distress, and agitation of Amanda could no longer be struggled with; she sunk beneath their violence, and for a week was confined to her bed by the fever which seized her in England, and had ever since lurked in her veins. The whole sisterhood, who took it in turn to attend her, vied with each other in kindness and care to the poor invalid. Their efforts for her recovery were aided by a skilful physician from the next town, who called, without being sent for, at the convent. He said he had known Captain Fitzalan, and that, hearing Miss Fitzalan was indisposed, he had come in hopes he might be of service to the daughter of a man he so much esteemed. He would accept of no fee, and the prioress, who was a woman of sagacity, suspected, as well as Amanda, that he came by the direction of Lord Mortimer. Nor were they mistaken, for, distracted with apprehensions about her, he had taken this method of lightening his fears, flattering himself, by the excellent advice he had procured, her recovery would be much expedited, and, of course, his suspense at least terminated. The doctor did not withdraw his visits when Amanda was able to rise; he attended her punctually, and often paid her long visits, which were of infinite service to her spirits, as he was a man of much information and cheerfulness. In a few days she was removed from her chamber into a pleasant room below stairs, which opened into the garden, where, leaning on the friendly doctor's arm, or one of the nuns', she walked at different times a few minutes each day Lord Mortimer, on hearing this, thought he might now solicit an interview, and accordingly wrote for that purpose:—

TO MISS FITZALAN.

Lord Mortimer presents his compliments to Miss Fitzalan, flatters himself she will allow him personally to express the sincere happiness her restoration to health has afforded him. He cannot think she will refuse so reasonable a request. He is almost convinced she would not hesitate a moment in granting it, could she form an idea of the misery he has experienced on her account, and the anxiety he feels, and must continue to feel, till some expressions in the last interview are explained.

Castle Carberry, 10th May

This letter greatly distressed Amanda. She had hoped the pain of again rejecting his visits and requests would have been spared her. She guessed at the expressions he alluded to in his letter; they were those she had dropped relative to her promise to her father, and from the impetuous and tender feelings of Lord Mortimer she easily conceived the agony he would experience when he found this promise inviolable. She felt more for his distress than her own. Her heart, seasoned in the school of adversity, could bear its sorrows with calmness; but this was not his case, and she paid the tribute of tears to a love so fervent, so faithful, and so hopeless.

She then requested Sister Mary to acquaint his messenger that she received no visits; that, as she was tolerably recovered, she entreated his lordship would not take the trouble of continuing his inquiries about her health, or to send her any more written messages, as she was unable to answer them. The prioress, who was present when she received the letter, commended her exceedingly for the fortitude and discretion she had manifested. Amanda had deemed it necessary to inform her, after the conversation she heard between her and Lord Mortimer, of the terms on which they stood with each other; and the prioress, who doubted whether his lordship was in reality as honorable as he professed himself, thought Amanda on the sure side in declining his visits.

The next morning the doctor called as usual. He told Amanda he had brought her an entertaining book, for no such thing could be procured at St. Catherine's, and, as she had expressed her regret at this, from the time she had been able to read he had supplied her from his library, which was extensive and well chosen.

He did not present it to her till he was retiring, and then said with a significant smile, she would find it contained something worthy of her particular attention. Amanda was alone, and immediately opened it. Great was her astonishment when a letter dropped from it into her lap. She snatched it up, and, perceiving the direction in Lord Mortimer's hand, she hesitated whether she should open a letter conveyed in this manner; but to return it unopened was surely a slight Lord Mortimer merited not, and she broke the seal with a trembling hand and a palpitating heart.—

Unkind Amanda, to compel me to use stratagems in writing to you, and destroy the delightful hopes which had sprung in my soul, at the prospect of being about to receive a reward for my sufferings. Am I ever to be involved in doubts and perplexity on your account? Am I ever to see difficulty succeeded by difficulty, and hope by disappointment?

You must be sensible of the anxiety I shall feel, until your ambiguous expressions are fully explained, and yet you refuse this explanation! But you have no pity for my feelings. Would it not be more generous in you to permit an interview than to keep me in suspense? To know the worst is some degree of ease; besides, I should then have an opportunity of perhaps convincing you that virtue, unlike vice, has its bounds, and that we may sometimes carry our notions of honor and generosity too far, and sacrifice our real happiness to chimerical ideas of them. Surely I shall not be too presumptuous in saying that, if the regard Amanda once flattered me with is undiminished, she will, by rejecting a union with me, leave me not the only sufferer.

Oh! do not, my dear and too scrupulous girl, think a moment longer of persevering in a resolution so prejudicial to your welfare. Your situation requires particular protection: young, innocent, and beautiful; already the object of licentious pursuits; your nearest relations your greatest enemies; your brother, from his unsettled line of life, unable to be near you. Oh! my Amanda, from such a situation what evils may accrue? Avoid them, by taking refuge in his arms, who will be to you a tender friend and faithful guardian. Before such evils, the obligations for keeping a promise to reject me, fade away, particularly when the motives which led to such a promise are considered. Captain Fitzalan, hurt by the unfortunate letter he received from my father, extended his resentment to his son, and called upon you without reflecting on the consequences of such a measure to give me up. This is the only reason I can conceive for his desiring such a promise, and had I but arrived while he could have listened to my arguments, I am firmly convinced, instead of opposing, he would have sanctioned our union, and given his beloved girl to a man who, in every instance, would study to evince his gratitude for such a gift, and to supply his loss.

Happiness, my dear Amanda, is in long arrears with us. She is now ready to make up for past deficiencies, if it is not our own faults; let us not frighten her from performing her good intentions, but hand in hand receive the lovely and long-absent guest to our bosoms.

You will not, cannot, must not, be inflexible; I shall expect, as soon as you read this, a summons to St. Catherine's, to receive the ratification of my hopes. In everything respecting our union I will be guided by you, except delaying it; what we have both suffered already from deceit makes me doubly anxious to secure you mine lest another vile scheme should be formed to effect our separation.

Oh! Amanda, the faintest prospect of calling you mine, gives to my heart a felicity no language can express. Refuse not being mine except you bring me an addition of fortune; already rich in every virtue, I shall, in obtaining you, obtain a treasure which the wealthiest, the proudest, and the vainest of the sons of men may envy me the possession of, and which the good, the sensible, and the elegant, must esteem the kindest gift indulgent heaven could bestow on me. Banish all uneasy doubts and scruples, my Amanda, from your mind, nor think a promise, which was demanded without reflecting on the consequences that must attend it, can be binding. The ingenuous soul of your father would have cancelled it in a moment, had those consequences been represented to him; and now, when our own reason convinces us of them, I make no doubt, if departed souls are permitted to view the transactions of this world, his spirit would behold our union with approbation. Yes, my Amanda, I repeat your father's approving spirit will smile upon an act which gives to his lovely and beloved orphan a faithful friend and steady protector, in her adoring MORTIMER

Castle Carberry, 11th May.

This letter deeply affected the sensibility, but could not shake the resolution of Amanda. She would not have answered it, as she considered any correspondence an infringement on the promises she had given her father to decline any further intimacy with him; but from the warmth and agitation displayed in his letter, it was evident to her that, if he did not receive an immediate answer to it, he would come to St. Catherine's and insist on seeing her; and she felt assured, that she could much better deliver her sentiments upon paper than to him; she accordingly wrote as follows:—

TO LORD MORTIMER.

MY LORD,—You cannot change my resolution; surely, when I solemnly declare to you it is unalterable, you will spare me any further importunity on so painful a subject. In vain, my Lord, would you, by sophistry, cloaked with tenderness for that purpose, try to influence me. The arguments you have made use of, I am convinced, you never would have adopted, had you not been mistaken in regard to those motives which prompted my father to ask a promise from me of declining any farther connection with you. It was not from resentment, my Lord; no, his death was then fast approaching, and he in charity for all mankind, forgave those who had wounded him by unjust reproach and accusation; it was a proper respect for his own character, and not resentment which influenced his conduct, as he was convinced if I consented to an alliance with you, Lord Cherbury would be confirmed in all the suspicions he entertained of his having entangled you with me, and consequently load his memory with contempt. Tenderness also for me actuated him; he was acquainted with the proud heart of Lord Cherbury, and knew that if, poor and reduced as I was, I entered his family, I should be considered and treated as a mean intruder. So thoroughly am I convinced that he did not err in this idea, that, whenever reason is predominant in my mind, I think, even if a promise did not exist for such a purpose, I should decline your addresses; for, though I could submit with cheerfulness to many inconveniences for your sake, I never could support indignities. We must part, my Lord; Providence has appointed different paths for us to pursue in life: yours smooth and flowery, if by useless regrets you do not frustrate the intentions of the benevolent Donor; mine rough and thorny; but both, though so different, will lead to the same goal, where we shall again meet to be no more separated.

Let not your lordship deem me either unkind or ungrateful; my heart disavows the justice of such accusations, and is but too sensible of your tenderness and generosity. Yes, my Lord, I will confess that no pangs can be more pungent than those which now rend it, at being obliged to act against its feelings; but the greater the sacrifice the greater the merit of submitting to it, and a ray of self-approbation is perhaps the only sunshine of the soul which will brighten my future days.

Never, my Lord, should I enjoy this, if my promise to my father was violated. There is but one circumstance which could set it aside, that is, having a fortune, that even Lord Cherbury might deem equivalent to your own to bring you; for then my father has often said he would approve our union; but this is amongst the improbabilities of this life, and we must endeavor to reconcile ourselves to the destiny which separates us.

I hope your lordship will not attempt to see me again; you must be sensible that your visits would be highly injurious to me. Even the holy and solitary asylum which I have found would not protect me from the malice which has already been so busy with my peace and fame. Alas! I now need the utmost vigilance—deprived as I am of those on whom I had claim of protection, it behooves me to exert the utmost circumspection in my conduct: he in whom I expected to have found a guardian, Oscar, my dear unfortunate brother, is gone, I know not whither, persecuted and afflicted by the perfidious monster who has been such a source of misery to me! Oh, my Lord, when I think what his sufferings may now be, my heart sinks within me. Oh! had I been the only sufferer I should not have felt so great a degree of agony as I now endure; but I will not despair about my dear Oscar. The Providence which has been so kind to his sister, which so unexpectedly raised her friends at the moment she deemed herself deprived of all earthly comfort, may to him have been equally merciful. I have trespassed a long time upon your lordship's attention but I wished to be explicit, to avoid the necessity of any further correspondence between us. You now know my resolves; you also know my feelings; in pity to them spare me any further conflicts. May the tranquil happiness you so truly deserve soon be yours! Do not, my Lord, because disappointed in one wish, lose your sense of the many valuable blessings with which you are surrounded, in fulfilling the claims which your friends, your country, have upon you; show how truly you merit those blessings, and banish all useless regrets from your heart. Adieu, my Lord!—suffer no uneasiness on my account. If Heaven prolongs my life, I have no doubt but I shall find a little comfortable shelter from the world, where, conscious I have acted according to my principles of right, I shall enjoy the serenity which ever attends self-approbation—a serenity which no changes or chances in this life will, I trust, ever wrest from AMANDA FITZALAN.

St. Catherine's, May 12th.

She despatched this by an old man who was employed in the garden at St. Catherine's; but her spirits were so much affected by writing it, she was obliged to go up and lie on the bed. She considered herself as having taken a final adieu of Lord Mortimer, and the idea was too painful to be supported with fortitude. Tender and fervent as his attachment was now to her, she believed the hurry and bustle of the world, in which he must be engaged, would soon eradicate it. A transfer of his affections, to one equal to himself in rank and fortune, was a probable event, and of course a total expulsion of her from his memory would follow. A deadly coldness stole upon her heart at the idea of being forgotten by him, and produced a flood of tears. She then began to accuse herself of inconsistency. She had often thought, if Lord Mortimer was restored to happiness, she should feel more tranquil. And now, when the means of effecting this restoration occurred, she trembled and lamented as if it would increase her misery. "I am selfish," said she to herself, "in desiring the prolongation of an affection which must ever be hopeless. I am weak in regretting the probability of its transfer, as I can never return it."

To conquer those feelings, she found she must banish Lord Mortimer from her thoughts. Except she succeeded in some degree in this, she felt she never should be able to exert the fortitude her present situation demanded. She now saw a probability of her existence being prolonged, and the bread of idleness or dependence could never be sweet to Amanda Fitzalan.

She had lain about an hour on the bed, and was about rising and returning to the parlor, when Sister Mary entered the chamber, and delivered her a letter. Ere Amanda looked at the superscription, her agitated heart foretold her whom it came from. She was not mistaken in her conjecture; but as she held it in her hand, she hesitated whether she should open it or not. "Yet," said she to herself, "it can be no great harm. He cannot, after what I have declared, suppose my resolution to be shaken. He writes to assure me of his perfect acquiescence to it." Sister Mary left her at the instant her deliberations ended, by opening the letter.

TO MISS FITZALAN.

Inexorable Amanda! but I will spare both you and myself the pain of farther importunity. All I now request is, that for three months longer at least, you will continue at St. Catherine's; or that, if you find a much longer residence there unpleasant, you will, on quitting it, leave directions where to be found. Ere half the above-mentioned period be elapsed, I trust I shall be able satisfactorily to account for such a request. I am quitting Castle Carberry immediately. I shall leave it with a degree of tranquillity that would perhaps surprise you, after what has so lately passed, if in this one instance you will oblige your ever faithful MORTIMER.

This laconic letter astonished Amanda. By its style it was evident Lord Mortimer had recovered his cheerfulness—recovered it not from a determination of giving her up, but from a hope of their again meeting, as they could both wish. A sudden transport rushed upon her heart at such an idea, but quickly died away when she reflected it was almost beyond the possibility of things to bring about a pleasing interview between them. She knew Lord Mortimer had a sanguine temper, and though it might mislead him, she resolved it should not mislead her. She could not form the most distant surmise of what he had now in agitation; but whatever it was, she firmly believed it would end in disappointment. To refuse every request of his was painful; but propriety demanded she should not accede to the last, for one step, she wisely considered, from the line of prudence she had marked out for herself to take, might plunge her in difficulties from which she would find it impossible to extricate herself. With an unsteady hand she returned the following answer:—

TO LORD MORTIMER.

MY LORD,—I cannot comply with your request. You may, if you please, repeat inexorable Amanda. I had rather incur the imputation of obstinacy than imprudence, and think it much better to meet your accusation, than deserve my own. How long I may reside at St. Catherine's is to myself unknown. When I quit it, I certainly will not promise to leave any directions where you may find me.

The obstacles which have rendered our separation necessary, are, I am convinced, beyond your lordship's power to conquer. Except they were removed, any farther interviews between us would be foolish and imprudent in the extreme. I rejoice to hear you are leaving the castle. I also rejoice, but am not surprised, to hear of your tranquillity. From your good sense I expected you would make exertions against useless regrets, and those exertions I knew would be attended with success; but, as some return for the sincere pleasure I feel for your restoration to tranquillity, seek not to disturb again that of AMANDA FITZALAN.

St. Catherine's, May 12th.

Scarcely had she sealed this letter when she was called to dinner; but though she obeyed the summons she could not eat. The exertions her writing to Lord Mortimer required, and the agitation his letter had thrown her into, quite exhausted her strength and spirits. The nuns withdrew soon after dinner, and left her alone with the prioress. In a few minutes after their departure, the old gardener returned from Castle Carberry, where he had been delivering her letter. After informing her he had put it safely into his lordship's hands, he added, with a look which seemed to indicate a fear lest she should be distressed, that he had received neither letter nor message from him, though he waited a long time in expectation of receiving either one or the other; but he supposed, he said, his lordship was in too great a hurry just then to give any answer, as a chaise and four was waiting to carry him to Dublin.

Amanda burst into tears as the man retired from the room. She saw she had written to Lord Mortimer for the last time, and she could not suppress this tribute of regret. She was firmly convinced, indeed, she should behold him no more. The idea of visiting her she was sure, nay, she hoped, he would relinquish, when he found, which she supposed would soon be the case, the schemes or hopes which now buoyed up his spirits impossible to be realized.

The prioress sympathized in her sorrow; though not from her own experience, yet from the experience of others, she knew how dangerous and bewitching a creature man is, and how difficult it is to remove the chains which he twines around the female heart To remove those which lay so heavy upon the delicate and susceptible heart of her young friend, without leaving a corrosive wound, was her sincere wish, and by strengthening her resolution, she hoped success would crown their endeavors.

Two hours were elapsed since her messenger's return from the castle, when Sister Mary entered the room with a large packet, which she put into Amanda's hands, saying, it was given her by Lord Mortimer's servant, who rode off the moment he delivered it

Sister Mary made no scruple of saying, she should like to know what such a weighty packet contained. The prioress chid her in a laughing manner for her curiosity, and drew her into the garden, to give Amanda an opportunity of examining the contents.

She was surprised, on breaking the seal, to perceive a very handsome pocket-book in a blank cover, and found unsealed, a letter to this effect:—

TO MISS FITZALAN.

I have put it out of your power to return this, by departing long ere you receive it. Surely, if you have the laudable pride you profess, you will not hesitate to use the contents of the pocket-book, as the only means of avoiding a weight of obligations from strangers. Though discarded as a lover, surely I may be esteemed as a friend, and with such a title I will be contented till I can lay claim to a tenderer one. You start at this last expression, and I have no doubt you will call me a romantic visionary, for entertaining hopes which you have so positively assured me can never be realized; but ere I resign them, I must have something more powerful than this assurance, my sweet Amanda, to convince me of their fallacy. I was inexpressibly shocked this morning to learn by your letter, that your brother had met with misfortune. My blood boils with indignation against the monster who has, to use your emphatical expression, been such a source of misery to you both. I shall make it my particular care to try and discover the place to which Mr. Fitzalan is gone, and in what situation. By means of the agents, or some of the officers belonging to the regiment, I flatter myself with being able to gain some intelligence of him. I need not add, that, to the utmost extent of my power, I will serve him. My success in this affair, as well as in that which concerns a much dearer being, you may be convinced you shall soon hear. Adieu, my Amanda; I cannot say, like Hamlet,

"Go, get you to a nunnery;" but I can say, "Stay there, I charge you." Seriously, I could wish, except you find your present situation very unpleasant and inconvenient, not to change it for a short time. I think, for a temporary abode, you could not find a more eligible one; and, as I shall be all impatience when I return to Ireland to see you, a search after you would be truly insupportable. You have already refused to inform me of your determination relative to this matter; surely I may venture to request it may be as I wish, when I assure you, that, except I can see you in a manner pleasing to both, I never will force into your presence him, who, let things turn out as they may, must ever continue Your faithful

MORTIMER.

"Gracious Heaven!" said Amanda to herself, "what can he mean? What scheme can he have in agitation which will remove the obstacles to our union? He here seems to speak of a certainty of success. Oh, grant, merciful Power!" she continued, raising her meek eyes to heaven, while a rosy blush stole upon her cheeks, "grant that indeed he may be successful. He talks of returning to Ireland; still," proceeded she, reading over the letter, "of requiring something more powerful than my assurance to convince him of the fallacy of his hopes. Surely, Lord Mortimer would not be so cruel as to raise expectations in my bosom without those in his own were well founded. No, dear Mortimer, I will not call you a romantic visionary, but the most amiable, the most generous of men, who for poor Amanda encounters difficulties and sacrifices every splendid expectation." She rejoiced at the intention he had declared of seeking out Oscar. She looked forward either to a speedy interview, or speedy intelligence of this beloved brother, as she knew Lord Mortimer would seek him with the persevering spirit of benevolence, and leave no means untried to restore him to her.

She now examined the contents of the pocket-book. It contained a number of small bills, to the amount of two hundred pounds,—a large present, but one so delicately presented, that even her ideas of propriety could scarcely raise a scruple against her accepting it. They did, however, suggest one. Uncertain how matters would yet terminate between her and Lord Mortimer, she was unwilling to receive pecuniary obligations from him. But when she reflected on his noble and feeling heart, she knew she should severely wound it by returning his present; she therefore resolved on keeping it, making a kind of compromise with her feelings about the matter, by determining that, except entitled to receive them, she would never more accept favors of this nature from his lordship. The present one, indeed, was a most seasonable relief, and removed from her heart a load of anxiety which had weighed on it. After paying her father's funeral expenses, the people with whom he lodged, and the apothecary who had attended him, she found herself mistress of but twenty guineas in the whole world, and more than half of this she considered as already due to the benevolent sisters of St. Catherine's, who were ill able to afford any additional expense.

She had resolved to force them to accept, what indeed she deemed a poor return for their kindness to her, and she then intended to retire to some obscure hovel in the neighborhood, as better suited to the state of her finances, and continue there till her health was sufficiently restored to enable her to make exertions for her livelihood. But she shuddered at the idea of leaving St. Catherine's and residing amongst a set of boors. She felt sensations something similar to those we may suppose a person would feel who was about being committed to a tempestuous ocean without any means of security.

Lord Mortimer had prevented the necessity which had prompted her to think of a removal, and she now resolved to reside at least for the time he had mentioned in the convent, during which she supposed her uncertainties relative to him would be over, and that, if it was not her fate to be his, she should, by the perfect re-establishment of her health, be enabled to use her abilities in the manner her situation required. Tears of heartfelt gratitude and sensibility flowed down her cheeks for him who had lightened her mind of the care which had so oppressed it.

She at length recollected the prioress had retired into the garden from complaisance to her, and yet continued in it, waiting no doubt to be summoned back by her. She hastily wiped away her tears, and folding up the precious letter which was bedewed with them, repaired to the garden, resolving not to communicate its contents, as the divulgement of expectations (considering how liable all human ones are to be disappointed) she ever considered a piece of folly.

She found the prioress and Sister Mary seated under a broken and ivy-covered arch. "Jesu! my dear," said the latter, "I thought you would never come to us. Our good mother has been keeping me here in spite of my teeth, though I told her the sweet cakes I made for tea would be burned by this time, and that, supposing you were reading a letter from Lord Mortimer, there could be no harm in my seeing you." Amanda relieved the impatient Mary, and she took her seat. The prioress cast her piercing eyes upon her. She perceived she had been weeping, and that joy rather than sorrow caused her tears. She was too delicate to inquire into its source; but she took Amanda's hand, and gave it a pressure, which seemed to say, "I see, my dear child, you have met with something which pleases you, and my heart sympathizes as much in your happiness as in your grief."

Amanda returned the affectionate pressure with one equally tender and a starting tear. They were soon called by Sister Mary to partake of her hot cakes, which she had made indeed in hopes of tempting Amanda to eat after her bad dinner. The whole community were assembled at tea when the doctor entered the parlor. Amanda blushed and looked grave at his first entrance; but he soon rallied her out of her gravity. And when the prioress and the nuns, according to custom, had withdrawn to evening vespers, he said, with a significant smile, "he feared she had not attended as much as he wished she should to the contents of the book he had last brought her." She saw by his manner he was acquainted with her situation relative to Lord Mortimer, and therefore replied by saying, "that perhaps, if he knew the motives which influenced her conduct, he would not think her wrong in disregarding what he had just mentioned." She also said, "she detested all kinds of stratagem, and was really displeased with him for practising one upon her." "In a good cause," he said, "he should never hesitate using one. Lord Mortimer was the finest young fellow he had ever seen, and had won his favor, and the best wishes of his heart, from the first moment that he beheld him. He made me contrive," continued the doctor, "a story to gain admission to your ladyship, and when I found him so dreadfully anxious about you, I gave you credit (as I had then no opportunity of judging for myself) for all the virtues and graces he ascribed to you, and which I have since perceived you to possess. You smile, and look as if you would call me a flatterer; seriously, I assure you I am not one. I really think you worthy of Lord Mortimer, and I assure you that is as great a compliment as could be paid any woman. His mind was troubled with grief; he revealed his troubles and perplexities to me, and, after hearing them, no good Christian ever prayed more devoutly for another than I prayed for your recovery, that all your sorrows, like a novel, might terminate in marriage." "You are obliging in your wishes," said Amanda, smiling. "Faith, I am sincere in them," exclaimed he, "and do not know when I have been so disconcerted as at things not turning out smoothly between you and his lordship; but I will not despair. In all my troubles, and Heaven has given me my share, I ever looked to the bright side of things, and shall always do so for my friends. I yet expect to see you settled at Castle Carberry, and to be appointed myself physician-general to your ladyship's household." The mention of an event yet so uncertain greatly agitated Amanda; she blushed and turned pale alternately, and convinced her good-natured but loquacious friend, he had touched a chord which could not bear vibration. He hastily changed the discourse, and as soon as he saw her composed rose to take his leave. Amanda detained him for a minute, to try and prevail on him to take a ten-guinea note; but he was inflexible, and said, with some archness, "till the disorder which preyed upon Lord Mortimer's heart was in some degree alleviated, he would receive no recompense for his visits, which he assured Amanda, from time to time, he would continue to pay her, adding, a certain person had enjoined him now and then to take a peep within the holy walls of St. Catherine's."

The next morning Amanda set about a temporary arrangement of her affairs. She presented thirty guineas to the sisterhood, which, with much difficulty, she forced them to accept, though, in reality, it was much required by them. But when she came to speak of paying for a continuance, they positively declared they would agree to no such thing, as she had already so liberally rewarded them for any expense they had incurred on her account. She told them that if they would not agree to be paid for lodging and board she would certainly leave them, though such a step was contrary to her inclinations; she assured them also she was at present well able to pay.

At last it was settled she should give them at the rate of forty pounds a year—a salary they thought extremely ample, considering the plain manner in which they lived. She then had all the things which belonged to her father and herself brought to the convent, and had the former, with whatever she did not immediately want, nailed up in a large chest, that on a short notice they might be removed. Her harp and guitar she had, in her distress, proposed sending back to the person in Dublin from whom they were purchased, to sell for her; but she now determined to keep those presents of her beloved father, except again urged by necessity to part with them. She had a variety of materials for painting and working, and proposed employing herself in executing pieces in each way, not only as a means of amusing her time, but as a resource on an evil day; thus wisely making use of the present sunshine, lest another storm should arise which she should not be so well able to struggle against.

CHAPTER XXXVII.

> "In struggling with misfortunes
> Lies the proof of virtue."—SHAKSPEARE.

THE turbulence of grief, and the agitation of suspense, gradually lessened in the mind of Amanda, and were succeeded by a soft and pleasing melancholy, which sprang from the consciousness of having always, to the best of her abilities, performed the duties imposed upon her, and supported her misfortunes with placid resignation. She loved to think on her father, for amidst her sighs for his loss were mingled the delightful ideas of having ever been a source of comfort to him, and she believed, if departed spirits were allowed to review this world, his would look down upon her with delight and approbation at beholding her undeviating in the path he had marked out for her to take. The calm derived from such meditations she considered as a recompense for many sorrows; it was such, indeed, as nothing earthly gives, or can destroy, and what the good must ever experience, though "amidst the wreck of matter and the crush of worlds."

She tried to prevent her thoughts from wandering to Lord Mortimer, as the surest means of retaining her composure, which fled whenever she reflected on the doubtful balance in which her fate yet hung concerning him.

The solitude of St. Catherine's was well adapted to her present situation and frame of mind. She was neither teased with impertinent or unmeaning ceremony, but perfect mistress of her own time and actions, read, worked, and walked, as most agreeable to herself. She did not extend her walks beyond the convent, as the scenes around it would awaken remembrances she had not sufficient fortitude to bear; but the space it covered was ample enough to afford her many different and extensive rambles. And of a still evening, when nothing but the lowing of the cattle, or the buzzing of the summer flies, was to be heard, she loved to wander through the solemn and romantic ruins, sometimes accompanied by a nun, but much oftener alone.

A fortnight had elapsed in this manner since Lord Mortimer's departure, when, one morning, a carriage was heard driving across the common and stopping at the outer gate of St. Catherine's. Amanda, who was sitting at work in the parlor with the prioress, started in a universal trepidation at the sound. It may be easily imagined the idea of Lord Mortimer was uppermost in her thoughts The door opened in a few minutes, and, to her great astonishment, Mrs. Kilcorban and her two daughters made their appearance.

Agitation and surprise prevented Amanda from speaking; she courtesied, and motioned them to be seated. The young ladies saluted her with an icy civility, and the mother treated her with a rude familiarity, which she thought herself authorized in using to one so reduced in circumstances as Amanda. "Dear me," cried she, "you can't think, child, how shocked we have all been to hear of your misfortunes. We only returned to the country yesterday, for we have been in town the whole winter, and to be sure a most delightful winter we have had of it—such balls, such routs, such racketings; but, as I was going to say, as soon as we came home I began, according to my old custom, to inquire after all my neighbors; and to be sure the very first thing I heard of was the poor Captain's death Don't cry, my dear, we must all go one time or another; those are things of course, as the doctor says in his sermon; so, when I heard of your father's death and your distress, I began to cast about in my brains some plan for helping you; and at last I hit upon one which, says I to the girls, will delight the poor soul, as it will give her an opportunity of earning decent bread for herself. You must know, my dear, the tutoress we brought to town would not come back with us—a dirty trollop, by the bye, and I think her place would be quite the thing for you. You will have the four young girls to learn French and work too, and I will expect you, as you have a good taste, to assist the eldest Miss Kilcorbans in making up their things and dressing. I give twenty guineas a year. When we have no company the tutoress always sits at the table, and gets, besides this, the best of treatment in every respect."

A blush of indignation had gradually conquered Amanda's paleness during Mrs. Kilcorban's long and eloquent speech. "Your intentions may be friendly, madam," cried she, "but I must decline your proposal." "Bless me, and why must you decline it? perhaps you think yourself not qualified to instruct; indeed, this may be the case, for people often get credit for accomplishments they do not possess. Well, if this is so, I am still content to take you, as you were always a decent behaved young body. Indeed, you cannot expect I should give you twenty guineas a year. No, no, I must make some abatement in the salary, if I am forced to get masters to help you in learning the girls." "Miss Fitzalan, madam," exclaimed the prioress, who had hitherto continued silent, "never got credit for accomplishments which she did not possess; her modesty has rather obscured than blazoned forth her perfections; she does not, therefore, madam, decline your offer from a consciousness of inability to undertake the office of an instructor, but from a conviction she never could support impertinence and folly; should her situation ever require her to exert her talents for subsistence, I trust she will never experience the mortification of associating with those who are insensible of her worth, or unwilling to pay her the respect she merits." "Hoity, toity," cried Mrs. Kilcorban, "what assurance! Why, madam, many a better man's child would be glad to jump at such an offer." "Dear madam," said Miss Kilcorban, "perhaps the young lady has a better settlement in view. We forget Lord Mortimer has been lately at Castle Carberry, and we all know his lordship is a friend to Captain Fitzalan's daughter." "Or perhaps," cried Miss Alicia, in a giggling tone, "she means to be a nun." "Indeed, I suppose she means to be nothing good," rejoined Mrs. Kilcorban; "and I suppose it was by some impertinence or other she had a tiff with Lady Greystock. Lord! (looking round the room), only see her music-books—her harp—her guitar—as if she had nothing to do but sing and thrum away the whole day. Well, miss (rising from her chair), you may yet be sorry your friend said so much about you. I did not come merely to offer to take you into my house, but to offer you also a good sum for your harp and guitar, supposing you had no business with such things now-a-days; but I dare say you would have refused this offer." "I certainly should, madam," said Amanda; "it must be strong necessity which compels me to part with my beloved father's presents." "Well, well, child, I wish this pride of thine may not yet be humbled." So saying, she flounced out of the room, followed by her daughters, who, under an affectation of contempt, evidently showed they were chagrined by the reception they had met.

The prioress indulged herself in a long fit of laughter at the passion into which she had thrown Mrs. Kilcorban; and Amanda, who considered the lady and her daughters as the most insignificant of beings, soon recovered from the discomposure their visit had occasioned. In the course of the evening a letter was delivered her by the servant, who said the messenger who brought it waited for an answer. Amanda, in a universal trepidation, broke the seal; but, instead of Lord Mortimer's as she expected, a hand, to her entirely new, struck her view:—

TO MISS FITZALAN

My dear Creature,—I think I never was so diverted in my life as at the account my mother and sisters gave of the reception they met with from you to-day at St. Catherine's. I vow to God it was excellent. Nor can I help still wondering at their absurdity, in thinking such a devilish fine girl as you are would sacrifice your time in instructing a parcel of chits, when it can be devoted to so much better a purpose! To be brief, my dear girl, I will take you immediately under my protection, if not your own fault, bring you to Dublin, settle you in elegant lodgings, with a handsome allowance, and not only make you, but declare you to be, the grand Sultana of my affection; a situation which, I can assure you, you will not be a little envied enjoying. In your answer to this, I shall expect to hear when I may have the felicity of bringing you from obscurity, to the brilliant scene you were formed to ornament. Adieu, my dear. Believe me your devoted,

B. KILCORBAN.

The indignation which filled Amanda's breast at reading this scrawl cannot be expressed. Her blood seemed to boil in her veins. It was some time ere she could sufficiently compose herself to acquaint the prioress with the cause of her agitation. It was then agreed that the letter should be returned, with the following lines written on it:—

The author of this effusion of ignorance and impertinence has already inspired all the contempt he merits. Should he repeat his insolence, something even more mortifying than contempt—chastisement—must ensue.

That a repetition of this kind would be the case, she did not believe. From Kilcorban she had no reason to suspect either the perseverance or designs of Belgrave. One was a libertine from principle, the other she believed from fashion; and that to pique his pride would be a sure method of getting rid of him.

But the calm she had for some time experienced was destined to be interrupted. The next morning brought Father O'Gallaghan, the little fat priest (of whom we have made mention before in our pages), to the convent. He was not the officiating priest; but, notwithstanding this, paid many visits to the sisterhood, with whom he was a great favorite; he had been much concerned about Amanda's illness. She was sitting alone in the parlor, drawing, when he entered it. He seated himself by her, and the expression of his countenance seemed to declare his heart was brimfull of something pleasant.

"You won't be offended now, my dear sowl," said he, smirking up in her face, "with a body for asking you how you would like to leave this dismal solitude and have a comfortable home of your own, where you might see your own friends, and have everything warm and cosy about you?" "Why," said Amanda, "though I do not consider this a dismal solitude, yet, to be sure, I should have no objection to a pleasant settled habitation." "Ay, I always thought you a sensible young body. Well, and what would you say to the person then who could point out such a habitation? Ay, you little rogue, who could say they had just such a one in their eye for you." Amanda stared at him with astonishment. She had at first believed him jesting, but now found him serious.

"Ay, faith, my dear creature," cried he, continuing his discourse, with a look of the most perfect satisfaction, "I have an offer to make you, which, I believe, would make many girls jump out of their skins with joy to hear. You remember the O'Flannaghans, I am sure, where you took tea last summer. Well, the eldest of the sons (as honest a lad as ever broke bread) cast a sheep's eye upon you then. But what with your going from the country, and some other matters, he thought there was no use then in revealing his flame; but now, when you are come plump in his way again, faith he plucked up his courage, and told his father all about it. Old Flannaghan is a good-natured sowl, and is very willing the match should take place. They have everything snug about them. The old man will give everything into your spouse's hands. The youngest son will live in the house till he gets married, and goes off to a farm of his own. The eldest daughter is married; the second will live with her, and the youngest will be a little handy assistant to you. So you see, you will not be tormented with a large family. There is one little matter which, to be sure, they are a little uneasy about, and that is your being of different persuasions; but says I to them, when this was started, faith, says I, you need not give yourself any trouble about it, for I know the young woman to be a discreet sowl, and I am sure she will make no hesitation about going to chapel instead of church, when she knows, too, it is for her own interest. So, my dear sowl, I hope soon to give you the nuptial benediction, and to be also your spiritual director."

Amanda had listened to this speech in silent amazement. She now rose, and would have quitted the room without speaking, to evince her contempt, had not an idea darted into her mind that such conduct perhaps might not be construed by the ignorant priest in the manner she wished. She therefore stopped, and turning to him said: "He could not wonder at her being offended at his pretending to answer so freely for her in matters so important as religion; but to prove how presumptuous he was in everything he said about her, she must assure him his embassy to her was equally fruitless and disagreeable; and that if Mr. O'Flannaghan consulted his own happiness, he would seek to unite himself with a woman brought up in his own sphere of life." So saying, she quitted the room with a look of dignity which quite confounded the poor priest, who snatched up his hat in a great hurry, and waddled away to the farm, to communicate the ill success of his visit, which had quite crushed his expectations of wedding presents and pudding feasts, which he had contemplated in idea with delight.

It was some time ere Amanda recovered from the discomposure into which the impertinence of the Kilcorbans and the priest had thrown her. From what she suffered in consequence of it, she was forcibly convinced how ill qualified she was to struggle with a world where she would be continually liable to such shocks. She had yet a hope of escaping them—a hope of being guarded by the tutelary care of Lord Mortimer, and of being one of the happiest of her sex.

CHAPTER XXXVIII.

"Lo! I am here to answer to your vows,
And be the meeting fortunate! I come
With joyful tidings; we shall part no more."—AKENSIDE.

BUT a shock more severe than those she had lately experienced was yet in store for our hapless heroine. About a fortnight after the visit of the Kilcorbans and the priest, as she was rambling one evening according to custom amongst the solitary ruins of St. Catherine's, indulging the pensive meditations of her soul, the figure of a man suddenly darted from under a broken arch, and discovered to her view the features of the hated Belgrave. Amanda gave a faint cry, and in unutterable dismay tottered back a few paces against a wall. "Cruel Amanda!" exclaimed Belgrave, while his look seemed to imply he would take advantage of her situation. His look, his voice, operated like a charm to rouse her from the kind of stupefaction into which she had fallen at first sight of him, and as he attempted to lay hold of her she sprang past him, and, with a swiftness which mocked his speed, flew through the intricate windings of the place till she reached the convent. Her pale and distracted look, as she rushed into the prioress's apartment, terrified the good old lady, who hastily interrogated her as to the cause of her disorder; but Amanda was unable to speak. The appearance of Belgrave she thought an omen of every ill to her. Her blood ran cold through her veins at his sight, and terror totally subdued her powers. The prioress summoned Sister Mary to her relief; drops and water were administered, and the overloaded heart of the trembling Amanda was relieved by tears. The prioress again asked the cause of her agitation, but perceiving Amanda did not like to speak before Sister Mary, she immediately pretended to think it proceeded from fatigue, and Mary, who was simplicity itself, readily credited the idea. The prioress soon sent her upon some pretext from the room, and then, in the gentlest terms, begged to know what had so cruelly alarmed her young friend. Amanda had already confided to the prioress the events of her life, so that the good lady, on hearing Belgrave now mentioned, no longer wondered at the agitation of Amanda; yet, as her fears she saw were too powérful for her reason, she endeavored to convince her they were unnecessary. She called to her remembrance the singular protection she had already experienced from Heaven, and the protection which, while she was innocent, she would still have a right to expect. She also mentioned the security of her present situation—encompassed by friends whose integrity could not be warped, and whose utmost zeal would be manifested in defeating any stratagems which might be laid against her.

Amanda grew composed as she listened to the prioress. She was cheered by the voice of piety and friendship, and her heart again felt firm and elevated. She acknowledged that after the singular, nay, almost miraculous interpositions of Providence she had experienced in her favor, to give way to terror or despair was sinful, since it showed a distrust of the Power who has promised with guardian care to watch the footsteps of the innocent. It was, however, agreed that Amanda should venture no more from the convent, but confine her rambles to the garden, which was enclosed with a high wall, and had no places of concealment. Five weeks yet remained of the period Lord Mortimer had requested her to stay at St. Catherine's. Before it was expired she trusted and believed Belgrave would be weary of watching her, and would decamp; if, then, she neither saw nor heard from Lord Mortimer, she resolved to relinquish all hope concerning him, and immediately think upon some plan which should put her in a way of procuring subsistence.

Her paintings and embroidery still went on. She had executed some elegant pictures in both, which, if obliged to dispose of, she was sure would bring a good price; yet, whenever compelled by reflection to this idea, the tear of tender melancholy would fall upon her lovely cheek—a tear which was ever hastily wiped away, while she endeavored to fortify her mind with pious resignation to whatever should be her future fate.

Three weeks more elapsed without any event to discompose their tranquillity; but as the termination of the destined period approached, the agitation of Amanda, in spite of all her efforts to the contrary, increased. She deemed the awful crisis of her fate at hand, and she trembled at the reflection. She now for the first time avoided solitude. She wanted to fly from herself, and sat constantly with the prioress, who had nothing of the gloomy recluse, save the habit, about her.

They were chatting together one evening after tea when Sister Mary entered the room, bearing a large packet, which she rather tossed than presented to Amanda, exclaiming, "From Lord Mortimer; I wish the troublesome fellow had not come back again; here we shall have him frisking or storming continually, and again plaguing us out of our lives." "From Lord Mortimer!" exclaimed Amanda, starting from her chair, and clasping the letter between her hands, "Oh, gracious Heaven!" She said no more, but flew from the room to her chamber. She tore open the seal. The envelope contained two letters. The first was directed in a hand unknown to her. Her heart sickened as she dropped it on the ground. The other was the superscription of Lord Mortimer. She opened it with revived spirits, and read as follows:—

TO MISS FITZALAN.

I am returned—returned to tell my Amanda that nothing but the awful fiat of Heaven shall part us more. Yes, my love, a sweet reward for all our difficulties, our trials—let me add, our persevering constancy—is at hand; and one name, one interest, one fate, I trust, will soon be ours.

Tears of joy gushed from Amanda as she exclaimed, "Can this, can this be true? Is Lord Mortimer, so long, so hopelessly beloved, indeed returned to tell me we shall part no more? 'Tis true, 'tis true, and never can my grateful heart sufficiently acknowledge the goodness it experiences; but how was this event brought about?" She wiped away her tears, and resumed the letter.

Your solemn refusal to unite yourself to me, threw me into agonies: but true love, like true courage, will never despair, will never yield to difficulties, without first trying every effort to conquer them. I soon, therefore, roused myself from the heavy weight which oppressed my spirits at your resolution, and ere long conceived a project so feasible, so almost certain of success, that my impatience to realize it cannot be described; yet you may conceive some idea of it from the abrupt manner in which I quitted Castle Carberry, without desiring to bid you adieu; but ere it could be accomplished I plainly saw I had many difficulties to encounter, difficulties which it was absolutely essential to overcome, that I might prove to the world I was not the dupe of love, but the friend, the lover, and the vindicator of real innocence and virtue. From what I have said, you may suppose the difficulties I allude to were such as I expected to encounter in my attempt to unravel the whole of the deep and execrable plot which involved you in a situation so distressing to your feelings, and injurious to your character; and, oh! with what mingled pride and pleasure did I meditate on being your champion, clearing your fame from each dark aspersion, and proving, clearly proving, that your mind was as lovely, as angelic, as your person!

I was happy, on my arrival in London, to find Lady Martha Dormer still at Lord Cherbury's house. I have already told you that I left town on pretence of a visit to my sister, in Wales. My father, I soon perceived, suspected that had not been the real motive of my departure; but I also perceived he did not desire to reveal his suspicions, as he asked some questions concerning Lady Araminta, which, you may be sure, I answered awkwardly enough, and, had a comic writer been present, he might have taken the hint of a good blundering scene from us both.

The Marquis of Roslin and his family, I learned, continued at his villa. Their absence from town rejoiced me, as it not only exempted me from society I abhorred, but, as it gave me an opportunity of interrogating their household, amongst whom, I was convinced, I should discover the trusty agents the amiable Marchioness had made use of in her scheme against you. The morning after my arrival, I accordingly set off to Portman Square. The man who opened the door knew me not, which I considered a lucky circumstance, for, not being able to mention my name to the housekeeper, whom I desired him to send to me, she was not as much on her guard as she would otherwise have been. She started as she entered the parlor, and lifted up her hands and eyes with unfeigned astonishment. Soon, however, recovering herself, she addressed me in the most obsequious manner, and spoke as if she supposed I was come purposely to inquire after her Lord and Lady, an artful way of trying to terminate her own suspense by learning the nature of my visit. I soon gave her to understand it was not of the most amicable kind to her. I came, I said, to demand either the letter, or an account of the letter, which I had intrusted to her care for Miss Fitzalan, which contained a note of large value, and which, I found, had never been received by that young lady. Her countenance in a moment condemned her—it spoke stronger than a thousand tongues against her. She first grew deadly pale, then fiery red; trembled, faltered, and hung her head, to avoid my eyes. Her looks, I told her, confirmed the suspicions I was forced to entertain of her integrity, yet, shocking as the action was which she had committed, being not only a breach of trust, but humanity, I was willing to come to an easy and private accommodation about it, provided she would truly and fully confess the part she had taken, or knew others to have taken, in injuring Miss Fitzalan, while she resided in the Marquis's house, by bringing Colonel Belgrave into it. I paused for her reply. She appeared as if considering how she should act. I thought I saw something yielding in her face, and, eager to take advantage of it, I proceeded: "What I have already said I am going again to repeat, that is, if you confess all you know relative to the plot which was contrived, and carried into execution, in this house, against Miss Fitzalan, I will settle everything relative to the letter and its contents in a manner pleasing to you. Her innocence is unquestioned by me; but it is essential to her peace that it should also be so to the rest of her friends, and they who regard her welfare will liberally reward those whose allegations shall justify her."

Upon this she turned to me, with a countenance of the utmost effrontery, and said she would not tell a lie to please any one. I will not shock you by repeating all she said. She ended, by saying, as to the letter she set me at defiance; true, I had given her one for Miss Fitzalan, but I might remember Miss Fitzalan was in a fit on the ground at the time, and she had called in other servants to her assistance, she said, and in the hurry and bustle which ensued, she knew not what became of it; others might as well be called upon as her. I could no longer command my temper. I told her she was a wretch, and only fit for the diabolical service in which she was employed. The note, which I enclosed in the letter I had given her for you, I had received from my father's agent in the country: as a post-note I had endorsed it, and taken the number in my pocket-book. I therefore left Portman Square, with a resolution of going to the bank, and, if not already received, stopping payment. I stepped into the first hackney-coach I met, and had the satisfaction of finding it had not been offered at the bank. I suspected she would be glad to exchange it for cash as soon as possible, and therefore left my direction, as well as a request for the detention of any person who should present it.

In consequence of this, a clerk came the following morning to inform me a woman had presented the note at the bank, and was, agreeably to my request, detained till I appeared. I immediately returned with him, and had the satisfaction of seeing the housekeeper caught in the snare. She burst into tears at my appearance, and coming up to me, in a low voice said, "If I would have mercy upon her, she would in return make a full confession of all she knew about the affair I had mentioned to her yesterday." I told her, though she deserved no mercy, yet, as I had promised on such condition to show her lenity, I would not violate my word. I received the note, sent for a coach, and handing the lady into it, soon conveyed her to Portman Square. She no sooner entered the parlor than she fell on her knees and besought my forgiveness. I bade her rise, and lose no time in revealing all she knew concerning the scheme against you. She then confessed that both she and Mrs. Jane, the attendant who had been placed about your person, were acquainted and concerned in all the contrivances the Marchioness had laid against you, who scrupled not in acknowledging to them the inveterate hatred she bore you. Their scruples—for they pretended to have some in abetting her schemes—were overruled, by knowing how much it was in her power to injure them in any future establishment, had they disobliged her, and by her liberal promises of reward, which the housekeeper added she had never kept. But this brief and uncircumstantial account was by no means satisfactory to me. I called for materials for writing, and insisted she should, to the best of her recollection, relate every word or circumstance which had ever passed between her and the Marchioness and their other associates relative to you. She hesitated at this. On those terms only I said I would grant her my forgiveness; and by her complying with them, not only that, but a liberal recompense should be hers. This last promise had the desired effect. She laid open, indeed, a scene of complicated iniquity; related the manner in which Colonel Belgrave was brought into the house by her and Mrs. Jane; how they had stationed themselves in a place of concealment to listen, by which means they knew what passed between you, which she now, in almost the very same words you made use of, repeated to me. As she spoke I wrote it, and made her sign the paper under a para graph, purporting that it was a true confession of the part she had taken, and knew others to have taken, in attempting to injure Miss Fitzalan.

I now mentioned Mrs. Jane, whose evidence I wished for to corroborate hers. This she assured me I might procure by promising a reward, as Mrs. Jane was much dissatisfied with the Marchioness and Lady Euphrasia, neither of whom had recompensed her as she expected for her faithful services to them. She was now at the villa; but the housekeeper added that she would strike out some expedient to bring her to town in the course of the week, and would inform me immediately of her arrival. I told her the affair of the note should be no more mentioned, and gave a bill for fifty pounds, as the reward I had promised, and she eagerly expected. I told her she might promise a similar one in my name to Mrs. Jane, provided she also told truth. I also told her I would take care she should suffer no distress by quitting the Marquis's family, which she lamented would be the consequence of what she had done.

Mrs. Jane did not come to town as soon as I expected. But on receiving a summons to inform me of her arrival, I hastened to the house like an inquisitor-general with my scroll, prepared to take the confession of the fair culprit, which exactly corresponded with the housekeeper's, and I had the felicity of seeing her subscribe her name to it. I gave her the promised recompense most cheerfully, as I had not half so much trouble in making her tell truth as I had with the housekeeper. Mrs. Jennings, your old landlady, and Lady Greystock's faithful friend, was the next and last person whose malice I wanted to refute. I made my servant inquire her character in the neighborhood, and learned it was considered a very suspicious one. I went to her one morning in my carriage, well knowing that the appearance of rank and splendor would have greater weight in influencing a being like her to justice than any plea of conscience. She appeared lost in astonishment and confusion at my visit, and I saw waited with trembling expectation to have the reason of it revealed. I kept her not long in suspense; I was the friend, I told her, of a young lady, whose character she had vilely and falsely aspersed. Her conscience, I believed, would whisper to her heart the name of this lady, and send its crimson current to her face at the mention of Miss Fitzalan.

The wretch seemed ready to sink to the earth. I repeated to her all she had said concerning you to Lady Greystock. I told her of the consequences of defamation, and declared she might expect the utmost rigor of the law, except she confessed her assertions were infamous falsehoods, and the motives which instigated her to them. She trembled with terror, and supplicated mercy. I desired her to deserve it by her confession. She then acknowledged she had grossly and cruelly wronged you by what she had said to Lady Greystock, and that she had many opportunities of being convinced, while you resided in her house, that your virtue and innocence were of the purest nature; but that she was provoked to speak maliciously against you from resentment at losing all the rich gifts Colonel Belgrave had promised her if she brought you to comply with his wishes. She related all the stratagems they had mutually concerted for your destruction, and she brought me some letters which I have kept, from him to you, and which she pretended you had received, lest she should lose the money he always gave when she was successful in delivering one. I bid her beware how she ever attempted to vilify innocence, lest the friends of those at whom she levelled the arrows of defamation should not be as merciful to her as Miss Fitzalan's had been; and was the tale of the slanderer thus ever to be minutely investigated, the evil might die away by degrees, and many hapless victims escape, who are daily sacrificed to malice, revenge, or envy.

Oh! my Amanda, I cannot express the transports I felt when I found the difficulties, which I dreaded as intervening between me and happiness, thus removed. I felt myself the happiest of men; my heart acknowledged your worth, I was convinced of your love, and in my hands I held the refutation of falsehood, and the confirmation of your innocence.

The period for mentioning my project was now arrived. I desired, the morning after my visit to Mrs. Jennings, to be indulged in a tête-à-tête in Lady Martha's dressing-room. I believe she half guessed what the subject of it would be; she saw by my countenance there was joyful news at hand. I shall not recapitulate our conversation; suffice it to say, that her excellent feeling heart participated largely in my satisfaction; it did more than participate, it wished to increase it, and ere I could mention my project, she declared my Amanda should henceforth be considered as her adopted daughter, and should from her receive such a fortune as such a title claimed. Yes, my Amanda, the fortune she ever destined for me, she said she should now consecrate to the purpose of procuring me a treasure the most valuable Heaven could bestow;—the richest—the most valuable indeed—a treasure dearer, far dearer to my soul for all the dangers it has encountered. I fell at Lady Martha's feet in a transport of gratitude, and acknowledged that she had anticipated what I was going to say, as I had been determined to throw myself on her generosity from the time I was convinced of your inflexible resolution, not to unite yourself to me without you brought a fortune.

It was now agreed we should keep Lord Cherbury a little longer ignorant of our intentions. We proposed taking the Marchioness and Lady Euphrasia by surprise, and hoped, by so doing, to be able to remove from his eyes the mist, which partiality had hitherto spread before them, to obscure the defects of the above-mentioned ladies.

He had hinted more than once his wishes for my paying my compliments at the Marquis's villa. I now proposed going thither myself the ensuing day. He looked equally surprised and pleased at this proposal: Lady Martha agreed to accompany me, and his lordship, you may be sure, determined to be one of the party, that he might supply the deficiencies of his son, which he had heretofore found pretty manifest in such society.

We had the happiness to find all the family at home when we reached the villa. The ladies all expressed themselves delighted at my unexpected appearance, and quite charmed by my recovered looks. The Marquis, with his usual sang froid, declared himself glad to see me. Ye smiling deceivers, I cried to myself, as I surveyed the Marchioness and Lady Euphrasia, your triumph over innocence and beauty will soon be over. After passing half an hour in uninteresting chitchat, I took the opportunity of one of those pauses in conversation, which so frequently happen, to commence my attack. It would be as painful to you as to me to recapitulate all which ensued in consequence of it. Rage, guilt, and confusion, were conspicuous in the Marchioness and Lady Euphrasia. The Marquis and Lady Greystock looked with astonishment, and my father seemed overwhelmed with surprise and consternation.

I said (addressing the Marchioness), I now trusted the resentment her ladyship had entertained against her unoffending niece was sufficiently appeased by what she had made her suffer, and that she would rather rejoice than regret the opportunity which presented itself of vindicating her fame. I wished, I said, as much as possible, to spare her ladyship's feelings, and provided she would clear Miss Fitzalan from the obloquy which the transactions in her house cast upon her, I was willing to conceal the share her ladyship had in them.

In a voice of smothered rage, and with a look into which she threw as much contempt as possible, she replied, "She thanked me for the attention I professed myself inclined to pay her feelings; but she fancied I had overlooked all inclination of this kind when I undertook to bribe her servants to asperse her character, that Miss Fitzalan's might be cleared. She was sorry," she said, "to find I could be capable of such complicated baseness and weakness. Miss Fitzalan, she perceived, had made me her dupe again; but this was not surprising, as she was the professed pupil of art. Too late I should behold her in her native colors, and find the disgrace, which, by artifice, I now attempted to remove from her character, thrown back upon her, perhaps, to overwhelm me also by its weight."

"She has infatuated him," said Lord Cherbury; "she will be the bane of his life, the destruction of my hopes." "Not Miss Fitzalan," cried I, assuming as much coolness as possible, though, like the Marchioness, I found it a difficult task; "not Miss Fitzalan, but the enemies of Miss Fitzalan deceived me. I own I was the dupe of the scheme contrived against her. Anything so horrid, so monstrous, so execrable, I did not think could have entered into the minds of those who were bound by the united ties of kindred and hospitality to protect her, and I rather believed I owed my misery to the frailty than to the turpitude of human nature." "You see, my Lord," exclaimed the Marchioness, turning to Lord Cherbury, "Lord Mortimer acknowledges his passion for this wretched girl." "I do," cried I, "I glory in confessing it. In loving Miss Fitzalan, I love virtue itself In acknowledging a passion for her, I violate no faith, I break no engagement; my heart ever resisted entering into any which it could not fulfil." "Unfortunate prepossession," said Lord Cherbury, sternly. "But why, why, when you believed her guilty, were you so infatuated as to follow her to Ireland? Why not calmly resign her to the infamy she merited?" "I followed her, my Lord," I replied, "in hope to withdraw her from her seducer's arms, and place her in her father's. I hoped, I trusted, I should be able also to alleviate the bitter destiny of poor Fitzalan. Alas! not in the arms of a gay, successful seducer, but apparently in the arms of death, did I find Amanda. I saw her at the solemn hour which consigned her parent to his grave, and to have doubted her protestations of innocence then would have been almost impious. Gracious Heaven! how impossible to disbelieve her truth at the very moment her gentle spirit seemed about to take its flight to heaven! From that period she has stood acquitted in my mind, and from that period I determined to develop, to the utmost of my power, the machinations which had made me doubt her innocence. My success in their development has been beyond my expectations; but Providence is on the side of suffering virtue, and assists those who stand up in its support." Contrary to my first intention, my dear Amanda, I have given you a sketch of part of our conversation. For the remainder, it shall suffice to say, that the Marchioness persevered in declaring I had bribed her servants to blacken her character, in order to clear Miss Fitzalan's, an attempt, she repeatedly assured me, I would find unsuccessful.

The Marquis talked in high terms of the dignity of his house, and how impossible it was the Marchioness should ever have disgraced it by such actions as I accused her of committing. I answered him in a manner equally warm, that my accusations were too well grounded and supported to dread refutation. That it was not only due to injured innocence, but essential to my own honor, which would soon be materially concerned in whatever related to Miss Fitzalan, to have those accusations made public, if her ladyship refused to contradict the aspersions which might be thrown upon Miss Fitzalan, in consequence of the scene which passed at his lordship's house.

This the Marchioness, with mingled rage and contempt, refused doing, and Lady Euphrasia, after the hint I gave of soon being united to you, left the room in convulsive agitation.

Lord Cherbury, I perceived, suspected foul play, by some speeches which dropped from him, such as, if there had been any misunderstanding between her ladyship and Miss Fitzalan, it was better surely to have it done away, or certainly, if any mistake was proved relative to the affair which happened in her ladyship's house, it was but justice to the young lady to have it cleared up.

Yet, notwithstanding the interest he felt in the cause of suffering innocence, it was obvious to me that he dreaded a rupture with the Marquis's family, and appeared shocked at the unequivocal declaration I had made of never being allied to it.

Lady Martha Dormer took up the cause. The testimony Lord Mortimer had received, she said, of Miss Fitzalan's innocence was incontrovertible, and exempted him alike from being stigmatized either as the dupe of art or love. Humanity, she was convinced, exclusive of every warmer feeling, would have influenced him to have undertaken Miss Fitzalan's cause; it was the cause of innocence and virtue—a cause in which every detester of scandal and treachery should join, since not only the defenceless orphan, but the protected child of rank and prosperity, was vulnerable to their shafts.

I again repeated the evidence of her servants, and the refutation of Mrs. Jennings to her former story. I produced, to strengthen it, the unopened letters of Colonel Belgrave—thus continuing to put proof upon proof of your innocence, as Sancho Panza says, upon the shoulders of demonstration.

The passions of the Marchioness rose at last to frantic violence. She persisted in alleging her integrity, and vilifying yours; but with a countenance so legibly impressed with guilt and confusion, that a doubt of her falsehood could not be entertained even by those who wished to doubt it.

The scene of violence we now became witness to was painful to me, and shocking to Lady Martha. I therefore ordered the horses immediately to her ladyship's chariot, in which, accompanied by me, she had preceded Lord Cherbury's coach, from the idea that our continuance at the villa might not be quite so long as his lordship's.

As we expected, his lordship stayed behind, with the hope, I perceived, of being able to calm the perturbations of the Marchioness, and lessen the breach between us. He returned the next day to town. I have so long dwelt upon disagreeable scenes, that to go over any others would be dreadful; nor should I hint to you that I had such scenes to encounter, was it not to excuse and account to you for my absence from Castle Carberry. Our difficulties (you see I already unite your interests with mine) began to decrease, and are at last happily overcome. Lady Martha made me write her intentions relative to you, and his lordship was quite satisfied with them. He authorizes me to assure you he longs to receive you into his family, at once a boast and acquisition to it, and he says, he shall consider himself under obligations to you, if you hasten, as much as possible, the period of becoming one of its members, thus giving him an opportunity of making early amends, by attention to the daughter, for the injustice he did the father.

Lady Martha Dormer's intentions I have only hinted to you; in the letter, which I have the pleasure of enclosing, she is more explicit concerning them. I have given you this long narrative on paper, that when we meet our conversation may be unembittered by any painful retrospect, and that we may enjoy uninterrupted the bright prospect which now lies before us.

But ere I close my letter, I must inform you that, knowing you could never be selfishly wrapped up in your own enjoyments, I made every possible inquiry relative to your brother, and was at length referred by the agent of his late regiment to an officer in it; with some difficulty I found he had quitted his quarters on leave of absence. I wrote immediately to his family residence, and after waiting long and impatiently for an answer to my letter, I despatched a special messenger to learn whether he was there or not. The courier returned with a polite note from the officer's father, informing me his son was gone on an excursion of pleasure with some friends, and that if he knew where to find him, he would have transmitted my letter, which I might depend on being answered the moment he returned. I have no doubt but we shall receive intelligence from him concerning Mr. Fitzalan. It shall then be our business, if his situation is not already pleasing, to change it, or render it as much so as possible to him. Keep up your spirits, therefore, about him, for by the time we arrive in England I expect a letter from his friend, and let me not be any more pained by seeing your countenance clouded with care or anxiety. As a reward for reining in my impatience to see you this evening, be propitious to my request for early admission to-morrow. If charitable, you will allow me to breakfast with you, for I shall take none except with you; and without an express command to the contrary, shall take it for granted I am expected. 'Tis said that contrast heightens pleasure, and I believe the saying—I believe that, without having felt pain in all its acuteness, as I have done, I never should have felt such pleasure as I now enjoy. After so often giving you up, so often lamenting you as lost for ever, to think I shall soon call you mine, is a source of transport which words cannot express. Mine, I may say, is the resurrection of happiness, for has it not been revived from the very grave of despair? But I forget that you have Lady Martha Dormer's letter still to peruse. I acknowledge that, for old friendship's sake, I supposed you would give mine the preference; but in all reason it is time I should resign my place to her ladyship. But ere I bid you adieu, I must tell you that Araminta is a sincere participator in our happiness. She arrived from Wales but a few minutes previous to my leaving London, and I would not allow her time, as she wished, to write to you. I almost forgot to tell you that the Marquis's family, amongst whom Lady Greystock is still numbered, instead of returning to town, set out for Brighthelmstone. I have learned, contrary to my and their expectations, that neither the housekeeper nor Mrs. Jane have been dismissed, but both sent to a distant seat of the Marquis's. As we know the Marchioness's revengeful disposition, it is plain she has some secret motive for not gratifying it immediately by their dismission; but what it is can be of little consequence for us to learn, since we are both too well guarded to suffer from any future plot of hers. Like every other which was formed against my dear Amanda, I trust they will ever prove abortive. I was disturbed within a few miles of Castle Carberry by a gentleman passing on horseback, who either strongly resembled, or was Colonel Belgrave. My blood boiled in my veins at his sight. I left the carriage, mounted one of my servant's horses, and endeavored to overtake him. He certainly avoided me by taking some cross-road, as his speed could not have outstripped mine

My efforts to discover his habitation were equally unsuccessful. As to your personal security I had no apprehensions, having heard constantly from my good friend the doctor about you; but I dreaded the wretch, if it were really him, might disturb your tranquillity, either by forcing into your presence, or writing. Thank Heaven, from all intrusions or dangers of this kind my Amanda will now be guarded. But again am I trespassing on the time you should devote to Lady Martha's letter. Adieu, and do not disappoint my hopes of being allowed to visit you early. MORTIMER.

Amanda perused this letter with emotions which can be better conceived than described. She could scarcely have parted with it without a second reading, had not Lady Martha's demanded her attention. She snatched it hastily from the ground where it hitherto lay neglected, and read to the following purpose:—

That I warmly and sincerely congratulate my dear and amiable Miss Fitzalan on the happy revolution in her affairs, she will readily believe, persuaded as she must be of the deep interest I take in whatever concerns a person on whom the happiness of him whom I have loved from childhood so materially—so entirely, I may say—depends.

Yet do not suppose me, my dear Miss Fitzalan, so selfish as not to be able to rejoice at your happiness on your own account, exclusive of every consideration relative to Lord Mortimer. Long since I was taught by description to esteem and admire you, and even when the hope of being connected with you became extinct, I could not so totally forego that admiration as to feel uninterested about you. Oh! how truly do I rejoice at the revival of the hope I have just mentioned, and at its revival with every prospect of its being speedily realized! I shall consider Lord Mortimer as one of the most fortunate of men in calling you his, and to think I have been able to promote his happiness gives me a satisfaction which never was, nor ever will be, equalled by any circumstance in my life.

Though I cannot give my adopted daughter a fortune by any means equal to that which Lady Euphrasia Sutherland will possess, Lord Cherbury is fully sensible that her perfections will abundantly make up for any deficiency in this respect. Ten thousand pounds, and one thousand a year, is at present to be her portion, and the reversion of the remainder of my fortune is to be secured to her and Lord Mortimer; the final adjustment of all affairs is to take place at my house in the country, whither I propose going immediately, accompanied by Lady Araminta, and where we shall both most impatiently expect your arrival, which, we mutually entreat, may be hastened as much as possible, consistent with your health and convenience. Lord Cherbury has promised to follow us in a few days, so that I suppose he will also be at Thornbury to receive you. Would to Heaven, my dear Miss Fitzalan, injured virtue and innocence may always meet with such champions to vindicate them as Lord Mortimer. Was that the case, we should see many lovely victims of scorn and reproach raising their heads with triumph and satisfaction. But pardon my involuntarily adverting to past scenes, though, at the same time, I think you have reason to rejoice at your trials, which served as so many tests and proofs of the estimable qualities you possess. Farewell, my dear Miss Fitzalan. I have been brief in my letter, because I know I should not be pardoned by a certain person, if I engrossed too much of your time. I told him I would give you a hint of the impetuosity of his disposition; but he told me, perhaps to prevent this, that you were already acquainted with it. In one instance I shall commend him for displaying it: that is, in hastening you to Thornbury, to the arms of your sincere and affectionate friend, MARTHA DORMER.

Amanda's happiness was now almost as great as it could be in this world; almost I say, for it received alloy from the melancholy consideration that her father, that faithful and affectionate friend who had shared her troubles, could not be a partaker of her joys; but the sigh of unavailing regret which rose in her mind she checked, by reflecting, that happiness all perfect was more than humanity could either support or expect, and with pious gratitude she bent to the Power who had changed the discolored prospect, by which she had been so long surrounded, into one of cheerfulness and beauty.

If her pride was wounded by the hint, though so delicately conveyed, which Lord Mortimer had given of the difficulties he encountered in gaining Lord Cherbury's approbation, it was instantly relieved by the flattering commendations of Lady Martha Dormer, and to be connected with her and Lady Araminta, she looked upon amongst the most valuable blessings she could enjoy.

To express what she felt for Lord Mortimer would be impossible—language could not do justice to her feelings—she felt love, gratitude, and admiration for him, all in the fullest extent, and all united, and she wept in the fulness of her heart over the joyful assurance of being his. With the two letters in her hand, she repaired to the prioress's apartment, whom she found alone. The good old lady saw the traces of tears on Amanda's face, and exclaimed, in a voice which evinced her sympathy in her concerns, "Oh! I fear, my child, something has happened to disturb you!" Amanda presented her the letters, and bid her judge from them whether she had not reason to be agitated. As the prioress read, her sudden and broken exclamations manifested her surprise and pleasure, and frequently were her spectacles removed to wipe from off them the tears of joy by which they were bedewed. When she finished the welcome packet, she turned to Amanda, who had been attentively watching the various turns in her countenance, and gave her a congratulatory embrace. "Lord Mortimer is worthy of you, my child," said the prioress, "and that is the highest eulogium I can pass on him." After commenting upon different parts of the letter, she asked Amanda a little archly, "whether she intended sending an express command to his lordship against coming early in the morning?" Amanda honestly confessed she had no such intention, and expressed her wish to behold him. The prioress said she would have breakfast prepared for them in the garden parlor, and that she would take care they should not be interrupted. She also promised to keep everything secret till matters were arranged for Amanda's removal from St. Catherine's.

CHAPTER XXXIX.

> "Thus let me hold thee to my heart,
> And every care resign;
> And shall we never—never part,
> Oh! thou my all that's mine."—GOLDSMITH.

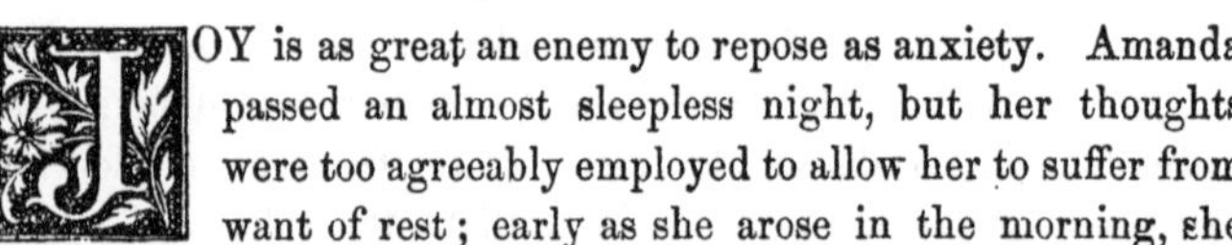

JOY is as great an enemy to repose as anxiety. Amanda passed an almost sleepless night, but her thoughts were too agreeably employed to allow her to suffer from want of rest; early as she arose in the morning, she was but a short time in the parlor before Lord Mortimer arrived. He appeared with all the transports of his soul beaming from his eyes, and was received by Amanda with tender and trembling emotion. He caught her to his heart as a treasure restored to him by the immediate hand of Heaven. He pressed her to it with silent ecstasy. Both for a few moments were unable to speak; but the tears which burst from Amanda, and those that stopped on the glowing cheeks of Lord Mortimer, expressed their feelings more forcibly than any language could have done.

Amanda at length found utterance, and began to thank his lordship for all the difficulties he had gone through in vindicating her fame. He hastily stopped those effusions of gratitude, by bidding her ask her heart whether he had not been serving himself as well as her by what he had done.

From the soft confusion into which his transports threw her Amanda endeavored to recover herself by repairing to the breakfast table, on which the good sisters had spread all the niceties (adapted for a morning repast) which the convent could produce: but her hand was unsteady, she spilt the tea in pouring it out, and committed twenty blunders in helping Lord Mortimer. He laughed a little archly at her embarrassment, and insisted on doing the honors of the table himself, to which Amanda, with a deep blush, consented; but breakfast was little attended to. Amanda's hand was detained in Lord Mortimer's, while his eyes were continually turning towards her, as if to assure his heart that, in the lovely evidence of his happiness, there was no deception; and the tenderness Amanda had no longer reason to restrain beamed from her looks, which also evinced her perfect sensibility of her present felicity—a felicity heightened by her approving conscience testifying she had merited it. The pure, the delightful satisfaction resulting from this reflection gave such radiance to her complexion, that Lord Mortimer repeatedly declared her residence at St. Catherine's had made her more beautiful than ever. Twelve o'clock struck, and found them still loitering over the breakfast table. "The nuns will think we have made a tolerable feast," cried Lord Mortimer, smiling, while Amanda rose with precipitation. "I need not," continued he, following her, "like Sterne, ask nature what has made the meal so delicious; I need only ask my own heart, and it will inform me, love and tenderness." Amanda blushed, and they went together into the garden. She would have walked before the windows of the convent, but Lord Mortimer forced her gently into a dark, sequestered alley. Here their conversation became more connected than it had been hitherto. The generous intentions of Lady Martha Dormer, and the arrangements she had made for the reception and nuptials of Amanda, were talked over. The marriage was to take place at Thornbury, Lady Martha's seat; they were to continue there for a month after its solemnization, and from thence to go to an estate of Lord Cherbury's for the remainder of the summer; a house in one of the squares was to be taken and prepared for their residence in winter, and Lady Martha Dormer had promised, whenever she came to town, which was but seldom, she would make their house her home, provided they would promise to spend every Christmas, and three months at least in summer, with her at Thornbury. Lord Mortimer said he had his choice of any of the Earl's seats, but chose none, from an idea of the Hall being more agreeable to Amanda. She assured him it was, and he proceeded to mention the presents which Lady Martha had prepared for her, also the carriages and retinue he had provided, and expected to find at Thornbury against she reached it, still asking if the arrangements he had made met her approbation.

Amanda was affected even to tears by the solicitude he showed to please her; and he, perceiving her emotions, changed the discourse to talk about her removal from St. Catherine's. He entreated her not to delay it longer than was absolutely necessary to adjust matters for it. She promised compliance to this entreaty, acknowledging that she but obeyed her inclinations in doing so, as she longed to be presented to her generous patroness, Lady Martha, and to her amiable and beloved Lady Araminta. Lord Mortimer, delicately considerate about all which concerned her, begged she would speak to the prioress to procure a decent female, who should be a proper attendant for her in her journey. They should travel together in one chaise, and he would follow them in another. Amanda promised she would lose no time in making this request, which, she had no doubt, would be successful.

Lord Mortimer presented her with a very beautiful embroidered purse, containing notes to the amount of five hundred pounds. Amanda blushed deeply, and felt her feelings a little hurt at the idea of being obliged to Lord Mortimer for everything. He pressed her hand, and in a voice of soothing tenderness, told her he should be offended if she did not, from this moment, consider her interest inseparable from his. The notes, he said, of right belonged to her, as they amounted to but the individual sum he had already devoted to her use. He requested she would not curb in the least her generous spirit, but, fulfil, to the utmost extent, all the claims which gratitude had upon her. The benevolent sisters of St. Catherine's were the foremost in the list of those who had conferred obligations upon her, and he desired she would not only reward them liberally at present, but promise them an annual stipend of fifty pounds.

Amanda was truly delighted at this. To be able to contribute to the comfort of those who had so largely promoted hers, was a source of exquisite felicity. Lord Mortimer presented her with his picture, which he had drawn in London for that purpose. It was a striking likeness, and most elegantly set with brilliants, which formed a cipher upon a plait of hair at the back. This was indeed a precious present to Amanda, and she acknowledged it was such. Lord Mortimer said, that "in return for it he should expect hers at some future time;" but added, smiling, "I shall not heed the shadow till I procure the substance." He also gave her a very beautiful ring, with an emblematical device, and adorned in the same manner as his picture, which Lady Martha had sent as a pledge of future friendship; and he now informed her, "that her ladyship, accompanied by Lady Araminta, intended meeting them at Holyhead, that all due honor and attention might be paid to her adopted daughter."

In the midst of their conversation the dinner bell rang from the convent. Amanda started, and declared she had not supposed it half so late. The arch smile which this speech occasioned in Lord Mortimer, instantly made her perceive it had been a tacit confession of the pleasure she enjoyed in their tête-à-tête.

She blushed, and telling him she could not stay another moment, was hurrying away. He hastily caught her, and holding both her hands, declared she should not depart, neither would he to his solitary dinner, till she promised he might return to her early in the evening. To this she consented, provided he allowed her to have the prioress and Sister Mary at least at tea. This was a condition Lord Mortimer by no means liked to agree to, and he endeavored to prevail on her to drop it; but finding her inflexible, he said she was a provoking girl, and asked her if she was not afraid that, when he had the power, he would retaliate upon her for all the trials she had put his patience to. But since she would have it so, why, it must be so to be sure, he said; but he hoped the good ladies would have too much conscience to sit out the whole evening with them. That was all chance, Amanda said. The bell again rang, and he was forced to depart.

She took the opportunity of being alone with the prioress for a few minutes, to speak to her about procuring a female to attend her in her journey. The prioress said she doubted not but she could procure her an eligible person from the neighboring town, and promised to write there that very evening, to a family who would be able to assist her inquiries.

Both she and Sister Mary were much pleased by being invited to drink tea with Lord Mortimer. He came even earlier than was expected. Poor Amanda was terrified, lest her companions should overhear him repeatedly asking her, whether they would not retire immediately after tea. Though not overheard, the prioress had too much sagacity not to know her departure was desired; she, therefore, under pretence of business, retired and took Mary along with her.

Amanda and Lord Mortimer went into the garden. He thanked her for not losing time in speaking to the prioress about her servant, and said that he hoped, at the end of the week at farthest, she would be ready to begin her journey. Amanda readily promised to use all possible dispatch. They passed some delightful hours in rambling about the garden, and talking over their felicity.

The prioress's expectation was answered relative to a servant. In the course of two days she produced one in every respect agreeable to Amanda, and things were now in such forwardness for her departure, that she expected it would take place as soon as Lord Mortimer had mentioned. His time was passed almost continually at St Catherine's, never leaving it except at dinner-time, when he went to Castle Carberry. His residence there was soon known, and visitors and invitations without number came to the castle, but he found means of avoiding them.

Amanda, laughing, would often tell him he retarded the preparations for her journey by being always with her; this, he said, was only a pretext to drive him away, for that he rather forwarded them by letting her lose no time.

Lord Mortimer, on coming to Amanda one evening as usual, appeared uncommonly discomposed, his face was flushed, and his whole manner betrayed agitation. He scarcely noticed Amanda; but seating himself, placed his arm upon a table, and leaned his head dejectedly upon it. Amanda was inexpressibly shocked—her heart panted with apprehension of ill; but she felt too timid to make any inquiry. He suddenly knit his brows, and muttered between his teeth, "Curse on the wretch!"

Amanda could no longer keep silence. "What wretch," she exclaimed, "or what is the meaning of this disorder?" "First tell me, Amanda," said he, looking very steadfastly at her, "have you seen any stranger here lately?" "Good Heaven!" replied she, "what can you mean by such a question? But I solemnly assure you I have not." "Enough," said he, "such an assurance restores me to quiet; but, my dear Amanda," coming over to her, and taking her hands in his, "since you have perceived my agitation, I must account to you for it. I have just seen Belgrave; he was but a few yards from me on the Common when I saw him; but the mean despicable wretch, loaded as he is with conscious guilt, durst not face me. He got out of my way by leaping over the hedge, which divides the Common from a lane with many intricate windings. I endeavored, but without success, to discover the one he had retreated through." "I see," said Amanda, pale and trembling, "he is destined to make me wretched. I had hoped indeed that Lord Mortimer would no more have suffered his quiet to be interrupted by him; it implies such a doubt," said she, weeping, "as shocks my soul! If suspicion is thus continually to be revived, we had better separate at once, for misery must be the consequence of a union without mutual confidence." "Gracious Heaven!" said Lord Mortimer, "how unfortunate I am to give you pain. You mistake entirely, indeed, my dearest Amanda, the cause of my uneasiness. I swear by all that is sacred, no doubt, no suspicion of your worth, has arisen in my mind. No man can think more highly of a woman than I do of you; but I was disturbed lest the wretch should have forced himself into your presence, and lest you, through apprehension for me, concealed it from me."

This explanation calmed the perturbation of Amanda. As so

atonement for the uneasiness he had given her, she wanted Lord Mortimer to promise he would not endeavor to discover Belgrave. This promise he avoided giving, and Amanda was afraid of pressing it, lest the spark of jealousy, which she was convinced existed in the disposition of Lord Mortimer, should be blown into a flame. That Belgrave would studiously avoid him she trusted, and she resolved that if the things that she had deemed it necessary to order from the neighboring town were not finished, to wait no longer for them, as she longed now more than ever to quit a place she thought dangerous to Lord Mortimer. The ensuing morning, instead of seeing his lordship at breakfast, a note was brought to her couched in these words:—

TO MISS FITZALAN.

I am unavoidably prevented from waiting on my dear Amanda this morning, but in the course of the day she may depend on either seeing or hearing from me again. She can have no excuse now on my account about not hastening the preparations for her journey, and when we meet, if I find that her time has not been employed for this purpose, she may expect a severe chiding from her faithful

MORTIMER.

This note filled Amanda with the most alarming disquiet. It was evident to her that he was gone in pursuit of Belgrave. She ran into the hall to inquire of the messenger about his master, but he was gone. She then hastened to the prioress and communicated her apprehensions to her.

The prioress endeavored to calm them, by assuring her she might be convinced that Belgrave had taken too many precautions to be discovered.

Amanda's breakfast, however, remained untouched, and her things unpacked, and she continued the whole morning the picture of anxiety, impatiently expecting the promised visit or letter. Neither came, and she resolved to send, after dinner, the old gardener to Castle Carberry to inquire about Lord Mortimer. While she was speaking to him for that purpose, the maid followed her into the garden, and told her there was a messenger in the parlor from Lord Mortimer. She flew thither, but what words can express her surprise when the supposed messenger, raising a large hat, which shadowed his face, and removing a handkerchief, which he had hitherto held up to it, discovered to her view the features of Lord Cherbury? She could only exclaim, "Gracious Heaven! has anything happened to Lord Mortimer?" ere she sunk into a chair in breathless agitation.

CHAPTER XL.

"My heavy heart,
The prophetess of woe, foretells some ill
At hand."

ORD CHERBURY hastened to support and calm her agitation, by assuring her Lord Mortimer was in perfect safety. Recovering a little by this assertion, she asked him "how he was assured of this?" He answered, "because he had seen him, though without being perceived by him, about an hour ago." Amanda, restored to her faculties by being assured he was uninjured, began to reflect on the suddenness of Lord Cherbury's visit. She would have flattered herself he came to introduce her to his family himself, had not his looks almost forbid such an idea. They were gloomy and disordered; his eyes were fastened on her, yet he appeared unwilling to speak.

Amanda felt herself in too awkward and embarrassing a situation to break the unpleasant silence. At last Lord Cherbury suddenly exclaimed, "Lord Mortimer does not, nor must not, know of my being here." "Must not!" repeated Amanda, in inconceivable astonishment.

"Gracious Heaven!" said Lord Cherbury, starting from the chair on which he had thrown himself opposite her, "how shall I begin, how shall I tell her? Oh! Miss Fitzalan," he continued, approaching her, "I have much to say, and you have much to hear which will shock you. I believed I could better in an interview have informed you of particulars, but I find I was mistaken. I will write to you." "My Lord," cried Amanda, rising, all pale and trembling, "tell me now; to leave me in suspense, after receiving such dreadful hints, would be cruelty. Oh! surely, if Lord Mortimer be safe—if Lady Martha Dormer—if Lady Araminta is well—I can have nothing so very shocking to hear."

"Alas!" replied he, mournfully, shaking his head, "you are mistaken Be satisfied, however, that the friends you have mentioned are all well. I have said I would write to you. Can you meet me this evening amongst the ruins?" Amanda gave an assenting bow "I shall then," pursued he, "have a letter ready to deliver you. In the mean time, I must inform you no person in the world knows of my visit here but yourself, and of all beings Lord Mortimer is the last I should wish to know it. Remember, then, Miss Fitzalan," taking her hand, which he grasped with violence, as if to impress his words upon her heart, "remember that on your secrecy everything most estimable in life, even life itself, perhaps, depends."

With these dreadful and mysterious words he departed, leaving Amanda a picture of horror and surprise. It was many minutes ere she moved from the attitude in which he left her, and when she did, it was only to walk in a disordered manner about the room, repeating his dreadful words. He was come, perhaps, to part her and Lord Mortimer, and yet, after consenting to their union, surely Lord Cherbury could not be guilty of such treachery and deceit. Yet, if this was not the case, why conceal his coming to Ireland from Lord Mortimer? Why let it be known only to her? And what could be the secrets of dreadful import he had to communicate?

From these self-interrogations, in which her reason was almost bewildered, the entrance of the prioress drew her.

She started at seeing the pale and distracted looks of Amanda, and asked, "if she had heard any bad tidings of Lord Mortimer?"

Amanda sighed heavily at this question, and said, "No." The secrecy she had been enjoined to she durst not violate, by mentioning the mysterious visit to her friend. Unable, however, to converse on any other subject, she resolved to retire to her chamber. She placed her illness and agitation to the account of Lord Mortimer, and said a little rest was absolutely necessary for her, and begged, if his lordship came in the course of the evening, he might be told she was too ill to see him.

The prioress pressed her to stay for tea. She refused, and, as she retired from the room, desired nothing might be said of the person who had just seen her to Lord Mortimer, saying, with a faint smile, "she would not make him vain by letting him know of her anxiety about him." She retired to her chamber, and endeavored to control her perturbations, that she might be the better enabled to support what she had so much reason to apprehend. Neither the prioress nor the nuns, in obedience to her injunctions, intruded upon her, and at the appointed hour she softly opened the chamber door, and, every place being clear, stole softly from the convent.

She found Lord Cherbury waiting for her amidst the solitary ruins. He had a letter in his hand, which he presented to her the moment she appeared.

"In this letter, Miss Fitzalan," said he, "I have opened to you my whole heart. I have disburthened it of secrets which have long oppressed it. I have intrusted my honor to your care. From what I have said, that its contents are of a sacred nature, you may believe, should they be considered in any other light by you, the consequence may, nay, must be fatal." He said this with a sternness that made Amanda shrink. "Meditate well on the contents of that letter, Miss Fitzalan," continued he, with a voice of deep solemnity, "for it is a letter which will fix your destiny and mine. Even should the request contained in it be refused, let me be the first acquainted with the refusal. Then indeed I shall urge you no more to secrecy, for what will follow, in consequence of such a refusal, must divulge all." "Oh! tell me, tell me," said Amanda, catching hold of his arm, "tell me what is the request or what it is I am to fear. Oh! tell me all at once, and rid me of the torturing suspense I endure." "I cannot," he cried, "indeed, I cannot. To-morrow night I shall expect your answer here at the same hour."

At this moment Lord Mortimer's voice calling upon Amanda was heard. Lord Cherbury dropped her hand, which he had taken, and instantly retired amongst the windings of the pile, from whence Lord Mortimer soon appeared, giving Amanda only time to hide the fatal letter.

"Good Heavens!" exclaimed he, "what could have brought you

35

hither, and who was the person who just departed from you?" It was well for Amanda that the twilight gave but an imperfect view of her face. She felt her color come and go; a cold dew overspread her forehead; she leaned against a rude fragment of the building, and faintly exclaimed, "the person——" "Yes," said Lord Mortimer, "I am sure I heard retreating footsteps." "You are mistaken," repeated Amanda, in the same faint accent. "Well," said he, "though you may dispute the evidence of my ears, you cannot the evidence of my eyes. I see you here, and I am astonished at it." "I came here for air," said Amanda. "For air!" repeated Lord Mortimer; "I own I should have thought the garden better adapted for such a purpose; but why come hither in a clandestine manner? Why, if you have the fears you would persuade me you have, expose yourself to danger from the wretch who haunts the place, by coming here alone. When I went to the convent I was told you were indisposed, and could not be disturbed. I could not depart, however, without making an effort to see you; but you can easier imagine than I describe the consternation I felt when you could not be found. It was wrong, indeed, Amanda, it was wrong to come here alone, and affect concealment." "Gracious Heaven!" said Amanda, raising her hands and eyes, and bursting into tears, "how wretched am I!"

She was indeed at this moment superlatively wretched. Her heart was oppressed by the dread of evil, and she perceived suspicions in Lord Mortimer which she could not attempt to remove, lest an intimation of the secret she was so awfully enjoined to keep should escape.

"Ah! Amanda," said Lord Mortimer, losing in a moment the asperity with which he had addressed her at first, "ah! Amanda, like the rest of your sex, you know too well the power of your tears not to use them. Forget, or at least forgive, all I have said. I was disappointed in not seeing you the moment I expected, and that put me out of temper. I know I am too impetuous, but you will in time subdue every unruly passion. I put myself into your hands, and you shall make me what you please."

He now pressed her to his bosom, and finding her tremble universally, again implored her forgiveness, as he imputed the agitation she betrayed entirely to the uneasiness he had given her.

She assured him, with a faltering voice, he had not offended her. Her spirits were affected, she said, by all she had suffered during the day. Lord Mortimer placing, as she wished, those sufferings to his own account, declared her anxiety at once pained and pleased him; adding, he would truly confess what detained him from her during the day as soon as they returned to the convent.

Their return to it relieved the sisterhood, who had also been seeking Amanda, from many apprehensions. The prioress and Sister Mary followed them into the parlor, where Lord Mortimer begged "they would have compassion on him, and give him something for his supper, as he had scarcely eaten anything the whole day." Sister Mary instantly replied, "he should be gratified, as Amanda was in the same predicament, and she hoped he would be now able to prevail on her to eat." The cloth was accordingly laid, and a few trifles placed upon it. Sister Mary would gladly have stayed, but the prioress had understanding enough to think the supper would be more palatable if they were absent, and accordingly retired.

Lord Mortimer now, with the most soothing tenderness, tried to cheer his fair companion, and make her take some refreshment; but his efforts for either of those purposes were unsuccessful, and she besought him not to think her obstinate, if she could not in a moment recover her spirits. To divert his attention a little from himself, she asked him to perform his promise, by relating what had kept him the whole day from St. Catherine's.

He now acknowledged "he had been in search of Belgrave; but the precautions he had taken to conceal himself baffled all inquiries, which convinces me," continued Lord Mortimer, "if I wanted conviction about such a matter, that he has not yet dropped his villanous designs upon you; but the wretch cannot always escape the vengeance he merits." "May he never," cried Amanda, fervently yet involuntarily, "meet it from your hands." "We will drop that part of the subject," said Lord Mortimer, "if you please. You must know," continued he, "after scouring the whole neighborhood, I fell in, about four miles hence, with a gentleman who had visited at the Marquis of Roslin's last summer. He immediately asked me to accompany him home to dinner. From his residence in the country I thought it probable he might be able to give some account of Belgrave, and therefore accepted the invitation; but my inquiries were as fruitless here as elsewhere When I found it so, I was on thorns to depart, particularly as all the gentlemen were set in for drinking, and feared I might be thrown into an improper situation to visit my Amanda. I was on the watch, however, and, to use their sporting term, literally stole away." "Thank Heaven!" said Amanda, "your inquiries proved fruitless. Oh! never, never repeat them. Think no more about a wretch so despicable." "Well," cried Lord Mortimer, "why don't you hurry me from the neighbourhood? Fix the day, the moment for our departure. I have been here already five days. Lady Martha's patience is, I dare say, quite exhausted by this time, and should we delay much longer, I suppose, she will think we have both become converts to the holy rites of this convent, and that I, instead of taking the vows which should make me a joyful bridegroom, am about taking those which shall doom me to celibacy. Seriously, what but want of inclination can longer detain you?" "Ah!" said Amanda, "you know too well that my departure cannot be retarded by want of inclination." "Then why not decide immediately upon the day?" Amanda was silent; her situation was agonizing; how could she fix upon a day, uncertain whether she did not possess a letter which would prevent her ever taking the projected journey!

"Well," said Lord Mortimer, after allowing her some time to speak, "I see I must fix the day myself; this is Tuesday—let it be Thursday." "Let us drop the subject this night, my Lord," said Amanda; "I am really ill, and only wait for your departure to retire to rest." Lord Mortimer obeyed her, but with reluctance, and soon after retired.

CHAPTER XLI.

"As one condemned to leap a precipice,
Who sees before his eyes the depth below,
Stops short, and looks about for some kind shrub
To break his dreadful fall."—DRYDEN.

MANDA went to her chamber the moment Lord Mortimer departed: the nuns were already retired to rest, so that the stillness which reigned through the house added to the awfulness of her feelings, as she sat down to peruse a letter which she had been previously informed would fix her fate.

TO MISS FITZALAN.

To destroy a prospect of felicity, at the very moment its enveloping glooms are dispersed, is indeed the source of pangs most dreadful; yet such are the horrors of my destiny, that nothing but intervening between you, Mortimer and happiness, can save me from perdition. Appalled at this dreadful assertion, the letter drops from your trembling hands; but oh! dear Miss Fitzalan, cast it not utterly aside till you peruse the rest of the contents, and fix the destiny of the most wretched of mankind, wretched in thinking he shall interrupt not only your peace, but the peace of a son so noble, so gracious, so idolized as Mortimer is by him; but I will not longer torture your feelings by keeping you in suspense; the preface I have already given is sufficient, and I will be explicit: gambling, that bane of fame and fortune, has been my ruin; but whilst I indulged, so well did I conceal my propensity for it, that even those I called my friends were ignorant of it. With shame I confess I was ever foremost to rail against this vice, which was continually drawing sums in secret from me, that would have given comfort and affluence to many a child of want. For some time my good and bad fortune were so equal, that my income suffered no considerable diminution. About five years ago a Mr. Freelove, a particular friend of mine, died, and left to my care his only son, whom, I dare say, you may recollect having seen at my house last winter. This young man's property was consigned to my care, to manage as much for his advantage as I could; it consisted of a large estate and fifty thousand pounds. At the period Freelove became my ward, I had had a constant run of ill-luck for many months. The ardor of gaming (unlike every other passion) is rather increased than diminished by disappointment. Without being warned, therefore, by ill-success, I still went on, till all I could touch of my own property was gone. Did I then retire, ashamed of my folly? No. I could not bear to do so, without another effort for recovering my losses, and in that effort risked something more precious than I had ever yet done—namely, my honor, by using the money which lay in my hands belonging to Freelove; the long period which was to elapse ere he came of age, emboldened me to this. Ere that period I trusted I should have retrieved my losses, and be enabled not only to discharge the principal, but whatever interest it would have brought, if applied to another purpose. I followed the bent of my evil genius, sum after sum taken up, and all alike buried in the accursed vortex which had already swallowed so much from me! But when I found all was gone, oh, Miss Fitzalan! I still tremble at the distraction of that moment.

All, as I have said before, that I could touch of my property was gone; the remainder was so settled I had no power over it, except joined by my son Great as was the injury that he would sustain by mortgaging it, I was confident he never would hesitate doing so if acquainted with my distress; but to let him know it was worse than a death of torture could be to me; his early excellence, the nobleness of his principles, mingled in the love I felt for him a degree of awe; to confess myself a villain to such a character, to acknowledge my life had been a scene of deceit; to be abashed, confounded in the presence of my son—to meet his piercing eye—to see the blush of shame mantle his cheeks for his father's crimes—Oh, horrible!—most horrible! I raved at the idea, and resolved, if driven by necessity to tell him of my baseness, not to survive the confession. At this critical juncture the Marquis of Roslin came from Scotland to reside in London. An intimacy which had been dormant for years between our families was then revived, and I soon found that an alliance between them would be pleasing. The prospect of it raised me from the very depth of despair. But my transports were of short continuance, for Mortimer not only showed but expressed the strongest repugnance to such a connection. Time and daily experience, I trusted, would so forcibly convince him of the advantages of it, as at last to conquer this repugnance. Nor did the hope of an alliance taking place entirely forsake my heart, till informed that his was already bestowed upon another object. My feelings at this information I shall not attempt to describe. All hope of saving myself from dishonor was now cut off; for though dutiful and attentive to me in the highest degree, I could not flatter myself that Mortimer would blindly sacrifice his reason and inclination to my will. The most fatal intentions again took possession of my mind; but the uncertainties he suffered on your account kept me in horrible suspense as to their execution. After some months of torture, I began again to revive, by learning that you and Mortimer were inevitably separated. And such is the selfish nature of vice; so abandoned is it to all feelings of humanity, that I rather rejoiced at, than lamented the supposed disgrace of the daughter of my friend. But the persevering constancy of Mortimer—rather let me say the immediate interposition of Providence—soon gave her reason to triumph over the arts of her enemies, and I was again reduced to despair. Mortimer, I dare say, from motives of delicacy, has concealed from you the opposition I gave to his wishes after your innocence was cleared, and the intentions of Lady Martha Dormer relative to you were made known. At last I found I must either seem to acquiesce in these wishes and intentions, or divulge my real motive for opposing them; or else quarrel with my son and sister, and appear in their eyes the most selfish of human beings. I, therefore, to appearance acquiesced, but resolved in reality to throw myself upon your mercy, believing that a character so tender, so perfect, so heroic-like as yours has been, through every scene of distress, would have compassion on a fallen fellow-creature. Was my situation otherwise than it now is—were you even portionless—I should rejoice at having you united to my family, from your own intrinsic merit. Situated as I now am, the fortune Lady Martha Dormer proposes giving you can be of no consequence to me. The projected match between you and Mortimer is yet a secret from the public—of course it has not lessened his interest with the Roslin family. I have already been so fortunate as to adjust the unlucky difference which took place between them, and remove any resentment they entertained against him; and I am confident the first overture he should make for a union with Lady Euphrasia would be successful. The fortune which would immediately be received with her is sixty thousand pounds, and five thousand a year. The first would be given up to me in place of the settlement I should make on Lord Mortimer; so that you see, my dear Miss Fitzalan, his marriage with Lady Euphrasia would at once extricate me from all my difficulties. Freelove in a few months will be of age, and the smallest delay in settling with him, after he attains that period, must brand me with dishonor. I stand upon the verge of a dreadful abyss, and it is in your power only to preserve me from plunging into it—you who, like an angel of mercy, may bid me live, and save me from destruction. Yet think not in resigning Lord Mortimer, if, indeed, such a resignation should take place, you sacrifice your own interest. No; it shall be my grateful care to secure to you independence; and I am confident, among the many men you must meet, sensible of your worth, and enraptured with your charms, you may yet select one as calculated to render you happy as Mortimer; while he, disappointed of the object of his affections, will, I have no doubt, without longer hesitation, accept the one I shall again propose to him. But should you determine on giving him up, you ask how, and by what means, you can break with him after what has passed, without revealing your real motive for doing so to him. That is indeed a difficulty; but after going so far, I must not hesitate in telling you how it can be removed. You must retire secretly from his knowledge, and leave no clue behind by which you can be traced. If you comply with the first of my requests, but stop short here, you will defeat all that your mercy, your pity, your compassion, would do to save me, since the consequence of any hesitation must be a full explanation, and I have already said it, and now repeat it in the most solemn manner, that I will not survive the divulgement of my secret—for never, no, never will I live humbled in the eyes of my son. If, then, you comply, comply not in part. Pardon me, dear Miss Fitzalan, if you think there is anything arbitrary in my style. I would have softened, if I could, all I had to say, but the time, the danger, the necessity, urged me to be explicit. I have now to you, as to a superior Being, opened my whole heart. It rests with you whether I shall live to atone for my follies, or by one desperate action terminate them. Should you show me mercy, unworthy as I am of it—should you, in compassion to poor Mortimer, comply with a request which can only save him from the pangs he would feel at a father's quitting life unbidden, my gratitude, my admiration, my protection whilst I live, will be yours, and the first act of my restored life will be to secure you a competence. I shall wait with trembling anxiety for your appearance to-morrow night. Till then, believe me Your sincere, though most unhappy friend,

CHERBURY.

The fatal letter fell from Amanda. A mist overspread her eyes, and she sunk senseless on her chair; but the privation of her misery was of short duration, and she recovered as if from a dreadful dream. She felt cold, trembling, and terrified. She looked round the room with an eye of apprehension and dismay, bewildered as to the cause of her wretchedness and terror, till the letter at her feet again struck her sight.

"Was there no way," she asked herself, as she again examined the contents, "was there no way by which the dreadful sacrifice it doomed her to could be avoided?" Lady Martha and Lord Mortimer would unite their efforts to save the honor of their wretched relative; they would soothe his feelings; they would compassionate his failings; they would——; but she started in the midst of these ideas—started as from ideas fraught with guilt and horror, as those fatal words rushed upon her mind—"I will not survive the divulgement of my secret;" and she found that to save the father she must resign the son. How unworthy of such a sacrifice! engaged as she was to Lord Mortimer, she began to doubt whether she had a right to make it. What a doubt! She shuddered for having conceived it, and reproached herself for yielding a moment to the suggestions of tenderness which had given rise to it. She resolved without a farther struggle to submit to reason and to virtue, convinced that, if accessory to Lord Cherbury's death, nothing could assuage her wretchedness, and that the unhappiness Lord Mortimer would suffer at losing her would be trifling compared to that he would feel if he lost his father by an act of suicide.

"In my fate," exclaimed she, in the low and broken accent of despair, "there is no alternative. I submit to it without a farther struggle; I dare not call upon one being to advise me. I resign him," therefore," she continued, as if Lord Cherbury was really present to hear her resignation; "I resign Lord Mortimer, but oh, my God!" raising her hands with agony to heaven, "give me fortitude to bear the horrors of my situation! Oh, Mortimer! dear, invaluable Mortimer! the hand of fate is against our union, and we must part, never, never more to meet! From the imputation of ingratitude and guilt I shall not be allowed to vindicate myself. No, I am completely the victim of Lord Cherbury—the cruel, perfidious Cherbury, whose treachery, whose seeming acquiescence in the wishes of his son, has given me joy but to render my misery more acute!"

That Lord Mortimer would impute withdrawing herself from him to an attachment for Belgrave she was convinced, and that her fame as well as peace should be sacrificed to Lord Cherbury, caused such a whirl of contending passions in her mind, that reason and reflection for a few minutes yielded to their violence, and she resolved to vindicate herself to Lord Mortimer. This resolution, however, was of short continuance. As her subsiding passions again gave her power to reflect, she was convinced that by trying to clear herself of an imaginary crime she should commit a real one—since to save her own character Lord Cherbury's must be stigmatized; and the consequence of such an act he had already declared—so that not only by the world, but by her own conscience, she should for ever be accused of accelerating his death.

"It must, it must be made!" she wildly cried; "the sacrifice must be made, and Mortimer is lost to me for ever." She flung herself on the bed, and passed the hours till morning in agonies too great for description. From a kind of stupefaction rather than sleep, into which she had gradually sunk towards morning, she was roused by a gentle tap at her chamber door, and the voice of Sister Mary informing her that Lord Mortimer was below, and impatient for his breakfast.

Amanda started from the bed, and bid her tell his lordship she would attend him immediately. She then adjusted her dress, tried to calm her spirits, and, with uplifted hands and eyes, besought Heaven to support her through the trials of the day.

Weak and trembling she descended to the parlor. The moment she entered it, Lord Mortimer, shocked and surprised by her altered looks, exclaimed, "Gracious Heaven! what is the matter?" Then feeling the feverish heat of her hands, continued, "Why, why, Amanda, had you the cruelty to conceal your illness? Proper assistance might have prevented its increasing to such a degree." With unutterable tenderness he folded his arms about her, and, while her drooping head sunk on his bosom, declared he would immediately send for the physician who had before attended her.

"Do not," said Amanda, while tears trickled down her cheeks, "do not," continued she, in a broken voice, "for he could do me no good." "No good!" repeated Lord Mortimer, in a terrified accent. "I mean," cried she, recollecting herself, "he would find it unnecessary to prescribe anything for me, as my illness only proceeds from the agitation I suffered yesterday. It made me pass an indifferent night, but quietness to-day will recover me."

Lord Mortimer was with difficulty persuaded to give up his intention; nor would he relinquish it till she had promised, if not better before the evening, to inform him, and let the physician be sent for.

They now sat down to breakfast, at which Amanda was unable either to preside or eat. When over, she told Lord Mortimer she must retire to her chamber, as rest was essential for her; but between nine and ten in the evening she would be happy to see him. He tried to persuade her that she might rest as well upon the sofa in the parlor as in her chamber, and that he might then be allowed to sit with her; but she could not be persuaded to this, she said, and begged he would excuse seeing her till the time she had already mentioned.

He at last retired with great reluctance, but not till she had several times desired him to do so.

Amanda now repaired to her chamber, but not to indulge in the supineness of grief, though her heart felt bursting, but to settle upon some plan for her future conduct. In the first place, she immediately meant to write to Lord Cherbury, as the best method she could take of acquainting him with her compliance, and preventing any conversation between them, which would now have been insupportable to her.

In the next place, she designed acquainting the prioress with the sudden alteration in her affairs, only concealing from her the occasion of that alteration, and, as but one day intervened between the present and the one fixed for her journey, meant to beseech her to think of some place to which she might retire from Lord Mortimer.

Yet such was the opinion she knew the prioress entertained of Lord Mortimer, that she almost dreaded she would impute her resignation of him to some criminal motive, and abandon her entirely. If this should be the case (and scarcely could she be surprised if it was), she resolved without delay to go privately to the neighboring town, and from thence proceed immediately to Dublin. How she should act there, or what would become of her, never entered her thoughts; they were wholly engrossed about the manner in which she should leave St. Catherine's.

But she hoped, much as appearances were against her, she should not be deserted by the prioress. Providence, she trusted, would be so compassionate to her misery, as to preserve her this one friend, who could not only assist but advise her.

As soon as she had settled the line of conduct she should pursue, she sat down to pen her renunciation of Lord Mortimer, which she did in the following words:—

TO THE EARL OF CHERBURY.

MY LORD,—To your wishes I resign my happiness; my happiness, I repeat, for it is due to Lord Mortimer to declare that a union with such a character as his must have produced the highest felicity. It is also due to my own to declare, that it was neither his rank nor his fortune, but his virtues, which influenced my inclination in his favor.

Happy had it been for us all, my Lord, but particularly for me, had you continued steady in opposing the wishes of your son. My reverence for paternal authority is too great ever to have allowed me to act in opposition to it. I should not then, by your seeming acquiescence to them, have been tempted to think my trials all over.

But I will not do away any little merit your lordship may perhaps ascribe to my immediate compliance with your request, by dwelling upon the suffer ings it entails on me. May the renunciation of my hopes be the means of realizing your lordship's, and may superior fortune bring superior happiness to Lord Mortimer!

I thank your lordship for your intentions relative to me; but whilst I do so, must assure you, both now and for ever, I shall decline having them executed for me.

I shall not disguise the truth. It would not be in your lordship's power to recompense the sacrifice I have made you; and, besides, pecuniary obligations can never sit easy upon a feeling mind, except they are conferred by those we know value us, and whom we value ourselves. I have the honor to be, your lordship's obedient servant,

AMANDA FITZALAN.

The tears she had with difficulty restrained while writing, now burst forth. She rose and walked to the window, to try if the air would remove the faintness which oppressed her. From it she perceived Lord Mortimer and the prioress in deep conversation, at a little distance from the convent. She conjectured she was their subject; for, as Lord Mortimer retired, the prioress, whom she had not seen that day before, came into her chamber. After the usual salutations—"Lord Mortimer has been telling me you were ill," said she. "I trusted a lover's fears had magnified the danger; but truly, my dear child, I am sorry to say this is not the case. Tell me, my dear, what is the matter? Surely now, more than ever, you should be careful of your health." "Oh, no!" said Amanda, with a convulsive sob. "Oh, no!" wringing her hands, "you are sadly mistaken." The prioress grew alarmed, her limbs began to tremble, she was unable to stand, and, dropping on the nearest chair, besought Amanda, in a voice expressive of her feelings, "to explain the reason of her distress."

Amanda knelt before her, she took her hands, she pressed them to her burning forehead and lips, and bedewed them with her tears, while she exclaimed, "she was wretched." "Wretched!" repeated the prioress. "For Heaven's sake be explicit—keep me no longer in suspense—you sicken my very heart by your agitation—it foretells something dreadful!"

"It does indeed," said Amanda. "It foretells that Lord Mortimer and I shall never be united!"

The prioress started, and surveyed Amanda with a look which seemed to say, "she believed she had lost her senses;" then, with assumed composure, begged "she would defer any farther explanation of her distress till her spirits were in a calmer state." "I will not rise," cried Amanda, taking the prioress's hand, which, in her surprise, she had involuntarily withdrawn. "I will not rise till you say that, notwithstanding the mysterious situation in which I am involved, you will continue to be my friend. Oh! such an assurance would assuage the sorrows of my heart."

The prioress now perceived that it was grief alone which disordered Amanda; but how she had met with any cause for grief, or what could occasion it, were matters of astonishment to her. "Surely my dear child," cried she, "should know me too well to desire such an assurance; but, however mysterious her situation may appear to others, she will not, I trust and believe, let it appear so to me. I wait with impatience for an explanation." "It is one of my greatest sorrows," exclaimed Amanda, "that I cannot give such an explanation. No, no," she continued in an agony, "a death-bed confession would not authorize my telling you the occasion of Lord Mortimer's separation and mine." The prioress now insisted on her taking a chair, and then begged, as far as she could, without farther delay, she would let her into her situation.

Amanda immediately complied. "An unexpected obstacle to her union with Lord Mortimer," she said, "had arisen, an obstacle which, while compelled to submit to it, she was bound most solemnly to conceal. It was expedient, therefore, she should retire from Lord Mortimer, without giving him the smallest intimation of such an intention, lest, if he suspected it, he should inquire too minutely, and by so doing, plunge not only her but himself into irremediable distress. To avoid this, it was necessary all but the prioress should be ignorant of her scheme: and by her means she hoped she should be put in a way of finding such a place of secrecy and security as she required. She besought the prioress, with streaming eyes, not to impute her resignation of Lord Mortimer to any unworthy motive; to that Heaven, which could alone console her for his loss, she appealed for her innocence. She besought her to believe her sincere; to pity, but not condemn her; to continue her friend now, when her friendship was most needful in this her deep distress, and she assured her, if it was withdrawn, she believed she could no longer struggle with her sorrows.

The prioress remained silent for a few minutes, and then addressed her in a solemn voice. "I own, Miss Fitzalan, your conduct appears so inexplicable, so astonishing, that nothing but the opinion I have formed of your character, from seeing the manner in which you have acted since left to yourself, could prevent my esteem from being diminished; but I am persuaded you cannot act from a bad motive, therefore, till that persuasion ceases, my esteem can know no diminution. From this declaration you may be convinced that, to the utmost of my power, I will serve you; yet, ere you finally determine and require such service, weigh well what you are about; consider in the eyes of the world you are about acting a dishonorable part, in breaking your engagement with Lord Mortimer without assigning some reason for doing so. Nothing short of a point of conscience should influence you to this." "Nothing short of it has," replied Amanda, "therefore pity, and do not aggravate my feelings, by pointing out the consequences which will attend the sacrifice I am compelled to make; only promise (taking the prioress's hand), only promise, in this great and sad emergency, to be my friend."

Her looks, her words, her agonies, stopped short all the prioress was going to say. She thought it would be barbarity any longer to dwell upon the ill consequences of an action, which she was now convinced some fatal necessity compelled her to, she therefore gave her all the consolation now in her power, by assuring her she would immediately think about some place for her to retire to, and would keep all that had passed between them a profound secret. She then insisted on Amanda's lying down, and trying to compose herself; she brought her drops to take, and drawing the curtains about her, retired from the room. In two hours she returned. Though she entered the chamber softly, Amanda immediately drew back the curtain, and appeared much more composed than when the prioress had left her. The good woman would not let her rise, but sat down on the bed to tell her what she had contrived for her.

"She had a relation in Scotland," she said, "who, from reduced circumstances, had kept a school for many years. But as the infirmities of age came on, she was not able to pay so much attention to her pupils as their friends thought requisite, and she had only been able to retain them by promising to get a person to assist her. As she thought her cousin (the prioress) more in the way of procuring such a one than herself, she had written to her for that purpose. A clever, well-behaved young woman, who would be satisfied with a small salary, was what she wanted. I should not mention such a place to you," said the prioress, "but that the necessity there is for your immediately retiring from Lord Mortimer leaves me no time to look out for another. But do not imagine I wish you to continue there. No indeed; I should think it a pity such talents as you possess should be buried in such obscurity. What I think is, that you can stay there till you grow more composed, and can look out for a better establishment." "Do not mention my talents," said Amanda; "my mind is so enervated by grief, that it will be long before I can make any great exertion, and the place you have mentioned is, from its obscurity, just such a one as I desire to go to." "There is, besides, another inducement," said the prioress, "namely, its being but a few miles from Port-Patrick, to which place a fair wind will bring you in a few hours from this. I know the master of a little wherry, which is perpetually going backwards and forwards. He lives in this neighborhood, and both he and his wife consider themselves under obligations to me, and will rejoice, I am sure, at an opportunity of obliging me. I shall therefore send for him this evening, informing him of the time you wish to go, and desire his care till he leaves you himself at Mrs. Macpherson's."

Amanda thanked the prioress, who proceeded to say, "that on the presumption of her going to her cousin's, she had already written a letter for her to take; but wished to know whether she would be mentioned by her own or a fictitious name."

Amanda replied, "By a fictitious one," and, after a little consideration, fixed on that of Frances Donald, which the prioress accordingly inserted, and then read the letter:—

TO MRS. MACPHERSON.

Dear Cousin,—The bearer of this letter, Frances Donald, is the young person I have procured you for an assistant in your school. I have known her some time, and can vouch for her cleverness and discretion. She is well born, and well educated, and has seen better days: but the wheel of fortune is continually turning, and she bears her misfortunes with a patience that to me is the best proof she could give of a real good disposition. I have told her you give but ten pounds a year. Her going proves she is not dissatisfied with the salary. I am sorry to hear you are troubled with rheumatic pains, and hope, when you have more time to take care of yourself, you will grow better. All the sisters join me in thanking you for your kind inquiries after them. We do tolerably well in the little school we keep, and trust our gratitude to Heaven for its present goodness will obtain a continuance of it. I beg to hear from you soon; and am, my dear cousin, your sincere friend and affectionate kinswoman,

ELIZABETH DERMOT.

St Catherine's.

"I have not said as much as you deserve," said the prioress; "but if the letter does not meet your approbation, I will make any alteration you please in it." Amanda assured her it did, and the prioress then said, "that Lord Mortimer had been again at the convent to inquire after her, and was told she was better." Amanda said, "she would not see him till the hour she had appointed for his coming to supper." The prioress agreed, that as things were changed, she was right in being in his company as little as possible, and, to prevent her being in his way, she should have her dinner and tea in her own room. The cloth was accordingly laid in it, nor would the good-natured prioress depart till she saw Amanda eat something. Sister Mary, she said, was quite anxious to come in, and perform the part of an attendant, but was prevented by her.

The distraction of Amanda's thoughts was now abated, from having everything adjusted relative to her future conduct, and the company of the prioress, who returned to her as soon as she had dined, prevented her losing the little composure she had with such difficulty acquired.

She besought the prioress not to delay writing after her departure, and to relate faithfully everything which happened in consequence of her flight. She entreated her not to let a mistaken compassion for her feelings influence her to conceal anything, as anything like the appearance of concealment in her letter would only torture her with anxiety and suspense.

The prioress solemnly promised she would obey her request, and

Amanda, with tears, regretted that she was now unable to recompense the kindness of the prioress and the sisterhood, as she had lately intended doing by Lord Mortimer's desire, as well as her own inclination. The prioress begged her not to indulge any regret on that account, as they considered themselves already liberally recompensed, and had, besides, quite sufficient to satisfy their humble desires.

Amanda said she meant to leave a letter on the dressing-table for Lord Mortimer, with the notes which he had given her enclosed in it. "The picture and the ring," said she, with a falling tear, "I cannot part with;" for the things which she had ordered from the neighboring town, she told the prioress she would leave money in her hands, also a present for the woman, who had been engaged to attend her to England, as some small recompense for her disappointment. She meant only to take some linen and her mourning to Scotland; the rest of her things, including her music and books, at some future and better period might be sent after her.

Amanda was in debt to the sisterhood for three months' board and lodging, which was ten guineas. Of the two hundred pounds, which Lord Mortimer had given her on leaving Castle Carberry, one hundred and twenty pounds remained, so that though unable to answer the claims of gratitude, she thanked Heaven she was able to fulfil those of justice. This she told the prioress, who instantly declared, "that, in the name of the whole sisterhood, she would take upon her to refuse anything from her." Amanda did not contest the point, being secretly determined how to act. The prioress drank tea with her. When over, Amanda said she would lie down, in order to try and be composed against Lord Mortimer come. The prioress accordingly withdrew, saying, "she should not be disturbed till then."

By this means Amanda was enabled to be in readiness for delivering her letter to Lord Cherbury at the proper hour. Her heart beat with apprehension as it approached. She dreaded Lord Mortimer again surprising her amongst the ruins, or some of the nuns following her to them. At last the clock gave the signal for keeping her appointment. She arose, trembling, from the bed, and opened the door She listened, and no noise announced any one's being near. The moments were precious. She glided through the gallery, and had the good fortune to find the hall door open. She hastened to the ruins, and found Lord Cherbury already waiting there. She presented him the letter in silence. He received it in the same manner; but when he saw her turning away to depart he snatched her hand, and, in a voice that denoted the most violent agitation, exclaimed: "Tell me, tell me, Miss Fitzalan, is this letter propitious?" "It is," replied she, in a faltering voice. "Then may Heaven eternally bless you," cried he, falling at her feet, and wrapping his arms about her. His posture shocked Amanda, and his detention terrified her.

"Let me go, my Lord," said she. "In pity to me, in mercy to yourself, let me go; for one moment longer and we may be discovered."

Lord Cherbury started up—"From whom," cried he, "can I hear about you?" "From the prioress of St. Catherine's," replied Amanda, in a trembling voice; "she only will know the secret of my retreat."

He again snatched her hand and kissed it with vehemence. "Farewell, thou angel of a woman!" he exclaimed, and disappeared amongst the ruins. Amanda hurried back, dreading every moment to meet Lord Mortimer; but she neither met him nor any other person. She had scarcely gained her chamber ere the prioress came to inform her his lordship was in the parlor. She instantly repaired to it. The air had a little changed the deadly hue of her complexion, so that from her looks he supposed her better, and her words strengthened the supposition. She talked with him, forced herself to eat some supper, and checked the tears from falling, which sprang to her eyes, whenever he mentioned the happiness they must experience when united, the pleasure they should enjoy at Thornbury, and the delight Lady Martha and Lady Araminta would experience whenever they met.

Amanda desired him not to come to breakfast the next morning, nor to the convent till after dinner, as she should be so busy preparing for her journey she would have no time to devote to him He wanted to convince her he should not retard her preparations by coming, but she would not allow this.

Amanda passed another wretched night. She breakfasted in

the morning with the nuns, who expressed their regret at losing her—a regret, however, mitigated by the hope of shortly seeing her again, as Lord Mortimer had promised to bring her to Castle Carberry as soon as she had visited his friends in England. This was a trying moment for Amanda. She could scarcely conceal her emotions, or keep herself from weeping aloud, at the mention of a promise never to be fulfilled. She swallowed her breakfast in haste, and withdrew to her chamber on pretence of settling her things. Here she was immediately followed by the nuns, entreating they might severally be employed in assisting her. She thanked them with her usual sweetness, but assured them no assistance was necessary, as she had but few things to pack, never having unlocked the chests which had come from Castle Carberry. They retired on receiving this assurance, and Amanda, fearful of another interruption, instantly sat down to write her farewell letter to Lord Mortimer.

TO LORD MORTIMER.

My Lord,—A destiny, which neither of us can control, forbids our union. In vain were obstacles encountered and apparently overcome; one has arisen to oppose it which we never could have thought of, and, in yielding to it, as I am compelled by dire necessity to do, I find myself separated from you, without the remotest hope of our ever meeting again—without being allowed to justify my conduct, or offer one excuse which might, in some degree, palliate the abominable ingratitude and deceit I may appear guilty of; appear, I say, for in reality my heart is a stranger to either, and is now agonized at the sacrifice it is compelled to make; but I will not hurt your lordship's feelings by dwelling on my own sufferings. Already have I caused you too much pain, but never again shall I cross your path to disturb your peace, and shade your prospect of felicity; no, my Lord, removed to a tedious distance, the name I love no more will sink upon my ear, the delusive form of happiness no more will mock me.

Had everything turned out according to my wishes, perhaps happiness, so great, so unexpected, might have produced a dangerous revolution in my sentiments, and withdrawn my thoughts too much from heaven to earth: if so, oh! blessed be the Power that snatched from my lips the cup of joy, though at the very moment I was tasting the delightful beverage.

I cannot bid you pity me, though I know myself deserving of compassion, I cannot bid you forbear condemning me, though I know myself undeserving of censure. In this letter I enclose the notes I received from your lordship; the picture and the ring I have retained; they will soon be my only vestiges of former happiness. Farewell, Lord Mortimer, dear and invaluable friend farewell for ever. May that peace, that happiness you so truly deserve to possess, be yours, and may they never again meet with such interruptions as they have received from the unfortunate

AMANDA M. FITZALAN.

This letter was blistered with her tears; she laid it in a drawer till evening, and then proceeded to pack whatever she meant to take with her in a little trunk. In the midst of this business the prioress came in to inform her she had seen the master of the wherry, and settled everything with him. He not only promised to be secret, but to sail the following morning at four o'clock, and conduct her himself to Mrs. Macpherson's. About three he was to come to the convent for her; he had also promised to provide everything necessary on board for her.

Matters being thus arranged, Amanda told the prioress, to avoid suspicion, she would leave the money she intended for the woman who had been engaged to accompany her to England on her dressing-table, with a few lines purporting who it was for. The prioress approved of her doing so, as it would prevent any one from suspecting she was privy to her departure. She was obliged to leave her directly, and Amanda took the opportunity of putting up fifteen guineas in a paper—five for the woman, and ten for the nuns. She wished to do more for them, but feared to obey the dictates of generosity, while her own prospect of provision was so uncertain. She wrote as follows to the prioress:—

TO MRS. DERMOT.

DEAR MADAM,—Was my situation otherwise than it now is, be assured I never should have offered the trifle you will find in this paper as any way adequate to the discharge of my debt; to you and your amiable companions, I regret my inability (more than I can express) of proving my gratitude to you and them for all your kindnesses—never will they be obliterated from my remembrance; and He, who has promised to regard those that befriend the orphan, will reward you for them. I have also left five guineas for the woman you were so good as to engage to attend me to England. I trust she will think them a sufficient recompense for any trouble or disappointment I may have occasioned her.

Farewell, dear Mrs. Dermot, dear and amiable inhabitants of St. Catherine's, farewell. As Amanda will never forget you in hers, so let her never be forgotten in your orisons, and never cease to believe her

Grateful, sincere, and affectionate,

A. M. FITZALAN.

By this time she was summoned to dinner. Her spirits were sunk in the lowest dejection at the idea of leaving the amiable women who had been so kind to her, and above all at the idea of the last sad evening she was to pass with Lord Mortimer.

His lordship came early to the convent. The dejected looks of Amanda immediately struck him, and renewed all his apprehensions about her health. She answered his tender inquiries by saying she was fatigued.

"Perhaps," said he, "you would like to rest one day, and not commence your journey to-morrow?"

"No, no," cried Amanda, "it shall not be deferred. To-morrow," continued she, with a smile of anguish, "I will commence it."

Lord Mortimer thanked her for a resolution, he imagined, dictated by an ardent desire to please him; but at the same time again expressed his fears that she was ill.

Amanda perceived that if she did not exert herself her dejection would lead him to inquiries she would find it difficult to evade; but as to exert herself was impossible, in order to withdraw his attention in some degree from herself, she proposed that, as this was the last evening they would be at the convent, they should invite the nuns to drink tea with them. Lord Mortimer immediately acquiesced in the proposal, and the invitation being sent was accepted.

But the conversation of the whole party was of a melancholy kind. Amanda was so much beloved among them, that the prospect of losing her filled them with a regret which even the idea of seeing her soon again could not banish. About nine, which was their hour for prayers, they rose to retire, and would have taken leave of Lord Mortimer, had he not informed them, that on Miss Fitzalan's account, he would not commence the journey next day till ten o'clock, at which time he would again have the pleasure of seeing them.

When they withdrew he endeavored to cheer Amanda, and besought her to exert her spirits. Of his own accord, he said, he would leave her early, that she might get as much rest as possible against the ensuing day. He accordingly rose to depart. What an agonizing moment for Amanda; to hear, to behold the man, so tenderly beloved, for the last time; to think that ere that hour the next night she should be far, far away from him, considered as a treacherous and ungrateful creature, despised, perhaps execrated, as a source of perpetual disquiet and sorrow to him! Her heart swelled at those ideas with feelings she thought would burst it: and when he folded her to his bosom, and bid her be cheerful against the next morning, she involuntarily returned the pressure, by straining him to her heart in convulsive agitation, whilst a shower of tears burst from her. Lord Mortimer, shocked and surprised at these tears and emotions, reseated her, for her agitation was contagious, and he trembled so much he could not support her; then throwing himself at her feet, "My Amanda! my beloved girl!" cried he, "what is the matter? Is any wish of your heart yet unfulfilled? If so, let no mistaken notion of delicacy influence you to conceal it—on your happiness you know mine depends; tell me, therefore, I entreat, I conjure you, tell me, is there anything I can do to restore you to cheerfulness?" "Oh, no!" said Amanda, "all that a mortal could do to serve me you have already done, and my gratitude, the fervent sense I have of the obligations I lie under to you, I cannot fully express. May Heaven," raising her streaming eyes, "may Heaven recompense your goodness by bestowing the choicest of its blessings on you!" "That," said Lord Mortimer, half smiling, "it has already done in giving you to me, for you are the choicest blessing it could bestow; but tell me, what has dejected you in this manner! something more than fatigue, I am sure."

Amanda assured him "he was mistaken;" and, fearful of his further inquiries, told him, "she only waited for his departure to retire to rest, which she was convinced would do her good."

Lord Mortimer instantly rose from his kneeling posture: "Farewell, then, my dear Amanda," cried he, "farewell, and be well and cheerful against the morning."

She pressed his hand between hers, and laying her cold wet cheek upon it: "Farewell," said she; "when we next meet I shall, I trust, be well and cheerful; for in heaven alone (thought she at that moment) we shall ever meet again."

On the spot in which he left her Amanda stood motionless, till she heard the hall-door close after him; all composure then for-sock her, and, in an agony of tears and sobs, she threw herself on the seat he had occupied. The good prioress, guessing what her feelings at this moment must be, was at hand, and came in with drops and water, which she forced her to take, and mingled the tears of sympathy with hers.

Her soothing attentions in a little time had the effect she desired. They revived in some degree her unhappy young friend, who exclaimed, "that the severest trial she could ever possibly experience was now over." "And will, I trust and believe," replied the prioress, "even in this life be yet rewarded."

It was agreed that Amanda should put on her habit, and be prepared against the man came for her. The prioress promised, as soon as the house was at rest, to follow her to her chamber. Amanda accordingly went to her apartment and put on her travelling dress. She was soon followed by the prioress, who brought in bread, wine, and cold chicken; but the full heart of Amanda would not allow her to partake of them, and her tears, in spite of her efforts to restrain them, again burst forth. "She was sure," she said, "the prioress would immediately let her know if any intelligence arrived of her brother, and she again besought her to write as soon as possible after her departure, and to be minute."

She left the letters—one for Lord Mortimer and the other for the prioress—on the table, and then with a kind of melancholy impatience waited for the man, who was punctual to the appointed hour of three, and announced his arrival by a tap at the window. She instantly rose and embraced the prioress in silence, who, almost as much affected as herself, had only power to say, "God bless you, my dear child, and make you as happy as you deserve to be."

Amanda shook her head mournfully, as if to say she expected no happiness, and then, softly stepping along the gallery, opened the hall door, where she found the man waiting. Her little trunk was already lying in the hall. She pointed it out to him, and as soon as he had taken it they departed.

Never did any being feel more forlorn than Amanda now did What she suffered when quitting the Marchioness's was comparatively happiness to what she now endured. She then looked forward to the protection. comfort, and support of a tender parent; now she had nothing in view which could in the least cheer or alleviate her feelings. She cast her mournful eyes around, and the objects she beheld heightened, if possible, her anguish. She beheld the old trees which shaded the grave of her father waving in the morning breeze, and oh! how fervently at that moment did she wish that by his side she was laid beneath their shelter!

She turned from them with a heart-rending sigh, which reached the ear of the man who trudged before her. He instantly turned, and, seeing her pale and trembling, told her he had an arm at her service, which she gladly accepted, being scarcely able to support herself. A small boat was waiting for them about half a mile above Castle Carberry. It conveyed them in a few moments to the vessel, which the master previously told her would be under weigh directly. She was pleased to find his wife on board, who conducted Amanda to the cabin, where she found breakfast laid out with neatness for her. She took some tea and a little bread, being almost exhausted with fatigue. Her companion, imputing her dejection to fears of crossing the sea, assured her the passage would be very short, and bid her observe how plainly they could see the Scottish hills, now partially gilded by the beams of the rising sun; but, beautiful as they appeared, Amanda's eyes were turned from them to a more interesting object,—Castle Carberry. She asked the woman if she thought the castle could be seen from the opposite coast? and she replied in the negative.

"I am sorry for it," said Amanda, mournfully. She continued at the window for the melancholy pleasure of contemplating it, till compelled by sickness to lie down on the bed. The woman attended her with the most assiduous care, and about four o'clock in the afternoon informed her they had reached Port-Patrick. Amanda arose, and sending for the master, told him, as she did not wish to go to an inn, she would thank him to hire a chaise to carry her directly to Mrs. Macpherson's. He said she should be obeyed; and Amanda having settled with him for her passage, he went on shore for that purpose, and soon returned to inform her a carriage was ready. Amanda, having thanked his wife for her kind attention, stepped into the boat, and entered the chaise the moment she landed. Her companion told her he was well acquainted with Mrs. Macpherson, having frequently carried packets from Mrs Dermot to her. She lived about five miles from Port-Patrick, he said, and near the sea coast. They accordingly soon reached her habitation. It was a small, low house, of a grayish color, situated in a field almost covered with thistles, and divided from the road by a rugged-looking wall. The sea lay at a little distance from it. The coast hereabouts was extremely rocky, and the prospect on every side wild and dreary in the extreme.

Amanda's companion, by her desire, went first into the house to prepare Mrs. Macpherson for her reception. He returned in a few minutes, and telling her she was happy at her arrival, conducted her into the house. From a narrow passage, they turned into a small gloomy-looking parlor, with a clay floor. Mrs. Macpherson was sitting in an old-fashioned arm-chair—her face was sharp and meagre—her stature low, and, like Otway's ancient Beldame, doubled with age; her gown was gray stuff, and, though she was so low, it was not long enough to reach her ankle; her black-silk apron was curtailed in the same manner, and over a little mob-cap she wore a handkerchief tied under her chin. She just nodded to Amanda on her entrance, and, putting on a pair of large spectacles, surveyed her without speaking. Amanda presented Mrs. Dermot's introductory letter, and then, though unbidden, seated herself on the window-seat till she had perused it. Her trunk, in the mean time, was brought in, and she paid for the carriage, requesting at the same time the master of the vessel to wait till she had heard what Mrs. Macpherson would say. At length the old lady broke silence, and her voice was quite as sharp as her face.

"So, child," said she, again surveying Amanda, and then elevating her spectacles to have a better opportunity of speaking, "why, to be sure I did desire my cousin to get me a young person, but not one so young, so very young, as you appear to be." "Lord bless you!" said the man, "if that is a fault, why, it is one will mend every day." "Ay, ay," cried the old dame, "but it will mend a little too slow for me. However, child, as you are so well recommended, I will try you. My cousin says something of your being well born, and having seen better days. However, child, I tell you beforehand, I shall not consider what you have been, but what you are now. I shall therefore expect you to be mild, regular, and attentive—no flaunting, no gadding, no chattering, but staid, sober, and modest." "Bless your heart," said the man, "if you look in her face you will see she'll be all you desire." "Ay, ay, so you may say; but I should be very sorry to depend upon the promise of a face—like the heart, it is often treacherous and deceitful; so pray, young woman, tell me, and remember I expect a conscientious answer, whether you think you will be able to do as I wish?" "Yes, madam," replied Amanda, in a voice almost choked by the variety of painful emotions she experienced.

"Well, then, we are agreed, as you know the salary I give." The master of the vessel now took his leave, never having been asked by Mrs. Macpherson to take any refreshment.

The heart of Amanda sunk within her from the moment she entered Mrs. Macpherson's door. She shuddered at being left with so unsocial a being in a place so wild and dreary. A hovel near St. Catherine's she would have thought a palace in point of real comfort to her present habitation, as she then could have enjoyed the soothing society of the tender and amiable nuns. The presence of the master of the vessel, from the pity and concern he manifested for her, had something consolatory in it, and when he left the room she burst into tears, as if then, and not till then, she had been utterly abandoned. She hastily followed him out. "Give my love, my best love," said she, sobbing violently, and laying her trembling hand on his, "to Mrs. Dermot, and tell her, oh! tell her to write directly, and give me some comfort."

"You may depend on my doing so," replied he; "but cheer up, my dear young lady; what though the old dame in the parlor is a little cranky, she will mend, no doubt; so Heaven bless you, and make you as happy as you deserve to be"

Sad and silent, Amanda returned to the parlor, and seating herself in the window, strained her eyes after the carriage which had brought her to this dismal spot.

CHAPTER XLII.

"Of joys departed, never to return,
How bitter the remembrance!"—BLAIR.

ELL, child," said Mrs. Macpherson, "do you choose to take anything?" "I thank you, madam," replied Amanda, "I should like a little tea." "Oh! as to tea, I have just taken my own, and the things are all washed and put by; but, if you like a glass of spirits and water, and a crust of bread, you may have it." Amanda said she did not. "Oh! very well," cried Mrs. Macpherson, "I shall not press you, for supper will soon be ready." She then desired Amanda to draw a chair near hers, and began torturing her with a variety of minute and trifling questions relative to herself, the nuns, and the neighborhood of St. Catherine's.

Amanda briefly said, "her father had been in the army, that many disappointments and losses had prevented his making any provision for her, and that on his death, which happened in the neighborhood of the convent, the nuns had taken her out of compassion, till she procured an establishment for herself." "Ay, and a comfortable one you have procured yourself, I promise you," said Mrs. Macpherson, "if it is not your own fault." She then told Amanda, "she would amuse her by showing her her house and other concerns." This indeed was easily done, as it consisted but of the parlor, two closets adjoining it, and the kitchen, on the opposite side of the entry; the other concerns were a small garden, planted with kail, and the field covered with thistles. "A good, comfortable tenement this," cried Mrs. Macpherson, shaking her head with much satisfaction, as she leaned upon her ebony-headed cane, and cast her eyes around. She bid Amanda admire the fine prospect before the door, and, calling to a red-haired and bare-legged girl, desired her to cut some thistles to put into the fire, and hasten the boiling of the kail. On returning to the parlor she unlocked a press, and took out a pair of coarse, brown sheets to air for Amanda. She herself slept in one closet, and in the other was a bed for Amanda, laid on a half-decayed bedstead, without curtains, and covered with a blue-stuff quilt. The closet was lighted by one small window, which looked into the garden, and its furniture consisted of a broken chair, and a piece of looking-glass stuck to the wall.

The promised supper was at length served. It consisted of a few heads of kail, some oaten bread, a jug of water, and a small phial half full of spirits, which Amanda would not taste, and the old lady herself took but sparingly. They were lighted by a small candle, which, on retiring to their closets, Mrs. Macpherson cut between them.

Amanda felt relieved by being alone. She could now without restraint indulge her tears and her reflections; that she could never enjoy any satisfaction with a being so ungracious in her manners and so contracted in her notions, she foresaw; but, disagreeable as her situation must be, she felt inclined to continue in it, from the idea of its giving her more opportunities of hearing from Mrs. Dermot than she could have in almost any other place, and by these opportunities alone could she expect to hear of Lord Mortimer; and to hear of him, even the most trifling circumstance, though divided, for ever divided from him, would be a source of exquisite though melancholy pleasure.

To think she should hear of him, at once soothed and fed her melancholy. It lessened the violence of sorrow, yet without abating its intenseness; it gave a delicious sadness to her soul she thought would be ill exchanged for any feelings short of those she must have experienced, if her wishes had been accomplished. She enjoyed the pensive luxury of virtuous grief, which mitigates the sharp

> "With gracious drops
> Of cordial pleasure,"

and which Akenside so beautifully describes; nor can I forbear quoting the lines he has written to illustrate this truth—

> "Ask the faithful youth
> Why the cold urn of her, whom long he loved,
> So often fills his arms, so often draws
> His lonely footsteps at the silent hour,
> To pay the mournful tribute of his tears?
> O, he will tell thee, that the wealth of worlds
> Should ne'er seduce his bosom to forego
> That sacred hour, when, stealing from the noise
> Of care and envy, sweet remembrance soothes
> With virtue's kindest looks his aching heart,
> And turns his tears to rapture."

Fatigued by the contending emotions she experienced, as well as the sickness she went through at sea, Amanda soon retired to her flock bed, and fell into a profound slumber, in which she continued till roused in the morning by the shrill voice of Mrs. Macpherson, exclaiming, as she rapped at the door, "Come, come, Frances, it is time to rise."

Amanda started from her sleep, forgetting both the name she had adopted and the place where she was; but Mrs. Macpherson again calling her to rise, restored her to her recollection. She replied she would attend her directly, and, hurrying on her clothes, was with her in a few minutes. She found the old lady seated at the breakfast-table, who, instead of returning her salutation, said, "that on account of her fatigue she excused her lying so long in bed this morning, for it was now eight o'clock; but in future she would expect her to rise before six in summer, and seven in winter, adding, as there was no clock, she would rap at her door for that purpose every morning."

Amanda assured her "she was fond of rising early, and always accustomed to it." The tea was now poured out; it was of the worst kind, and sweetened with coarse brown sugar; the bread was oaten, and there was no butter. Amanda, unused to such unpalatable fare, swallowed a little of it with difficulty, and then, with some hesitation, said "she would prefer milk to tea." Mrs. Macpherson frowned exceedingly at this, and, after continuing silent a few minutes, said, "she had really made tea for two people, and she could not think of having it wasted; besides, she added, the economy of her house was so settled she could not infringe it for any one." She kept no cow herself, and only took in as much milk as served her tea and an old tabby-cat.

Amanda replied, "it was of no consequence," and Mrs. Macpherson said, indeed she supposed so, and muttered something of people giving themselves airs they had no pretensions to. The tea table was removed before nine, when the school began; it consisted of about thirty girls, most of them daughters to farmers in the neighborhood. Amanda and they being introduced to each other (and she being previously informed what they were taught), was desired to commence the task of instructing them entirely herself that day, as Mrs. Macpherson wanted to observe her manner—a most unpleasant task indeed for poor Amanda, whose mind and body were both harassed by anxiety and fatigue. As she had undertaken it, however, she resolved to go through it with as much cheerfulness and alacrity as possible. She accordingly acquitted herself to the satisfaction of Mrs. Macpherson, who only found fault with her too great gentleness, saying, the children would never fear her. At two the school broke up, and Amanda, almost as delighted as the children to be at liberty, was running into the garden to try if the air would be of use to a very violent headache; when she was called back to put the forms and other things in order. She colored, and stood motionless, till, recollecting, that if she refused to obey Mrs. Macpherson a quarrel would probably ensue, which, circumstanced as she was, without knowing where to go to, would be dreadful, she silently performed what she had been desired to do Dinner was then brought in; it was as simple and as sparing as a Braman could desire it to be. When over, Mrs. Macpherson composed herself to take a nap in the large chair, without making any kind of apology to Amanda.

Left at liberty, Amanda would now have walked out; but it had just begun to rain, and everything looked dreary and desolate. From the window in which she pensively sat she had a view of the sea; it looked black and tempestuous, and she could distinguish its awful and melancholy roaring as it dashed against the rocks. The little servant girl, as she cleaned the kitchen, sung a dismal Scotch ditty, so that all conspired to oppress the spirits of Amanda with a dejection greater than she had before ever experienced; all hope was now extinct, the social ties of life seemed broken, never more to be reunited. She had now no father, no friend, no lover, as heretofore, to soothe her feelings, or alleviate her sorrows. Like the poor Belvidera she might have said,

"There was a time
Her cries and sorrows
Were not despised, when, if she chanced to sigh,
Or but look sad, a friend or parent
Would have taken her in their arms,
Eased her declining head upon their breasts,
And never left her till they found the cause;
But now let her weep seas,
Cry till she rend the earth, sigh till she burst
Her heart asunder, she is disregarded."

Like a tender sapling, transplanted from its native soil, she seemed to stand alone, exposed to every adverse blast. Her tears gushed forth, and fell in showers down her pale cheeks. She sighed forth the name of her father: "Oh! dear and most benignant of men," she exclaimed, "my father and my friend; were you living, I should not be so wretched; pity and consolation would then be mine. Oh! my father, one of the dreariest caverns in yonder rocks would be an asylum of comfort were you with me; but I am selfish in these regrets, certain as I am that you exchanged this life of wretchedness for one of eternal peace, for one where you were again united to your Malvina."

Her thoughts adverted to what Lord Mortimer, in all probability, now thought of her; but this was too dreadful to dwell upon, convinced as she was, that, from appearances, he must think most unfavorably of her. His picture which hung in her bosom, she drew out. She gazed with agonizing tenderness upon it. She pressed it to her lips, and prayed for its original. From this indulgence of sorrow she was disturbed by the waking of Mrs. Macpherson. She hastily wiped away her tears, and hid the beloved picture. The evening passed most disagreeably. Mrs. Macpherson was tedious and inquisitive in her discourse, and it was almost as painful to listen as to answer her. Amanda was happy when the hour for retiring to bed arrived, and relieved her from what might be called a kind of mental bondage.

Such was the first day Amanda passed in her new habitation, and a week elapsed in the same manner without any variation, except that on Sunday she had a cessation from her labors, and went to the kirk with Mrs. Macpherson. At the end of the week she found herself so extremely ill from the fatigue and confinement she endured, as Mrs. Macpherson would not let her walk out, saying, "gadders were good for nothing"—that she told her, except allowed to go out every evening, she must leave her, as she could not bear so sedentary a life. Mrs. Macpherson looked disconcerted, and grumbled a good deal; but as Amanda spoke in a resolute manner she was frightened lest she should put her threats into execution, she was so extremely useful in the school; and at last told her she might take as much exercise as she pleased every day after dinner.

Amanda gladly availed herself of this permission. She explored all the romantic paths about the house; but the one she chiefly delighted to take was that which led to the sea. She loved to ramble about the beach; when fatigued to sit down upon the fragment of a rock and look towards the opposite shore. Vainly then would she try to discover some of the objects she knew so well Castle Carberry was utterly undistinguishable, but she knew the spot on which it stood, and derived a melancholy pleasure from looking that way. In these retired rambles she would freely indulge her tears, and gaze upon the picture of Lord Mortimer. She feared no observation; the rocks formed a kind of recess about her, and in going to them she seldom met a creature.

A fortnight passed in this way, and she began to feel surprise and uneasiness at not hearing from Mrs. Dermot. If much longer silent, she resolved on writing, feeling it impossible to endure much longer the agony her ignorance of Lord Mortimer's proceedings gave her. The very morning previous to the one she had fixed for writing she saw a sailor coming to the house, and believing he was the bearer of a letter to her, she forgot everything but her feelings at the moment, and starting from her seat ran from the room. She met him a few yards from the house, and then perceived he was one of the sailors of the vessel she had come over in. "You have a letter for me, I hope?" said Amanda. The man nodded, and fumbling in his bosom for a moment, pulled out a large packet, which Amanda snatched with eager transport from him; and knowing she could not attempt to bring him into the house for refreshment, gave him a crown to procure it elsewhere, which he received with thankfulness, and departed. She then returned to the parlor, and was hastening to her closet to read the letter, when Mrs. Macpherson stopped her. "Hey-day," cried she, "what is the matter?—what is all this fuss about? Why, one would think that was a love letter, you are so very eager to read it." "It is not, then, I can assure you," said Amanda. "Well, well; and who is it from?" Amanda reflected, that if she said from Mrs. Dermot, a number of impertinent questions would be asked her. She therefore replied: "From a very particular friend." "From a very particular friend! Well, I suppose there is nothing about life or death in it, so you may wait till after dinner to read it; and pray sit down now, and hear the children their spelling lessons." This was a tantalizing moment to Amanda. She stood hesitating whether she should obey, till reflecting that if she went now to read the packet, she should most probably be interrupted ere she had got through half the contents, she resolved on putting it up till after dinner. The moment at last came for Mrs. Macpherson's usual nap, and Amanda instantly hastened to a recess amongst the rocks, where seating herself, she broke the seal. The envelope contained two letters. The first she cast her eyes upon was directed in Lord Cherbury's hand. She trembled, tore it open, and read as follows:—

TO MISS FITZALAN.

In vain, my dear madam, do you say you never will receive pecuniary favors from me. It is not you, but I, should lie under obligations from their acceptance. I should deem myself the most ungrateful of mankind if I did not insist on carrying this point. I am but just returned to London, and shall immediately order my lawyer to draw up a deed entitling you to three hundred pounds a year, which, when completed, I shall transmit to the prioress (as I have this letter) to send to you. I am sensible, indeed, that I never can recompense the sacrifice you have made me. The feelings it has excited I shall not attempt to express, because language could never do them justice; but you may conceive what I must feel for the being who has preserved me from dishonor and destruction. I am informed Lord Mortimer has left Ireland, and therefore daily expect him in town. I have now not only every hope, but every prospect, of his complying with my wishes. This, I imagine, will be rather pleasing to you to hear, that you may know the sacrifice you have made is not made in vain, but will be attended with all the good consequences I expected to derive from it. I should again enjoy a tolerable degree of peace, were I assured you were happy; but this is an assurance I will hope soon to receive; for if you are not happy, who has a right to expect being so?—you, whose virtue is so pure, whose generosity is so noble, so heroic, so far superior to any I have ever met with!

That in this world, as well as the next, you may be rewarded for it, is, dear madam, the sincere wish of him who has the honor to subscribe himself your most grateful, most obliged, and most obedient, humble servant,

CHERBURY.

"Unfeeling man!" exclaimed Amanda, "how little is your heart interested in what you write, and how slight do you make of the sacrifice I have made you; how cruelly mention your hopes, which are derived from the destruction of mine! No, sooner would I wander from door to door for charity, than be indebted to your ostentatious gratitude for support—you, whose treachery and vile deceit have ruined my happiness." She closed the letter, and committing it to her pocket, took up the other, which she saw by the direction was from her dear Mrs. Dermot.

TO MISS DONALD.

Ah! my dear child, why extort a promise from me of being minute in relating everything which happened in consequence of your departure—a promise so solemnly given that I dare not recede from it; yet most unwillingly do I keep it, sensible as I am that the intelligence I have to communicate will but aggravate your sorrows. Methinks I hear you exclaim at this: "Surely, my dear Mrs. Dermot, you who know my disposition and temper so well, might suppose I would receive such intelligence with a fortitude and patience that would prevent its materially injuring me." Well, my dear, hoping this will be the case, I begin, without further delay, to communicate particulars. You left me, you may remember, about three o'clock. I then went to bed, but so fatigued and oppressed I could scarcely sleep, and was quite unrefreshed by what I did get. After prayers I repaired to the parlor, where the assiduous care of Sister Mary had already prepared everything for your breakfast and Lord Mortimer's. I told the sisters not to appear till they were sent for. I had not been long alone when Lord Mortimer came in—cheerful, blooming, animated. Never did I see happiness so strongly impressed in any countenance as in his. He looked, indeed, the lover about receiving the precious reward of constancy. He asked me had I seen you? I answered, No. He soon grew impatient, said you were a lazy girl, and feared you would make a bad traveller. He then rang the bell, and desired the maid to go and call you. Oh! my dear girl, my heart almost died within me at this moment. I averted my head, and pretended to be looking at the garden to conceal my confusion. The maid returned in a few minutes, and said you were not above. "Well," said Lord Mortimer, "she is in some other apartment; pray search, and hasten her hither." In a few minutes after she departed, Sister Mary, all pale and breathless, rushed into the room. "Oh, heavens!" cried she, "Miss Fitzalan cannot be found; but here are two letters I found on her dressing-table—one for you, madam, and one for Lord Mortimer." I know not how he looked at this instant, for a guilty consciousness came over my mind, which prevented my raising my eyes to his. I took the letter in silence, opened, but had no power to read it. Sister Mary stood by me, wringing her hands and weeping, as she exclaimed, "What—what does she say to you?" I could neither answer her nor move, till a deep sigh, or rather groan, from Lord Mortimer roused me. I started from my seat, and perceived him pale and motionless, the letter open in his hand, upon which his eyes were riveted. I threw open the garden door to give him air. This a little revived him. "Be comforted, my Lord," said I. He shook his head mournfully, and waving his hand for me neither to speak nor follow him, passed into the garden. "Blessed Heaven!" said Sister Mary again, "what does she say to you?" I gave her your letter, and desired her to read it aloud, for the tears which flowed at the affecting situation of Lord Mortimer quite obscured my sight. And here, my dear child, I must declare that you have been too generous, and also, that the sum you betrayed us into taking is but considered as a loan by us. But, to return to my first subject. The alarm concerning you now became general, and the nuns crowded into the room—grief and consternation in every countenance. In about half an hour I saw Lord Mortimer returning to the parlor, and I then dismissed them He had been endeavoring to compose himself, but his efforts for doing so were ineffectual. He trembled, was pale as death, and spoke with a faltering voice. He gave me your letter to read, and I put mine into his hand. "Well, my Lord," said I, on perusing it, "we must rather pity than condemn her." "From my soul," cried he, "I pity her—I pity such a being as Amanda Fitzalan, for being the slave, the prey of vice. But she has been cruel to me; she has deceived, inhumanly deceived me, and blasted my peace for ever!" "Ah, my Lord!" I replied, "though appearances are against her, I can never believe her guilty. She, who performed all the duties of a child, as Amanda Fitzalan did, and who, to my certain knowledge, was preparing herself for a life of poverty, can never be a victim to vice." "Mention her no more," cried he; "her name is like a dagger to my heart. The suspicions which, but a few nights ago, I could have killed myself for entertaining, are now confirmed. They intruded on my mind from seeing Belgrave haunting this place, and from finding her secreted amidst the ruins at a late hour. Ah, heavens! when I noticed her confusion, how easily did she exculpate herself to a heart prepossessed like mine in her favor! Unhappy, unfortunate girl! sad and pitiable is thy fate! but may an early repentance snatch thee from the villain who now triumphs in thy ruin; and may we, since thus separated, never meet again. So well," continued he, "am I convinced of the cause of her flight, that I shall not make one inquiry after her." I again attempted to speak in your justification, but he silenced me. I begged he would allow me to get him breakfast. He could touch nothing, and said he must return directly to Castle Carberry, but promised, in the course of the day, to see me again. I followed him into the hall. At the sight of your corded boxes, he started, and shrunk back, with that kind of melancholy horror which we involuntarily feel when viewing anything that belonged to a dear, lost friend. I saw his emotions were agonizing. He hid his face with his handkerchief, and, with a hasty step, ascended to his carriage, which, with a travelling chaise, was waiting at the door.

I own I was often tempted, in the course of conversation, to tell him all I knew about you; but the promise I had given you still rose to my view, and I felt, without your permission, I could not break it; yet, my dear, it is shocking to me to have such imputations cast on you. We cannot blame Lord Mortimer for them. Situated as you were with him, your conduct has naturally excited the most injurious suspicions. Surely, my child, though not allowed to solve the mystery which has separated you from him, you may be allowed to vindicate your conduct. The sacrifice of fame and happiness is too much. Consider and weigh well what I say, and, if possible, authorize me to inform Lord Mortimer that I know of your retreat, and that you have retired neither to a lover nor a friend; but to indigence and obscurity, led thither by a fatal necessity which you are bound to conceal, and feel more severely from that circumstance. He would, I am confident, credit my words; and then, instead of condemning, would join me in pitying you. The more I reflect on your unaccountable separation, the more am I bewildered in conjectures relative to it, and convinced more strongly than ever of the frailty of human joy, which, like a summer cloud, is bright, but transitory in its splendor. Lord Mortimer had left the convent about two hours, when his man arrived to dismiss the travelling chaise and attendants. I went out and inquired after his lord. "He is very bad, madam," said he, "and this has been a sad morning for us all." Never, my dear Miss Fitzalan, did I, or the sisterhood, pass so melancholy a day. About five in the afternoon, I received another visit from Lord Mortimer. I was alone in the parlor, which he entered with an appearance of the deepest melancholy; one of his arms was in a sling. I was terrified, lest he and Belgrave had met. He conjectured, I fancy, the occasion of the terror my countenance expressed, for he immediately said he had been ill on returning to Castle Carberry, and was bled. He was setting off directly for Dublin, he said, from whence he intended to embark for England. "But I could not depart, my dear, good friend," continued he, "without bidding you farewell; besides, I wanted to assure you, that any promise which the unfortunate girl made you in my name I shall hold sacred." I knew he alluded to the fifty pounds which he had desired you to tell me should be annually remitted to our house. I instantly, therefore, replied, that we had already been rewarded beyond our expectation or desires for any little attention we showed Miss Fitzalan; but his generous resolution was not to be shaken. He looked weak and exhausted. I begged permission to make tea for him ere he commenced his journey. He consented. I went out of the room to order in the things. When I returned, he was standing at the window which looked into the garden, so absorbed in meditation that he did not hear me. I heard him say, "Cruel Amanda! is it thus you have rewarded my sufferings?" I retreated, lest he should be confused by supposing himself overheard, and did not return till the maid brought in the tea things.

When he arose to depart, he looked wavering and agitated, as if there was something on his mind he wanted courage to say. At last, in a faltering voice, while the deadly paleness of his complexion gave way to a deep crimson, he said, "I left Miss Fitzalan's letter with you." Ah, my dear! never did man love woman better than he did, than he now loves you. I took the letter from my pocket, and presented it to him. He put it in his bosom, with an emotion that shook his whole frame. I hailed this as a favorable opportunity for again speaking in your favor. I bid him retrospect your past actions, and judge from them whether you could be guilty of a crime——. He stopped me short. He begged me to drop a subject he was unable to bear. Had he been less credulous, he said, he should now have been much happier; then wringing my hand, he bid me farewell, in a voice, and with a look, that drew tears from me. "Ah, my dear madam!" cried he, "when this day commenced, how differently did I think it would have terminated!"

I attended him to his carriage. He was obliged to lean upon his man as he ascended to it, and his looks and agitation proclaimed the deepest distress. I have sent repeatedly to Castle Carberry since his departure to inquire about him, and have been informed, that they expect to hear nothing of him till Lord Cherbury's agent comes into the country, which will not be these three months.

I have heard much of the good he did in the neighborhood. He has a bounteous and benevolent spirit indeed. To our community he has been a liberal benefactor, and our prayers are daily offered up for his restoration to health and tranquillity. Amongst his other actions, when in Dublin, about three months ago, he ordered a monument to the memory of Captain Fitzalan, which has been brought down since your departure, and put up in the parish church, where he is interred. I sent Sister Mary and another of the nuns the other evening to see it, and they brought me a description of it. It is a white marble urn, ornamented with a foliage of laurel, and standing upon a pedestal of gray, on which the name of the deceased, and words to the following effect, are inscribed, namely: "That he whose memory it perpetuates, performed the duties of a Christian and a soldier, with a fidelity and zeal that now warrants his enjoying a blessed recompense for both."

I know this proof of respect to your father will deeply affect you; but I would not omit telling it, because, though it will affect, I am confident it will also please you. The late events have cast a gloom over all our spirits. Sister Mary now prays more than ever; and you know I have often told her she was only fit for a religious vocation. It is a bad world, she says, we live in, and she is glad she has so little to say to it.

I am longing to hear from you. Pray tell me how you like Mrs. Macpherson. I have not seen her since her youth, and years often produce as great a change in the temper as the face. At any rate, your present situation is too obscure for you to continue in, and, as soon as your thoughts are collected and composed, you must look out for another. I hope you will be constant in writing; but I tell you beforehand, you must not expect me to be punctual in my answers—I have been so long disused to writing, and my eyes are grown so weak. This letter has been the work of many days; besides, I have really nothing interesting to communicate; whenever I have, you may be assured I shall not lose a moment in informing you.

The woman was extremely thankful for the five guineas you left her. Lord Mortimer sent her five more by his man; so that she thinks herself well rewarded for any trouble or disappointment she experienced. If you wish to have any of your things sent to you, acquaint me: you know I shall never want an opportunity by the master of the vessel. He speaks largely of your generosity to him, and expresses much pity at seeing so young a person in such melancholy. May Heaven, if it does not remove the source, at least lessen this melancholy.

If possible, allow me to write to Lord Mortimer, and vindicate you from the unworthy suspicions he entertains of you. I know he would believe me and I should do it without discovering your retreat. Farewell, my dear girl. I recommend you constantly to the care of Heaven, and beg you to believe you will ever be dear and interesting to the heart of

ELIZABETH DERMOT.

St. Catherine's.

Poor Amanda wept over this letter. "I have ruined the health, the peace of Lord Mortimer," she exclaimed, "and he now execrates me as the source of his unhappiness. Oh! Lord Cherbury, how severely do I suffer for your crime!" She began to think her virtue had been too heroic in the sacrifice she had made. But this was a transient idea, for when she reflected on the disposition of Lord Cherbury, she was convinced the divulgement of his secret would have been followed by his death; and, great as was her present wretchedness, she felt it light compared to the horrors she knew she would experience could she accuse herself of being accessory to such an event. She now drank deeply of the cup of misery, but conscious rectitude, in some degree, lessened its noxious bitterness. She resolved to caution Mrs. Dermot against mentioning her in any manner to Lord Mortimer. She was well convinced he would believe no asseveration of her innocence. And even if he did, what end could it answer? Their union was opposed by an obstacle not to be surmounted, and if he sought and discovered her retreat, it would only lead to new sorrows, perhaps occasion some dreadful catastrophe. "We are separated," cried she, folding her hands together, "for ever separated in this world, but in Heaven we shall again be re-united."

Absorbed in the reflections and sorrow this letter gave rise to, she remained in her seat till Mrs. Macpherson's little girl suddenly appeared before her, and said her mistress had made tea, and was wondering what kept her out so long.

Amanda instantly arose, and carefully putting up the letter, returned to the house, where she found Mrs. Macpherson in a very bad humor. She grumbled exceedingly at Amanda's staying out so long, and taking notice of her eyes being red and swelled, said, "indeed, she believed she was right in supposing she had got a love letter." Amanda made no reply, and the evening passed away in peevishness on one side and silence on the other.

The charm which had hitherto rendered Amanda's situation tolerable was now dissolved, as Mrs. Dermot had said she could write but seldom, and scarcely expected to have anything interesting to relate. She would gladly, therefore, have left Mrs. Macpherson immediately, but she knew not where to go. She resolved, however, ere winter had entirely set in, to request Mrs. Dermot to look out for some other place for her: as she had connections in Scotland, she thought she might recommend her to them as a governess, or a fit person to do fine works for a lady. She rose long before her usual hour the next morning, and wrote a letter expressive of her wishes and intentions to Mrs. Dermot, which she sent by a poor man, who lived near the house, to the post town, rewarding him liberally for his trouble.

CHAPTER XLIII.

"Who knows the joys of friendship,
The trust, security, and mutual tenderness,
The double joys, where each is glad for both;
Friendship, our only wealth, our last retreat and strength,
Secure against ill fortune and the world?"—ROWE.

MONG Mrs. Macpherson's pupils were two little girls, who pleased and interested Amanda greatly. Their father, for whom they were in mourning, had perished in a violent storm, and their mother had pined in health and spirits ever since the fatal accident. The kindness with which Amanda treated them, they repaid with gratitude and attention. It had a double effect upon their little hearts, from being contrasted with the sour austerity of Mrs. Macpherson. They told Amanda, in a whisper, one morning, that their mamma was coming to see their dear, good Frances Donald.

Accordingly, in the course of the day, Mrs. Duncan came. She was young and pleasing in her appearance; her weeds and deep dejection rendered her a most interesting object. She sat by Amanda, and took an opportunity, while Mrs. Macpherson was engaged with some of the children, to tell her, in a low voice, "she was truly obliged to her for the great attention and kindness she showed her little girls, so unlike their former treatment at the school." "The task of instructing them was hers," she said, "till her declining health and spirits rendered her no longer able to bear it." Amanda assured her, "it was a pleasure to instruct minds so docile and sweet tempered as theirs." Mrs. Duncan, as she rose to depart, asked her and Mrs. Macpherson to tea that evening, which invitation was instantly accepted by Mrs. Macpherson, who was extremely fond of being sociable everywhere but in her own house. Mrs. Duncan lived at but a little distance, and everything in and about her house was neat and comfortable. She had an old neighbor in the parlor, who kept Mrs. Macpherson in chat, and gave her an opportunity of conversing freely with Amanda. She remarked the delicacy of her looks, and said "She believed she was ill qualified to endure so fatiguing a life as her present one." She mentioned her own lonely and melancholy life, and the happiness she would derive from having such a companion, and expressed her hopes of often enjoying her society. Amanda said this would be impossible without disobliging Mrs. Macpherson; and Mrs. Duncan, on reflection, allowed it would be so. She then inquired if she ever walked? Amanda replied she did; and was asked where she generally rambled? By the sea-side, she answered. Mrs. Duncan sighed deeply, and her eyes filled with tears. "It is there I generally ramble too," said she. This led to the mention of her late loss. "Mr. Duncan had been the kindest, best of husbands," she said; "the first years of their marriage were attended with difficulties, which were just removed, when he was lost on a party of pleasure, with several others. It was some consolation, however," continued Mrs. Duncan, "that the body was cast upon the shore, and I had the power of paying the last rites of decency and respect to him." In short, between her and Amanda there appeared a mutual sympathy, which rendered them truly interesting to each other. From this period they generally met every evening, and passed many hours on the "sea-beat shore," talking, and often weeping, over joys departed, never to return! Mrs. Duncan was too delicate to inquire into Amanda's former situation; but was well convinced it had been very different from her present one. Amanda, however, of her own accord, told her what she had told Mrs. Macpherson respecting herself. Mrs. Duncan lamented her misfortunes; but since she had met them, blessed the happy chance which conducted her near her habitation.

A month passed in this manner, when one evening, at the usual place of meeting, Mrs. Duncan told her, "that she believed she should soon be quitting that part of the country." Amanda started, and turned pale at this disagreeable intelligence. She had received no answer to her letter from Mrs. Dermot, consequently dreaded that necessity would compel her to remain in her present situation, and on Mrs. Duncan's society she had depended for rendering it bearable to her.

"I have been invited, my dear girl," said Mrs. Duncan, leaning on her arm as they walked up and down the beach, "to reside with an aunt, who has always been kind, and was particularly so to me in my distress. She lives about ten miles from this, at an old place called Dunreath Abbey, of which she is housekeeper. Have you ever heard of it?" Amanda's agitation at hearing her mother's native habitation mentioned, is not to be described. Her heart palpitated; she felt her color change, and said Yes and No to Mrs. Duncan, without knowing what she answered. Then recollecting herself, she replied, "she had heard of it." "Well, then, my dear," continued Mrs. Duncan, "my aunt, as I have already told you, is housekeeper there. She lives in great grandeur, for it is a magnificent old seat, and has the absolute command of everything, as none of the family have resided at it since the Earl of Dunreath's decease. My aunt is lately grown weary of the profound solitude in which she lives, and has asked me, in a letter which I received this morning, to go immediately and take up my residence with her, promising, if I do, she will leave everything she is worth to me and my children; and as her salary is very good, I know she must have saved a good deal. This is a very tempting offer, and I am only withheld from accepting it directly by the fear of depriving my children of the advantages of education." "Why," said Amanda, "what they learn at Mrs. Macpherson's they could easily learn anywhere else." "But I intended, when they were a little older," replied Mrs. Duncan, "to go to some one of the neighboring towns with them. If I once go to my aunt, I must entirely relinquish such an idea, and to a boarding-school I could not send them, for I have not fortitude to bear a separation from them. What I wish, therefore, is to procure a person who would be at once a pleasing companion for me, and an eligible governess for them. With such a person, the solitude of Dunreath Abbey would be rather agreeable than irksome to me."

She looked earnestly at Amanda as she spoke, and Amanda's heart began to throb with hope and agitation. "In short, my dear girl," continued she, "you of all others, to be explicit, are the person I would choose to bring along with me. Your sweet society would alleviate my sorrows, and your elegant accomplishments give to my children all the advantages I desire them to possess." "I am not only flattered, but happy by your prepossession in my favor," replied Amanda.

"I am pleased we agree in point of inclination," said Mrs. Duncan; "but I must now inform you that my aunt has always been averse to admit any strangers to the Abbey. Why, I know not, except it is by the commands of the family; and she tells me in her letter, that if I accept her invitation, I must not on any account let it be known where I am removing to. I dare not, therefore, bring you with me without her permission; but I shall write immediately and request it. In the course of a day or two I may expect an answer. In the mean time give Mrs. Macpherson no intimation of our present intentions, lest they should be defeated." Amanda promised she would not, and they separated.

She was now in a state of the greatest agitation, at the probability there was that she might visit the seat of her ancestors She dreaded a disappointment, and felt that, if she went there as the companion of Mrs. Duncan, she should be better situated than a few hours before she had ever expected to be again. Two evenings after her conversation with Mrs. Duncan, on going to the beach to meet her, she saw her approaching with an open letter in her hand, and a smile on her face, which informed her its contents were pleasing. They were so indeed, as they gave permission to have Amanda brought to the Abbey, provided she promised inviolable secrecy as to where she was going. This Amanda cheerfully did, and Mrs. Duncan said she had some affairs to settle, which would prevent their departure for a few days. At whatever time she appointed, her aunt was to send a carriage for them, and it was now agreed that Mrs. Macpherson should be informed Mrs. Duncan was leaving that part of the country, and had engaged Amanda as a governess to her children.

Mrs. Duncan then mentioned her own terms. Amanda assured her an idea of them had never entered her thoughts. Mrs. Duncan said she was sure of that, but at the same time thought between the most intimate friends exactness should be preserved. Everything being settled to their mutual satisfaction, they separated, and the following day, after school broke up, Amanda informed Mrs. Macpherson of her intended departure. The old dame was thunderstruck, and for some time unable to speak; but when she recovered the use of her tongue, she expressed the utmost rage and indignation against Amanda, Mrs. Duncan, and the prioress. Against the first for thinking of leaving her, the second for inveigling her away, and the third for recommending a person who could serve her in such a manner. When she stopped, exhausted by her violence, Amanda took the opportunity of assuring her that she had no reason to condemn any of them; as for her part, previous to Mrs. Duncan's offer, she intended to leave her, being unable to bear a life of such fatigue; that as her removal would not be immediate, Mrs. Macpherson could suffer no inconvenience by it, there being time enough to look out for another person ere it took place. But the truth now broke from Mrs. Macpherson; angry as she was with Amanda, she could not help confessing, that she never again expected to meet with a person so well qualified to please her, and a torrent of bitter reproaches again burst forth for her quitting her.

Amanda resented them not, but did all in her power to mollify her; as the most effectual method of doing so, she declared she meant to take no recompense for the time she had been with her, and added, if she had her permission, she would write that evening to Mrs. Dermot about a woman she had seen at the convent, whom she thought well qualified to be an assistant in her school. This was the woman who had been engaged to attend her to England. Mrs. Macpherson at last consented she should write for her, as her wrath had gradually subsided from the moment Amanda declared she would take no payment. Amanda accordingly wrote to Mrs. Dermot, and informed her of the agreeable change there was about taking place in her situation; also of Mrs. Macpherson's displeasure, and her own wish that a person might immediately be procured to fill the place she was resigning. She mentioned the woman already spoken of as a proper person, but requested, if she consented to come, she might not be allowed to do so till she had left Mrs. Macpherson's, else who she really was would be betrayed. She now thought little of the tedious and disagreeable days she spent, as the eagerness with which she saw Mrs. Duncan preparing for their departure promised so speedily to change them. She received an answer from Ireland even sooner than she expected. Mrs. Dermot congratulated her on having met with so amiable a friend as Mrs. Duncan, said the woman accepted the offer made in Mrs. Macpherson's name, but should not depart till she had written for that purpose, and concluded her letter by saying, there was no intelligence yet of Lord Mortimer. Mrs. Macpherson was pleased to find she should not be long without a companion, and two days after the receipt of the letter Mrs. Duncan told Amanda their journey was fixed for the ensuing day, and begged Amanda to sleep at her house that night, to which she gladly consented; accordingly after dinner she took leave of Mrs. Macpherson, who grumbled out a farewell, and a hope that she might not have reason to repent quitting her, for the old lady was so incensed to have the place Mrs. Duncan was going to concealed from her that all her ill-humor had returned. Amanda, with a pleasure she could scarcely conceal, quitted her inhospitable mansion, and, attended by a man who carried her trunk, soon found herself at Mrs. Duncan's, where she was received with every demonstration of joy. The evening passed sociably away; they rose early in the morning, and had just breakfasted when the expected carriage from Dunreath Abbey arrived. It was a heavy, old-fashioned chaise, on whose faded panels the arms of the Dunreath family were still visible. Mrs. Duncan's luggage had been sent off the preceding day, so that there was nothing now to delay them. Mrs. Duncan made Amanda and the children go into the chaise before her, but, detained by an emotion of the most painful nature, she lingered some time after them upon the threshold. She could not indeed depart from the habitation where she had experienced so many happy days with the man of her tenderest affections without a flood of tears, which spoke the bitterness of her feelings. Amanda knew too well the nature of those feelings to attempt restraining them; but the little children, impatient to begin their journey, called out to their mamma to come into the carriage. She started when they spoke, but instantly complied with their desire; and when they expressed their grief at seeing her cheeks wet with tears, kissed them both, and said she would soon recover her spirits. She accordingly exerted herself for that purpose, and was soon in a condition to converse with Amanda. The day was fine and serene; they travelled leisurely, for the horses had long outlived their mettlesome days, and gave them an opportunity of attentively viewing the prospects on each side, which were various, romantic, and beautiful; the novelty of the scenes, the disagreeable place she had left, and the idea of the one she was going to, helped a little to enliven the pensive soul of Amanda, and she enjoyed a greater degree of tranquillity than she had before experienced since her separation from Lord Mortimer.

CHAPTER XLIV.

"My listening powers
Were awed, and every thought in silence hung
And wondering expectation."—AKENSIDE.

Y dear Fanny," said Mrs. Duncan, addressing our heroine by her borrowed name, "if at all inclined to superstition, you are now going to a place which will call it forth. Dunreath Abbey is gothic and gloomy in the extreme, and recalls to one's mind all the stories they ever heard of haunted houses and apparitions. The desertion of the native inhabitants has hastened the depredations of time, whose ravages are unrepaired, except in the part immediately occupied by the domestics. Yet what is the change in the building compared to the revolution which took place in the fortunes of her who once beheld a prospect of being its mistress. The Earl of Dunreath's eldest daughter, as I have often heard from many, was a celebrated beauty, and as good as she was handsome, but a malignant stepmother thwarted her happiness, and forced her to take shelter in the arms of a man who had everything but fortune to recommend him—but, in wanting that, he wanted everything to please her family. After some years of distress, she found means to soften the heart of her father; but here the invidious stepmother again interfered, and prevented her experiencing any good effects from his returning tenderness, and, it was rumored, by a deep and iniquitous scheme, deprived her of her birthright. Like other rumors, however, it gradually died away; perhaps from Lady Malvina and her husband never hearing of it, and none but them had a right to inquire into its truth. But if such a scheme was really contrived, woe be to its fabricator; the pride and pomp of wealth can neither alleviate nor recompense the stings of conscience. Much rather," continued Mrs. Duncan, laying her hands upon her children's heads as they sat at her feet, "much rather would I have my babes wander from door to door, to beg the dole of charity than live upon the birthright of the orphan. If Lady Dunreath, in reality, committed the crime she was accused of, she met, in some degree, a punishment for it. Soon after the Earl's death she betrayed a partiality for a man every way inferior to her.

which partiality, people have not scrupled to say, commenced and was indulged to a criminal degree during the lifetime of her husband. She would have married him, had not her daughter, the Marchioness of Roslin, interfered. Proud and ambitious, her rage, at the prospect of such an alliance, knew no bounds, and, seconded by the Marquis, whose disposition was congenial to her own, they got the unfortunate mother into their power, and hurried her off to a convent in France. I know not whether she is yet living; indeed, I believe there are few either know or care, she was so much disliked for her haughty disposition. I have sometimes asked my aunt about her, but she would never gratify my curiosity. She has been brought up in the family, and no doubt thinks herself bound to conceal whatever they choose. She lives in ease and plenty, and is absolute mistress of the few domestics that reside at the Abbey. But of those domestics I caution you in time, or they will be apt to fill your head with frightful stories of the Abbey, which sometimes, if one's spirits are weak, in spite of reason, will make an impression on the mind. They pretend that the Earl of Dunreath's first wife haunts the Abbey, venting the most piteous moans, which they ascribe to grief for the unfortunate fate of her daughter, and that daughter's children being deprived of their rightful patrimony. I honestly confess, when at the Abbey a few years ago, during some distresses of my husband, I heard strange noises one evening at twilight as I walked in a gallery. I told my aunt of them, and she was quite angry at the involuntary terror I expressed, and said it was nothing but the wind whistling through some adjoining galleries which I heard. But this, my dear Fanny," said Mrs. Duncan, who on account of her children had continued the latter part of her discourse in a low voice, "is all between ourselves; for my aunt declared she would never pardon my mentioning my ridiculous fears, or the yet more ridiculous fears of the servants, to any human being."

Amanda listened in silence to Mrs. Duncan's discourse, fearful that if she spoke she should betray the emotions it excited.

They at last entered between the mountains that enclosed the valley on which the Abbey stood. The scene was solemn and solitary. Every prospect, except one of the sea, seen through an aperture in one of the mountains, was excluded. Some of these mountains were bare, craggy, and projecting. Others were skirted with trees, robed with vivid green, and crowned with white and yellow furze. Some were all a wood of intermingled shades, and others covered with long and purple heath. Various streams flowed from them into the valley. Some stole gently down their sides in silver rills, giving beauty and vigor wherever they meandered. Others tumbled from fragment to fragment, with a noise not undelightful to the ear, and formed for themselves a deep bed in the valley, over which trees, that appeared coeval with the building, bent their old and leafy heads.

At the foot of what to the rest was called a gently swelling hill lay the remains of the extensive gardens which had once given the luxuries of the vegetable world to the banquets of the Abbey; but the buildings which had nursed those luxuries were all gone to decay, and the gay plantations were overrun with the progeny of neglect and sloth.

The Abbey was one of the most venerable looking buildings Amanda had ever beheld; but it was in melancholy grandeur she now saw it—in the wane of its days, when its glory was passed away, and the whole pile proclaimed desertion and decay. She saw it when, to use the beautiful language of Hutchinson, its pride was brought low, when its magnificence was sinking in the dust, when tribulation had taken the seat of hospitality, and solitude reigned, where once the jocund guest had laughed over the sparkling bowl, whilst the owls sang nightly their strains of melancholy to the moonshine that slept upon its mouldering battlements.

The heart of Amanda was full of the fond idea of her parents, and the sigh of tender remembrance stole from it. "How little room," thought she, "should there be in the human heart for the worldly pride which so often dilates it, liable as all things are to change! the distress in which the descendants of noble families are so often seen, the decline of such families themselves, should check that arrogant presumption with which so many look forward to having their greatness and prosperity perpetuated through every branch of their posterity.

"The proud possessors of this Abbey, surrounded with affluence, and living in its full enjoyment, never perhaps admitted the idea as at all probable, tha⁴ one of their descendants should ever ap proach the seat of her ancestors without that pomp and elegance which heretofore distinguished its daughters. Alas! one now approaches it neither to display nor contemplate the pageantry of wealth, but meek and lowly; not to receive the smile of love, or the embrace of relatives, but, afflicted and unknown, glad to find a shelter, and procure the bread of dependence, beneath its decaying roof."

Mrs. Duncan happily marked not Amanda's emotion as she gazed upon the Abbey. She was busily employed in answering her children's questions, who wanted to know whether she thought they would be able to climb up the great big hills they saw.

The carriage at last stopped before the Abbey. Mrs. Bruce was already at the door to receive them. She was a little, smart old woman, and welcomed her niece and the children with an appearance of the greatest pleasure. On Amanda's being presented to her, she gazed steadfastly in her face a few minutes, and then exclaimed, "Well, this is very strange; though I know I could never have seen this young lady before, her face is quite familiar to me."

The hall into which they entered was large and gloomy, paved with black marble, and supported by pillars, through which the arched doors that led to various apartments were seen. Rude implements, such as the Caledonians had formerly used in war and hunting, were ranged along the walls. Mrs. Bruce conducted them into a spacious parlor, terminated by an elegant saloon This, she told them, had once been the banqueting-room. The furniture, though faded, was still magnificent, and the windows, though still in the gothic style, from being enlarged considerably beyond their original dimensions, afforded a most delightful view of the domain.

"Do you know," said Mrs. Duncan, "this apartment, though one of the pleasantest in the Abbey in point of situation, always makes me melancholy. The moment I enter it I think of the entertainments once given in it, and then its present vacancy and stillness almost instantly reminds me that those who partook of these entertainments are now almost all humbled with the dust!" Her aunt laughed, and said, "she was very romantic."

The solemnity of the Abbey was well calculated to heighten the awe which stole upon the spirit of Amanda from her first view of it. No noise was heard throughout it, except the hoarse creaking of the massy doors, as the servants passed from one room to another, adjusting Mrs. Duncan's things, and preparing for dinner. Mrs. Duncan was drawn into a corner of the room by her aunt, to converse, in a low voice, about family affairs, and the children were rambling about the hall, wondering and inquiring about everything they saw.

Thus left to herself, a soft languor gradually stole over the mind of Amanda, which was almost exhausted from the emotions it had experienced. The murmuring sound of waterfalls, and the buzzing of the flies that basked in the sunny rays which darted through the casements, lulled her into a kind of pensive tranquillity.

"Am I really," she asked herself, "in the seat of my ancestors? Am I really in the habitation where my mother was born—where her irrevocable vows were plighted to my father? I am; and oh! within it may I at last find an asylum from the vices and dangers of the world; within it may my sorrowing spirit lose its agitation, and subdue, if not its affections, at least its murmurs, at the disappointment of those affections."

The appearance of dinner interrupted her. She made exertions to overcome any appearance of dejection, and the conversation, if not lively, was at least cheerful. After dinner Mrs. Duncan, who had been informed by Amanda of her predilection for old buildings, asked her aunt's permission to show her the Abbey. Mrs. Bruce immediately arose, and said she would have that pleasure herself. She accordingly led the way. Many of the apartments yet displayed the sumptuous taste of those who had furnished them. "It is astonishing to me," said Mrs. Duncan, "that so magnificent a pile as this should be abandoned, as I may say, by its possessors." "The Marquis of Roslin's castle is a more modern structure than this," said Mrs. Bruce, "and preferred by them on that account." "So, like the family monument," rejoined Mrs. Duncan, "they are merely satisfied with permitting this to stand, as it may help to transmit the Marchioness's name to posterity." "How far does the Marquis live from this?" asked Amanda. "About twelve miles," replied Mrs. Bruce, who did not appear pleased with her niece's conversation, and led the way to a long gallery, ornamented with portraits of the family. This gallery Amanda knew well by description. This was the gallery in which her father had stopped to contemplate the picture of her mother, and her heart throbbed with impatience and anxiety to see that picture.

Mrs. Bruce, as she went before her, told her the names of the different portraits. She suddenly stopped before one. "That," cried she, "is the Marchioness of Roslin's, drawn for her when Lady Augusta Dunreath." Amanda cast her eyes upon it, and perceived in the countenance the same haughtiness as still distinguished the Marchioness. She looked at the next panel, and found it empty.

"The picture of Lady Malvina Dunreath hung there," said Mrs. Bruce; "but after her unfortunate marriage it was taken down." "And destroyed," exclaimed Amanda mournfully. "No; but it was thrown into the old chapel, where, with the rest of the lumber (the soul of Amanda was struck at these words), it has been locked up for years." "And is it impossible to see it?" asked Amanda. "Impossible, indeed," replied Mrs. Bruce. "The chapel, and the whole eastern part of the Abbey, have long been in a ruinous situation, on which account it has been locked up." "This is the gallery," whispered Mrs. Duncan, "in which I heard the strange noises; but not a word of them to my aunt." Amanda could scarcely conceal the disappointment she felt at finding she could not see her mother's picture. She would have entreated the chapel might be opened for that purpose, had she not feared exciting suspicions by doing so.

They returned from the gallery to the parlor; and in the course of conversation Amanda heard many interesting anecdotes of her ancestors from Mrs. Bruce. Her mother was also mentioned, and Mrs. Bruce, by dwelling on her worth, made amends, in some degree, to Amanda for having called her picture lumber. She retired to her chamber with her mind at once softened and elevated by hearing of her mother's virtues. She called upon her, upon her father's spirit, upon them whose kindred souls were re-united in heaven, to bless their child, to strengthen, to support her in the thorny path marked out for her to take; nor to cease their tutelary care till she was joined to them by Providence

CHAPTER XLV.

> "Such on the ground the fading rose we see,
> By some rude blast torn from the parent tree!
> The daffodil so leans his languid head,
> Newly mown down upon his grassy bed!"—LEE.

XPERIENCE convinced Amanda that the change in her situation was, if possible, more pleasing than she expected it would be. Mrs. Duncan was the kindest and most attentive of friends. Mrs. Bruce was civil and obliging, and her little pupils were docile and affectionate. Could she have avoided retrospection, she would have been happy; but the remembrance of past events was too deeply impressed upon her mind to be erased; it mingled in the visions of the night, in the avocations of the day, and in the meditations of her lonely hours, forcing from her heart the sighs of regret and tenderness. Her mornings were devoted to her pupils, and in the evenings she sometimes walked with Mrs. Duncan, sometimes read aloud whilst she and her aunt were working; but whenever they were engaged in chatting about family affairs, or at a game of piquet (which was often the case), as Mrs. Bruce neither loved walking nor working, she always took that opportunity of retiring from the room, and either rambled through the dark and intricate windings of the Abbey, or about the grounds contiguous to it. She sighed whenever she passed the chapel which contained the picture of her mother; it was in a ruinous condition, but a thick foliage of ivy partly hid while it proclaimed its decay; the windows were broken in many places, but all too high to admit the possibility of her gaining admittance through them, and the door was strongly secured by massy bars of iron, as was every door which had a communication with the eastern part of the Abbey. A fortnight passed away at the Abbey without anything happening to disturb the tranquillity which reigned in it. No one approached it, except a few of the wandering children of poverty, and its inhabitants seemed perfectly content with their seclusion from the world. Amanda, by Mrs. Duncan's desire, had told Mrs. Dermot to direct her letters to a town about five miles from the Abbey; thither a man went every day, but constantly returned without one for her.

"Why," she asked herself, "this anxiety for a letter, this disappointment at not receiving one, when I neither expect to hear anything interesting or agreeable? Mrs. Dermot has already said she had no means of hearing about Lord Mortimer; and, even if she had, why should I desire such intelligence, torn as I am from him for ever?"

At the expiration of another week an incident happened, which again destroyed the composure of our heroine. Mrs. Bruce one morning hastily entered the room, where she and Mrs. Duncan were sitting with the little girls, and begged they would not stir from it till she had told them to do so, as the Marquis of Roslin's steward was below stairs, and if he knew of their residence at the Abbey, she was confident he would reveal it to his lord, which she had no doubt would occasion her own dismission from it. The ladies assured her they would not leave the apartment, and she retired, leaving them astonished at the agitation she betrayed.

In about two hours she returned, and said she came to release them from confinement, as the steward had departed. "He has brought unexpected intelligence," said she; "the Marquis and his family are coming down to the castle. The season is so far advanced, I did not suppose they would visit it till next summer. I must, therefore," continued she, addressing her niece, "send to the neighboring town to procure lodgings for you till the family leave the country, as no doubt some of them will come to the Abbey, and to find you in it would, I can assure you, be attended with unpleasant consequences to me."

Mrs. Duncan begged she would not suffer the least uneasiness on her account, and proposed that very day leaving the Abbey. "No," Mrs. Bruce replied, "there is no necessity for quitting it for a few days longer; the family," continued she, "are coming down upon a joyful occasion, to celebrate the nuptials of the Marquis's daughter, Lady Euphrasia Sutherland." "Lady Euphrasia's nuptials!" exclaimed Amanda, in an agitated voice, and forgetting her own situation. "To whom is she going to be married?" "To Lord Mortimer," Mrs. Bruce replied, "the Earl of Cherbury's only son; a very fine young man. I am told the affair has been long talked of; but——" Here she was interrupted by a deep sigh, or rather groan, from the unfortunate Amanda, who at the same moment fell back on her chair, pale, and without motion Mrs. Duncan screamed, and flew to her assistance. Mrs. Bruce, equally frightened, though less affected, ran for restoratives, and the children clasped her knees and wept. From her pensive look and manner, Mrs. Duncan suspected, from their first acquaintance, that her heart had experienced a disappointment of the tenderest nature. Her little girls, too, had told her that they had seen Miss Donald crying over a picture. Her suspicions concerning such a disappointment were now confirmed by the sudden emotion and illness of Amanda. But she had all the delicacy which belongs to true sensibility, and determined never to let Amanda know she conjectured the source of her sorrows, certain as she was that they had never originated from any misconduct.

Mrs. Bruce's drops restored Amanda's senses; but she felt weak and trembling, and begged she might be supported to her room, to lie down on the bed. Mrs. Bruce and Mrs. Duncan accordingly led her to it. The former almost immediately retired, and the tears of Amanda now burst forth. She wept a long time without intermission; and as soon as her sobs would permit her to speak, begged Mrs. Duncan to leave her to herself. Mrs. Duncan knew too well the luxury of secret grief to deny her the enjoyment of so melancholy a feast, and directly withdrew.

The wretched Amanda then asked herself, "if she had not known before that the sacrifice she made Lord Cherbury would lead to the event she now regretted?" It was true she did know it. But whenever an idea of its taking place occurred, she had so sedulously driven it from her mind, that she at last almost ceased to think about it. Were he to be united to any other woman than Lady Euphrasia, she thought she would not be so wretched. "Oh, Mortimer! beloved of my soul!" she cried, "were you going to be united to a woman sensible of your worth, and worthy of your noble heart, in the knowledge of your happiness my misery would be lessened. But what a union of misery must minds so uncongenial as yours and Lady Euphrasia's form! Alas! am I not wretched enough in contemplating my own prospect of unhappiness, but that yours, also, must be obtruded on me?" "Yet perhaps," she continued, "the evils that I dread on Lord Mortimer's account may be averted. Oh, that they may!" said she, with fervor, and raising her hands and eyes. "Soften, gracious Heaven! soften the flinty nature of Lady Euphrasia. Oh, render her sensible of the blessing you bestow in giving her Lord Mortimer! and render her not only capable of inspiring, but of feeling tenderness. May she prove to him the tender friend, the faithful, the affectionate companion the unfortunate Amanda would have been! Oh, may she build her happiness on his! and may his be great as his virtues—extensive as his charities! and may the knowledge of it soothe my afflicted heart!"

Her spirits were a little elevated by the fervency of her language. But it was a transient elevation. The flush it spread over her cheeks soon died away, and her tears again began to flow. "Alas!" she cried, "in a few days it will be criminal to think of Lord Mortimer as I have hitherto done; and I shall blush," continued she, gazing at his picture, "to contemplate this dear shadow, when I reflect its original is the husband of Lady Euphrasia."

The dinner-bell now sounded through the Abbey, and almost at the same minute she heard a tap at her door. She started, and reflected for the first time that her deep dejection would naturally excite suspicions as to its source, if longer indulged. Shocked at the idea of incurring them, she hastily wiped away her tears, and opening the door, found her friend Mrs. Duncan at it, who begged she would come down to dinner. Amanda did not refuse, but was obliged to use the supporting arm of her friend to reach the parlor. She could not eat. With difficulty could she restrain her tears, or answer the inquiries Mrs. Bruce made, after what she supposed a mere bodily indisposition. She forced herself, however, to continue in the parlor till after tea, when cards being produced, she had an opportunity of going out, and indulging her anguish without fear of interruption. Unable, however, to walk far, she repaired to the old chapel, and sitting down by it, leaned her head against its decayed and ivy-covered walls. She had scarcely sat in this manner a minute, when the stones gave way, with a noise which terrified her, and she would have fallen backwards had she not caught at some projecting wood. She hastily rose, and found that the ivy entirely concealed the breach. She examined it, however, and perceived it large enough to admit her into the chapel. A sudden pleasure pervaded her heart at the idea of being able to enter it, and examine the picture she had so long wished to behold. There was nothing to oppose her entrance but the ivy. This she parted with difficulty, but so as not to strip it from the wall, and after stepping over the fallen rabbish, she found herself in the body of the chapel. The silent hour of twilight was now advanced, but the moonbeams that darted through the broken roof prevented the chapel from being involved in utter darkness. Already had the owls begun their strains of melancholy on its mouldering pillars, while the ravens croaked amongst the luxuriant trees that rustled round it. Dusty and moth-eaten banners were suspended from the walls, and rusty casques, shields, and spears were promiscuously heaped together, the useless armor of those over whose remains Amanda now trod with a light and trembling foot. She looked for the picture, and perceived one reclined against the wall near the altar. She wiped away the dust, and perceived this was indeed the one she sought, the one her father had so often described to her. The light was too imperfect for her to distinguish the features, and she resolved, if possible, to come at an earlier hour the ensuing evening. She felt impressed with reverential awe as she stood before it. She recollected the pathetic manner in which her father had mentioned his emotions as he gazed upon it, and her tears began to flow for the disastrous fate of her parents and her own. She sunk in an agony of grief, which mournful remembrances and present calamities excited, upon the steps of that altar, where Fitzalan and Malvina had plighted their irrevocable vows. She leaned her arm on the rails, but her face was turned to the picture, as if it could see and would pity her distress. She remained in this situation till the striking of the Abbey clock warned her to depart. In going towards the entrance she perceived a small arched door at the opposite side. As the apartments Lady Malvina had occupied were in this part of the building, she resolved on visiting them before she left the Abbey, lest the breach in the wall should be discovered ere she returned to it. She returned to the parlor ere the ladies had finished their game of piquet, and the next evening, immediately after tea, repaired to the chapel, leaving them engaged as usual at cards. She stood a few minutes before it, to see if any one was near; but perceiving no object she again entered it. She had now sufficient light to examine the picture; though faded by the damp, it yet retained that loveliness for which its original was so admired, and which Amanda had so often heard eloquently described by her father. She contemplated it with awe and pity. Her heart swelled with the emotions it excited, and gave way to its feelings in tears. To weep before the shade of her mother, seemed to assuage the bitterness of those feelings. She pronounced the name of her parents, she called herself their wretched orphan, a stranger, and a dependant in the mansion of her ancestors. She pronounced the name of Lord Mortimer in the impassioned accents of tenderness and distress. As she thus indulged the sorrows of her soul in tears and lamentations, she suddenly heard a faint noise, like an advancing footstep near her. She started up, for she had been kneeling before her mother's picture, terrified lest her visit to the chapel had been discovered, which she knew, if the case, would mortally disoblige Mrs. Bruce, though why she should be so averse to any one's visiting it she could not conceive. She listened in trembling anxiety a few minutes. All again was still, and she returned to the parlor, where she found the ladies as she had left them, determined, notwithstanding her late fright, to return the next evening to the chapel, and visit the apartments that were her mother's.

CHAPTER XLVI.

"What beckoning ghost along the moonlight shade,
Invites my steps?"—POPE.

HE next evening Amanda's patience was put to the test; for after tea Mrs. Duncan proposed a walk, which seemed to cut off her hopes of visiting the chapel that evening; but after strolling some time about the valley, complaisance for her aunt made Mrs. Duncan return to the parlor, where she was expected to take her usual hand at piquet. The hour was late, and the sky so gloomy, that the moon, though at its full, could scarcely penetrate the darkness; notwithstanding all this, Amanda resolved on going to the chapel, considering this as, in all probability, the only opportunity she would have of visiting the apartments her mother had occupied (which she had an irrepressible desire to enter), as in two days she was to accompany Mrs. Duncan to lodgings in the neighboring town; she accordingly said she had a mind to walk a little longer. Mrs. Bruce bade her beware of catching cold, and Mrs. Duncan said she was too fond of solitary rambles; but no opposition being made to her intention she hurried to the chapel, and, entering the little arched door, found herself in a lofty hall, in the centre of which was a grand staircase, the whole enlightened by a large gothic window at the head of the stairs. She ascended them with trepidation, for her footsteps produced a hollow echo, which added something awful to the gloom that enveloped her. On gaining the top of the stairs she saw two large folding doors on either side, both closed. She knew the direction to take, and, by a small exertion of strength, pulled the one on the left side open, and perceived a long gallery, which she knew was terminated by the apartments she wanted to visit. Its almost total darkness, however, nearly conquered her wish, and shook her resolution of proceeding; but ashamed, even to herself, to give way to superstitious fears, or turn back without gratifying her inclination after going so far, she advanced into the gallery, though with a trembling step, and as she let the door out of her hand, it shut to with a violence that shook the whole building. The gallery on one side had a row of arched doors, and on the other an equal number of windows; but so small, and placed so high, as scarcely to admit a ray of light. Amanda's heart began to beat with unusual quickness, and she thought she should never reach the end of the gallery. She at last came to a door, it was closed, not fastened; she pushed it gently open, and could just discern a spacious room. This, she supposed, had been her mother's dressing-room. The moonbeams, as if to aid her wish of examining it, suddenly darted through the casements. Cheered by the unexpected light, she advanced into the room at the upper end of it something in white attracted her notice. She concluded it to be the portrait of Lady Malvina's mother, which she had been informed hung in this room. She went up to examine it; but her horror may be better conceived than described, when she found herself not by a picture, but by the real form of a woman, with a death-like countenance! She screamed wildly at the terrifying spectre, for such she believed it to be, and quick as lightning flew from the room. Again was the moon obscured by a cloud, and she involved in utter darkness. She ran with such violence, that, as she reached the door at the end of the gallery, she fell against it. Extremely hurt, she had not power to move for a few minutes; but while she involuntarily paused she heard approaching footsteps. Wild with terror, she instantly recovered her faculties, and attempted opening it; but it resisted all her efforts. "Protect me, Heaven!" she exclaimed, and at the moment felt an icy hand upon hers! Her senses instantly receded, and she sunk to the floor. When she recovered from her insensibility she perceived a glimmering light around her. She opened her eyes with fearfulness, but no object appeared, and to her great joy she saw the door standing open, and found that the light proceeded from the large window. She instantly rose, and descended the staircase with as much haste as her trembling limbs could make; but again, what was her horror when, on entering the chapel, the first object she beheld was the same that had already alarmed her so much! She made a spring to escape through the entrance, but the apparition, with a rapidity equal to her own, glided before her, and with a hollow voice, as she waved an emaciated hand, exclaimed, "Forbear to go."

A deadly faintness again came over Amanda; she sunk upon a broken seat, and put her hand over her eyes to shut out the frightful vision.

"Lose," continued the figure, in a hollow voice, "lose your superstitious fears, and in me behold not an airy inhabitant of the other world, but a sinful, sorrowing, and repentant woman."

The terrors of Amanda gave way to this unexpected address; but her surprise was equal to what these terrors had been; she withdrew her hand, and gazed attentively on the form before her.

"If my eye, if my ear deceives me not," it continued, "you are a descendant of the Dunreath family. I heard you last night, when you imagined no being near, call yourself the unfortunate orphan of Lady Malvina Fitzalan." "I am indeed her child," replied Amanda. "Tell me, then, by what means you have been brought hither. You called yourself a stranger, and a dependant in the house of your ancestors." "I am both," said Amanda; "my real name is concealed, from circumstances peculiarly distressing, and I have been brought to the Abbey as an instructress to two children related to the person who takes care of it." "My prayers at length," exclaimed the ghastly figure, raising her hollow eyes and emaciated hands, "my prayers have reached the Throne of Mercy, and, as a proof that my repentance is accepted, power is given me to make reparation for the injuries I have committed. Oh! thou," she cried, turning to Amanda, "whose form revives in my remembrance the youth and beauty blasted by my means, if thy mind as well as face, resembles Lady Malvina's, thou wilt, in pity to my sufferings, forbear to reproach my crimes. In me," she continued, "you behold the guilty but contrite widow of the Earl of Dunreath."

Amanda started. "Oh, gracious Heaven!" she exclaimed, "can this be possible?" "Have you not been taught to execrate my name?" asked the unhappy woman. "Oh! no," replied Amanda. "No," replied Lady Dunreath, "because your mother was an angel. But did she not leave a son?" "Yes," said Amanda. "And does he live?" "Alas! I do not know," replied Amanda, melting into tears; "distress separated us, and he is not more ignorant of my destiny than I am of his." "It is I," exclaimed Lady Dunreath, "have been the cause of this distress. It is I, sweet and sainted Malvina, have been the cause of calamity to your children; but, blessed be the wonder-working hand of Providence," she continued, "which has given me an opportunity of making some amends for my cruelty and injustice. But," she proceeded, "as I know the chance which led you to the chapel, I dread to detain you longer, lest it should lead to a discovery. Was it known that you saw me, all my intentions would be defeated. Be secret, then, I conjure you, more on your account than my own, and let not Mrs. Bruce have the smallest intimation of what has passed; but return to-morrow night, and you shall receive from me a sacred deposit, which will, if affluence can do it, render you completely happy. In the mean time do you throw upon paper a brief account of your life, that I may know the incidents which so providentially brought you to the Abbey." Amanda promised to obey her in every respect and the unfortunate woman, unable longer to speak, kissed her hand, and retired through the little arched door. Amanda left the chapel, and, full of wonder, pity, and expectation, moved mechanically to the parlor. Mrs. Bruce and Mrs. Duncan had just risen from cards, and both were instantly struck with her pallid and disordered looks. They inquired if she was ill. Their inquiries roused her from a deep reverie. She recollected the danger of exciting suspicions, and replied, "she was only fatigued with walking, and begged leave to retire to her chamber." Mrs. Duncan attended her to it, and would have sat with her till she saw her in bed, had Amanda allowed; but it was not her intention, indeed, to go to bed for some time. When left to herself, the surprising and interesting discovery she had made had so agitated her that she could scarcely compose herself enough to take up a pen to narrate the particulars of her life, as Lady Dunreath had requested. She sketched them in a brief yet hasty manner, sufficiently strong, however, to interest the feelings of a sympathetic heart; the tender and peculiar sorrows of her own she omitted; her life was represented sufficiently calamitous, without mentioning the incurable sorrow which disappointed love had entailed upon it. She was glad she had executed her task with haste, as Mrs. Duncan called upon her in the course of the next day to assist in packing for their removal to the neighboring town. The evening was far advanced ere she had an opportunity of repairing to the chapel, where she found the unfortunate Lady Dunreath resting in an attitude of deep despondence, against the rails of the altar.

Her pale and woe-worn countenance—her emaciated form—her solitary situation—all inspired Amanda with the tenderest compassion, and she dropped a tear upon the cold and withered hand which was extended to hers, as she approached. "I merit not the tear of pity," said the unhappy woman, "yet it casts a gleam of comfort on my heart to meet with a being who feels for its sorrows. But the moments are precious" She then led Amanda to the altar, and, stooping down, desired her assistance in removing a small marble flag beneath it. This being effected, with difficulty, Amanda perceived an iron box, which she also assisted in raising. Lady Dunreath then took a key from her bosom, with which she opened it, and took from thence a sealed paper. "Receive," said she, presenting it to Amanda, "receive the will of your grandfather, a sacred deposit, intrusted to your care for your brother, the rightful heir of the Earl of Dunreath. Oh! may its restoration, and my sincere repentance, atone for its long detention and concealment. Oh! may the fortune it will bestow upon you, as well as your brother, be productive to both of the purest happiness." Trembling with joyful surprise, Amanda received the paper. "Gracious Heaven!" exclaimed she, "is it possible? Do I really hold the will of my grandfather—a will which will entitle my brother to affluence? Oh! Providence, how mysterious are thy ways! Oh! Oscar, beloved of my heart," she continued, forgetting at that moment every consideration of self, "could thy sister have possibly foreseen her sorrows would have led to such a discovery, half their bitterness would have been allayed. Yes, my father, one of thy children may at least be happy, and in witnessing that happiness the other will find a mitigation of misery." Tears burst from her as she spoke, and relieved the strong emotions that swelled her heart, almost to bursting.

"Oh! talk not of your misery," said Lady Dunreath, with a convulsive sigh, "lest you drive me to despair. For ever must I accuse myself of being the real source of calamity to Lady Malvina and her children." "Excuse me," cried Amanda, wiping her eyes, "I should be ungrateful to Heaven and to you if I dwelt upon my sorrows; but let me not neglect this opportunity," she continued, "of inquiring if there is any way in which I can possibly serve you. Is there no friend to whom I could apply in your name, to have you released from this cruel and unjustifiable confinement?" "No," said Lady Dunreath, "no such friend exists. When I had the power to do so, I never conciliated friendship; and if I am still remembered in the world, it is only with contempt and abhorrence. The laws of my country would certainly liberate me at once; but if things turn out as I expect, there will be no occasion for an application to them, and any step of that kind at present might be attended with the most unpleasant consequences. Your future prosperity, my present safety, all depend on secrecy for a short period. In this paper (drawing one from her pocket and presenting it to Amanda) I have explained my reason for desiring such secrecy." Amanda put it with the will into her bosom, and gave in return the little narrative she had sketched They both assisted in replacing the box and flag, and then seated themselves on the steps of the altar. Amanda informed Lady Dunreath of her intended departure the next day from the Abbey, and the occasion of it Lady Dunreath expressed the utmost impatience to have everything put in a proper train for the avowal of the will, declaring that the sight of the rightful heir in possession of the Abbey would calm the agitations of a spirit which, she believed, would soon forsake its earthly habitation. Tears of compassion fell from Amanda at these words, and she shuddered to think that the unfortunate woman might die abandoned, and bereft of comfort. Again she urged her to think of some expedient for procuring immediate liberty, and again Lady Dunreath assured her it was impossible. Absorbed in a kind of sympathetic melancholy, they forgot the danger of delay till the Abbey clock chimed half an hour past ten—which was later than Mrs. Bruce's usual hour of supper—startled and alarmed them both. "Go! go!" cried Lady Dunreath, with a wild expression of fear; "go! or we are undone!" Amanda pressed her hand in silence, and, trembling, departed from the chapel. She stopped at the outside to listen; for by her ear alone could she now receive any intimation of danger, as the night was too dark to permit any object to be discerned; but the breeze sighing amongst the trees of the valley, and the melancholy murmur of waterfalls, were the only sounds she heard. She groped along the wall of the chapel to keep in the path, which wound from it to the entrance of the Abbey, and in doing so passed her hand over the cold face of a human being. Terrified, an involuntary scream burst from her, and she faintly articulated: "Defend me, Heaven!" In the next moment she was seized round the waist, and her senses were receding, when Mrs. Duncan's voice recalled them. She apologized to Amanda for giving her such a fright; but said, "that her uneasiness was so great at her long absence that, attended by a servant, she had come in quest of her."

Mrs. Duncan's voice relieved Amanda from the horror of thinking she had met with a person who would insult her; but it had given rise to a new alarm. She feared she had been traced to the chapel, that her discourse with Lady Dunreath had been overheard.

and of course the secret of the will discovered, and that Mrs. Duncan, amiable as she was, might sacrifice friendship to interest and consanguinity. This idea overwhelmed her with anguish; her deep and heavy sighs, her violent trembling, alarmed Mrs. Duncan, who hastily called the servant to assist her in supporting Amanda home; drops were then administered, but they would have wanted their usual efficacy with the poor night wanderer had she not soon been convinced by Mrs. Duncan's manner she had not made the dreaded discovery.

Amanda would have retired to her chamber before supper, but that she feared distressing Mrs. Duncan by doing so, who would have imputed her indisposition to her fright. She accordingly remained in the parlor, but with a mind so occupied by the interesting events of the evening, that she soon forgot the purpose for which she sat down to table, and neither heeded what was doing or saying. From this reverie she was suddenly roused by the sound of a name for ever dear and precious, which in a moment had power to recall her wandering ideas. She raised her eyes, and with a sad intenseness fixed them on Mrs. Bruce, who continued to talk of the approaching nuptials of Lord Mortimer. Tears now fell from Amanda in spite of her efforts to restrain them, and while drooping her head to wipe them away, she caught the eyes of Mrs. Duncan fastened on her with an expression of mingled pity and curiosity. A deep crimson suffused the face of Amanda, at the consciousness of having betrayed the secret of her heart; but her confusion was inferior to her grief, and the rich suffusion of the one soon gave place to the deadly hue of the other. "Ah!" thought she, "what is now the acquisition of wealth, when happiness is beyond my reach!" Yet scarcely had she conceived the thought ere she wished it buried in oblivion. "Is the comfort of independence, the power of dispensing happiness to others, nothing?" she asked herself. "Do they not merit gratitude of the most pure thankfulness, of the most fervent nature to Providence? They do," she cried, and paid them at the moment in the silence of her heart. It was late ere the ladies separated for the night, and as soon as Amanda had secured the door of her chamber, she drew from her bosom the papers so carefully deposited there, and sat down to peruse the narrative of Lady Dunreath.

CHAPTER XLVII.

"For true repentance never comes too late;
As soon as born she makes herself a shroud,
The weeping mantle of a fleecy cloud,
And swift as thought her airy journey takes,
Her hand Heaven's azure gate with trembling strikes.
The stars do with amazement on her look:
She tells her story in so sad a tone,
That angels start from bliss, and give a groan."—LEE.

NARRATIVE OF LADY DUNREATH.

ADORING the Power who has given me means of making restitution for my injustice, I take up my pen to disclose to your view, oh! lovely orphan of the injured Malvina, the frailties of a heart which has long been tortured with the retrospect of past and the pressure of present evil. Convinced, as I have already said, that if your mind, as well as form, resembles your mother's, you will, while you condemn the sinner, commiserate the penitent, and, touched by that penitence, offer up a prayer to Heaven (and the prayers of innocence are ever availing) for its forgiveness unto me. Many years are now elapsed since the commencement of my confinement, years which diminished my hope of being able to make reparation for the injustice and cruelty I had done Lady Malvina Fitzalan, but left unabated my desire of doing so.

Ah! sweet Malvina! from thy soft voice I was doomed never to hear my pardon pronounced; but from thy child I may, perhaps, have it accorded; if so, from that blissful abode where thou now enjoyest felicity, if the departed souls of the happy are allowed to view the transactions of this world, thine, I am convinced, will behold, with benignancy and compassion, the wretch who covers herself with shame to atone for her injuries to thee. But I must restrain these effusions of my heart, lest I encroach too much upon the limited time allotted to make what I may call my confession, and inform you of particulars necessary to be known.

My cruelty and insolence to Lady Malvina you no doubt already know. In my conduct to her I forgot the obligations her mother had conferred upon me, whose patronage and kind protection laid the foundation of my prosperity. I rejoiced at her marriage wit.

Captain Fitzalan, as a step that would deprive her of her father's favor, and place her in that state of poverty which would conceal charms I detested for being superior to my daughter's. The Earl's resentment was violent at first; but with equal surprise and concern I soon perceived it gradually subsiding. The irrevocableness of the deed, the knowledge that he wanted no acquisition of fortune, above all, Fitzalan's noble descent, and the graces and virtues he possessed, worthy of the highest station, dwelt upon the Earl's imagination, and pleaded strongly in extenuation of his daughter. Alarmed lest my schemes against her should be rendered abortive, like an evil spirit, I contrived to rekindle by means of my agents, the Earl's resentment. They represented the flagrant, the daring contempt Lady Malvina had shown to paternal authority, and that too easy a forgiveness of it might influence her sister to similar conduct with a person perhaps less worthy, and more needy, if possible, than Fitzalan. This last suggestion had the desired effect, and Lady Malvina he declared in future should be considered as an alien to his family.

I now hoped my ambitious views, relative to my daughter, would be accomplished. I had long wished her united to the Marquis of Roslin; but he had for years been Lady Malvina's admirer, and was so much attached to her, that on her marriage he went abroad. My arts were then tried to prevail on the Earl to make a will in Lady Augusta's favor; but this was a point I could not accomplish, and I lived in continual apprehension lest his dying intestate should give Lady Malvina the fortune I wanted to deprive her of. Anxious, however, to procure a splendid establishment for my daughter, I everywhere said there was no doubt but she would be sole heiress to the Earl. At the expiration of three years the Marquis returned to his native country. His unfortunate passion was subdued; he heard and believed the reports I circulated, and stimulated by avarice, his leading propensity, offered his hand to my daughter and was accepted. The Earl gave her a large portion in ready money; but notwithstanding all my endeavors, would not make a settlement of any of his estates upon her. I, however, still hoped, and the Marquis, from what I said, believed that she would possess all his fortune. My daughter's nuptials added to my natural haughtiness. They also increased my love of pleasure, by affording me more amply the means of gratifying it at the sumptuous entertainments at the Marquis's castle. Engaged continually in them, the Earl, whose infirmities confined him to the Abbey, was left to solitude and the care of his domestics. My neglect, you will say, was impolitic, whilst I had any point to carry with him; but Providence has so wisely ordained it that vice should still defeat itself. Had I always acted in uniformity with the tenderness I once showed the Earl, I have little doubt but what at last I should have prevailed on him to act as I pleased; but, infatuated by pleasure, my prudence —no, it deserves not such an appellation—forsook me. Though the Earl's body was a prey to the infirmities of age, his mind knew none of its imbecilities, and he sensibly felt and secretly resented my neglect. The more he reflected on it, the more he contrasted it with the attention he was accustomed to receive from his banished Malvina, and the resentment I had hitherto kept alive in his mind against her gradually subsided, so that he was well prepared to give a favorable reception to the little innocent advocate she sent to plead her cause. My terror, my dismay, when I surprised the little Oscar at the knee of his grandfather, are not to be described. The tears which the agitated parent shed upon the infant's lovely cheek seemed to express affection for its mother, and regret for his rigor to her. Yet amidst those tears I thought I perceived an exulting joy as he gazed upon the child, which seemed to say, "Thou wilt yet be the pride, the prop, the ornament, of my ancient house." After-circumstances proved I was right in my interpretation of his looks. I drove the little Oscar from the room with frantic rage. The Earl was extremely affected. He knew the violence of my temper, and felt too weak to enter into any altercation with me. He therefore reserved his little remaining strength and spirits to arrange his affairs, and by passiveness seemed yielding to my sway; but I soon found, though silent, he was resolute.

My preventing your brother from again gaining access to his grandfather, and my repulsing your mother when she requested an interview with the Earl, I suppose you already know. Gracious Heaven! my heart sickens, even at this remote period, when I reflect on the night I turned her from her paterna home—from that mansion under whose roof her benevolent mother had sheltered my tender years from the rude storms of adverse life. Oh, black and base ingratitude! dire return for the benefits I had received; yet, almost at the very instant I committed so cruel an action she was avenged. No language can describe my horrors, as conscience represented to me the barbarity of my conduct. I trembled with involuntary fears. Sounds had power to terrify. Every blast which shook the Abbey (and dreadful was the tempest of that night), made me shrink as if about to meet with an instantaneous punishment.

> "I trembled at my undivulged crimes
> Unwhipped of justice——"

I knew the Earl expected either to see or hear from your mother. He was ignorant of the reception she had met from me, and I was determined, if possible, he should continue so. As soon as certified of Lady Malvina's departure from the neighborhood of the Abbey, I contrived a letter in Captain Fitzalan's name to the Earl, filled with the most cutting and insolent reproaches to him for his conduct to his daughter, and imputing her precipitate departure from Scotland to it. These unjust reproaches, I trusted, would irritate the Earl, and work another revolution in his mind; but I was disappointed. He either believed the letter a forgery, or else resolved the children should not suffer for the fault of the parent. He accordingly sent for his agent, an eminent lawyer in one of the neighboring towns. This man was lately deceased, but his son, bred to his profession, obeyed the summons to the Abbey. I dreaded his coming; but scarcely had I seen him, ere this dread was lost in emotions, till then unknown. A soft, a tender, an ardent passion took possession of my heart, on beholding a man, in the very prime of life, adorned with every natural and acquired grace that could please the eye and ear. Married at an early period, possessed of all the advantages of art, said and believing myself to be handsome, I flattered myself I might on his heart make an impression equal to that he had done on mine. If so, I thought how easily could the Earl's intentions in favor of his daughter be defeated, for that love will readily make sacrifices I had often heard. A will was made but my new ideas and schemes divested me of uneasiness about it. Melross continued at the Abbey much longer than he need have done, and when he left it, his absence was of short continuance. The Earl's business was his pretext for his long and frequent visits. But the real motive of them he soon discovered to me, encouraged, no doubt, by the partiality I betrayed.

I shall not dwell upon this part of my story; but I completed my crime by violating my conjugal fidelity, and we entered into an engagement to be united whenever I was at liberty, which, from the infirm state of the Earl, I now believed would shortly be the case. In consequence of this, Melross agreed to put into my hands the Earl's will, which had been intrusted to his care, and, he acknowledged, drawn up entirely in favor of Lady Malvina Fitzalan and her offspring. It was witnessed by friends of his, whom he had no doubt of bribing to silence. You may wonder that the will was not destroyed as soon as I had it in my possession. But to do so never was my intention. By keeping it in my hands, I trusted I should have a power over my daughter, which duty and affection had never yet given me. Violent and imperious in her disposition, I doubted not but she and the Marquis, who nearly resembled her in these particulars, would endeavor to prevent, from pride and selfishness, my union with Melross. But to know they were in my power would crush all opposition, I supposed, and obtain their most flattering notice for him—a notice, from my pride, I found essential to my tranquillity. The Earl requested Melross to inquire about Lady Malvina, which he promised to do, but, it is almost unnecessary to say, never fulfilled such a promise.

In about a year after the commencement of my attachment for Melross the Earl expired, and the Marchioness inherited his possessions by means of a forged will executed by Melross. Ignorant, indeed, at the time, that it was by iniquity she obtained them, though her conduct since that period has proved she would not have suffered any compunction from such a knowledge, I removed from the Abbey to an estate about fifteen miles from it, which the Earl had left me, and here, much sooner than decency would have warranted, avowed my intention of marrying Melross, to the Marquis and Marchioness of Roslin. The consequences of this avowal were pretty much what I expected. The Marquis, more by looks than words expressed his contempt; but the Marchioness openly declared her indignation. To think of uniting myself to a being so low in life and fortune, she said, as Melross, was an insult to the memory of her father, and a degradation to his illustrious house; it would also be a confirmation of the scandalous reports which had already been circulated to the prejudice of my character about him. Her words roused all the violence of my soul. I upbraided her with ingratitude to a parent, who had stepped beyond the bounds of rigid propriety to give her an increase of fortune. My words alarmed her and the Marquis. They hastily demanded an explanation of them. I did not hesitate in giving one, protesting at the same time that I would no longer hurt my feelings on their account, as I found no complaisance to my wishes, but immediately avow Lady Malvina Fitzalan the lawful heiress of the Earl of Dunreath. The Marquis and Marchioness changed color; I saw they trembled lest I should put my threats into execution, though with consummate art they pretended to disbelieve that such a will as I mentioned existed.

"Beware," cried I, rising from my chair to quit the room, "lest I give you too convincing a proof of its reality; except I meet with the attention and complaisance I have a right to expect, I shall no longer act contrary to the dictates of my conscience by concealing it. Unlimited mistress of my own actions, what but affection for my daughter could make me consult her upon any of them? Her disapprobation proceeds alone from selfishness, since an alliance with Melross, from his profession, accomplishments, and birth, would not disgrace a house even more illustrious than the one she is descended from or connected to."

I retired to my chamber, secretly exulting at the idea of having conquered all opposition, for I plainly perceived by the Marquis and Marchioness's manner, they were convinced it was in my power to deprive them of their newly-acquired possessions, which, to secure, I doubted not their sacrificing their pride to my wishes. I exulted in the idea of having my nuptials with Melross celebrated with that splendor I always delighted in, and, the prospect of having love and vanity gratified, filled me with a kind of intoxicating happiness.

In a few hours after I had retired to my room, the Marchioness sent to request an interview with me, which I readily granted.

She entered the apartment with a respectful air, very unusual to her, and immediately made an apology for her late conduct. She acknowledged I had reason to be offended, but a little reflection had convinced her of her error, and both she and the Marquis thanked me for consulting them about the change I was about making in my situation, and would pay every attention in their power to the man I had honored with my choice. That I did not think the Marchioness sincere in her professions you may believe, but complaisance was all I required. I accompanied her to the Marquis; a general reconciliation ensued, and Melross was presented to them. In about two days after this the Marchioness came into my dressing-room one morning, and told me she had a proposal to make, which she hoped would be agreeable to me to comply with. It was the Marquis's intention and hers to go immediately to the continent, and they had been thinking, if Melross and I would favor them with our company, that we had better defer our nuptials till we reached Paris, which was the first place they intended visiting, as their solemnization in Scotland so soon after the Earl's decease might displease his friends, by whom we were surrounded, and, on their return, which would be soon, they would introduce Melross to their connections as a man every way worthy of their notice. After a little hesitation I agreed to this plan, for where it interfered not with my own inclinations, I wished to preserve an appearance of propriety to the world, and I could not avoid thinking my marrying so soon after the Earl's death would draw censure upon me, which I should avoid by the projected tour, as the certain time of my nuptials could not then be ascertained. Melross submitted cheerfully to our new arrangements, and it was settled farther, to preserve appearances, that he should go before us to Paris. I supplied him with everything requisite for making an elegant appearance, and he departed in high spirits at the prospect of his splendid establishment for life.

I counted the moments with impatience for rejoining him, and, as had been settled, we commenced our journey a month after his departure. It was now the middle of winter, and ere we stopped for the night, darkness, almost impenetrable, had veiled the earth. Fatigued, and almost exhausted by the cold, I followed the Marquis through a long passage, lighted by a glimmering lamp, to a parlor which was well lighted and had a comfortable fire. I started with amazement on entering it at finding myself in a place I thought familiar to me; my surprise, however, was but for an instant, yet I could not help expressing it to the Marquis. "Your eyes, madam," cried he, with a cruel solemnity, "have not deceived you, for you are now in Dunreath Abbey." "Dunreath Abbey!" I repeated: "Gracious Heaven! what can be the meaning of this?" "To hide your folly, your imprudence, your deceit from the world," he exclaimed; "to prevent your executing the wild projects of a depraved and distempered mind, by entering into a union at once contemptible and preposterous, and to save those, from whom alone you derive your consequence by your connection with them, farther mortification on your account."

To describe fully the effect of this speech upon a heart like mine is impossible; the fury which pervaded my soul would, I believe, have hurried me into a deed of dire revenge, had I had the power of executing it; my quivering lips could not express my strong indignation.

"And do you then, in a country like this," I cried, "dare to think you can deprive me of my liberty?" "Yes," replied he, with insulting coolness, "when it is known you are incapable of making a proper use of that liberty. You should thank me," he continued, "for palliating your late conduct, by imputing it rather to an intellectual derangement than to total depravity. From what other source than the former could you have asserted that there was a will in Lady Malvina Fitzalan's favor?"

These words at once developed the cause of his unjustifiable conduct, and proved that there is no real faith between the guilty. From my disposition the Marquis was convinced that I would assume a haughty sway over him, in consequence of the secret of the will. He also dreaded that passion or caprice might one day induce me to betray that secret, and wrest from him his unlawful possessions. Thus pride and avarice tempted and determined him, by confining me, to rid himself of these fears. "Oh! would to Heaven," cried I, replying to the last part of his speech, "I had proved my assertion; had I done justice to others, I should not have been entangled in the snare of treachery." "Prove the assertion now," said he, "by showing me the will, and you may, perhaps," he continued, in a hesitating accent, "find your doing so attended with pleasing consequences."

Rage and scorn flashed from my eyes at these words. "No," cried I, "had you the power of torturing, you should not tear it from me. I will keep it to atone for my sins, and expose yours to view by restoring it to the right owner." I demanded my liberty, I threatened, supplicated, but all in vain. The Marquis told me I might as well compose myself, for my fate was decided. "You know," cried he, with a malicious look, "you have no friends to inquire or interfere about you, and, even if you had, when I told them what I believe to be the case, that your senses were disordered, they would never desire to have you released from this confinement." I called for my daughter. "You will see her no more;" he replied, "the passions she has so long blushed to behold she will no more witness." "Rather say," I exclaimed, "that she dare not behold her injured parent; but let not the wretch who has severed the ties of nature hope to escape unpunished. No, my sufferings will draw a dreadful weight upon her head, and may, when least expected, torture her heart with anguish."

Convinced that I was entirely in the Marquis's power, convinced that I had nothing to hope from him or my daughter, rage, horror, and agony, at their unjust and audacious treatment, kindled in my breast a sudden frenzy, which strong convulsions only terminated. When I recovered from them I found myself on a bed in a room which, at the first glance, I knew to be the one the late Lady Dunreath had occupied, to whose honors I so unworthily succeeded. Mrs. Bruce, who had been housekeeper at the Abbey before my marriage, sat beside me; I hesitated a few minutes whether I should address her as a suppliant or a superior; the latter, however, being most agreeable to my inclinations, I bid her, with a haughty air, which I hoped would awe her into obedience, assist me in rising, and procure some conveyance from the Abbey without delay. The Marquis entered the chamber as I spoke. "Compose yourself, madam," said he, "your destiny, I repeat, is irrevocable; this Abbey is your future residence, and bless those who have afforded your follies such an asylum. It behooves both the Marchioness and me indeed to seclude a woman who might cast imputations on our characters, which those unacquainted with them might believe." I started from the bed, in the loose dress in which they had placed me on it, and stamping round the room, demanded my liberty. The Marquis heard my demand with contemptuous silence, and quitted the room. I attempted to rush after him, but he pushed me back with violence, and closed the door. My feelings again brought on convulsions, which terminated in a delirium and fever. In this situation the Marquis and Marchioness abandoned me, hoping, no doubt, that my disorder would soon lay me in a prison even more secure than the one they had devoted me to. Many weeks elapsed ere I showed any symptom of recovery. On regaining my senses, I seemed as if awaking from a tedious sleep, in which I had been tortured with frightful visions. The first object my eyes beheld, now blessed with the powers of clear perception, was Mrs. Bruce bending over my pillow, with a look of anxiety and grief, which implied a wish, yet a doubt, of my recovery.

"Tell me," said I, faintly, "am I really in Dunreath Abbey—am I really confined within its walls by order of my child?"

Mrs. Bruce sighed. "Do not disturb yourself with questions now," said she; "the reason Heaven has so mercifully restored would be ill employed in vain murmurs." "Vain murmurs!" I repeated, and a deep, desponding sigh burst from my heart. I lay silent a long time after this. The gloom which encompassed me at length grew too dreary to be borne, and I desired Mrs Bruce to draw back the curtains of the bed and windows. She obeyed, and the bright beams of the sun, darting into the room, displayed to my view an object I could not behold without shuddering—this was the portrait of Lady Dunreath, exactly opposite the bed. My mind was softened by illness, and I felt in that moment as if her sainted spirit stood before me to awaken my conscience to remorse and my heart to repentance. The benevolence which had irradiated the countenance of the original with a celestial expression was powerfully expressed upon the canvas, and recalled, oh! how affectingly to my memory, the period in which this most amiable of women gave me a refuge in her house, in her arms, from the storms of life; and yet her child, I groaned, her child, I was accessory in destroying. Oh! how excruciating were my feelings at this period of awakened conscience! I no longer inveighed against my sufferings. I considered them in the light of retribution, and felt an awful resignation take possession of my soul. Yes, groaned I to myself, it is fit that in the very spot in which I triumphed in deceit and cruelty I should meet the punishment due to my misdeeds.

The change in my disposition produced a similar one in my temper, so that Mrs. Bruce found the task of attending me easier than she had imagined it would be; yet I did not submit to confinement without many efforts to liberate myself through her means; but her fidelity to her unnatural employers was not to be shaken. Blushing, however, at my past enormities, I should rather have shrunk from than solicited admission again into the world, had not my ardent desire of making reparation to the descendants of Lady Dunreath influenced me to desire my freedom. Oh! never did that desire cease—never did a morning dawn, an evening close, without entreating Heaven to allow me means of restoring to the injured their inheritance. Mrs. Bruce, though steady, was not cruel, and nursed me with the tenderest attention till my health was re-established. She then ceased to see me, except at night, but took care I should always be amply stocked with necessaries. She supplied me with religious and moral books; also, materials for writing, if I chose to amuse myself with making comments on them. To those books am I indebted for being able to endure, with some degree of calmness, my long and dreadful captivity. They enlarged my heart, they enlightened its ideas concerning the Supreme Being, they impressed it with awful submission to His will, they convinced me more forcibly of my transgressions, yet without exciting despair; for, while they showed the horrors of vice, they proved the efficacy of repentance. Debarred of the common enjoyments of life, air, exercise, and society, in vain my heart assured me my punishment was inadequate to my crimes; nature repined, and a total languor seized me. Mrs. Bruce at last told me I should be allowed the range of that part of the building in which I was confined (for I had hitherto been limited to one room), and consequently air from the windows, if I promised to make no attempt for recovering my freedom,—an attempt, she assured me, which would prove abortive, as none but people at tached to the Marquis lived in or about the Abbey, who would immediately betray me to him; and if he ever detected such a step, it was his determination to hurry me to France.

Certain that he would be capable of such baseness, touched by the smallest indulgence, and eager to procure any recreation, I gave her the most solemn assurances of never attempting to make known my situation. She accordingly unlocked the several doors that had hitherto impeded my progress from one apartment to another, and removed the iron bolts which secured the shutters of the windows. Oh! with what mingled pain and pleasure did I contemplate the rich prospect stretched before them, now that I was debarred from enjoying it. At liberty, I wondered how I could ever have contemplated it with a careless eye; and my spirits, which the air had revived, suddenly sunk into despondence, when I reflected I enjoyed this common blessing but by stealth; yet who (cried I, with agony) can I blame but myself? The choicest gifts of Heaven were mine, and I lost them by my own means. Wretch as I was, the first temptation that assailed warped me from integrity, and my error is marked by the deprivation of every good. With eager, with enthusiastic delight, I gazed on scenes which I had so often before regarded with a careless eye; it seemed as if I had only now perception to distinguish their beauties: the season's difference made a material change to me, as all the windows were shut up in winter, except those of the apartment I occupied, which only looked into a gloomy court. Ah! how welcome to me, then, was the return of spring, which again restored to me the indulgence of visiting the windows. How delightful to my eyes the green of the valley, and the glowing bloom of the mountain shrubs just bursting into verdure. Ah! how soothing to my ear the lulling sound of waterfalls, and the lively carol of the birds; how refreshing the sweetness of the air, the fragrance of the plants. which friendly zephyrs, as if pitying my confinement, wafted through the windows. The twilight hour was also hailed by me with delight; it was then I turned my eyes from earth to heaven, and, regarding its blue and spangled vault but as a thin covering between me and myriads of angels, felt a sweet sensation of mingled piety and pleasure, which for the time had power to steep my sorrows in forgetfulness! But, in relating my feelings, I wander from the real purpose of my narrative, and forget that I am describing those feelings to a person who, from my injurious actions, can take but little interest in them.

The will I shall deliver to you to-night. I advise you, if your brother cannot immediately be found, to put it into the hands of some man on whose abilities and integrity you can rely; but till you meet with such a person, beware of discovering you have it in your possession, lest the Marquis who, I am sorry to say, I believe capable of almost any baseness, should remove from your knowledge the penitent, whose testimony to the validity of the deed will be so cheerfully given, and is so materially essential. Be secret, then, I again conjure you, till everything is properly arranged for the avowal of your rights; and, oh! may the restoration of all those rights you shall claim, be to you and to your brother productive of every felicity. From your hands may the wealth it puts into them bestow relief and comfort on the children of adversity; thus yielding to your hearts a pure and permanent satisfaction, which the mere possession of riches, or their expenditure on idle vanities, never can bestow. As much as possible I wish to have my daughter saved from public disgrace. From me you will say she merits not this lenient wish; but, alas! I hold myself accountable for her misconduct. Intrusted to my care by Providence, I neglected the sacred charge, nor ever curbed a passion or laid the foundation of a virtue. Ah! may her wretched parent's prayers be yet availing; may penitence, ere too late, visit her heart, and teach her to regret and expiate her errors! Had she been united to a better man, I think she never would have swerved so widely from nature and from duty; but the selfish soul of the Marquis taught her to regard self as the first consideration in life.

Mrs. Bruce informed me that the Marquis had written to Melross, informing him that I had changed my mind, and would think no more about him, and she supposed he had procured some pleasant establishment in France, as no one had ever heard of his returning from it. She made several attempts to prevail on me to give up the will to her, but I resisted all her arts, and was rejoiced to think I had concealed it in a place which would never be suspected. My narrative now concluded, I wait with even trembling impatience for your expected visit—for that moment in which I shall make some reparation for my injuries to your mother. I am also anxious for the moment in which I shall receive the promised narrative of your life. From your tears, your words, your manner, I may expect a tale of sorrow; ah! may it be only that gentle sorrow which yields to the influence of time, and the sweets of friendship and conscious innocence.

I cannot forbear describing what I felt on first hearing your voice—a voice so like in its harmonious tones to one I knew had long been silent. Impressed with an awful dread, I stood upon the stairs, which I was descending to visit the chapel, as was my constant custom at the close of day. Shivering and appalled, I had not for a few minutes power to move—but when I at last ventured nearer to the door, and saw you kneeling before the dust-covered shade of her I had injured, when I heard you call yourself her wretched orphan, ah! what were my emotions? An awful voice seemed sounding in my ear—"Behold the hour of restitution is arrived! Behold a being, whom the hand of Providence has conducted hither to receive reparation for the injustice you did her parents! Adore that mighty hand which thus affords you means of making atonement for your offences!" I did adore it. I raised my streaming eyes, my trembling hands to Heaven, and blessed the gracious Power which had granted my prayer. The way by which I saw you quit my retirement, proved to me your entrance into it was unknown. With an impatience bordering on agony, I waited for the next evening—it came without bringing you, and no language can express my disappointment. Dejected, I returned to my chamber, which you entered soon after, and where you received so great a fright, yet, be assured, not a greater one than I experienced, for the gleam of moonlight which displayed me to you gave you full to my view, and I beheld the very form and face of Lady Malvina. In form and face may you alone resemble her; different, far different, be your destiny from hers. Soon may your brother be restored to your arms. Should he then shudder at my name, oh! teach him, with a mercy like your own, to accord me forgiveness.

Ye sweet and precious descendants of this illustrious house!—ye rightful heirs of Dunreath Abbey!—may your future joys amply recompense your past sorrows! May those sorrows be forgotten, or only remembered to temper prosperity, and teach it pity for the woes of others! May your virtues add to the renown of your ancestors, and entail eternal peace upon your souls! May their line by you be continued, and continued as a blessing to all around! May your names be consecrated to posterity by the voice of gratitude, and excite in others an emulation to pursue your courses!

Alas! my unhappy child! why do I not express such a wish for you? I have expressed it—I have prayed for its accomplishment—I have wept in bitterness at the idea of its being unavailing; lost to the noble propensities of nature, it is not from virtue, but from pomp and vanity you seek to derive pleasure.

Oh! lovely orphans of Malvina, did you but know, or could you but conceive, the bitter anguish I endure on my daughter's account, you would think yourselves amply avenged for all your injuries.

Oh, God! ere my trembling soul leaves its frail tenement of clay, let it be cheered by the knowledge of my child's repentance.

Oh! you young and tender pair, who are about entering into the dangerous possession of riches, learn from me that their misapplication, the perversion of our talents, and the neglect of our duties, will, even in this world, meet their punishment.

Resolute in doing justice to the utmost of my power, I am ready, whenever I am called upon, to bear evidence to the validity of the will I shall deliver into your possession. Soon may all it entitles you to be restored, is the sincere prayer of her who subscribes herself, the truly penitent

ANNABELLA DUNREATH.

CHAPTER XLVIII.

"Cease, then, ah! cease, fond mortal, to repine
At laws, which Nature wisely did ordain;
Pleasure, what is it? rightly to define,
'Tis but a short-lived interval from pain:
Or rather each alternately renewed,
Gives to our lives a sweet viciss tude."—Browne

HE emotions Amanda experienced from reading this narrative deeply affected but gradually subsided from her mind, leaving it only occupied by pity for the penitent Lady Dunreath, and pleasure at the prospect of Oscar's independence—a pleasure so pure, so fervent, that it had power to steal her from her sorrows; and when the recollection of them again returned, she endeavored to banish it by thinking of the necessity there was for immediately adopting some plan for the disclosure of the will Lady Dunreath had advised her to put into the hands of a friend of integrity and abilities.

"But where," cried the desolate Amanda, "can I find such a friend?" The few, the very few who she had reason to think regarded her, had neither power nor ability to assist her in what would probably be an arduous demand for restitution. After sitting a considerable time in deep meditation, the idea of Rushbrook suddenly occurred, and she started, as if in joyful surprise at the remembrance. She considered that, though almost a stranger to him, an application of such a nature must rather be regarded as a compliment than a liberty, from the great opinion it would prove she had of his honor by intrusting him with such a secret. From his looks and manner, she was well convinced he would not only deeply feel for the injured, but ably advise how those injuries should be redressed. From his years and situation there could be no impropriety in addressing him, and she already in imagination beheld him her friend, advocate, and adviser. He also, she trusted, would be able to put her in a way of making inquiries after Oscar. Oh! how delightful the prospect of discovering that brother—of discovering, but to put him in possession of even a splendid independence! Ah! how sweet the idea of being again folded to a heart interested in her welfare, after being so long a solitary mourner treading the rugged path of life, and bending as she went beneath its adverse storm! Ah! how sweet again to meet an eye which should beam with tenderness on hers, an ear which should listen with attentive rapture to her accents, and a voice that would soothe with softest sympathy her sorrows! It is only those who, like her, have known the social ties of life in all their sweetness; who, like her, have mourned their loss with all the bitterness of anguish, that can possibly conceive her feelings as these ideas occurred to her mind. "Oh, Oscar! oh, my brother!" she exclaimed, while tears wet her pale cheeks, "how rapturous the moment which restores you to me! How delightful to think your youth will no more experience the chill of poverty—your benevolence no longer suffer restraints! Now will your virtues shine forth with full lustre, dignifying the house from which you have descended, doing service to your country, and spreading diffusive happiness around."

The morning surprised Amanda in the midst of her meditations She opened the shutters, and hailed its first glories in the eastern hemisphere; the sunbeams, exhaling the mists of the valley, displayed its smiling verdure, forming a fine contrast to the deep shadows that yet partially enveloped the surrounding mountains. The morning breeze gently agitated the old trees, from whose bending heads unnumbered birds arose, and in their matin notes seemed to consecrate the first return of day to the Great Author of life and light!

Spontaneous praise burst from the lips of Amanda, and she felt all that calm and sweet delight which ever pervades a mind of religion and sensibility on viewing the rural beauties of nature. She left the charming scene to try and get a little rest, but she thought not of undressing; she soon sunk into a gentle sleep, and awoke with renovated spirits near the breakfast hour.

Mrs. Bruce expressed the utmost regret at the necessity there was for parting with her guests; but added, that "she believed, as well as hoped, their absence from her would be but short, as she was sure the Marquis's family would leave Scotland almost immediately after Lady Euphrasia's nuptials." In vain did Amanda struggle for fortitude to support the mention of those nuptials; her frame trembled, her heart sickened. whenever they were talked of; the spirits she had endeavored to collect from the idea, that they would all be requisite in the important affair she must undertake, fleeted away at Mrs. Bruce's words, and a heavy languor took possession of her.

They did not leave the Abbey till after tea in the evening, and the idea that she might soon behold her brother the acknowledged heir of that Abbey, cast again a gleam of pleasure on the sad heart of Amanda; a gleam, I say, for it faded before the almost instantaneous recollection, that ere that period Lord Mortimer and Lady Euphrasia would be united. Sunk in a profound melancholy, she forgot her situation, heeded not the progress of the carriage, or remarked any object. A sudden jolt roused her from her reverie, and she blushed as she thought of the suspicions it might give rise to in the mind of Mrs. Duncan, whose intelligent eye on the preceding night had more than half confessed her knowledge of Amanda's feelings. She now, though with some embarrassment, attempted to enter into conversation, and Mrs. Duncan, who with deep attention had marked her pensive companion, with much cheerfulness rendered the attempt a successful one. The chaise was now turning from the valley, and Amanda leaned from her window to take another view of Dunreath Abbey. The sun was already sunk below the horizon, but a tract of glory still remained that marked the spot in which its daily course was finished; a dubious lustre yet played around the spires of the Abbey, and while it displayed its vast magnificence by contrast added to its gloom—a gloom heightened by the dreary solitude of its situation, for the valley was entirely overshaded by the dark projection of the mountains, on whose summits a few bright and lingering beams yet remained, that showed the wild shrubs waving in the evening breeze. A pensive spirit seemed now to have taken possession of Mrs. Duncan, a spirit congenial to the scene; and the rest of the little journey was passed almost in silence. Their lodgings were at the entrance of the town, and Mrs. Bruce had taken care they should find every requisite refreshment within them. The woman of the house had already prepared a comfortable supper for them, which was served up soon after their arrival. When over, Mrs. Duncan, assisted by Amanda, put the children to bed, as she knew, till accustomed to her, they would not like the attendance of the maid of the house. Neither she nor Amanda felt sleepy; it was a fine moonlight night, and they were tempted to walk out upon a terrace, to which a glass door from the room opened. The terrace overhung a deep valley which stretched to the sea, and the rocky promontory that terminated it was crowned with the ruins of an ancient castle; the moonbeams seemed to sleep upon its broken battlements, and the waves that stole murmuring to the shore cast a silvery spray around it. A pensive pleasure pervaded the hearts of Mrs. Duncan and Amanda, and conversing on the charms of the scene they walked up and down, when suddenly upon the floating air they distinguished the sound of a distant drum beating the tattoo. Both stopped, and leaned upon a fragment of a parapet wall, which had once stretched along the terrace; and Mrs. Duncan, who knew the situation of the country, said, that the sounds they heard proceeded from a fort near the town. They ceased in a short time, but were almost immediately succeeded by martial music; and Amanda soon distinguished an admired march of her father's. Ah! how affectingly did it remind her of him! She recalled the moments in which she had played it for him, whilst he hung over her chair with delight and tenderness; she wept at the tender remembrance it excited—wept at listening to the sounds which had so often given to his pale cheek the flush of ardor. They did not return to the house till convinced by a long interval of silence that the music had ceased for the night.

Amanda having formed a plan relative to the will, determined not to delay executing it. She had often mentioned to Mrs. Duncan her uneasiness concerning her brother, as an excuse for the melancholy that lady, in a half-serious, half-jesting manner, so often rallied her about; and she now intended to assign her journey to London (which she was resolved should immediately take place) to her anxious wish of discovering, or at least inquiring about him. The next morning she accordingly mentioned her intention. Mrs. Duncan was not only surprised, but concerned, and endeavored to dissuade her from it by representing, in the most forcible manner, the dangers she might experience in so long a journey without a protector.

Amanda assured her she was already aware of these, but the

apprehensions they excited were less painful than the anxiety she suffered on her brother's account, and ended by declaring her resolution unalterable.

Mrs. Duncan, who, in her heart, could not blame Amanda for such a resolution, now expressed her hopes that she would not make a longer stay in London than was absolutely necessary, declaring that her society would be a loss she could scarcely support.

Amanda thanked her for her tenderness, and said, "she hoped they should yet enjoy many happy days together." She proposed travelling in a chaise to the borders of England, and then pursuing the remainder of the journey in a stage coach. The woman of the house was sent for, and requested to engage a carriage for her against the morning, which she promised to do; and the intervening time was almost entirely passed by Mrs. Duncan in lamenting the approaching loss of Amanda's society, and in entreaties for her to return as soon as possible. Till this period she did not know, nor did Amanda conceive, the strength of her friendship. She presented her purse to our heroine, and in the impassioned language of sincerity, entreated her to consider it as the purse of a sister, and take from it whatever was necessary for her long journey and uncertain stay.

Amanda, who never wished to lie under obligations, when she could possibly avoid them, declined the offer; but with the warmest expressions of gratitude and sensibility, declaring (what she thought indeed would be the case), that she had more than sufficient for all her purposes; all, therefore, she would accept was what Mrs. Duncan owed her.

Mrs Duncan begged her to take a letter from her to a family, near whose house her first day's journey would terminate. They were relations of Mr. Duncan's, she said, and had been extremely kind to him and her. She had kept up a correspondence with them till her removal to Dunreath Abbey, when she dropped it, lest her residence there should be discovered; but such an opportunity of writing to them, by a person who would answer all their inquiries concerning her, she could not neglect; besides, she continued, they were the most agreeable and hospitable people she had ever known, and she was convinced would not suffer Amanda to sleep at an inn, but would probably keep her a few days at their house, and then escort her part of the way.

Averse to the society of strangers, in her present frame of mind, Amanda said she would certainly take the letter, but could not possibly present it herself. She thanked Mrs. Duncan for her solicitous care about her; but added, whether she lodged at an inn or private house for one night was of little consequence; and as to her journey being retarded, it was what she never could allow.

Mrs. Duncan declared she was too fond of solitude, but did not argue the point with her. She wrote the letter, however.

They took leave of each other at night, as the chaise was ordered at an early hour. As Mrs. Duncan folded Amanda to her heart, she again besought her to hasten back, declaring that neither she nor her little girls would be themselves till she returned.

At an early hour Amanda entered the chaise; and, as she stepped into it, could not forbear casting a sad and lingering look upon a distant prospect, where, the foregoing evening, a dusky grove of firs had been pointed out to her, as encompassing the Marquis of Roslin's Castle. Ah! how did her heart sicken at the idea of the event which either had or was soon to take place in that Castle! Ah! how did she tremble at the idea of her long and lonesome journey, and the difficulties she might encounter on its termination! How sad, how solitary, did she feel herself! Her mournful eyes filled with tears as she saw the rustic families hastening to their daily labors; for her mind involuntarily drew a comparison between their situation and her own. And, ah! how sweet would their labor be to her, she thought, if she, like them, was encompassed with the social ties of life. Fears, before unthought of, rose in her mind, from which her timid nature shrunk appalled. Should Rushbrook be absent from London, or should he not answer her expectations; but, "I deserve disappointment," cried she, "if I thus anticipate it. Oh! let me not be over-exquisite

'To cast the fashion of uncertain evils,'

oppressed as I already am with real ones." She endeavored to exert her spirits. She tried to amuse them by attending to the objects she passed, and gradually they lost somewhat of their heaviness. On arriving in London, she designed going to the haberdasher's, where, it may be remembered, she had once met Miss Rushbrook; here she hoped to procure lodgings, also a direction to Rushbrook. It was about five when she stopped for the night, as the shortened days of autumn would not permit a longer journey, had the tired horses, which was not the case, been able to proceed. They stopped at the inn, which Mrs. Duncan had taken care to know would be the last stage of the first day's journey; a small, but neat and comfortable house, romantically situated at the foot of a steep hill, planted with ancient firs, and crowned with the straggling remains of what appeared to have been a religious house, from a small cross which yet stood over a broken gateway. A stream trickled from the hill, though its murmurs through the thick underwood alone denoted its rising there, and winding round the inn, flowed in meanders though a spacious vale, of which the inn was not the lone inhabitant, for cottages appeared on either side, and one large mansion stood in the centre, whose superior size and neat plantations proclaimed it master of the whole. This was really the case, for immediately on entering the inn Amanda had inquired about the Macqueen family, to whom Mrs. Duncan's letter was directed, and learned that they inhabited this house, and owned the grounds to a large extent surrounding it. Amanda gave Mrs. Duncan's letter to the landlady, and begged she would send it directly to Mrs. Macqueen. The inn was without company; and its quiet retirement, together with the appearance of the owners, an elderly pair, soothed the agitated spirits of Amanda. Her little dinner was soon served up; but when over and she was left to herself, all the painful ideas she had sedulously, and with some degree of success, attempted to banish from he mind in the morning, by attending to the objects she passed, now returned with full, or rather aggravated force. Books, those pleasing and, in affliction, alleviating resources, she had forgotten to bring along with her, and all that the inn contained she had been shown on a shelf in the apartment she occupied, but without finding one that could possibly fix her attention or change her melancholy ideas; a ramble, though the evening was uninviting, she preferred to the passive indulgence of her sorrow; and having ordered tea against her return. and invited the landlady to it, she was conducted to the garden of the inn, from whence she ascended the hill by a winding path. She made her way with difficulty through a path, which, seldom trodden, was half-choked with weeds and brambles; the wind blew cold and sharp around her, and the gloom of closing day was heightened by thick and lowering clouds that involved the distant mountains in one dark shade. Near those mountains she knew the domain of Roslin lay; and from the bleak summit of the hill she surveyed them as a lone mourner would survey the sad spot in which the pleasure of his heart was buried. Forgetting the purpose for which she had walked out, she leaned in melancholy reverie against a fragment of the ruined building, nor heard approaching footsteps till the voice of her host suddenly broke upon her ear. She started, and perceived him accompanied by two ladies, who he directly informed her were Mrs. and Miss Macqueen. They both went up to Amanda, and after the usual compliments of introduction were over, Mrs. Macqueen took her hand, and with a smile of cordial good-nature, invited her to her house for the night, declaring that the pleasure she received from Mrs. Duncan's letter was heightened by being introduced through its means to a person that lady mentioned as her particular friend. Miss Macqueen seconded her mother's invitation, and said, "the moment they had read the letter they had come out for the purpose of bringing her back with them." "Ay, ay," said the host, good-humoredly (who was himself descended from one of the inferior branches of the Macqueens), "this is the way, ladies, you always rob me of my guests. In good faith, I think I must soon change my dwelling, and go higher up the valley."

Conscious from her utter dejection that she would be unable, as she wished, to participate in the pleasures of conversation, Amanda declined the invitation, alleging, as an excuse for doing so, her intention of proceeding on her journey the next morning by dawn of day.

Mrs. Macqueen declared that she should act as she pleased in that respect, and both she and her daughter renewed their entreaties for her company with such earnestness, that Amanda could no longer refuse them; and they returned to the inn, where Amanda begged they would excuse her absence a few minutes; and retired to pay her entertainers, and repeat her charges to the postilion to be at the house as soon as he should think any of the family stirring. She then returned to the ladies, and attended them to their mansion, which might well be termed the seat of hospitality. The family consisted of Mr. and Mrs. Macqueen, four sons, and six daughters, now all past childhood, and united to one another by the strictest ties of duty and affection. After residing a few years at Edinburgh, for the improvement of the young people, Mr. and Mrs. Macqueen returned to their mansion in the valley, where a large fortune was spent in the enjoyment of agreeable society, and acts of benevolence. Mrs. Macqueen informed Amanda, during the walk, that all her family were now assembled together, as her sons, who were already engaged in different professions and businesses in various parts of the king dom, made it a constant rule to pay a visit every autumn to their friends. It was quite dark before the ladies reached the house, and the wind was sharp and cold, so that Amanda found the light and warmth of the drawing-room, to which she was conducted, extremely agreeable. The thick window curtains and carpeting, and the enlivening fire, bid defiance to the sharpness of the mountain blast which howled without, and rendered the comforts within more delectable by the effect of contrast. In the drawing-room were assembled Mr. Macqueen, two of his daughters, and half a dozen ladies and gentlemen, to whom Amanda was presented, and they in return to her. In the countenance of Mr. Macqueen, Amanda perceived a benevolence equal to that which irradiated his wife's. Both were past the prime of life; but in him only was its decline visible. He was lately grown so infirm as to be unable to remove without assistance. Yet was his relish for society undiminished; and in his arm-chair, his legs muffled in flannel, and supported by pillows, he promoted as much as ever the mirth of his family, and saw with delight the dance go on in which he had once mixed with his children. Mrs. Macqueen appeared but as the eldest sister of her daughters; and between them al Amanda perceived a strong family likeness. They were tall, well, but not delicately made; handsome, yet more indebted to the animation of their countenances than to regularity of features for beauty, which was rendered luxuriant by a quantity of rich auburn hair, that, unrestrained by superfluous ornaments, fell in long ringlets on their shoulders, and curled with a sweet simplicity on their white polished foreheads.

"So the boys and girls are not yet returned," said Mrs. Macqueen, addressing one of her daughters. "I am afraid they have taken their friends too far." She had scarcely spoken, when a party was heard under the windows laughing and talking, who ascended the stairs immediately in a kind of gay tumult. The drawing-room door opened, and a lady entered (of a most prepossessing appearance, though advanced in life), and was followed by a number of young people.

But, oh! what were the powerful emotions of Amanda's soul, when amongst them she beheld Lady Araminta Dormer and Lord Mortimer! Shocked, confused, confounded, she strained an eye of agony upon them, as if with the hope of detecting an illusion, then dropped her head, anxious to conceal herself, though she was fatally convinced she could be but a few minutes unobserved by them. Never, amidst the many trying moments of her life, had she experienced one more dreadful. To behold Lord Mortimer, when she knew his esteem for her was lost, at a period, too, when he was hastening to be united to another woman, oh! it was agony, torture in the extreme! Vainly did she reflect she deserved not to lose his esteem. This consciousness could not at present inspire her with fortitude. Her heart throbbed as if it would burst; her bosom, her frame trembled, and she alternately experienced the glow of confusion and the chill of dismay—dismay at the idea of meeting the silent but expressive reproach of Lord Mortimer's eye for her imaginary errors—dismay at the idea of meeting the contempt of his aunt (who was the lady that first entered the room) and sister.

CHAPTER XLIX.

"It would raise your pity but to see the tears
Force through her snowy lids their melting course,
To lodge themselves on her red murm'ring lips,
That talk such mournful things; when straight a gale
Of starting sighs carry those pearls away,
As dews by winds are wafted from the flowers."—LEE.

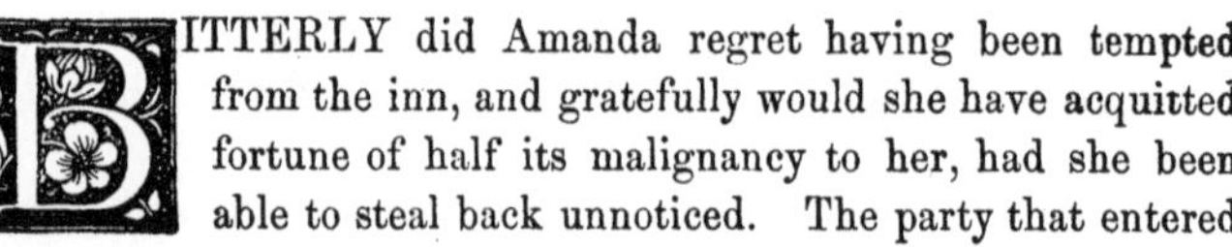

BITTERLY did Amanda regret having been tempted from the inn, and gratefully would she have acquitted fortune of half its malignancy to her, had she been able to steal back unnoticed. The party that entered engaged in talking to those they found in the drawing-room—laughing and describing their ramble, which Lady Araminta said was in the style of Will-o'-the-Wisp (over breaks and through briers)—were some time before they observed Amanda; but soon, ah! how much too soon, did she perceive Mrs. Macqueen approaching to introduce those of her family who were just returned.

"The trying moment is come!" cried Amanda. "Oh! let me not by my confusion look as if I really was the guilty thing I am supposed to be." She endeavored to collect herself, and rose to meet the young Macqueens, by a timid glance perceiving that they yet hid her from the eyes she most dreaded to encounter. She was unable, however, to return their compliments, except by a faint smile, and was again sinking upon her seat—for her frame trembled universally—when Mrs. Macqueen, taking her hand, led her forward, and presented her to Lady Martha and Lady Araminta Dormer. It may be remembered that Lady Martha had never before seen Amanda. She therefore gave her, as Miss Donald, a benignant smile, which, had she supposed her Miss Fitzalan, would have been lost in a contemptuous frown. Seldom, indeed, had she seen a form more interesting than our heroine's. Her mourning habit set off the elegance of her form and the languid delicacy of her complexion, whilst the sad expression of her countenance denoted that habit but the shadow of the unseen grief which dwelt within her soul. Her large blue eyes were half concealed by their long lashes, but the beams that stole from beneath those fringed curtains were full of sweetness and sensibility. Her fine hair discomposed by the jolting of the carriage and the blowing of the wind, had partly escaped the braid on which it was turned under her hat, and hung in long ringlets of glossy brown upon her shoulders and careless curls about her face, giving a sweet simplicity to it, which heightened its beauty. How different was the look she received from Lady Araminta to that she had received from Lady Martha! In the expressive countenance of the former she read surprise, contempt, and anger; her cheeks were flushed with unusual color, her eyes sparkled with uncommon lustre, and their quick glances pierced the palpitating heart of Amanda, who heard her repeat, as if involuntarily, the name of Donald. Ah! how dreadful was the sound to her ear! Ah! how sad a confirmation did it convey—that every suspicion to her prejudice would now be strengthened. "Ah! why, why," said she to herself, "was I tempted to take this hated name? Why did I not prefer incurring any danger to which my own might have exposed me, rather than assume anything like deceit?" Happily the party were too much engrossed by one another to heed the words or manner of Lady Araminta.

Amanda withdrew her hand from Mrs. Macqueen, and moved tremblingly to her seat; but that lady, with a politeness poor Amanda had reason to think officious, stopped her. "Miss Donald—Lord Mortimer!" said she. Amanda raised her head, but not her eyes, and neither saw nor heard his lordship. The scene she had dreaded was over, and she felt a little relieved at the idea. The haughty glance of Lady Araminta dwelt upon her mind, and, when agitation had a little subsided, she stole a look at her, and saw Mrs. Macqueen sitting between her and Lady Martha; and from the altered countenance of the latter, she instantly conjectured she had been informed by her niece of her real name. She also conjectured, from the glances directed towards her, that she was the subject of conversation, and concluded it was begun for the purpose of discovering whether Mrs. Macqueen knew anything of her real history.

From these glances she quickly withdrew her own, and one of the young Macqueens, drawing a chair near hers, began a conversation with all that spirit and vivacity which distinguished his family. The mind of Amanda was too much occupied by its concerns to be able to attend to anything foreign to them. She scarcely knew what he said, and when she did reply it was only by monosyllables. At last a question, enforced with peculiar earnestness, roused her from this inattention, and, blushing for it, she looked at the young man, and perceived him regarding her with something like wonder. She now, for the first time, considered the strange appearance she must make amongst the company, if she did not collect and compose her spirits. The family, too, to whom she was (she could not help thinking) so unfortunately introduced, from their hospitality, merited attention and respect from her. She resolved, therefore, to struggle with her feelings, and, as an apology for her absent manner, complained, and not without truth, of a headache.

Young Macqueen, with friendly warmth, said he would acquaint his mother, or one of his sisters, with her indisposition, and procure some remedy for it; but she insisted he should on no account disturb the company, assuring him she would soon be well; she then endeavored to support a conversation with him; but, ah! how often did she pause in the midst of what she was saying, as the sweet, insinuating voice of Mortimer reached her ear, who, with his native elegance and spirit, was participating in the lively conversation then going forward. In hers, with young Macqueen, she was soon interrupted by his father, who in a good-humored manner told his son he would no longer suffer him to engross Miss Donald to himself, and desired him to lead her to a chair near his.

Young Macqueen immediately arose, and taking Amanda's hand, led her to his father, by whom he seated her; and by whom on the other side sat Lady Martha Dormer; then with a modest gallantry declared it was the first time he ever felt reluctance to obey his father's commands, and hoped his ready acquiescence to them would be rewarded with speedy permission to resume his conversation with Miss Donald. Amanda had hitherto prevented her eyes from wandering, though they could not exclude the form of Lord Mortimer; she had not yet seen his face, and still strove to avoid seeing it Mr. Macqueen began with various inquiries relative to Mrs. Duncan, to which Amanda, as she was prepared for them, answered with tolerable composure. Suddenly he dropped the subject of his relation, and asked Amanda from what branch of the Donalds she was descended. A question so unexpected shocked, dismayed, and overwhelmed her with confusion. She made no reply till the question was repeated, when, in a low and faltering voice, her face covered with blushes, and almost buried in her bosom, she said she did not know.

"Well," cried he, again changing his discourse, after looking at her a few minutes, "I do not know any girl but yourself would take such pains to hide such a pair of eyes as you have. I suppose you are conscious of the mischief they have the power of doing, and therefore it is from compassion to mankind you try to conceal them."

Amanda blushed yet more deeply than before at finding her downcast looks were noticed. She turned hers with quickness to Mr. Macqueen, who having answered a question of Lady Martha's thus proceeded: "And so you do not know from which branch of the Donalds you are descended? Perhaps now you only forget, and if I was to mention them one by one, your memory might be refreshed; but first let me ask your father's surname, and what countrywoman he married, for the Donalds generally married amongst each other?"

Oh! how forcibly was Amanda at this moment convinced (if indeed her pure soul wanted such conviction) of the pain, the shame of deception, let the motive be what it may which prompts it. Involuntarily were her eyes turned from Mr. Macqueen as he paused for a reply to his last question, and at the moment encountered those of Lord Mortimer, who sat directly opposite to her, and with deep attention regarded her, as if anxious to hear how she would extricate herself from the embarrassments her assumed name had plunged her into.

Her confusion, her blushes, her too evident distress, were all imputed by Mrs. Macqueen to fatigue at listening to such tedious inquiries. She knew her husband's only foible was an eager desire to trace every one's pedigree. In order, therefore, to relieve Amanda from her present situation, she proposed a party of whist, at which Mr. Macqueen often amused himself, and for which the table and cards were already laid before him. As she took up the cards to hand them to those who were to draw, she whispered Amanda to go over to the tea-table.

Amanda required no repetition now, and thanking Mrs. Mac

queen in her heart for the relief she afforded her, went to the table around which almost all the young people were crowded; so great was the mirth going on amongst them, that Miss Macqueen, the gravest of the set, in vain called upon her sisters to assist her in serving the trays, which the servants handed about, and Mrs. Macqueen had more than once called for. Miss Macqueen made room for Amanda by herself, and Amanda, anxious to do anything which could keep her from encountering the eyes she dreaded, requested to be employed in assisting her, and was deputed to fill out the coffee. After the first performance of her task, Miss Macqueen, in a whispering voice, said to Amanda, "Do you know we are all here more than half in love with Lord Mortimer. He is certainly very handsome, and his manner is quite as pleasing as his looks, for he has none of that foppery and conceit which handsome men so generally have, and nothing but the knowledge of his engagement could keep us from pulling caps about him. You have heard, to be sure, of Lady Euphrasia Sutherland, the Marquis of Roslin's daughter; well, he is going to be married to her immediately; she, and the Marquis and the Marchioness, were here the other day. She is not to be compared to Lord Mortimer, but she has what will make her be considered very handsome in the eyes of many—namely, a large fortune. They only stopped to breakfast here, and ever since we have been on the watch for the rest of the party, who arrived this morning, and were, on Lady Martha's account, whom the journey had fatigued, prevailed on to stay till to-morrow. I am very glad you came while they were here. I think both ladies charming women, and Lady Araminta quite as handsome as her brother; but see," she continued, touching Amanda's hand, "the conquering hero comes!" Lord Mortimer with difficulty made his way round the table, and accepted a seat by Miss Macqueen, which she eagerly offered him, and which she contrived to procure by sitting closer to Amanda. To her next neighbor, a fine lively girl, Amanda now turned, and entered into conversation with her; but from this she was soon called by Miss Macqueen, requesting her to pour out a cup of coffee for Lord Mortimer.

Amanda obeyed, and he rose to receive it; her hand trembled as she presented it. She looked not in his face, but she thought his hand was not quite steady. She saw him lay the cup on the table, and bend his eyes to the ground. She heard Miss Macqueen address him twice ere she received an answer, and then it was so abrupt that it seemed the effect of sudden recollection. Miss Macqueen now grew almost as inattentive to the table as her sisters, and Mrs. Macqueen was obliged to come over to know what they were all about. At length the business of the tea-table was declared over; and almost at the same moment the sound of a violin was heard from an adjoining room, playing an English country dance, in which style of dancing the Macqueens had been instructed in Edinburgh, and chose this evening in compliment to their guests. The music was a signal for universal motion—all in a moment was bustle and confusion. The young men instantly selected their partners, who seemed ready to dance from one room to another. The young Macqueen, who had been so assiduous about Amanda, now came, and taking her hand, as if her dancing was a thing of course, was leading her after the rest of the party, when she drew back, declaring she could not dance. Surprised and disappointed, he stood looking on her in silence, as if irresolute whether he should not attempt to change her resolution. At last he spoke, and requested she would not mortify him by a refusal.

Mrs. Macqueen hearing her son's request came forward and joined it. Amanda pleaded her headache.

"Do, my dear," said Mrs. Macqueen, "try one dance; my girls will tell you dancing is a sovereign remedy for everything." It was painful to Amanda to refuse; but, scarcely able to stand, she was utterly unable to dance; had even her strength permitted her so to do, she could not have supported the idea of mingling in the set with Lord Mortimer, the glance of whose eye she never caught without a throb in her heart, which shook her whole frame. One of the Miss Macqueens ran into the room, exclaiming: "Lord, Colin, what are you about? Lord Mortimer and my sister have already led off; do, pray, make haste and join us," and away she ran again.

"Let me no longer detain you," said Amanda, withdrawing her hand. Young Macqueen finding her inflexible, at length went off to seek a partner. He was as fond of dancing as his sisters, and feared he should not procure one; but luckily there were fewer gentlemen than ladies present, and a lady having stood up with his youngest sister, he easily prevailed on her to change her partner.

"We will go into the dancing room, if you please," said Mrs. Macqueen to Amanda; "that will amuse without fatiguing you.' Amanda would rather not have gone, but she could not say no; and they proceeded to it. Lord Mortimer had just concluded the dance, and was standing near the door in a pensive attitude, Miss Macqueen being too much engrossed by something she was saying to the young lady next to her, to mind him. The moment he perceived Amanda enter, he again approached his partner, and began chatting in a lively manner to her. Amanda and Mrs. Macqueen sat down together, and in listening to the conversation of that lady, Amanda found herself insensibly drawn from a too painful attention to surrounding objects. On expressing the pleasure which a mind of sensibility must feel on witnessing such family happiness as Mrs. Macqueen possessed, that lady said she had reason indeed to be grateful to Heaven, and was truly so for her domestic comforts. "You see us now," she continued, "in our gayest season, because of my sons' company; but we are seldom dull. Though summer is delightful, we never think the winter tedious. Yet, though we love amusement, I assure you we dislike dissipation. The mornings are appropriated to business, and the evenings to recreation. All the work of the family goes through the hands of my daughters, and they wear nothing ornamental which they do not make themselves. Assisted by their good neighbors, they are enabled to diversify their amusements; the dance succeeds the concert; sometimes small plays, and now and then little dramatic entertainments. About two years ago they performed the Winter's Tale; their poor father was not then in his present situation." Mrs. Macqueen sighed, paused a minute, and then proceeded—"Time must take something from us; but I should and do bless, with heartfelt gratitude, the power which only, by its stealing hand, has made me feel the lot of human nature. Mr. Macqueen," continued she, "at the time I mentioned, was full of spirits, and performed the part of Autolycus. They made me take the character of the good Paulina. By thus mixing in the amusements of our children, we have added to their love and reverence perfect confidence and esteem, and find, when our presence is wanting, the diversion, let it be what it may, wants something to render it complete. They are now about acting the Gentle Shepherd. Several rehearsals have already taken place n our great barn, which is the theatre. On these occasions one of my sons leads the band, another paints the scenes, and Colin, your rejected partner, acts the part of prompter." Here this conversation, so pleasing to Amanda, and interesting to Mrs. Macqueen, was interrupted by a message from the drawing-room, to inform the latter the rubber was over, and a new set wanted to cut in.

"I will return as soon as possible," said Mrs. Macqueen, as she was quitting her seat. If Amanda had not dreaded the looks of Lady Martha almost as much as those of Lord Mortimer or Lady Araminta, she would have followed her to the drawing-room. As this was the case, she resolved on remaining in her present situation It was some time ere she was observed by the young Macqueens. At last Miss Macqueen came over to her—"I declare," said she, "you look so sad and solitary, I wish you could be prevailed on to dance. Do try this; it is a very fine lively one, and take Flora for your partner, who, you see, has sat in a corner quite discomposed since she lost her partner, and by the next set Colin will be disengaged."

Amanda declared she could not dance, and Miss Macqueen being called to her place at the instant, she was again left to herself. Miss Macqueen, however, continued to come and chat with her whenever she could do so without losing any part of the dance. At last Lord Mortimer followed her. The eyes of Amanda were involuntarily bent to the ground when she saw him approach:—"You are an absolute runaway," cried he to Miss Macqueen; "how do you suppose I will excuse your frequent desertions?"

"Why, Miss Donald is so lonely," said she.

"See," cried he, with quickness, "your sister beckons you to her. Suffer me (taking her hand) to lead you to her."

Amanda looked up as they moved from her, and saw Lord Mortimer's head half turned back; but the instant she perceived him he averted it, and took no further notice of her. When the set was finished, Miss Macqueen returned to Amanda, and was fol lowed by some of her brothers and sisters. Some of the gentlemen also approached Amanda, and requested the honor of her hand, but she was steady in refusing all. Rich wines, sweetmeats, and warm lemonade, were now handed about in profusion, and the strains of the violin were succeeded by those of the bagpipe, played by the family musician, venerable in his appearance, and habited in the ancient Highland dress. With as much satisfaction to himself as his Scotch auditors, he played a lively Scotch reel, which in a moment brought two of the Miss Macqueens and two gentlemen forward, and they continued the dance till politeness induced them to stop, that one might be begun in which the rest of the party could join. Dancing continued in this manner with little intermission, but whenever there was an interval, the young Macqueens paid every attention to Amanda; and on her expressing her admiration of the Scotch music, made it a point that she should mention some favorite airs that they might be played for her; but these airs, the lively dances, the animated conversation, and the friendly attentions paid her, could not remove her dejection, and with truth they might have said—

> "That nothing could a charm impart
> To soothe the stranger's woe."

The entrance of Mrs. Macqueen was the signal for the dance being ended. She made the young people sit down to refresh themselves before supper, and apologized to Amanda for not returning to her; but said Lady Martha Dormer had engaged her in a conversation which she could not interrupt. At last they were summoned to supper, which, on Mr. Macqueen's account, was laid out in a room on the same floor. Thither without ceremony whoever was next the door first proceeded. Mr. Macqueen was already seated at the table in his arm-chair, and Lady Martha Dormer on his right hand. The eldest son was deputed to do the honors of the foot of the table. The company was chequered, and Amanda found herself seated between Lord Mortimer and Mr. Colin Macqueen; and in conversing with the latter, Amanda sought to avoid noticing, or being noticed by Lord Mortimer; and his lordship, by the particular attention which he paid Miss Macqueen, who sat on the other side, appeared actuated by the same wish

The sports of the morning had furnished the table with a variety of the choicest wild fowl, and the plenty and beauty of the confectionery denoted at once the hospitable spirit and elegant taste of the mistress of the feast. Gaiety presided at the board, and there was scarcely a tongue, except Amanda's, which did not utter some lively sally. The piper sat in the lobby, and if his strains were not melodious, they were at least cheerful. In the course of supper, Lord Mortimer was compelled to follow the universal example in drinking Amanda's health. Obliged to turn her looks to him, oh! how did her heart shrink at the glance, the expressive glance of his eye, as he pronounced Miss Donald. Unconscious whether she had noticed in the usual manner his distressing compliment, she abruptly turned to young Macqueen, and addressed some scarcely articulate question to him. The supper things removed, the strains of the piper were silenced, and songs, toasts, and sentiments succeeded. Old Mr. Macqueen set the example by a favorite Scotch air, and then called upon his next neighbor. Between the songs, toasts were called for. At last it came to Lord Mortimer's turn. Amanda suddenly ceased speaking to young Macqueen. She saw the glass of Lord Mortimer filled, and in the next moment heard the name of Lady Euphrasia Sutherland. A feeling like wounded pride stole into the soul of Amanda. She did not decline her head as before, and she felt a faint glow upon her cheek. The eyes of Lady Martha and Lady Araminta she thought directed to her with an expressive meaning. "They think," cried she, "to witness mortification and disappointment in my looks, but they shall not (if, indeed, they are capable of enjoying such a triumph) have it."

At length she was called upon for a song. She declined he call; but Mr. Macqueen declared, except assured she could not sing, she should not be excused. This assurance, without a breach of truth, she could not give. She did not wish to appear ungrateful to her kind entertainers, or unsocial in the midst of mirth, by refusing what she was told would be pleasing to them and their company. She also wished, from a sudden impulse of pride, to appear cheerful in those eyes she knew were attentively observing her, and therefore, after a little hesitation, consented to sing. The first song which occurred to her was a little simple, but pathetic air, which her father used to delight in, and which Lord Mortimer more than once had heard from her; but indeed she could recollect no song which at some time or other she had not sung for him. The simple air she had chosen seemed perfectly adapted to her soft voice, whose modulations were inexpressibly affecting. She had proceeded through half the second verse, when her voice began to falter. The attention of the company became, if possible, more fixed; but it was a vain attention; no rich strain of melody repaid it, for the voice of the songstress had totally ceased. Mrs. Macqueen, with the delicacy of a susceptible mind, feared increasing her emotion by noticing it, and, with a glance of her expressive eye, directed her company to silence. Amanda's eyes were bent to the ground. Suddenly a glass of water was presented to her by a trembling hand—by the hand of Mortimer himself. She declined it with a motion of hers, and, reviving a little, raised her head. Young Macqueen then gave her an entreating whisper to finish the song. She thought it would look like affectation to require farther solicitation, and, faintly smiling, again began in strains of liquid melody, strains that seemed to breathe the very spirit of sensibility, and came over each attentive ear,

> "Like a sweet sound
> That breathes upon a bank of violets
> Stealing and giving odor."

The plaudits she received from her singing gave to her cheeks such a faint tinge of red as is seen in the bosom of the wild rose. She was now authorized to call for a song, and, as if doomed to experience cause for agitation, Lord Mortimer was the person from whom, in the rotation of the table, she was to claim it. Thrice she was requested to do this ere she could obey. At last she raised her eyes to his face, which was now turned towards her, and she saw in it a confusion equal to that she herself trembled under. Pale and red by turns, he appeared to her to wait in painful agitation for the sound of her voice. Her lips moved, but she could not articulate a word. Lord Mortimer bowed, as if he had heard what they would have said, and then turning abruptly to Miss Macqueen, began speaking to her.

"Come, come, my Lord," said Mr. Macqueen, "we must not be put off in this manner."

Lord Mortimer laughed, and attempted to rally the old gentleman; but he seemed unequal to the attempt, for, with a sudden seriousness, he declared his inability of complying with the present demand. All farther solicitation on the subject was immediately dropped. In the round of toasts, they forgot not to call upon Amanda for one. If she had listened attentively when Lord Mortimer was about giving one, no less attentively did he now listen to her. She hesitated a moment, and then gave Sir Charles Bingley. After the toast had passed, "Sir Charles Bingley," repeated Miss Macqueen, leaning forward, and speaking across Lord Mortimer. "Oh! I recollect him very well. His regiment was quartered about two years ago at a little fort some distance from this—and I remember his coming with a shooting party to the mountains, and sleeping one night here. We had a delightful dance that evening, and all thought him a charming young man. Pray, are you well acquainted with him?" "Yes—No," replied Amanda.

"Ah! I believe you are, sly girl," cried Miss Macqueen, laughing. "Pray, my Lord, does not that blush declare Miss Donald guilty?" "We are not always to judge from the countenance," said he, darting a penetrating yet quickly-withdrawn glance at Amanda. "Experience," continued he, "daily proves how little dependence is to be placed on it." Amanda turned hastily away, and pretended, by speaking to young Macqueen, not to notice a speech she knew directly pointed at her; for often had Lord Mortimer declared that, "in the lineaments of the human face divine, each passion of the soul might be well traced."

Miss Macqueen laughed, and said she always judged of the countenance, and that her likings and dislikings were always the effects of first sight.

The company broke up soon after this, and much earlier than their usual hour, on account of the travellers. All but those then immediately belonging to the family having departed, some maids of the house appeared, to show the ladies to their respective chambers. Lady Martha and Lady Araminta retired first Amanda was following them, when Mrs. Macqueen detained her, to try and prevail on her to stay two or three days along with them. The Miss Macqueens joined their mother; but Amanda assured them she could not comply with their request, though she felt with gratitude its friendly warmth. Old Mr. Macqueen had had his chair turned to the fire, and his sons and Lord Mortimer were surrounding it. "Well, well," said he, calling Amanda to him, and taking her hand, "if you will not stay with us now, remember, on your return, we shall lay an embargo on you. In the meantime, I shall not lose the privilege which my being an old married man gives me." So saying, he gently pulled Amanda to him, and kissed her cheek. She could only smile at this innocent freedom, but she attempted to withdraw her hand to retire. "Now," said Mr. Macqueen, still detaining it, "are all these young men half mad with envy?" The young Macqueens joined in their father's gallantry, and not a tongue was silent except Lord Mortimer's. His head rested on his hand, and the cornice of the chimney supported his arm. His hair, from which the dancing had almost shaken all the powder, hung negligently about his face, and added to its paleness and sudden dejection. One of the young Macqueens, turning from his brothers, who were yet continuing their mirth with their father, addressed some question to his lordship, but received no answer. Again he repeated it. Lord Mortimer then suddenly started, as if from a profound reverie, and apologised for his absence.

"Ay, ah, my lord," exclaimed old Mr. Macqueen, jocosely, "we may all guess where your lordship was then travelling in idea—a little beyond the mountains, I fancy. Ay, we all know where your heart and your treasure now lie." "Do you?" said Lord Mortimer, with a tone of deep dejection, and a heavy sigh, with an air, also, which seemed to declare him scarcely conscious of what he said. He recollected himself, however, at the instant, and began rallying himself, as the surest means of preventing others doing so. The scene was too painful to Amanda. She hastily withdrew her hand, and, faintly wishing the party a good night, went out to the maid, who was waiting for her in the lobby, and was conducted to her room. She dismissed the servant at the door, and, throwing herself into a chair, availed herself of solitude to give vent to the tears whose painful suppression had so long tortured her heart. She had not sat long in this situation when she heard a gentle tap at the door. She started, and believing it to be one of the Miss Macqueens, hastily wiped away her tears, and opened the door. A female stranger appeared at it, who courtseying, respectfully said, "Lady Martha Dormer, her lady, desired to see Miss Donald for a few minutes, if not inconvenient to her." "See me!" repeated Amanda, with the utmost surprise; "can it be possible?" She suddenly checked herself, and said, "she would attend her ladyship immediately." She accordingly followed the maid, a variety of strange ideas crowding upon her mind. Her conductress retired as she shut the door of the room into which she showed Amanda. It was a small ante-chamber adjoining the apartment Lady Martha was to lie in. Here, with increasing surprise, she beheld Lord Mortimer pacing the room in an agitated manner. His back was to the door as she entered, but he turned round with quickness, approached, looked on her a few moments, then, striking his hand suddenly against his forehead, turned from her with an air of distraction.

Lady Martha, who was sitting at the head of the room, and only bowed as Amanda entered it, motioned for her to take a chair; a motion Amanda gladly obeyed, for her trembling limbs could scarcely support her.

All was silent for a few minutes. Lady Martha then spoke in a grave voice:—"I should not, madam, have taken the liberty of sending for you at this hour, but that I believe so favorable an opportunity would not again have occurred of speaking to you on a subject particularly interesting to me—an opportunity which has so unexpectedly saved me the trouble of trying to find you out, and the necessity of writing to you."

Lady Martha paused, and her silence was not interrupted by Amanda. "Last summer," continued Lady Martha—again she paused. The throbbings of Amanda's heart became more violent. "Last summer," said she again, "there were some little gifts presented to you by Lord Mortimer. From the events which followed their acceptance, I must presume they are valueless to you: from the events about taking place, they are of importance elsewhere." She ceased, but Amanda could make no reply.

"You cannot be ignorant," said Lady Martha, with something of severity in her accent, as if offended by the silence of Amanda, "you cannot be ignorant, I suppose, that it is the picture and ring I allude to. The latter, from being a family one of particular value, I always destined for the wife of Lord Mortimer; I therefore claim it in my own name. The picture, I have his lordship's approbation and authority to demand; and to convince you I have,—indeed, if such a conviction be necessary,—have prevailed on him to be present at this conversation." "No, madam, such a conviction was not necessary," cried Amanda. "I should——" She could utter no more at the moment, yet tried to suppress the agonizing feeling that tumultuously heaved her bosom.

"If not convenient to restore them immediately," said Lady Martha, "I will give you a direction where they may be left in London, to which place Mrs. Macqueen has informed me you are going." "It is perfectly convenient now to restore them, madam," replied Amanda, with a voice perfectly recovered, animated with conscious innocence and offended pride, which always gave her strength. "I shall return," continued she, moving to the door, "with them immediately to your ladyship."

The picture was suspended from her neck, and the ring in its case lay in her pocket; but by the manner in which they had been asked, or rather demanded from her, she felt amidst the anguish of her soul a sudden emotion of pleasure that she could directly give them back. Yet, when in her own room she hastily untied the picture from her neck, pulled the black ribbon from it, and laid it in its case, her grief overcame every other feeling, and a shower of tears fell from her. "Oh, Mortimer! dear Mortimer!" she sighed, "must I part even with this little shadow! must I retain no vestige of happier hours! Yet, why—why should I wish to retain it, when the original will so soon be another's? Yes, if I behold Mortimer again, it will be as the husband of Lady Euphrasia."

She recollected she was staying beyond the expected time, and wiped away her tears. Yet, still she lingered a few minutes in the chamber, to try to calm her agitation. She called her pride to her aid; it inspired her with fortitude, and she proceeded to Lady Martha, determined that lady should see nothing in her manner which she could possibly construe into weakness or meanness. Never did she appear more interesting than at the moment she re-entered the apartment. The passion she had called to her aid gave a bright glow to her cheeks, and the traces of the tears she had been shedding appeared upon those glowing cheeks like dew on the silken leaves of the rose ere the sunbeams of the morning have exhaled it. Those tears left an humble lustre in her eyes, even more interesting than their wonted brilliancy. Her hair hung in rich and unrestrained luxuriance—for she had thrown off her hat on first going to her chamber—and gave to the beauty of her face, and the elegance of her form, a complete finishing.

"Here, madam, is the ring," cried she, presenting it to Lady Martha, "and here is the picture," she would have added, but her voice faltered, and a tear started from her eye. Determined to conceal, if possible, her feelings, she hastily dashed away the pearly fugitive. Lady Martha was again extending her hand when Lord Mortimer suddenly started from a couch on which he had thrown himself, and snatching the picture from the trembling hand that held it, pulled it from its case, and flinging it on the floor, trampled it beneath his feet. "Thus perish," exclaimed he, "every memento of my attachment to Amanda! Oh, wretched, wretched girl!" cried he, suddenly grasping her hand, and as suddenly relinquishing it, "Oh, wretched, wretched girl! you have undone yourself and me!" He turned abruptly away, and instantly quitted the room. Shocked by his words, and terrified by his manner, Amanda had just power to gain a chair. Lady Martha seemed also thunderstruck; but, from the musing attitude in which she stood, the deep convulsive suffocating sobs of Amanda soon called her. She went to her, and finding her unable to help herself, loosened her cravat, bathed her temples with lavender, and gave her water to drink. These attentions, and the tears she shed, revived Amanda. She raised herself in her chair, on which she had fallen back, but was yet too much agitated to stand.

"Poor, unhappy young creature!" said Lady Martha, "I pity you from my soul! Ah! if your mind resembled your person, what a perfect creature had you been! How happy had then been my poor Mortimer!"

Now, now was the test, the shining test of Amanda's virtue, agonized by knowing she had lost the good opinion of those whom she loved with such ardor, esteemed with such reverence. She knew by a few words she could explain the appearances which had deprived her of his good opinion, and fully regain it—regain, by a few words, the love, the esteem of her valued, her inestimable Mortimer—the affection, the protection, of his amiable aunt and sister. She leaned her head upon her hand, the weight on her bosom became less oppressive; she raised her head. "Of my innocence I can give such proofs," cried she. Her lips closed, a mortal paleness overspread her face; the sound of suicide seemed piercing through her ear; she trembled; the solemn, the dreadful declaration Lord Cherbury had made of not surviving the disclosure of his secret, her promise of inviolably keeping it, both rushed upon her mind. She beheld herself on the very verge of a tremendous precipice, and about plunging herself and a fellow-creature into it, from whence, at the tribunal of her God, she would have to answer for accelerating the death of that fellow-creature. "And is it by a breach of faith?" she asked herself, "I hope to be re-established in the opinion of Lord Mortimer and his relations. Ah! mistaken idea, and how great is the delusion passion spreads before our eyes, even if their esteem could be thus regained? Oh! what were that, or what the esteem, the plaudits of the world, if those of my own heart were gone for ever! Oh! never!" cried she, still to herself, and raising her eyes to Heaven, "Oh! never may the pang of self-reproach be added to those which now oppress me!" Her heart at the moment formed a solemn vow never, by any wilful act, to merit such a pang. "And, oh, my God!" she cried, "forgive thy weak creature who, assailed by strong temptation, thought for a moment of wandering from the path of truth and integrity, which can alone conduct her to the region where peace and immortal glory will be hers."

Amanda, amidst her powerful emotions, forgot she was observed, except by that Being to whom she applied for pardon and future strength. Lady Martha had been a silent spectator of her emotions, and, thinking as she did of Amanda, could only hope that they proceeded from contrition for her past conduct, forcibly awakened by reflecting on the deprivations it had caused her.

When she again saw Amanda able to pay attention, she addressed her: "I said I was sorry for witnessing your distress; I shall not repeat the expression, thinking as I now do; I hope that it is occasioned by regret for past errors: the tears of repentance wash away the stains of guilt, and that heart must indeed be callous which the sigh of remorse will not melt to pity." Amanda turned her eyes with earnestness on Lady Martha as she spoke, and her cheeks were again tinged with a faint glow.

"Perhaps I speak too plainly," cried Lady Martha, witnessing this glow, and imputing it to resentment; "but I have ever liked the undisguised language of sincerity. It gave me pleasure," she continued, "to hear you had been in employment at Mrs. Duncan's, but that pleasure was destroyed by hearing you were going to London, though to seek your brother; Mrs. Duncan has informed Mrs. Macqueen. If this were indeed the motive, there are means of inquiring without taking so imprudent a step." "Imprudent!" repeated Amanda, involuntarily. "Yes," cried Lady Martha, "a journey so long, without a protector, to a young, I must add, a lovely woman, teems with danger, from which a mind of delicacy would shrink appalled. If, indeed, you go to seek your brother, and he regards you as he should, he would rather have you neglect him (though that you need not have done by staying with Mrs. Duncan), than run into the way of insults. No emergency in life should lead us to do an improper thing; as trying to produce good by evil is impious, so trying to produce pleasure by imprudence is folly; they are trials, however flatteringly they may commence, which are sure to end in sorrow and disappointment.

"You will," continued Lady Martha, "if indeed anxious to escape from any farther censure than what has already fallen upon you, return to Mrs. Duncan, when I inform you (if indeed you are already ignorant of it) that Colonel Belgrave passed this road about a month ago, on his way from a remote part of Scotland to London, where he now is." "I cannot help," said Amanda, "the misconstructions which may be put on my actions; I can only support myself under the pain they inflict by conscious rectitude. I am shocked, indeed, at the surmises entertained about me, and a wretch whom my soul abhorred from the moment I knew his real principles."

"If," said Lady Martha, "your journey is really not prompted by the intention of seeing your brother, you heighten every other by duplicity." "You are severe, madam," exclaimed Amanda, in whose soul the pride of injured innocence was again reviving.

"If I probe the wound," cried Lady Martha, "I would also

wish to heal it. It is the wish I feel of saving a young creature from further error, of serving a being once so valued by him who possesses my first regard, that makes me speak as I now do. Return to Mrs. Duncan's, prove in one instance at least you do not deserve suspicion. She is your friend, and in your situation a friend is too precious a treasure to run the risk of losing it with her; as she lives retired, there will be little danger of your history or real name being discovered, which I am sorry you dropped, let your motive for doing so be what it may, for the detection of one deception makes us suspect every other. Return, I repeat, to Mrs. Duncan's, and if you want any inquiries made about your brother, dictate them, and I will take care they shall be made, and that you shall know their result."

Had Amanda's motive for a journey to London been only to seek her brother, she would gladly have accepted this offer, thus avoiding the imputation of travelling after Belgrave, or of going to join him, the hazard of encountering him in London, and the dangers of so long a journey; but the affair of the will required expedition, and her own immediate presence—an affair the injunction of Lady Dunreath had prohibited her disclosing to any one who could not immediately forward it, and which, if such an injunction never existed, she could not with propriety have divulged to Lady Martha, who was so soon to be connected with a family so materially concerned in it, and in whose favor, on account of her nephew's connection with them, it was probable she might be biassed.

Amanda hoped and believed that in a place so large as London, and with her assumed name (which she now resolved not to drop till in a more secure situation), she should escape Belgrave. As to meeting him on the road she had not the smallest apprehension concerning that, naturally concluding that he never would have taken so long a journey as he had lately done, if he could have stayed but a few weeks away. Time, she trusted, would prove the falsity of the inference, which she already was informed would be drawn from her persevering in her journey. She told Lady Martha "that she thanked her for her kind offer, but must decline it, as the line of conduct she had marked out for herself rendered it unnecessary whose innocence would yet be justified," she added

Lady Martha shook her head; the consciousness of having excited suspicions which she could not justify, had indeed given to the looks of Amanda a confusion when she spoke which confirmed them in Lady Martha's breast. "I am sorry for your determination," said she, "but notwithstanding it is so contrary to my ideas of what is right, I cannot let you depart without telling you that, should you at any time want or require services, which you would, or could not, ask from strangers, or perhaps expect them to perform, acquaint me, and command mine; yet, in doing justice to my own feelings, I must not do injustice to the noble ones of Lord Mortimer. It is by his desire, as well as my own inclination, I now speak to you in this manner, though past events, and the situation he is about entering into, must for ever preclude his personal interference in your affairs. He could never hear the daughter of Captain Fitzalan suffered inconveniency of any kind, without wishing, without having her, indeed, if possible extricated from it." "Oh! madam," cried Amanda, unable to repress her gushing tears, "I am already well acquainted with the noble feelings of Lord Mortimer, already oppressed with a weight of obligations." Lady Martha was affected by her energy; her eyes grew humid, and her voice softened. "Error in you will be more inexcusable than in others," cried Lady Martha, "because, like too many unhappy creatures, you cannot plead the desertion of all the world. To regret past errors, be they what they may, is to insure my assistance and protection, if both, or either, are at any time required by you. Was I even gone, I should take care tc leave a substitute behind me who should fulfil my intentions towards you, and by so doing at once soothe and gratify the feelings of Lord Mortimer." "I thank you, madam," cried Amanda, rising from her chair, and, as she wiped away her tears, summoning all her fortitude to her aid, "for the interest you express about me; the time may yet come, perhaps, when I shall prove I never was unworthy of exciting it—when the notice now offered from compassion may be tendered from esteem—then," continued Amanda, who could not forbear this justice to herself, "the pity of Lady Martha Dormer will not humble but exalt me, because then I shall know that it proceeded from that generous sympathy which one virtuous mind feels for another in distress." She moved to the door. "How lamentable," said Lady Martha, "to have such talents misapplied!" "Ah! madam," cried Amanda, stopping, and turning mournfully to her, "I find you are inflexible."

Lady Martha shook her head, and Amanda had laid her hand upon the lock, when Lady Martha said suddenly, "There were letters passed between you and Lord Mortimer." Amanda bowed "They had better be mutually returned," said Lady Martha. "Do you seal up his and send them to Lord Cherbury's house in London, directed to me, and I will pledge myself to have yours returned." "You shall be obeyed, madam," replied Amanda, in a low, broken voice, after the pause of a moment. Lady Martha then said she would no longer encroach upon her rest, and she retired.

In her chamber, the feelings she had so long, so painfully tried to suppress, broke forth without again meeting opposition. The pride which had given her transient animation was no more; for, as past circumstances arose to recollection, she could not wonder at her being condemned from them. She no longer accused Lady Martha in her mind of severity—no longer felt offended with her; but, oh! Mortimer, the bitter tears she shed fell not for herself alone; she wept to think thy destiny, though more prosperous, was not less unhappy than her own; for in thy broken accents, thy altered looks, she perceived a passion strong and sincere as ever for her, and well she knew Lady Euphrasia not calculated to soothe a sad heart, or steal an image from it which corroded its felicity. Rest, after the incidents of the evening, was not to be thought of, but nature was exhausted, and insensibly Amanda sunk upon the bed in a deep sleep—so insensibly, that when she awoke, which was not till the morning was pretty far advanced, she felt surprised at her situation. She felt cold and unrefreshed from having lain in her clothes all night, and when she went to adjust her dress at the glass, was surprised at the pallidness of her looks. Anxious to escape a second painful meeting, she went to the window to see if the chaise was come, but was disappointed on finding that she had slept at the back of the house. She heard no noise, and concluding the family had not yet risen after the amusements of the preceding night, sat down by the window which looked into a spacious garden, above which rose romantic hills that formed a screen for some young and beautiful plantations that lay between them and the garden; but the misty tops of the hills, the varied trees which autumn spread over the plantations, nor the neat appearance of the garden, had power to amuse the imagination of Amanda. Her patience was exhausted after sitting some time, and going to the door she softly opened it, to try if she could hear any one stirring. She had not stood long, when the sound of footsteps and voices rose from below. She instantly quitted her room, and descended the stairs into a small hall, across which was a folding door; this she gently opened, and found it divided the hall she stood in from the one that was spacious and lofty, and which her passing through the preceding night before it was lighted up, had prevented her taking notice of. Here, at a long table, were the men servants belonging to the family, and the guests assembled at breakfast, the piper at the head, like the king of the feast. Amanda stepped back the moment she perceived them, well knowing Lord Mortimer's servants would recollect her, and was ascending the stairs to her room to ring for one of the maids, when a servant hastily followed her, and said the family were already in the breakfast-room. At the same moment, Mr. Colin Macqueen came from a parlor which opened into the little hall, and paying Amanda, in a lively and affectionate manner, the compliments of the morning, he led her to the parlor, where not only all the family guests who had lain in the house, but several gentlemen, who had been with them the preceding night, were assembled. Doctor Johnson has already celebrated a Scotch breakfast, nor was the one at which Mrs. Macqueen and her fair daughters presided inferior to any he had seen. Besides chocolate, tea, and coffee, with the usual appendages, there were rich cakes, choice sweetmeats, and a variety of cold pastry, with ham and chickens, to which several of the gentlemen did honor. The dishes were ornamented with sweet herbs and wild flowers, gathered about the feet of the mountains and in the valley, and by every guest was placed a fine bouquet from the green-house, with little French mottoes on love and friendship about them, which, being opened and read, added to the mirth of the company.

"I was just going to send one of the girls for you," said Mrs. Macqueen, when Amanda had taken a place at the table, "and would have done so before, but wished you to get as much rest as possible, after your fatiguing journey." "I assure you, madam," said Amanda, "I have been up this long time, expecting every moment a summons to the chaise." "I took care of that last night," said Mrs. Macqueen, "for I was determined you should not depart, at least without breakfasting." Amanda was seated between Mr. Colin Macqueen and his eldest sister, and sought, by conversing with the former, for the latter was too much engrossed by the general gaiety to pay much attention to any one, to avoid the looks she dreaded to see. Yet the sound of Lord Mortimer's voice affected her as much almost as his looks.

"Pray, Lady Martha," said the second Miss Macqueen, a lively, thoughtless girl, "will your ladyship be so good as to guarantee a promise Lord Mortimer has just made me, or rather that I have extorted from him, which is the cause of this application?" "You must first, my dear," answered Lady Martha, "let me know what the promise is." "Why, gloves and bridal favors; but most unwillingly granted, I can assure your ladyship." Amanda was obliged to set down the cup she was raising to her lips, and a glance stole involuntarily from her towards Lord Mortimer—a glance instantly withdrawn when she saw his eyes in the same direction. "I declare," continued Miss Phœbe Macqueen, "I should do the favor all due honor." "I am sure," cried Lord Mortimer, attempting to speak cheerfully, "your acceptance of it would do honor to the presenter." "And your lordship may be sure, too," said one of her brothers, "it is a favor she would wish with all her heart to have an opportunity of returning." "Oh! in that she would not be singular," said a gentleman. "What do you think, Miss Donald," cried Colin Macqueen, turning to Amanda, "do you imagine she would not?" Amanda could scarcely speak. She tried, however, to hide her agitation, and, forcing a faint smile, with a voice nearly as faint, said, "that was not a fair question." The Miss Macqueens took upon themselves to answer it, and Amanda, through their means, was relieved from farther embarrassment.

Breakfast over, Amanda was anxious to depart, and yet wanted courage to be the first to move. A charm seemed to bind her to the spot where, for the last time, she should behold Lord Mortimer, at least the last time she ever expected to see him unmarried.

Her dread of being late on the road—and she heard the destined stage for the night was at a great distance—at last conquered her reluctance to move, and she said to Mr. Colin Macqueen it was time for her to go. At that moment Lord Mortimer rose, and proposed to the young Macqueens going with them to see the new plantations behind the house, which old Mr. Macqueen had expressed a desire his lordship should give his opinion of.

All the young gentlemen, as well as the Macqueens, Colin excepted, attended his lordship; nor did they depart without wishing Amanda a pleasant journey.

Silent and sad, she continued in her chair for some minutes after they quitted the room, forgetful of her situation, till the loud laugh of the Miss Macqueens restored her to a recollection of it. She blushed, and, rising hastily, was proceeding to pay her farewell compliments, when Mrs. Macqueen, rising, drew her to the window, and in a low voice repeated her request for Amanda's company a few days. This Amanda again declined, but gratefully expressed her thanks for it, and the hospitality she had experienced. Mrs. Macqueen said, on her return to Scotland, she hoped to be more successful. She also added, that some of her boys and girls would gladly have accompanied Amanda a few miles on her way, had not they all agreed, ere her arrival, to escort Lord Mortimer's party to an inn at no great distance, and take an early dinner with them. She should write that day, she said, to Mrs. Duncan, and thank her for having introduced to her family a person whose acquaintance was an acquisition. Amanda, having received the affectionate adieus of this amiable woman and her daughters, courtseyed, though with downcast looks, to Lady Martha and Lady Araminta, who returned her salutation with coolness.

Followed by two of the Miss Macqueens, she hurried through the hall, from which the servants and the breakfast things were already removed; but how was she distressed, when the first object she saw outside the door was Lord Mortimer, by whom stood Colin Macqueen—who had left the parlor to see if the chaise was ready—and one of his brothers. Hastily would she have stepped forward to the chaise, had not the gallantry of the young men impeded her way. They expressed sorrow at her not staying longer among them, and hopes on her return she would.

"Pray, my Lord," cried the Miss Macqueens, while their brothers were thus addressing Amanda, "pray, my Lord," almost in the same breath, "what have you done with the gentlemen?" "You should ask your brother," he replied; "he has locked them up in the plantation." A frolic was at all times pleasing to the light-hearted Macqueens, and to enjoy the present one off they ran directly, followed by their brothers, all calling, as they ran, to Amanda not to stir till they came back, which would be in a few minutes; but Amanda, from the awkward, the agitating situation in which they had left her, would instantly have relieved herself, could she have made the postilion hear her; but, as if enjoying the race, he had gone to some distance to view it, and none of the servants of the house were near. Conscious of her own emotions, she feared betraying them, and stepped a few yards from the door, pretending to be engrossed by the Macqueens. A heavy sigh suddenly pierced her ears. "Amanda," in the next moment said a voice to which her heart vibrated. She turned with involuntary quickness and saw Lord Mortimer close by her. "Amanda," he repeated; then suddenly clasping his hands together, exclaimed, with an agonized expression, while he turned abruptly from her, "Gracious Heaven! what a situation! Amanda," said he, again looking at her, "the scene which happened last night was distressing. I am now sorry on your account that it took place. Notwithstanding past events, I bear you no ill-will. The knowledge of your uneasiness would give me pain. From my heart I forgive you all that you have caused—that you have entailed upon me. At this moment I could take you to my arms, and weep over you—like the fond mother over the last darling of her hopes—tears of pity and forgiveness."

Amanda, unutterably affected, covered her face to hide the tears which bedewed it.

"Let me have the pleasure of hearing," continued Lord Mortimer, "that you forgive the uneasiness and pain I might have occasioned you last night." "Forgive!" repeated Amanda. "Oh, my Lord," and her voice sunk in the sobs which heaved her bosom. "Could I think you were, you would be happy—" Lord Mortimer stopped, overcome by strong emotions.

"Happy!" repeated Amanda; "oh! never—never!" continued

she, raising her streaming eyes to heaven; "oh, never—never in this world!"

At this moment the Macqueens were not only heard but seen running back, followed by the gentlemen whom they had been prevailed on to liberate. Shocked at the idea of being seen in such a situation, Amanda would have called the postilion, but he was too far off to hear her weak voice, had she then even been able to exert that voice. She looked towards him, however, with an expression which denoted the feelings of her soul. Lord Mortimer, sensible of those feelings, hastily pulled open the door of the chaise, and taking the cold and trembling hand of Amanda with one equally cold and trembling, assisted her into the chaise, then pressing the hand he held between both his, he suddenly let it drop from him, and closing the door without again looking at Amanda, called to the driver, who instantly obeyed the call, and had mounted ere the Macqueens arrived. Oh, what a contrast did their looks, blooming with health and exercise, their gaiety, their protected situation, form to the wan, dejected, desolate Amanda! With looks of surprise they were going up to the chaise, when Lord Mortimer, still standing by it, and anxious to save his unhappy, lost Amanda the pain of being noticed in such agitation, gave the man a signal to drive off, which was instantly obeyed.

Thus did Amanda leave the mansion of the Macqueens, where sorrow had scarcely ever before entered without meeting alleviation, a mansion, where the stranger, the wayfaring man, and the needy, were sure of a welcome, cordial as benevolence and hospitality themselves could give; and where happiness, as pure as in this sublunary state can be experienced, was enjoyed. As she drove from the door, she saw the splendid equipages of Lord Mortimer and Lady Martha driving to it. She turned from them with a sigh, at reflecting they would soon grace the bridal pomp of Lady Euphrasia. She pursued the remainder of her journey without meeting anything worthy of relation. It was in the evening she reached London. The moment she stopped at the hotel she sent for a carriage, and proceeded in it to Mrs. Connel's, in Bond Street.

CHAPTER L.

"Dissembling hope, her cloudy front she clears,
And a false vigor in her eyes appears."—DRYDEN.

HE alighted from the carriage when it stopped at the door, and entered the shop, where, to her inexpressible satisfaction, the first object she beheld was Miss Rushbrook, sitting pensively at one of the counters. The moment she saw Amanda she recollected her, and, starting up, exclaimed, as she took her hand, "Ah! dear madam, this is indeed a joyful surprise! Ah! how often have I wished to meet you again to express my gratitude." The affectionate reception she met, and the unexpected sight of Miss Rushbrook, seemed to promise Amanda that her wishes relative to Rushbrook would not only be accelerated, but crowned with success. She returned the fervent pressure of Miss Rushbrook's hand, and inquired after her parents—the inquiry appeared distressing, and she was answered with hesitation, that they were indifferent. The evident embarrassment her question excited prevented her renewing it at this time. The mistress of the house was not present, and Amanda requested, if she was within, she might see her directly. Miss Rushbrook immediately stepped to a parlor behind the shop, and almost instantly returned, followed by the lady herself, who was a little fat Irish woman, past her prime, but not past her relish for the good things of this life. "Dear madam," said she, courtseying to Amanda, "you are very welcome. I protest I am very glad to see you, though I never had that pleasure but once before; but it is no wonder I should be so, for I have heard your praises every day since, I am sure, from that young lady," looking at Miss Rushbrook. Amanda bowed, but her heart was too full of the purpose of this visit to allow her to speak about anything else. She was just come from the country, she told Mrs. Connel, where (she sighed as she spoke) she had left her friends, and, being unwilling to go amongst total strangers, she had come to her house in hopes of being able to procure lodgings in it.

"Dear ma'am," said Mrs. Connel, "I protest I should have

been happy to have accommodated you, but at present my house is quite full."

The disappointment this speech gave Amanda rendered her silent for a moment, and she was then going to ask Mrs. Connel if she could recommend her to a lodging, when she perceived Miss Rushbrook whispering her. "Why, madam," cried the former, who, by a nod of her head, seemed to approve of what the latter had been saying, "since you dislike so much going among strangers, which, indeed, shows your prudence, considering what queer kind of people are in the world, Miss Emily says, that if you condescend to accept of part of her little bed, till you can settle yourself more comfortably in town, you shall be extremely welcome to it; and I can assure you, madam, I shall do everything in my power to render my house agreeable to you." "Oh, most joyfully, most thankfully, do I accept the offer," said Amanda, whose heart had sunk at the idea of going amongst strangers. "Any place," she continued, speaking in the fulness of that agitated heart, "beneath so reputable a roof, would be an asylum of comfort I should prefer to a palace, if utterly unacquainted with the people who inhabited it." Her trunk was now brought in, and the carriage discharged. "I suppose, ma'am," said Mrs. Connel, looking at the trunk on which her assumed name was marked, "you are Scotch by your name, though, indeed, you have not much of the accent about you." "I declare," cried Emily, also looking at it, "till this moment I was ignorant of your name."

Amanda was pleased to hear this, and resolved not to disclose her real one, except convinced Rushbrook would interest himself in her affairs. She was conducted into the parlor, which was neatly furnished, and opened into the shop by a glass door. Mrs. Connel stirred a declining fire into a cheerful blaze, and desired to know if Amanda would choose anything for dinner. "Speak the word only, my dear," said she, "and I think I can procure you a cold bone in the house. If you had come two hours sooner, I could have given you a bit of nice veal for your dinner." Amanda assured her she did not wish to take anything till tea-time.

"Well, well," cried Mrs. Connel, "you shall have a snug cup of tea by-and-by, and a hot muffin with it. I am very fond of tea myself. though poor Mr. Connel, who is dead and gone, used often and often to say, 'I that was so nervous should never touch tea;' 'but, Biddy,' he would say, and he would laugh so, poor dear man, 'you and all your sex are like your mother Eve, unable to resist temptation.' "

Emily retired soon after Amanda entered; but returned in a few minutes with her hat and cloak on, and said, nothing but a visit she must pay her parents should have induced her to forego, for the first evening, at least, the pleasure of Miss Donald's society. Amanda thanked her for her politeness, but assured her if considered as a restraint she should be unhappy.

"I assure you," said Mrs. Connel, as Emily departed, "she is very fond of you." "I am happy to hear it," replied Amanda, "for I think her a most amiable girl." "Indeed she is," cried the other; "all the fault I find with her is being too grave for her time of life. Poor thing, one cannot wonder at that, however, considering the situation of her parents." "I hope," interrupted Amanda, "it is not so bad as it was." "Bad! Lord! it cannot be worse; the poor Captain has been in jail above a year." "I am sorry," said Amanda, "to hear this. Has any application been made to Lady Greystock since his confinement?" "To Lady Greystock! why, Lord! one might as well apply to one of the wild beasts in the Tower! Ah! poor gentleman, if he was never to get nothing but what she gave him, I believe he would not long be a trouble to any one. It is now about fourteen years since my acquaintance with him first commenced. My poor husband, that is no more, and I kept a shop in Dublin, where the Captain's regiment was quartered, and he being only a Lieutenant had not room enough for his family in the barracks, so he took lodgings at our house, where Mrs. Rushbrook lay in, and I being with her now and then during her confinement, a kind of friendship grew up amongst us. They had not left us long to go to America, when a relation of my husband, who owned this house and shop, having lost his wife, and being lonesome, without either chick or child, invited us to come and live with him, promising us if we did, to settle us in his business, and leave us everything he had. Well, such offers do not come every day; so, to be sure, we took him at his word; and here we had not long been when the poor man bid adieu to all mortal care, and was soon followed by Mr. Connel. Well, to be sure, I was sad and solitary enough; but when I thought how irreligious it was to break one's heart with grief, I plucked up my spirits and began to hold up my head again. So, to make a short story of a long one, about six years ago Mrs. Rushbrook and Miss Emily came one day into the shop to buy something, little thinking they should see an old friend. It was, to be sure, a meeting of joy and sorrow, as one may say. We told all our griefs to each other, and I found things were very bad with the poor Captain. Indeed, I have a great regard for him and his family, and when he was confined, I took Emily home as an assistant in my business. The money she earned was to go to her parents, and I agreed to give her her clothes gratis; but that would have gone but a little way in feeding so many mouths, had I not procured plain work for Mrs. Rushbrook and her daughters. Emily is a very good girl, indeed, and it is to see her parents she is now gone. But while I am gabbling away I am sure the kettle is boiling." So saying, she started up, and ringing the bell, took the tea-things from a beaufet where they were kept. The maid having obeyed the well-known summons, then retired; and as soon as the tea was made, and the muffins buttered, Mrs. Connel made Amanda draw her chair close to the table, that she might, as she said, look snug, and drink her tea comfortably.

"I assure you, madam," cried she, "it was a lucky hour for Miss Emily when she entered my house." "I have no doubt of that," said Amanda. "You must know, madam," proceeded Mrs. Connel, "about a month ago a gentleman came to lodge with me, who I soon found was making speeches to Miss Emily. He was one of those wild looking sparks, who, like Ranger in the play, looked as if they would be popping through every one's doors and windows, and playing such tricks as made poor Mr. Strickland so jealous of his wife. Well, I took my gentleman to task one day unawares. 'So, Mr. Sipthorpe,' says I, 'I am told you have cast a sheep's eye upon one of my girls; but I must tell you she is a girl of virtue and family, so if you do not mean to deal honorably with her, you must either decamp from this, or speak to her no more.' Upon this he made me a speech as long as a member of parliament's upon a new tax. 'Lord, Mr. Sipthorpe,' said I, 'there is no occasion for all this oratory, a few words will settle the business between us.'

Well, this was coming close to the point, you will say, and he told me then he always meant to deal honorably by Miss Emily, and told me all about his circumstances; and I found he had a fine fortune, which indeed I partly guessed before from the appearance he made, and he said he would not only marry Miss Emily, but take her parents out of prison, and provide for the whole family. Well, now comes the provoking part of my story. A young clergyman had been kind at the beginning of their distress to them, and he and Miss Emily took it into their heads to fall in love with each other. Well, her parents gave their consent to their being married, which to be sure I thought a very foolish thing, knowing the young man's inability to serve them. To be sure he promised fair enough; but, Lord! what could a poor curate do for them, particularly when he got a wife and a house full of children of his own? I thought; so I supposed they would be quite glad to be off with him, and to give her to Mr. Sipthorpe; but no such thing I assure you. When I mentioned it to them, one talked of honor, and another of gratitude, and as to Miss Emily, she fairly went into fits. Well, I thought I would serve them in spite of themselves, so, knowing the curate to be a romantic young fellow, I writes off to him, and tells him what a cruel thing it would be, if, for his own gratification, he kept Miss Emily to her word, and made her lose a match, which would free her family from all their difficulties; and, in short, I touched upon his passion not a little, I assure you, and, as I hoped, a letter came from him, in which he told her he gave her up. Well, to be sure there was sad work when it came—with her, I mean, for the Captain and his wife were glad enough of it, I believe, in their hearts; so at last everything was settled for her marriage with Mr. Sipthorpe, and he made a number of handsome presents to her, I assure you, and they are to be married in a few days. He is only waiting for his rents in the country to take the Captain out of prison; but here is Miss Emily, instead of being quite merry and joyful, is as dull and as melancholy as if she was going to be married to a frightful old man." "Consider," said Amanda, "you have just said her heart was pre-engaged." "Lord!" cried Mrs. Connel, "a girl at her time of life can change her love as easily as her cap." "I sincerely hope," exclaimed Amanda, "that she either has, or may soon be able to transfer hers." "And now, pray, madam," said Mrs. Connel, with a look which seemed to say Amanda should be as communicative as she had been, "may I ask from whence you have travelled?" "From a remote part of Scotland." "Dear, what a long journey!—Lord! they say that is a very desolate place, without never a tree or a bush in it." "I assure you it wants neither shade nor verdure," replied Amanda. "Really; well, Lord, what lies some people tell! Pray, ma'am, may I ask what countrywoman you are?" "Welsh," said Amanda. "Really; well, I suppose, ma'am, you have had many a scramble up the mountains, after the goats, which they say are marvellous plenty in that part of the world." "No, indeed," replied Amanda. "Are you come to make any long stay in London, ma'am?" "I have not determined." "I suppose you have come about a little business, ma'am?" resumed Mrs. Connel. "Yes," replied Amanda. "To be sure, not an affair of great consequence, or so young a lady would not have undertaken it." Amanda smiled, but made no reply, and was at length relieved from these tiresome and inquisitive questions by Mrs. Connel's calling in her girls to tea; after which she washed the tea-things, put them into the beaufet, and left the room to order something comfortable for supper. Left to herself, Amanda reflected that at the present juncture of Rushbrook's affairs, when his attention and time were engrossed by the approaching settlement of his daughter, an application to him, on her own account, would be not only impertinent, but unavailing; she therefore determined to wait till the hurry and agitation produced by such an event had subsided, and most sincerely did she hope that it might be productive of felicity to all. Mrs. Connel was not long absent, and Emily returned almost at the moment she re-entered the room. "Well, miss," said Mrs. Connel, addressing her ere she had time to speak to Amanda, "I have been telling your good friend here all about your affairs."

"Have you, ma'am?" cried Emily, with a faint smile, and a dejected voice. Amanda looked earnestly in her face, and saw an expression of the deepest sadness in it. From her own heart she readily imagined what her feelings must be at such a disappointment as Mrs. Connel had mentioned, and felt the sincerest pity for her Mrs Connel's volubility tormented them both; supper happily terminated it, as she was then much better employed in her own opinion, than she could possibly have been in talking. Amanda pleaded fatigue for retiring early. Mrs. Connel advised her to try a few glasses of wine as a restorative, but she begged to be excused, and was allowed to retire with Emily. The chamber was small but neat, and enlivened by a good fire, to which Amanda and Emily sat down while undressing. The latter eagerly availed herself of this opportunity to express the gratitude of her heart. Amanda tried to change the discourse, but could not succeed. "Long, madam," continued Emily, "have we wished to return our thanks for a benefaction so delicately conveyed as yours, and happy were my parents to-night when I informed them I could now express their grateful feelings." "Though interested exceedingly in your affairs," said Amanda, making another effort to change the discourse, "be assured I never should have taken the liberty of inquiring minutely into them, and I mention this, lest you might suppose from what Mrs. Connel said, that I had done so." "No, madam," replied Emily, "I had no such idea, and an inquiry from you would be rather pleasing than otherwise, because I should then flatter myself you might be induced to listen to griefs which have long wanted the consolation of sympathy—such, I am sure, as they would receive from you." "Happy should I be," cried Amanda, "had I the power of alleviating them." "Oh! madam, you have the power," said Emily, "for you would commiserate them, and commiseration from you would be balm to my heart; you would strengthen me in my duties—you would instruct me in resignation; but I am selfish in desiring to intrude them on you." "No," replied Amanda, taking her hand, "you flatter me by such a desire." "Then, madam, whilst you are undressing, I will give myself the melancholy indulgence of relating my little story."

CHAPTER LI.

"Take heed, take heed, thou lovely maid,
Nor be by glittering ills betrayed."

TO open our hearts to those we know will commiserate our sorrows, is the sweetest consolation those sorrows can receive; to you, then, madam, I divulge mine, sure at least of pity. At the time I first had the happiness of seeing you, the little credit my father had was exhausted, and his inability to pay being well known, he was arrested one evening as he sat by the bed-side of my almost expiring mother! I will not pain your gentle nature by dwelling on the horrors of that moment, on the agonies of a parent, and a husband torn from a family so situated as was my father's. Feeble, emaciated, without even sufficient clothing to guard him from the inclemency of the weather, he leaned upon the arm of one of the bailiffs, as he turned his eyes from that wife he never more expected to behold. She fainted at the moment he left the room, and it was many minutes ere I had power to approach her. The long continuance of her fit at length recalled my distracted thoughts; but I had no restoratives to apply, no assistance to recover her, for my eldest brother had followed my father, and the rest of the children, terrified by the scene they had witnessed, wept together in a corner of the room. I at last recollected a lady who lived nearly opposite to us, and from whom I hoped to procure some relief for her. Nothing but the present emergency could have made me apply to her, for the attention she had paid us on first coming to Mr Heathfield's was entirely withdrawn after his death. Pride, however, was forgotten at the present moment, and I flew to her house The servant showed me into a parlor, where she, her daughters, and a young clergyman I had never before seen, were sitting at tea. I could not bring myself to mention my distress before a stranger, and accordingly begged to speak to her in another room· but she told me in a blunt manner I might speak there. In a low and faltering voice, which sighs and tears often impeded, I acquainted her of what had happened, the situation of my mother and requested a cordial for her. How great was my confusion when she declared aloud all I had told her, and turning to her daughter, bid her give me part of a bottle of wine. 'Ay, ay, cried she, 'I always thought things would turn out so. It was really very foolish of Mr. Heathfield to bring you to his house, and lead you all into such expenses!' I listened to no more, but taking the wine with a silent pang, retired.

"I had not been many minutes returned, and was kneeling by the bed-side of my mother, who began to show some symptoms of returning life, when a gentle knock came to the hall door. I supposed it my brother, and bade one of the children fly to open it. What was my surprise when in a few minutes she returned, followed by the young clergyman I had just seen. I started from my kneeling posture, and my looks expressed my wonder. He approached, and in the soft accent of benevolence, apologized for his intrusion; but said he came with a hope and a wish that he might be serviceable. Oh! how soothing was his voice! Oh! how painfully pleasing the voice of tenderness to the wretched! The tears which pride and indignation had suspended but a few moments before again began flowing.

"But I will not dwell upon my feelings; suffice it to say, that every attention which could mitigate my wretchedness, he paid, and that his efforts, aided by mine, soon restored my mother. His looks, his manner, his profession, all conspired to calm her spirits, and she blessed the power which so unexpectedly had given us a friend. My brother returned from my father merely to inquire how we were, and to go back to him directly. The stranger requested permission to accompany him; a request most pleasing to us, as we trusted his soothing attention would have the same effect upon his sorrowing heart as it had upon ours. Scarcely were they gone ere a man arrived from a neighboring hotel with a basket loaded with wine and provisions. But to enumerate every instance of this young man's goodness would be encroaching upon your patience. In short, by his care, my mother in a few days was able to be carried to my father's prison. Mrs. Connel, who, on the first intimation of our distress, had come to us, took me into the house at a stated salary, which was to be given to my parents, and the rest of the children were to continue with them. My mother desired me one evening to take a walk with the children to Kensington, as she thought them injured by constant confinement. Our friend attended us, and in our way thither, informed me that he must soon leave town, as he was but a country curate, and his leave of absence from his rector was expired. It was above a month since we had known him, during which time his attentions were unremitting, and he was a source of comfort to us all. A sudden chill came over my heart as he spoke, and every sorrow at that moment seemed aggravated. On entering Kensington gardens, I seated myself on a little rising mount, for I felt trembling and fatigued, and he sat beside me. Never had I before felt so oppressed, and my tears gushed forth in spite of my efforts to restrain them. Something I said of their being occasioned by the recollection of the period when my parents enjoyed the charming scene I now contemplated along with him. 'Would to Heaven,' cried he, 'I could restore them again to the enjoyment of it.'

"'Ah,' said I, 'they already lie under unreturnable obligations to you. In losing you,' added I, involuntarily, 'they would lose their only comfort.' 'Since then,' cried he, 'you flatter me by saying it is in my power to give them comfort, oh! let them have a constant claim upon me for it! Oh! Emily!' he continued, taking my hand, 'let them be my parents as well as yours; then will their too scrupulous delicacy be conquered, and they will receive as a right what they now consider as a favor.' I felt my cheeks glow with blushes, but still did not perfectly conceive his meaning. 'My destiny is humble,' he continued; 'was it otherwise, I should long since have entreated you to share it with me. Could you be prevailed on to do so, you would give it pleasures it never yet experienced.' He paused for a reply, but I was unable to give one.

"Ah! madam, how little necessity either was there for one; my looks, my confusion, betrayed my feelings. He urged me to speak, and at last I acknowledged I should not hesitate to share his destiny, but for my parents who, by such a measure, would lose my assistance. 'Oh! do not think,' cried he, 'I would ever wish to tempt you into any situation which should make you neglect them.' He then proceeded to say that, though unable at present to liberate them, yet he trusted that if they consented to our union, he should by economy be enabled to contribute more essentially to their support than I could do, and also be able in a short time to discharge their debts. His proposals were made known to them, and met their warmest approbation. The pleasure they derived from them was more on my account than their own, as the idea of having me so settled removed a weight of anxiety from their minds; some of my brothers and sisters should live with us, he said, and promised my time should be chiefly spent in doing fine works, which should be sent to Mrs. Connel to dispose of for my parents; and also that, from time to time, I should visit them till I had the power of bringing them to my cottage, for such he described his residence.

"He was compelled to go to the country, but it was settled he should return in a short time, and have everything finally settled. In about a week after his departure, as I was returning one morning from a lady's, where I had been on a message from Mrs. Connel, a gentleman joined me in the street, and with a rude familiarity endeavored to enter into conversation with me. I endeavored to shake him off, but could not succeed, and hastened home with the utmost expedition, whither I saw he followed me. I thought no more of the incident till about two days after I saw him enter the shop, and heard him inquire of Mrs. Connel about her lodgings, which to my great mortification he immediately took, for I could not help suspecting he had some improper motive for taking them. I resolved, however, if such a motive really existed, to disappoint it by keeping out of his way; but all my vigilance was unavailing; he was continually on the watch for me, and I could not go up or down stairs without being insulted by him. I at length informed Mrs. Connel of his conduct, and entreated her to fulfil the sacred trust her friends reposed in her, when they gave me to her care, by terminating the insults of Mr. Sipthorpe. Alas! could I have possibly foreseen the consequences that would have followed my application to her, I should have borne those insults in silence. She has already informed you of them. Oh! madam! when the letter came which dissolved a promise so cheerfully, so fondly given, every prospect of felicity was in a moment overshadowed! For a long time I resisted every effort that was made to prevail on me to marry Sipthorpe; but when at last my mother said she was sorry to find my feelings less than his, who had so generously resigned me that my father might be extricated from his difficulties, I shrunk with agony at the rebuke. I wondered, I was shocked, how I could have so long hesitated to open the prison gates of my father, and determined from that moment to sacrifice myself for him; for oh! Miss Donald, it is a sacrifice of the most dreadful nature I am about making. Sipthorpe is a man I never could have liked, had my heart even been disengaged."

Amanda felt the truest pity for her young friend, who ended her narrative in tears; but she did not, by yielding entirely to that pity (as too many girls with tender hearts, but weak heads, might have done), heighten the sorrow of Miss Rushbrook. She proved her friendship and sympathy more sincerely than she could have done by mere expressions of condolement, which feed the grief they commiserate, in trying to reconcile her to a destiny that seemed irrevocable. She pointed out the claims a parent had upon a child, and dwelt upon the delight a child experienced when conscious of fulfilling those claims. She spoke of the rapture attending the triumph of reason and humanity over self and passion, and mentioned the silent plaudits of the heart as superior to all gratification or external advantages. She spoke from the real feelings of her soul. She recollected the period at which, to a father's admonition, she had resigned a lover, and had that father been in Captain Rushbrook's situation, and the same sacrifice been demanded from her as from Emily, she felt, without hesitation, she would have made it. She was indeed a monitress that had practised, and would practise (was there a necessity for so doing) the lessons she gave, not as poor Ophelia says—

> "Like some ungracious pastors,
> Who show the steep and thorny path to heaven,
> But take the primrose one themselves."

The sweet consciousness of this gave energy, gave more than usual eloquence to her language; but whilst she wished to inspirit her young friend, she felt from the tenderness of her nature, and the sad situation of her own heart, what that friend must feel from disappointed affection and a reluctant union. Scarcely could she refrain from weeping over a fate so wretched, and which she was tempted to think as dreadful as her own; but a little reflection soon convinced her she had the sad pre-eminence of misery; for in her fate there were none of those alleviations as in Emily's, which she was convinced must, in some degree, reconcile her to it. Her sufferings, unlike Emily's, would not be rewarded by knowing that they contributed to the comfort of those dearest to her heart.

"Your words, my dear madam," said Emily, "have calmed my spirits; henceforth I will be more resolute in trying to banish regrets from my mind. But I have been inconsiderate to a degree in keeping you so long from rest, after your fatiguing journey." Amanda indeed appeared at this moment nearly exhausted, and gladly hastened to bed. Her slumbers were short and unrefreshing; the cares which clung to her heart when waking were equally oppressive while sleeping. Lord Mortimer mingled in the meditations of the morning, in the visions of the night, and when she awoke she found her pillow wet with the tears she had shed on his account. Emily was already up, but on Amanda's drawing back the curtain she laid down the book she was reading, and came to her. She saw she looked extremely ill, and, imputing this to fatigue, requested she would breakfast in bed; but Amanda, who knew her illness proceeded from a cause which neither rest nor assiduous care could cure, refused complying with this request, and immediately dressed herself.

As she stood at the toilet, Emily suddenly exclaimed, "If you have a mind to see Sipthorpe, I will show him to you now, for he is just going out." Amanda went to the window, which Emily gently opened; but, oh! what was the shock of that moment, when in Sipthorpe she recognised the insidious Belgrave! A shivering horror ran through her veins, and recoiling a few paces she sunk half fainting on a chair. Emily, terrified by her appearance, was flying to the bell to ring for assistance, when, by a faint motion of her hand, Amanda prevented her. "I shall soon be better," said she, speaking with difficulty; "but I will lie down on the bed for a few minutes, and I beg you may go to your breakfast." Emily refused to go, and entreated, that instead of leaving her, she might have breakfast brought up for them both. Amanda assured her she could take nothing at present, and wished for quiet. Emily therefore reluctantly left her. Amanda now endeavored to compose her distracted thoughts, and quiet the throbbings of her agonizing heart, that she might be able to arrange some plan for extricating herself from her present situation, which appeared replete with every danger to her imagination; for, from the libertine principles of Belgrave, she could not hope that a new object of pursuit would detach him from her, when he found her so unexpectedly thrown in his way. Unprotected as she was, she could not think of openly avowing her knowledge of Belgrave. To discover his baseness, required therefore caution and deliberation, lest in saving Emily from the snare spread for her destruction, she should entangle herself in it. To declare at once his real character, must betray her to him; and though she might banish him from the house, yet, unsupported as she was by her friends or kindred—unable to procure the protection of Rushbrook, in his present situation, however willing he might be to extend it—she trembled to think of the dangers to which, by thus discovering, she might expose herself—dangers which the deep treachery and daring effrontery of Belgrave would, in all probability, prevent her escaping. As the safest measure, she resolved on quitting the house in the course of the day; but without giving any intimation that she meant not to return to it. She recollected a place where there was a probability of her getting lodgings which would be at once secret and secure; and by an anonymous letter to Captain Rushbrook, she intended to acquaint him of his daughter's danger, and refer him to Sir Charles Bingley, at whose agent's he could receive intelligence of him for the truth of what she said. Her plan concerted, she grew more composed, and was able, when Emily entered the room with her breakfast, to ask, in a seemingly careless manner, when Mr. Sipthorpe was expected back.

"It is very uncertain, indeed," answered she.

"I must go out in the course of the day," said Amanda, "about particular business; I may therefore as well prepare myself at once for it." She accordingly put on her habit, and requested materials for writing from Emily, which were immediately brought, and Emily then retired till she had written her letter. Amanda, left to herself, hastily unlocked her little trunk, and taking from it two changes of linen, and the will and narrative of Lady Dunreath, she deposited the two former in her pocket, and the two latter in her boscm, then sat down and wrote the following letter to Captain Rushbrook:—

A person who esteems the character of Captain Rushbrook, and the amiable simplicity of his daughter, cautions him to guard that simplicity against the danger which now threatens it, from a wretch who, under the sacred semblance of virtue, designs to fix a sharper sting in the bosom of affliction than adversity ever yet implanted. The worth of Sipthorpe is not more fictitious than his name. His real one is Belgrave. His hand is already another's, and his character for many years past marked with instances of deceit, if not equal, at least little inferior to the present. For the truth of these assertions, the writer of the letter refers Captain Rushbrook to Sir Charles Bingley, of ——— regiment, from whose agent a direction may be procured to him, certain, from his honor and sensibility, he will eagerly step forward to save worth and innocence from woe and destruction.

Amanda's anxiety about Emily being equal to what she felt for herself, she resolved to leave this letter at Rushbrook's prison, lest any accident should happen if it went by any other hands. She was anxious to be gone, but thought it better to wait till towards evening, when there would be the least chance of meeting Belgrave, who at that time would probably be fixed in some place for the remainder of the day. Emily returned in about an hour, and finding Amanda disengaged, requested permission to sit with her. Amanda, in her present agitation, would have preferred solitude, but could not decline the company of the affectionate girl, who, in conversing with her, sought to forget the heavy cares which the dreadful idea of a union with Sipthorpe had drawn upon her. Amanda listened with a beating heart to every sound, but no intimation of Belgrave's return reached her ear. At length they were summoned to dinner; but Amanda could not thing of going to it, lest she should be seen by him. To avoid this risk, and also the particularity of a refusal, she determined immediately to go out, and, having told Emily her intention, they both descended the stairs together. Emily pressed her exceedingly to stay for dinner, but she positively refused, and left the house with a beating heart, without having answered Emily's question, who desired to know if she would not soon return. Thus perpetually threatened with danger, like a frighted bird again was she to seek a shelter for her innocent head She walked with quickness to Oxford Street, where she directly procured a carriage, but was so weak and agitated the coachman was almost obliged to lift her into it. She directed it to the prison, and on reaching it sent for one of the turnkeys, to whom she gave her letter for Rushbrook, with a particular charge to deliver it immediately to him. She then ordered the carriage to Pall Mall, where it may be remembered she had once lodged with Lady Greystock. This was the only lodging-house in London she knew, and in it she expected no satisfaction but what would be derived from thinking herself safe, as its mistress was a woman of a most unpleasant temper. She had once been in affluent circumstances, and the remembrance of those circumstances soured her temper, and rendered her, if not incapable of enjoying, at least unwilling to acknowledge, the blessings she yet possessed. On any one in her power she vented her spleen. Her chief pursuit was the gratification of a most insatiate curiosity, and her first delight relating the affairs, good or bad, which that curiosity dived into. Amanda, finding she was within, dismissed the coach, and was shown by the maid into the back parlor, where she sat. "Oh dear!" cried she, with a supercilious smile, the moment Amanda entered, without rising from her chair to return her salute, "When did you return to London?—and pray, may I ask what brought you back to it?"

Amanda was convinced from Mrs. Hansard's altered manner, who had once been servile to a degree to her, that she was perfectly acquainted with her destitute condition, and a heavy sigh burst from her heart at the idea of associating with a woman who had the meanness to treat her ill because of that condition. A chillness crept through her frame when she reflected her sad situation might long compel her to this. Sick, weak, exhausted, she sunk upon a chair, which she had neither been offered nor desired to take. "Well, miss, and pray what is your business in town?" again asked Mrs. Hansard, with an increased degree of pertness.

"My business, madam," replied Amanda, "can be of no consequence to a person not connected with me. My business with you is to know whether you can accommodate me with lodgings?"

"Really. Well, you might have paid me the compliment of saying you would have called at any rate to know how I did. You may guess how greatly flattered an humble being like me would be by the notice of so amiable a young lady."

These words were pronounced with a kind of sneer that, by rousing the pride of Amanda, a little revived her spirits. "I should be glad, madam," said she, with a composed voice, while a faint glow stole over her cheek, "to know whether you can, or choose, to accommodate me with lodgings?" "Lord, my dear," replied Mrs. Hansard, "do not be in such a wondrous hurry—take a cup of tea with me, and then we will settle about that business." These words implied that she would comply with the wish of Amanda; and, however disagreeable the asylum, yet to have secured one cheered her sinking heart. Tea was soon made, which to Amanda, who had touched nothing since breakfast—and but little then—would have been a pleasant refreshment, had she not been tormented and fatigued by the questions of Mrs. Hansard, who laid a thousand baits to betray her into a full confession of what had brought her to London. Amanda, though a stranger in herself to every species of art, from fatal experience was aware of it in others, and therefore guarded her secret. Mrs. Hansard, who loved what she called a gossipping cup of tea, sat a tedious time over the tea-table. Amanda, at last mortified and alarmed by some expressions which dropped from her, again ventured to ask if she could be lodged under her roof.

"Are you really serious in that question?" said Mrs. Hansard. There was a certain expression of contempt in her features as she spoke, which shocked Amanda so much that she had not power to reply; "because if you are, my dear," continued Mrs. Hansard, "you have more assurance than I thought you were possessed of, though I always gave you credit for a pretty large share. Do you think I would ruin my house, which lodges people of the first rank and character, by admitting you into it? you, who, it is well known, obtained Lady Greystock's protection from charity, and lost it through misconduct. Poor lady—I had the whole story from her own mouth. She suffered well from having anything to say to you. I always guessed how it would be. Notwithstanding your demure look, I saw well enough how you would turn out. I assure you, to use your own words, if I could accommodate you in my house, it would not answer you at all, for there are no convenient closets in it in which a lady of your disposition might now and then want to hide a smart young fellow. I advise you, if you have had a tiff with any of your friends, to make up the difference; though, indeed, if you do not, in such a place as London, you can never be at a loss for such friends. Perhaps you are now beginning to repent of your evil courses, and, if I took you into my house, I should suffer as much in my pocket, I suppose, as in my character."

The terrified and distressed look with which Amanda listened to this speech, would have stopped Mrs. Hansard in the middle of it, had she possessed a spark of humanity, even if she believed her (which was not the case) guilty. But lost to the noble, the gentle feelings of humanity, she exulted in the triumph of malice, and rejoiced to have an opportunity of piercing the panting heart of helpless innocence with the sharp darts of insult and unmerited reproach. Amidst the various shocks Amanda had experienced in the short but eventful course of her life, one greater than the present she had never felt. Petrified by Mrs. Hansard's words, it was some time ere she had power to speak. "Gracious Heaven!" exclaimed she, at last, looking up to that Heaven she addressed, and which she now considered her only refuge from evil, "to what trials am I continually exposed! Persecuted, insulted, shocked! Oh! what happiness to lay my feeble frame, my woe-struck heart, within that low asylum where malice could no more annoy, deceit no more betray me! I am happy," she continued, starting up, and looking at Mrs. Hansard, "that the accommodation I desired in this house you refused me, for I am now well convinced, from the knowledge of your disposition, that the security my situation requires I should not have found within it." She hastily quitted the room; but on entering the hall her spirits entirely forsook her, at the dreadful idea of having no home to go to. Overcome with horror, she sunk in a flood of tears upon one of the hall chairs. A maid, who had probably been listening to her mistress's conversation, now came from a front parlor, and as Mrs. Hansard had shut the door after Amanda, addressed her without fear of being overheard. "Bless me, miss," said she, "are you crying? Why, Lord! surely you would not mind what old Blouzy in the parlor says? I promise you, if we minded her, we should have red eyes

46

here every day in the week. Do, pray, miss, tell me if I can be of any service to you?"

Amanda, in a voice scarcely articulate, thanked her, and said in a few minutes she should be better able to speak. To seek lodgings at this late hour was not to be thought of, except she wished to run into the very dangers she had wanted to avoid, and Mrs. Connel's house returned to her recollection, as the impossibility of procuring a refuge in any other was confirmed in her mind. She began to think it could not be so dangerous as her fears in the morning had represented it to be. Ere this she thought Belgrave (for since the delivery of the letter there had been time enough for such a proceeding) might be banished from it; if not, she had a chance of concealing herself, and, even if discovered, she believed Mrs. Connel would protect her from his open insults, whilst she trusted her own precautions would, under Heaven, defeat his secret schemes, should he again contrive any. She therefore resolved, or rather necessity compelled her—for could she have avoided it she would not have done so—to return to Mrs. Connel's; she accordingly requested the maid to procure her a carriage, and rewarded her for her trouble. As she was returning to Mrs. Connel's, she endeavored to calm her spirits, and quell her apprehensions. When the carriage stopped, and the maid appeared, she could scarcely prevent herself ere she alighted from inquiring whether any one but the family was within; conscious, however, that such a question might create suspicions, and that suspicions would naturally excite inquiries, she checked herself, and re-entered, though with trembling limbs, that house from whence in the morning she had fled with such terror.

CHAPTER LII.

"Why, thou poor mourner, in what baleful corner
Hast thou been talking with that witch, the night?
On what cold stone hast thou been stretched along,
Gathering the grumbling winds about thy head,
To mix with theirs the accents of thy woes?"—OTWAY.

MANDA had not reached the parlor when the door opened, and Mrs. Connel came from it. "Oh! oh! miss," cried she, "so you are returned. I protest I was beginning to think you had stolen a march upon us." There was a rude bluntness in this speech which confounded Amanda; and her mind misgave her that all was not right. "Come," continued Mrs. Connel, "come in, miss, I assure you I have been very impatient for your return." Amanda's fears increased. She followed Mrs. Connel in silence into the parlor, where she beheld an elderly woman, of a pleasing but emaciated appearance, who seemed in great agitation and distress. How she could possibly have anything to say to this woman, she could not conjecture, and yet an idea that she had, instantly darted into her mind; she sat down, trembling in every limb, and waited with impatience for an explanation of this scene. After a general silence of a few minutes, the stranger, looking at Amanda, said, "My daughter, madam, has informed me we are indebted to your bounty; I am therefore happy at an opportunity of discharging the debt." These words announced Mrs. Rushbrook, but Amanda was confounded at her manner; its coolness and formality were more expressive of dislike and severity than of gentleness or gratitude. Mrs. Rushbrook rose as she spoke, and offered a note to her. Speechless from astonishment, Amanda had not power either to decline or accept it, and it was laid on a table before her.

"Allow me, madam," said Mrs. Rushbrook, as she resumed her seat, "to ask if your real name is Donald?" Amanda's presentiment of under-hand doings was now verified; it was evident to her that their author was Belgrave, and that he had been too successful in contriving them.

Amanda now appeared to have reached the crisis of her fate. In all the various trials she had hitherto experienced, she had still some stay, some hope, to support her weakness, and soothe her sorrows. When groaning under the injuries her character sustained by the success of an execrable plot, she had the consolation to think an idolizing father would shelter her from further insult. When deprived of that father, tender friends stepped forward, who mingled tears of sympathy with hers, and poured the balm of pity on her sorrowing heart. When torn from the beloved object enshrined within that heart, while her sick soul languished under the heavy burthen of existence, again did the voice of friendship penetrate its gloom, and, though it could not remove, alleviated its sufferings. Now helpless, unprotected, she saw a dreadful storm ready to burst over her devoted head, without one hope to cheer, one stretched-out arm to shield her from its violence. Surrounded by strangers prejudiced against her, she could not think that her plain, unvarnished tale would gain their credence, or prevail on them to protect her from the wretch whose machinations had ruined her in their estimation. The horrors of her situation all at once assailed her mind, overpowered its faculties; a kind of mental sickness seized her, she leaned her throbbing head upon her hand, and a deep groan burst from her agonizing heart.

"You see," said Mrs. Connel, after a long silence, "she cannot brave this discovery."

Amanda raised her head at these words; she had grown a little more composed. "The Being in whom I trust," she said to herself, "and whom I never wilfully offended, will still, I doubt not, as heretofore, protect me from danger." Mrs. Rushbrook's unanswered question still sounded in her ear. "Allow me, madam," she cried, turning to her, "to ask your reason for inquiring whether my real name is Donald?" "Oh, Lord! my dear!" said Mrs. Connel, addressing Mrs. Rushbrook, "you need not pester yourself or her with any more questions about the matter; her question is an answer in itself." "I am of your opinion, indeed," exclaimed Mrs. Rushbrook, "and think any farther inquiry needless." "I acknowledge, madam," said Amanda, whose voice grew firmer from the consciousness of never having acted improperly, "that my name is not Donald. I must also do myself the justice to declare (let me be credited or not) that my real one was not concealed from any motive which could deserve reproach or censure.

My situation is peculiarly distressing. My only consolation amidst my difficulties is the idea of never having drawn them upon myself by imprudence." "I do not want, madam," replied Mrs. Rushbrook, "to inquire into your situation; you have been candid in one instance, I hope you will be equally so in another. Pray, madam," handing to Amanda the letter she had written to Rushbrook, "is this your writing?" "Yes, madam," answered Amanda, whose pride was roused by the contempt she met, "it is my writing." "And pray," said Mrs. Rushbrook, looking steadfastly at her, while her voice grew more severe, "what was your motive for writing this letter?" "I think, madam," cried Amanda, "the letter explains that." "A pretty explanation, truly!" exclaimed Mrs. Connel; "and so you would try to vilify the poor gentleman's character; but, miss, we have had an explanation you little dream of; ay, we found you out, notwithstanding your slyness in writing, like one of the madams in a novel, a bit of a letter without ever a name to it. Mr. Sipthorpe knew directly who it came from. Ah! poor gentleman, he allowed you wit enough; a pity there is not more goodness with it; he knows you very well to his cost." "Yes," said Amanda, "he knows I am a being whose happiness he disturbed, but whose innocence he never triumphed over. He knows that like an evil genius, he has pursued my wandering footsteps, heaping sorrow upon sorrow on me by his machinations; but he also knows, when encompassed with those sorrows, perplexed with those machinations, I rose superior to them all, and with uniform contempt and abhorrence rejected his offers." "Depend upon it," cried Mrs. Connel, "she has been an actress." "Yes, madam," said Amanda, whose struggling voice confessed the anguish of her soul, "upon a stage where I have seen a sad variety of scenes." "Come, come," exclaimed Mrs. Connel, "confess all about yourself and Sipthorpe; full confession will entitle you to pardon." "It behooves me, indeed," said Amanda, "to be explicit; my character requires it, and my wish," she continued, turning to Mrs. Rushbrook, "to save you from a fatal blow demands it." She then proceeded to relate everything she knew concerning Belgrave; but she had the mortification to find her short and simple story received with every mark of incredulity. "Beware, madam," said she to Mrs. Rushbrook, "of this infatua tion; I adjure you beware of the consequences of it. Oh! doom not your innocent, your reluctant Emily to destruction; draw not upon your own head by such a deed horrible and excruciating anguish. Why does not Mr. Sipthorpe, if I must call him so, appear, and in my presence support his allegations?" "I asked him to do so," replied Mrs. Rushbrook; "but he has feeling, and he wished not to see your distress, however merited it might be." "No, madam," cried Amanda, "he refused, because he knew that without shrinking he could not behold the innocent he has so abused; because he knew the conscious coloring of his cheek would betray the guilty feelings of his soul. Again, I repeat, he is not what he appears to be. I refer you for the truth of my words to Sir Charles Bingley. I feel for you, though you have not felt for me. I know, from false representations, you think me a poor misguided creature; but was I even so, my too evident anguish might surely have excited pity. Pardon me, madam, if I say your conduct to me has been most unkind. The gentle virtues are surely those best fitting a female breast. She that shows leniency to a fallen fellow-creature, fulfils the Divine precept. The tear she sheds over her frailties is consecrated in the sight of Heaven, and her compassion draws a blessing on her own head. Oh! madam, I once looked forward to a meeting with you, far, far different from the present one. I once flattered myself, that from the generous friendship of Mr. and Mrs. Rushbrook, I should derive support and consolation; but this, like every other hope, is disappointed." Amanda's voice faltered at these last words, and tears again trickled down her lovely cheeks. A faint glow tinged the pale cheek of Mrs. Rushbrook at Amanda's accusation of unkindness. She bent her eyes to the ground as if conscious it was merited, and it was many minutes ere she could again look on the trembling creature before her. "Perhaps," said she, at last, "I may have spoken too severely, but it must be allowed I had great provocation. Friendship and gratitude could not avoid resenting such shocking charges as yours against Sipthorpe." "For my part, I wonder you spoke so mildly to her," exclaimed Mrs. Connel; "I protest in future I shall be guarded who I admit into my house. I declare she seemed so distressed at the idea of going amongst strangers, that, sooner than let her do so, I believe, if Miss Emily had not, I should have offered her part of my bed; but this distress was all a pretext to get into the house with Mr. Sipthorpe, that she might try to entangle him in her snares again. Well, I am determined she shall not stay another night under my roof. Ay, you may stare as you please, miss, but you shall march directly. You are not so ignorant about London, I dare say, as you pretend to be."

Mrs. Connel rose as she spoke, and approached her with a look which seemed to say she would put her threat into execution. It was Amanda's intention to quit the house the next morning, but to be turned from it at such an hour, a wanderer in the street, the idea was replete with horror! She started up, and retreating a few paces, looked at Mrs. Connel with a kind of melancholy wildness. "Yes," repeated Mrs. Connel, "I say you shall march directly." The wretched Amanda's head grew giddy, her sight failed, her limbs refused to support her, and she would have fallen to the ground had not Mrs. Rushbrook, who perceived her situation, timely caught her. She was replaced in a chair, and water sprinkled on her face. "Be composed, my dear," said Mrs. Rushbrook, whose softened voice proclaimed the return of her compassion, "you shall not leave this house to-night, I promise, in the name of Mrs. Connel. She is a good-natured woman, and would not aggravate your distress." "Ay, Lord knows, good nature is my foible," exclaimed Mrs. Connel. "So, miss, as Mrs. Rushbrook has promised, you may stay here to-night." Amanda, opening her languid eyes, and raising her head from Mrs. Rushbrook's bosom, said in a low, tremulous voice, "To-morrow, madam, I shall depart. Oh! would to Heaven," cried she, clasping her hands together, and bursting into an agony of tears, "before to-morrow I could be rid of the heavy burthen that oppresses me!" "Well, we have had wailing and weeping enough to-night," said Mrs. Connel, "so, miss, you may take one of the candles off the table, and go to your chamber if you choose."

Amanda did not require to have this permission repeated. She arose, and taking the light, left the parlor. With feeble steps she ascended to the little chamber; but here all was dark and solitary, no cheerful fire sent forth an animating blaze; no gentle Emily, like the mild genius of benevolence, appeared to offer with undis sembled kindness her little attentions. Forsaken, faint, the pale child of misery laid down the candle, and seating herself at the foot of the bed, gave way to deep and agonizing sorrow.

"Was I ever," she asked herself, "blessed with friends who valued my existence as their own, who called me the beloved of their hearts? Oh! yes," she groaned, "once such friends were mine, and the sad remembrance of them aggravates my present misery. Oh! happy is our ignorance of futurity. Oh! my father, had you been permitted to read the awful volume of fate, the page marked with your Amanda's destiny would have rendered your existence miserable, and made you wish a thousand times the termination of hers.

"Oh, Oscar! from another hand than mine must you receive the deed which shall entitle you to independence. My trials sink me to the grave, to that grave where, but for the sweet hope of again seeing you, I should long since have wished myself." The chamber door opened. She turned her eyes to it in expectation of seeing Emily, but was disappointed on perceiving only the maid of the house. "Oh! dear ma'am," cried she, going up to Amanda, "I declare it quite grieves me to see you in such a situation. Poor Miss Emily is just in as bad a plight. Well, it is no matter, but I think both the old ladies will be punished for plaguing you in this manner. Madam Rushbrook will be sorry enough, when, after giving her daughter to Mr. Sipthorpe, she finds he is not what he seems to be." Amanda shrunk with horror from the idea of Emily's destruction, and by a motion of her hand, signified to the maid her dislike to the subject. "Well, ma'am," she continued, "Miss Emily, as I was saying, is quite in as bad a plight as yourself. They have clapped her into my mistress's chamber, which she durst not leave without running the risk of bringing their tongues upon her. However, she contrived to see me, and sent you this note." Amanda took it and read as follows:—

"I hope my dear Miss Donald will not doubt my sincerity, when I declare that all my sorrows are heightened by knowing I have been the occasion of trouble to her. I have heard of the unworthy treatment she has received in this house, and her intention of quitting it to-morrow. Knowing her averseness to lodge in a place she is unacquainted with, I have been speaking to the maid about her, and had the satisfaction to hear, that, through ner means, my dear Miss Donald might be safely accommodated for a short time; long enough, however, to permit her to look out for an eligible situation. I refer her for particulars of the conversation to the maid, whose fidelity may be relied on. To think it may be useful to my dear Miss Donald, affords me the only pleasure I am now capable of enjoying. In her esteem may I ever retain the place of a sincere and affectionate friend.

"E. R."

"And where is the place I can be lodged in?" eagerly asked Amanda. "Why, ma'am," said the maid, "I have a sister who is housemaid, at a very grand place, on the Richmond Road. All the family are now gone to Brighton, and she is left alone in the house, where you would be very welcome to take up your residence till you could get one to your mind. My sister is a sage, sober body, and would do everything in her power to please and oblige you, and you would be as snug and secure with her as in a house of your own; and poor Miss Emily begged you would go to her, till you could get lodgings with people whose characters you know. And, indeed, ma'am, it is my humble opinion, it would be safe and pleasant for you to do so; and, if you consent, I will conduct you there to-morrow morning; and I am sure, ma'am, I shall be happy if I have the power of serving you." Like the Lady in Comus, Amanda might have said—

"I take thy word,
And trust thy honest offered courtesy;
For in a place
Less warranted than this, or less secure
I cannot be, that I should fear to change it:
Eye me, blest Providence, and square my trial
To my proportioned strength."

To take refuge in this manner, in any one's house, was truly repugnant to the feelings of Amanda; but sad necessity conquered her scrupulous delicacy, and she asked the maid at what hour in the morning she should be ready for her.

"I shall come to you, ma'am," answered she, "as soon as I think there is a carriage on the stand, and then we can go together to get one. But I protest, ma'am, you look sadly. I wish you would allow me to assist in undressing you, for I am sure you want a little rest. I dare say, for all my mistress said, if you choose it, I could get a little wine from her to make whey for you." Amanda refused this, but accepted her offer of assistance, for she was so overpowered by the scenes of the day, as to be almost unequal to any exertion. The maid retired after she had seen her to bed Amanda entreated her to be punctual to an early hour, and also requested her to give her most affectionate love to Miss Rushbrook, and her sincere thanks for the kind solicitude she had expressed about her. Her rest was now, as on the preceding night, broken and disturbed by frightful visions. She arose pale, trembling, and unrefreshed. The maid came to her soon after she was dressed, and she immediately accompanied her down stairs, trembling as she went, lest Belgrave should suddenly make his appearance, and either prevent her departure, or follow her to her new residence. She left the house, however, without meeting any creature, and soon obtained the shelter of a carriage.

As they proceeded, Amanda besought the maid, who seemed perfectly acquainted with everything relative to Belgrave, to tell Miss Rushbrook to believe her assertions against him if she wished to save herself from destruction. The maid assured her she would, and declared she always suspected Mr. Sipthorpe was not as good as he should be. Amanda soon found herself at the end of her little journey. The house was elegant and spacious, with a short avenue before it planted with chestnuts. The maid's sister was an elderly plain-looking woman, who received Amanda with every appearance of respect, and conducted her into a handsome parlor, where a neat breakfast was laid out. "I took care, ma'am," said the maid, smiling, "to apprise my sister last night of the honor she was to have this morning; and I am sure she will do everything in her power to oblige you." "I thank you both," cried Amanda, with her usual sweetness, but while she spoke a straggling tear stole down her lovely cheek at the idea of that forlorn situation which had thus cast her upon the kindness of strangers—strangers who were themselves the children of poverty and dependence. "I hope, however," she continued, "I shall not long be a trouble to either, as it is my intention immediately to look out for a lodging amongst the cottages in this neighborhood, till I can settle my affairs to return to my friends. In the mean time I must insist on making some recompense for the attention I have received, and the expense I have put you to." She accordingly forced a present upon each, for both the women appeared unwilling to accept them, and Mrs. Deborah, the maid's sister, said it was quite unnecessary at present to think of leaving the house, as the family would not return to it for six weeks. Amanda, however, was resolved on doing what she had said, as she could not conquer her repugnance to continue in a stranger's house. Mrs. Con ne.'s maid departed in a few minutes. Of the breakfast prepared for her, Amanda could only take some tea. Her head ached violently, and her whole frame felt disordered. Mrs. Deborah, seeing her dejection, proposed showing her the house and garden, which were very fine, to amuse her, but Amanda declined the proposal at present, saying she thought if she lay down she should be better. She was immediately conducted to an elegant chamber, where Mrs. Deborah left her, saying she would prepare some little nice thing for her dinner, which she hoped would tempt her to eat. Amanda now tried to compose her spirits by reflecting she was in a place of security; but their agitation was not to be subdued from the sleep into which mere fatigue threw her. She was continually starting in inexpressible terrors. Mrs. Deborah came up two or three times to know how she was, and at last appeared with dinner. She laid a small table by the bedside, and besought Amanda to rise and try to eat. There was a friendliness in her manner which recalled to Amanda's recollection her faithful nurse Edwin, and she sighed to think that the shelter of her humble cottage she could no more enjoy (should such a shelter be required) from its vicinity to Tudor Hall, near which every feeling of propriety and tenderness must forbid her residing; the sad remembrance of which, now reviving in her mind, drew tears from her, and rendered her unable to eat. She thanked Mrs. Deborah for her attention, but, anxious to be alone, said she would no longer detain her; yet no sooner was she alone than she found solitude insupportable. She could not sleep, the anguish of her mind was so great, and arose with the idea that a walk in the garden might be of use to her. As she was descending the stairs, she heard, notwithstanding the door was shut, a man's voice from a front parlor. She started, for she thought it was a voice familiar to her ear. With a light foot and a throbbing heart she turned into a parlor at the foot of the stairs which communicated with the other Here she listened, and soon had her fears confirmed by recollecting the voice to be that of Belgrave's servant, whom she had often seen in Devonshire. She listened with that kind of horror which the trembling wretch may be supposed to feel when about hearing a sentence he expects to be dreadful.

"Ay, I assure you," cried the man, "we are blown up at Mrs. Connel's, but that is of little consequence to us; the Colonel thinks the game now in view better than that he has lost, so to-night you may expect him in a chaise and four to carry off your fair guest." "I declare, I am glad of it," said Mrs. Deborah, "for I think she will die soon." "Die soon!" repeated he. "Oh! yes, indeed, great danger of that—" and he added something else, which, being delivered with a violent burst of laughter, Amanda could not hear. She thought she heard them moving towards the door; she instantly slipped from the parlor, and, ascending the stairs in breathless haste, stopped outside the chamber door to listen. In a few minutes she heard them coming into the hall, and the man softly let out by Mrs. Deborah. Amanda now entered the chamber and closed the door, and, knowing a guilty conscience is easily alarmed, she threw herself on the bed, lest Mrs. Deborah, if she found her up, should have her suspicions awakened. Her desperate situation inspired her with strength and courage, and she trusted by presence of mind to be able to extricate herself from it. It was her intention, if she effected her escape, to proceed directly to London, though the idea of entering it, without a certain place to go to, was shocking to her imagination; yet she thought it a more secure place for her than any of the neighboring cottages, which she thought might be searched. Mrs Deborah, as she expected, soon came up to her. Amanda involuntarily shuddered at her appearance, but, knowing her safety depended on the concealment of her feelings, she forced herself to converse with the treacherous creature. She at last arose from the bed, declaring she had indulged her languor too much, and, after a few turns about the room, went to the window, and pretended to be engrossed in admiring the garden. "There is a great deal of fruit in the garden," said she, turning to Mrs. Deborah; "if I did not think it encroached too much on your kindness, I should ask for a nectarine or two." "Dear ma'am," replied Miss Deborah, "you are heartily welcome. I declare I should have offered them to you, only I thought you would like a turn in the garden and pull them yourself." "No," said Amanda, "I cannot at present." Mrs. Deborah went off, and Amanda watched at the window till she saw her at the very end of the garden; she then snatched up her hat, and tied it on with a handkerchief, the better to conceal her face, then hastily descended the stairs, and locked the back door to prevent an immediate pursuit. She ran down the avenue, nor flagged in her course till she had got some paces from it; she was then compelled to do so, as much from weakness as from fear of attracting notice, if she went on in such a wild manner. She started at the sound of every carriage, and hastily averted her head as they passed; but she reached London without any alarm but what her own fears gave her. The hour was now late and gloomy, and warned Amanda of the necessity there was for exertions to procure a lodging. Some poor women she saw retiring from their little fruit-stands drew a shower of tears from her, to think her situation was more wretched than theirs, whom but a few days before she should have considered as objects of compassion. She knew at such an hour she would only be received into houses of an inferior description, and looked for one in which she could think there might be a chance of gaining admittance. She at last came to a small, mean-looking house. "This humble roof, I think," cried she, "will not disdain to shelter an unhappy wanderer!" She turned into the shop, where butter and cheese were displayed, and where an elderly woman sat knitting behind the counter. She arose immediately, as if from surprise and respect at Amanda's appearance, who in universal agitation leaned against the door for support, unable for some minutes to speak. At last, in faltering accents, whilst over her pale face a crimson blush was diffused, she said, "I should be glad to know if you have any lodgings to let?"

The woman instantly dropped into her seat, and looked steadfastly at Amanda. "This is a strange hour," cried she, "for any decent body to come looking for lodgings!" "I am as sensible of that as you can be," said Amanda, "but peculiar circumstances have obliged me to it; if you can accommodate me, I can assure you you will not have reason to repent doing so." "Oh! I do not know how that may be," cried she; "it is natural for a body to speak a good word for themselves; however, if I do let you a room, for I have only one to spare, I shall expect to be paid for it beforehand." "You shall, indeed," said Amanda. "Well, I will show it you," said she. She accordingly called a little girl to watch the shop, and, taking a candle, went up, before Amanda, a narrow, winding flight of stairs, and conducted her into a room, whose dirty, miserable appearance made her involuntarily shrink back, as if from the den of wretchedness itself. She tried to subdue the disgust it inspired her with, by reflecting that, after the imminent danger she had escaped, she should be happy to procure any asylum she could consider safe. She also tried to reconcile herself to it, by reflecting that in the morning she should quit it.

"Well, ma'am," said the woman, "the price of the room is neither more nor less than one guinea per week, and if you do not like it, you are very welcome not to stay." "I have no objection to the price," replied Amanda; "but I hope you have quiet people in the house." "I flatter myself, ma'am," said the woman, drawing up her head, "there is never a house in the parish can boast a better name than mine." "I am glad to hear it," answered Amanda; "and I hope you are not offended by the inquiry." She now put her hand in her pocket for the purse, to give the expected guinea, but the purse was not there. She sat down on the side of the bed, and searched the other, but with as little success. She pulled out the contents of both, but no purse was to be found "Now—now," cried she, clasping her hands together, in an agony which precluded reflection, "now—now, I am lost indeed! My purse is stolen," she continued, "and I cannot give you the promised guinea." "No, nor never could, I suppose," exclaimed the woman. "Ah! I suspected all along what you were;—and so you was glad my house had a good name? I shall take care it does not lose that name by lodging you." "I conjure you," cried Amanda, starting up, and laying her hand on the woman's, "I conjure you to let me stay this night; you will not—you shall not lose by doing so. I have things of value in a trunk in town, for which I will this instant give you a direction." "Your trunk!" replied the woman in a scornful tone. "Oh! yes, you have a trunk with things of value in it, as much as you have a purse in your pocket. A pretty story, indeed. But I know too much of the ways of the world to be deceived now-a-days—so march directly."

Amanda again began to entreat, but the woman interrupted her, and declared, if she did not depart directly, she would be sorry for it. Amanda instantly ceased her importunities, and in trembling silence followed her down stairs. Oppressed with weakness, she involuntarily hesitated in the shop, which the woman perceiving, she rudely seized her, and pushing her from it, shut the door. Amanda could not now, as in former exigencies, consider what was to be done. Alas! if even capable of reflection, she could have suggested no plan, which there was a hope of accomplishing. The powers of her mind were overwhelmed with horror and anguish. She moved mechanically along, nor stopped, till from weakness, she sunk upon the step of a door, against which she leaned her head in a kind of lethargy; but from this she was suddenly roused by two men who stopped before her. Death alone could have conquered her terrors of Belgrave. She instantly concluded these to be him and his man. She started up, uttered a faint scream, and calling upon Heaven to defend her, was springing past them, when her hand was suddenly caught. She made a feeble but unsuccessful effort to disengage it, and overcome by terror and weakness fell, though not fainting, unable to support herself, upon the bosom of him who had arrested her course. "Gracious Heaven!" cried he, "I have heard that voice before."

Amanda raised her head. "Sir Charles Bingley!" she exclaimed. The feelings of joy, surprise, and shame, that pervaded her whole soul, and thrilled through her frame, were, in its present weak state, too much for it, and she again sunk upon his shoulder. The joy of unexpected protection—for protection she was convinced she should receive from Sir Charles Bingley—was conquered by reflecting on the injurious ideas her present situation must excite in his mind—ideas she feared she should never be able to remove so strongly were appearances against her.

"Gracious Heaven!" exclaimed Sir Charles, "is this Miss Fitzalan? Oh, this," he cried, in a tone of deep dejection, "is indeed a meeting of horror!" A deep convulsive sob from Amanda alone proclaimed her sensibility, for she lay motionless in his arms—arms which involuntarily encircled and enfolded her to a heart that throbbed with intolerable anguish on her account. His friend stood all this time a silent spectator of the scene, the raillery which he had been on the point of uttering at seeing Amanda, as he thought, so premeditatedly fall into the arms of his companion, was stopped by the sudden exclamation of Sir Charles. Though the face of Amanda was concealed, the glimmering of a lamp over their heads gave him a view of her fine form, and the countenance of Sir Charles as he bent over her, full of sorrow and dismay. "Miss Fitzalan," cried Sir Charles, after the silence of a minute, "you are ill; allow me to have the pleasure of seeing you home." "Home!" repeated Amanda, in the slow and hollow voice of despair, and raising her languid head, "alas! I have no home to go to."

Every surmise of horror which Sir Charles had formed from seeing her in her present situation was now confirmed. He groaned, he shuddered, and, scarcely able to stand, was obliged to lean with the lovely burden he supported against the rails. He besought his friend either to procure a chair or coach in which he might have her conveyed to a house where he knew he could gain her admittance. Touched by his distress, and the powerful impulse of humanity, his friend instantly went to comply with his request.

The silence of Amanda Sir Charles imputed to shame and illness, and grief and delicacy forbade him to notice it. His friend returned in a few minutes with a coach, and Sir Charles then found that Amanda's silence did not altogether proceed from the motives he had ascribed it to; for she had fainted on his bosom. She was lifted into the carriage, and he again received her in his arms. On the carriage stopping, he committed her to the care of his friend, whilst he stepped into the house to procure a reception. In a few minutes he returned with a maid, who assisted him in carrying her up stairs. But on entering the drawing-room, how great was his amazement, when a voice suddenly exclaimed, "Oh, merciful Powers! this is Miss Donald!" It was indeed to Mrs. Connel's house, and to the care of the Rushbrooks, whom his bounty had released from prison, he had brought her. He had previously informed them of the situation in which he found her, little suspecting, at the time, she was the Miss Donald they mentioned being under such obligations to.

"It is I, it is I," cried Mrs. Rushbrook, gazing on her with mingled horror and anguish, "it is I have been the occasion of her distress, and never shall I forgive myself for it." "Oh, my preserver, my friend, my benefactress!" said Emily, clasping her in an agony of tears to her bosom, "is it thus your Emily beholds you?" Amanda was laid upon a couch, and her hat being removed, displayed a face which, with the paleness of death, had all the wildness of despair—a wildness that denoted more expressively than language could have done, the conflicts her spirit had endured; heavy sighs announced her having recovered from her fainting fit; but her eyes still continued closed, and her head, too weak to be self-supported, rested against the arm of the couch. Mrs. Rushbrook and her daughter hung over her in inexpressible agonies. If they were thus affected, oh! how was Sir Charles Bingley distressed—oh! how was his heart, which loved her with the most impassionate tenderness, agonized! As he bent over the couch, the big tear trickled down his manly cheek, and fell upon the cold, pale face he contemplated. He softly asked himself, Is this Amanda? Is this she, whom but a short time ago I beheld moving with unequalled elegance, adorned with unrivalled beauty, whom my heart worshipped as the first of women, and sought to unite its destiny to, as the surest means of rendering that destiny happy? Oh! what a change is here! How feeble is that form! how hollow is that cheek! how heavy are those eyes whose languid glance speak incurable anguish of soul! Oh, Amanda, was the being present who first led you into error, what horror and remorse must seize his soul at seeing the consequence of that error! "Has this unhappy young creature," asked Rushbrook, who had approached the couch and viewed her with the truest pity, "no connections that could be prevailed on to save her?" "None that I know of," replied Sir Charles; "her parents are both dead." "Happy are the parents," resumed Rushbrook, "who, shrouded in the dust, cannot see the misfortunes of their children—the fall of such a child as this!" glancing his tearful eyes as he spoke on his daughters.

"And pray, sir," said Mrs. Connel, who was chafing her temples with lavender, "if she recovers, what is to become of her?" "It shall be my care," cried Sir Charles, "to procure her an asylum Yes, madam," he continued, looking at her with an expression of mingled tenderness and grief, "he that must for ever mourn thy fate, will try to mitigate it; but does she not want medical assistance?" "I think not," replied Mrs. Connel; "it is want of nourishment and rest has thrown her into her present situation." "Want of nourishment and rest!" repeated Sir Charles. "Good Heavens!" continued he, in the sudden agony of his soul, and walking from the couch, "is it possible that Amanda was a wanderer in the streets, without food, or a place to lay her head in? Oh, this is dreadful! Oh! my friends," he proceeded, looking around him, whilst his eyes beamed the divine compassion of his soul, "be kind, be careful of this poor creature; but it is unnecessary to exhort you to this, and excuse me for having done so. Yes, I know you will delight in binding up a broken heart, and drying the tears of a wretched outcast. A short time ago, and she appeared——" he stopped, overcome by his emotions, and turned away his head to wipe away his tears. "A short time ago," he resumed, "and she appeared all that the heart of man could desire, all that a woman should wish and ought to be. Now she is fallen, indeed, lost to herself and to the world!" "No," cried Emily, with generous warmth, starting from the side of the couch, at which she had been kneeling, "I am confident she never was guilty of an error." "I am inclined, indeed, to be of Emily's opinion," said Mrs. Rushbrook. "I think the monster, who spread such a snare for her destruction, traduced Miss Donald in order to drive her from those who would protect her from his schemes." "Would to Heaven the truth of your conjecture could be proved," exclaimed Sir Charles. Again he approached the couch. Amanda remained in the same attitude, but seeing her eyes open, he took her cold hand, and in a soothing voice assured her she was safe; but the assurance had no effect upon her. Hers, like the "dull, cold ear of death," was insensible of sound. A faint spark of life seemed only quivering through her woe-worn frame. "She is gone!" cried Sir Charles, pressing her hand between his; "she is gone, indeed! Oh! sweet Amanda, the mortal bounds that enclose thy afflicted spirit will soon be broken!" "I trust not, sir," exclaimed Captain Rushbrook His wife and daughter were unable to speak. "In my opinion she had better be removed to bed."

Amanda was accordingly carried to a chamber, and Sir Charles remained in the drawing-room till Mrs. Rushbrook had returned to it. She informed him Miss Donald continued in the same state. He desired a physician might be sent for, and departed in inexpressible dejection.

CHAPTER LIII.

"Love, gratitude, and pity wept at once."—THOMSON.

E shall now account for the incidents in the last chapter. Amanda's letter to the Rushbrooks filled them with surprise and consternation. Mrs. Rushbrook directly repaired to Mrs. Connel, who, without hesitation, gave it as her opinion that the whole was a fabrication, invented by malice to ruin Sipthorpe in their opinion, or else by envy to prevent their enjoying the good fortune which he offered to their acceptance. Mrs. Rushbrook was inclined to be of the same opinion. Her mind was sensibly affected by the favors Sipthorpe had conferred on her family, and, yielding to its gratitude, she resolved to be guided implicitly by her friend, who advised her to show the letter to him. She considered this the best measure she could pursue. If innocent, he would be pleased by the confidence reposed in his honor; if guilty, his confusion must betray him. But Belgrave was guarded against detection. His servant had seen Amanda as she was alighting from the coach the evening she arrived in town. He inquired from the maid concerning her, and learned that she was to lodge in the house, and go by her assumed name. These circumstances he related to his master the moment he returned home, who was transported at the intelligence. From her change of name, he supposed her not only in deep distress, but removed from the protection of her friends, and he determined not to lose so favorable an opportunity as the present for securing her in his power. He instantly resolved to relinquish his designs on Emily—designs which her beautiful simplicity and destitute condition had suggested, and to turn all his thoughts on Amanda, who had ever been the first object of his wishes. His pride, as well as love, was interested in again ensnaring her, as he had been deeply mortified by her so successfully baffling his former stratagems; he knew not of the manner she had left the house. Half distracted at what he supposed her escape from it, he had followed her to Ireland, and remained incognito near the convent, till the appearance of Lord Mortimer convinced him any schemes he formed against her must prove abortive; but to concert a plan for securing her required some deliberation. Ere he could devise one he was summoned to Mrs. Connel's parlor to peruse the letter, and from the hand as well as purport, instantly knew Amanda to be its author. With the daring effrontery of vice, he directly declared she was a discarded mistress of his, who from jealousy had taken this step, to prevent, if possible, his union. He assured them her real name was not Donald, bid them tax her with that deceit, and judge from her confusion whether she was not guilty of that, as well as everything else he alleged against her. His unembarrassed manner had the appearance of innocence to his too credulous auditors, prejudiced as they were already in his favor, and in their minds he was now fully acquitted of his imputed crimes. He was now careless whether Amanda saw him or not (for he had before stolen into the house), being well convinced nothing she could allege against him would be credited. When night approached without bringing her, he grew alarmed lest he had lost her again At last her return relieved him from this fear. The conversation which passed in the parlor he heard through the means of his servant, who had listened to it. The mention of Amanda's removal in the morning made him immediately consult his servant about measures for securing her, and he, with the assistance of the maid contrived the scheme which has been already related, having forged a letter in Emily's name. But how inadequate is language to describe the rage that took possession of his soul, when, going at the appointed hour to carry Amanda off, he found her already gone. He raved, cursed, stamped, and accused the woman and his servant of being privy to her escape. In vain Mrs. Deborah told him of the trick she had played on her, and how she had been obliged to get into the house through the window. He continued his accusations, which so provoked his servant, conscious of their unjustness, that he at last replied to them with insolence. This. in the present state of Belgrave's mind, was not to be borne, and he immediately struck him over the forehead with his sword, and with a violence which felled him to the earth. Scarcely had he obeyed ere he repented his impulse of passion, which seemed attended with fatal consequences, for the man gave no symptoms of existence. Consideration for his own safety was more prevalent in his mind than any feelings of humanity, and he instantly rushed from the house, ere the woman was sufficiently recovered from her horror and amazement to be able to call to the other servants, as she afterwards did, to stop him. He fled to town, and hastened to an hotel in Pall Mall, from whence he determined to hire a carriage for Dover, and thence embark for the continent. Ascending the stairs he met a man, of all others he would have wished to avoid, namely, Sir Charles Bingley. He started, but it was too late to retreat. He then endeavored to shake off his embarrassment, from a faint hope that Sir Charles had not heard of his villanous design upon Miss Rushbrook; but this hope vanished the moment Sir Charles addressed him, who with coldness and contempt said he would be glad to speak to him for a few minutes. But ere we relate their conversation, it is necessary to relate a few particulars of the Rushbrooks.

Captain Rushbrook, from knowing more of the deceits of mankind than his wife, was less credulous. The more he reflected on the letter the more he felt doubts obtruding on his mind, and he resolved sooner to forfeit the friendship of Sipthorpe than permit any further intercourse between him and his daughter till those doubts were removed. He sent his son to Sir Charles's agent, and had the satisfaction of hearing he was then in town, and lodged at an hotel in Pall Mall. He immediately wrote to Sir Charles, and requested to see him whenever he was at leisure; adding, he was well convinced his benevolence would excuse the liberty he had taken, when informed of the purpose for which his visit was requested. Sir Charles was fortunately within. and directly attended little Rushbrook to the prison. The letter had filled him with surprise, but that surprise gave way, the moment he entered the wretched apartment of Rushbrook, to the powerful emotions of pity. A scene more distressing he had never seen, or could not have conceived. He saw the emaciated form of the soldier, for such his dress announced him, seated beside a dying fire, his little children surrounding him, whose faded countenances denoted their keen participation of his grief, and the sad partner of his misery bending her eyes upon those children with mingled love and sorrow.

Rushbrook was unable to speak for a few minutes after his entrance. When he recovered his voice, he thanked him for the kind attention he had paid his request, briefly informed him of the motives for that request, and ended by putting Amanda's letter into his hand. Sir Charles perused it with horror and amazement. "Gracious Heaven!" he exclaimed, "what a monster! I know not the lady who has referred you to me, but I can testify the truth of her allegations. I am shocked to think such a monster as Belgrave exists."

Shocked at the idea of the destruction she was so near devoting her daughter to, disappointed in the hopes she entertained of having her family liberated from prison, and struck with remorse for her conduct to Amanda, Mrs. Rushbrook fell fainting to the floor, overpowered by her painful emotions. Sir Charles aided in raising her from it, for the trembling hand of Rushbrook refused its assistance. "Unhappy woman!" he exclaimed, "the disappointment of her hopes is too much for her feeble frame" Water, the only restorative in the room, being sprinkled on her face, she slowly revived, and the first object she beheld was the pale and weeping Emily, whom her father had insisted on being brought to the prison. "Oh, my child," she cried, clasping her to her bosom, "can you forgive the mother who was so near devoting you to destruction? Oh! my children, for your sake, how near was I sacrificing this dear, this precious girl! I blush! I shudder! when I reflect on my conduct to the unhappy young creature, who, like a guardian angel, interposed between my child and ruin. But these dreary walls," she continued, bursting into an agony of tears, "which now we must never hope to pass, will hide my shame and sorrows together!" "Do not despair, my dear madam," said Sir

Charles, in the soft accent of benevolence, "nor do you," continued he, turning to Rushbrook, "deem me impertinent in inquiring into those sorrows." His accent, his manner, were so soothing, that these children of misery, who had long been strangers to the voice of kindness, gave him, with tears and sighs, a short relation of their sorrows. He heard them with deep attention, and, when he departed, gave them such a smile as, we may suppose, would beam from an angel, if sent by Heaven to pour the balm of comfort and mercy over the sorrows of a bursting heart.

He returned early in the morning. How bright, how animated was his countenance! Oh, ye sons of riot and extravagance! ye children of dissipation! never did ye experience a pleasure equal to his, when he entered the apartment of Rushbrook to inform him he was free; when, in the impassioned, yet faltering accents of sensibility, he communicated the joyful tidings, and heard the little children repeat his words, while their parents gazed on each other with surprise and rapture.

Rushbrook at length attempted to pour out the fulness of his heart, but Sir Charles stopped him. "Blessed with a fortune," cried he, "beyond my wants, to what nobler purpose could superfluous wealth be devoted, than to the enlargement of a man who has served his country, and who has a family which he may bring up to act as he has done? May the restoration of liberty be productive of every happiness! Your prison gates, I rejoice to repeat, are open. May the friendship which commenced within these walls be lasting as our lives!" To dwell longer on this subject is unnecessary. The transported family were conveyed to Mrs. Connel's, where he had been the preceding night to order everything for their reception. He then inquired about Sipthorpe, or rather Belgrave, whom he meant to upbraid for his cruel designs against Miss Rushbrook; but Belgrave, as soon as his plan was settled about Amanda, had quitted Mrs. Connel's. The joy of the Rushbrooks was greatly damped the next morning on hearing of the secret departure of Amanda. What Belgrave had said against her they never would have credited, but for the appearance of mystery which enveloped her. Still, her amiable attention to them merited their truest gratitude; they wished to have expressed that gratitude to her, and offer her their services. Much as appearances were against Amanda, yet from the very moment Mrs. Rushbrook declared it her idea that Belgrave had traduced her for the purpose of depriving her of protection, a similar idea started in Sir Charles's mind, and he resolved to seek Belgrave, and never rest till he had discovered whether there was any truth in his assertions against Amanda. Their meeting at the hotel was considered as fortunate as unexpected by him; yet could he not disguise for a moment the contempt his character inspired him with. He reproached him as soon as they entered an apartment, for his base designs against Miss Rushbrook; designs in every respect degrading to his character, since he knew the blow he levelled at the peace of her father, could not, from the unfortunate situation of that father, be resented. "You are," continued Sir Charles, "not only the violator, but the defamer of female innocence. I am well convinced from reflection on past and present circumstances, that your allegations against Miss Fitzalan were as false as vile." "You may doubt them, Sir Charles," replied Belgrave, "if it is agreeable to you; but yet, as a friend, I advise you not to let every one know you are her champion." "Oh, Belgrave!" cried Sir Charles, "can you think without remorse, of having destroyed not only the reputation, but the existence of an amiable young creature?" "The existence!" repeated Belgrave, starting, and with a kind of horror in his look. "What do you mean?" "I mean that Amanda Fitzalan, involved through your means in a variety of wretchedness she was unable to support, is now on her death-bed!" Belgrave changed color, trembled, and in an agitated voice, demanded an explanation of Sir Charles's words.

Sir Charles saw his feelings were touched, and trusting they would produce the discovery he wished, briefly gave him the particulars he asked for.

Amanda was the only woman that had ever really touched the heart of Belgrave. His mind, filled with horror and enervated with fear at the idea of the crime he had recently committed, could make no opposition to the grief he experienced on hearing of her situation—a grief heightened almost to distraction, by reflecting that he was accessory to it. "Dying!" he repeated, "Amanda Fitzalan dying! but she will be happy! Hers will be a pure and ministering spirit in heaven, when mine lies howling.

The angels are not purer in mind and person than she is!" "Then you are an execrable villain," cried Sir Charles, laying his hand on his sword. "Strike," exclaimed Belgrave, with an air of wildness; "death will rid me of horrors. Death from you will be better than the ignominious one which now stares me in the face; for I have, oh, horrible! this night I have committed murder!"

Astonished and dismayed, Sir Charles gazed on him with earnestness. "It is true!" continued he, in the same wild manner, "it is true! therefore strike! but against you I will not raise my hand; it were impious to touch a life like yours, consecrated to the purposes of virtue. No, I would not deprive the wretched of their friend." Sir Charles, still shuddering at his words, demanded an explanation of them; and the tortured soul of Belgrave, as if happy to meet any one it could confide in, after a little hesitation, divulged at once its crimes and horrors. "No," cried Sir Charles, when he had concluded, "to raise a hand against him over whom the arm of justice is uplifted, were cruel as well as cowardly. Go, then, and may repentance, not punishment, overtake you." To describe the raptures Sir Charles experienced at the acquittal of Amanda, is impossible. Not a fond father rejoicing over the restored fame of a darling child, could experience more exquisite delight. The next morning, as soon as he thought it possible he could gain admittance, he hastened to Mrs. Connel's, and had the satisfaction of hearing from Mrs. Rushbrook that Amanda was then in a sweet sleep, from which the most salutary consequences might be expected. With almost trembling impatience he communicated the transports of his heart, and his auditors rejoiced as much at these transports on Amanda's account as on his. Mrs. Rushbrook and Emily had sat up with her the preceding night, which she passed in a most restless manner, without any perception of surrounding objects. Towards morning she fell into a profound sleep, which they trusted would recruit her exhausted frame. Mrs. Rushbrook then withdrew to her husband. It was past noon ere Amanda awoke. At first a pleasing languor was diffused through her frame, which prevented her from having an idea of her situation; but gradually her recollection returned, and with it anxiety to know where she was. She remembered, too, the moment she had met Sir Charles, but no further. She gently opened the curtain, and beheld—oh! how great the pleasure of that moment—Emily sitting by the bedside, who, instantly rising, kissed her cheek in a transport of affection, and inquired how she did. Oh! how delightful, how soothing was that gentle voice to the ears of Amanda! The softest music could not have been more grateful. Her heart vibrated to it with an exquisite degree of pleasure, and her eyes feasted on the rays of benevolence which streamed from those of Emily. At last, in a faint voice, she said: "I am sure I am safe, since I am with Emily."

Mrs. Rushbrook entered at that instant. Her delight at the restored faculties of Amanda was equal to her daughter's; yet the recollection of her own conduct made her almost reluctant to approach her. At last, advancing, "I blush, yet I rejoice—oh! how truly rejoice—to behold you," she exclaimed; "that I could be tempted to harbor a doubt against you fills me with regret; and the vindication of your innocence can scarcely yield you more pleasure than it yields me." "The vindication of my innocence!" repeated Amanda, raising her head from the pillow. "Oh, gracious Heaven! is it then vindicated? Tell me, I conjure you, how, and by what means."

Mrs. Rushbrook hastened to obey her, and related all she had heard from Sir Charles. The restoration of her fame seemed to reanimate the soul of Amanda, yet tears burst from her, and she trembled with emotion. Mrs. Rushbrook was alarmed, and endeavored to compose her. "Do not be uneasy," said Amanda, "those tears will never injure me. It is long, it is very long, since I have shed tears of joy!" She implored Heaven's choicest blessings on Sir Charles for his generosity to her, his benevolence to the Rushbrooks. Her heart, relieved of a heavy burthen of anxiety on her own account, now grew more anxious than ever to learn something of her poor Oscar; and notwithstanding Mrs. Rushbrook's entreaties to the contrary, who feared she was exerting herself beyond her strength, she arose in the afternoon for the purpose of going to the drawing-room, determined, as Sir Charles's generous conduct merited her confidence, to relate to him as well as to Mrs. Rushbrook the motives which had brought her to town; the particulars of her life necessary to be known; and to request their assistance in trying to learn intelligence of her brother. Emily helped her to dress, and supported her to the drawing-room. Sir Charles had continued in the house the whole day, and met her as she entered with mingled love and pity; for in her feeble form, her faded cheek, he witnessed the ravages of grief and sickness. His eyes more than his tongue expressed his feelings, yet in the softest accent of tenderness did he pour forth those feelings, whilst his hand trembled as it pressed hers to his bosom. "My feelings, Sir Charles," said she, "cannot be expressed; but my gratitude to you will cease but with my existence."

Sir Charles besought her to be silent on such a subject. "He was selfish," he said, "in everything he did for her, for on her happiness his depended."

Rushbrook approached to offer his congratulations. He spoke of her kindness, but, like Sir Charles, the subject was painful to her, and dropped at her request. The idea of being safe, the soothing attentions she experienced, gave to her mind a tranquillity it had long been a stranger to, and she looked back on her past dangers but to enjoy more truly her present security. As she witnessed the happiness of the Rushbrooks, she could scarcely forbear applauding aloud the author of that happiness; but she judged of his heart by her own, and therefore checked herself by believing he would prefer the silent plaudits of that heart to any praise whatsoever. After tea, when only Sir Charles, Mr. and Mrs. Rushbrook, and Emily, were present, she entered upon the affairs she wished to communicate. They heard her with deep attention, wonder, and pity, and, when she concluded, both Sir Charles and Rushbrook declared their readiness to serve her. The latter, who had betrayed strong emotions during her narrative, assured her he doubted not, nay, he was almost convinced, he should soon be able to procure her intelligence of her brother.

This was a sweet assurance to the heart of Amanda, and, cheered by it, she soon retired to bed. Her strength being exhausted by speaking she sunk into a tranquil slumber, and next morning she arose for breakfast. "Well," said Rushbrook to her as they sat at it, "I told you last night I should soon be able to procure you intelligence of your brother, and I was not mistaken." "Oh, heavens!" cried Amanda, in trembling emotion, "have you really heard anything of him?" "Be composed, my dear girl," said he, taking her hand, in the most soothing, most affectionate manner, "I have heard of him, but——" "But what?" interrupted Amanda, with increased emotion. "Why, that he has experienced some of the trials of life. But let the reflection that these trials are over, prevent your suffering pain by hearing of them." "Oh! tell me, I entreat," said Amanda, "where he is! Tell me, I conjure you; shall I see him?" "Yes," replied Rushbrook, "you shall see him, to keep you no longer in suspense. In that dreary prison, from which I have been just released, he has languished for many months." "Oh, my brother!" exclaimed Amanda, while tears gushed from her.

"I knew not," continued Rushbrook, "from the concealment of your name, that he was your brother, till last night. I then told Sir Charles, and he is gone this morning to him; but you must expect to see him somewhat altered. The restoration of liberty, and the possession of fortune, will no doubt soon re-establish his health. Hark! I think I hear a voice on the stairs."

Amanda started, arose, attempted to move, but sunk again upon her chair. The door opened, and Sir Charles entered, followed by Oscar. Though prepared for an alteration in his looks, she was not by any means prepared for an alteration which struck her the moment she beheld him. Pale and thin, even to a degree of emaciation, he was dressed, or rather wrapped, in an old regimental great-coat, his fine hair wildly dishevelled. As he approached her, Amanda rose. "Amanda, my sister!" said he, in a faint voice. She tottered forward, and falling upon his bosom, gave way in tears to the mingled joy and anguish of the moment. Oscar pressed her to his heart. He gazed on her with the fondest rapture—yet a rapture suddenly checked, by surveying the alteration in her appearance, which was as striking to him, as his was to her. Her pale and woe-worn countenance, her sable dress, at once declared her sufferings, and brought most painfully to recollection the irreparable loss they had sustained since their last meeting.

"Oh, my father!' groaned Oscar, unable to control the strong emotions of his mind—"Oh, my father! when last we met we were blessed with your presence." He clasped Amanda closer to his heart as he spoke, as if doubly endeared to him by her desolate situation.

"To avoid regretting him is indeed impossible," said Amanda; "yet, had he lived, what tortures would have wrung his heart in witnessing the unhappiness of his children, when he had not the power of removing it!" "Come," cried Captain Rushbrook, whose eyes, like those of every person present, confessed his sympathetic feelings, "let us not cloud present blessings by the retrospection of past misfortunes. In this life we must all expect to meet with such losses as you lament." As soon as Oscar and Amanda grew composed, they were left to themselves, and Oscar then satisfied the anxious and impatient heart of his sister, by informing her of all that had befallen him. He began with his attachment for Adela, and the disappointment of that attachment; but as this part of his story is already known, we shall pass it over in silence, and merely relate the occasion of his quarrel with Belgrave.

CHAPTER LIV.

> "But thou who, mindful of the unhonored dead,
> Dost in these lines their artless tale relate,
> If chance, by lonely contemplation led,
> Some kindred spirit should lament thy fate,
> Haply some hoary headed swain may say,
> Oft have I seen him, at the peep of dawn,
> Brushing with hasty steps the dews away,
> To meet the sun upon the upland lawn."

I LEFT Enniskellen," said Oscar, "in the utmost distress of mind, for I left it with the idea that I might no more behold Adela. Yet, dear and precious as was her sight to my soul, I rejoiced she had not accompanied the regiment, since to have beheld her but as the wife of Belgrave would have been insupportable. Had the disappointment of my passion been occasioned by its not meeting a return, pride would have assisted me to conquer it; but to know it was tenderly returned, at once cherished and, if possible, increased it. The idea of the happiness I might have attained, rendered me insensible of any that I might still have enjoyed. I performed the duties of my situation mechanically, and shunned society as much as possible, unable to bear the raillery of my gay companions on my melancholy.

"The summer you came to Ireland the regiment removed to Bray, whose romantic situation allowed me to enjoy many delightful and solitary rambles. It was there a man enlisted, whose manner and appearance were for many days subjects of surprise and conversation to us all. From both, it was obvious he had been accustomed to one of the superior situations in life. A form more strikingly elegant I never beheld. The officers made many attempts to try and discover who he really was; but he evaded all their inquiries, yet with the utmost agitation. What rendered him, if possible, more interesting, was his being accompanied by a young and lovely woman, who, like him, appeared sunk beneath her original state; but to their present one both conformed, if not with cheerfulness, at least with resignation.

"Mary obtained work from almost all the officers; Henry was diligent in his duties; and both were universally admired and respected. Often, in my lonely rambles, have I surprised this unfortunate pair, who, it was evident, like me, sought solitude for the indulgence of sorrow, weeping together as if over the remembrance of happier hours. Often have I beheld them gazing with mingled agony and tenderness on the infant which Mary nursed, as if shuddering at the idea of its destiny.

"The loveliness of Mary was too striking not to attract the notice of Belgrave; and from her situation he flattered himself she would be an easy prey. He was, however, mistaken. She repulsed his overtures with equal abhorrence and indignation. She wished to conceal them from her husband, but he heard of them through the means of his fellow-soldiers, who had several times seen the Colonel following his wife. It was then he really felt the bitterness of a servile situation. Of his wife he had no doubt; she had already given him a convincing proof of constancy, but he dreaded the insults she might receive from the Colonel. The united vigilance of both prevented, however, for some time, a repetition of those insults. Exasperated by their vigilance, the Colonel at last concerted one of the most diabolical plans which could have entered into the heart of man. A party of the soldiers were ordered to the sea-side, to watch there for smuggled goods. Henry was named to be of the party, but when the soldiers were drawn out he was not to be found. Belgrave's servant, the vile agent of his master, had informed him that the Colonel meant to take advantage of his absence, and visit his wife. He trembled for her safety, resolved to run every risk, sooner than leave her unguarded, and accordingly absconded till the departure of the party. The consequence of this was, that on his reappearance he was put under an arrest for disobedience of orders, tried the next day, and sentenced to be flogged on the following one. The very officers that passed the sentence regretted it, but the strictness of military discipline rendered it unavoidable.

"I shall not attempt to describe the situation of the unhappy young couple; they felt for each other more than for themselves, and pride heightened the agonies of Henry.

"Pale, weeping, with a distracted air, Mary flew to my apartment, and, sinking at my feet, with uplifted hands besought me to interpose in favor of her husband. I raised the poor mourner from the ground, and assured her, yet with a sigh, from the fear of proving unsuccessful, that I would do all in my power to save him. I therefore hastened to the Colonel, to ask for another that favor I should have disdained to desire for myself; but to serve this wretched couple, I felt I could almost humble myself to the earth.

"The Colonel was on the parade; and, as if aware of my intention, appeared sedulous to avoid me. But I would not be repulsed by this, and followed him, entreating his attention for a few minutes. 'Despatch your business then in haste, sir,' said he, with an unusual haughtiness. 'I shall, sir,' cried I, endeavoring to repress the indignation his manner excited, 'and I also hope with success.' 'What is your business, sir?' demanded he. ''Tis the business of humanity,' I replied, 'and 'tis only for others I could ask a favor.'

"I then proceeded to mention it. Rage and malice inflamed his countenance as I spoke. 'Never,' exclaimed he, 'shall the wretch receive pardon from me; and I am astonished at your presumption in asking it.' 'Yet not half so astonished,' replied I, 'as I am at your obduracy. Though, why do I say so? from your past actions, I should not be surprised at any act you may commit.'

"His passion grew almost to frenzy; he asked me if I knew who I was addressing. 'Too well,' I replied; 'I know I am addressing one of the completest villains upon earth.'

"He raised a small rattan he held, at these words, in a threatening manner. I could no longer oppose my indignation. I rushed upon him, wrested it from his hand, broke it, and flung it over his head. 'Now,' cried I, laying my hand upon my sword, 'I am ready to give you the satisfaction you may desire for my words—words whose truth I will uphold with my life.' 'No,' said he, with the coolness of deliberate malice; ''tis a far different satisfaction I shall expect to receive.' Some of the officers had by this time gathered round us, and attempted to interfere, but he commanded their silence in a haughty manner, and ordered me under an immediate arrest. My fate I then knew decided, but I resolved to bear that fate with fortitude, nor let him triumph in every respect over me. I was confined to my room, and Henry the next morning was brought forth to receive his punishment. I will not, my sister, pain your gentle heart by describing to you, as it was described to me by an officer, his parting from his wife. Pride, indignation, tenderness, and pity, were struggling in his heart, and visible in his countenance. He attempted to assume composure, but when he reached the destined spot, he could no longer control his feelings. The idea of being exposed, disgraced, was too much for his noble soul. The paleness of his face increased. He tottered, fell into the arms of a soldier, and expired groaning forth the name of Mary. Four days after this melancholy event a court-martial was held on me, when, as I expected, I was broken, for contempt to my superior officer. I retired to a solitary inn near Bray, in a state of mind which baffles description, destitute of friends and fortune. I felt in that moment as if I had no business in the world. I was followed to the inn by a young lieutenant with whom I had been on an intimate footing. The grief he expressed at my situation roused me from almost a stupefaction that was stealing on me. The voice of friendship will penetrate the deepest gloom, and I felt my sorrows gradually allayed by it. He asked me had I fixed on any plan for myself

I replied I had not, for it was vain to fix on plans when there were no friends to support them. He took my hand, and told me I was mistaken. In a few days he trusted to procure me letters to a gentleman in London who had considerable possessions in the West Indies, if such a thing was agreeable to me. It was just what I wished for, and I thanked him with the sincerest gratitude

"In the evening I received a message from the unfortunate Mary, requesting to see me directly. The soldier who brought it said she was dying. I hastened to her. She was in bed, and supported by a soldier's wife. The declining sunbeams stole into the apartment, and shed a kind of solemn glory around her. The beauty that had caused her misfortunes was faded, but she looked more interesting than when adorned with that bloom of beauty. Sighs and tears impeded her words for some minutes after I approached her. At last, in a faint voice, she said, 'I sent for you, sir, because I knew your goodness, your benevolence would excuse the liberty. I knew you would think that no trouble which could soothe the last sad moments of a wretched woman.'

"She then proceeded to inform me of the motives which made her send—namely, to convey her infant to her father, a person of fortune in Dublin, and to see her remains, ere I did so, laid by those of her husband. Her unfortunate Henry, she added, had been son to a respectable merchant. Their families were intimate, and an attachment which commenced at an early period between them was encouraged. Henry's father experienced a sudden reverse of fortune, and hers, in consequence of it, forbade their ever thinking more of each other; but they could not obey his commands, and married clandestinely, thus forfeiting the favor of all their friends, as Henry's thought he wanted spirit, and hers deemed her deficient in respect to her father. They were therefore compelled by necessity to a state of life infinitely beneath them. 'But in my grave,' continued she, 'I trust my father will bury all his resentment, and protect this little orphan.'

"I promised a religious observance to her commands, and she expired in about an hour after I quitted her. Mournful were the tasks she enjoined me. I attended her remains to the grave, and then conveyed her child to Dublin.

"Startled, amazed, distressed, her father too late regretted his rigor, and received her infant to his arms with floods of repentant tears.

"I now procured my recommendatory letters, and sailed for England, having first written farewell ones to my father and Mrs. Marlowe, in which I informed both I was about quitting the kingdom. As soon as I had procured cheap lodgings in London, I repaired to the gentleman to whom I was recommended; but conceive my consternation when I heard he was himself gone to the West Indies. I turned into a coffee-house, with an intention of communicating this intelligence to my friend. While the waiter was getting me materials for writing, I took up a newspaper, and cast my eyes carelessly over it. Oh! my Amanda, what was the shock of that moment, when I read my father's death: grief for him, anxiety for you, both assailed my heart too powerfully for its feelings. My head grew giddy, my sight failed me, and I fell back with a deep groan. When recovered, by the assistance of some gentlemen, I requested a carriage might be sent for, but I was too weak to walk to it. On returning to my lodgings, I was compelled to go to bed, from which I never rose for a fortnight. During my illness all the little money I had brought along with me was expended, and I was besides considerably in debt with the people of the house for procuring me necessaries. When able to sit up they furnished their accounts, and I candidly told my inability to discharge them. In consequence of this I was arrested, and suffered to take of my clothes but a change or two of linen. The horrors of what I imagined would be a lasting captivity were heightened by reflecting on your unprotected situation. A thousand times was I on the point of writing to inquire into that situation, but still checked myself by reflecting that, as I could not aid you, I should only add to any griefs you might be oppressed with by acquainting you of mine. The company of Captain Rushbrook alleviated in some degree the dreariness of my time. I knew I should sustain an irreparable loss in losing him, but I should have detested myself if any selfish motives had prevented my rejoicing at his enlargement. Oh! little did I think his liberation was leading the way to mine. Early this morning he returned, and introduced Sir Charles Bingley to me. Gently, and by degrees, they broke the joyful intelligence they had to communicate. With truth I can aver that the announcement of a splendid fortune was not so pleasing to my heart as the mention of my sister's safety. Of my poor Adela I know nothing since my confinement; but I shudder to think of what she may have suffered from being left solely in the power of such a man as Belgrave, for the good old General died soon after I left Enniskellen.

"'Regret not too bitterly, my dear Oscar,' said Mrs. Marlowe, in one of her letters, 'the good man's death; rather rejoice he was removed ere his last hours were embittered by the knowledge of his darling child's unhappiness.'

"Oh! my sister!" continued Oscar, with a heavy sigh, while tears fell from him, and mingled with those Amanda was shedding, "in this world we must have still something to wish and sigh for."

Oscar here concluded his narrative with such an expression of melancholy as gave to Amanda the sad idea of his passion for Adela being incurable. This was indeed the case; neither reason, time, nor absence could remove or lessen it, and the acquisition of liberty or fortune lost half their value by brooding over her loss.

When their friends returned to the drawing-room and again offered their congratulations, Oscar's dejection would not permit him to reply to them. When Mr. and Mrs. Rushbrook spoke of the happiness he might now enjoy, he listened to their recapitulation of it as to a fulsome tale, to which his heart in secret gave the lie. An innate sense of piety, however, recalled him to a proper recollection of the blessings so unexpectedly declared to be his He accused himself of ingratitude to Heaven in yielding to murmurs, after so astonishing a reverse in his situation. Perfect happiness he had been early taught—and daily experience confirmed the truth of the remark—was rarely to be met with; how presumptuous in him, therefore, to repine at the common lot of humanity: to be independent, to have the means of returning the obligations Sir Charles Bingley had conferred upon him; to be able to comfort and provide for his lovely and long-afflicted sister; and to distribute relief amongst the children of indigence, were all blessings which would shortly be his—blessings which demanded his warmest gratitude, and for which he now raised his heart with thankfulness to their divine Dispenser. His feelings grew composed; a kind of soft and serene melancholy stole over his mind. He still thought of Adela, but not with that kind of distracting anguish he had so recently experienced; it was with that kind of tender regret which a soul of sensibility feels when reflecting on a departed friend, and to him Adela was as much lost, as if already shrouded in her native clay. "Yes, my love," he said, as if her gentle spirit had already forsaken its earthly mansion, "in that happy world we shall be reunited, which only can reward thy goodness and thy sufferings."

He could now enter into conversation with his friends about the measures which should be taken to forward his pretensions. It was the opinion of Captain Rushbrook and Sir Charles, that to make known his claim to the Marquis of Roslin was all that was necessary; a claim which they did not imagine he would or could dispute, when such proofs of its validity as the testimony of Lady Dunreath, and the will, could be produced. Was it disputed, it was then time enough to apply elsewhere for justice.

Sir Charles knew the Marquis personally, and was also well acquainted in his neighborhood, and declared he would accompany Oscar to Scotland. Oscar thanked him for his intention. The support of a person so well known, and universally esteemed, he was convinced, would essentially serve him. Sir Charles said, regimental business required his presence in Ireland, which, however, would occasion no great delay, as he should have it transacted in a few days; and as his regiment lay near Donaghadee, they could cross over to Port-Patrick, and, in a few hours after, reach the Marquis of Roslin's Castle.

The day after the next he had fixed for commencing his journey, and he asked Oscar if it would be agreeable and convenient to accompany him then. Oscar instantly assured him it was both Amanda's heart fluttered at the idea of a journey to Ireland. It was probable, she thought, that they would take Wales in their way; and her soul seemed already on the wing to accompany them thither, and be left at the cottage of nurse Edwin, from whence she could again wander through the shades of Tudor Hall, and take a last, a sad farewell of them; for she solemnly determined from the moment she should be apprised of Lord Mortimer's return to England to visit them no more. In such a farewell she believed she should find a melancholy consolation that would soothe her spirits. She imagined there was no necessity for accompanying her brother into Scotland, and except told there was an absolute one, she determined to decline the journey if she should be asked to undertake it. To go to the very spot where she would hear particulars of Lord Mortimer's nuptials, she felt would be too much for her fortitude, and might betray to her brother a secret she had resolved carefully to conceal from him, as she well knew the pain he would feel from knowing that the pangs of a hopeless attachment were entailed upon her life, and would defeat whatever flattering hopes he entertained for her. Exclusive of the above-mentioned objections, she could not bear to go to a place where she might perhaps witness the pain which Lord Mortimer must unavoidably feel from having any disgrace befall a family he was so nearly connected with. Oh, how her heart swelled at the idea that ere Oscar reached Scotland, the interest of the Marquis of Roslin and Lord Mortimer would be but one! From her apprehensions of being asked to undertake a journey so truly repugnant to her feelings, she was soon relieved by Oscar's declaring that, except she wished it, he would not ask her to take so fatiguing a one, particularly as her presence he could not think at all necessary.

Sir Charles Bingley assured him it was not; though in a low voice he said to her, it was against his own interest he spoke.

She would now have mentioned her wish of going to Wales, had not a certain consciousness checked her. She feared her countenance would betray her motives for such a wish. While she hesitated about mentioning it, Sir Charles Bingley told Captain Rushbrook, that he had applied to a friend of his in power for a place for him, and had been fortunate enough to make application at the very time there was one of tolerable emolument vacant, at ——, about seventy miles distant from London, whither it would be necessary he should go as soon as possible. He therefore proposed that he and Mrs. Rushbrook should begin preparations for their journey the ensuing morning, and exert themselves to be able to undertake it in the course of the week.

They were all rapture and gratitude at this intelligence, which opened a prospect of support through their own means, as the bread of independence, however hardly earned, which here was not the case, must ever be sweet to souls of sensibility.

Oscar looked with anxiety at his sister, on the mention of the Rushbrooks' removal from town, as if to say, to whose care then can I intrust you? Mrs. Rushbrook interpreted his look, and instantly requested that Miss Fitzalan might accompany them, declaring her society would render their felicity complete. This was the moment for Amanda to speak. She took courage, and mentioned her earnest wish of visiting her faithful nurse, declaring she could not lose so favorable an opportunity as now offered for the gratification of that wish, by accompanying her brother into Wales. Emily pleaded, but Amanda, though with the utmost gratitude and tenderness, as if to soften her refusal, was steady. Oscar was pleased with his sister's determination, as he trusted going into what might be called her native air, joined to the tender care of nurse Edwin, would recruit her health. Sir Charles was in raptures at the idea of having her company so far on their way.

Everything relative to the proceedings of the whole party was arranged before dinner, at which Sir Charles presided, giving pleasure to all around him, by the ineffable sweetness of his manners. He withdrew at an early hour at night, and his friends soon after retired to their respective chambers. On entering the breakfast-room next morning, Amanda found not only her brother and the Rushbrooks, but Sir Charles Bingley there. Immediately after breakfast, he drew Oscar aside, and in the most delicate terms insisted on being his banker at present, to which Oscar gratefully consented. As soon as this affair was settled, he put a note into his sister's hands to purchase whatever she should deem necessary; and she went out with the Rushbrooks, who, according to Sir Charles's directions, began preparations for their journey this day. After their return, Sir Charles found an opportunity of again making an offer of his hand to Amanda.

The sincere friendship she had conceived for him made her determine to terminate his suspense on her account. "Was I to accept your generous proposal, Sir Charles," said she, "I should be unworthy of that esteem which it will be my pride to retain and my pleasure to return, because beyond esteem I cannot go myself. It is due to your friendship," cried she, after the hesitation of a moment, whilst a rosy blush stole over her lovely face, and as quickly faded from it, "to declare, that ere I saw you, the fate of my heart was decided."

Sir Charles turned pale. He grasped her hands in a kind of silent agony to his bosom, then exclaimed: "I will not, Miss Fitzalan, after your generous confidence, tease you with further importunity."

CHAPTER LV.

"——— I solitary court
The inspiring breeze."—THOMSON.

HE ensuing morning, Oscar, Amanda, and Sir Charles began their journey The Rushbrooks, who regarded Amanda as the cause of their present happiness, took leave of her with a tender sorrow that deeply affected her heart. The journey to Wales was pleasant and expeditious, the weather being fine, and relays of horses being provided at every stage. On the evening of the third day they arrived about sunset at the village which lay contiguous to Edwin's abode; from whence, as soon as they had taken some refreshment, Amanda set off, attended by her brother, for the cottage, having ordered her luggage to be brought after her. She would not permit the attendance of Sir Charles, and almost regretted having travelled with him, as she could not help thinking his passion seemed increased by her having done so. "How dearly," cried he, as he handed her down stairs, "shall I pay for a few short hours of pleasure, by the unceasing regret their remembrance will entail upon me."

Amanda withdrew her hand, and, bidding him farewell, hurried on. Oscar proceeded no farther than the lane, which led to the cottage, with his sister. He had no time to answer the interrogations which its inhabitants might deem themselves privileged to make. Neither did he wish his present situation to be known to any others than those already acquainted with it. Amanda therefore meant to say she had taken the opportunity of travelling so far with two particular friends who were going to Ireland. Oscar promised to write to her immediately from thence, and from Scotland, as soon as he had seen the Marquis. He gave her a thousand charges concerning her health, and took a tender farewell. From his too visible dejection, Amanda rejoiced she had not revealed her own sorrows to him. She trusted it would be in her power, by soothing attentions, by the thousand little nameless offices of friendship, to alleviate his. To pluck the thorn from his heart which rankled within it was beyond her hopes. In their dispositions, as well as fates, there was too great a similitude to expect this.

Amanda lingered in the walk as he departed. She was now in the very spot that recalled a thousand fond and tender remembrances. It was here she had given a farewell look to Tudor Hall; it was here her father had taken a last look at the spire of the church where his beloved wife was interred; it was here Lord Mortimer used so often to meet her. Her soul sunk in the heaviest sadness. Sighs burst from her overcharged heart, and with difficulty she prevented her tears from falling. All around was serene and beautiful; but neither the serenity nor the beauty of the scene could she now enjoy. The plaintive bleating of the cattle that rambled about the adjacent hills only heightened her melancholy, and the appearance of autumn, which was now far advanced, only made her look back to the happy period when admiring its luxuriance had given her delight. The parting sunbeams yet glittered on the windows of Tudor Hall. She paused involuntarily to contemplate it. Hours could she have continued in the same situation, had not the idea that she might be observed from the cottage made her at last hasten to it.

The door lay open. She entered, and found only the nurse within, employed at knitting. Her astonishment at the appearance of Amanda is not to be described. She started, screamed, surveyed her a minute, as if doubting the evidence of her eyes, then, running to her, flung her arms about her neck, and clasped her to her bosom. "Good gracious!" cried she; "well, to pe sure, who ever would have thought such a thing? Well, to pe sure, you are as welcome as the flowers in May. Here we have peen in such a peck of troubles about you. Many and many a time has my good man said, that if he knew where you were, he would go to you." Amanda returned the embraces of her faithful nurse, and they both sat down together.

"Ah! I fear," said the nurse, looking tenderly at her for a few minutes, "you have been in a sad way since I last saw you. The poor tear Captain, alack! little did I think when he took you away from us, I should never see him more." Amanda's tears could no longer be suppressed; they gushed in torrents from her, and deep sobs spoke the bitterness of her feelings. "Ay," said the nurse, wiping her eyes with the corner of her apron, "gentle or simple, sooner or later, we must all go the same way; so, my tear chilt, don't take it so much to heart. Well, to pe sure, long pefore this I thought I should have seen or heard of your being greatly married; put I pelieve it is true enough, that men are like the wind—always changing. Any one that had seen Lord Mortimer after you went away, would never have thought he could prove fickle. He was in such grief, my very heart and soul pitied him. To pe sure, if I had known where you were, I should have told him. I comforted myself, however, by thinking he would certainly find you out, when, Lort! instead of looking for you, here he's going to be married to a great lady, with such a long, hard name—a Scotch heiress, I think they call her. Ay, golt is everything in these days. Well, all the harm I wish him is, that she may plague his life out."

This discourse was too painful to Amanda. Her tears had subsided, and she endeavored to change it, by asking after the nurse's family. The nurse, in a hasty manner, said they were well, and thus proceeded: "Then there is Parson Howel. I am sure one would have thought him as steady as Penmaenmawr, but no such thing. I am sure he has changed, for he does not come to the cottage half so often to ask about you as he used to do."

Amanda, notwithstanding her dejection, smiled at the nurse's anger about the curate, and again requested to hear particulars of her family. The nurse no longer hesitated to comply with her request. She informed her they were all well, and then at a little distance at the mill in the valley. She also added, that Ellen was married to her faithful Chip; had a comfortable cottage, and a fine little girl she was nursing, and to whom, from her love to her tear young laty, she would have given the name of Amanda, but that she feared people would deem her conceited, to give it so fine a one. The nurse said she often regretted having left her young laty, and then even Chip himself could not console her for having done so. Tears again started in Amanda's eyes, at hearing of the unabated attachment of her poor Ellen. She longed to see and congratulate her on her present happiness. The nurse, in her turn, inquired of all that had befallen Amanda since their separation and shed tears at hearing of her dear child's sufferings since that period. She asked about Oscar, and was briefly informed he was well. The family soon returned from the dance; and it would be difficult to say whether surprise or joy was most predominant at seeing Amanda. One of the young men ran over for Ellen, and returned in a few minutes with her, followed by her husband, carrying his little child. She looked wild with delight. She clasped Amanda in her arms, as if she would never let her depart from them, and wept in the fulness of her heart. "Now, now," cried she. "I shall be quite happy; but, oh! why, my dear young laty, did you not come amongst us before? you know all in our power we would have done to render you happy." She now recollected herself, and modestly retired to a little distance. She took her child and brought it to Amanda, who delighted her extremely by the notice she took of it and Chip. If Amanda had had less cause for grief, the attentions of these affectionate cottagers would have soothed her mind; but at present nothing could diminish her dejection. Her luggage was by this time arrived. She had brought presents for all the family, and now distributed them. She tried to converse about their domestic affairs, but found herself unequal to the effort, and begged to be shown to her chamber. The nurse would not suffer her to retire to it till she had tasted her new cheese and Welsh ale. When alone within it, she found fresh objects to remind her of Lord Mortimer, and consequently to augment her grief. Here lay the book-case he had sent her. She opened it with trembling impatience; but scarcely a volume did she examine in which select passages were not marked, by his hand, for her particular perusal. Oh! what mementos were those volumes of the happy hours she had passed at the cottage! The night waned away, and still she continued weeping over them.

She could with difficulty bring herself to close the book-case; and when she retired to rest her slumbers were short and unrefreshing The next morning as she sat at breakfast, assiduously attended by the nurse and her daughters (for Ellen had come over early to inquire after her health), Howel entered to pay her a visit. The previous intimation she had received of the alteration in his sentiments rendered his visit more pleasing than it would otherwise have been to her. His pleasure was great at seeing her, but it was not the wild and extravagant delight of a lover, but the soft and placid joy of a friend. After his departure, which was not soon, she accompanied Ellen to view her cottage, and was infinitely pleased by its neatness and romantic situation. It lay on the side of a hill which commanded a beautiful prospect of Tudor Hall. Everything she beheld reminded Amanda of Lord Mortimer, even the balmy air she breathed, on which his voice had so often floated.

The sad indulgence of wandering through the shades of Tudor Hall, which she had so eagerly desired, and fondly anticipated, she could not long deny herself. The second evening after her arrival at the cottage, she turned her solitary steps to them; their deep embowering glens, their solitude, their silence, suited the pensive turn of her feelings. Here, undisturbed and unobserved, she could indulge the sorrows of her heart; and oh! how did recollection augment those sorrows by retracing the happy hours she had spent within those shades. A cold, a death-like melancholy pervaded her feelings, and seemed repelling the movements of life. Her trembling limbs were unable to support her, and she threw herself on the ground. For some minutes she could scarcely breathe. Tears at length relieved her painful oppression, she raised her languid head, she looked around, and wept with increasing violence at beholding what might be termed mementos of former happiness. She repeated in soft and tremulous accents the name of Mortimer; but as the beloved name vibrated on her ear, how did she start at recollecting that she was then calling upon the husband of Lady Euphrasia. She felt a momentary glow upon her cheeks. She arose, and sighed deeply. "I will strive to do right," she cried; "I will try to wean my soul from remembrances no longer proper to be indulged." Yet still she lingered in the wood. The increasing gloom of evening rendered it, if possible, more pleasing to her feelings, whilst the breeze sighed mournfully through the trees, and the droning bat fluttered upon the air, upon which the wild music of a harp, from one of the neighboring cottages, softly floated.

Amanda drew nearer to it. It looked dark and melancholy. She sighed—she involuntarily exclaimed, "Oh, how soon will it be enlivened by bridal pomp and festivity!" She now recollected the uneasiness her long absence might create at the cottage, and as soon as the idea occurred, hastened to it. She met Edwin in the lane, who had been despatched by his wife in quest of her. The good woman expressed her fears, that such late rambles would injure the health of Amanda; "it was a sad thing," she said, "tc see young people giving way to dismal fancies."

Amanda did not confine her rambles entirely to Tudor Hall; she visited all the spots where she and Mortimer used to ramble together. She went to the humble spot where her mother lay interred. Her feelings were now infinitely more painful than when she had first seen it. It recalled to her mind, in the most agonizing manner, all the vicissitudes she had experienced since that period. It recalled to view the calamitous closure of her father's life—the sorrows, the distresses of that life, and she felt overwhelmed with grief. Scarcely could she prevent herself from falling on the grave, and giving way in tears and lamentations to that grief. Deprived of the dearest connections of life, blasted in hopes and expectations—"Oh! well had it been for me," she cried, "had this spot at once received the mother and child; and yet," she exclaimed, after a minute's reflection; "oh! what, my God, am I, that I should dare to murmur or repine at thy decrees? Oh! pardon the involuntary expressions of a woe-worn heart, of a heart that feels the purest gratitude for thy protection through past dangers. Oh! how presumptuous," she continued, "to repine at the common lot of humanity, as the lot of her," she continued, casting her tearful eyes upon the grave, where the last flowers of autumn were now withering, "who reposes in this earthly bed who, in life's meridian, in beauty's prime, sunk, the sad victim of sorrow, into the arms of death! Oh, my parents, how calamitous were your destinies! even your ashes were not permitted to moulder together, but, in a happier region, your kindred spirits are now united. Blessed spirits, your child will strive to imitate your example; in patient resignation to the will of Heaven, she will endeavor to support life. She will strive to live, though not from an idea of enjoying happiness, but from an humble hope of being able to dispense it to others."

Such were the words of Amanda at the grave of her mother, from which she turned like a pale and drooping lily, surcharged with tears. At the end of a week, she heard from Oscar, who told her in the course of a few days he expected to embark for Scotland. Amanda had brought materials for drawing with her, and she felt a passionate desire of taking views of Tudor Hall; views which, she believed, would yield her a melancholy pleasure when she should be far and for ever distant from the spots they represented.

This desire, however, she could not gratify without the assistance of her nurse, for she meant to take her views from the library, and she feared if she went there without apprising the housekeeper, she should be liable to interruption. She, therefore, requested her nurse to ask permission for her to go there. The nurse shook her head, as if she suspected Amanda had a motive for the request she did not divulge. She was, however, too anxious to gratify her dear child to refuse complying with it, and accordingly lost no time in asking the desired permission, which Mrs. Abergwilly readily gave, saying—" Miss Fitzalan was welcome to go to the library whenever she pleased, and should not be interrupted."

Amanda did not delay availing herself of this permission, but it was some time after she entered the library, ere she could compose herself sufficiently for the purpose which had brought her to it. In vain did nature appear from the windows, displaying the most beautiful and romantic scenery to her view, as if to tempt her to take up the pencil. Her eyes were dimmed with tears as she looked upon this scenery, and reflected that he who had once pointed out its various beauties was lost to her for ever. By degrees, however, her feelings grew composed, and every morning she repaired to the library, feeling, whilst engaged within it, a temporary alleviation of sorrow.

Three weeks passed in this manner, and at the expiration of that period, she received a letter from Oscar. She trembled in the most violent agitation as she broke the seal, for she saw by the post-mark he was in Scotland ; but how great was her surprise and joy at the contents of this letter, which informed her everything relative to the important affair so lately in agitation, was settled in the most amicable manner ; that the avowal of his claim occasioned not the smallest litigation ; that he was then in full possession of the fortune bequeathed him by the Earl, and had already received the congratulations of the neighboring families on his accession, or rather restoration to it. He had not time, he said, to enumerate the many particulars which rendered the adjustment of affairs so easy, and hoped the pleasing intelligence his letter communicated would atone for his brevity ; he added, he was then preparing to set off for London with Sir Charles Bingley, of whose friendship he spoke in the highest terms, to settle some affairs relative to his new possessions, and particularly about the revival of the Dunreath title, which not from any ostentatious pride, he desired to obtain, as he was sure she would suppose, but from gratitude and respect to the wishes of his grandfather, who in his will had expressed his desire that the honors of his family should be supported by his heir. When everything was finally settled, he proceeded to say, he would hasten on the wings of love and impatience to her, for in her sweet society alone he found any balm for the sorrows of his heart, sorrows which could not be eradicated from it, though fortune had been so unexpectedly propitious ; and he hoped, he said, he should find her then gay as the birds, blooming as the flowerets of spring, and ready to accompany him to the venerable mansion of their ancestors.

The joyful intelligence this letter communicated she had not spirits at present to mention to the inhabitants of this cottage ; the pleasure it afforded was only damped by reflecting on what Lord Mortimer must feel from a discovery which could not fail of casting a dark shade of obloquy upon his new connections. She was now doubly anxious to finish her landscapes, from the prospect there was of her quitting Wales so soon. Every visit she now paid the library was paid with the sad idea of its being the last. As she was preparing for going there one morning, immediately after breakfast, the nurse, who had been out some time previous to her rising, entered the room with a look of breathless impatience. which seemed to declare she had something wonderful to communicate. "Goot lack-a-taisy," cried she, as soon as she had re covered her breath, lifting up her head from the back of the chair on which she had thrown herself, "goot lack-a-taisy, well, to pe sure there is nothing but wonderful things happening in this world! Here, old Dame Abergwilly sent in such a hurry for me this morning; to pe sure I was surprised, but what was that to the surprise I felt when I heard what she had sent to me for." It was now Amanda's turn to feel breathless impatience. "Good heavens!" she exclaimed, "what did she tell you?" "Ay, I knew," cried the nurse, "the commotion you would be in when I told you the news; if you were guessing from this time till this time to-morrow you would never stumble over what it is." "I dare say I should not," cried Amanda, "so do be brief." "Why, you must know,—but Lort, my tear child, I am afraid you made but a bad breakfast, for you look very pale; inteed I made no great one myself, for I was in such a hurry-flurry with what Mrs. Abergwilly told me, that though she made some nice green tea, and we had a slim cake, I could scarcely touch anything." "Well," said Amanda, tortured with anxiety and impatience, "what did she tell you?" "Why, my tear child, down came a special messenger from London last night, to let them know that Lort Cherbury was tead, and that Lort Mortimer had sold Tudor Hall; and the steward is ordered to pay all the servants off, and to discharge them; and to have everything in readiness against the new lantlort comes down to take possession. Oh! Lort, there is such weeping and wailing at the Hall; the poor creatures who had grown old in the service, hoped to have finished their tays in it; it is not that they are in any fear of want—the young Lort has taken care of that, for he has settled something yearly upon them all—but that they are sorry to quit the family. Poor Mrs. Abergwilly, nothing can comfort the old soul; she has neither chick nor child, and she told me she loved the very chairs and tables, to which, to pe sure, her hand has given many a polishing rub. She says she thinks she will come and lodge with me; put if she does, she says I must not put her into a room from whence she can have a view of Tudor Hall; for she says she will never be able to look at it when once it gets a new master. So this, my tear child, is the sum totem of what I have heard."

Amanda was equally astonished and affected by what she heard. She wished to know if the nurse had received any intelligence of Lord Mortimer's marriage, but she could not bring herself to ask the question. Besides, upon reflection, she was convinced she should have heard it had it been the case. With Lord Cherbury died all hopes of the restoration of her fame in the opinion of his son. "Yet why," she asked herself, "should I regret this? since thus separated, it is better, perhaps, he had ceased to esteem me, as undoubtedly it must lessen his feelings on my account." Why he should part with Tudor Hall she could not conceive, except it was to humor some caprice of Lady Euphrasia's, who, it was probable, she imagined, knew that the attachment between Lord Mortimer and her had there commenced.

"Ah!" cried Amanda, "she never could have relished its beauties—beauties which, if Lord Mortimer thinks as I do, would, if reviewed, only have augmented his sorrows—sorrows which propriety now demands his repelling." She hastened to the Hall, but was some time there ere she could commence her employment, so much had she been agitated. The landscape she was finishing was taken from the little valley which lay beneath the windows of the music-room. The romantic ruins of an old castle overhung an eminence at its extremity; and of the whole scene she had taken a most accurate copy; it wanted but one charm to please her, and that charm was the figure of Lord Mortimer, with whom she had often wandered round the ruins. Her hand was ready in obeying the impulse of her heart, and she soon beheld, sketched in the most striking manner, the elegant features of him so ardently beloved. She gazed with rapture upon them, but it was a short-lived rapture. She started, as if conscious she had committed a crime, when she reflected on the situation in which he now stood with another woman; her trembling hand hastened to atone for its error, by expunging the dangerous likeness, and the warm, involuntary tear she shed at the moment, aided her design. "Oh! how unnecessary," she cried, as she made this sacrifice to delicacy, "to sketch features which are indelibly engraven on my heart." As she spoke, a deep and long-drawn sigh reached her ear. Alarmed, confounded at the idea of being overheard, and, of course, the feelings of her heart discovered, she started with precipitation from her seat, and looked round her with a kind of wild confusion. But, gracious Heavens! who can describe the emotions of her soul when the original of that picture so fondly sketched, so hastily obliterated, met her eye. Amazed, unable to speak, to move, almost to breathe, she stood motionless and aghast, the pale statue of Surprise, as if she neither durst nor could believe the evidence of her eyes. Well, indeed, might she have doubted them, for in the pale countenance of Lord Mortimer scarce a vestige of his former self (except in the benignancy of his looks) remained. His faded complexion, the disorder of his hair, his mourning habit, all heightened the sad expression of his features—an expression which declared that he and happiness were never so disunited as at the present moment. The first violence of Amanda's feelings in a little time abated, she somewhat recovered the use of her faculties, and hastily snatching up her drawings, moved with weak and trembling steps to the door. She had nearly reached it, when the soft, the tremulous voice of Lord Mortimer arrested her course. "You go, then, Miss Fitzalan," cried he, "without one adieu. You go, and we never more shall meet." The agonizing manner in which these words were pronounced, struck a death-like chill upon the heart of Amanda. She stopped, and turned around involuntarily, as if to receive that last, that sad adieu, which she was half reproached for avoiding. Lord Mortimer approached her, he attempted to speak, but his voice was inarticulate; a gust of sorrow burst from his eyes, and he hastily covered his face with a handkerchief, and walked to a window.

Amanda, unutterably affected, was unable to stand; she sunk upon a chair, and watched with a bursting heart the emotions of Lord Mortimer. Oh! with what difficulty at this moment did she confine herself within the cold, the rigid rules of propriety; with what difficulty did she prevent herself from flying to Lord Mortimer; from mingling tears with his, and lamenting the cruel destiny which had disunited them for ever. Lord Mortimer in a few minutes was sufficiently recovered again to approach her "I have long wished for an opportunity of seeing you," said he, "but I had not courage to desire an interview. How little did I imagine this morning, when, like a sad exile, I came to take a last farewell of a favorite residence, that I should behold you! Fate, in granting this interview, has for once befriended me. To express my horror—my remorse—my anguish—not only for the error a combination of events led me into concerning you, but for the conduct that error influenced me to adopt, will, I think, a little lighten my heart. To receive your pardon will be a sweet, a sad consolation; yet," continued he, after a moment's pause, "why do I say it will be a consolation? Alas! the sweetness that may lead you to accord it will only heighten my wretchedness at our eternal separation." Here he paused. Amanda was unable to speak. His words seemed to imply he was acquainted with the injuries she had sustained through his father's means, and she waited in trembling expectation for an explanation of them. "The purity of your character," exclaimed Lord Mortimer, "was at length fully revealed to me. Good Heaven! under what afflicting circumstances? by that being, to whom you so generously made a sacrifice of what then you might have considered your happiness." "Did Lord Cherbury, then," said Amanda, with inexpressible eagerness, "did he then, at last, justify me?" "Yes," cried Lord Mortimer, "he proved you were indeed the most excellent, the most injured of human beings; that you were all which my fond heart had once believed you to be; but, oh! what were the dreadful emotions of that heart to know his justification came too late to restore its peace. Once there was a happy period, when, after a similar error being removed, I had hoped, by a life for ever devoted to you, to have made some reparation, some atonement, for my involuntary injustice; but, alas! no reparation, no atonement can now be made."

Amanda wept. She raised her streaming eyes to heaven, and again cast them to the earth.

"You weep," cried Lord Mortimer, in a tone expressive of surprise, after surveying her some minutes in silence. "My love, my Amanda," continued he, suddenly seizing her hand, while he surveyed her with a most rapturous fondness, a crimson glow mantling his cheek, and a beam of wonted brilliancy darting from his eye,

"What am I to imagine from those tears? are you, then, indeed, unaltered?"

Amanda started. She feared the emotions she betrayed had convinced Lord Mortimer of the continuance, the unabated strength of her affection. She felt shocked at her imprudence, which had alone, she was convinced, tempted Lord Mortimer to address her in such a manner. "I know not, my Lord," cried she, "in what sense you ask whether I am unchanged; but of this be assured, a total alteration must have taken place in my sentiments, if I could remain a moment longer with a person who seems at once forgetful of what is due to his own situation and mine." "Go, then, madam," exclaimed Lord Mortimer, in an accent of displeasure, "and pardon my having thus detained you—pardon my involuntary offence—excuse my having disturbed your retirement, and obtruded my sorrows on you."

Amanda had now reached the door. Her heart recoiled at the idea of parting in such a manner from Lord Mortimer, but prudence bade her hasten as fast as possible from him. Yet slow and lingering she pursued her way. Ere she had gone many yards she was overtaken by Lord Mortimer. His pride was inferior to his tenderness, which drove him to despair at the idea of parting in displeasure from her. "Oh! my Amanda," cried he, seizing her hand, and almost breathless with emotion, "add not, by your anger, to the bitterness of this sad hour. Since we must part, oh! let us part in amity, as friends that regard each other. You have not yet (if, indeed, it is possible for you to do so) pronounced your forgiveness of the persecutions you underwent on my account. You have not yet granted your pardon for the harshness, the cruelty with which a dreadful error tempted me to treat you." "Oh! my Lord," said Amanda, again yielding to the softness of her soul, while tears trickled down her cheeks, "why torture me by speaking in this manner? How can I pronounce forgiveness when I never was offended? When wretched and deserted, I appeared to stand upon the great theatre of life, without one hand to offer me assistance, your ready friendship came to my relief, and poured the balm of comfort over the sorrows of my heart! when deprived by deceit and cruelty of your good opinion, even then your attention and solicitude pursued my wandering footsteps, and strove to mark a path of comfort for me to take! these, these are the obligations that never can be forgotten, that demand, that possess, my eternal gratitude, my——." A warmer expression rose to her lips, but was again buried in her heart. She sighed, and after a pause of a minute, thus went on:—"For your happiness, my warmest, purest prayers are daily offered up; oh! may it yet be equal to your virtues; greater I cannot wish it."

Lord Mortimer groaned in the excruciating agony of his soul. "Oh! Amanda," he said, "where, where can I receive consolation for your loss? Never, never in this world!" He took her hands within his, he raised them to Heaven, as if supplicating its choicest blessings on her head. "For my happiness you pray," he exclaimed; "ah! my love, how unavailing is the prayer!"

Amanda now saw more than ever the necessity of hastening away. She gently withdrew her hands, and hurried on as fast as her trembling limbs could carry her. Still Lord Mortimer attended her. "Yet, Amanda," cried he, "a little moment. Tell me," he continued, again seizing her hand, "do not these shades remind you of departed hours? Oh! what blissful ones have we not passed beneath their foliage, that foliage which I shall never more behold expanding to the breath of spring."

Amanda trembled. This involuntary but sad declaration of the loss of a seat so valued by him, overpowered her. Her respiration grew faint, she could not support herself, and made a motion to sit down upon the grass, but Lord Mortimer eagerly caught her to his bosom. She had not strength to resist the effort, and her head reclined upon his shoulder. But who can speak her feelings as she felt the beating heart of Mortimer, which, from its violent palpitations, seemed as if it would burst his bosom to find a passage to her feet. In a few minutes she was a little recovered, and, sensible of the impropriety of her situation, was now resolutely determined to quit Lord Mortimer. "We must part, my Lord," cried she, disengaging herself from his arms, notwithstanding a gentle effort he made to retain her. "We must part, my Lord," she repeated, "and part for ever." "Tell me, then," he exclaimed, still impeding her course, "tell me whether I may hope to live in your remembrance; whether I may hope not to be obliterated from your memory by the happiness which will shortly surround you? Promise I shall at times be thought of with your wonted, though, alas! unavailing wishes for my happiness, and the promise will, perhaps, afford me consolation in the solitary exile I have doomed myself to." "Oh! my Lord," said Amanda, unable to repress her feelings, "why do I hear you speak in this manner? In mentioning exile, do you not declare your intentions of leaving unfulfilled the claims which situation, family, and society have upon you? Oh! my Lord, you shock—shall I say more—you disappoint me! Yes, I repeat it, disappoint the idea I had formed of the virtue and fortitude of him, who, as a friend, I shall ever regard. To yield thus to sorrow, to neglect the incumbent duties of life, to abandon a woman to whom so lately you plighted your solemn vows of love and protection. Oh! my Lord, what will her friends, what will Lady Euphrasia herself say to such cruel, such unjustifiable conduct?" "Lady Euphrasia!" repeated Lord Mortimer, recoiling a few paces. "Lady Euphrasia!" he again exclaimed, in tremulous accents, regarding Amanda with an expression of mingled horror and wildness. "Gracious Heaven! is it, can it be possible you are ignorant of the circumstances which lately happened? Yes, your words, your looks, declare you are so."

It was now Amanda's turn to repeat his words. She demanded, with a wildness of countenance equal to that he had just displayed, what were the circumstances he alluded to?

"First tell me," cried he, "was the alteration in your manner produced by your supposing me the husband of Lady Euphrasia?" "Supposing you her husband?" repeated Amanda, unable to answer his question in a moment of such torturing suspense. "And are you not so?" "No," replied Lord Mortimer; "I never had the misfortune to offer vows which my heart could not ratify. Lady Euphrasia made another choice. She was your enemy; but I know your gentle spirit will mourn her sad and sudden fate." He ceased, for Amanda had no longer power to listen. She sunk, beneath surprise and joy, into the expanded arms of her beloved Mortimer. It is ye alone, who, like her, have stood upon the very brink of despair—who, like her, have been restored, unexpectedly restored to hope, to happiness, that can form any judgment of her feelings at the present moment. At the moment when recovering from her insensibility, the soft accent of Lord Mortimer saluted her ear, and made her heart, without one censure from propriety respond to rapture, as he held her to his bosom. As he gazed on her with tears of impassioned tenderness, he repeated his question, whether the alteration in her manner was produced alone by the supposition of his marriage; but he repeated it with a sweet, a happy consciousness of having it answered according to his wishes.

"These tears, these emotions, oh! Mortimer, what do they declare?" exclaimed Amanda. "Ah! do they not say my heart never knew a diminution of tenderness, that it never could have forgotten you? Yes," she continued, raising her eyes, streaming with tears of rapture, to heaven, "I am now recompensed for all my sufferings. Yes, in this blissful moment, I meet a full reward for them." Lord Mortimer now led her back to the library, to give an explanation of the events which had produced so great a reverse of situation; but it was long ere he could sufficiently compose himself to commence his narrative. Alternately he fell at the feet of Amanda, alternately he folded her to his bosom, and asked his heart if its present happiness was real. A thousand times he questioned her whether she was indeed unaltered--as often implored her forgiveness for one moment doubting her constancy. Amanda exerted her spirits to calm her own agitation, that she might be enabled to soothe him into tranquillity. At length she succeeded, and he terminated her anxious impatience by giving her the promised relation.

CHAPTER LVI.

"By suffering well, our torture we subdue,
Fly when she frowns, and when she calls, pursue."

OVERWHELMED with grief and disappointment at the supposed perfidy of Amanda, Lord Mortimer had returned to England, acquainting Lord Cherbury and Lady Martha of the unhappy cause of his returning alone; entreating them, in pity to his wounded feelings, never to mention the distressing subject before him. His dejection was unconquerable; all his schemes of felicity were overthrown, and the destruction of his hopes was the destruction of his peace. It was not in these first transports of bitter sorrow that Lord Cherbury ventured to speak his wishes to his son. He waited till, by slow degrees, he saw a greater degree of composure in his manner, though it was a composure attended with no abatement of melancholy. At first he only hinted those wishes—hints, however, which Lord Mortimer appeared designedly insensible of. At last the Earl spoke plainer. He mentioned his deep regret at beholding a son, whom he had ever considered the pride of his house, and the solace of his days, wasting his youth in wretchedness, for an ungrateful woman, who had long triumphed in the infatuation which bound him to her. "It filled his soul with anguish," he said, "to behold him lost to himself, his family, and the world, thus disappointing all the hopes and expectations which the fair promise of his early youth had given rise to in the bosom of his friends concerning the meridian of his day."

Lord Mortimer was unutterably affected by what his father said. The Earl beheld his emotion, and blessed it as a happy omen. His pride, as well as sensibility, he continued, were deeply wounded at the idea of having Lord Mortimer still considered the slave of a passion which had met so base a return. "Oh! let not the world," added he, with increasing energy, "triumph in your weakness; try to shake it off, ere the finger of scorn and ridicule is pointed at you as the dupe of a deceitful woman's art."

Lord Mortimer was inexpressibly shocked. His pride had frequently represented as weakness the regret he felt for Amanda; and the Earl now stimulating that pride, he felt at the moment as if he could make any sacrifice which should prove his having triumphed over his unfortunate attachment. But when his father called on him to make such a sacrifice, by uniting himself to Lady Euphrasia, he shrunk back, and acknowledged he could not give so fatal a proof of fortitude. He declared his total repugnance at present to any alliance. Time, and the efforts of reason, he trusted, would subdue his ill-placed attachment, and enable him to comply with the wishes of his friends.

Lord Cherbury would not, could not drop the subject next his heart—a subject so important, so infinitely interesting to him. He exerted all his eloquence, he entreated, he implored his son not for ever to disappoint his wishes. He mentioned the compliance he had so recently shown to his, though against his better judgment, in the useless consent he had given to his marriage with Miss Fitzalan.

Lord Mortimer, persecuted by his arguments, at length declared that, was the object he pointed out for his alliance any other than Lady Euphrasia Sutherland, he would not perhaps be so reluctant to comply with his wishes; but she was a woman he could never esteem, and must consequently for ever refuse. She had given such specimens of cruelty and deceit, in the schemes she had entered into with the Marchioness against (he blushed, he faltered, as he pronounced her name) Miss Fitzalan, that his heart felt unutterable dislike to her.

The Earl was prepared for this; he had the barbarity to declare, in the most unhesitating manner, he was sorry to find him still blinded by the art of that wretched girl. He bade him reflect on her conduct, and then consider whether any credence was to be given to her declaration of Belgrave's being admitted to the house without her knowledge.

Lord Mortimer was startled. Her conduct, indeed, as his father said, might well make him doubt her veracity. But still the evidence of the servants; they acknowledged having been instruments in forwarding the scheme which she said was laid against her. He mentioned this circumstance. The Earl was also prepared for it; the servants, he declared, had been examined in his presence, when with shame and contrition they confessed, that seeing the strong anxiety of Lord Mortimer for the restoration of Miss Fitzalan's fame, and tempted by the large bribes he offered, if they could or would say anything in her justification, they had at last made the allegation so pleasing to him.

Lord Mortimer sighed deeply. "On every side," cried he, "I find I have been the dupe of art; but it was only the deceit of one could agonize my soul." Still, however, he was inexorable to all his father could say relative to Lady Euphrasia.

Lady Martha was at last called in as an auxiliary; she was now as strenuous for the connection as ever Lord Cherbury had been. A longer indulgence of Lord Mortimer's grief, she feared, would completely undermine his health, and either render him a burden to himself, or precipitate him to an early grave. Whilst he continued single, she knew he would not consider any vigorous exertions for overcoming that grief necessary; but if once united, she was convinced, from the rectitude and sensibility of his disposition, he would struggle against his feelings, in order to fulfil the incumbent duties he had imposed upon himself. Thus did she deem a union requisite to rouse him to exertion; to restore his peace, and in all probability to save his life. She joined in her brother's arguments and entreaties, with tears she joined in them, and besought Mortimer to accede to their wishes. She called him the last hope of their house. He had long, she said, been the pride, the delight of their days; their comfort, their existence were interwoven in his; if he sunk, they sunk with him.

The yielding soul of Mortimer could not resist such tenderness and he gave a promise of acting as they wished. He imagined he could not be more wretched; but scarcely had this promise passed his lips, ere he felt an augmentation of misery. To enter into new engagements, to resign the sweet though melancholy privilege of indulging his feelings, to fetter at once both soul and body, were ideas that filled him with unutterable anguish. A thousand times was he on the point of retracting his regretted and reluctant promise, had not honor interposed, and showed the inability of doing so, without an infringement on its principles. Thus entangled, Mortimer endeavored to collect his scattered thoughts, and in order to try and gain some composure, he altered his former plan of acting, and mingled as much as possible in society. He strove to fly from himself, that by so doing he might fly from the corrosive remembrances which embittered his life. But who shall paint his agonies at the unexpected sight of Amanda at the Macqueens? The exertions he had for some time before compelled himself to make, had a little abated the pain of his feelings; but that pain returned with redoubled violence at her presence, and every idea of present composure, or of future tranquillity, vanished. He felt with regret, with anguish, that she was as dear as ever to his soul, and his destined union became more hateful than ever to him. He tried, by recollecting her conduct, to awaken his resentment; but, alas! softness, in spite of all his efforts to the contrary, was the predominant feeling of his soul Her pallid cheek, her deep dejection, seemed to say she was the child of sorrow and repentance. To soothe that sorrow, to strengthen that repentance, oh! how delightful unto him; but either he durst not do, situated as he then was.

With the utmost difficulty Lady Martha Dormer prevailed on him to be present when she demanded the picture from Amanda. That scene has already been described; also his parting one with her; but to describe the anguish he endured after this period is impossible. He beheld Lady Euphrasia with a degree of horror; his faltering voice refused even to pay her the accustomed compliments of meeting; he loathed the society he met at the castle, and, regardless of what would be thought of him, regardless of health, or the bleakness of the season, wandered for hours together in the most unfrequented parts of the domain, the veriest son of wretchedness and despair.

The day, the dreaded day, at length arrived which was to complete his misery. The company were all assembled in the great hall of the castle, from whence they were to proceed to the chapel, and every moment expected the appearance of the bride. The Marquis, surprised at her long delay, sent a messenger to request her immediate presence, who returned in a few minutes with a letter, which he presented to the Marquis, who broke the seal in visible trepidation, and found it from Lady Euphrasia.

She had taken a step, she said, which she must depend on the kind indulgence of her parents to excuse; a step which nothing but a firm conviction that happiness could not be experienced in a union with Lord Mortimer, should have tempted her to. His uniform indifference had at last convinced her that motives of the most interested nature influenced his addresses to her; and if her parents inquired into his, or, at least, Lord Cherbury's conduct, they would find her assertion true, and would, consequently, she trusted, excuse her for not submitting to be sacrificed at the shrine of interest. In selecting Mr. Freelove for her choice, she had selected a man whose addresses were not prompted by selfish views, but by a sincere affection, which he would openly have avowed, had he not been assured, in the present situation of affairs, it would have met with opposition. To avoid, therefore, a positive act of disobedience, she had consented to a private union. To

Lord Mortimer and Lord Cherbury, she said, she deemed no apology necessary for her conduct, as their hearts, at least Lord Cherbury's, would at once exculpate her, from his own consciousness of not having acted either generously or honorably to her.

The violent transports of passion the Marquis experienced are not to be described. The Marchioness hastily perused the letter, and her feelings were not inferior in violence to his. Its contents were soon known, and amazement sat on every countenance. But, oh! what joy did they inspire in the soul of Lord Mortimer; not a respite, or rather a full pardon to the condemned wretch, at the very moment when preparing for death, could have yielded more exquisite delight; but to Lord Cherbury, what a disappointment! It was, indeed, a death-stroke to his hopes. The hints in Lady Euphrasia's letter concerning him plainly declared her knowledge of his conduct; he foresaw an immediate demand from Freelove; foresaw the disgrace he should experience when his inability to discharge that demand was known. His soul was shaken in its inmost recesses, and the excruciating anguish of his feelings was indeed as severe a punishment as he could suffer. Pale, speechless, aghast, the most horrid ideas took possession of his mind, yet he sought not to repel them, for anything was preferable to the shame he saw awaiting him.

Lord Mortimer's indignation was excited by the aspersions cast upon his father, aspersions he imputed entirely to the malice of Lady Euphrasia, and which, from the character of Lord Cherbury, he deemed it unnecessary to attempt refuting. But alas! what a shock did his noble, his unsuspicious nature receive, when, in a short time after the perusal of her letter, one from Freelove was brought him, which fully proved the truth of her assertions. Freelove, in his little, trifling manner, expressed his hopes that there would be no difference between his lordship and him, for whom he expressed the most entire friendship, on account of the fair lady who had honored him with her regard; declared her partiality was quite irresistible; and, moreover, that in love, as in war, every advantage was allowable; begged to trouble his lordship with his compliments to Lord Cherbury, and a request that everything might be prepared to settle matters between them, on his return from his matrimonial expedition. An immediate compliance with this request, he was convinced, could not be in the least distressing; and it was absolutely essential to him, from the eclat with which he designed Lady Euphrasia Freelove should make her bridal entry into public. As to the report, he said, which he had heard relative to Lord Cherbury's losing the fortune which was intrusted to his care for him at the gaming-table, he quite disbelieved it.

The most distressing, the most mortifying sensations took possession of Lord Mortimer at this part of the letter. It explained the reasons of Lord Cherbury's strong anxiety for an alliance with the Roslin family, which Lord Mortimer, indeed, had often wondered at, and he at once pitied, condemned, and blushed for him. He stole a glance at his father, and his deep, despairing look filled him with horror. He resolved, the first opportunity, to declare his knowledge of the fatal secret which oppressed him, and his resolution of making any sacrifice which could possibly remove or lessen his inquietude.

Lord Cherbury was anxious to fly from the now hated castle, ere further confusion overtook him. He mentioned his intention of immediately departing—an intention opposed by the Marquis, but in which he was steady, and also supported by his son.

Everything was ready for their departure, when Lord Cherbury, overwhelmed by the dreadful agitation he experienced, was seized with a fit of the most violent and alarming nature. He was carried to a chamber, and recourse was obliged to be had to a physician, ere the restoration of his senses was effected; but he was then so weak that the physician declared if not kept quiet, a return of his disorder might be expected. Lord Mortimer, tenderly impatient to lighten the burden on his father's mind, dismissed the attendants as soon as he possibly could, and then, in the most delicate terms, declared his knowledge of his situation.

Lord Cherbury at this started up in the most violent paroxysm of anguish, and vowed he would never survive the discovery of his being a villain. With difficulty could Lord Mortimer compose him; but it was long ere he could prevail on him to hear what he wished to say.

Few there were, he said, who at some period of their lives, he believed, were not led into actions which, upon reflection, they had reason to regret. He thought not, he meant not, to speak slightly of human nature, he only wished to prove that, liable as we all are to frailty—a frailty intended no doubt to check the arrogance of pride and presumption, we should not suffer the remembrance of error, when once sincerely repented of, to plunge us into despair, particularly when, as far as in our power, we meant to atone for it. Thus did Lord Mortimer attempt to calm the dreadful conflicts of his father's mind, who still continued to inveigh against himself.

The sale of Tudor Hall, Lord Mortimer proceeded, and mortgages upon Lord Cherbury's estates, would enable his father to discharge his debt to Mr. Freelove. He knew, he said, it was tenderness to him which had prevented him ere this from adopting such a plan; but he besought him to let no further consideration on his account make him delay fulfilling immediately the claims of honor and justice. He besought him to believe his tranquillity was more precious to him than anything in life; that the restoration of his peace was far more estimable to him than the possession of the most brilliant fortune—"a possession which," continued Lord Mortimer, deeply sighing, "I am well convinced will not alone yield happiness. I have long," said he, "looked with an eye of cool indifference on the pomps, the pageantries of life. Disappointed in my tenderest hopes and expectations, wealth, merely on my own account, has been long valueless to me. Its loss, I make no doubt—nay, I am convinced—I shall have reason to consider as a blessing. It will compel me to make those exertions which its possession would have rendered unnecessary, and by so doing, in all probability, remove from my heart that sadness which has so long clung about it, and enervated all its powers. A profession lies open to receive me, which, had I been permitted at a much earlier period, I should have embraced; for a military life was always my passion. At the post of danger, I may perhaps have the happiness of performing services for my country, which, while loitering supinely in the shade of prosperity, I never could have done. Thus, my dear father," he continued, "you see how erroneous we are in opinions we often form of things, since what we often consider as the bitterest evil leads to the most supreme good. We will, as soon as possible, hasten everything to be prepared for

51

Freelove, and thus, I make no doubt, disappoint the little malice of his soul.

"My aunt, my sister are unacquainted with your uneasiness, nor shall an intimation o: it from me ever transpire to them. Of fortune, sufficient will remain to allow, though not the splendors, the comforts and elegancies of life. As for me, the deprivation of what is considered, and falsely termed, my accustomed indulgences, will be the most salutary and efficacious thing that could possibly happen to me. In short, I believe that the realization of my plan will render me happy, since, with truth I can assure you, its anticipation has already given more pleasure to my soul than I thought it would ever have again enjoyed."

Lord Cherbury, overcome by the tenderness, the virtue of his son, by the sacrifice he so willingly offered, so strenuously insisted on making, of his paternal fortune, could not for some minutes speak. At length the struggling emotions of his soul found utterance.

"Oh! Virtue," he exclaimed, while tears of love, of gratitude, of contrition, flowed from his eyes, and fell upon the hand of his son, clasped within his—"Oh! Virtue, I cannot say, like Brutus, thou art but a shade; no, here, in this invaluable son, thou art personified—this son, whom I so cruelly deceived, so bitterly distressed! Oh! gracious powers, would not that heroic, that heaven-born disposition, which now leads him to sign away his paternal fortune for my sake have also led him to a still greater resignation, the sacrifice of his Amanda, had I entrusted him with my wretched situation. Oh! had I confided in him, what an act of baseness should I have avoided! What pangs, what tortures, should I have prevented his experiencing! But, to save my own guilty confusion, I drew wretchedness upon his head. I wrung every fibre of his heart with agony, by making him believe its dearest, its most valuable object unworthy of its regards."

Mortimer started; he gasped—he repeated, in faltering accents, these last words. His soul seemed as if it would burst its mortal bounds, and soar to another region to hear an avowal of his Amanda's purity.

"Oh! Mortimer," cried the Earl, in the deep, desponding tone of anguish, "how shall I dare to lift my eyes to thine, after the avowal of the injustice I have done one of the most amiable and loveliest of human beings?" "Oh! tell me," cried Mortimer, in breathless, trembling agitation, "tell me if, indeed, she is all my fond heart once believed her to be? In mercy, in pity, delay not to inform me."

Slowly, in consequence of his weakness, but with all the willingness of a contrite spirit, anxious to do justice to the injured, did Lord Cherbury reveal all that had passed between him and Amanda. "Poor Fitzalan," cried he, as he finished his relation, "poor, unhappy friend! From thy cold grave, couldst thou have known the transactions of this world, how must thy good and feeling spirit have reproached me for my barbarity to thy orphan in robbing her of the only stipend thy adverse fortune had power to leave her—a pure and spotless fame?"

Lord Mortimer groaned with anguish. Every reproachful word he had uttered to Amanda darted upon his remembrance, and were like so many daggers to his heart. It was his father that oppressed her. This knowledge aggravated his feelings, but stifled his reproaches; it was a father contrite, perhaps at that very moment stretched upon a death-bed, therefore he forgave him. He cast his eyes around, as if in that moment he had hoped to behold her, have an opportunity of falling prostrate at her feet and imploring her forgiveness. He cast his eyes around, as if imagining he should see her, and be allowed to fold her to his beating heart, and ask her soft voice to pronounce his pardon.

"Oh! thou lovely mourner," he exclaimed to himself, while a gush of sorrow burst from his eyes. "Oh! thou lovely mourner, when I censured, reviled, upbraided you, even at that very period your heart was suffering the most excruciating anguish. Yes, Amanda, he who would willingly have laid down life to yield thee peace, even he was led to aggravate thy woes. With what gentleness, what unexampled patience didst thou bear my reproaches! No sudden ray of indignation for purity so insulted, innocence so arraigned, flashed from thy eyes; the beams of meekness and resignation alone stole from underneath their tearful lids.

"No sweet hope of being able to atone, no delightful idea of being able to make reparation for my injustice, now alleviates the poignancy of my feelings; since fate interposed between us in the hour of prosperity, I cannot, in the bleak and chilling period of adversity, seek to unite your destiny with mine. Now almost the child of want myself, a soldier of fortune, obliged by the sword to earn my bread, I cannot think of leading you into difficulties and dangers greater than you ever before experienced. Oh! my Amanda, may the calm shade of security be for ever thine; thy Mortimer, thy ever-faithful ever-adoring Mortimer, will not, from any selfish consideration, seek to lead thee from it. If thy loss be agonizing, oh! how much more agonizing to possess but to see thee in danger or distress. I will go, then, into new scenes of life with only thy dear, thy sweet, and worshipped idea to cheer and support me--an idea I shall lose but with life, and which to know I may cherish, indulge, adore, without a reproach from reason for weakness in so doing, is a sweet and soothing consolation."

The indulgence of feelings such as his language expressed, he was obliged to forego, in order to fulfil the wish he felt of alleviating the situation of his father; but his attention was unable to lighten the anguish which oppressed the mind of Lord Cherbury; remorse for his past conduct, mortification at being lessened in the estimation of his son, sorrow for the injury he was compelled to do him, to be extricated from the power of Freelove, all preyed upon his mind, and produced the most violent agitations, and an alarming repetition of fits.

Things remained in this situation for a few days, during which time no intelligence had been received of Euphrasia, when one morning, as Lord Mortimer was sitting for a few minutes with the Marquis and Marchioness, a servant entered the apartment, and informed his lord that a gentleman had just arrived at the castle, who requested to be introduced to his presence. The Marquis and Marchioness instantly concluded this was some person sent as an intercessor from Lady Euphrasia, and they instantly admitted him, in order to have an opportunity of assuring her ladyship, through his means, it must be some time (if indeed at all) ere they could possibly forgive her disrespect and disobedience. Lord Mortimer would have retired, but was requested to stay, and complied, prompted indeed by curiosity to hear what kind of apology or message Lady Euphrasia had sent. A man of a most pleasing appearance entered, and was received with the most frigid politeness.

He looked embarrassed, agitated, even distressed. He attempted several times to speak, but the words still died away undistinguished. At length the Marchioness, yielding to the natural impetuosity of her soul, hastily desired he would reveal what had procured them the honor of his visit.

"A circumstance of the most unhappy nature, madam," he replied in a hesitating voice. "I came with the hope, the expectation of being able to break it by degrees, so as not totally to overpower; but I find myself unequal to the distressing task." "I fancy, sir," cried the Marchioness, "both the Marquis and I are already aware of the circumstance you allude to." "Alas! madam," said the stranger, fixing his eyes with a mournful earnestness on her face, "I cannot think so. If you were, it would not be in human, in parent nature to appear as you now do." He stopped, he turned pale, he trembled, his emotions became contagious.

"Tell me," said the Marquis, in a voice scarcely articulate, "I beseech you, without delay, the meaning of your words."

The stranger essayed to speak, but could not; words indeed were scarcely necessary to declare that he had something shocking to reveal. His auditors, like old Northumberland, might have said, "The paleness on thy cheek is apter than thy tongue to tell thy errand." "Something dreadful has happened to my child," said the Marchioness, forgetting in that agonizing moment all displeasure. "Alas! madam," cried the stranger, while a trickling tear denoted his sensibility for the sorrows he was about giving rise to. "Alas! madam, your fears are too well founded; to torture you with longer suspense would be barbarity. Something dreadful has happened, indeed—Lady Euphrasia in this world will never more be sensible of your kindness." A wild, a piercing, agonizing shriek burst from the lips of the Marchioness, as she dropped senseless from her seat. The Marquis was sinking from his, had not Lord Mortimer, who sat by him, timely started up, and, though trembling himself with horror, caught him in his arms. The servants were summoned, the still insensible Marchioness was carried to her chamber; the wretched Marquis, reviving in a few minutes—if that could be called reviving, which was only a keener perception of misery—demanded, in a tone of anguish, the whole particulars of the sad event. Yet scarcely had the stranger begun to comply with his request, ere, with all the wild inconsistency of grief, he bade him forbear, and, shuddering, declared he could not listen to the dreadful particulars. But it were needless, as well as impossible, to describe the feelings of the wretched parents, who in one moment beheld their hopes, their wishes, their expectations finally destroyed. Oh! what an awful lesson did they inculcate of the instability of human happiness, of the insufficiency of rank or riches to retain it. This was one of the events which Providence, in its infinite wisdom, makes use of to arrest the thoughtless in their career of dissipation, and check the arrogance of pride and vanity. When we behold the proud, the wealthy, the illustrious, suddenly surprised by calamity, and sinking beneath its stroke, we naturally reflect on the frail tenure of earthly possessions, and, from the reflection, consider how we may best attain that happiness which cannot change. The human heart is in general so formed as to require something great and striking to interest and affect it. Thus a similar misfortune happening to a person in a conspicuous, and to one in an obscure situation, would not, in all probability, equally affect or call home the wandering thoughts to sadness and reflection. The humble floweret, trampled to the dust, is passed with an eye of careless indifference; but the proud oak torn from the earth, and levelled by the storm, is viewed with wonder and affright. The horrors of the blow which overwhelmed the Marquis and Marchioness, were augmented by the secret whispers of conscience, that seemed to say it was a blow of retribution from a Being all righteous and all just, whose most sacred laws they had violated, in oppressing the widow and defrauding the orphan. Oh! what an augmentation of misery is it to think it merited! Remorse, like the vengeance of Heaven, seemed now awakened to sleep no more. No longer could they palliate their conduct, no longer avoid retrospection—a retrospection which heightened the gloomy horrors of the future. In Lady Euphrasia, all the hopes and affections of the Marquis and Marchioness were centered. She alone had ever made them feel the tenderness of humanity, yet she was not less the darling of their love than the idol of their pride. In her they beheld the being who was to support the honors of their house, and transmit their names to posterity. In her they beheld the being who gave them an opportunity of gratifying the malevolent, as well as the tender and ambitious passions of their souls. The next heir to the Marquis's title and fortune had irreconcilably disobliged him. As a means, therefore, of disappointing him, if on no other account, Lady Euphrasia would have been regarded by them. Though she had disappointed and displeased them by her recent act of disobedience, and though they had deemed it essential to their consequence to display that displeasure, yet they secretly resolved not long to withhold forgiveness from her, and also to take immediate steps for ennobling Freelove.

For Lady Euphrasia they felt indeed a tenderness her heart for them was totally a stranger to. It seemed, indeed, as if, cold and indifferent to all mankind, their affections were stronger for being confined in one channel. In the step she had taken, Lady Euphrasia only considered the gratification of her revenge. Freelove, as the ward of Lord Cherbury, in honor to him, had been invited to the nuptials. He accepted the invitation, but, instead of accompanying, promised to follow the bridal party to the castle. A day or two ere he intended setting out, by some accidental chance, he got into company with the very person to whom Lord Cherbury had lost so much, and on whose account he had committed an action which had entailed the most excruciating remorse upon him. This person was acquainted with the whole transaction. He had promised to keep his knowledge a secret, but the promises of the worthless are of little avail. A slight expression, which, in a moment of anxiety, had involuntarily dropped from Lord Cherbury, had stung him to the soul, because he knew too well its justice, and inspired him with the most inveterate hatred and rancorous desire of revenge. His unexpectedly meeting Freelove afforded him an opportunity of gratifying both these propensities, and he scrupled not to avail himself of it. Freelove was astonished, and, when the first violence of astonishment was over, delighted.

To triumph over the proud soul of Lord Cherbury and his son, was indeed an idea which afforded rapture. Both he had ever disliked, the latter particularly. He disliked him from the superiority which he saw in every respect he possessed over himself. A stranger to noble emulation, he sought not, by study or imitation, to aspire to any of those graces or perfections he beheld in Lord Mortimer. He sought alone to depreciate them, and, when he found that impossible, beheld him with greater envy and malignity than ever. To wound Lord Mortimer through the bosom of his father, to overwhelm him with confusion, by publicly displaying the error of that father, were ideas of the most exquisite delight—ideas which the wealth of worlds would scarcely have tempted him to forego,—so sweet is any triumph, however accidental or imaginary, over a noble object, to an envious mind, which ever hates that excellence it cannot reach. No fear of self-interest being injured checked his pleasure. The fortune of Lord Cherbury he knew sufficient to answer for his violated trust. Thus had he another source of triumph in the prospect of having those so long considered as the proud rivals of his wealth and splendor, cast into the shade. His pleasure, however, from this idea, was short lived, when he reflected that Lord Mortimer's union with Lady Euphrasia would totally exempt him from feeling any inconvenience from his father's conduct. But could not this union be prevented? Freelove asked himself. He still wanted a short period of being of age, consequently had no right, at present, to demand a settlement of his affairs from Lord Cherbury. He might, however, privately inform Lady Euphrasia of the affair so recently communicated to him. No sooner did he conceive this scheme, than he glowed with impatience to put it into execution. He hastened to the Marquis's, whither, indeed, the extravagant and foppish preparations he had made for the projected nuptials had before prevented his going, and took the first opportunity which offered of revealing to Lady Euphrasia, as if from the purest friendship, the conduct of Lord Cherbury, and the derangement of his affairs.

Lady Euphrasia was at once surprised and incensed. The reason for a union between her and his son being so ardently desired by Lord Cherbury, was now fully explained, and she beheld herself as an object addressed merely from a view of repairing a ruined fortune; but this view she resolved to disappoint. Such was the implacable nature of her disposition, that had this disappointment occasioned the destruction of her own peace, it would not have made her relinquish it. But this was not the case. In sacrificing all ideas of a union with Lord Mortimer to her offended pride she sacrificed no wish or inclination of her soul. Lord Mortimer, though the object of her admiration, had never been the object of her love. She was, indeed, incapable of feeling that passion. Her admiration had, however, long since given place to resentment, at the cool indifference with which he regarded her. She would have opposed a marriage with him, but for fear that he might, thus freed, attach himself to Amanda. The moment, however, she knew a union with her was necessary for the establishment of his fortune, fear, with every consideration which could oppose it, vanished before the idea of disappointing his views, and retaliating upon him that uneasiness he had, from wounded pride, made her experience by his cold and unalterable behavior to her.

She at first determined to acquaint the Marquis of what she had heard, but a little reflection made her drop this determination. He had always professed a warm regard for Lord Cherbury, and she feared that regard would still lead him to insist on the nuptials taking place. She was not long in concerting a scheme to render such a measure impracticable, and Freelove she resolved to make an instrument for forwarding, or rather executing her revenge. She hesitated not to say she had always disliked Lord Mortimer; that, in short, there was but one being she could ever think, ever hope to be happy with. Her broken sentences, her looks, her affected confusion, all revealed to Freelove that he was that object. The rapture this discovery inspired he could not conceal. The flattering expressions of Lady Euphrasia were repaid by the most extravagant compliments, the warmest professions, the strongest assurances of never-dying love. This soon led to what she desired, and, in a short space, an elopement was agreed to, and everything relative to it settled. Freelove's own servants and equipage were at the Castle, and consequently but little difficulty attended the arrangement of their plan. In Lady Euphrasia's eyes Freelove had no other value than what he now merely derived from being an instrument in gratifying the haughty and revengeful passions of her nature. She regarded him, indeed, with sovereign contempt; his fortune, however, she knew would give him consequence in the world, and she was convinced she should find him quite that easy, convenient husband which a woman of fashion finds so necessary;

in short, she looked forward to being the uncontrolled mistress of her own actions, and without a doubt but that she should meet many objects as deserving of her admiration, and infinitely more grateful for it, than ever Lord Mortimer had been.

Flushed with such a pleasing prospect, she quitted the Castle—that castle she was destined never more to see. At the moment, the very moment, she smiled with joy and expectation, the shaft, the unerring shaft, was raised against her breast.

The marriage ceremony over, they hastened to the vicinity of the Castle, in order to send an apologizing letter, as usual on such occasions. The night was dark and dreary, the road rugged and dangerous; the postilions ventured to say it would be better to halt for the night, but this was opposed by Lady Euphrasia. They were within a few miles of the destined termination of their journey, and, pursuant to her commands, they proceeded. In a few minutes after this, the horses, startled by a sudden light which gleamed across the path, began plunging in the most alarming manner. A frightful precipice lay on one side, and the horses, in spite of all the efforts of the postilions, continued to approach it. Freelove, in this dreadful moment, lost all consideration but for himself; he burst open the chariot door, and leaped into the road. His companion was unable to follow his example; she had fainted at the first intimation of danger. The postilions with difficulty dismounted. The other servants came to their assistance, and endeavored to restrain the horses; every effort was useless, they broke from their hold, and plunged down the precipice. The servants had heard the chariot-door open; they therefore concluded, for it was too dark to see, that both their master and Lady Euphrasia were safe. But who can describe their horror, when a loud shriek from him declared her situation? Some of them immediately hastened, as fast as their trembling limbs could carry them, to the house adjoining the road, from whence the fatal light had gleamed which caused the sad catastrophe. They revealed it in a few words, and implored immediate assistance. The master of the house was a man of the greatest humanity. He was inexpressibly shocked at what he had heard, and joined himself in giving the assistance that was desired. With lanterns they proceeded down a winding path cut in the precipice, and soon discovered the objects of their search. The horses were already dead—the chariot was shattered to pieces. They took up some of the fragments, and discovered beneath them the lifeless body of the unfortunate Lady Euphrasia. The stranger burst into tears at the sight of so much horror; and, in a voice scarcely audible, gave orders for her being conveyed to his house. But when a better light gave a more perfect view of the mangled remains, all acknowledged that, since so fatal an accident had befallen her, Heaven was merciful in taking a life whose continuance would have made her endure the most excruciating tortures

Freelove was now inquired for. He had fainted on the road, but in a few minutes after he was brought in, recovered his senses. and the first use he made of them was to inquire whether he was dead or alive. Upon receiving the comfortable assurance of the latter, he congratulated himself, in a manner so warm, upon his escape, as plainly proved self was his whole and sole consideration. No great preparations, on account of his feelings, were requisite to inform him of the fate of Lady Euphrasia. He shook his head on hearing it; said it was what he already guessed, from the devilish plunge of the horses; declared it was a most unfortunate affair, and expressed a kind of terror at what the Marquis might say to it, as if he could have been accused of being accessory to it.

Mr. Murray, the gentleman whose house had received him, offered to undertake the distressing task of breaking the affair to Lady Euphrasia's family, an offer Freelove gladly accepted, declaring he felt himself too much disordered in mind and body to be able to give any directions relative to what was necessary to be done.

How Mr. Murray executed his task is already known; but it was long ere the emotions of the Marquis would suffer him to say he wished the remains of Lady Euphrasia to be brought to the Castle, that all the honors due to her birth should be paid them. This was accordingly done; and the Castle, so lately ornamented for her nuptials, was hung with black, and all the pageantries of death.

The Marquis and Marchioness confined themselves, in the deepest anguish, to their apartments; their domestics, filled with terror and amazement, glided about like pale spectres. and all was a scene of solemnity and sadness. Every moment Lord Mortimer could spare from his father he devoted to the Marquis. Lady Euphrasia had ever been an object of indifference, nay, of dislike to him; but the manner of her death, notwithstanding, shocked him to the soul: his dislike was forgotten; he thought of her only with pity and compassion, and the tears he mingled with the Marquis were the tears of unfeigned sympathy and regret.

Lady Martha and Lady Araminta were equally attentive to the Marchioness; the time not spent with Lord Cherbury was devoted to her. They used not unavailing arguments to conquer a grief which nature, as her rightful tribute, demands; but they soothed that grief by showing they sincerely mourned its source.

Lord Cherbury had but short intervals of reason; those intervals were employed by Lord Mortimer in trying to compose his mind; and by him in blessing his son for those endeavors, and congratulating himself on the prospect of approaching dissolution. His words unutterably affected Lord Mortimer; he had reason to believe they were dictated by a prophetic spirit; and the dismal peal which rung from morning till night for Lady Euphrasia sounded in his ear as the knell of his expiring father.

Things were in this situation in the Castle when Oscar and his friend Sir Charles Bingley arrived at it, and, without sending in their names, requested immediate permission to the Marquis's presence, upon business of importance. Their request was complied with, from an idea that they came from Freelove, to whom the Marquis and Marchioness, from respect and affection to the memory of their daughter, had determined to pay every attention.

The Marquis knew, and was personally known to Sir Charles; he was infinitely surprised by his appearance, but how much was that surprise increased when Sir Charles, taking Oscar by the hand, presented him to the Marquis as the son of Lady Fitzalan, the rightful heir of the Earl of Dunreath! The Marquis was confounded; he trembled at these words; and his confusion, had such a testimony been wanting, would have been sufficient to prove his guilt. He at last, though with a faltering voice, desired to know by what means Sir Charles could justify or support his assertion.

Sir Charles for Oscar was too much agitated to speak, as briefly as possible related all the particulars which had led to the discovery of the Earl's will; and his friend, he added, with the generosity of a noble mind, wished as much as possible to spare the feelings and save the honor of those with whom he was connected; a wish, which nothing but a hesitation in complying with his just and well-supported claim could destroy.

The Marquis's agitation increased; already was he stripped of happiness, and he now saw himself on the point of being stripped of honor. An hour before he had imagined his wretchedness could not be augmented; he was now convinced human misery cannot be complete without the loss of reputation. In the idea of being esteemed, of being thought undeserving our misfortunes, there is a sweet, a secret balm, which meliorates the greatest sorrow. Of riches, in his own right, the Marquis ever possessed more than sufficient for all his expenses: those expenses would now, comparatively speaking, be reduced within very narrow bounds; for the vain pride which had led him to delight in pomp and ostentation died with Lady Euphrasia. Since, therefore, of his fortune such a superabundance would remain, it was unnecessary as well as unjust to detain what he had no pretensions to; but he feared tamely acquiescing to this unexpected claim, would be to acknowledge himself a villain. 'Tis true, indeed, that his newly-felt remorse had inspired him with a wish of making reparation for his past injustice, but false shame starting up, hitherto opposed it; and even now, when an opportunity offered of accomplishing his wish, still continued to oppose it, lest the scorn and contempt he dreaded should at length be his portion for his long injustice.

Irresolute how to act, he sat for some time silent and embarrassed, till at last, recollecting his manner was probably betraying what he wished to conceal, namely, the knowledge of the will, he said, with some sternness, "That, till he inspected into the affair so recently laid before him, he could not, nor was it to be expected he should, say how he would act; an inspection which, under present melancholy circumstances, he could not possibly make for some time. Had Mr. Fitzalan," he added, "possessed in reality that generosity Sir Charles's partiality ascribed to him, he would not, at a period so distressing, have appeared to make such a claim. To delicacy and sensibility the privileges of grief were ever held sacred. Those privileges they had both violated. They had intruded on his sorrows; they had even insulted him, by appearing on such a business before him, ere the last rites were paid to his lamented child." Sir Charles and Oscar were inexpressibly shocked. Both were totally ignorant of the recent event.

Oscar, as he recovered from the surprise the Marquis's words had given him, declared, in the impassioned language of a noble mind, hurt by being thought destitute of sensibility, "That the Marquis had arraigned him unjustly. Had he known of his sorrows," he said, "nothing should have tempted him to intrude upon them. He mourned, he respected them; he besought him to believe him sincere in what he uttered." A tear, an involuntary tear, as he spoke, starting into his eye, and trickling down his cheek, denoted his sincerity. The Marquis's heart smote him as he beheld this tear; it reproached him more than the keenest words could have done, and operated more in Oscar's favor than any arguments, however eloquent. "Had this young man," thought he, "been really illiberal when I reproached him for want of sensibility, how well might he have retaliated upon me my more flagrant want of justice and humanity; but no, he sees I am a son of sorrow, and he will not break the reed which Heaven has already smitten." Tears gushed from his eyes. He involuntarily extended his hand to Oscar. "I see," said he, "I see, indeed, I have unjustly arraigned you; but I will endeavor to atone for my error. At present, rest satisfied with an assurance, that whatever is equitable shall be done; and that, let events turn out as they may, I shall ever feel myself your friend." Oscar again expressed his regret for having waited on him at such a period, and requested he would dismiss for the present the subject they had been talking of from his mind. The Marquis, still more pleased with his manner, desired his direction, and assured him he should hear from him sooner than he expected.

As soon as they retired, his agitation decreased, and, of course, he was better qualified to consider how he should act. That restitution his conscience prompted, but his false ideas of shame had prevented, he now found he should be compelled to make; how to make it, therefore, so as to avoid total disgrace, was what he considered. At last he adopted a scheme, which the sensibility of Oscar, he flattered himself, would enable him to accomplish. This was to declare, that by the Earl of Dunreath's will, Mr. Fitzalan was heir to his estates, in case of the death of Lady Euphrasia; that in consequence, therefore, of this event, he had come to take possession of them; that Lady Dunreath (whose residence at Dunreath Abbey he could not now hope to conceal) was but lately returned from a convent in France, where for many years she had resided. To Oscar he intended saying, from her ill conduct he and the Marchioness had been tempted to sequester her from the world, in order to save her from open shame and derision; and that her declaration of a will they had always believed the mere fabrication of her brain, in order, as he supposed, to give them uneasiness. This scheme once formed, his heart felt a little relieved of the heavy burden of fear and inquietude. He repaired to the Marchioness's apartment, and broke the affair gently to her, adding, at the same time, that, sensible as they must now be of the vanities and pursuits of human life, it was time for them to endeavor to make their peace with Heaven. Affliction had taught penitence to the Marchioness, as well as her husband. She approved of his scheme, and thought, with him, that the sooner their intention of making restitution was known the greater would be the probability of its being accomplished Oscar, therefore, the next day received a letter from the Marquis, specifying at once his intention and his wishes. With those wishes Oscar generously complied. His noble soul was superior to a triumph over a fallen enemy; and he had always wished rather to save from, than expose the Marquis to disgrace. He hastened as soon as possible to the Castle, agreeably to a request contained in the letter, to assure the Marquis his conduct throughout the whole affair would be regulated according to his desire.

Perhaps, at this moment, public contempt could not have humbled the Marquis more than such generosity, when he drew a comparison between himself and the person he had so long injured. The striking contrast wounded his very soul, and he groaned at the degradation he suffered in his own eyes. He told Oscar, as soon as the last sad duties were performed to his daughter, he would settle everything with him, and then perhaps be able to introduce him to the Marchioness. He desired he might take up his residence in the Castle, and expressed a wish that he would attend the funeral of Lady Euphrasia as one of the chief mourners Oscar declined the former, but promised, with a faltering voice, to comply with the latter request. He then retired, and the Marquis, who had been roused from the indulgence of his grief by a wish of preserving his character, again relapsed into its wretchedness. He desired Oscar to make no secret of his now being heir to the Earl of Dunreath, and said he would mention it himself in his family. Through this medium, therefore, did this surprising intelligence reach Lord Mortimer, and his heart dilated with sudden joy at the idea of his Amanda and her brother at last enjoying independence and prosperity.

In a few hours after this the sufferings of Lord Cherbury were terminated. His last faltering accents pronounced blessings on his son. Oh! how sweet were those blessings! How different were the feelings of Lord Mortimer from the callous sons of dissipation, who seem to watch with impatience the last struggles of a parent, that they may have more extensive means of gratifying their inordinate desires. The feelings of Lord Mortimer were soothed by reflecting he had done everything in his power for restoring the tranquillity of his father, and his regret was lessened by the conviction that Lord Cherbury, after the discovery of his conduct, could never more in this life have experienced happiness. He therefore, with tender piety, resigned him to his God; humbly trusting that his penitence had atoned for his frailties, and insured him felicity.

He now bade adieu to the Castle and its wretched owners, and accompanied Lady Martha and his sister to Thornbury, at which the burying-place of the family lay. Here he continued till the remains of his father arrived, and were interred. He then proceeded to London to put into execution the plan he had projected for his father. He immediately advertised the Tudor estate. A step of this kind could not be concealed from Lady Martha; but the mortgages on the other estates he resolved carefully to guard from her knowledge, lest suspicions prejudicial to the memory of his father should arise in her mind. But, during this period, the idea of Amanda was not absent from his soul Neither grief nor business could banish it a moment; and, again, a thousand fond and flattering hopes concerning her had revived, when a sudden blow dispersed them all, and plunged him, if possible, into greater wretchedness than he had ever before experienced. He heard it confidently reported that the Earl of Dunreath's sister (for Oscar by this time had claimed, and been allowed to take the title of his grandfather) was to be married to Sir Charles Bingley. The friendship which he knew subsisted between the Earl and Sir Charles rendered this too probable. But if a doubt concerning it still lingered in his mind, it was destroyed when Sir Charles waited on him to treat about the purchase of Tudor Hall; it instantly occurred to him that this purchase was made by the desire of Amanda Unable to command his feelings, he referred Sir Charles to his agent, and abruptly retired. He called her cruel and ungrateful. After all his sufferings on her account, did he deserve so soon to be banished from her remembrance—so soon supplanted in her affections by another—by one, too, who never had, who never would have, an opportunity of giving such proofs as he had done of constancy and love. She is lost, then, he sighed; she is lost for ever! Oh! what avails the vindication of her fame? Is it not an augmentation of my misery? Oh! my father, of what a treasure did you despoil me! But let me not disturb the sacred ashes of the dead—rest, rest in peace, thou venerable author of my being! and may the involuntary expression of heart-rending anguish be forgiven! Amanda, then, he continued, after a pause, will indeed be mistress of Tudor Hall; but never will a sigh for him who once was its owner heave her bosom. She will wander beneath those shades, where so often she has heard my vows of unalterable love—vows which, alas! my heart has too fully observed —and listen to similar ones from Sir Charles: well, this is the last stroke fate can level at my peace.

Lord Mortimer (or, as in future we must style him, Lord Cherbury) had indeed imagined that the affections of Amanda, like his own, were unalterable; he had therefore indulged the rapturous idea, that, by again seeking an union with her, she should promote the happiness of both. It is true he knew she would possess a fortune infinitely superior to what he had now a right to expect; but after the proofs he had given of disinterested attachment, not only she, but the world, he was convinced, would acquit him of any selfish motives in the renewal of his addresses. His hopes destroyed —his prospects blasted by what he had heard, he resolved, as soon as affairs were settled, to go abroad. The death of his father had rendered his entering the army unnecessary, and his spirits were too much broken, his health too much impaired, for him voluntarily now to embrace that destiny.

On the purchase of Tudor Hall being completed by Sir Charles, it was necessary for Lord Cherbury to see his steward. He preferred going to sending for him, prompted indeed by a melancholy wish of paying a last visit to Tudor Hall, endeared to his heart by a thousand fond remembrances. On his arrival he took up his abode at the steward's for a day or two. After a strict injunction to him of concealing his being there, it was after a ramble through every spot about the demesne which he had ever trodden with Amanda, that he repaired to the library and discovered her. He was ignorant of her being in the country. Oh! then, how great was her surprise—how exquisite his emotions, at seeing her in such unexpected circumstances!

I shall not attempt to go over the scene I have already tried to describe; suffice it to say, that the desire she betrayed of hastening from him he imputed to the alteration of her sentiments with respect to him and Sir Charles. When undeceived in this respect, his rapture was as great as ever it had before been at the idea of her love, and, like Amanda, he declared his sufferings were now amply rewarded.

CHAPTER LVII.

> "No, never from this hour to part,
> We'll live and love so true;
> The sigh that rends thy constant heart,
> Shall break thy lover's too."

UT, my love," cried Lord Cherbury, as he wiped away the tears which pity and horror at the fate of Lady Euphrasia had caused Amanda to shed, "will your brother, think you, sanction our happiness? Will he, who might aspire so high for a sister thus at once possessed of beauty and fortune, bestow her on one whose title may now almost be considered an empty one?" "Oh! do not wrong his noble nature by such a doubt," exclaimed Amanda. "Yes, with pride, with pleasure, with delight, will he bestow his sister upon the esteemed, the beloved of her heart; upon him, who, unwarped by narrow prejudice or selfish interest, sought her in the low shade of obscurity, to lay, all friendless and forlorn as she was, his fortune at her feet. Could he indeed be ungrateful to such kindness, could he attempt to influence me to another choice, my heart would at once repulse the effort, and avow its fixed determination; but he is incapable of such conduct; my Oscar is all that is generous and feeling: need I say more, than that a spirit congenial to yours animates his breast."

Lord Cherbury clasped her to his heart. "Dearest, loveliest of human beings," he exclaimed, "shall I at length call you mine? After all my sorrows, my difficulties, shall I indeed receive so precious a reward? Oh! wonder not, my Amanda, if I doubt the reality of so sudden a reverse of situation; I feel as if under the influence of a happy dream; but, good Heaven! a dream from which I should never wish to be awakened."

Amanda now recollected, that if she stayed much longer from the cottage she would have some one coming in quest of her. She informed Lord Cherbury of this, and rose to depart; but he would not suffer her to depart alone, neither did she desire it. The nurse and her daughter Betsey were in the cottage at her return to it. To describe the surprise of the former at the appearance of Lord Cherbury is impossible—a surprise mingled with indignation, at the idea of his falsehood to her darling child; but when undeceived in that respect, her transports were of the most extravagant nature.

"Well, she thanked Heaven," she said, "she should now see her tear child hold up her head again, and look as handsome as ever. Ay, she had always doubted," she said, "that his lortship was not one of the false-hearted men she had so often heard her old grandmother talk of." "My good nurse," said Lord Cherbury, smiling, "you will then give me your dear child with all your heart?" "Ay, that I will, my lort," she replied, "and this very moment too, if I could." "Well," cried Amanda, 'his lordship will be satisfied at present with getting his dinner from you." She then desired the things to be brought to the little arbor, already described at the beginning of this book, and proceeded to it with Lord Cherbury. The mention of dinner threw nurse and her daughter into universal commotion.

"Good lack! how unfortunate it was she had nothing hot or nice to lay pefore his lortship! How could she think he could dine upon cold lamb and salad! Well, this was all Miss Amanda's fault, who would never let her do as she wished." With the utmost difficulty she was persuaded he could dine upon these things. The cloth was laid upon the flowery turf, beneath the spreading branches of the arbor. The delicacies of the dairy were added to their repast, and Betsey provided a dessert of new filberts.

Never had Lord Cherbury partaken of so delicious a meal—never had he and Amanda experienced such happiness. The pleasure, the tenderness of their souls, beamed in expressive glances from their eyes, and they were now more convinced than ever that the humble scenes of life were best calculated for the promotion of felicity. Lord Cherbury felt more reconciled than he had been before to the diminution of his fortune; he yet retained sufficient for the comforts, and many of the elegancies of life. The splendor he lost was insignificant in his eyes; his present situation proved happiness could be enjoyed without it, and he knew it was equally disregarded by Amanda. He asked himself,

"—— — What was the world to them—
Its pomps, its pleasures, and its nonsense all,
Who in each other clasp, whatever fair
High fancy forms, or lavish hearts can wish?"

All nature looked gay and smiling around him. He inhaled the balmy breath of opening flowers, and through the verdant canopy he sat beneath, he saw the bright azure of the heavens, and felt the benignant influence of the sun, whose potent beams heightened to glowing luxuriance the beauties of the surrounding landscape. He expressed his feelings to Amanda; he heard her declare the similarity of hers; heard her, with all the sweet enthusiasm of a refined and animated mind, expatiate on the lovely scene around them. Oh! what tender remembrances did it awaken, and what delightful plans of felicity did they sketch! Lord Cherbury would hear from Amanda all she had suffered since their separation; and could his love and esteem have been increased, her patient endurance of the sorrows she related would have increased them. They did not leave the garden till a dusky hue had overspread the landscape. Oh! with what emotions did Amanda watch the setting sun, whose rising beams she had beheld with eyes obscured by tears of sorrow! As they sat at tea in the room, she could not avoid noticing the alteration in the nurse's dress who attended. She had put on all her holiday finery; and, to evince her wish of amusing her guests, had sent for the blind harper, whom she stationed outside the cottage. His music drew a number of the neighboring cottagers about him, and they would soon have led up a dance in the vale, had not the nurse prevented them, lest they should disturb her guests. Lord Cherbury, however, insisted on their being gratified, and, sending for his servant, ordered him to provide refreshments for them, and to reward the harper. He would not leave Amanda till he had her permission to come early next morning, as soon as he could hope to see her. Accordingly the first voice she heard on rising was his chatting to the nurse. We may believe she did not spend many minutes at her toilet. The neat simplicity of her dress never required she should do so, and in a very short time she joined him. They walked out till breakfast was ready.

> "Together trod the morning dews, and gathered
> In their prime fresh blooming sweets."

Amanda, in hourly expectation of her brother's arrival, wished, ere he came, to inform the inhabitants of the cottage of the alteration of his fortune. This, with the assistance of Lord Cherbury, she took an opportunity of doing in the course of the day to the nurse. Had she been sole relator, she feared she should have been overwhelmed with questions. Joy and wonder were excited in an extreme degree by this relation, and nothing but the nurse's hurry and impatience to communicate it to her family, could have prevented her from asking again and again a repetition of it.

Lord Cherbury now, as on the foregoing day, dined with

Amanda. Her expectations relative to the speedy arrival of her brother were not disappointed. While sitting after dinner with Lord Cherbury in the garden, the nurse, half breathless, came running to tell them that a superb coach and four, which to be sure must be my Lort Dunreath's, was coming down the road.

Lord Cherbury colored with emotion. Amanda did not wish he and her brother should meet, till she had explained everything relative to him. By her desire he retired to the valley, to which a winding path from the garden descended, whilst she hurried to the cottage to receive and welcome her beloved brother. Their meeting was at once tender and affecting. The faithful Edwins surrounded Oscar with delight and rapture, pouring forth, in their simple style, congratulations on his happy fortune, and their wishes for his long enjoying it. He thanked them with a starting tear of sensibility. He assured them that their attentions to his dear sister, his lamented parents, his infant years, entitled them to a lasting gratitude. As soon as he and Amanda could disengage themselves from the good creatures, without wounding their feelings, they retired to her room, where Oscar related, as we have already done, all that passed between him and the Marquis of Roslin.

As soon as the funeral of Lady Euphrasia was over, the Marquis settled everything with him, and put him into formal possession of Dunreath Abbey. By the Marquis's desire, he then waited upon Lady Dunreath, to inform her she was at liberty, and to request she would not contradict the assertion of having been abroad. Mrs. Bruce had previously informed her of the revolution of affairs. "I own," continued Oscar, "from the cruelty to my mother, and the depravity of her conduct, I was strongly prejudiced against her, attributing, I acknowledge, her doing justice to us, in some degree, to her resentment against the Marquis; but the moment I entered her apartment this prejudice vanished, giving place to the softer emotions of pity and tenderness, while a thorough conviction of her sincere repentance broke upon my soul. Though prepared to see a form reduced by affliction and confinement, I was not by any means prepared to see a form so emaciated, so death-like—a faint motion of her head, as I entered, alone proved her existence. Had the world been given me to do so, I think I could not have broken a silence so awful. At length she spoke, and in language that pierced my heart, implored my forgiveness for the sufferings she had caused me to endure. Repeatedly I assured her of it; but this rather heightened than diminished her agitation, and tears and sobs spoke the anguish of her soul. 'I have lived,' she cried, 'to justify the ways of Providence to men, and prove that, however calamity may oppress the virtuous, they or their descendants shall at last flourish. I have lived to see my contrite wish accomplished, and the last summons will now be a welcome release.' She expressed an ardent desire to see her daughter. 'The pitying tears of a mother,' she exclaimed, 'may be as balm to her wounded heart. Oh! my prophetic words, how often have I prayed that the punishment I then denounced against her might be averted!'

"I signified her desire," continued Oscar, "to the Marquis. I found the Marchioness at first reluctant to it, from a secret dread, I suppose, of seeing an object so injured; but she at last consented, and I was requested to bring Lady Dunreath from the Abbey, and conduct her to the Marchioness's room. I will not attempt to describe the scene which passed between affection on the one hand, and penitence on the other. The Marchioness indeed seemed truly penitent: remorse and horror were visible in her countenance, as she gazed upon her injured parent. I begged Lady Dunreath, if agreeable to her, still to consider the Abbey as her residence. This, however, she declined, and it was determined she should continue with her daughter. Her last moments may, perhaps, be soothed by closing in the presence of her child; but till then, I think, her wretchedness must be aggravated by beholding that of the Marquis and his wife. Theirs is that situation where comfort can neither be offered nor suggested—hopeless and incurable is their sorrow—for, to use the beautiful and emphatic words of a late celebrated writer, 'The gates of death are shut upon their prospects.'"

Amanda now, after a little hesitation, proceeded to inform Oscar of her real situation, and entreated him to believe that she never would have had a concealment from him, but for the fear of giving him uneasiness. He folded her to his bosom as she ceased speak ing, declaring he rejoiced and congratulated her on having found an object so well qualified to make her happy.

"But where is this dear creature?" cried Oscar, with some gaiety; "am I to search for him, like a favorite sylph, in your bouquet; or, with more probability of success, seek him amongst the shades of the garden? Come," said he, "your looks confess our search will not be troublesome." He led her to the garden Lord Cherbury, who had lingered near it, saw them approaching. Amanda motioned him to meet them. He sprang forward, and was instantly introduced by her to Lord Dunreath. The reception he met was the most flattering proof he could receive of his Amanda's affections; for what but the most animated expressions in his favor could have made Lord Dunreath, at the first introduction, address him with all the fervency of friendship? Extremes of joy and sorrow are difficult to describe. I shall, therefore, as perfectly conscious of my inability to do justice to the scene which followed this introduction, pass it over in silence. Lord Dunreath had ordered his equipage and attendants to the village inn, where he himself intended to lodge. But this was prevented by Lord Cherbury, who informed him he could be accommodated at his steward's. It was here, when they had retired for the night, that, Lord Cherbury having intimated his wishes for an immediate union with Amanda, all the necessary preliminaries were talked over and adjusted; and it was agreed that the marriage should take place at the cottage, from whence they should immediately proceed to Lady Martha's, and that, to procure a license, they should both depart the next morning. At breakfast, therefore, Amanda was apprised of their plan, and though the glow of modesty overspread her face, she did not with affectation object to it.

With greater expedition than Amanda expected, the travellers returned from the journey they had been obliged to take, and a their earnest and united request, without any affectation of modesty though with its real feelings, Amanda consented that the marriage should take place the day but one after their return. Howel was sent for, and informed of the hour his services would be required. His mild eyes evinced to Amanda his sincere joy at the termination of her sorrows.

On the destined morning, Lord Dunreath and his friend went over to the cottage, and in a few minutes were joined by Amanda, the perfect model of innocence and beauty. She looked, indeed, the child of sweet simplicity, arrayed with the unstudied elegance of a village maid; she had no ornaments but those which could never decay, namely, modesty and meekness.

Language was inadequate to express the feelings of Lord Cherbury. His fine eyes alone could do them justice—alone reveal what might be the sacred triumph of his soul at gaining such a woman. A soft shade of melancholy stole over the fine features of Lord Dunreath, as he witnessed the happiness of Lord Cherbury; for as his happiness, so might his own have been, but for the blackest perfidy.

As Lord Cherbury took the trembling hand of Amanda, to lead her from the cottage, she gave a farewell sigh to a place where, it might be said, her happiness had commenced and was completed. They walked to the church, followed by the nurse and her family. Some kind hand had strewed Lady Malvina's grave with the gayest flowers, and when Amanda reached it she paused involuntarily for a moment, to invoke the spirits of her parents to bless her union.

Howel was already in the church, waiting to receive them, and the ceremony was begun without delay. With the truest pleasure did Lord Dunreath give his lovely sister to Lord Cherbury, and with the liveliest transport did he receive her as the choicest gift Heaven could bestow. Tears of sweet sensibility fell from Amanda, as Lord Cherbury folded her to his bosom as his own Amanda. Nor was he less affected; joy of the most rapturous kind agitated his whole soul at the completion of an event so earnestly desired, but so long despaired of. He wiped away her tears, and, when she had received the congratulations of her brother, presented her to the rest of the little group. Their delight, particularly the nurse's, was almost too great for expression.

"Well," she said, sobbing, "thank Cot her wish was fulfilled. It had peen her prayer, night, noon, and morn, to see the taughter of her tear, tear Captain Fitzalan greatly married." Poor Ellen wept—"Well, now she should be happy," she said, "since she knew her tear young laty was so." Amanda, affected by the artless testimonies of affection she received, could only smile upon the faithful creatures.

Lord Cherbury, seeing her unable to speak, took her hand, and said—"Lord Cherbury never would forget the obligations conferred upon Miss Fitzalan." Bridal favors and presents had already been distributed among the Edwins. Howel was handsomely complimented on the occasion, and received some valuable presents from Lord Cherbury, as proofs of his sincere friendship; also money to distribute among the indigent villagers. His lordship then handed Amanda into his coach, already prepared for its journey to Thornbury, and the little bridal party were followed by the most ardent blessings. After proceeding a quarter of a mile, they reached Tudor Hall.

"I wish, my Lord," cried Oscar, as they were driving round the wood, "you would permit me to stop and view the Hall, and also accompany me to it." Lord Cherbury looked a little embarrassed. He felt a strong reluctance to visit it, when no longer his, yet he could not think of refusing the Earl. Amanda knew his feelings, and wished her brother had not made such a request. No opposition, however, being shown to it, they stopped at the great gate which opened into the avenue, and alighted. This was a long, beautiful walk, cut through the wood, and in a direct line with the house. On either side were little grassy banks, now covered with a profusion of gay flowers, and a thick row of trees, which, waving their old fantastic branches on high, formed a most delightful shade. Honey-suckles twined around many of the trunks, forming in some places luxuriant canopies, and with a variety of aromatic shrubs quite perfumed the air. It was yet an early hour; the dew, therefore, still sparkled upon the grass, and everything looked in the highest verdure. Through vistas in the wood, a fine clear river was seen, along whose sides beautiful green slopes were stretched, scattered over with flocks, that spread their swelling treasures to the sun. The birds sung sweetly in the embowering recesses of the woods, and so calm, so lovely did the place appear, that Lord Cherbury could not refrain a sigh for its loss. "How delighted," cried he, casting his fine eyes around, "should I have been still to have cherished those old trees, beneath whose shades some of my happiest hours were passed." They entered the hall, whose folding door they found open. It was large and gothic; a row of arched windows were on either side, whose recesses were filled with myrtles, roses, and geraniums, which emitted a delicious perfume, and, contrasted with the white walls, gave an appearance of the greatest gaiety to the place.

Oscar led the way to a spacious parlor at the end of the hall. But how impossible to describe the surprise and pleasure of Lord and Lady Cherbury, on entering it, at beholding Lady Martha and Lady Araminta Dormer! Lord Cherbury stood transfixed like a statue. The caresses of his aunt and his sister, which were shared between him and his bride, restored him to animation; but while he returned them, he cast his eyes upon Oscar, and demanded an explanation of the scene. "I shall give no explanation, my Lord," cried Oscar, "till you welcome your friends to your house."

"My house!" repeated Lord Cherbury, staring at him. Lord Dunreath approached. Never had he appeared so engaging. The benignant expression his countenance assumed was such as we may suppose an angel sent from heaven, on benevolent purposes to man, would wear.

"Excuse me, my dear Cherbury," said he, "for suffering you to feel any uneasiness which I could remove. I only did so from an idea of increasing your pleasure hereafter. In Scotland I was informed of your predilection for my sister by Lady Greystock, whom, I fancy, you have both some reason to remember, in consequence of which, on seeing Tudor Hall advertised, I begged Sir Charles Bingley to purchase it for me, in his own name, from a presentiment I had, that the event I now rejoice at would take place; and from my wish of having a nuptial present for my sister worthy of her acceptance. Let me," continued he, taking a hand of each and joining them together, "let me, in this respected mansion, and in the dear presence of those you love, again wish you a continuance of every blessing. May this seat, as heretofore, be the scene of domestic happiness; may it ever be a pleasing abode to the prosperous, and an asylum of comfort to the afflicted."

Lord Cherbury's heart was too full for words. He turned aside to wipe away his starting tears. At last, though in a broken voice, he said, "I cannot speak my feelings." "Pain me not," cried

Oscar, "by attempting to do so. From this moment forget that Tudor Hall was ever out of your possession; or, if you must remember it, think it restored to you with an encumbrance, which half the fashionable men in England would give an estate to get rid of, and this will conquer your too refined feelings."

Lord Cherbury smiled as he looked at the lovely encumbrance which Oscar alluded to. "And what shall I say to my brother?" cried Amanda, throwing herself into his arms. "Why, that you will compose your spirits, and endeavor to give a proper welcome to your friends." He presented her to Lady Martha and Lady Araminta, who again embraced and congratulated her He then led her to the head of the breakfast-table, which was elegantly laid out. The timid bride was assisted in doing the honors by her brother and Lord Cherbury. Lady Martha beheld the youthful pair with the truest delight. Never had she before seen two, from equal merit and loveliness, so justly formed to make each other happy; never had she seen either to such advantage. The beautiful coloring of health and modesty tinged the soft cheeks of Amanda, and her eyes, through their long lashes, emitted mild beams of pleasure; its brightest glow mantled the cheeks of Lord Cherbury, and his eyes were again illumined with all their wonted radiancy.

Oscar was requested to tell particularly how he had arranged his plan; which he accordingly did. He had written to the ladies at Thornbury, informing them of his scheme, and requesting their presence, and on the preceding night they had arrived at the Hall. Lord Dunreath also added, that from a certainty of its being agreeable to Lord Cherbury, he had directed the steward to reinstate the old servants in their former stations, and also to invite the tenants to a nuptial feast. Lord Cherbury assured him he had done what was truly grateful to his feelings. A ramble about the garden and shrubberies was proposed, and agreed to, after breakfast. In the hall and avenue the servants and tenants were already assembled. Lord Cherbury went among them all, and the grateful joy they expressed at having him again for a master and a landlord deeply affected his feelings. He thanked them for their regard, and received their congratulations on his present happiness with that sweetness and affability which ever distinguished his manners. The ramble was delightful. When the sun had attained its meridian, they sought the cool shade, and retired to little romantic arbors, overcanopied with woodbines, where, as if by the hand of enchantment, they found refreshments laid out. They did not return to the house till they received a summons to dinner, and had then the pleasure of seeing the tenants seated at long tables in the wood, enjoying with unbounded mirth the profusion with which they were covered, and Lord Cherbury begged Amanda to observe her nurse seated at the head of one of these tables, with an air of the greatest self-importance. The pride and vanity of this good woman (and she always possessed a large share of both) had been considerably increased from the time her cottage was honored with such noble guests. When she received an invitation from the steward to accompany the rest of the tenants to the Hall to celebrate its restoration to Lord Cherbury, her joy and exultation knew no bounds; she took care to walk with the wives of some of the most respectable tenants, describing to them all that had passed at the ceremony, and how the Earl had first fallen in love with his bride at her cottage, and what trials they had undergone, no toubt, to prove their constancy. "Cot pless their hearts," she said to her eager auditors; "she could tell them of such tangers and tifficulties, and tribulations, as would surprise the very souls in their poties. Well, well, it is now her tear child's turn to hold up her head with the highest in the land, and to pe sure she might now say, without telling a lie, that her tear latyship would now make somepoty of herself, and, please Cot, she hoped and pelieved, she would not tisgrace or tisparage a petter situation." When she came near the Countess, she took care to press forward for a gracious look; but this was not all; she had always envied the consequence of Mrs. Abergwilly in having so great a house as the Hall entirely under her management, and she now determined, upon the strength of her favor with Lady Cherbury, to have something to say to it, and, of course, increase her consequence among her neighbors. There was nothing on earth she so much delighted in as bustle, and the present scene was quite adapted to her taste, for all within and without the house was joyous confusion. The first specimen she gave of her intention was, in helping to distribute refreshments among the tenants; she then proceeded to the dinner-parlor, to give her opinion, and assistance, and direction about laying out the table. Mrs. Abergwilly, like the generality of those accustomed to absolute power, could not tamely submit to any innovation on it. She curbed her resentment, however, and civilly told Mrs. Edwin she wanted no assistance; "thank Cot," she said, "she was not come to this time of tay without peing able to give proper tirections about laying out a table." Mrs. Edwin said, "To be sure Mrs. Abergwilly might have a very pretty taste, but then another person might have as good a one." The day was intensely hot; she pinned back her gown, which was a rich silk that had belonged to Lady Malvina, and, without further ceremony, began altering the dishes, saying, she knew the taste of her tear laty, the Countess, petter than any one else, and that she would take an early opportunity of going through the apartments, and telling Mrs. Abergwilly how to arrange the furniture.

The Welsh blood of the housekeeper could bear no more, and she began abusing Mrs. Edwin, though in terms scarcely articulate, to which she replied with interest. In the midst of this fracas, old Edwin entered. "For the love of Cot," he asked, "and the mercy of Heaven, could they choose no other time or tay than the present to pegin to fight, and scold, and abuse each other like a couple of Welsh witches? What would the noble Earl and the Countess say? Oh, Lort! oh, Lort! he felt himself blushing all over for their misdemeanors." His remonstrance had an immediate effect; they were both ashamed of their conduct; their rage abated; they became friends, and Mrs. Edwin resigned the direction of the dinner-table to Mrs. Abergwilly, satisfied with being allowed to preside among the tenants.

The bridal party found Howel in the dining parlor, and his company increased their pleasure. After dinner the rustics commenced dancing in the avenue, to the strains of the harp, and afforded a delightful scene of innocent gaiety to their benevolent entertainers who smiled to see

"The dancing pair that simply sought renown
By holding out to tire each other down:
The bashful virgin's side-long looks of love,
The matron's glance that would those looks reprove."

After tea the party went out amongst them, and the gentlemen, for a short time, mingled in the dance. Long it could not detain Lord Cherbury from his Amanda. Oh! with what ecstasy did he listen to the soft accents of her voice, while his fond heart assured him she was now his! The remembrance of past difficulties but increased his present felicity. In the course of the week all the neighboring families came to pay their congratulations at Tudor Hall; invitations were given and received, and it again became the seat of pleasure and hospitality; but Amanda did not suffer the possession of happiness to obliterate one grateful remembrance from her mind. She was not one of those selfish beings, who, on being what is termed settled for life, immediately contract themselves within the narrow sphere of their own enjoyments; still was her heart as sensible as ever to the glow of friendship and compassion. She wrote to all the friends she had ever received kindnesses from, in terms of the warmest gratitude, and her letters were accompanied by presents sufficiently valuable to prove her sincerity. She sent an invitation to Emily Rushbrook, which was immediately accepted. And now a discovery took place which infinitely surprised and pleased Amanda, namely, that Howel was the young clergyman Emily was attached to. He had gone to London on a visit to the gentleman who patronized him. Her youth, her simplicity, above all, her distress, affected his heart; and in the hope of mitigating that distress (which he was shocked to see had been aggravated by the ladies she came to), he had followed her. To soothe the wretched, to relieve the distressed, was not considered more a duty than a pleasure by Howel. And the little favors he conferred upon the Rushbrooks afforded, if possible, more pleasure to him than they did to them; so sweet are the feelings of benevolence and virtue. But compassion was not long the sole motive of his interest in their affairs—the amiable manners, the gentle conversation of Emily, completely subdued his unfortunate passion for Amanda, and in stealing her image from his heart she implanted her own in its place. He described, in a romantic manner, the little rural cottage he invited her to share; he anticipated the happy period when it should become an asylum to her parents; when he, like a second father, should assist their children through the devious paths of life. These fond hopes and expectations vanished the moment he received Mrs. Connel's letter. He could not think of sacrificing the interest of Rushbrook to the consideration of his own happiness, and therefore generously, but with the most agonizing conflicts, resigned his Emily to a more prosperous rival. His joy at finding her disengaged, still his own unaltered Emily, can better be conceived than described. He pointed out the little sheltered cottage which again he hoped she would share, and blessed, with her, the hand that had opened her father's prison gates. Lord and Lady Cherbury were delighted tc think they could contribute to the felicity of two such amiable beings; and the latter wrote to Captain and Mrs. Rushbrook on the subject, who immediately replied to her letter, declaring that their fondest wish would be gratified in bestowing their daughter on Howel. They were accordingly invited to the Hall, and in the same spot where a month before he ratified the vows of Lord Cherbury and Amanda, did Howel plight his own to Emily, who from the hand of Lady Cherbury received a nuptial present sufficient to procure every enjoyment her humble and unassuming spirit aspired to. Her parents, after passing a few days in her cottage, departed, rejoicing at the happiness of their beloved child, and truly grateful to those who had contributed to it.

And now did the grateful children of Fitzalan amply reward the Edwins for their past kindnesses to their parents and themselves. An annual stipend was settled on Edwin by Lord Dunreath, and the possessions of Ellen were enlarged by Amanda. Now was realized every scheme of domestic happiness she had ever formed; but even that happiness could not alleviate her feelings on Oscar's account, whose faded cheek, whose languid eye, whose total abstraction in the midst of company, evidently proved the state of his heart; and the tear of regret, which had so often fallen for her own sorrows, was now shed for his. He had written to Mrs. Marlowe a particular account of everything which had befallen him since their separation. She answered his letter immediately, and, after congratulating him in the warmest terms on the change in his situation, informed him that Adela was then at one of Belgrave's seats in England, and that he was gone to the continent. Her style was melancholy, and she concluded her letter in these words: "No longer, my dear Oscar, is my fireside enlivened by gaiety or friendship; sad and solitary I sit within my cottage till my heart sickens at the remembrance of past scenes, and if I wander from it, the objects without, if possible, add to the bitterness of that remembrance. The closed windows, the grass-grown paths, the dejected servants of Woodlawn, all recall to my mind those hours when it was the mansion of hospitality and pleasure. I often linger by the grave of the General; my tears fall upon it, and I think of that period when, like him, I shall drop into it. But my last hours will not close like his; no tender child will bend over my pillow, to catch my last sigh, to soothe my last pang. In vain my closing eyes will look for the pious drops of nature, or of friendship. Unfriended I shall die, with the sad consciousness of doing so through my own means; but I shall not be quite unmourned. You, and my Adela, the sweet daughter of my care, will regret the being whose affection, whose sympathy for you both, can only be obliterated with life."

CHAPTER LVIII.

"The modest virtues mingled in her eyes,
Still on the ground dejected, darting all
Their humid beams into the opening flowers·
Or when she thought—
Of what her faithless fortune promised once,
They, like the dewy star
Of evening, shone in tears."—THOMSON.

DELA, on the death of her father, was taken by Belgrave to England, though the only pleasure he experienced in removing her was derived from the idea of wounding her feelings, by separating her from Mrs. Marlowe, whom he knew she was tenderly attached to. From his connections in London, she was compelled to mix in society—compelled, I say, for the natural gaiety of her soul was quite gone, and that solitude, which permitted her to brood over the remembrance of past days, was the only happiness she was capable of enjoying. When the terrors of Belgrave drove him from the kingdom, he had her removed to Woodhouse, to which, it may be remembered, he had once brought Amanda, and from which the imperious woman who then ruled was removed; but the principal domestic was equally harsh and insolent in her manner, and to her care the unfortunate Adela was consigned, with strict orders that she should not be allowed to receive any company, or correspond with any being. Accustomed from her earliest youth to the greatest tenderness, this severity plunged her in the deepest despondency, and life was a burden she would gladly have resigned. Her melancholy, or rather her patient sweetness, at last softened the flinty nature of her governante, and she was permitted to extend her walks beyond the gardens, to which they had hitherto been confined; but she availed herself of this permission only to visit the churchyard belonging to the hamlet, whose old yew-trees she had often seen waving from the windows. Beneath their solemn gloom she loved to sit, while evening closed around her; and in a spot sequestered from every human eye, weep over the recollection of that father she had lost, that friend she was separated from. She remained in the churchyard one night beyond her usual hour. The soft beams of the moon alone prevented her from being involved in darkness, and the plaintive breathings of a flute from the hamlet just stole upon her ear. Lost in sadness, her head resting upon her hand, she forgot the progress of time, when suddenly she beheld a form rising from a neighboring grave. She started up, screamed, but had no power to move. The form advanced to her. It was the figure of a venerable man, who gently exclaimed, "Be not afraid!" His voice dissipated the involuntary fears of Adela; but still she trembled so much she could not move. "I thought," cried he, gazing on her, "this place had been alone the haunt of wretchedness and me." "If sacred to sorrow," exclaimed Adela, "I well may claim the privilege of entering it." She spoke involuntarily, and her words seemed to affect the stranger deeply. "So young," said he; "it is melancholy, indeed; but still the sorrows of youth are more bearable than those of age, because, like age, it has not outlived the fond ties, the sweet connections of life." "Alas!" cried Adela, unable to repress her feelings, "I am separated from all I regarded." The stranger leaned pensively against a tree for a few minutes, and then again addressed her: "'Tis a late hour," said he; "suffer me to conduct you home, and also permit me to ask if I may see you here to-morrow night? Your youth, your manner, your dejection, all interest me deeply. The sorrows of youth are often increased by imagination. You will say that nothing can exceed its pains; 'tis true, but it is a weakness to yield to them—a weakness which, from a sensible mind, will be eradicated the moment it hears of the real calamities of life. Such a relation I can give you, if you meet me to-morrow night in this sad, this solitary spot —a spot I have visited every closing evening, without ever before meeting a being in it."

His venerable looks, his gentle, his pathetic manner, affected Adela inexpressibly. She gazed on him with emotions somewhat similar to those with which she used to contemplate the mild features of her father. "I will meet you," cried she, "but my sorrows are not imaginary." She refused to let him attend her home; and in this incident there was something affecting and romantic, which soothed and engrossed the mind. She was punctual the next evening to the appointed hour. The stranger was already in the churchyard. He seated her at the head of the grave from which she had seen him rise the preceding night, and which was only distinguished from the others by a few flowering shrubs planted round it, and began his promised narrative. He had not proceeded far ere Adela began to tremble with emotion—as he continued it increased. At last, suddenly catching his hand with wildness, she exclaimed, "She lives—the wife so bitterly lamented still lives, a solitary mourner for your sake. Oh, never! never did she injure you, as you suppose. Oh, dear, inestimable Mrs. Marlowe, what happiness to the child of your care, to think that through her means you will regain the being you have so tenderly regretted—regain him with a heart open to receive you." The deep convulsive sobs of her companion now pierced her ear. For many minutes he was unable to speak—at last, raising his eyes. "Oh, Providence! I thank Thee," he exclaimed; "again shall my arms fold to my heart its best beloved object. Oh, my Fanny, how have I injured thee! Learn from me," he continued, turning to Adela, "Oh! learn from me never to yield to rashness. Had I allowed myself time to inquire into the particulars of my wife's conduct; had I resisted, instead of obeying, the violence of pas sion, what years of lingering misery should I have saved us both! But tell me where I shall find my solitary mourner, as you call her?" Adela gave him the desired information, and also told him her own situation. "The wife of Belgrave!" he repeated; "then I wonder not," continued he, as if involuntarily, "at your sorrows." It was, indeed, to Howel, the unfortunate father of Juliana, the regretted husband of Mrs. Marlowe, that Adela had been addressing herself. He checked himself, however, and told her that the being, by whose grave they sat, had been hurried, through the villany of Belgrave, to that grave. Adela told him of the prohibition against her writing; but at the same time assured him, ere the following night, she would find an opportunity of writing a letter, which he should bring to Mrs. Marlowe, who by its contents would be prepared for his appearance, as it was to be sent in to her. But Adela was prevented from putting her intention into execution by an event as solemn as unexpected.

The ensuing morning she was disturbed from her sleep by a violent noise in the house, as of people running backwards and forwards in confusion and distress. She was hurrying on her clothes to go and inquire into the occasion of it, when a servant rushed into the room, and in a hasty manner told her that Colonel Belgrave was dead. Struck with horror and amazement, Adela stood petrified, gazing on her. The maid repeated her words, and added that he had died abroad, and his remains were brought over to Woodhouse for interment, attended by a French gentleman, who looked like a priest. The various emotions which assailed the heart of Adela at this moment were too much for her weak frame, and she would have fallen to the floor but for the maid. It was some time ere she recovered her sensibility, and when she did regain it, she was still so agitated as to be unable to give those directions, which the domestics, who now looked up to her in a light very different from they had hitherto done, demanded from her. All she could desire was that the steward should pay every respect and attention to the gentleman who had attended the remains of his master, and have every honor that was due shown to those remains. To suppose she regretted Belgrave would be unnatural; but she felt horror, mingled with a degree of pity, for his untimely fate, at the idea of his dying abroad, without one connection, one friend near him. His last moments were indeed more wretched than she could conceive. Overwhelmed with terror and grief, he had quitted England—terror at the supposition of a crime which in reality he had not committed, and grief for the fate of Amanda. He sought to lose his horrors in inebriety; but this, joined to the agitations of his mind, brought on a violent fever by the time he had landed at Calais, in the paroxysms of which, had the attendants understood his language, they would have been shocked at the crimes he revealed. His senses were restored a short time before he died; but what excruciating anguish, as well as horror, did he suffer from their restoration! He knew from his own feelings, as well as from the looks of his attendants, that his last moments were approaching; and the recollection of past actions made him shudder at those moments. Oh, Howel! now were you amply avenged for all the pangs he made you suffer. Now did the pale image of your shrouded Juliana seem to stand beside his bed reproaching his barbarity. Every treacherous action now rose to view, and, trembling, he groaned with terror at the spectres which a guilty conscience raised around him. Death would have been a release, could he have considered it an annihilation of all existence; but that future world he had always derided, that world was opening in all its awful horrors to his view. Already he saw himself before its sacred Judge, surrounded by the accusing spirits of those he had injured. He desired a clergyman to be brought to him. A priest was sent for. Their faiths were different, but still, as a man of God, Belgrave applied to him for an alleviation of his tortures. The priest was superstitious, and ere he tried to comfort he wished to convert; but scarcely had he commenced the attempt ere the wretched being before him clasped his hands together, in a strong convulsion, and expired. The English servant who attended Belgrave informed the people of the hotel of his rank and fortune, and the priest offered to accompany his remains to England. He was, by the direction of Adela, who had not resolution to see him, amply rewarded for his attention: and in two days after their arrival at Woodhouse, the remains of Belgrave were consigned to their kindred earth. From a sequestered corner of the churchyard Howel witnessed his interment. When all had departed, he approached the grave of his daughter—"He is gone!" he exclaimed; "my Juliana, your betrayer is gone; at the tribunal of his God he now answers for his cruelty to you. But, oh! may he find mercy from that God; may He pardon him, as in this solemn moment I have done—my enmity lives not beyond the grave."

Adela now sent for Howel; and, after their first emotions had subsided, informed him she meant immediately to return to Ireland. The expectation of her doing so had alone prevented his going before. They accordingly commenced their journey the ensuing day, and in less than a week reached the dear and destined spot so interesting to both. They had previously settled on the manner in which the discovery should be revealed to Mrs. Marlowe, and Adela went alone into her cottage. Sad and solitary, as Mrs. Marlowe said in her letter to Oscar, did Adela find her in her parlor; but it was a sadness which vanished the moment she beheld her. With all the tenderness of a mother she clasped Adela to her breast, and, in the sudden transports of joy and surprise, for many minutes did not notice her dress; but when she did observe it, what powerful emotions did it excite in her breast! Adela, scarcely less agitated than she was, could not for many minutes relate all that had happened. At last the idea of the state in which she had left Howel made her endeavor to compose herself. Mrs. Marlowe wept while she related her sufferings; but when she mentioned Howel, surprise suspended her tears—a surprise, increased when she began the story; but when she came to that part where she herself had betrayed such emotion while listening to Howel, Mrs. Marlowe started and turned pale. "Your feelings are similar to mine," said Adela; "at this period I became agitated. Yes," she continued, "it was at this period I laid my trembling hand on his, and exclaimed, she lives!" "Merciful Heaven!" cried Mrs. Marlowe, "what do you mean?" "Oh, let me now," cried Adela, clasping her arms round her, "repeat to you the same expression. He lives! that husband, so beloved and regretted, lives!" "Oh, bring him to me!" said Mrs. Marlowe, in a faint voice; "let me behold him while I have reason myself to enjoy the blessing." Adela flew from the room. Howel was near the door. He approached, he entered the room, he tottered forward, and in one moment was at the feet and in the arms of his wife, who, transfixed to the chair, could only open her arms to receive him. The mingled pain and pleasure of such a reunion cannot be described. Both, with tears of grateful transport, blessed the Power which had given such comfort to their closing days. "But, my children," exclaimed Mrs. Marlowe, suddenly, "ah! when shall I behold my children? Why did they not accompany you? Ah! did they deem me then unworthy of bestowing a mother's blessing?" Howel trembled and turned pale. "I see," said Mrs. Marlowe, interpreting his emotion, "I am a wife, but not a mother." Howel, recovering his fortitude, took her hand and pressed it to his bosom. "Yes," he replied, "you are a mother; one dear, one amiable child remains, Heaven be praised!" He paused, and a tear fell to the memory of Juliana. "But Heaven," he resumed, "has taken the other to its eternal rest. Inquire not concerning her at present, I entreat; soon will I conduct you to the grave; there will I relate her fate, and together will we mourn it. Then shall the tears that never yet bedewed her grave, the precious tears of a mother, embalm her sacred dust." Mrs. Marlowe wept, but she complied with her husband's request. She inquired, in a broken voice, about her son, and the knowledge of his happiness gradually cheered her mind.

Adela consented to stay that night in the cottage; but the next day she determined on going to Woodlawn. To think she should again wander through it, again linger in the walks she had trodden with those she loved, gave to her mind a melancholy pleasure. The next morning, attended by her friend, she repaired to it, and was inexpressibly affected by reviewing scenes endeared by the tender remembrance of happier hours. The house, from its closed windows, appeared quite neglected and melancholy, as if pleasure had forsaken it with the poor departed General. Standard, his favorite horse, grazed in the lawn; and beside him, as if a secret sympathy endeared them to each other, stood the dog that had always attended the General in his walks. It instantly recollected Adela, and running to her, licked her hand, and evinced the utmost joy. She patted him on the head, while her tears burst forth at the idea of him who had been his master. The transports of the old domestics, particularly of the gray-headed butler, at her unexpected return, increased her tears. But when she entered the parlor, in which her father usually sat, she was quite overcome, and motioning with her hand for her friends not to mind her, she retired to the garden. There was a little romantic root-house at the termination of it, where she and Oscar had passed many happy hours together. Thither she repaired, and his idea, thus revived in her mind, did not lessen its dejection. While she sat within it indulging her sorrow, her eye caught some lines inscribed on one of its windows. She hastily arose, and examining them, instantly recollected the hand of Oscar. They were as follows:—

"Adieu, sweet girl, a last adieu!
We part to meet no more;
Adieu to peace, to hope, to you,
And to my native shore.

"If fortune had propitious smiled,
My love had made me blest;
But she, like me, is Sorrow's child,
By sadness dire opprest.

"I go to India's sultry clime,
Oh! never to return;
Beneath some lone embowering lime
Will be thy soldier's urn.

"No kindred spirit there shall weep,
Or, pensive, musing stray;
My image thou alone wilt keep,
And Grief's soft tribute pay."

Oscar, previous to his going to England, with the expectation of being sent to the West Indies, had paid a secret visit to Woodlawn, to review and bid adieu to every well-known and beloved spot, and had, one morning at early day, inscribed these lines on a window in the root-house, prompted by a tender melancholy he could not resist.

"His love is then unfortunate," said Adela, pensively, leaning her head upon her hand. "Oh, Oscar! how sad a similitude is there between your fate and mine!" She returned to the house Mr. and Mrs. Howel (for so we shall in future call Mr. and Mrs. Marlowe, that name being only assumed while her husband had a prospect of inheriting his uncle's fortune) had consented to stay some time with her. Oscar's lines ran in her head the whole day; and in the evening she again stole out to read them.

She had been absent some time, when Mrs. Howel came out to her. Adela blushed and started at being caught at the window.

"'Tis a long time, my dear Adela," said Mrs. Howel, "since we had a ramble in this delightful garden together. Indulge me in taking one, and let us talk of past times." "Past times," cried Adela, with a faint smile, "are not always the pleasantest to talk about." "There are some, at least one friend," cried Mrs. Howel, "whom you have not yet inquired after." Adela's heart suddenly palpitated; she guessed who that one friend was. "Oscar Fitzalan, surely," continued Mrs. Howel, "merits an inquiry. I have good news to tell you of him; therefore, without chiding you for any seeming neglect, I will reveal it." She accordingly related his late reverse of situation. Adela heard her with deep attention. "Since fortune, then, is propitious at last," cried she, "his love will no longer be unfortunate." "'Tis time, indeed," said Mrs. Howel, looking at her with pleasure, "that love, so pure, so constant as his, should be rewarded. Oh! Adela," she continued, suddenly taking her hand, "sweet daughter of my care, how great is my happiness at this moment, to think of that about to be your portion." "My happiness!" exclaimed Adela in a dejected voice. "Yes," replied Mrs. Howel, "in your union with a man every way worthy of possessing you; a man who, from the first moment he beheld you, has never ceased to love—in short, with Oscar Fitzalan himself." "Impossible!" cried Adela, trembling with emotion as she spoke. "Did not—how humiliating is the remembrance—did not Oscar Fitzalan reject me, when the too generous and romantic spirit of my beloved father offered my hand to his acceptance?" "For once," said Mrs. Howel, "I must disturb the sacred ashes of the dead, to prevent the innocent from being unhappy. Oh! Adela, you were cruelly deceived: and the moment which gave you to Belgrave, rendered Oscar the most wretched of mankind. My heart was the repository of all his griefs, and how many are the bitter tears I have shed over them! Be composed," continued she, seeing Adela's agitation, "and a few moments will explain everything to you." She then led her back to the root-house, and in a most explicit manner informed her of Belgrave's treachery. Adela burst into tears as she concluded. She wept on Mrs. Howel's bosom, and acknowledged she had removed a weight of uneasiness from her mind. "Poor Oscar!" she continued, "how much would the knowledge of his misery have aggravated mine!" "He acted nobly," said Mrs. Howel, "in concealing it; and amply will he be rewarded for such conduct." She then proceeded to inform Adela that she soon expected a visit from him. There was something in her look and manner which instantly excited the suspicion of Adela, who, blushing, starting, trembling, exclaimed—"He is already come!" Mrs. Howel smiled, and a tear fell from her upon the soft hand of Adela. "He is already come," she repeated, "and he waits, oh! how impatiently, to behold his Adela."

We may believe his patience was not put to a much longer test. But when Adela in reality beheld him as she entered the parlor where she had left Mr. Howel, and where he waited for the reappearance of her friend, she sunk beneath her emotion, upon that faithful bosom which had so long suffered the most excruciating pangs on her account; and it was many minutes ere she was sensible of the soft voice of Oscar. Oh! who shall paint his transports, after all his sufferings, to be thus rewarded! But in the midst of his happiness, the idea of the poor General, who had so generously planned it, struck upon his heart with a pang of sorrow. "Oh, my Adela!" he cried, clasping her to his heart, as if doubly endeared by the remembrance, "is Oscar at last permitted to pour forth the fulness of his soul before you, to reveal its tenderness, to indulge the hope of calling you his—a hope which affords the delightful prospect of being able to contribute to your felicity?" "Yes, most generous of friends!" he exclaimed, raising his eyes to a picture of the General, "I will endeavor to evince my gratitude to you by my conduct to your child." Oh! how did the tear he shed to the memory of her father interest the heart of Adela! her own fell with it, and she felt that the presence of that being to whom they were consecrated was alone wanting to complete their happiness. It was long ere she was sufficiently composed to inquire the reason of Oscar's sudden appearance, and still longer ere he could inform her. Mrs. Marlowe's melancholy letter, he at last said, had brought him over, with the hope of being able to cheer her solitude, and also, he acknowledged, his own dejection, by mutual sympathy; from her cottage he had been directed to Woodlawn, and at Woodlawn received particulars, not only of her happiness, but his own. Adela, who had never yet deviated from propriety, would not now infringe it, and resolutely determined, till the expiration of her mourning, not to bestow her hand on Oscar; but permitted him to hope, that in the intervening space, most of his time might be devoted to her. It was necessary, however, to sanction that hope by having proper society. She could not flatter herself with much longer retaining Mr. and Mrs. Howel, as the latter particularly was impatient to behold her son. Oscar therefore requested, and obtained permission from Adela, to write in her name to Lord and Lady Cherbury, and entreat their company at Woodlawn, promising she would then accompany them to Castle Carberry, and from thence to Dunreath Abbey, a tour which, previous to Oscar's leaving Wales, had been agreed on. The invitation was accepted, and in a few days Oscar beheld the two beings most valued by him in the world introduced to each other. Tears of rapture started to his eyes, as he saw his Adela folded to the bosom of his lovely sister, who called her the sweet restorer of her brother's happiness! Lord Cherbury was already acquainted with her, and, next to his Amanda, considered her the loveliest of human beings; and Lady Martha and Lady Araminta, who were also invited to Woodlawn, regarded her in the same light. A few days after their arrival Mrs. Howel prepared for her departure. Adela, who considered her as a second mother, could not behold those preparations without tears of real regret. "Oh, my Adela!" she exclaimed, "these tears flatter, yet distress me. I am pleased to think the child of my care regards me with such affection, but I am hurt to think she should consider my loss such an affliction. Oh, my child! may the endearments of the friends who surround you steal from you all painful remembrances! nature calls me from you; I sigh to behold my child; I sigh," she continued, with eyes suffused in tears, "to behold the precious earth which holds another."

About three weeks after her departure the whole party proceeded to Castle Carberry. Amanda could not re-enter it without emotions of the most painful nature. She recollected the moment in which she had quitted it, oppressed with sorrow and sickness, to attend the closing period of a father's life. She wept, and sighed to think, that the happiness he had prayed for he could not behold. Lord Cherbury saw her emotions, and soothed them with the softest tenderness; it was due to that tenderness to conquer her dejection, and in future the remembrance of her father was only attended with a pleasing melancholy. She did not delay visiting the convent. The good-natured nuns crowded around her, and cried, laughed, and wished her joy, almost in the same moment; particularly Sister Mary. The prioress's pleasure was of a less violent, but more affecting nature. An almost constant scene of gaiety was kept up at the Castle, a gaiety, however, which did not prevent Lord and Lady Cherbury from inspecting into the situation of their poor tenants, whose wants they relieved, whose grievances they redressed, and whose hearts they cheered, by a promise of spending some months in every year at the Castle. After continuing at it six weeks, they crossed over to Port Patrick, and from thence proceeded to Dunreath Abbey, which had been completely repaired, and furnished in a style equally modern and elegant; and here it was determined they should remain till the solemnization of Lord Dunreath's nuptials. The time which intervened till the period appointed for them was agreeably diversified by parties amongst the neighboring families, and excursions about the country; but no hours were happier than those which the inhabitants of the Abbey passed when free from company, so truly were they united to each other by affection. Lord Dunreath, soon after his return, waited upon the Marquis of Roslin, and, by his sister's desire, signified to him that if a visit from her would be agreeable to the Marquis she would pay it. This, however, was declined; and about the same period Lady Dunreath died. Mrs. Bruce, whom from long habit she was attached to, then retired to another part of Scotland, ashamed to remain where her conduct was known—a conduct which deeply affected her niece, whom Amanda visited immediately after her arrival, and found settled in a neat house near the town she had lodged in. She received Lady Cherbury with every demonstration of real pleasure, and both she and her little girls spent some time with her at the Abbey.

The happy period for completing the felicity of Oscar at last arrived. In the chapel where his parents were united, he received from the hand of Lord Cherbury the lovely object of his long-tried affections. The ceremony was only witnessed by his own particular friends; but at dinner all the neighboring families were assembled, and the tenants were entertained in the great hall, where dancing commenced at an early and was continued till a late hour.

And now having (to use the words of Adam) brought our story to the sum of earthly bliss, we shall conclude, first giving a brief account of the characters connected with it.

Lady Greystock, as one of the most distinguished, we shall first mention. After the death of Lady Euphrasia, she found her company no longer desired at the Marquis's, and accordingly repaired to Bath. Here she had not been long ere she became acquainted with a set of female Puritans, who soon wrought a total change (I will not say a reformation) in her ladyship's sentiments; and to give a convincing proof of this change, she was prevailed on to give her hand to one of their spruce young preachers, who shortly taught her, what indeed she had long wanted to learn, the doctrine of repentance; for most sincerely did she repent putting herself into his power. Vexation, disappointment, and grief, brought on a lingering illness, from which she never recovered When convinced she was dying, she sent for Rushbrook, and made a full confession of her treachery and injustice to him, in consequence of which he took immediate possession of his uncle's fortune; and thus, in the evening of his life, enjoyed a full recompense for the trials of its early period. Lady Greystock died with some degree of satisfaction at the idea of disappointing her husband of the fortune she was convinced he had married her for.

Mrs. Howel, after visiting her son, retired to her husband's cottage, where their days glide on in a kind of pleasing melancholy. The happiness of that son, and his Emily, is as perfect as happiness can be in this sublunary state.

Sir Charles Bingley, after studiously avoiding Lord and Lady Cherbury for above two years, at last, by chance, was thrown in their way, and then had the pleasure of finding he was not so agitated by the sight of Amanda as he had dreaded. He did not refuse the invitations of Lord Cherbury. The domestic happiness he saw him enjoying, rendered his own unconnected and wandering life more unpleasant than ever to him. Lady Araminta Dormer was almost constantly in his company. No longer fascinated by Amanda, he could now see and admire her perfections. He soon made known his admiration. The declaration was not ungraciously received, and he offered his hand, and was accepted —an acceptance which put him in possession of happiness fully equal to Lord Cherbury's.

The Marquis and Marchioness of Roslin pass their days in gloomy retirement, regretful of the past and hopeless of the future. Freelove flutters about every public place, boasts of having carried off a Scotch heiress, and thinks, from that circumstance, he may now lay siege to any female heart with a certainty of being successful.

To return once more to the sweet descendants of the Dunreath family. The goodness of heart, the simplicity of manners which ever distinguished them, they still retain. From having been children of sorrow themselves, they feel for all who come under that denomination, and their charity is at once bestowed as a tribute from gratitude to Heaven, and from humanity to want; from gratitude to that Being who watched their unsheltered youth, who guarded them through innumerable perils, who placed them on the summit of prosperity, from whence, by dispensing His gifts around, they trust to be translated to a still greater height of happiness. Lady Dunreath's wish is fulfilled. To use her words, their past sorrows are only remembered to teach them pity for the woes of others. Their virtues have added to the renown of their ancestors, and entailed peace upon their own souls. Their children, by all connected with them, are considered as blessings. Gratitude has already consecrated their names, and their example inspires others with emulation to pursue their courses.

Lightning Source UK Ltd.
Milton Keynes UK
UKHW04f2042240818
327707UK00012B/33/P

9 781434 414656